ScienceSaurus™

A Student Handbook

Great Source

A Division of Houghton Mifflin Company

Acknowledgments

We gratefully acknowledge the following teachers, science supervisors, and professors who helped make *ScienceSaurus* a reality.

Ron Bonnstetter, Ph.D.
University of Nebraska

Bonnie J. Brunkhorst, Ph.D.
Past President, National Science Teacher's Association
California State University, *San Bernardino, CA*

Herbert K. Brunkhorst, Ph.D.
California State University, *San Bernardino, CA*

James Cowden
Chicago, IL

Jim Cronin
Centennial, CO

Patrick Curtin
Oakland, CA

William Daniels
Beaumont, TX

D'Ann Douglas
Beaumont, TX

Nina S. Guthrie
Carriere, MS

Terry L. Johnson
Springville, UT

Patty Kincaid
Englewood, CO

Nancy F. Knop, Ph.D.
Oakland, CA

Patsy Magee
Beaumont, TX

Sharon McCue
Wichita, KS

Thomas Medcalf
West Palm Beach, FL

Russell J. Rapose
Warwick, RI

Kenneth Russell Roy, Ph.D.
Glastonbury, CT

Michael C. Shackleford, Ed.D.
Hendersonville, TN

Terry Starr-Klein
Brockton, MA

K. J. Walsh
Los Angeles, CA

Development and Illustration credits start at item 542.

Printed in the United States of America

International Standard Book Number: 978-0-669-00527-1 (hardcover)
1 2 3 4 5 6 7 8 9 0 RRDC 09 08 07

TABLE OF CONTENTS

H
H
O

How This Book Is Organized

ScienceSaurus is a resource book. That means you are not expected to read it from cover to cover. Instead, you will want to keep it handy for those times when you are not clear about a science topic and need a place to look up definitions, procedures, explanations, and diagrams.

Because this is a resource book, and because there may be more than one topic on a page, we have given each topic a number. So, when you are looking up a specific topic, look for its number.

052

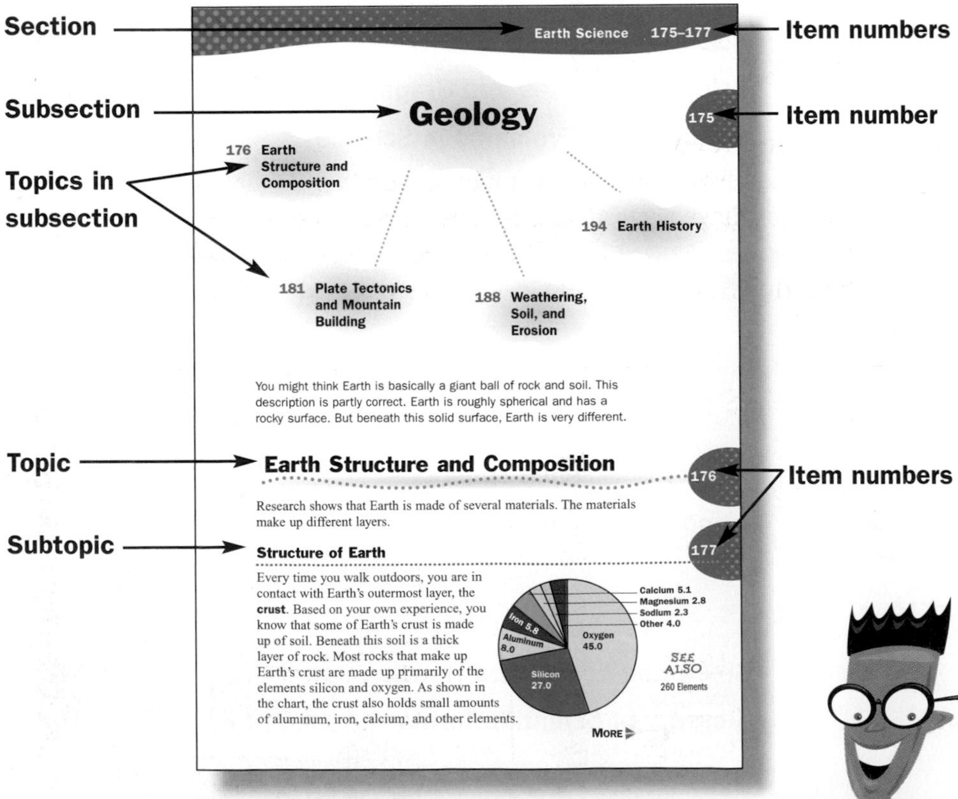

Section
Earth Science 175–177
Item numbers
Subsection
Geology
175
Item number
Topics in subsection
176 Earth Structure and Composition
194 Earth History
181 Plate Tectonics and Mountain Building
188 Weathering, Soil, and Erosion
You might think Earth is basically a giant ball of rock and soil. This description is partly correct. Earth is roughly spherical and has a rocky surface. But beneath this solid surface, Earth is very different.
Topic
Earth Structure and Composition
176
Item numbers
Research shows that Earth is made of several materials. The materials make up different layers.
Subtopic
Structure of Earth
177
Every time you walk outdoors, you are in contact with Earth's outermost layer, the crust. Based on your own experience, you know that some of Earth's crust is made up of soil. Beneath this soil is a thick layer of rock. Most rocks that make up Earth's crust are made up primarily of the elements silicon and oxygen. As shown in the chart, the crust also holds small amounts of aluminum, iron, calcium, and other elements.
Calcium 5.1
Magnesium 2.8
Sodium 2.3
Other 4.0
Iron 5.8
Aluminum 8.0
Oxygen 45.0
Silicon 27.0
SEE ALSO
260 Elements
MORE

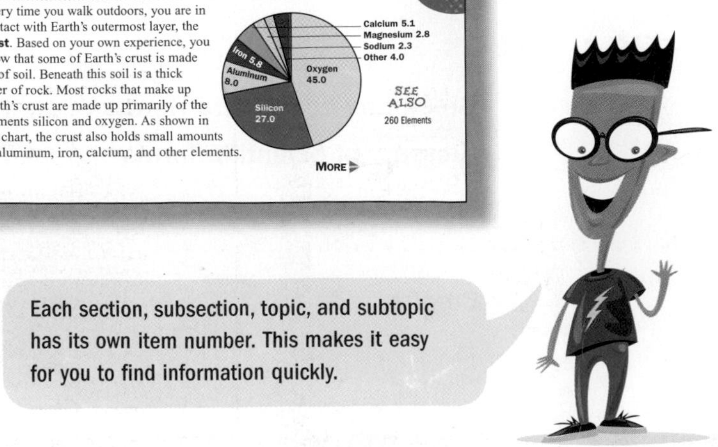

Each section, subsection, topic, and subtopic has its own item number. This makes it easy for you to find information quickly.

A good way to get started in this book is to thumb through the pages. Find these parts:

Table of Contents

This lists the major sections and subsections of the book.

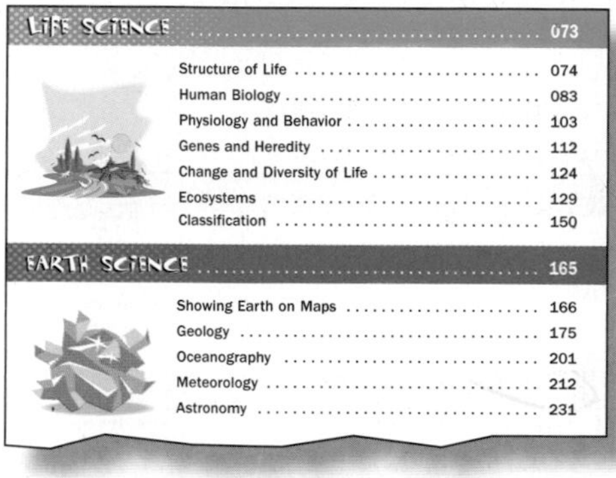

Sections and Subsections

Each section of the handbook has an organizer so you know what is in the section. Sections have several subsections, and each of these also has its own organizer. Notice the colored areas across the top of the pages. Each section has a different color to make it easy to find.

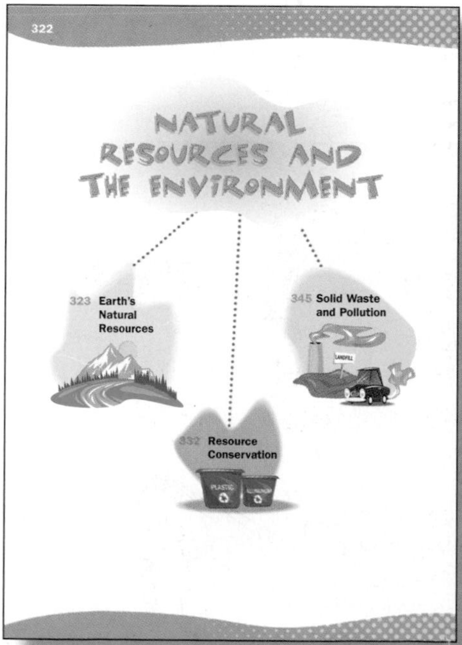

322

NATURAL RESOURCES AND THE ENVIRONMENT

323 Earth's Natural Resources

345 Solid Waste and Pollution

332 Resource Conservation

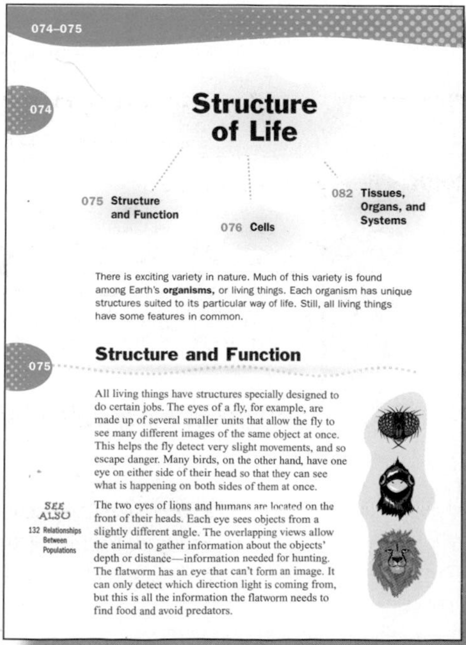

074–075

074

Structure of Life

075 Structure and Function

076 Cells

082 Tissues, Organs, and Systems

There is exciting variety in nature. Much of this variety is found among Earth's **organisms,** or living things. Each organism has unique structures suited to its particular way of life. Still, all living things have some features in common.

075

Structure and Function

All living things have structures specially designed to do certain jobs. The eyes of a fly, for example, are made up of several smaller units that allow the fly to see many different images of the same object at once. This helps the fly detect very slight movements, and so escape danger. Many birds, on the other hand, have one eye on either side of their head so that they can see what is happening on both sides of them at once.

SEE ALSO
132 Relationships Between Populations

The two eyes of lions and humans are located on the front of their heads. Each eye sees objects from a slightly different angle. The overlapping views allow the animal to gather information about the objects' depth or distance—information needed for hunting. The flatworm has an eye that can't form an image. It can only detect which direction light is coming from, but this is all the information the flatworm needs to find food and avoid predators.

Almanac

The Almanac includes some helpful guidelines for making tables and graphs, using mathematics for science, researching information, organizing your time and your work groups, and taking tests. It also includes some useful maps and tables. Check out all the Almanac entries—you will want to refer to them often.

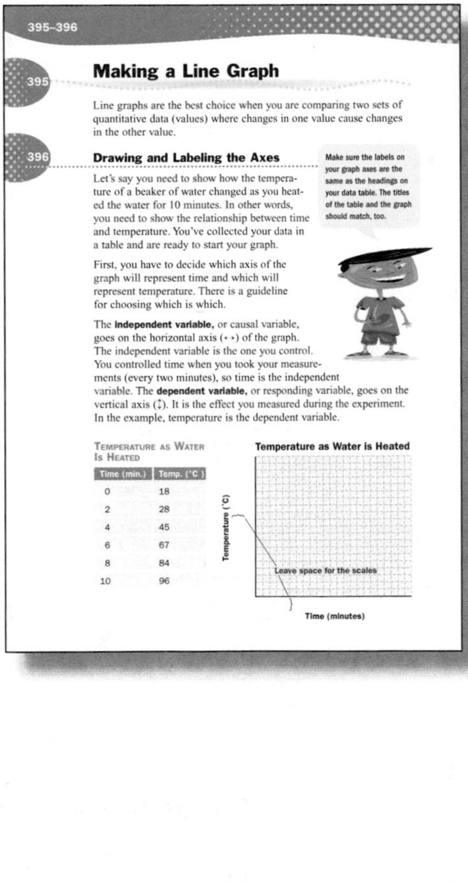
395–396

Making a Line Graph

395 Line graphs are the best choice when you are comparing two sets of quantitative data (values) where changes in one value cause changes in the other value.

396 **Drawing and Labeling the Axes**

Let's say you need to show how the temperature of a beaker of water changed as you heated the water for 10 minutes. In other words, you need to show the relationship between time and temperature. You've collected your data in a table and are ready to start your graph.

First, you have to decide which axis of the graph will represent time and which will represent temperature. There is a guideline for choosing which is which.

The **independent variable,** or causal variable, goes on the horizontal axis (↔) of the graph. The independent variable is the one you control. You controlled time when you took your measurements (every two minutes), so time is the independent variable. The **dependent variable,** or responding variable, goes on the vertical axis (↕). It is the effect you measured during the experiment. In the example, temperature is the dependent variable.

Make sure the labels on your graph axes are the same as the headings on your data table. The titles of the table and the graph should match, too.

TEMPERATURE AS WATER IS HEATED

Time (min.)	Temp. (°C)
0	18
2	28
4	45
6	67
8	84
10	96

Yellow Pages

This part of the handbook includes a **History of Science Time Line,** which shows when important events in the history of science and technology occurred. It also includes information about a few of the many **Famous Scientists** you may read about in your study of science. In **Scientific Terms,** you will find a glossary of terms that your teachers, textbooks, and other science sources use. Use it to look up new and unfamiliar words that you hear or read in science.

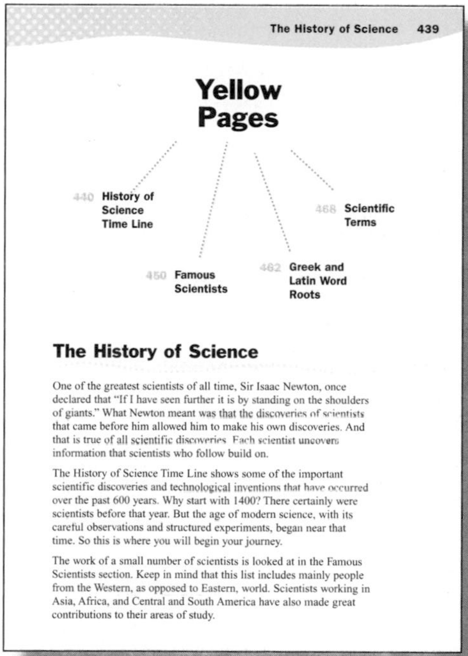
The History of Science 439

Yellow Pages

440 History of Science Time Line

450 Famous Scientists

462 Greek and Latin Word Roots

468 Scientific Terms

The History of Science

One of the greatest scientists of all time, Sir Isaac Newton, once declared that "If I have seen further it is by standing on the shoulders of giants." What Newton meant was that the discoveries of scientists that came before him allowed him to make his own discoveries. And that is true of all scientific discoveries. Each scientist uncovers information that scientists who follow build on.

The History of Science Time Line shows some of the important scientific discoveries and technological inventions that have occurred over the past 600 years. Why start with 1400? There certainly were scientists before that year. But the age of modern science, with its careful observations and structured experiments, began near that time. So this is where you will begin your journey.

The work of a small number of scientists is looked at in the Famous Scientists section. Keep in mind that this list includes mainly people from the Western, as opposed to Eastern, world. Scientists working in Asia, Africa, and Central and South America have also made great contributions to their areas of study.

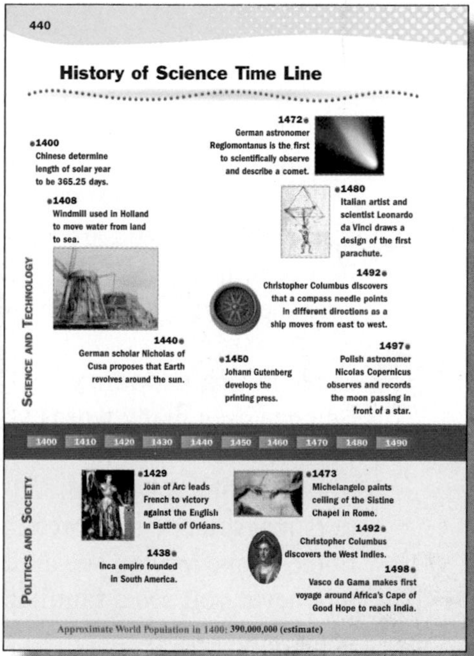
440

History of Science Time Line

Science and Technology

1400 Chinese determine length of solar year to be 365.25 days.

1408 Windmill used in Holland to move water from land to sea.

1440 German scholar Nicholas of Cusa proposes that Earth revolves around the sun.

1450 Johann Gutenberg develops the printing press.

1472 German astronomer Regiomontanus is the first to scientifically observe and describe a comet.

1480 Italian artist and scientist Leonardo da Vinci draws a design of the first parachute.

1492 Christopher Columbus discovers that a compass needle points in different directions as a ship moves from east to west.

1497 Polish astronomer Nicolas Copernicus observes and records the moon passing in front of a star.

1400 1410 1420 1430 1440 1450 1460 1470 1480 1490

Politics and Society

1429 Joan of Arc leads French to victory against the English in Battle of Orléans.

1438 Inca empire founded in South America.

1473 Michelangelo paints ceiling of the Sistine Chapel in Rome.

1492 Christopher Columbus discovers the West Indies.

1498 Vasco da Gama makes first voyage around Africa's Cape of Good Hope to reach India.

Approximate World Population in 1400: 390,000,000 (estimate)

Index

This is at the very end of the book. Use it to find topics in the book.

Inside Back Cover

Here you will find the steps to follow in a scientific investigation, and a table showing metric (SI) prefixes and their meanings. You'll use this information often, so we placed it where it's easy to find.

How to Use This Book

There are three ways to find information about a topic:

1 Look in the Index

We listed topics in the Index using any word we thought you might use to describe the topic. For example, if you want to find information about cell division, you will find the item numbers listed under both "cell" and "mitosis."

Cell, 076–081
animal, 077
cell division, 080
discovery of, 076, 442
eukaryotic, 076

Mitosis, 080

Remember that you are being directed to item numbers, not page numbers. Use the item numbers at the top of each page to help you find the section that your topic is in.

2 Look in the Glossary

Science uses many words you may not have heard before. It also uses familiar words—like "work"—in unfamiliar ways. Think of this Glossary as your personal science interpreter. Turn to this part of the book whenever you see an unfamiliar word, or whenever you see a familiar word being used in a new way.

Most Glossary entries will give you an item number to refer to if you want more information about the topic.

work: occurs when a force is used to move an object through a distance; measured in **joules (J) (287)**

3 Look in the Table of Contents

All the major topics covered in this book are listed in the Table of Contents. If you are looking for a general topic, such as Ecosystems, rather than a very specific one, such as Food Chains, the Table of Contents is a quick way to find it. Notice that the color of each section's title in the Table of Contents matches the color that's across the top of each page in that section. This makes it easy to locate a section.

How to Use *sci*LINKS

Sometimes you want to know more about a topic than you can find in a book. *Sci*LINKS can help. *Sci*LINKS is a way to link science textbooks with sites on the Internet. *Sci*LINKS was developed and is maintained by the National Science Teachers Association.

Look for the *sci*LINKS name on certain pages throughout this book. Next to the *sci*LINKS name, you will find information that will help you get to the linked sites for that topic.

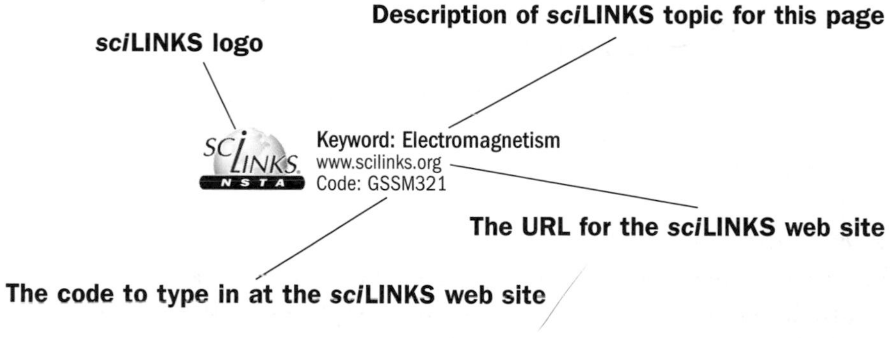

To use *sci*LINKS, first go to the *sci*LINKS web site. Sign in, then type the code from the page you are reading. You will receive a list of URLs for that topic. Click on the URL for the site you wish to visit, and *sci*LINKS will take you there. If you need more information, go back to the *sci*LINKS page and try another URL from the list. The sites you reach through *sci*LINKS have already been checked out by science teachers and scientists, so you know you're getting the best the Internet has to offer for that topic.

sciLINKS are constantly being updated, so you don't have to worry about dead links or outdated information.

SCIENTIFIC INVESTIGATION

001

Have you ever wondered what the moon's surface is like, why rocks have different colors and textures, or how birds and airplanes can fly? If so, you have thought about science. The goal of science is to answer questions about the natural world. Scientific investigations give you information you can use to answer these questions.

002 Scientific Inquiry

- 003 **Asking Scientific Questions**
- 007 **Testing Hypotheses**
- 011 **Analyzing and Concluding**
- 014 **Communicating Results**
- 016 **Identifying Questions for Further Investigation**

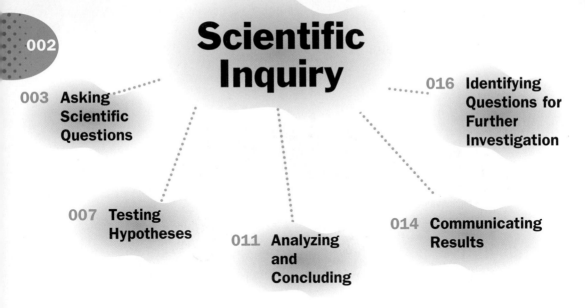

Scientific Inquiry is a fancy way of describing how scientists go about finding answers to questions about the natural world. Scientific inquiry begins when you ask questions. It continues as you look for answers to these questions.

The goal of scientific inquiry is to understand and explain the natural world. Scientific inquiry draws from two main sources when attempting to answer questions: scientific observations and scientific ideas.

Word Watch!

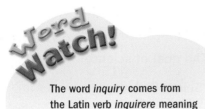

The word *inquiry* comes from the Latin verb *inquirere* meaning "to seek."

SCILINKS NSTA

Keyword: Scientific Inquiry
www.scilinks.org
Code: GSSM002

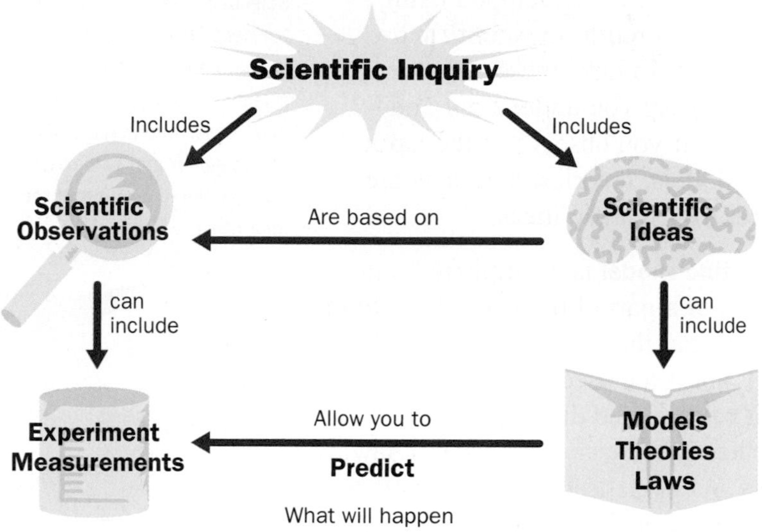

Scientific observations involve using your senses to describe the natural world. For example, you may open a package of bread and see patches of green or black fuzz. You may also note that the bread has a strange odor. These observations tell you that mold has started to grow on the bread.

SEE ALSO
008 Designing an Experiment

Observations are often made during experiments. An **experiment** is a test or trial that produces evidence you can use to help answer a question. For example, you may wonder: Does temperature affect mold growth on bread? To answer this question, you could do an experiment to compare how much mold grows on bread stored at different temperatures.

Not all observations come from experiments. Sometimes you get information about the world just by observing it and taking measurements. A **measurement** describes a quantity, such as time, length, distance, mass, volume, or temperature. Measurements always include a number and a unit.

SEE ALSO
053 Measurement

MORE ▶

Scientific ideas are developed using evidence gathered from scientific observations. In turn, these ideas can be used to help you understand and explain what you observe in the natural world. Models, theories, and laws are all types of scientific ideas.

Scientific ideas can never be "proven." They can only be supported or unsupported by scientific observations. The more observations you and others gather that agree with an idea, the more support the idea gains.

SEE ALSO
006 Forming a Hypothesis
013 Drawing Conclusions

A **scientific model** is a simplified representation of a part of the natural world that explains what that part looks like or how it works. Models are often used to represent things that cannot be observed directly, like individual water molecules or the center of Earth. Drawings, objects, mathematical equations, and computer simulations can all be models.

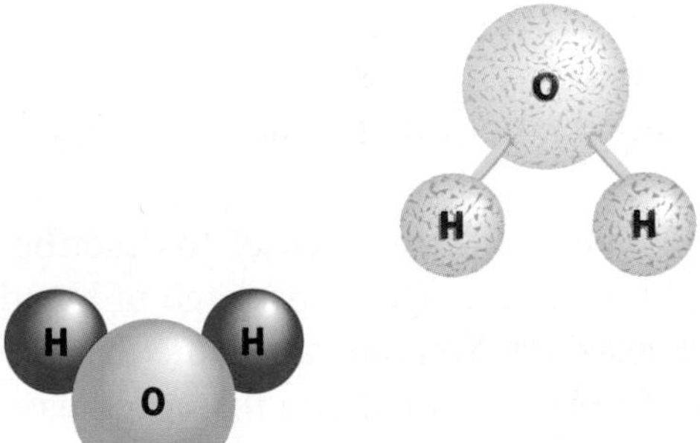

Water molecule models

If observations do not support a scientific theory, the theory must be changed. Observations should never be changed to match scientific theories!

SEE ALSO
276 Gravity

A **theory** is a set of ideas that tie together many observations. For example, the theory that the universe is expanding is based on many observations showing that objects in space are moving farther and farther away from one another. Theories are based on ideas that have been tested and shown to be true over time.

A **law** describes how some part of nature acts under certain conditions. For example, the law of universal gravitation explains how the force of gravity affects all objects in the universe. Like theories, laws are based on ideas that have been tested by observations and experimentation. Both theories and laws are used to explain nature.

A **prediction** is a statement of what you think will happen under certain conditions based on what you know from observations or research. For instance, if you observed that mold grew on bread stored in a warm place but not on bread stored in a cold place, you might predict that storing bread in the refrigerator would keep mold from growing, or at least slow it down. You might make the same prediction if you read that more types of mold are found in warm areas of Earth than in cold areas. In either case, you use your prior knowledge to predict what you might observe in an experiment.

Working in science is like working with puzzles. There is no single way to do science, just as there is no single way to solve a puzzle. The methods you use to answer a question depend partly on what the question is. How do you decide the best way to find an answer to a particular question? You use a combination of reasoning, common sense, imagination, intuition, and guesswork—just like when you try to solve a puzzle. This is how most work in science is done.

Did You Know?

Albert Einstein described science this way: "The whole of science is nothing more than a refinement of everyday thinking."

You will find it helpful to become familiar with each of the following procedures when performing a scientific investigation. Remember that you will not use all of these steps for every investigation.

Scientific Investigation
Ask a question
Do research
Form a hypothesis
Design an experiment
Gather data
Analyze data and draw conclusions
Communicate results
Identify questions for further investigation

Asking Scientific Questions

003

Your work in science will likely include doing experiments. You may design your own experiment, or do an experiment that is assigned to you. Either way, your experiment should be based on a scientific question that you want to answer.

Asking a Question

004

All scientific investigations begin with a question. At what temperature does glass melt? What effect does weathering have on rocks? What are the stages of an insect's life cycle?

Suppose you are interested in devices used to measure time. You come across a pendulum clock and wonder: "How does a pendulum work?"

You can find out how a pendulum works by reading about pendulums. Or, you can do an experiment to see for yourself. But first you need a testable question.

Parts of a Pendulum

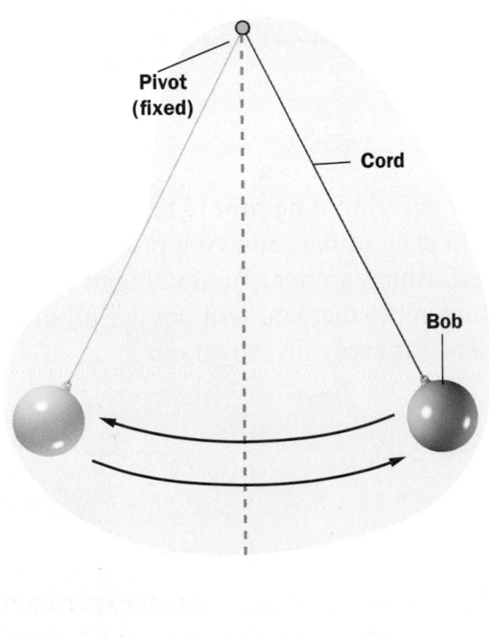

Experiments can only answer testable questions. For example, an experiment cannot answer the question, "How does a pendulum work?" Here are some testable questions about pendulums:

SEE ALSO
414 Asking Questions

- Does the time it takes a pendulum to swing back and forth depend on the length of the pendulum cord?
- Does the time it takes a pendulum to swing back and forth depend on how heavy the bob is?
- Does the time it takes a pendulum to swing back and forth depend on how wide the pendulum swings?

Doing Research

005

Before you design and carry out any experiment, you should find out what is already known about the topic you are investigating.

Suppose you want to do an experiment with pendulums. First, you should find out what is known about pendulums—what the parts of a pendulum are, how pendulums are built, and if there are different kinds of pendulums. The more you learn about your subject, the better your chances of designing a good experiment!

As you do research, you may discover that other people have already done experiments on a topic that interests you. You may decide to do a similar experiment to see if you get the same results. Repeating an experiment that's already been done may not sound very exciting to you, but the results can be just as valuable. You see, the more times we repeat an experiment and get the same results, the more certain we can be of those results.

SEE ALSO
420 Researching Information

Or, you may plan an original experiment—one that has never been done. In this case, you can use information you found about similar or related experiments to develop your own experiment.

006 Forming a Hypothesis

A **hypothesis** is an idea that can be tested by an experiment. All experiments should have a hypothesis. The hypothesis might be a positive statement ("All objects fall at the same speed"), or a negative statement ("Plants will not grow in the dark").

Many hypotheses turn out to be wrong. However, even wrong hypotheses are useful because they help you rule out some ideas.

Let's look at an example of how you might form a hypothesis.

Word Watch!

The plural of *hypothesis* is *hypotheses*.

Consider an experiment with a pendulum. After doing research and thinking about pendulums, you might propose this hypothesis: The time it takes for one back-and-forth swing (period) of a pendulum depends on the length of pendulum cord, but not on the weight of the bob, or the angle from which the bob is released. Your experiment should be designed to test this hypothesis.

SEE ALSO
002 Scientific Inquiry
013 Drawing Conclusions
279 Friction

Sometimes a hypothesis includes a model. A **scientific model** is a simplified version of some part of nature. In thinking about a pendulum, you might assume that the cord has no weight and that the pivot has no friction. This is your model of a pendulum.

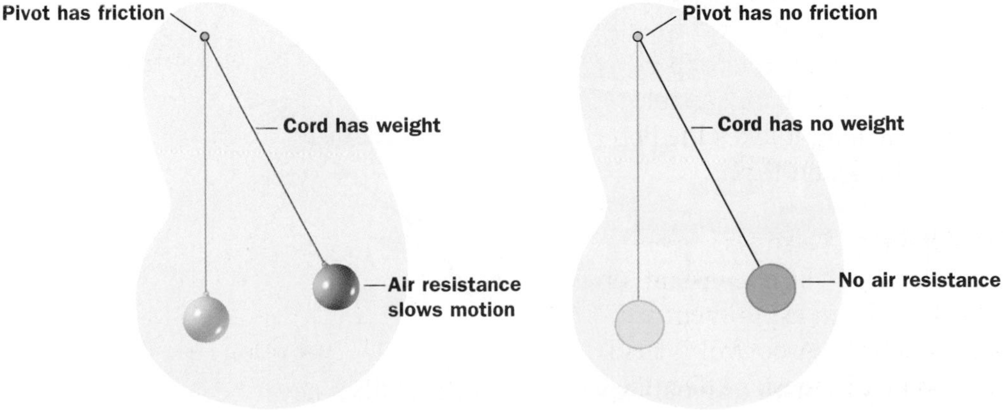

Testing Hypotheses

007

Once you have done research and formed a hypothesis, you are ready to design and carry out an investigation to find the answer to your question.

Designing an Experiment

008

An **experiment** is a set of steps you follow to test a hypothesis. In order for the results of an experiment to be meaningful, the experiment must be carefully designed.

Start out by writing down how your experiment will be set up. Once you have a plan, collect your materials and start your experiment.

Identifying Variables

Variables are factors that can affect the results of an experiment. Before you begin any experiment, you must identify variables that can affect your results. You then need to decide which variables to control and which to vary.

Variables Affecting Pendulum Period

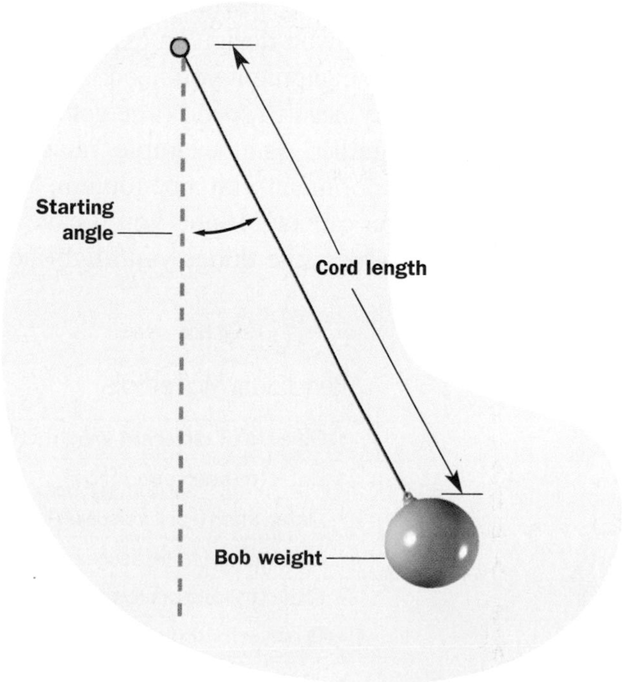

Suppose you do an experiment with a pendulum. Your variables might be cord length, bob weight, and starting angle. Your experiment might test which variable affects how long it takes the bob to swing back and forth.

Establishing Controls

The factors you keep constant, or hold fixed, in an experiment are called **controls.** A control is held fixed so that it doesn't affect the outcome of the experiment.

MORE ▶

How can you find which variable—cord length, bob weight, or starting angle—affects how long it takes a pendulum to swing back and forth? You separately test the effect of each variable on the pendulum's period. You do this by keeping two variables the same while changing the third. To test all three variables, you would perform the following three tests:

1. Vary cord length, but keep bob weight and starting angle fixed.

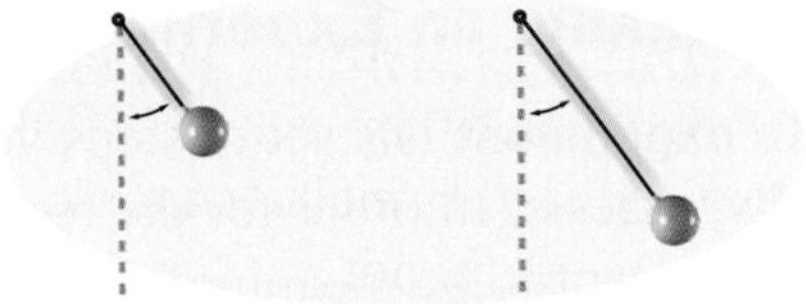

2. Vary bob weight, but keep cord length and starting angle fixed.

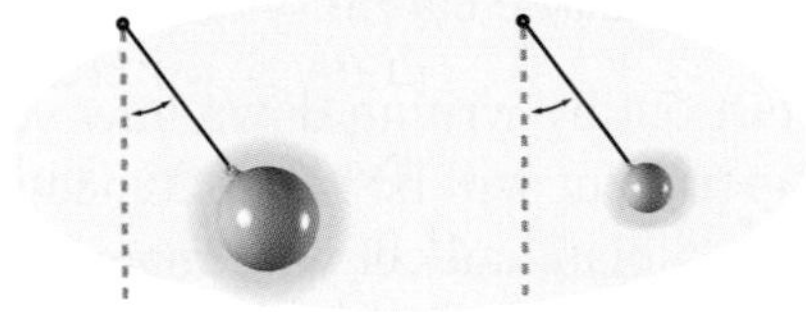

3. Vary starting angle, but keep cord length and bob weight fixed.

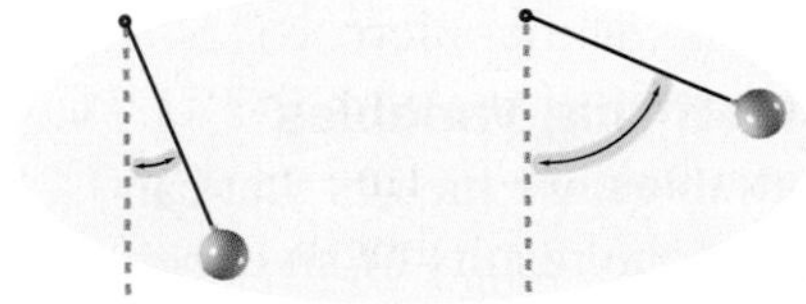

SEE ALSO
411 Managing Your Time

Gathering Materials and Equipment

When you design an experiment, you must figure out what materials and equipment you need. Sometimes, this is easy. Other times, you may need to spend time gathering materials and then putting them together. As an example, imagine that you want to carry out an experiment with a pendulum. You may have a ready-made pendulum you can use. If not, you'll have to build your own. Here's a list of some of the things you might need to build a pendulum.

Pendulum Materials

- Objects of different weights (for use as pendulum bobs)
- Hook (to hang cord from)
- Meter stick (for measuring cord length)
- Stopwatch (to measure period)
- Scale (to measure bob weight)
- Protractor (to measure starting angle)
- Tools: hammer, nails, pliers, wood block, dowel, etc. (to build pendulum)

Plan how you will build your pendulum. Anticipate any problems your pendulum might have. For example, you need to make sure the bob won't fall off the cord. How will you attach the bob to the cord?

Gathering Data

009

Information you gather during an experiment is called **data.** Sometimes data include numbers (10 plant leaves) or measurements (0.12 cm). Other times they include simple observations (the mineral did not scratch the glass). As you search for answers to scientific questions, you will gather data in many different ways.

Word Watch!

Data is the plural of *datum.*

Using Tools and Technology Tools and technology can be used to help you gather and organize data. You can use a telescope to view objects in the sky, while microscopes let you look at things too small to see with the unaided eye. You can use a balance to find an object's mass or a meter stick to find its length.

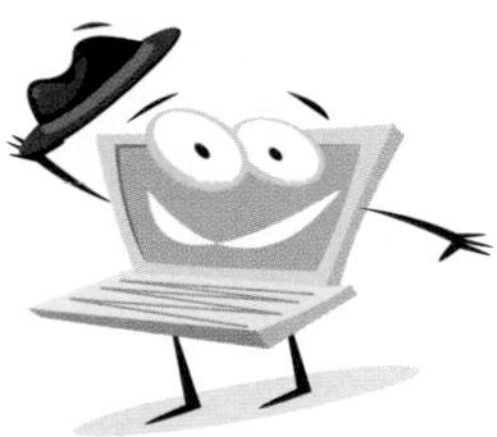

SEE ALSO

389 Recording Data Electronically

Computers, calculators, graphing calculators, and data probes are other useful tools. Hand-held calculators can be used to make quick and accurate calculations. Computers can be used to do research, store data, and make graphs, tables, and charts. A graphing calculator can be used to convert raw data into a graph.

Using Math Mathematics is an important science tool. Measurements, for example, are expressed as numbers and units, such as 40 grams or 34°C. Ratios are used to write chemical formulas. Many laws of physics are expressed in the language of mathematics. Charts and graphs are used to display, understand, and communicate scientific data.

SEE ALSO

375 Scientific Numbers

10÷2=5

Repeating Measurements Carpenters often say, "Measure twice, cut once." The more measurements you make, the more reliable your results. When possible, you should repeat measurements several times, and then average the results. Each set of repeated measurements is called a **trial.**

010 Recording Data

After you design an experiment, you are ready to carry it out. As you do so, it is important to record your data in a sensible, orderly way. If you scribble notes all over the place, you might forget what your data mean.

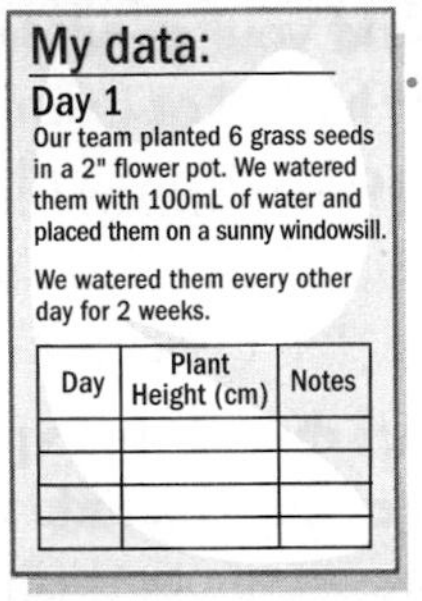

My data:
Day 1
Our team planted 6 grass seeds in a 2" flower pot. We watered them with 100mL of water and placed them on a sunny windowsill.
We watered them every other day for 2 weeks.
Day
Plant Height (cm)
Notes

Good data sheet

Poor data sheet

SEE ALSO
375 Scientific Numbers
053 Measurement

General observations can be recorded like diary entries in a science journal. For observations that include numbers or measurements, however, tables are the best way to organize the data.

Imagine you conduct an experiment with a pendulum. You measure the pendulum's period (the time it takes for one back-and-forth swing of the bob) as you change the cord length (while keeping the bob weight and starting angle fixed). You might set up your data table as follows:

SEE ALSO
386 Organizing Data Tables

Period vs. Cord Length

	Time (s)			
Cord Length (cm)	Trial 1	Trial 2	Trial 3	Average
10	0.5	0.6	0.6	0.6
20	1.0	1.0	0.8	0.9
30	0.9	1.1	1.0	1.0
40	1.1	1.3	1.4	1.3
50	1.4	1.4	1.5	1.4
60	1.7	1.6	1.6	1.6
70	1.8	1.5	1.9	1.7
80	1.6	1.9	2.0	1.8
90	1.9	1.8	1.9	1.9
100	2.0	2.1	2.0	2.0

You could use similar tables to record your data for bob weight vs. period and starting angle vs. period.

Analyzing and Concluding

011

Data collected from an experiment must be analyzed in order to be meaningful. Analyzed data can then be used to help you draw a conclusion about what you learned in your scientific investigation.

Analyzing Data

012

After you do an experiment, you need to decide what your data mean. This process is called analyzing your data. How you analyze your data depends on your experiment. For example, you may need to make calculations or graph your data.

Suppose you did an experiment to find out how cord length, bob weight, and starting angle affect how long it takes a pendulum to swing back and forth. It would make sense to graph these data. In this case, you would draw three graphs: period vs. cord length, period vs. bob weight, and period vs. starting angle.

SEE ALSO
390 Kinds of Graphs
395 Making a Line Graph

You should make each graph easy for someone else to read and understand by including a title, labeling the axes, showing your data points, and drawing the best line that fits those points.

Looking at this graph should help you understand how cord length affects swing time. The great thing about a graph is that it gives you a picture of your data, allowing you to uncover patterns you might not otherwise notice.

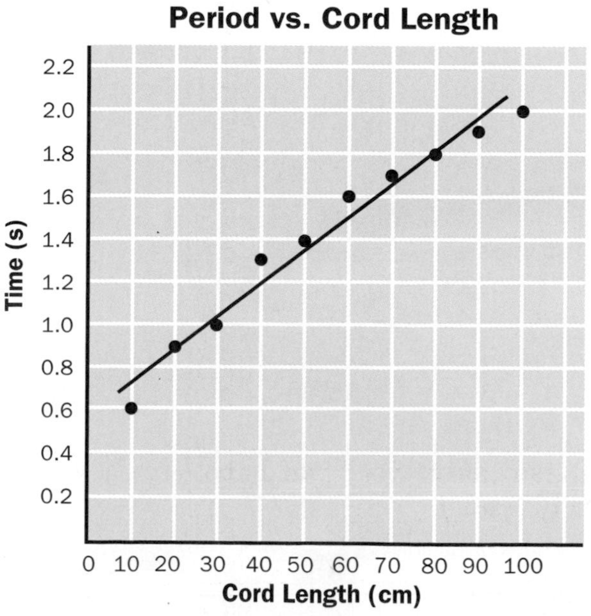

When you analyze your data carefully, you might discover things you didn't expect. For example, you might not only observe that period increases with cord length; you may also be able to figure out exactly how it increases.

013 Drawing Conclusions

Always question your data and conclusions. Ask yourself if errors in measurement or other factors may have affected your results. If so, redesign your experiment and try it again. This shows you're thinking like a scientist.

Conclusions are explanations that are based on evidence from observations. The main question to be answered in any experiment is: "Do my observations support my hypothesis?" Let's ask this question for a pendulum experiment in which your hypothesis was this: The period of a pendulum—the time it takes for one back-and-forth swing—depends on the length of the cord, but not on the weight of the bob, or the angle from which the bob is released.

Suppose your graphs show that the pendulum's period increases as its cord length increases, but that the period does not change greatly as bob weight or starting angle changes. In this case, your results support your hypothesis. If your results did not support your hypothesis, you would have to rethink your idea.

Making Inferences You will often make inferences to reach a conclusion or judgment based on your data. An **inference** is an explanation of information that is based on facts, but not direct observation. Imagine you are in a movie theater. When you leave, you see that the ground is wet. You conclude that it rained while you were in the theater. This conclusion is an example of an inference. You reached your conclusion based on the fact that the ground is wet, even though you did not observe it raining.

Scientific Models

Sometimes it is helpful to develop a model to explain what you found out in an experiment. **Scientific models**—which can be physical objects, detailed drawings, or equations—explain how a system works. For example, a cell model made out of clay, string, and beads can be used to show how chemicals flow in and out of the cell through small openings in the cell membrane. You can use a map to show the living and nonliving parts of a backyard ecosystem.

In the case of a pendulum experiment looking at the effect of cord length on period (the time it takes the bob to swing back and forth one time), a simplified model can be used to show the relationship that exists.

SEE ALSO
002 Scientific Inquiry
006 Forming a Hypothesis
077 Animal Cell
078 Plant Cell
129 Ecosystems

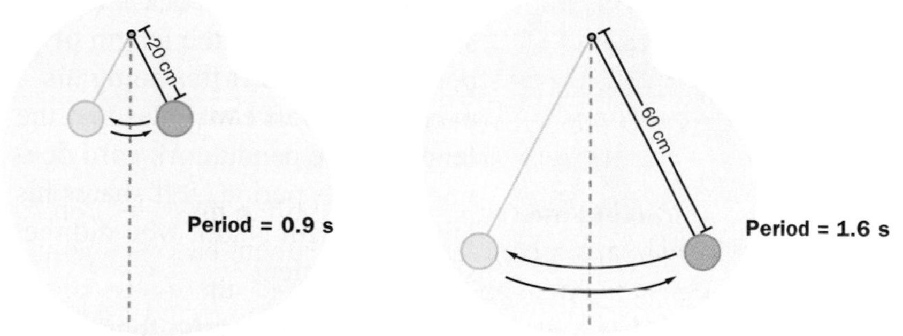

As cord length increases, so does period.

As scientists conduct more experiments, they gain new information about relationships that exist in nature. This information can be used to update and improve existing models. For example, hundreds of years ago, people believed that the sun revolved around Earth. But through careful observation and experimentation, scientists later discovered that Earth actually revolves around the sun, and not vice versa. Thus a new model of the solar system was developed.

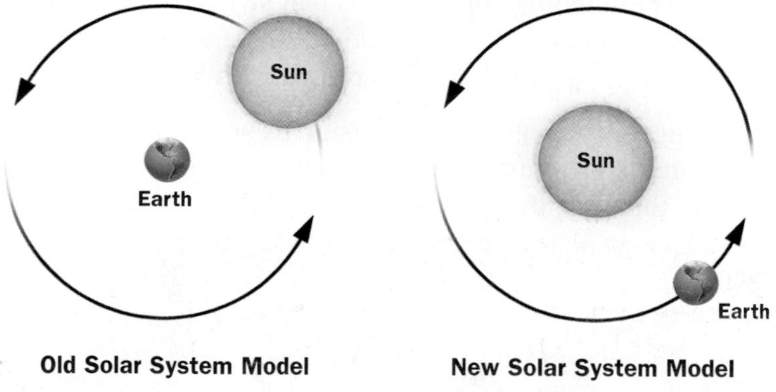

Communicating Results

014

Jeff finishes his lab report.

Both as you are doing an experiment and afterward, you should communicate your questions, ideas, and results with others. This allows them to evaluate and understand your experiment. Let's look at an example:

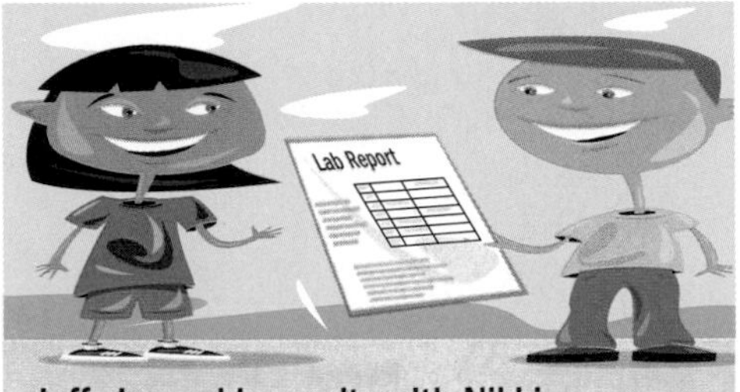

Jeff shares his results with Nikki.

Suppose Jeff does an experiment to test the following hypothesis: The period of a pendulum (the time it takes for one back-and-forth swing) depends on the length of the pendulum's cord. After doing his experiment, Jeff concludes that the length of the pendulum's cord does not affect its period. Jeff shares his lab report with Nikki, who did the same experiment.

Nikki compares her results to Jeff's.

Nikki tells Jeff that she found that swing time does depend on cord length. Nikki reads through Jeff's lab report. She checks his procedure, his data, and his analysis. She suspects that Jeff may have incorrectly measured his cord lengths, and discusses her findings with him.

Jeff does his experiment again and finds that swing time does depend on cord length. Jeff may not have found out there was a problem with his experiment if he hadn't shared his results with Nikki.

Communicating your results with others gives you a chance to see if any mistakes were made in experimental design, calculations, or analysis. In this way, the quality of everyone's work is improved. Sharing results may also give you new ideas for other topics to investigate.

Writing a Lab Report

015

It is important to share your ideas and findings in science with others. Communication allows you to learn from work done by others and gives others a chance to learn from your work. It may also provide you with new ideas for study. You can share your lab results by talking with other people. You can also write a report. A **lab report** is a written summary of how you did your work and the results you obtained. This report should be clear enough so whoever reads it can repeat your experiment.

Let's look at the parts of a lab report using an experiment with a pendulum as an example.

Purpose
The purpose describes what you were trying to find out in your experiment. A purpose may also include an explanation of why you did your experiment.

Title
The title briefly tells the reader your investigation topic.

Does a Pendulum's Period Depend Only On the Length of Its Cord?

Purpose: To determine what factors (cord length, bob weight, or starting angle) affect the period of a pendulum (the time it takes a pendulum to make one back-and-forth swing).

Hypothesis: The period of a pendulum (the time it takes for one back-and-forth swing) is affected by cord length, but not by bob weight or starting angle.

Hypothesis
State your hypothesis here. In your pendulum experiment, the hypothesis was that cord length affects the pendulum's period, while bob weight and starting angle do not. In a lab report, you should always tell the reader what hypothesis you were trying to test.

SEE ALSO
006 Forming a Hypothesis

MORE ▶

Materials and Equipment
This section lists all the materials needed for your experiment. It should also explain how the materials are put together. Drawings or sketches can also show the reader how materials are set up.

Materials and Equipment: wooden dowel, two chairs, masking tape, hook, string, scissors, clay (used for bobs), meter stick, spring scale, protractor, stopwatch, hammer, pliers

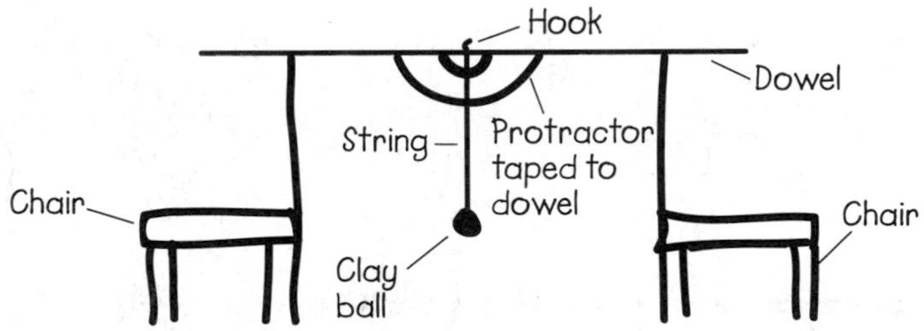

SEE ALSO
008 Designing an Experiment

Procedure:

1. The pendulum was built using the materials and setup shown in the Materials and Equipment section of this report.

2. Ten different lengths of cord were cut, from 10 cm to 100 cm. A meter stick was used to measure the cord lengths.

3. The 10 cm cord was attached to the ball of clay. The cord was set in motion using a starting angle of 25°. A stopwatch was used to measure the period of one swing and the time was recorded. This process was repeated three times. The average of the three swing times was then calculated.

4. Step 3 was repeated for each of the other cord lengths.

5. Bob weight was tested next...

Procedure
The procedure is a step-by-step description of how you carried out your experiment. The procedure should allow the reader to reproduce your results in a new experiment.

Data
All the data collected during the experiment is shown here. This allows the reader to determine if your data make sense.

Data:

Steps 3 and 4 of the procedure produced the following data:

Table 1: Period vs. Cord Length				
Cord Length (cm)	Trial 1 (s)	Trial 2 (s)	Trial 3 (s)	Average (s)
10	0.5	0.6	0.6	0.6
20	1.0	1.0	0.8	0.9

Analysis of Data
The analysis section explains how you analyze, or make sense of, your data. This section might include graphs and calculations. It should tell why you analyzed your data as you did.

Analysis of Data:

Data collected for period vs. cord length, bob weight, and starting angle were graphed.

The cord length graph is shown here:

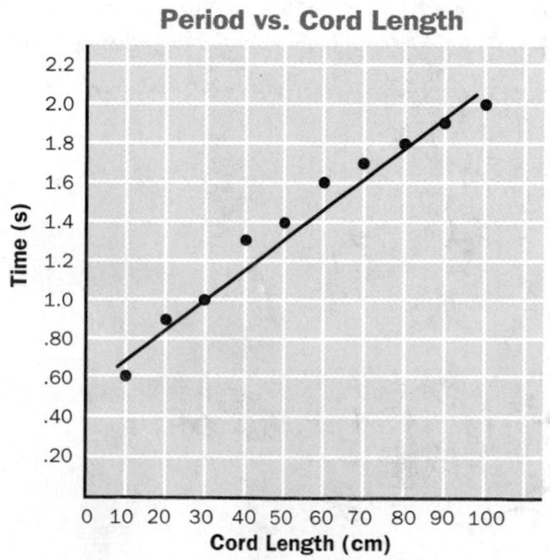

The bob weight graph is shown here:

SEE ALSO

009 Gathering Data
010 Recording Data
012 Analyzing Data
386 Organizing Data Tables
395 Making a Line Graph

MORE ▶

Conclusions Based on Data
Here you summarize what you learned from your experiment. Restate your hypothesis, tell if it was supported or not, and explain your conclusion.

Conclusions Based on Data:

The data collected (see graphs) showed that bob weight and starting angle did not have a significant effect on the period of the pendulum. The data also showed that cord length did have an effect on pendulum period. Thus, the data support this hypothesis: The period of a pendulum (the time it takes for one back-and-forth swing) is affected by cord length, but not by bob weight or starting angle.

The data also show...

SEE ALSO
013 Drawing Conclusions

Include any other conclusions you reach while doing your experiment. For example, if you find a mathematical equation that describes the motion of a pendulum, include that data. Include any observations that may be useful to someone reading your report.

Your conclusion section should also discuss limitations of your experiment—and all experiments have limitations. Here are some issues to consider.

SEE ALSO
006 Forming a Hypothesis

- Did you think of all the factors that could affect your results? For example, can you be sure that cord length was the only variable affecting the pendulum's period? How do you know the change in period was not also affected by air resistance or by friction in the pendulum's pivot?
- Do you have to redo your experiment in order to take these factors into account?

Always have some skepticism about your work. This helps you make sure you have not overlooked things that may affect your experimental results.

Be sure to discuss the limitations of your experiments with others. To acknowledge limitations is not a weakness—it is part of what science is all about.

Identifying Questions for Further Investigation

016

When you conduct an experiment, the observations you make may lead you to ask new questions. Suppose you do an experiment to see how temperature affects the rate of mold growth on bread. As you are doing your experiment, you accidentally spill water on one of the samples stored at room temperature. You observe that mold grows more rapidly on this sample than on the other samples kept at the same temperature. You wonder: Does moisture affect how much mold grows on bread? You decide to do an experiment to compare how adding different amounts of moisture to bread samples stored at room temperature affects the amount of mold that grows on the bread.

Here are some other mold growth questions you could investigate, either by doing research or new experiments.

- Does light affect the growth of bread mold? For example, if you store bread at room temperature in a dark place and in a well-lighted place, will the amount of mold that grows on the bread differ?
- Does mold grow more rapidly on home-made bread than on packaged bread that contains preservatives?

017

Designing Your Own Investigations

018 Sample Investigations

019 Students Doing Science

Here's a checklist you might follow as you do investigations in science.

Scientific Investigation Review

Step or Method	What It Includes
Ask a question	Ask a question you can answer by performing an experiment.
Do research	Learn as much as you can about the experiment topic. Research may be needed before and after you decide what to do in your experiment.
Form a hypothesis	Suggest an idea that can be tested by an experiment.
Design an experiment	Decide what steps you need to do to test your hypothesis. Figure out what equipment you need. Create a model if necessary. Identify the variables for your experiment.
Gather data	Record your observations. This may include making measurements, drawings, or tables.
Analyze data and draw conclusions	Examine data to see if the hypothesis is supported. Create a model that explains your results.
Communicate results	Share results with others and get feedback.
Identify questions for further investigation	Can your experiment be improved? Does it lead you to ask more questions?

SEE ALSO
004 Asking a Question
005 Doing Research
006 Forming a Hypothesis
008 Designing an Experiment
009 Gathering Data
012 Analyzing Data
013 Drawing Conclusions
014 Communicating Results
015 Writing a Lab Report
016 Identifying Questions for Further Investigation

Keep in mind that doing experiments is only one way to find answers to your questions about nature. Other kinds of investigations make use of only some of the steps included in the list. Let's look at an example.

While on a hike, you see an unusual bird. You want to know what kind of bird it is.

Ask a question. What kind of bird is that?

Gather data. Observe the bird and make a list of some of its features. You may estimate the bird's size, describe its color, and record what it eats or what sounds it makes.

Do research. Use a field guide to birds, an encyclopedia, or do Internet research to find information on different types of birds.

Analyze data and draw conclusions. Compare your notes to what you found during your research. Use this information to identify the bird.

Sample Investigations

018

Here are some ideas for investigations you can do. Notice that these examples follow the steps laid out in the Scientific Investigation Review.

Falling Objects

SEE ALSO
004 Asking a Question
005 Doing Research
006 Forming a Hypothesis
008 Designing an Experiment

SEE ALSO
276 Gravity

1. **Ask a question.** Most objects, when you let them go, fall to the ground. (Some, such as helium balloons, do not.) What causes objects to fall to the ground? If you think "gravity," you are correct. But here's a question you may wish to investigate further: Do heavy objects fall faster than light objects?
2. **Do research.** By doing some research, you find out that weight and mass are related, but different. For example, you have the same mass on Earth as you do on the moon because you are made up of the same amount of matter in both places. But you weigh more on Earth than you do on the moon because Earth's gravity is greater than the moon's gravity.
3. **Form a hypothesis.** Your research motivates you to make this hypothesis: The amount of time it takes an object to fall to the ground has nothing to do with the object's mass.
4. **Design an experiment.** How would you design an experiment to test this hypothesis? You might gather an assortment of objects, drop them from the same height, and see how long each takes to strike the ground.

Think more about this experiment. What factors might affect its results? Perhaps air may slow an object's fall. To control this variable, you can make sure all the objects you drop have the same shape. This way air resistance should affect all the objects the same way.

Try to think of all the factors that can affect your results. Then, find a way to control all the factors except mass—the variable you want to test.

Keyword: Scientific Inquiry
www.scilinks.org
Code: GSSM002

Earth-Moon-Sun Model

1. **Use scientific models.** Why are there moon phases? Here's a chance to see how useful models are. Perhaps you have learned that the moon orbits Earth, and Earth orbits the sun. That's a useful scientific model. But, like all scientific models, it is only approximately true. It is more accurate to say that the moon, Earth, sun, and all other objects in the solar system orbit a point called the center of mass of the solar system. Are you curious about what that means? Why not do some research to satisfy your curiosity?

   For now, let's discuss how to use a simple Earth-moon-sun model to investigate moon phases.

SEE ALSO
002 Scientific Inquiry
013 Drawing Conclusions

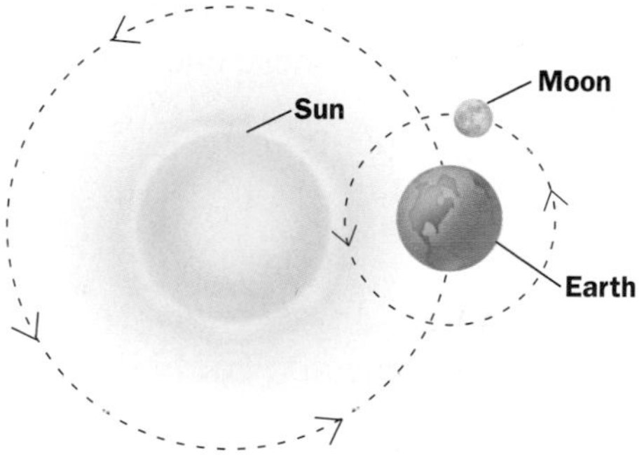

A **scientific model** is an idea used to help understand or explain some part of nature. This idea can be turned into a physical model. You can make a physical model of the Earth-moon-sun system by using a baseball to represent the moon, a basketball to represent Earth, and a lightbulb to represent the sun.

2. **Gather and analyze data.** Make the moon of your model go around the Earth, in the same way the real moon goes around Earth. Imagine someone is watching the moon from Earth. What patterns of light and dark would this person see? These are the moon phases predicted by your model. Test your model with observations of real moon phases: Do the predictions you made using your model match the real moon phases?

SEE ALSO
009 Gather Data
012 Analyzing Data

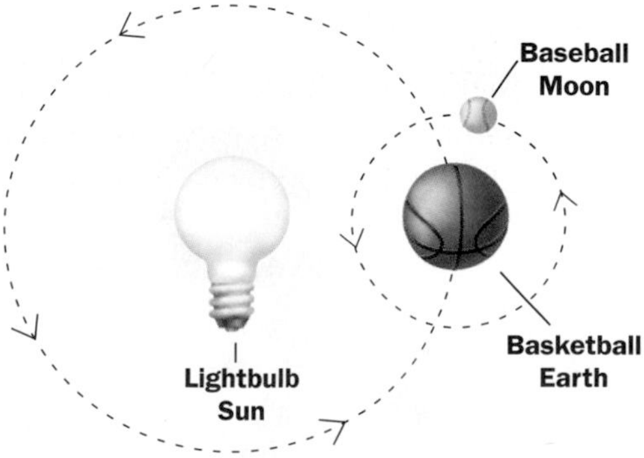

Students Doing Science

019

Students like you sometimes get the chance to work on special science projects. Following are descriptions of some science experiments done by students around the country as part of the Discovery Channel Young Scientist Challenge.™*

To learn more about the contest, go to www.sciserv.org and click on Discovery Channel Young Scientist Challenge.

Megan M. Jackson
St. Louis School, Waco, Texas
Project title: To Boldly Go Where No Ant Has Gone Before

One day Megan noticed that Red Harvester ants had invaded the livestock food in her family's barn. Megan wanted to find a way to stop the ants. Unfortunately, most commercial ant repellants contain toxic, or poisonous, chemicals. Megan knew that spraying these chemicals near livestock feed was a bad idea.

So Megan decided to try using naturally fragrant materials to head off the ants. She chose to experiment with bay leaves, mint, peppermint, and garlic. After testing each material, Megan concluded that mint and peppermint did the best job of turning the ants away.

Thomas R. Saldin
Tanque Verde Elementary School, Tucson, Arizona
Project title: What Is the Effect of Inflation Pressure on the Distance a Soccer Ball Can Be Kicked?

Thomas knows science doesn't stop at the classroom door. He used a scientific experiment to help improve his soccer game.

To find out what level of air pressure would allow a kicked soccer ball to travel the farthest, Thomas set up an experiment where air pressure was a variable, and kicking strength was held constant. How did he do that? By designing a kicking machine that kicked each ball with equal strength. What Thomas observed was that soccer balls traveled farther at a lower air pressure than at a higher air pressure.

*This contest is sponsored by Discovery Communications, Inc.

Kathleen E. Murray
Leawood Middle School, Leawood, Kansas
Project title: Heavy Metal Veggies

After learning that old, inner-city houses were often painted with lead-based paint, Kathleen wondered if vegetables grown in inner-city soil would also be contaminated with lead. Because even tiny amounts of lead can be poisonous to children, Kathleen worried about the kids eating food grown in these areas.

To find out if the vegetables would be contaminated, Kathleen designed an experiment in which she grew different vegetables in both clean soil and lead-contaminated soil. She then tested the vegetables for lead content. What she found shocked even members of the United States Food and Drug Administration: the peppers and tomatoes she grew in contaminated soil contained unsafe levels of lead. Kathleen concluded that vegetables should not be grown near houses that contain lead-based paints.

Prishantha C. Dunstan
St. Mary's School of Oak Ridge, Oak Ridge, Tennessee
Project title: Strength and Durability of Fibers

Prishantha wanted to see how natural fibers compared to synthetic fibers in terms of strength and ability to withstand exposure to the elements. So he designed an experiment to test several natural and synthetic fibers under a variety of conditions.

Prishantha added weights to each fiber to see how much they could hold before breaking. He then exposed each fiber to salt, bleach, acid, and flames to see which would break down and which would hold up.

After analyzing his data, Prishantha concluded that synthetic fibers, especially polyester, are stronger and more durable than natural fibers.

020

WORKING IN THE LAB

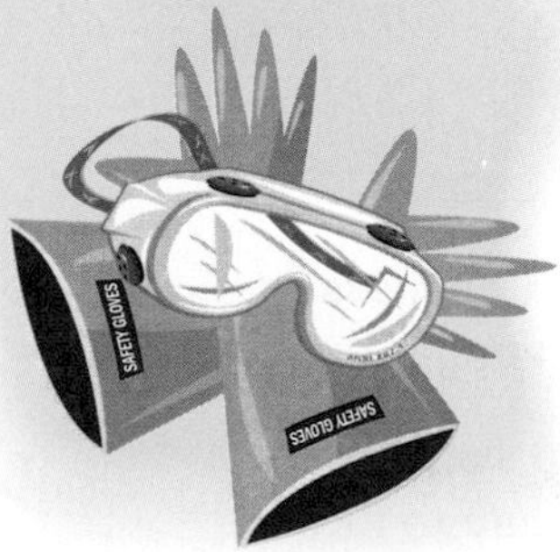

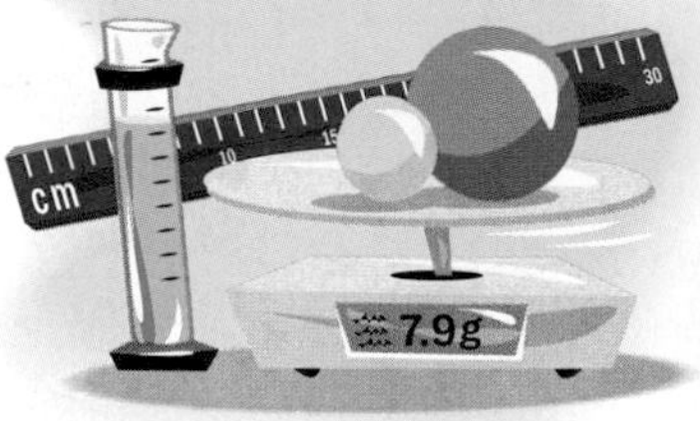

020

Tina and Juan's hours of experimenting pay off–the perfect s'more.

As you study science, you will likely do some activities and experiments. Any time you do a science activity, you are in a science laboratory. Your laboratory may be in a park or at a stream. It may be in your kitchen or in a special laboratory room. Wherever your laboratory is located, you will need to follow certain rules to make sure your experiments are safe and your results are reliable. You may also need to learn how to use some new kinds of equipment. The items in this part of the handbook will help you work safely in the lab as you brush up on your laboratory skills.

021

Laboratory Safety

Working in a laboratory can be an exciting way to learn. It can also be dangerous, but by following proper safety procedures and rules of behavior, you can reduce the chance of accidents.

SEE ALSO

436 Almanac, Laboratory Safety Contract

Rules for Working in the Laboratory

1. **NEVER** work in the laboratory unless an adult is present.
2. Follow all directions you are given.
3. **ONLY** do activities that are approved by the adult in charge.
4. If you don't understand any directions or how to use a piece of equipment, ask an adult to help you.
5. **NEVER** fool around in the lab.
6. **ONLY** use equipment in the way it is meant to be used.
7. Wear appropriate clothing.
8. Keep the laboratory clean and free of clutter.
9. Learn how to properly use laboratory equipment.
10. Learn what to do if you or someone else is hurt or if a piece of equipment is broken.

To learn more about working safely in the lab, review the items on the following pages.

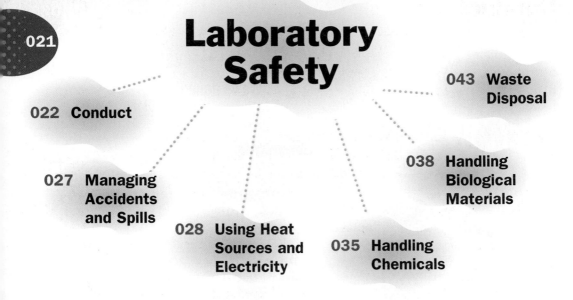

Conduct

Your conduct and attitude, or how you behave, is the most important part of laboratory safety. Whenever you are doing a science activity, **BE CAREFUL.** Even when using simple, everyday materials, you must follow safety guidelines.

Safe lab behavior includes activities such as walking instead of running in the lab. It also means that you never throw objects. You should not touch any equipment until you are told to do so by an adult. Never push others or play practical jokes in a laboratory. Such behavior may seem fun, but hurting yourself or someone else will quickly ruin your good time.

If you and your lab partner have trouble acting responsibly, ask to change lab partners. It is safer to work with someone you do not know than to work with a friend who wants to joke around.

One way to stay safe in a lab is to follow directions you are given. NEVER carry out any laboratory work unless you are given directions to do so. It is important to listen to or to read all directions before you begin any lab activity. Doing so prepares you for the activity. It also gives you a chance to ask questions if you don't understand something.

- **Oral Directions** are spoken. Listen to and follow all oral directions given to you by the adult in the lab. Ask for more information if you are not sure you understand.
- **Written Directions** are directions you must read and follow. These directions may be in a lab manual (or other book), on loose sheets of paper handed out to you, or on a chalkboard or overhead transparency.

"Lets see what happens when you add three drops of phenolphthalein to the vinegar in the beaker."
"I want to put the whole dropper in to see what happens, but that isn't safe."
vinegar
phenolp

023 Protective Clothing

Firefighters wear protective clothing—helmets, coats, and boots—for a reason. This clothing can protect them from injury. Working in a lab is not as dangerous as fighting a fire, but you should adopt the same attitude as firefighters and wear the right clothing.

Some types of protective clothing, such as safety goggles, aprons, and gloves, will help keep you safe and healthy in the lab. In addition to wearing protective clothing, you should also leave bulky jackets, coats, and backpacks in your locker or set them out of the way in the laboratory room. Do not place them on your lab table or chair, or on the floor under your lab table where you may trip on them.

Safety Goggles

Wearing **safety goggles** protects your eyes as you work in the lab. Some goggles protect your eyes from splashing chemicals. Others, such as those worn by factory workers, protect your eyes from flying objects. Some goggles are made to protect your eyes from both chemicals and flying objects. These goggles are stamped with the code ANSI Z87.1. The code may appear on the rim of the goggles or somewhere else. The goggles you wear in the lab should have this code.

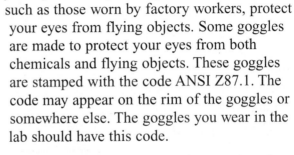

Always wear protective equipment when told to, no matter how you think it makes you look. You will look worse wearing bandages for weeks than wearing goggles or gloves for an hour.

You should wear safety goggles any time that a lab activity calls for them, even if someone else in the room is doing that activity. If you wear eyeglasses, wear the goggles over your eyeglasses. Make sure the goggles you use are clean and in good repair. The elastic band should be fresh and stretchy. Clean your goggles after each use to prevent the spread of germs. Cleaning your goggles with goggle sanitizer, alcohol wipes, or dish detergent will help keep you and others in the lab safe.

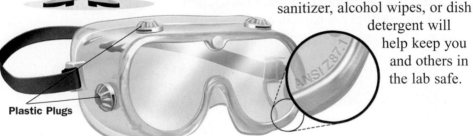

Lab Coats and Aprons

Wearing a lab coat or apron helps protect your body and your clothing from chemicals. A lab coat covers both the front and back of your body as well as your arms and the upper part of your legs. A lab apron covers only the front and sides of your body and the upper part of your legs.

SEE ALSO
038 Handling Biological Materials

Gloves

In the laboratory, you may need to wear gloves to protect your hands from chemicals and germs, such as harmful bacteria and molds. Latex and polyethylene gloves will protect you from germs and chemicals.

CAUTION! If you are allergic to latex, wear only non-latex gloves in the lab. Early symptoms of a latex allergy are red, swollen skin, a rash, and maybe itching. If you are allergic and you keep wearing latex, you might even have trouble breathing.

Tie back long hair. This will help keep your hair away from chemicals or open flames.
Wear splash-proof safety goggles. Goggles protect your eyes from chemicals that splash and from flying objects.
Wear a laboratory coat or apron. This protects your body and your clothing from spilled chemicals, stains, and burns.
Wear shoes that cover your feet completely. This is very important if you are working with chemicals, sharp objects, glassware, or equipment that is heavy.

Did You Know?

If your mouth itches after you eat bananas, chestnuts, or avocados, you may have a latex allergy. If you have these symptoms, don't wear latex gloves. It's better to be safe than sorry.

024 Keep Your Work Area Clean

Keep your work area free of things you do not need for the lab activity, such as papers, books, backpacks, and clothing. These items can be in your way as you work or they can fall onto the floor, where they can cause someone to trip and fall. Items in your work area may also be stained or ruined by spills. A messy work area can also cause a "confusion hazard" by making it difficult for you to find items you need to do your work.

Right way

Wrong way

025 No Food or Drinks in Lab

You should NEVER eat, drink, taste, touch, or smell anything while in a science lab, unless told to do so by an adult. Many chemicals could be **toxic,** or poisonous. When you work with chemicals, food and drinks can become contaminated with those chemicals. Any chewing gum in your mouth can become contaminated, even if you never take it out. Contaminated food or gum may make you sick. To avoid this problem, throw away all food (including gum, mints, and snacks) before you enter a lab area. For the same reason, never use lab equipment for cooking or as a plate or a cup. To further protect yourself, always wash your hands thoroughly before leaving the lab.

Another reason to keep food and drinks out of the lab is to prevent spilling these things onto lab equipment. Besides messing up your experiment, spills can be dangerous to people and equipment.

Washing Your Hands

026

At the end of any lab session, always wash your hands thoroughly. Washing your hands helps keep you healthy by removing germs or other materials from your skin that could make you sick.

Washing your hands thoroughly means more than wetting them with water. To correctly wash your hands, follow these steps.

Hand-Washing Instructions

1. Wet your hands with warm water. Then apply soap to your hands.
2. Rub your hands together to work the soap into a lather. Be sure to rub the soap onto all parts of your hand, including around and under your fingernails. Continue scrubbing your hands this way for at least 20 seconds.
3. Rinse your hands completely with warm water.
4. Use a fresh paper towel to dry your hands. Then use the same towel to shut off the water.
5. Throw the paper towel in the trash.

027 Managing Accidents and Spills

Many types of accidents can take place in a laboratory. Burns can result from contact with fire, heat sources, and spilled chemicals. Cuts can occur if you work with sharp objects. You can stay safe in the laboratory by preventing accidents, by being aware that accidents can occur, and by being prepared to take action if they do.

SEE ALSO
436 Almanac, Laboratory Safety Contract

Type of Accident	What to Do (after telling adult)
Water spill	Mop up spill immediately to avoid risk of slips and falls.
Chemical spill on floor	Keep others away. Ask adult what to do; exact procedure depends on chemical.
Broken glassware 	Ask adult whether you may clean it up. While wearing gloves and goggles, use a brush and dustpan to sweep up all pieces. Put all pieces in sturdy paper bag or cardboard box and close securely. Label the bag or box "Broken Glass." Follow adult's instructions for disposal.
Minor heat burn	Run cold water over burned skin for 5 minutes, or apply ice or cold pack to affected area.
Fire at work station	Tell the adult in charge and get away. DO NOT use water on an electrical fire. DO NOT try to "blow out" a fire by fanning it—you will only make the fire bigger.
Person on fire	Drop to floor and roll from side to side to smother flames. Roll person in fire blanket if available.

Safety equipment can help you respond to accidents in the lab. Find out where each piece of equipment is located in the lab you work in. It should be easy to see from every part of the lab.

Laboratory Safety Equipment

Fire Extinguisher

- Used to put out chemical fires, electrical fires, and gas and grease fires.
- Each extinguisher is marked with a code showing the kinds of fires it can be used for.

Fire Blanket

- Used to smother small fires on surfaces.
- Used to wrap person who is on fire.

Eye Wash Shower

- Used to rinse eyes if a chemical gets into them.
- Eyes should be rinsed with tepid water for at least 15 minutes according to instructions posted on equipment.

Shower

- Use if chemicals are spilled directly onto skin or if they seep through clothing onto skin.
- Remove contaminated clothing. Rinse yourself under running water for at least 15 minutes.
- Put on clean, uncontaminated clothing.

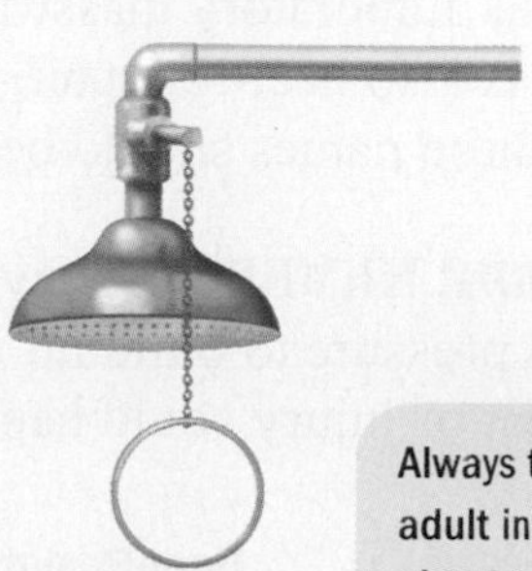

Always tell the adult in charge about accidents before you do anything else!

In addition to knowing where safety equipment is kept in the lab, you must also know how to get out of the lab quickly if there is an emergency such as a fire. Review the fire drill procedures with the adult in charge of the lab. Also know the location of the nearest phone in case you have to call for help. In many areas, the phone number for emergency help is **911**.

028 Using Heat Sources and Electricity

There are different ways to heat materials. No matter which method you use, there is one rule that always applies: NEVER leave a heat source unattended. A serious accident could be the result!

"Can you watch the beaker while I get the test tubes?"
"Sure, no problem."
H_2O

029 Heating a Container

Many experiments require you to heat materials in containers. Before using a container to heat a substance, you must make sure the container is heat-resistant. A heat-resistant container is one that does not melt or crack when used on a hot plate or over a flame. Some heat-resistant containers, like pots and pans used for cooking, are made of metal. A few kinds of lab equipment are made of heat-resistant porcelain. Laboratory glassware with the brand names **Pyrex**® and **Kimax**® is also heat-resistant. Only glassware clearly labeled with one of these names should be used for heating substances.

CAUTION! NEVER heat any substance in a closed container. Heat causes pressure to build up inside a closed container. A serious accident or injury could happen!

Heat-Resistant Containers

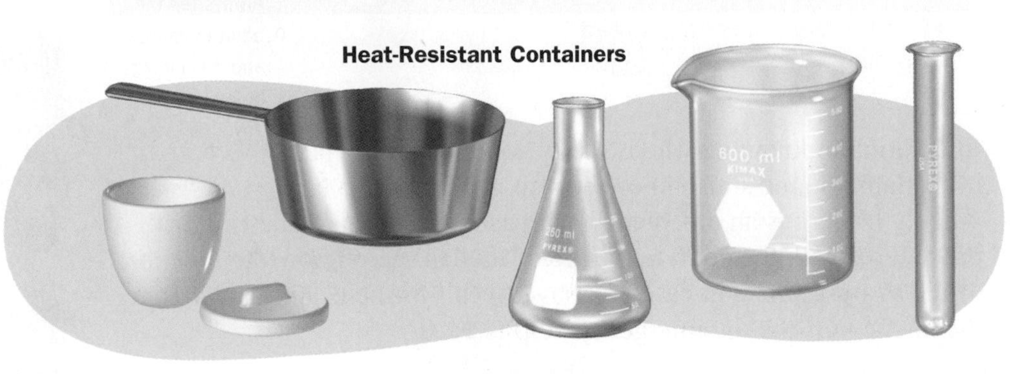

Handling Hot Containers

030

Your work in the lab may require you to handle hot containers. When doing this, you must protect your hands. You can use heat-resistant mitts to protect your hands when you handle hot containers. Heat-resistant mitts are like hot mitts at home, and you wear them like mittens. After putting a mitt onto each hand, you can safely grasp a hot object.

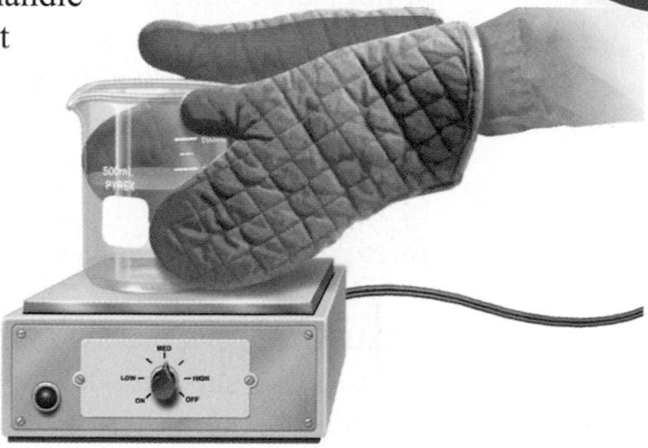

Another way to protect your hands is to use tongs. The tongs you will use are designed for picking up objects or small dishes. (Do not use them for picking up beakers or test tubes.) Tongs open and close like scissors. To use tongs, first open them wide enough to fit around the edge of the container you want to grasp. Then squeeze the tongs closed around the container. Once the tongs are closed firmly on the container, you can lift and move the container.

Hot and cold dishes look alike! Always assume that a beaker or dish is hot whenever anyone has been using a heat source.

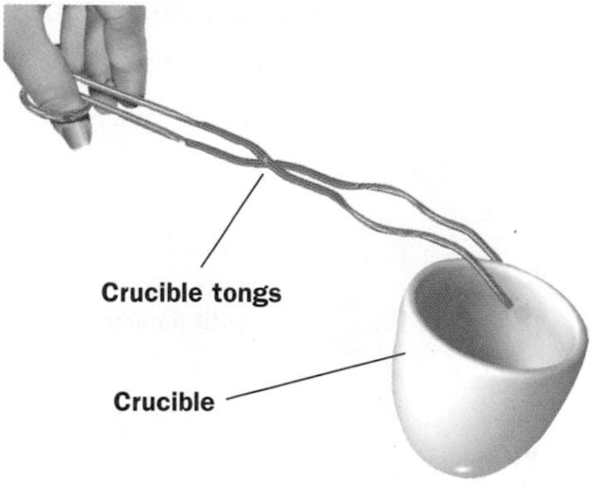
Crucible tongs
Crucible

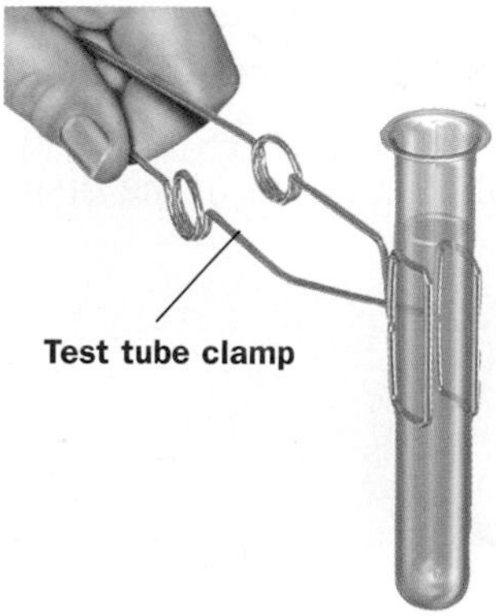
Test tube clamp

Hot test tubes are handled using test tube clamps. Using test tube clamps takes less practice than using tongs. Instead of opening and closing like scissors, test tube clamps work by squeezing the two sides of the clamp together. This makes the clamp open. After you fit the open clamp around the test tube, gently release your grip until the clamp closes securely around the test tube.

031

Using a Hot Plate

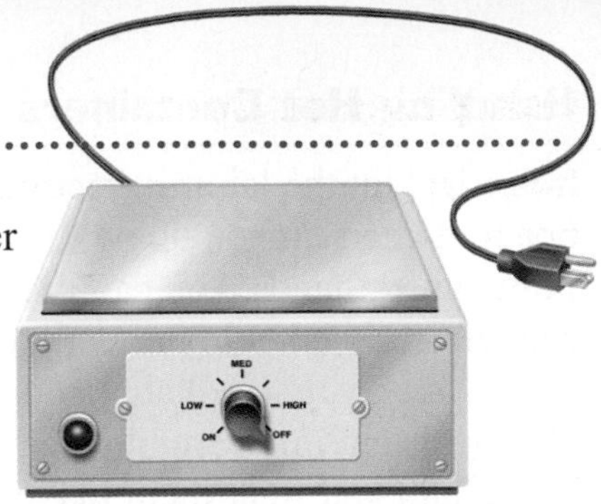

A hot plate is like a miniature electric stove. Like an electric stove, the burner of a hot plate is heated by electricity. A dial on the hot plate allows you to control its temperature. The container of water being heated is placed directly on the hot plate.

CAUTION! A hot plate is an electrical appliance. Before you use a hot plate, make sure the socket you plan to use is at least 6 feet from a source of water or is a ground-fault circuit interrupter (GFCI) outlet.

SEE ALSO
029 Heating a Container

Some substances cannot be heated safely if you put them directly on a heat source. One way to heat these substances is by using a hot water bath. In a hot water bath, the hot water heats other substances indirectly. A hot water bath heats more evenly than direct heating.

Suppose you need to heat two test tubes that contain liquids. To do this, heat a water-filled beaker on a hot plate. Then place the test tubes of liquid inside the beaker. The hot plate heats the water in the beaker. The hot water in the beaker heats the liquids in the test tubes.

Sometimes, you might use the steam from a hot-water bath to heat another substance. In this case, place the dish on top of a beaker containing water that is being heated. (Make sure that there is a space for steam to escape.) As the water in the beaker is heated, the rising steam heats the liquid in the dish.

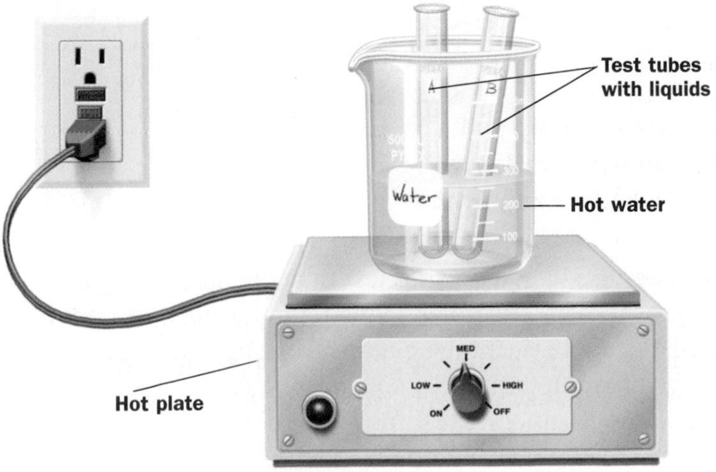

Using Electricity

In the laboratory, you might use equipment that has to be plugged into an electrical socket, or outlet. If you do not use electricity carefully, you can place yourself and others in danger. Here are some guidelines for how to use electrical equipment safely.

Check all electrical cords to make sure they are in good shape. The cord should not be cracked, worn, melted, or damaged in any way. NEVER use an appliance with a damaged cord or plug. A damaged cord can cause a short circuit, which can lead to a fire. If you find a damaged cord, tell the adult in charge immediately.

Before you use an electrical socket, be sure it is at least 6 feet from a source of water or that it is a **ground-fault circuit interrupter** (GFCI) outlet. Also, never place a grounded 3-prong plug into a 2-prong socket (such as those found on some extension cords).

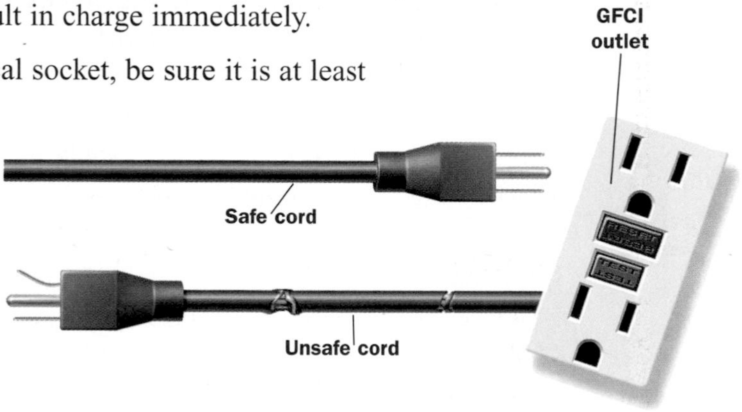

Before you put a plug into a socket, make sure the plug is not wet. Likewise, if a liquid is spilled on electrical equipment that is plugged in, stay away from the equipment. Ask an adult for help. The equipment must be unplugged before anyone goes near it, because of the risk of electric shock.

Be sure to place electrical wires in a safe position. Wires should not be easy to trip over. Nor should it be easy to accidentally pull a wire in a way that will knock over a piece of electrical equipment.

Always unplug an electrical appliance when you are done using it.

CAUTION! NEVER use water to put out an electrical fire, which is any fire that involves electrical equipment. Electrical fires must be put out with proper equipment, such as a carbon dioxide (CO_2) fire extinguisher. As with any type of fire, immediately ask an adult for help.

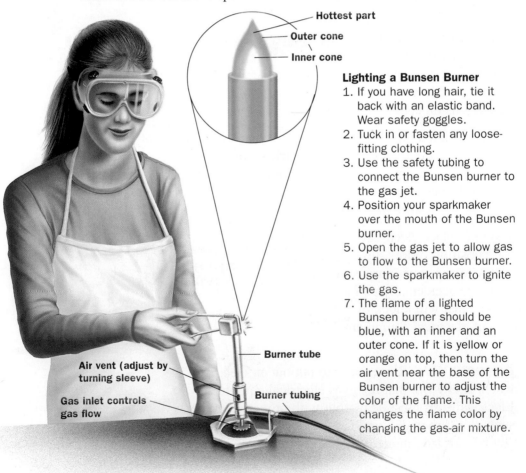

033 Using a Bunsen Burner

Unlike a hot plate, a **Bunsen burner** produces heat with an open flame. The Bunsen burner is a useful scientific tool. But it is a dangerous tool if you don't use it correctly.

The gas used for a Bunsen burner is either natural gas or bottled gas. It is not liquid gasoline, like you use in a car.

A Bunsen burner looks like a tower with a base. Air and gas flow into a Bunsen burner at its base. The gas comes in through a special safety tube you connect securely to the burner and to a gas jet. Air enters the Bunsen burner through holes near its base. The air and gas mixture then flows up through the tube of the Bunsen burner.

Lighting a Bunsen burner is not difficult. But to do it safely, you must follow certain steps in order.

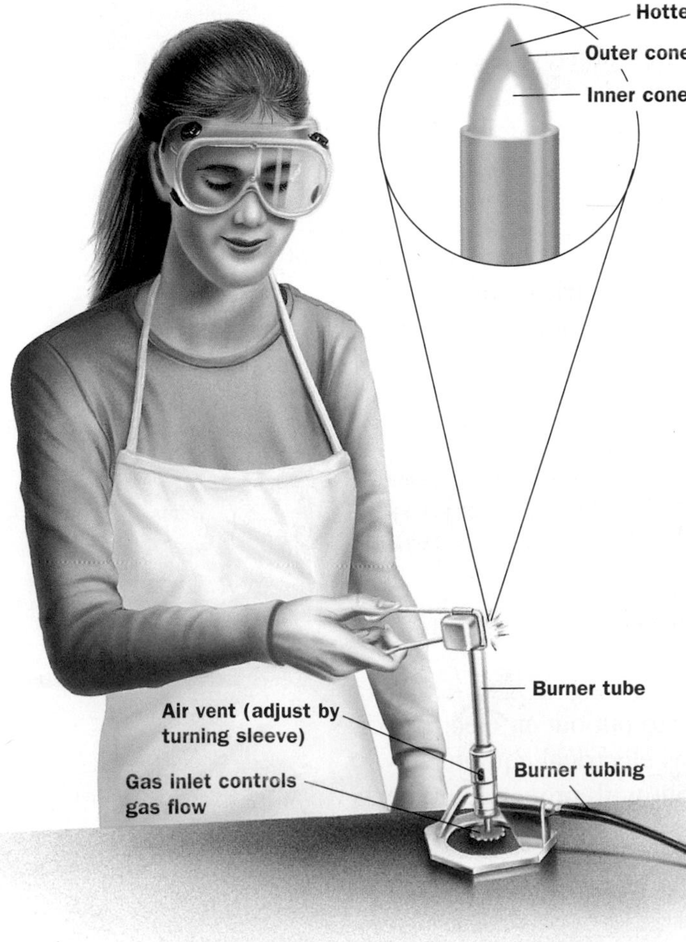

Lighting a Bunsen Burner

1. If you have long hair, tie it back with an elastic band. Wear safety goggles.
2. Tuck in or fasten any loose-fitting clothing.
3. Use the safety tubing to connect the Bunsen burner to the gas jet.
4. Position your sparkmaker over the mouth of the Bunsen burner.
5. Open the gas jet to allow gas to flow to the Bunsen burner.
6. Use the sparkmaker to ignite the gas.
7. The flame of a lighted Bunsen burner should be blue, with an inner and an outer cone. If it is yellow or orange on top, then turn the air vent near the base of the Bunsen burner to adjust the color of the flame. This changes the flame color by changing the gas-air mixture.

When you finish using a Bunsen burner, turn off the gas at the gas jet. Then close the gas valve at the bottom of the burner. If an accident occurs while Bunsen burners are in use, the adult in charge must shut off all gas in the room at the master shut-off control.

Ring Stands and Tripods

If you use a Bunsen burner, you also need a piece of equipment, such as a ring stand or a tripod stand, to hold the object that is being heated.

A ring stand is a vertical metal pole with a base. A metal ring is attached to a ring stand. On top of the ring goes a wire screen square or a triangle made of wire and clay. You place your beaker, or other container for heating, on top of the screen or triangle. The lit Bunsen burner is placed beneath the metal ring on the base of the ring stand.

Word Watch!

The word *tripod* is made up of the prefix *tri-*, meaning three, and the word *pod*, meaning leg or foot.

A tripod may also be used to hold objects that are being heated with a Bunsen burner. As with the ring stand, place a wire screen square or triangle on top of the tripod. Place the object being heated on a wire screen square or triangle on top of the ring. Place the lit Bunsen burner beneath the tripod.

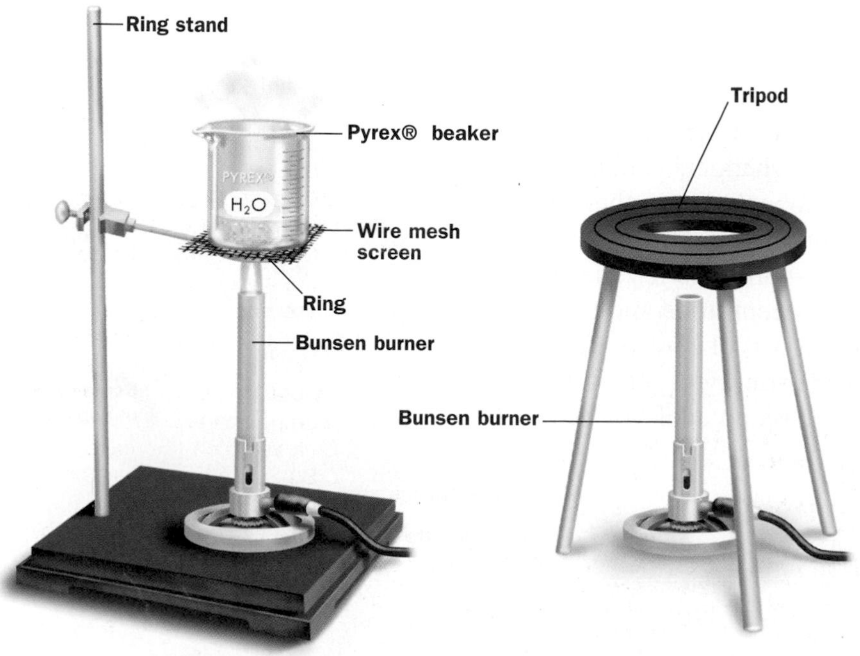

035 Handling Chemicals

You know that some chemicals you may use in the laboratory can be harmful. Handling, storing, and disposing of chemicals safely is important to your health.

036 Labels and Containers

Always label a container before adding a chemical to the container. Suppose you add a chemical to a container and then get called away. When you return, you do not remember what chemical is in the container. You cannot safely use a chemical if you don't know what it is. Many chemicals look alike, but have major differences. You can't know what a chemical is if its container is not correctly labeled.

NEVER assume that any clear, colorless liquid is water.

There are two main ways to label a container:

- Write directly on the container. Most glassware comes with a white section for labeling that you can write on in pencil. You can also write on other parts of the container with a wax pencil.
- Write your information on a piece of masking tape or a self-stick label. Place the tape or label on the container you are labeling.

Whatever way you label a container, be sure to remove the label when you are finished.

To be useful, a label must contain certain information. When you label a chemical container, be sure to include the chemical name, chemical formula, or common name—all three if you can—plus the concentration and today's date. If you don't know all of the information you need for your label, ask an adult for help.

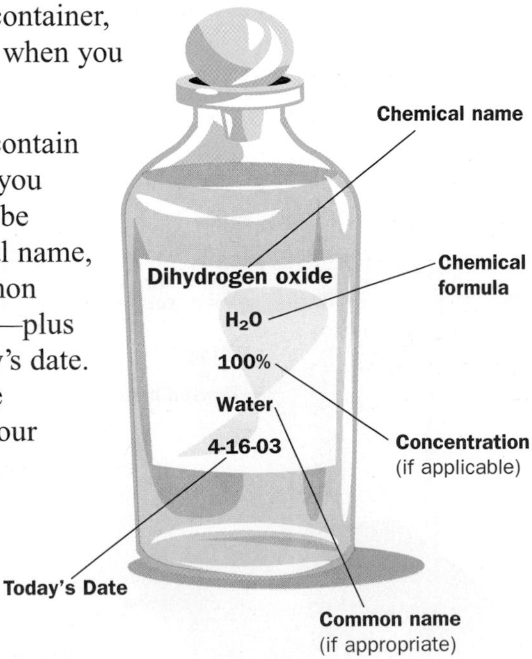

A used chemical may be contaminated with other chemicals—that is, it may have other chemicals in it. For this reason, you should never pour a chemical back into its original container. For the same reason, try not to take more of a chemical than you need from a container.

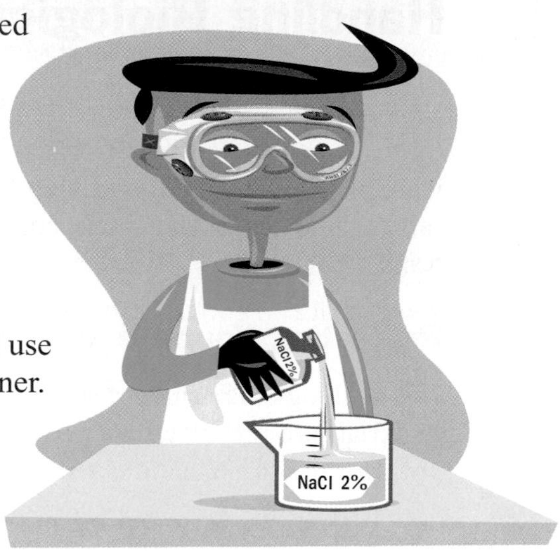

Many chemicals look alike. NEVER use a chemical from an unlabeled container. When a container is unlabeled, you cannot be sure what chemical it contains. If you are not sure what chemical you are handling, you cannot be sure how to safely handle that chemical.

Smelling Chemicals

Odor, or smell, is a characteristic you can observe. ONLY observe the odor of a chemical when an adult in charge tells you. NEVER observe the odor of a chemical by placing your nose to the chemical's container and inhaling. You could be hurt by the fumes. Instead, smell a chemical by wafting it. To **waft** a chemical, hold the container at least 15 cm away (6 inches away) and gently wave your hand over the open container. This motion allows the chemical vapors to come to you.

Wafting

Handling Biological Materials

038

Biology is the study of living things. When you learn about living things, you will handle **biological materials,** materials that are or were once alive. Handling living things or once-living materials raises some health and safety concerns, because such materials can transmit disease.

039 Protecting Yourself from Biological Specimens

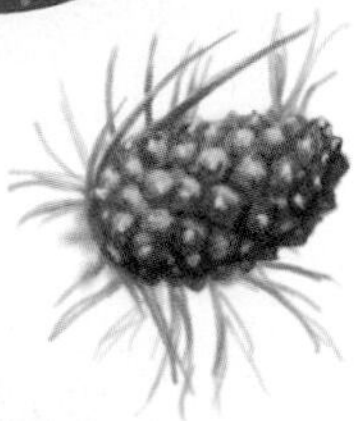

Living things may carry disease-causing germs. Some once-living materials are preserved with chemicals. Unpreserved specimens are not. In either case, handle a specimen carefully to protect yourself.

- Wear gloves to avoid infections that animals can carry.
- If you have allergies to animals or plants, let the adult in charge know. Do not handle animals or plants you are allergic to.
- Handle animals carefully to avoid injuries caused by bites and scratches.
- Wear gloves, laboratory coats or aprons, and goggles when handling preserved plant or animal specimens. This equipment can help prevent hazardous chemicals from getting on your skin or in your eyes.

040 Protecting Biological Specimens from Harm

Here are ways you can responsibly study and care for animals as you learn about them.

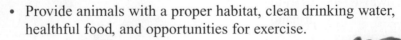

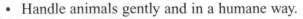

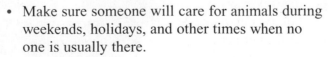

- The care you give an animal must be right for the species.
- Provide animals with a proper habitat, clean drinking water, healthful food, and opportunities for exercise.
- Handle animals gently and in a humane way.
- Make sure someone will care for animals during weekends, holidays, and other times when no one is usually there.
- All lab work and science projects involving animals should be done under the supervision of a qualified professional.

Source: National Science Teacher's Association

Using Sealed Containers 041

Biological materials such as mold and bacteria may cause you or others to become sick. For this reason, these materials might be kept in sealed containers. These containers include Petri dishes and self-sealing plastic bags. NEVER open a sealed container that contains biological materials unless you are told to do so by an adult. Instead, you can look at these materials through the containers they are kept in.

After you finish working with biological materials, dispose of them as instructed by an adult. You should never release living things into your local environment. Doing so can cause harm to local ecosystems. Small animals, such as snails and earthworms, should be kept in the lab. Plants must be kept or destroyed. Containers with bacteria or mold need to be treated with heat before disposal. This may be done in a microwave oven or special laboratory sanitizer.

Handling Sharp Instruments 042

Knives are useful for studying plant specimens and preparing slides of plant material. Always use sharp instruments carefully, and only use ones permitted in your school. Use the following information as a guide to using sharp instruments such as scissors, knives, and scalpels.

- Always hold sharp instruments by their handles, not by the sharp parts. You should also hold the handles of sharp objects with a firm grip.
- If you must pass a sharp object to another person, always offer the handle, not the blade. Do not hold the blade in your hand.
- NEVER run while holding a sharp instrument.
- Sit down to use a knife. Position yourself so you will not cut yourself. Be especially careful to protect your hands.
- Always cut in a direction away from your body and away from others.
- NEVER leave sharp objects lying around. Do not lay a sharp object on a chair—not even for a second.

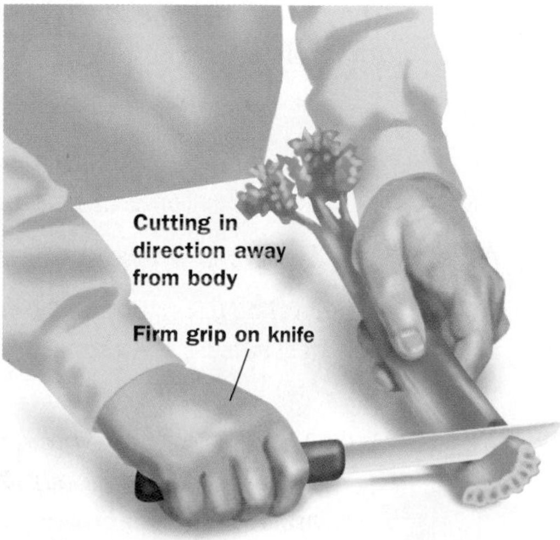

Waste Disposal

043

Some lab investigations produce **waste**, material that is of no use to you. **Hazardous wastes** are materials that can harm living things. They can also affect the environment in such a way that living things can be harmed. Non-hazardous wastes do not threaten living things directly but may cause other problems. All waste must be disposed of properly to avoid these and other hazards.

044

Non-hazardous Waste

Although they are not generally harmful, non-hazardous wastes must also be disposed of properly. Non-hazardous wastes include things such as paper, paper towels, sand, clay, soil, plaster of Paris, and pieces of wood. Many of these wastes (paper, paper towels) can be thrown in a waste can, unless they are contaminated with hazardous waste. Paper towels used to wipe up a chemical spill must be handled like that chemical. Soil, clay, sand, and plaster of Paris must be placed in a separate container—NEVER poured down a drain. Ask the adult in charge how to dispose of them.

Correct way to dispose of wastes.

Listen to the directions you are given for disposing of each kind of waste, because directions may be different for different materials.

Hazardous Waste

045

There are six types of hazardous wastes. You must dispose of hazardous wastes in a way that an adult tells you to. NEVER dispose of hazardous wastes in a way that can threaten living things—either directly by poisoning them, or indirectly by affecting the environment. For example, never pour chemicals that may be hazardous waste down the drain of a sink or into a toilet bowl. Dispose of hazardous wastes in an approved, labeled container given to you by an adult. People trained in waste disposal will then take care of safely disposing of the waste.

Symbol	Type of Hazardous Waste	Waste Examples
	**Flammable Waste**	Rubbing alcohol, solvents, some hand cleaners, gasoline
	**Corrosive Chemical Waste**	Acids, bases, discarded wet-cell batteries
	**Toxic Waste**	Poisonous chemicals, some cleaning products, some solutions
	**Biological/Medical**	Dead animals, mold, used Petri dishes, animal waste from cages, blood and blood contaminated materials, infectious lab wastes
	**Sharp Objects and Glassware**	Broken glass, objects with blades or points, or the blades themselves
	**Radioactive Waste**	Used x-ray equipment, medical or laboratory equipment contaminated with radiation

046

Glassware and Microscopes

SEE ALSO
028 Using Heat Sources and Electricity
053 Measurement

Some laboratory equipment is described in the Lab Safety portion of this book. Tools for measuring are described in the measurement section. Descriptions of glassware and microscopes, and instructions for using them, are covered here.

047

Glassware and Stoppers

In your lab work, you will use several kinds of glassware. Some kinds are used for many purposes, other kinds for just a few.

Beakers are containers used to hold liquids. Most have spouts for pouring. Beakers may be made of glass or plastic and are marked on the sides to show the amount of liquid they hold. A **flask** has an opening that is narrower than its base. A flask's narrow opening means that you can seal it with a stopper. Like beakers, flasks come in different sizes and are usually marked on the side. Markings on beakers and flasks are approximate. When you need to measure a precise quantity of a liquid, use a graduated cylinder.

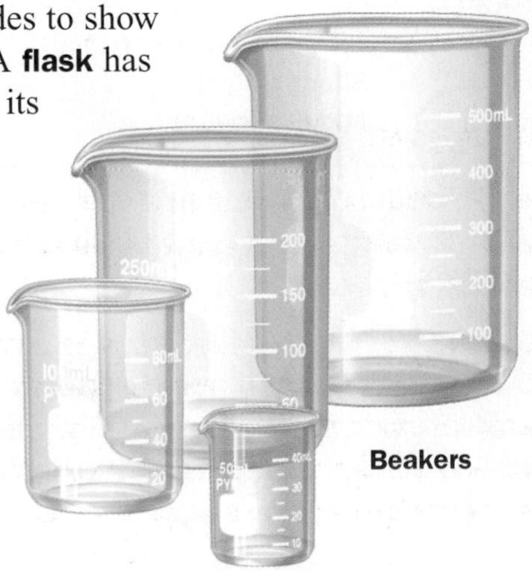

Beakers

SEE ALSO
060 Measuring Liquid Volume

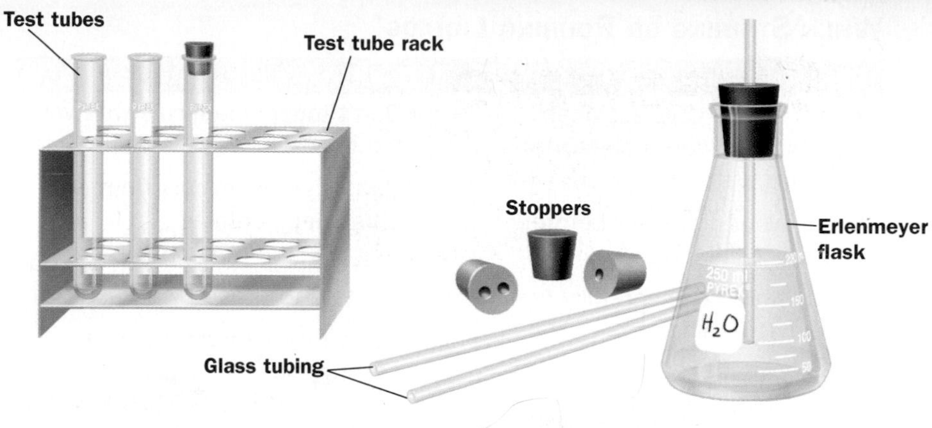

Test tubes are cylinders of glass closed at one end. Test tubes are used to hold small amounts of liquids. Test tube racks give you a place to put test tubes when you are not holding them.

Remember:

- Only use glassware labeled Pyrex® or Kimax® for heating.
- NEVER heat a closed container.

Stoppers are used to seal test tubes and flasks, and come in as many sizes as there are sizes of test tubes and flasks. Most laboratory stoppers are rubber. Some stoppers are solid; others have holes in them. The only time you may heat a container with a stopper in it is when the stopper has an open hole. Often the stopper hole will have a piece of glass tubing in it. The tubing lets you connect the flask or test tube to other pieces of equipment.

CAUTION! Ask the adult in charge to insert glass tubing into a stopper, bore a hole in a stopper, or cut and bend glass tubing. You may be injured if you try to do these things yourself.

Stirring and Pouring 048

Lab work often requires that you pour liquids from one container into another. You also may need to stir substances to make sure they are completely mixed.

A **stirring rod** is a glass rod that is used to stir a liquid. Stirring rods are fragile. Stir slowly and carefully. If you break a stirring rod, tell an adult immediately. Clean up the broken glass per the adult's instructions. Because stirring rods are so fragile, you may be asked to stir with a spoon, spatula, or wooden stirrer instead of a stirring rod.

MORE ▶

When Stirring or Pouring Liquids

Do	Don't
• Wear safety goggles, a lab apron, and gloves suited for working with chemicals. • Label your container before adding a liquid to it. • Pour slowly and carefully to avoid splashing. • Use a funnel to prevent splashing of chemicals. • Have paper towels available in case of spills.	• Don't touch chemicals with your hands. • Don't use chemicals from an unlabeled container. • Don't mix chemicals unless you are told to do so by an adult. • Don't use a thermometer as a stirring rod.

Use a **funnel** to make sure that a liquid goes into a container when you pour it. The wide part of the funnel catches the liquid. The tube-shaped stem of the funnel directs the liquid into the container. Filter paper is used with a funnel to remove solid particles from a liquid. As a mixture is poured into the filter paper, the liquid passes through the paper. Solids are trapped by the filter paper.

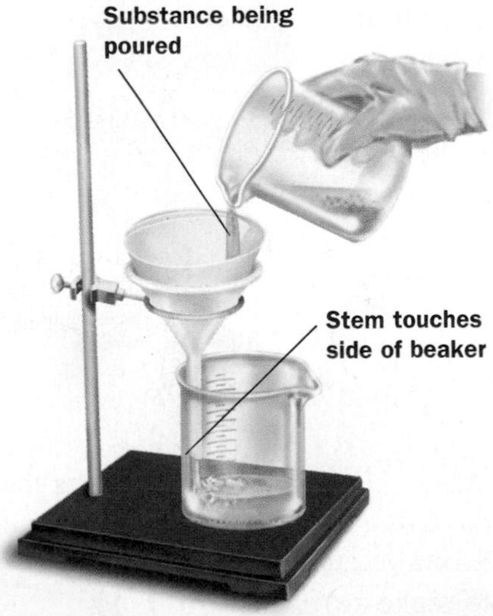

How to Use a Funnel

1. Place container on base of ring stand.
2. Set funnel into ring so stem is in container.
3. If you need filter paper, fold as shown and place in funnel.
4. Slowly pour liquid down side of funnel.

How to Fold Filter Paper

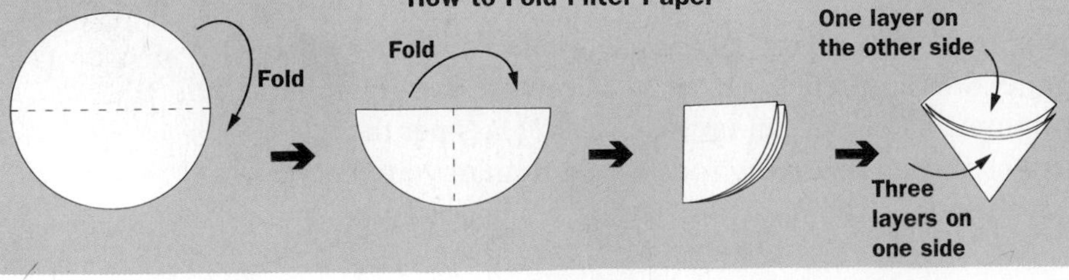

Microscopes and Slides

A **microscope** is an instrument that is used to magnify, or enlarge, the features of objects.

The microscope you are most likely to use is the compound microscope. A compound microscope has two or more lenses.

Word Watch!

The eyepiece is sometimes called the ocular lens. Ocular comes from the Latin word *oculus*, meaning eye.

PARTS OF A COMPOUND MICROSCOPE

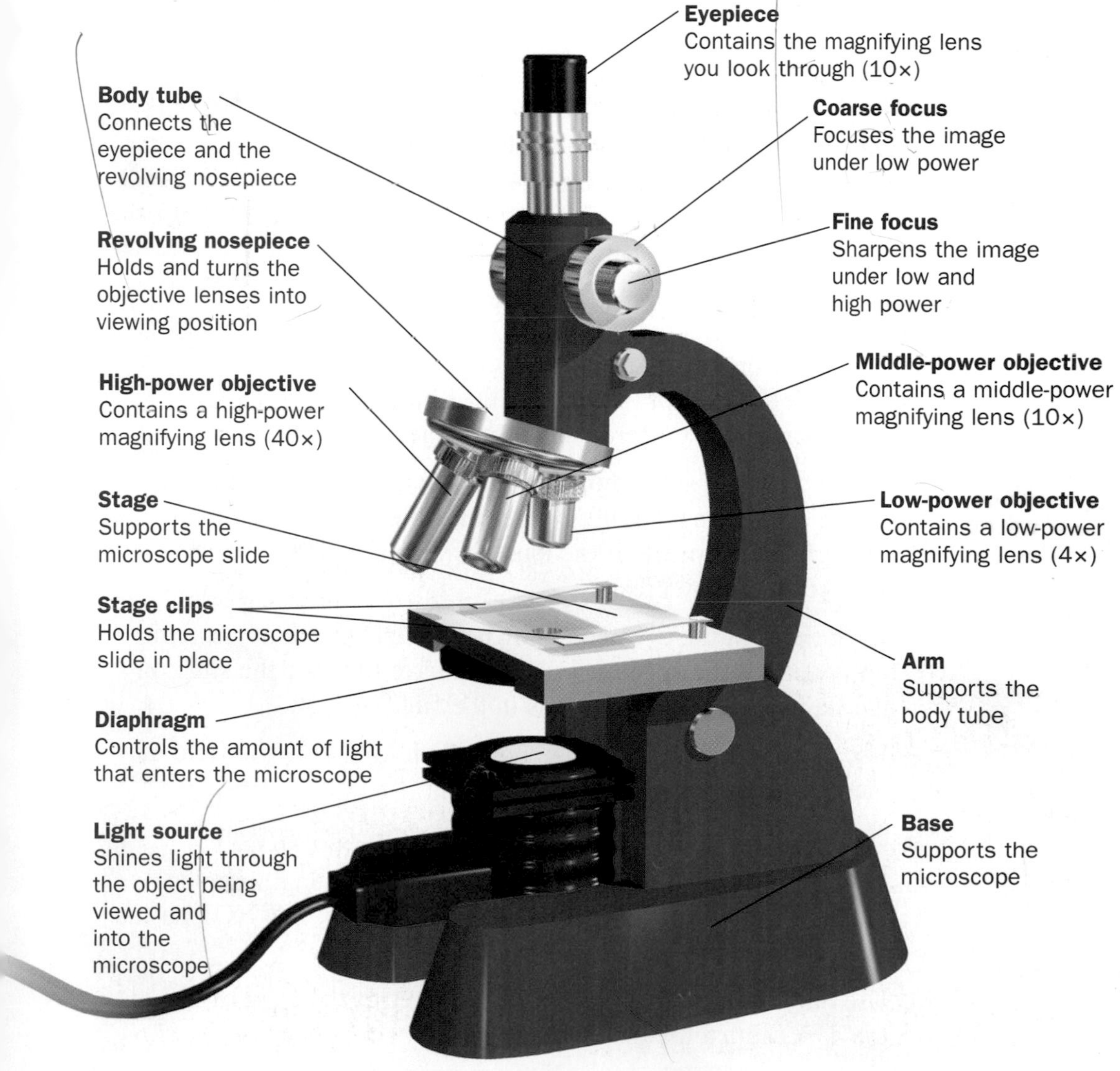

Eyepiece
Contains the magnifying lens you look through (10×)
Body tube
Connects the eyepiece and the revolving nosepiece
Coarse focus
Focuses the image under low power
Fine focus
Sharpens the image under low and high power
Revolving nosepiece
Holds and turns the objective lenses into viewing position
High-power objective
Contains a high-power magnifying lens (40×)
Middle-power objective
Contains a middle-power magnifying lens (10×)
Stage
Supports the microscope slide
Low-power objective
Contains a low-power magnifying lens (4×)
Stage clips
Holds the microscope slide in place
Arm
Supports the body tube
Diaphragm
Controls the amount of light that enters the microscope
Light source
Shines light through the object being viewed and into the microscope
Base
Supports the microscope

050 Using a Microscope

Following these steps will keep your microscope safe and will help you get the most out of using it.

1. Carry the microscope by holding the arm in one hand and the base in the other. Place the microscope on a table, away from the edge, with the arm facing you.
2. Turn the coarse focus to raise the body tube above the stage.
3. Rotate the revolving nosepiece until the low-power objective is in line with the body tube. Listen for a click as the objective locks into position.
4. Look through the eyepiece. The lighted area you see is the **field of view.** Adjust the light source and the diaphragm so that the field of view is bright.

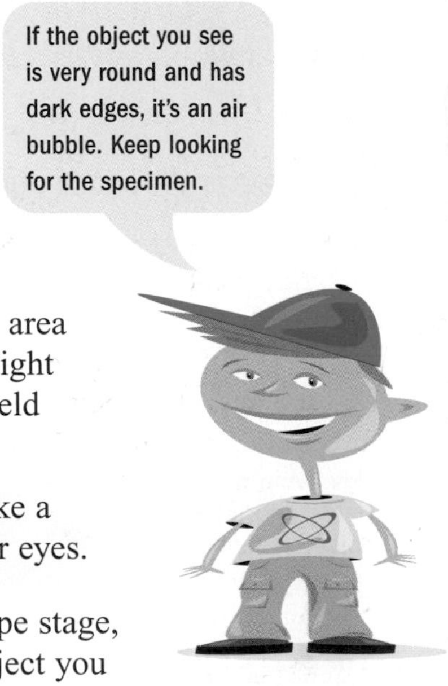

If the object you see is very round and has dark edges, it's an air bubble. Keep looking for the specimen.

CAUTION! DO NOT let direct sunlight strike a microscope mirror. You could damage your eyes.

5. Fasten a prepared slide to the microscope stage, using the stage clips. Make sure the object you are looking at is centered under the objective.
6. Watch from the side while you turn the coarse focus. Lower the objective lens. NEVER lower the objective while looking through the eyepiece. If the lens hits the slide, both the lens and the slide may break.
7. Look through the eyepiece. Slowly turn the coarse adjustment until you see the specimen. You may have to move the slide on the stage until the specimen is in the field of view.
8. Use the diaphragm to change how much light is in the field of view if necessary.
9. Sharpen the focus by gently turning the fine adjustment.
10. Watch from the side while you move the revolving nosepiece until the high-power objective clicks into place. DO NOT let the lens hit the slide.
11. Use only the fine focus under high power. If the field of view is too dark, adjust the diaphragm.

Magnification

Magnification is how large the image of an object appears, compared to the object's actual size. For example, if a microscope makes a daphnia look 40 times bigger than it really is, the microscope has a magnification of 40 (written as 40×). When you use a microscope, you can sketch, or draw, what you observe. Always label your sketches with the magnification you are using when you draw them.

You can figure out the magnification of a compound microscope by multiplying the magnifying power of the eyepiece lens by the magnifying power of the objective lens you use. These magnifying powers are marked on the eyepiece and objective lenses.

When you use the high-power objective, you will see much less of the specimen you are viewing. However, the parts you do see will have much more detail.

EXAMPLE: The eyepiece lens has a magnifying power of 10×. The objective lens being used has a magnifying power of 4×. To find the total magnification, multiply these two numbers:

eyepiece magnification	×	objective magnification	=	total magnification
10×	×	4×	=	40×

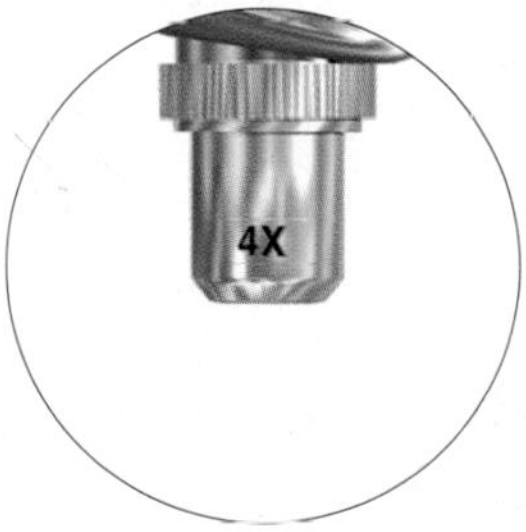

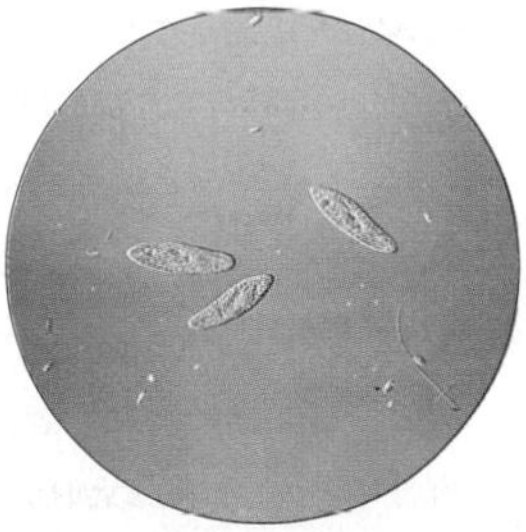

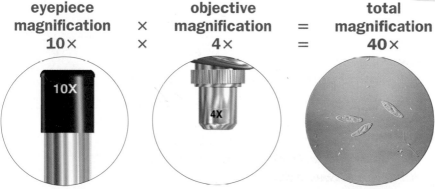

What is the magnification for the same microscope if you are using the middle-power objective and its magnifying power is 10×?

10×	×	10×	=	100×

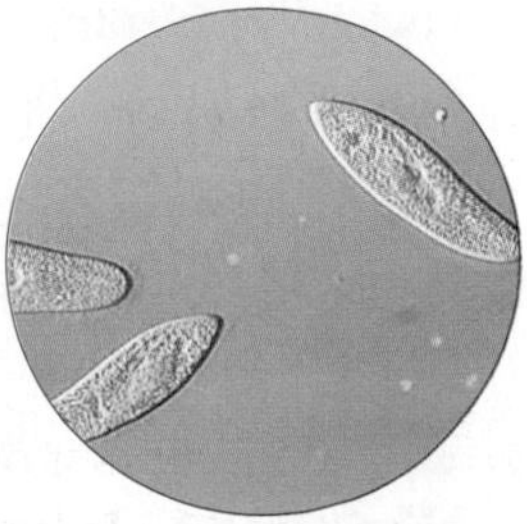

052 Microscope Slides

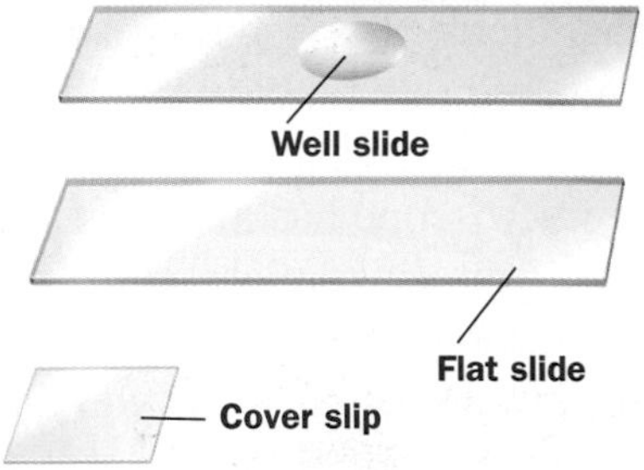

Before you can view objects with a compound microscope, they must be placed on a slide. Some slides are already prepared, and you just view them. Other slides, you need to prepare. If you prepare your own slide, you can use either a flat slide or a well slide. A flat slide is simply a flat piece of glass. A well slide, or depression slide, has a bowl-shaped well. The well is good for holding bulky specimens, such as an insect, that are too thick to fit under a cover slip on a flat slide. A cover slip is a small glass square that goes over a specimen on a slide.

When you prepare a slide, you must decide whether to use a wet mount or a dry mount. A **wet mount** is a slide that is prepared by adding a drop or two of water to the specimen. A **dry mount** is a slide that is prepared without adding water.

Preparing a Wet Mount Slide

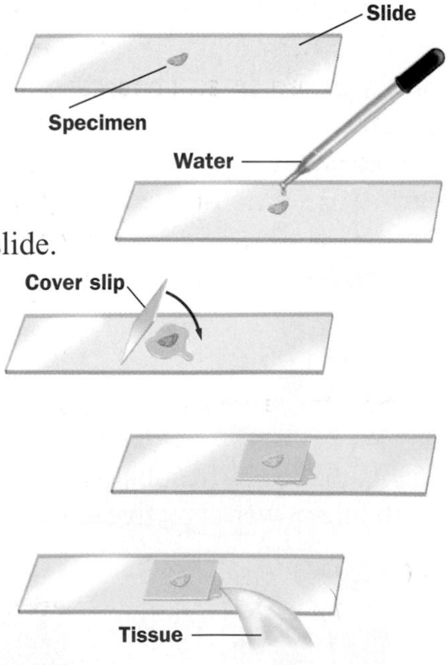

1. Wash and dry slide and cover slip.
2. Place slide on a flat surface.
3. Place specimen near center of slide.
4. Use dropper to add a drop or two of water to specimen.
5. Set edge of cover slip on slide, to one side of specimen.
6. Gently lower cover slip until it covers specimen.
7. Check for air bubbles under coverslip. Gently tap edge of slip to get them out.
8. Use tissue at edge of cover slip to sip up extra water.
9. Carefully place slide beneath stage clips. Then focus microscope to view specimen.
10. To prepare a dry mount slide, follow these same guidelines, but skip steps 4, 7, and 8.

053

Measurement

055 SI System of Measurement

058 Length and Distance

059 Volume

063 Mass

068 Finding Density

069 Time and Temperature

A **measurement** is a repeatable observation of a quantity that includes a number and a unit. An **estimate** is a reasonable guess at a quantity based on an observation. Bob, Shari, and Louisa observed the same pot, but their statements about what they saw differed. Bob gave his opinion about the time it took for the water to boil ("a long time"). Shari gave an estimate ("about a quarter hour"). Louisa measured the time ("18 minutes"): she used a measuring device (the clock) to give a number (18) and a unit (minutes) to a quantity (time).

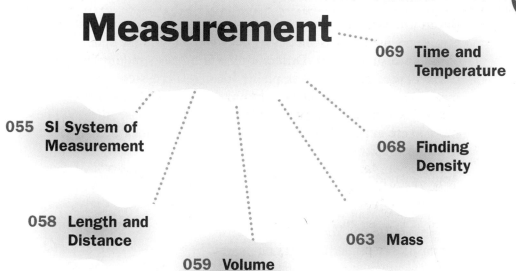

054 Precision and Accuracy

When you make measurements, you need to be concerned with two things: precision and accuracy. **Precision** refers to how detailed or exact a measurement is. Different measuring tasks require different levels of precision. For example, if you take a cross-country trip, you may describe the total distance to only the nearest 10 kilometers. However, if you give someone directions to your house, they will be more likely to get there if you use a more precise measurement such as tenths of a kilometer.

Accuracy refers to the correctness of a measurement. Have you ever set your watch 10 minutes fast? Your watch may give the time to the nearest second. Your watch is precise (to the nearest second), but it's not accurate. Unless you know how many minutes fast it is, and correct for that time difference, your watch will not be useful (unless you tend to run late, in which case setting it ahead is a good idea!).

055 SI System of Measurement

Scientists worldwide have agreed to use the **SI system** of measurement in their work. SI stands for "Système International," which is French for International System. Each type of measurement in SI has a base unit, such as the meter for distance or the second for time. Prefixes are added to the base unit to show multiples of that unit (such as the kilometer) or fractions of that unit (such as the centimeter). All multiples and fractions used in the SI system are powers of ten.

Word Watch!

The SI system is sometimes called the metric system. The metric system was invented about 200 years ago. SI is an updated version of it.

Science Alert!

When you make and record measurements, you must also record the units that describe the measurements. Otherwise, measurements have no meaning. Remember: A measurement is not just a number; it is a measure of a real quantity that needs a unit to describe it.

SI Base Units and Prefixes

056

The first table shows quantities you are likely to measure in your lab work, and the units that describe those quantities.

Quantity	Unit used in SI (symbol)*
length or distance	meter (m)
volume or capacity	liter (L)
mass	gram (g)
density	gram per cubic centimeter (g/cm^3)
time	second (s)
temperature	degrees Celsius (°C)

* Strictly speaking, some units are not SI, or are not base units. The distinction is not important to your lab work.

Prefixes are added to base units to create larger and smaller units for that quantity. There are as many SI units for a quantity as there are unit prefixes (such as centi-, kilo-). You will use some of these units more often than others.

The table below shows common prefixes used in SI measurements and the multiples or fractions of a unit they stand for. In your science work, you will use some of these units more often than others.

Prefix	Multiple or fraction of a unit	Symbol	Example
kilo- (KIH-loh)	1000	k	km
hecto- (HEK-toh)	100	h	hm
deka- (DEK-uh)	10	da	dam
(none)	1.0		m
deci- (DEH-sih)	0.1	d	dm
centi- (SEN-tih)	0.01	c	cm
milli- (MIH-lih)	0.001	m	mm
micro- (MYK-roh)	0.000001	μ (greek letter, pronounced "mew")	μm

SCI LINKS NSTA
Keyword: SI Units
www.scilinks.org
Code: GSSM056

057 Converting Between Units in SI

Suppose you want to change a measurement from one SI length unit to another, or from one mass unit to another, or any other quantity. How do you do it?

Here is an easy way to convert SI units. Because SI units are based on powers of 10, you can simply move the decimal point to convert the unit. To get the right answer doing it this way, you need to keep two questions in mind:

1. In which direction do you move the decimal point?
2. How many places do you move the decimal point?

To answer the first question, figure out whether you need to multiply or divide to convert the units.

- When the unit you are changing to is smaller, then there will be more of those units and the number will get larger. The number is getting larger, so you are multiplying. Move the decimal point to the right to multiply.
- When the unit you are changing to is larger, then there will be fewer of those units and the number will get smaller. The number is getting smaller, so you are dividing. Move the decimal point to the left to divide.

SEE ALSO
056 SI Base Units and Prefixes

To answer the second question, use the prefix chart to figure out how many steps there are between the unit you have and the unit you want. Then move the decimal point that number of steps. To do this, you will sometimes need to add zeros before or after the measurement.

EXAMPLE : Convert 12.2 meters into centimeters.

12.2 m = ? cm

1. There will be more centimeters than meters because centimeters are a smaller unit than meters. So the number will be getting bigger. If the number is getting bigger move the decimal place to the right (multiply).

2. There are 100 centimeters to 1 meter, so you multiply by 100. Multiplying by 100 means the decimal point moves 2 places to the right (2 steps on the prefix table). To do this, you may need to add zeroes.

12.2 m = 12.20 cm

The answer is 1220 cm.

Why does it work to move the decimal point? Here is the math behind it.

You know: 1 meter = 100 centimeters, or 1 m = 100 cm

Write: $12.2 \text{ m} = 12.2 \text{ m} \times \dfrac{100 \text{ cm}}{1 \text{ m}}$

Note: $\frac{100 \text{ cm}}{1 \text{ m}}$ is not the same as the fraction, $\frac{100}{1}$. The units make the difference. The numerical value of the fraction is one. In other words,

$$\frac{100 \text{ cm}}{1 \text{ m}} = 1$$

Because the fractions equal 1, you can put them into an equation without changing its value. So why insert them? The fractions are set up to make the same units cancel, and give you the unit you want.

Observe:

$12.2 \text{ m} \times \dfrac{100 \text{ cm}}{1 \text{ m}} = ? \text{ cm}$	Write equation including fractions to cancel units
$12.2 \cancel{\text{m}} \times \dfrac{100 \text{ cm}}{1 \cancel{\text{m}}} = ? \text{ cm}$	Cancel similar units
$= 12.2 \times 100 \text{ cm} = ? \text{ cm}$	Simplify the calculation
$= 1200 \text{ cm}$	Calculate the final answer

058 Length and Distance

The SI base unit for length and distance is the **meter** (m). The table gives the name of some other SI length units that are based on the meter. Each unit listed is equal to 1 meter multiplied by some power of 10, or 1 meter divided by some power of 10. The units of length you will use most often are the kilometer, the meter, the centimeter, and the millimeter.

SI Units of Length

Unit Name	Symbol	Multiple of a meter	Example
kilometer	km	1000	1 kilometer is equal to the length of about 10 soccer fields.
hectometer	hm	100	A 100-m dash could be called a hectometer dash!
dekameter	dam	10	The distance from the 0-yard line to the 11-yard line on a football field is about 1 dekameter.
meter	**m**	1	A meterstick is exactly 1 meter long.
decimeter	dm	0.1	The short side of a video cassette tape is about 1 dm.
centimeter	cm	0.01	Your little finger is about 1 cm wide.
millimeter	mm	0.001	A dime is about 1 mm in thickness.

You can use several different tools to measure length. One measuring tool for length is a metric ruler. It is marked in centimeters and millimeters. A metric ruler is useful for measuring lengths under one-half meter along a straight line.

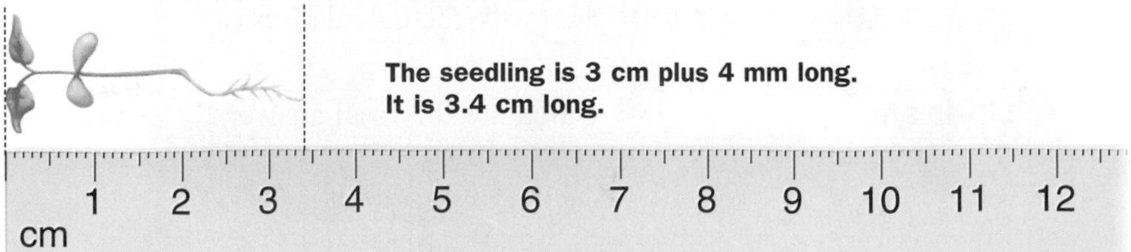

The seedling is 3 cm plus 4 mm long. It is 3.4 cm long.

The **meter stick** is similar to the metric ruler. "Meter stick" is a good name for this device, since it is a stick that is 1 meter long! Because it is longer than a metric ruler, a meter stick is used to measure greater distances along a straight line.

A ruler with a broken or worn edge does not give you a precise measurement. You can still use it—just start measuring at 1 cm, and then subtract 1 cm from your result to get the right measurement.

Suppose you want to measure the **circumference,** or distance around, a ball. What you need is a measuring tape. Wrap the tape around the ball, starting at the zero end of the tape. Read the measurement where the zero end overlaps the tape. When you use a measuring tape, make sure the tape lays flat. If it is folded or twisted along its length, you will not get a precise measurement.

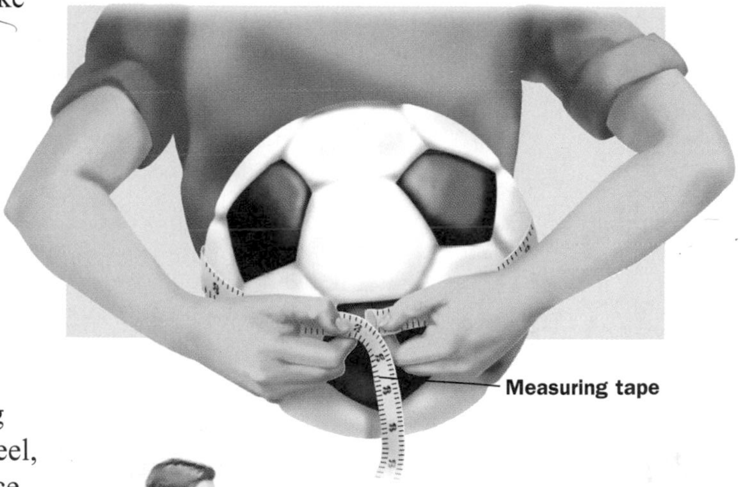

A **trundle wheel** or measuring wheel is used to measure distances of several meters or more, such as the length of a winding path. To use a trundle wheel, roll the wheel of the device along a surface and count the clicks you hear. Each click equals 1 meter.

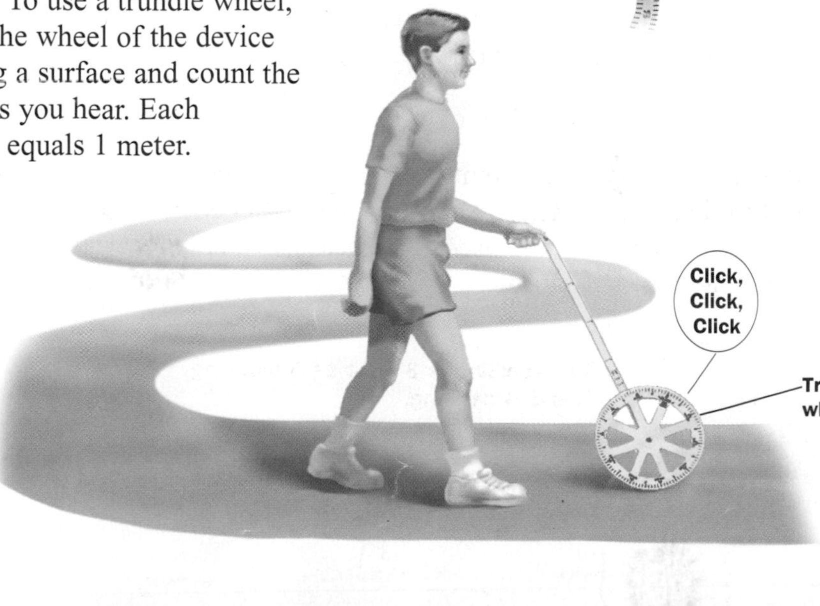

Volume

059

Volume is a quantity that describes an amount of space. When you measure volume, you want to know one of two things:

Either - How much space does an object take up?

Or - How much empty space is in a container?

The empty space in a container is also called **capacity.**

A unit of volume used with SI prefixes is the **liter** (L). The table lists volume units based on a liter. These units are often used to describe the volumes of liquids and gases.

SI Units of Volume

Unit Name	Symbol	Multiple of a liter	Example
kiloliter	kL	1000	You could fit 1 kiloliter of material in a box measuring 1 meter long, 1 meter high, and 1 meter wide.
hectoliter	hL	100	A hectoliter of water is enough to give 100 marathon runners a 1-liter bottle of water each.
dekaliter	daL	10	A dekaliter equals five 2-liter bottles of soda pop.
liter	**L**	1	Soda pop and water are sold in 1-liter and 2-liter bottles.
deciliter	dL	0.1	If you drink one-half pint of milk, then you drink a little more than 2 deciliters of milk.
centiliter	cL	0.01	A sip of water is about 1 centiliter (or 10 mL).
milliliter	mL	0.001	A teaspoon holds about 5 milliliters of a liquid.

Science Alert!

A milliliter (mL) is equal in value to 1 cm^3 and 1 cc. As a general rule, use mL to record liquid volumes (except in medicine where cc is commonly used). When recording the volume of a solid, use cm^3.

Measuring Liquid Volume

A **graduated cylinder** is a narrow container used to measure the volume of liquids. As its name suggests, the cylinder is graduated, or marked, with units of volume. Some graduated cylinders are made of glass. Others are made of clear or cloudy plastic.

Glass graduated cylinders have a plastic bumper, or cylinder guard, that slides up and down the cylinder. The bumper helps to keep the cylinder from breaking if it falls over. It should be about one-quarter the way down from the top of the cylinder to work.

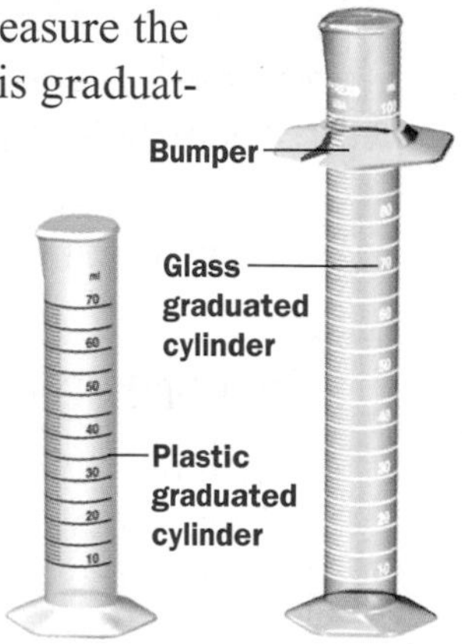

How to Use a Graduated Cylinder

1. Pour liquid into the graduated cylinder.
2. Move your head so the top of the liquid in the cylinder is at eye level.
3. Look for the meniscus (meh-NIHS-kus), the curved surface of the liquid. You may find it easier to see the meniscus if you hold a sheet of white paper behind the graduated cylinder.
4. A water meniscus is about as thick as a nickel. Read the volume at the bottom of the meniscus. If the volume is between two marks on the cylinder, estimate the volume.

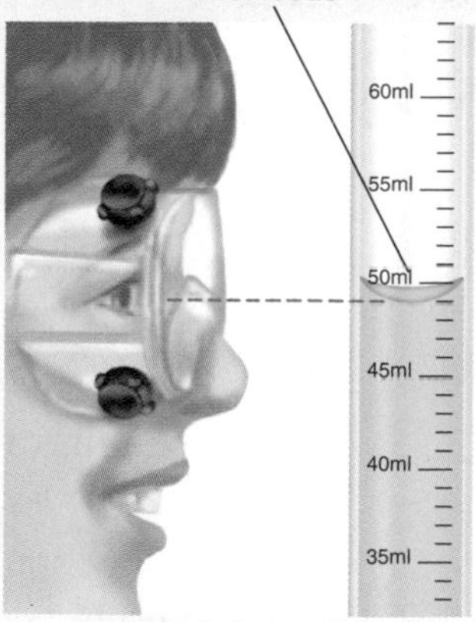

Volume = 49 mL

Did You Know?

A meniscus forms because the liquid sticks to the inside surface of the container. Liquids form a meniscus in glass graduated cylinders. No matter what liquid you have, always read a meniscus at the bottom of the curve.

061 Volume of Rectangular Solids

One way to describe volume is to take a length unit and make a cube. The cubic centimeter (cm^3 or cc) is a common unit of volume. It is usually used to measure the volume or capacity of a rectangular solid, or box. The volume of a box equals its length times its width times its height. In mathematical language, you can write:

Volume = length × width × height

$$V = l \times w \times h$$

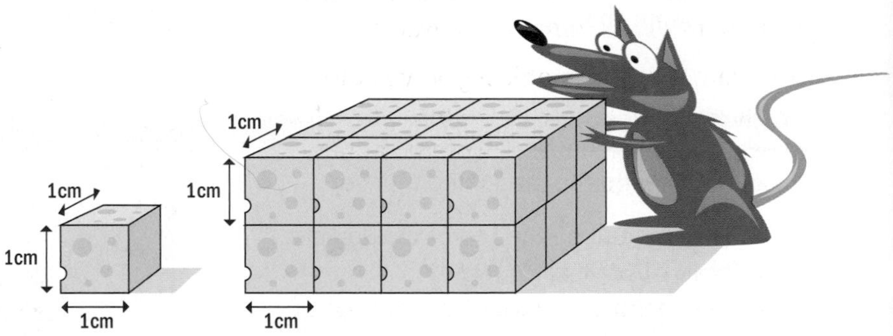

EXAMPLE: The length, width, and height of a stack of mini cheese cubes is 4 cm, 2 cm, and 3 cm, respectively. Volume = length × width × height, so to calculate its volume, multiply:

4 cm × 2 cm × 3 cm = 24 cubic centimeters

Notice that the volume unit makes sense, since cm × cm × cm = centimeter cubed, or a cubic centimeter (written as cm^3).

The stack of cheese cubes takes up 24 cubic centimeters of space. Each cube has a volume of 1 cubic centimeter.

Did You Know?

A liter equals exactly 1 cubic decimeter. A milliliter equals exactly 1 cubic centimeter.

Volume of Irregularly Shaped Solids

Have you ever noticed that when you get into a tub filled with water, the water level rises? The water rises as it is **displaced,** or pushed away. The volume of water pushed away is equal to the volume of the part of your body that is underwater.

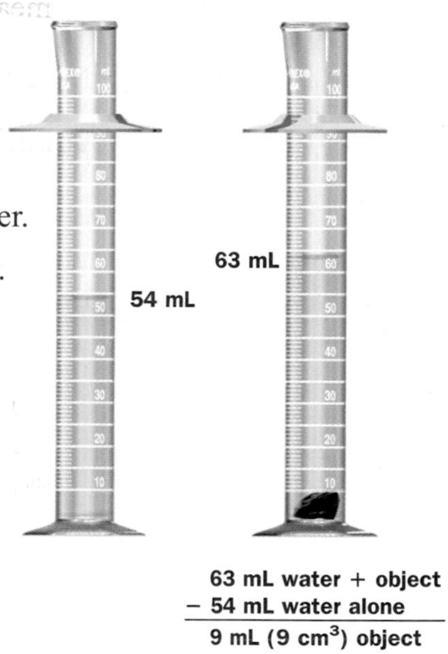

You can use the displacement of water to find the volume of an object that does not have a regular shape, if the object sinks in water.

1. Partly fill a graduated cylinder with water. Record the volume of the water.
2. Gently lower the object you want to measure into the water. This makes the water rise. Record the volume at the new water level.
3. Subtract your first volume reading (the volume of only the water) from your second volume reading (the volume of the water and the object).
4. The difference in volume is equal to the volume of the object you are measuring.

Some objects won't fit into a graduated cylinder. Water displacement can be used to find the volume of these solids, but the procedure differs a bit. Here's how you do it.

1. Fill an overflow can to the top with water. Let extra water run out of spout. (You can use a large beaker instead of an overflow can.)
2. Hold a beaker under the spout of the overflow can.
3. Place the object you want to measure into the overflow can. This will cause water to flow from the spout into the beaker.
4. Use a graduated cylinder to measure the amount of water collected in the beaker.

063

Mass

Mass is a measure of the amount of matter in a solid, liquid, or gas. All solids, liquids, and gases have mass because they are all made of matter (rather than energy). The mass of an object is measured using a laboratory balance. Mass is recorded in units such as kilograms (kg), grams, or milligrams. The **gram** (g) is the unit of mass that is used with SI prefixes to create other units.

SEE ALSO
250 Matter
276 Gravity

SI Units of Mass

Unit Name	Symbol	Multiple of a gram	Example
kilogram	kg	1000	One liter of water has a mass of 1 kilogram.
hectogram	hg	100	A baseball has a mass of about 1.5 hectograms.
dekagram	dag	10	Two U.S. state quarters have a mass of just over 1 dekagram.
gram	g	1	A one-dollar bill has a mass of about 1 gram.
decigram	dg	0.1	A paper clip has a mass of about 5 decigrams.
centigram	cg	0.01	A large black ant has a mass of about 1 centigram.
milligram	mg	0.001	One dekagram of table salt contains about 1 milligram of iodine.

064

Using a Triple-Beam Balance

One measuring device for mass is the **triple-beam balance.** On one side of the balance is a pan (or platform) on which you place the object to be measured. On the other side are three beams. Each beam has a sliding weight called a rider. The first beam might be marked in intervals of 10 grams; the second in 100 grams; and the third in tenths (0.1) of a gram up to 10 grams.

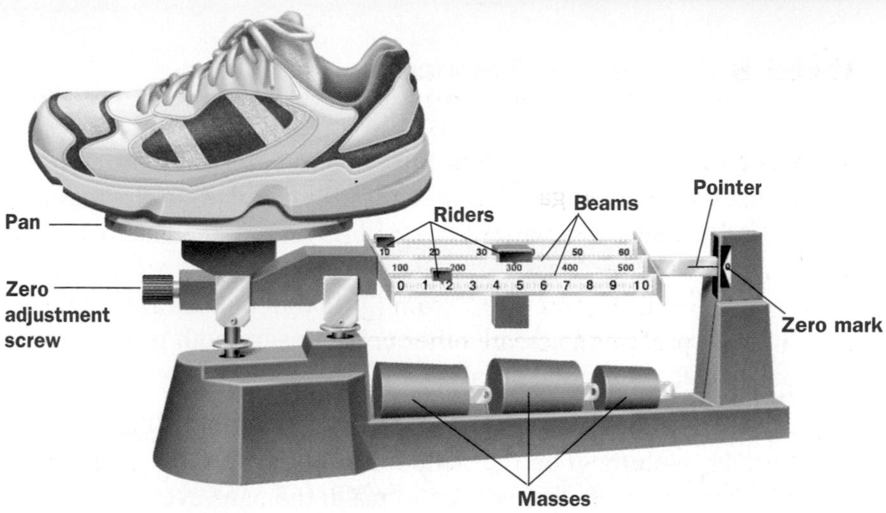

How to use a triple-beam balance:

1. Set the balance on a level surface. Make sure the pan of the balance is clean and empty.
2. Move all riders to zero. Make sure the two largest riders rest in the notches in the beams.
3. Look at the pointer to make sure it reads zero. If it does not, you must zero the balance. Turn the zero adjustment screw just a teeny bit at a time until the line on the pointer comes to rest at the zero mark on the scale. Turning the screw clockwise lowers the pointer; counterclockwise raises it.
4. Place the object you want to measure on the pan. This causes the pointer to rise.
5. Gently slide the largest rider across the beam until the pointer drops below the zero mark on the scale. When you reach this point, back the rider up one notch.
6. Slide the next-sized rider as you did in step 5. Again, back the rider up one notch when the pointer mark drops below the scale line.
7. Slide the smallest rider along its beam. If the rider causes the pointer to drop below the zero mark, begin sliding it in the opposite direction. Continue sliding the rider back and forth until the pointer lines up exactly with the zero mark on the scale.
8. Record the mass by adding the sum of the measures indicated by the riders. Make sure that you are adding all the same unit.
9. Remove your object from the balance. Slide all riders back to zero.

Always make sure that your measuring device reads zero when there is no mass on the pan. If it does not read zero, you must adjust the device to get an accurate measurement.

065 Using a Double-Pan Balance

Another measuring device for mass is a double-pan balance. A **double-pan balance** has a pan (or platform) on each side of the balance. This type of balance measures mass by comparing the mass of an object to standard known masses placed on the opposite pan.

Here's how you use a double-pan balance.

1. Set the balance on a level surface. Make sure both pans of the balance are clean and empty.
2. Make sure the pans are even and that the pointer, if there is one, lines up with the 0 on the scale mark. If they are not even, use the adjustment on the balance to make the pans even.
3. Place the object you wish to measure on one pan of the balance.
4. Add masses to the other pan of the balance until the pans are again even and the pointer lines up with the mark.
5. Add up the total mass, in grams, of all the masses. The total is equal to the mass of the object.

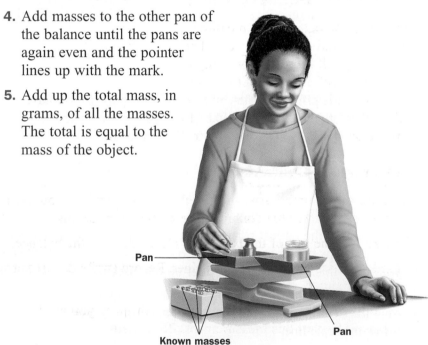

Science Alert!

Do not count the standard masses to find the total mass. Instead, add the gram values printed on each standard mass.

Electronic Balances

066

An **electronic balance** is quick and easy to use. The electronic balances that you are most likely to use give mass measurements to the nearest tenth of a gram (0.1 gram) in a digital display. To use an electronic balance, first make sure the pan is clean and dry and that the balance is resting on a flat, level surface. Check that the balance is turned on and that it reads 0.0 grams. (If it does not read 0.0, press the zero button.) Place the object you are measuring on the pan. Wait for the numbers to stop changing, and record the measurement shown on the display.

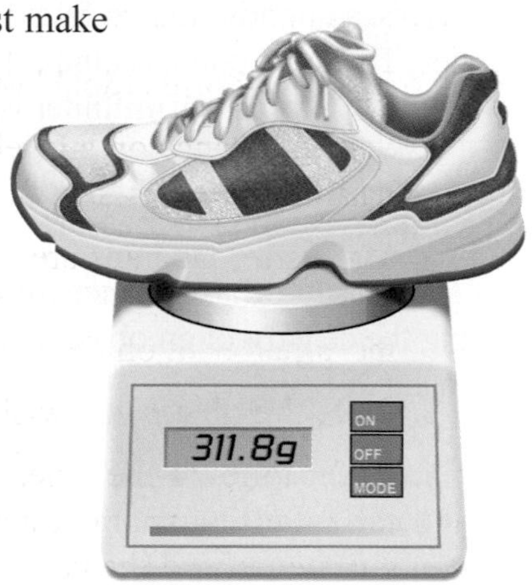

Every electronic balance can measure only up to a certain mass. This could be as low as one-half kilogram, or as high as 2 kilograms. Look for the limit of your balance, which is printed somewhere near the display. If you have an object that has a mass greater than the limit of your balance, use a triple-beam or double-pan balance to find its mass.

Correcting for Container

067

If you are measuring the mass of something in a container, you must correct for the mass of the container. Here's how you do this.

1. Make sure the pan of the balance is clean and zero the balance.
2. Find the mass of the empty container. Record (write down) this measurement. **5 grams**
3. Find the mass of the container plus the substance you want to measure. Record this measurement. **20 grams**
4. Subtract the mass of the empty container (your first measurement) from the mass of both the substance and the container (your second measurement). The difference is the mass of the substance.

20 g container + substance
− 5 g container
15 g substance

068 Finding Density

Density is a measurement of how much matter is packed into a certain volume of a substance. Density is an example of a derived quantity—that is, a quantity that is found by using measurements of other quantities. The most common unit of density is grams per cubic centimeter (g/cm^3). Grams per milliliter is also common. Note that $1\ cm^3 = 1\ mL$.

To find the density of an object, you must first measure its mass and its volume. Divide the mass by the volume to find the object's density.

The density of a substance mostly stays the same. For this reason, knowing the density of an object may give you a clue as to what the object is made of.

EXAMPLE: Pure 24-karat gold has a density of 19.3 g/cm^3. A person at a cart is selling "pure gold" bracelets for a very low price. You doubt they are pure gold and decide to check one out. The mass of the bracelet is 26.7 grams. Its volume is 3 cm^3. What is the bracelet's density? Is the bracelet pure gold?

$$\text{density} = \frac{\text{mass}}{\text{volume}} \quad \text{or} \quad d = \frac{m}{v}$$

$$\text{density} = \frac{26.7\ g}{3\ cm^3}$$

$$\text{density} = \frac{8.9\ g}{cm^3}$$

The bracelet is not pure gold.

Density is also useful for predicting if something will sink or float in water. Pure water has a density of 1 g/cm^3. Materials with a density greater than water sink in water. Gold, with a density of 19.3 g/cm^3, sinks in water. Materials with a density less than water float in water. Corn oil, with a density of only 0.93 g/cm^3, floats in water.

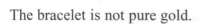

Science Alert!

The density of a material changes with temperature. Ice (0.9 g/cm^3), for example, is less dense than liquid water (1.0 g/cm^3). For most other materials, density increases as temperature decreases.

Time and Temperature

069

People ask about time and temperature many times a day. Usually, an estimated answer is enough for people to go about their day. In science, precise time and temperature readings are useful data for understanding events and conditions.

Measuring Time

070

There are two questions you can ask about time. (1) At what time did something happen? (2) How long did something last? Most of your time measurements in a lab will answer the second question. Outdoor observations, such as moonrise and moonset, may answer the first.

Use a timepiece that measures in seconds when you want to measure 1-minute intervals. Your results will be more precise.

The SI unit of time is the **second.** Other common units of time are the minute, hour, day, and year. Some measurements are made in fractions of a second (milliseconds, microseconds, or nanoseconds). Your measurements probably will not need to be that precise.

Clocks show time in different ways. Dial clocks have hour, minute, or second hands that rotate around a common center. Digital clocks show time as numbers (digits).

You can use a wall clock with a second hand for some science investigations. For example, imagine you need to take a temperature reading of a substance every 60 seconds. Note the position of the second hand when you take your first measurement. When the second hand reaches that point again, take the next reading. Repeat this process until you have all your readings.

Suppose you want to find out how long it takes a ball to roll down a ramp. A stopwatch is just what you need. Some wristwatches have stopwatches built in, or you may use a separate stopwatch. At the moment the ball is released press the "start" button on the stopwatch. At the moment the ball reaches the bottom of the ramp, stop the watch by pressing the stop button (the same button may be used to start and stop the watch).

Stopwatch

071 Temperature

You experience temperature differences as the feeling of hot and cold, but this is not a repeatable way to describe temperature. Try holding your left hand in warm water and your right hand in cold water for a few minutes. Then place both hands in room temperature water. To your left hand, the water will feel cold; to your right hand, the water may feel warm! In your lab work, you need a more precise way of comparing temperature. You need a thermometer marked with a temperature scale.

There are two commonly used temperature scales: the Celsius scale and the Fahrenheit scale. Scientists generally measure temperature in **degrees Celsius** (°C).

SEE ALSO
302 Temperature versus Heat

The Celsius temperature scale is used in science labs, but you will find Fahrenheit temperature readings used in many weather reports. Here are some useful equations that let you convert between the Celsius and Fahrenheit temperature scales:

$$°F = \frac{9}{5}(°C) + 32$$

$$°C = \frac{5}{9}(°F - 32)$$

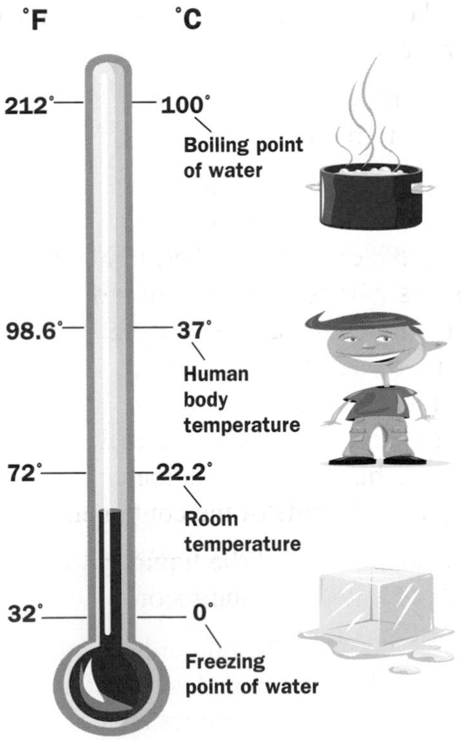

Did You Know?

The SI unit of temperature is the **Kelvin.** Kelvin equals a Celsius reading minus 273. Kelvins are used in chemistry and physics starting at the high school level.

Taking Temperature Readings

Temperature is measured with a thermometer. A liquid **thermometer** is a clear tube filled with a liquid that expands when heated and contracts when cooled. When you place the liquid thermometer in contact with a substance or object, the thermometer reaches the same temperature as the substance. The level of the liquid in the thermometer shows the temperature of its liquid, which is also the temperature of the object or substance.

CAUTION! Use only a non-mercury thermometer in your science work. Mercury is a toxic chemical. If the liquid is red or blue, the thermometer is okay. If the liquid is silver, put the thermometer away.

Here's how you use a thermometer to measure the temperature of a substance.

1. Stir the substance using a stirring rod or spoon.
2. Carefully lower the bulb end of the thermometer into the container. Hold the thermometer so its bulb is near the center of the liquid you are measuring (not resting on the bottom; temperature can vary at the sides and bottom). Be careful not to bump the thermometer against the side of the container.
3. Read the level of the liquid in the thermometer and record the temperature.

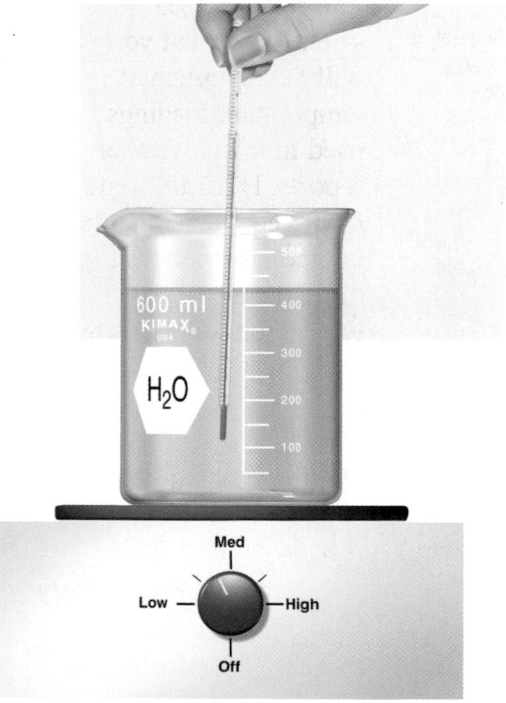

Did You Know?

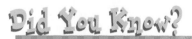

Some thermometers measure temperature using a coil made of two different metals, instead of a liquid.

LIFE SCIENCE

074 **Structure of Life**

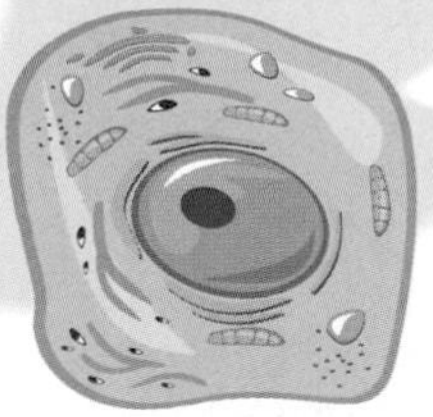

083 **Human Biology**

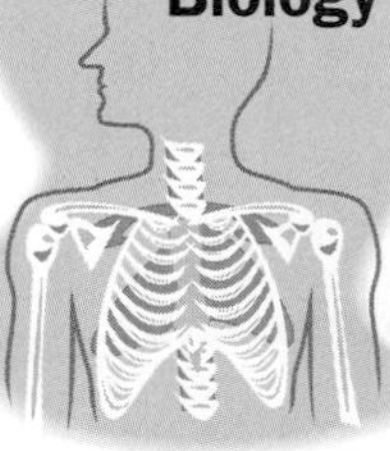

103 **Physiology and Behavior**

112 **Genes and Heredity**

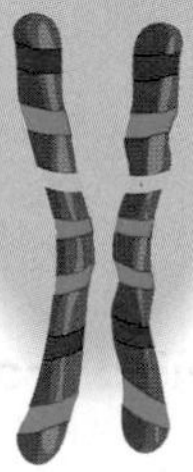

124 **Change and Diversity of Life**

129 **Ecosystems**

150 **Classification**

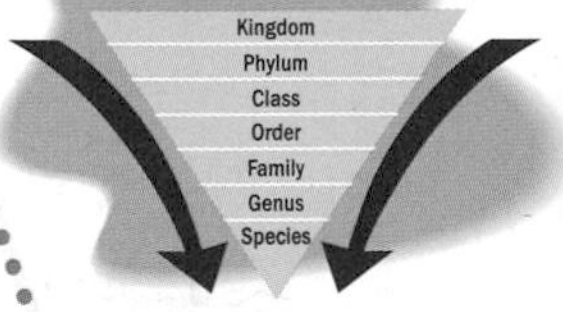

What do mold, seaweed, fleas, trees, and snakes have in common? All are living things. The branch of science that deals with the study of living things is called **biology,** or life science. Biologists are interested in similarities and differences among living things. They're also interested in how organisms interact with their environment, and how the human body works.

074

Structure of Life

There is exciting variety in nature. Much of this variety is found among Earth's **organisms,** or living things. Each organism has unique structures suited to its particular way of life. Still, all living things have some features in common.

075

Structure and Function

All living things have structures specially designed to do certain jobs. The eyes of a fly, for example, are made up of several smaller units that allow the fly to see many different images of the same object at once. This helps the fly detect very slight movements, and so escape danger. Many birds, on the other hand, have one eye on either side of their head so that they can see what is happening on both sides of them at once.

The two eyes of lions and humans are located on the front of their heads. Each eye sees objects from a slightly different angle. The overlapping views allow the animal to gather information about the objects' depth or distance—information needed for hunting. The flatworm has an eye that can't form an image. It can only detect which direction light is coming from, but this is all the information the flatworm needs to find food and avoid predators.

SEE ALSO
132 Relationships Between Populations

Different organisms may use different structures to do the same job. For example, tiny hair-like cilia surround the microscopic organism known as a paramecium. The cilia move back-and-forth like the oars of a boat to move the paramecium through water. Some bacteria, on the other hand, use whiplike structures called flagella to move through water. The flagella spin rapidly, moving the bacteria much like a propeller moves a boat through water.

Word Watch! The term *bacteria* is used to refer to members of the kingdom *eubacteria.* A single bacteria is called a *bacterium.*

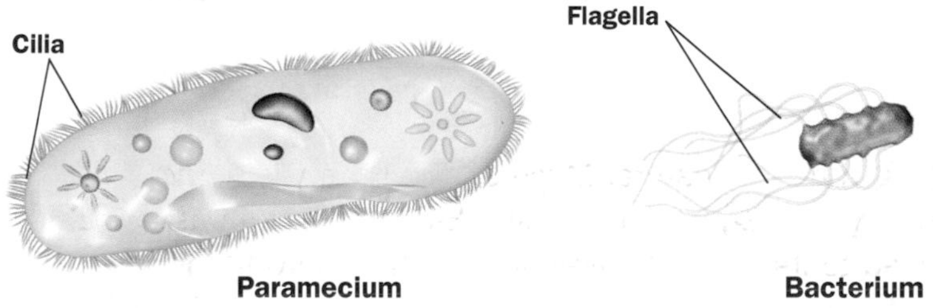

Different structures may serve the same function.

SEE ALSO
156 Protist Kingdom
157 Archaebacteria and Eubacteria Kingdoms

Like microscopic organisms, animals have different kinds of structures to help them move. Birds, bats, and many insects, for example, have wings that allow them to fly through the air. Whales and fish have fins that move them through water. Still other animals, including you, use legs to move from one place to another. Wings, fins, and legs all serve the same function. But each structure is suited to movement in a different type of environment.

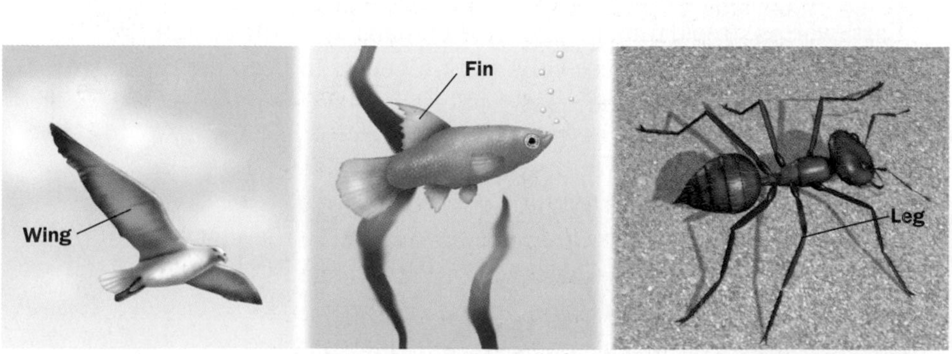

Animals have different structures for moving through air, through water, and on land.

Cells

076

A feature shared by all organisms is that they are made up of one or more cells. A **cell** is the basic unit of structure and function of life. This is a fancy way of saying that cells make up living things and carry out the activities that keep a living thing alive. A cell is itself a living unit. So, cells are able to make more cells like themselves. In fact, new cells can come only from existing cells.

SEE ALSO
079 Cell Processes
080 Cell Division

All cells have some things in common. For example, all are surrounded by a membrane that holds the contents together, and all use energy to do the work of staying alive.

There are many different kinds of cells. Differences between cells can be used to categorize various cell types. For example, most cells contain structures that are enclosed by a membrane. But the cell of a bacterium does not have structures surrounded by membranes. Cells that do not have membrane-bound structures are called **prokaryotic** (PRO-care-ee-AH-tic) cells. Cells that have membrane-bound structures are called **eukaryotic** (YOU-care-ee-AH-tic) cells. All organisms except archaebacteria and eubacteria are made up of eukaryotic cells.

SEE ALSO
160 Prokaryotes and Eukaryotes

Many organisms are **unicellular,** or made of only one cell. The cell of a unicellular organism has structures to help the organism move, get food, reproduce, and respond to its surroundings. So, the single cell carries out all the activities that keep the organism alive and allow it to reproduce, or make more of its own kind.

SEE ALSO
113 Reproduction

Earthworms, trees, mushrooms, and humans are **multicellular,** or made of many cells. These cells work together to keep the organism alive and help it reproduce.

Word Watch!

Bacteria is the plural of *bacterium.*

Many cells in multicellular organisms are specialized to do only certain jobs. For example, the root cells of a plant have tiny hairlike projections that absorb water. Leaf cells do not have these projections. Your nerve cells have long spidery branches that help relay information quickly between your body and your brain. Each specialized cell in a multicellular organism works with other similar cells to carry out a specific job. Having specialized cells for different jobs allows multicellular organisms to perform more functions than unicellular organisms.

SEE ALSO
095 Nervous System

Science Alert!

Large organisms have cells that are about the same size as those in small organisms, but large organisms have more cells than small organisms.

Cells come in all sizes and shapes, but most are **microscopic,** or so tiny you need a microscope to see them.

Your red blood cells are among the smallest cells in your body. About 2000 red blood cells would be needed to form a line across your thumbnail.

Word Watch!

The word *cell* comes from the Latin word *cella,* meaning "chamber."

The British scientist Robert Hooke was the first person to observe cells. In the 1660s, Hooke looked at cork from the bark of an oak tree through a microscope. The cork looked like it was made up of small chambers, or rooms. These reminded Hooke of the cells in which monks lived. For this reason, Hooke named the structures that made up the cork *cells.*

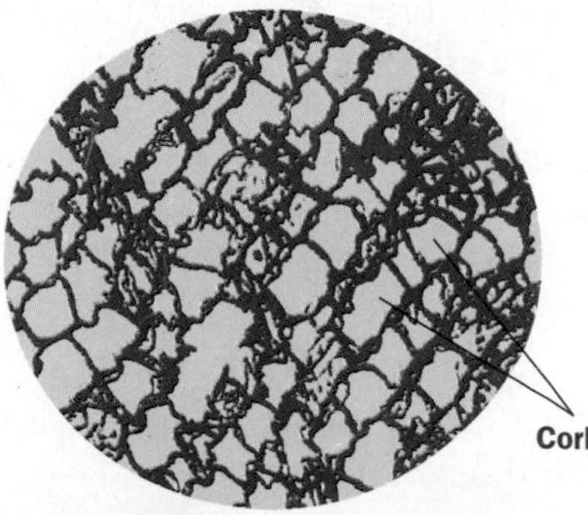

077 Animal Cell

SEE ALSO
078 Plant Cell

Animals are made up of many different types of cells. The diagram below shows some of the structures found in a typical animal cell. Not all animal cells contain all the structures shown.

Animal cell

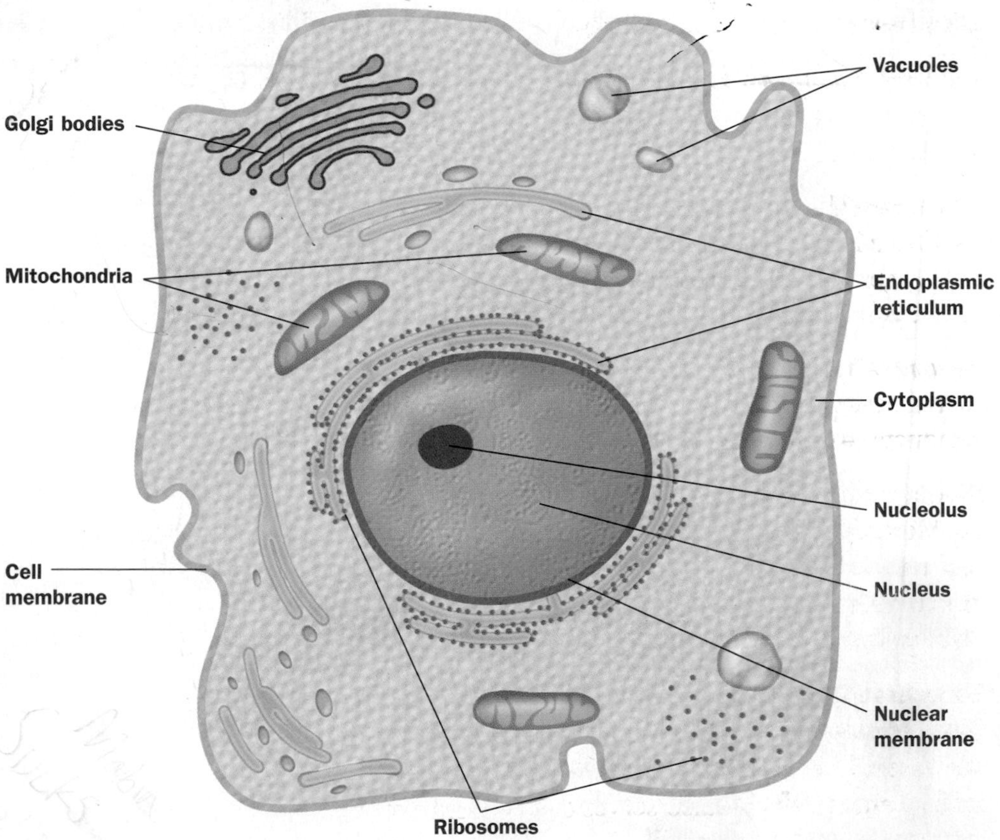

Cell membrane The cell membrane encloses the cell. It acts like a gatekeeper—allowing some materials to pass through it, but not others.

SEE ALSO
082 Tissues, Organs, and Systems

Cytoplasm A gel-like fluid called cytoplasm takes up most of the space inside a cell. Cytoplasm is mostly water, with other substances dissolved in it. Scattered throughout the cytoplasm are many structures called **organelles.** Organelles carry out the activities that keep the cell alive.

Word Watch!

Organelle means "little organ." Like the organs that make up your body, each kind of organelle is specialized to carry out a specific function within a cell.

Nucleus The nucleus is a structure usually located near the center of an animal cell. The nucleus is home to the cell's **chromosomes,** genetic structures that contain the information used to direct cell activity and make new cells. Chromosomes are made of **DNA.**

DNA stands for "deoxyribonucleic acid." The traits that make organisms different from one another are coded for in their DNA.

SEE ALSO
080 Cell Division
116 Genes
121 Heredity
115 DNA

Nuclear membrane The nuclear membrane surrounds and protects the nucleus.

Nucleolus This structure, found inside the nucleus, is responsible for making ribosomes, which are then transported to the cytoplasm.

Vacuoles These fluid-filled structures temporarily store different substances needed by the cell. Some are specialized for storing waste products. Animal cells often have many small vacuoles.

Mitochondria Mitochondria use oxygen to transform the energy in food to a form the cell can use to carry out its activities. These structures are sometimes called the "powerhouses" of the cell.

Word Watch!

Mitochondria is the plural of *mitochondrion.*

Endoplasmic reticulum and **Ribosomes** These organelles produce important products for the cell, including proteins and lipids. The endoplasmic reticulum also serves as an internal delivery system for the cell.

Golgi bodies Golgi bodies help package products from the endoplasmic reticulum and distribute them around the cell or outside of it.

Science Alert!

Many organelles are too small for you to see using a classroom microscope. But you should be able to find the cell membrane, nucleus, and cytoplasm.

SCILINKS NSTA
Keyword: Cell Structures
www.scilinks.org
Code: GSSM076

078 Plant Cell

SEE ALSO

077 Animal Cell
079 Cell Processes
107 Plant Physiology

Plant cells have all the structures animal cells do. But they also have some structures not found in animal cells. These structures include a cell wall and chloroplasts.

Plant cell

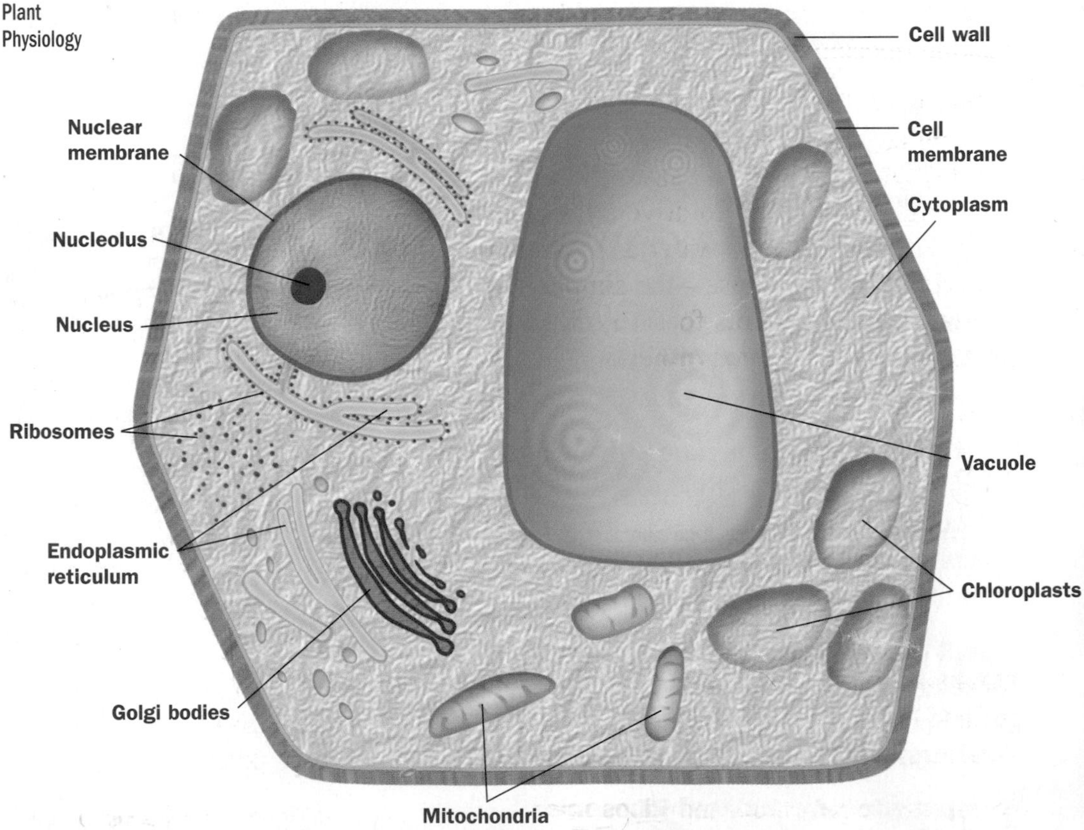

Cell wall This outer barrier provides extra support for the cell and gives it a shape. In plants, the cell wall is made mostly of cellulose, a fiber that is the main component of wood and paper.

Cell membrane The cell membrane encloses the cell and controls what materials enter and leave the cell.

Cytoplasm This gel-like fluid fills much of the inside of the cell. The **organelles** that carry out the cell's activities are scattered throughout the cytoplasm.

Nucleus The nucleus is a structure usually located to one side of a plant cell. The nucleus is home to the cell's **chromosomes,** genetic structures that contain the information used to direct cell activity and make new cells. Chromosomes are made of **DNA.**

SEE ALSO
080 Cell Division
116 Genes
121 Heredity
115 DNA

Nuclear membrane The nuclear membrane surrounds and protects the nucleus.

Nucleolus This structure, found inside the nucleus, is responsible for making ribosomes, which are then transported to the cytoplasm.

Chloroplasts These food-making structures of plant cells contain the green pigment, **chlorophyll.** Chlorophyll captures the energy of sunlight and uses it to drive a chemical reaction that combines water and carbon dioxide to make glucose—the simple sugar plants use as food. This food-making process is called **photosynthesis.**

Word Watch!

The word *photosynthesis* is made from the prefix *photo-* meaning "light," and the root *synthesis* meaning "to put together." During photosynthesis, plants use sunlight to put together the atoms that make glucose (their food).

Science Alert!

Not all plant cells have chloroplasts. Cells in the roots of plants, for example, are not exposed to sunlight and therefore have no need for chloroplasts.

SEE ALSO
079 Cell Processes
107 Plant Physiology

Mitochondria Mitochondria use oxygen to transform the energy in food to a form the cell can use to carry out its activities. These structures are sometimes called the "powerhouses" of the cell.

Endoplasmic reticulum and **Ribosomes** These structures produce important products for the cell, including proteins and lipids. The endoplasmic reticulum also serves as an internal delivery system for the cell.

Unlike animal cells, plant cells often have only one large vacuole. It takes up much of the space in the cell.

Golgi bodies In plant cells, cellulose is made in the Golgi bodies. Cellulose is used in the cell wall.

Vacuole The vacuole acts as a storage structure for the cell.

SciLINKS NSTA
Keyword: Cell Structures
www.scilinks.org
Code: GSSM076

079

Cell Processes

SEE ALSO

077 Animal Cell
078 Plant Cell
090 Excretory System
093 Circulatory System

Every cell is a busy place in which many chemical activities occur. These activities include releasing energy from food, making chemicals the cell needs, and getting rid of wastes. A cell is well designed to carry out these activities. The fluid cytoplasm, for example, allows materials to move through the cell. A cell also has organelles that make or break down different substances. Together, all the activities carried out by a cell make up its **metabolism.**

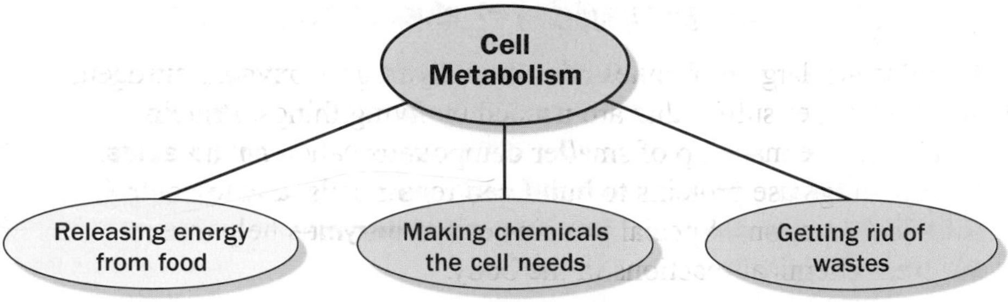

A summary of metabolism

SEE ALSO

105 Animal Physiology
107 Plant Physiology
267 Chemical Formulas
269 Chemical Reactions

Most chemical activities that take place in a cell need an energy source to drive them. Mitochondria release this energy from food through cellular respiration. **Cellular respiration** is the process in which oxygen (O_2) is chemically combined with food molecules (sugar) in the cell to release energy.

Both plant and animal cells get energy in the form they need (**ATP**) through cellular respiration. Because respiration is a chemical process, it can be shown in a chemical equation. The general equation for cellular respiration is written this way:

glucose (sugar) + $O_2 \rightarrow CO_2 + H_2O$ + energy (as ATP)

Notice that in addition to releasing energy, cellular respiration also produces carbon dioxide (CO_2) and water (H_2O).

You might also know the term *respiration* as it is commonly used to describe the process of breathing, or bringing oxygen into the body.

Photosynthesis is the food-making process of plants and some other organisms. Plant cells contain the green pigment **chlorophyll.** Chlorophyll molecules trap energy from the sun and use it to transform carbon dioxide gas (CO_2) and water (H_2O) into a simple sugar called **glucose.** Plants (and other living things) use glucose as a food source. Oxygen (O_2) is also produced during photosynthesis.

Photosynthesis can be summarized in a chemical equation. The general equation for photosynthesis is written this way:

$$CO_2 + H_2O + \text{energy (sunlight)} \rightarrow \text{glucose (sugar)} + O_2$$

SEE ALSO

078 Plant Cell
156 Protist Kingdom
157 Archaebacteria and Eubacteria Kingdoms

Proteins are large molecules of carbon, hydrogen, oxygen, nitrogen, and sometimes sulfur, that are needed by living things. Protein molecules are made up of smaller compounds called **amino acids.** Living things use proteins to build and repair cells, and to control chemical reactions. Special proteins called **enzymes** help direct different chemical reactions in the body.

SEE ALSO

265 Periodic Table
259 Elements, Molecules, and Compounds
089 Digestive System

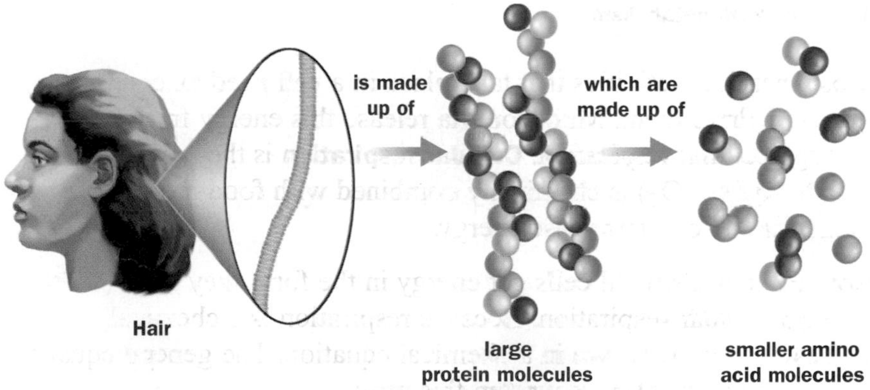

Proteins are made up of many amino acids joined together.

Ribosomes are the protein factories of a cell. An individual cell may have 500,000 ribosomes dotted throughout the membranes of the cell's endoplasmic reticulum and floating freely in the cytoplasm. The endoplasmic reticulum has a lot of surface area to which ribosomes can attach. Once ribosomes get their "work plans" (from the nucleus) to make a specific protein, they combine amino acids to form giant protein molecules. Some proteins are transported to different parts of the cell by the endoplasmic reticulum. Golgi bodies move other proteins to the cell membrane where they can be transported out of the cell.

SEE ALSO

077 Animal Cell
078 Plant Cell

080 Cell Division

Weeds can grow pretty fast. In fact, the stem and roots of a fast-growing plant seem to get longer over night. Where do the new stem and root parts come from? They are made when existing cells divide to form new cells. This process is called **cell division.** Cell division allows organisms to grow larger. Cell division also helps organisms replace injured cells.

The cells formed through cell division are called *daughter cells.* The daughter cells form from the parent cell.

SEE ALSO

076 Cells
077 Animal Cell
078 Plant Cell
081 Stages of Cell Division

Before a eukaryotic cell (a cell with a true nucleus) divides, the genetic material in the nucleus of the cell copies itself. When the cell divides, the nuclear material splits in half so that each daughter cell gets genetic material that is the same as that of the parent cell. The dividing of the nuclear material is known as **mitosis.** In the last stage of cell division, the cytoplasm divides as well. There are now two complete cells where there used to be one.

Science Alert!

The terms *mitosis* and *cell division* are sometimes used interchangeably. But mitosis really refers only to the dividing of the nuclear material. Cell division is the complete process of copying and dividing the whole cell.

Stages of Cell Division

Cell division in eukaryotic cells (cells with a true nucleus) occurs in a predictable set of stages or phases. These steps ensure that the new daughter cells are the same as the cell from which they formed.

SEE ALSO
077 Animal Cell
078 Plant Cell

1. **Interphase** is the stage before cell division starts. As a cell prepares to divide, each chromosome in the nucleus makes an exact copy of itself.

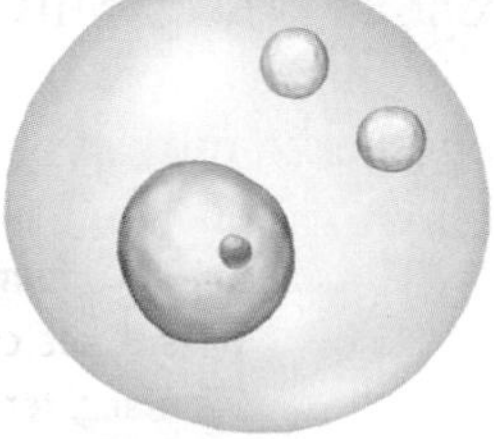

2. During **prophase,** the nucleus prepares for cell division. The genetic material shortens and thickens. The chromosome copies are held together at their centers, so they form a sort of "X."

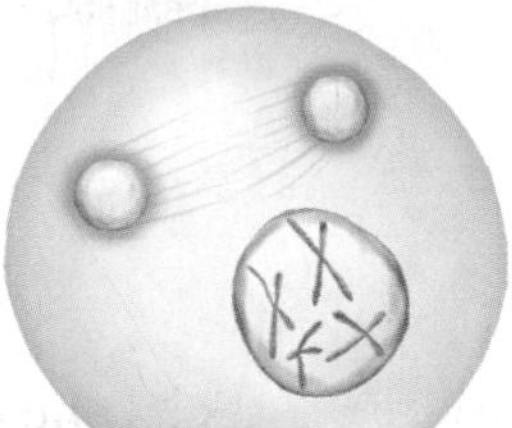

3. During **metaphase,** the two copies of each chromosome line up in the center of the cell.

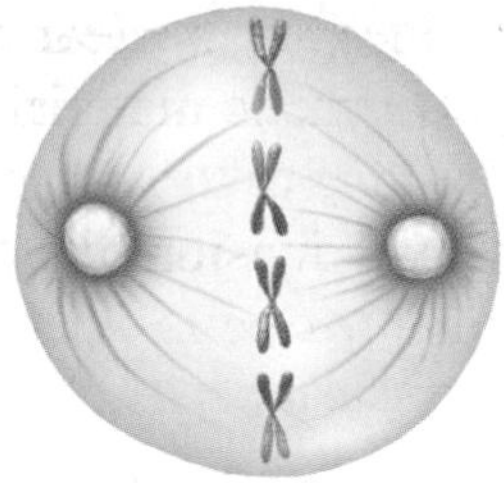

4. During **anaphase,** the copies separate. One complete set of chromosomes is pulled to one side of the cell. The other complete set is pulled to the other side of the cell.

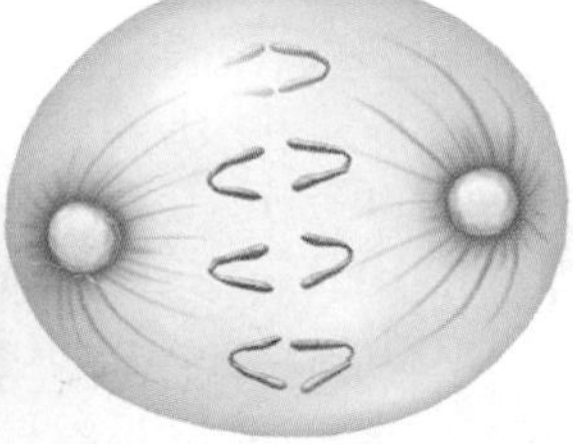

5. **Telophase** is the final stage of cell division. During this stage, the cytoplasm pinches in at the center of the cell, dividing the original cell in half. When cell division is complete, two new daughter cells are formed. The daughter cells are identical to the parent cell.

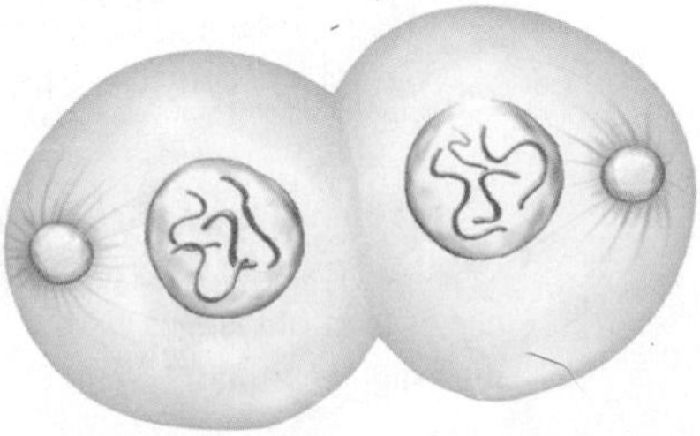

Tissues, Organs, and Systems

082

Groups of cells that work together to do a specific job are called tissues. Your body, like that of many other animals, is made up of several types of **tissue.** Blood, for example, is a tissue that includes different kinds of blood cells and platelets in a liquid. This tissue works to move substances throughout your body and protect you from illness. You also have muscle tissue and nerve tissue that work together to move your body. Cells of the muscle tissue contract or relax to allow your body to move. But this movement does not occur until direction is given by cells of the nervous tissue.

SEE ALSO
076 Cells
093 Circulatory System
087 Muscular System
095 Nervous System

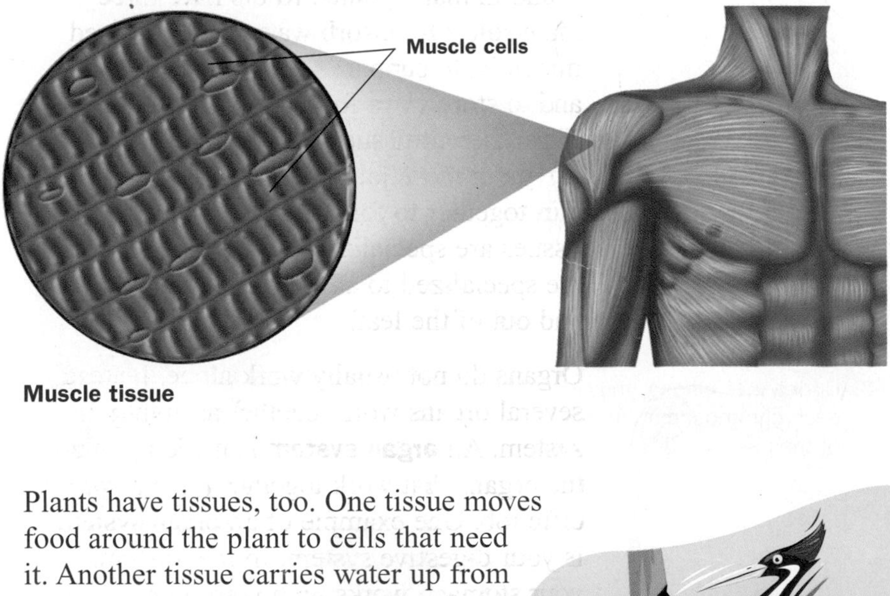

Muscle tissue

Plants have tissues, too. One tissue moves food around the plant to cells that need it. Another tissue carries water up from the plant's roots to its leaves. Still another plant tissue forms the hard outer covering of trees known as bark. Bark is a tissue that acts as a protective covering for woody plants.

SEE ALSO
107 Plant Physiology

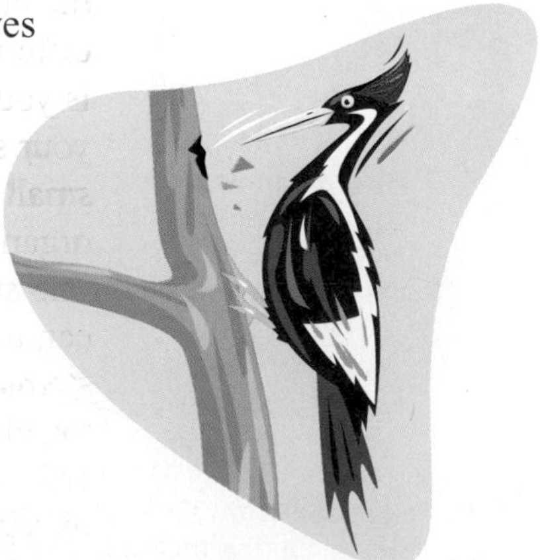

A woodpecker must work hard to break through the protective outer tissue, or bark, of a tree.

Word Watch!

Tissues are made up of cells woven together into webs. The word *tissue* comes from Old French *tissu,* meaning "woven."

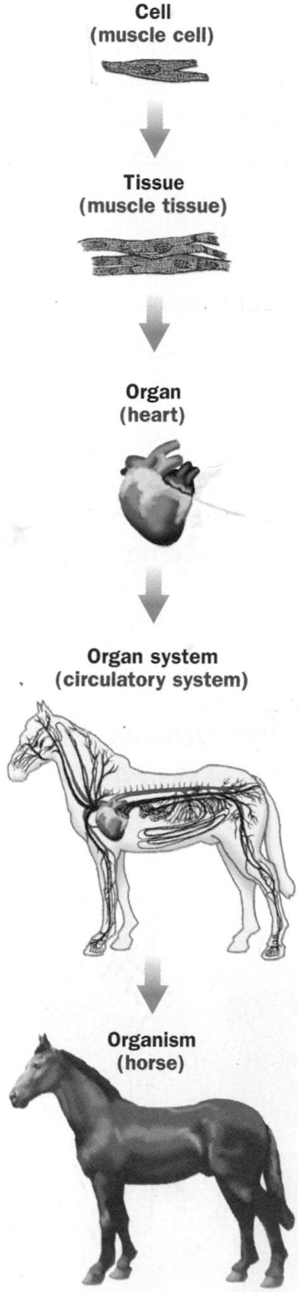

Just as cells join together to form tissues, different tissues join together to form organs. An **organ** is a structure made up of two or more tissues that work together to carry out a specific job. Your stomach is an organ that is made of several types of tissue. For example, muscle tissue allows your stomach to churn and grind food. A tissue that lines your stomach produces chemicals that help break down and digest food.

Roots, stems, and leaves are three organs found in many plants. Roots have three main roles: to absorb water and dissolved minerals, to support and anchor a plant, and to store extra food made by the plant. The different tissues that make up a root carry out these jobs. Other tissues in a plant join together to form leaves. Some of these tissues are specialized to make food. Others are specialized to allow gases to move into and out of the leaf.

SEE ALSO
162 Vascular and Nonvascular Plants

Organs do not usually work alone. Instead, several organs work together as an organ system. An **organ system** is made up of all the organs that work together to do a specific job. One example of an organ system is your digestive system. In this system, your stomach works with your liver, small and large intestines, and other organs to break down food into substances your cells can use. A plant's leaves, stems, and roots work together to make, transport, and store food. At each level of organization, cells depend on other cells to keep the system running smoothly.

SEE ALSO
089 Digestive System
097 Endocrine System

Some organs are part of more than one organ system. Your pancreas, for example, is part of both your digestive system and your endocrine system.

083

Human Biology

SEE ALSO

082 Tissues, Organs, and Systems

The trillions of cells that make up your body are organized into tissues, organs, and organ systems that work together to keep you alive and healthy. In this section, you will explore some of the organ systems of the human body.

The Human Body

SEE ALSO
104 Physiology

Your body is quite a piece of work. Its trillions of cells are organized into the tissues, organs, and organ systems that keep conditions inside your body stable, even when conditions outside are changing. This maintenance of stable conditions inside your body is called **homeostasis** (HOME-ee-oh-STAY-sis). One example of homeostasis is your body's ability to maintain a temperature of about 37°C (98.6°F) even when temperatures outside are warmer or cooler.

Your body's cells are made mostly of water, which means you are made mostly of water, too. In fact, about two thirds of your total mass comes from water. You don't dry out because your skin does a great job of keeping your bones, blood, muscles, and brain wrapped up in the tidy package that is you. Skin is made up of a tissue called epithelial tissue. Epithelial tissue is one of the four main tissue types found in your body.

Main Tissue Types

Tissue		Description	Examples
Epithelial		covers the outside of the body and lines inner surfaces of the body	skin
Connective	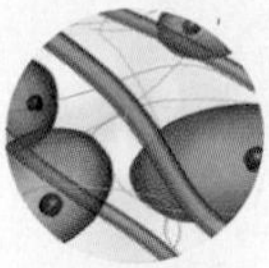	fills in spaces and connects other tissues together; supports, protects, nourishes, and insulates organs	ligaments, cartilage, blood
Muscular		contracts and relaxes to allow movement; makes up some organs	diaphragm, heart, biceps, triceps
Nervous	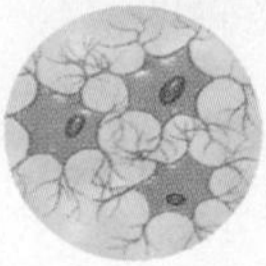	transmits messages through the body	brain, spinal cord, nerves

085

Skeletal and Muscular Systems

Your body has two organ systems that work together to help you move—the skeletal system and the muscular system. The **skeletal system** is made up of the bones and cartilage that form the framework of your body. The **muscular system** includes the muscles that help you move, and muscles that help things inside your body move.

086

Skeletal System

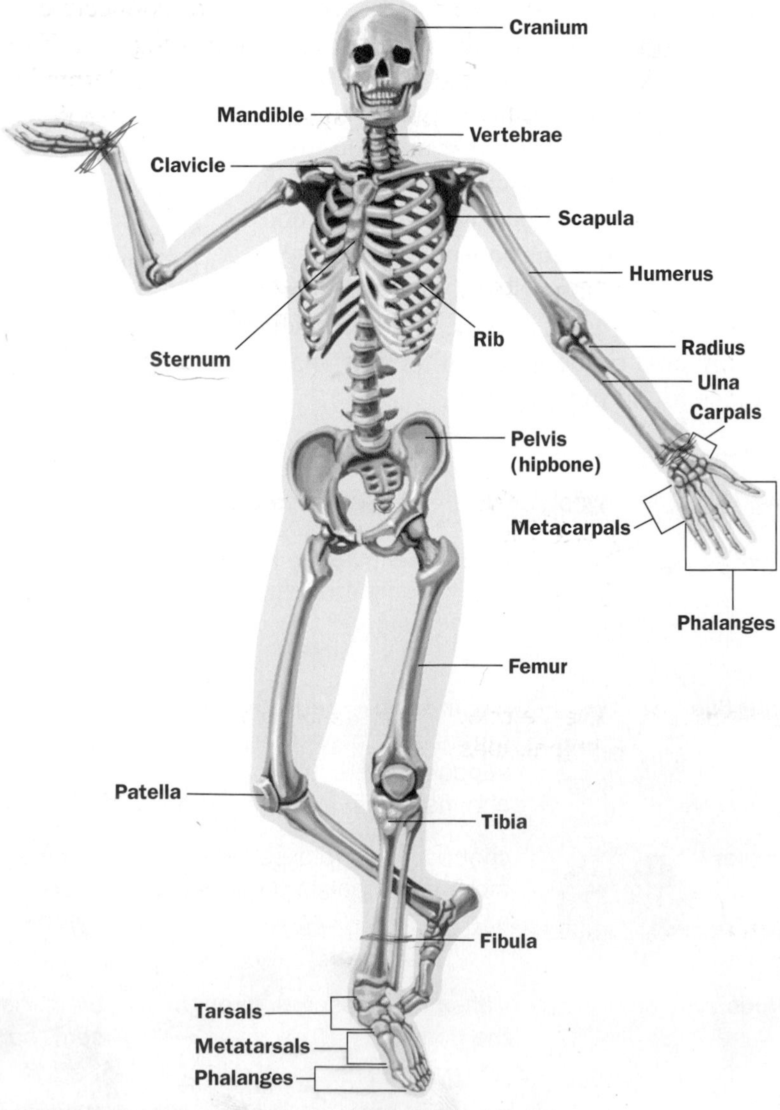

Your skeleton is made up of about 206 individual bones.

All humans have a stiff inner **skeleton** made of bone and a hard, but flexible tissue called **cartilage.** The bones of your skeleton have four main jobs:

- to support your body and give it shape
- to protect your internal organs
- to provide a scaffolding for your muscles, allowing you to move
- to store minerals and make blood cells

SEE ALSO
082 Tissues, Organs, and Systems

Your knees, elbows, and hips are examples of joints. **Joints** are parts of the body where two or more bones meet. Bands of connective tissue called **ligaments** hold the bones of many joints together. The joints in your skull are fixed and do not allow movement. Joints in other parts of your body allow only certain kinds of movements.

Some Joints of the Human Body

Joint Type	Where Found	Movement	Example
Pivot joint	neck, elbow	bones rotate around each other	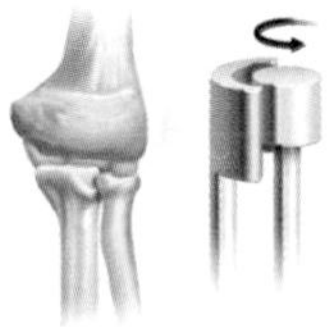
Gliding joint	wrist, ankle, vertebrae	bones slide over each other	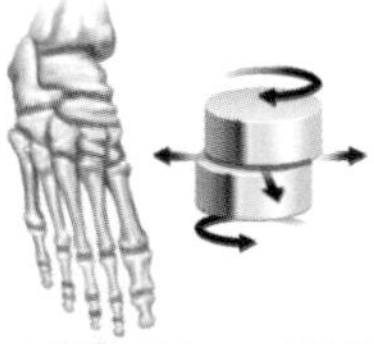
Hinge joint	knee, elbow, fingers, toes	back-and-forth	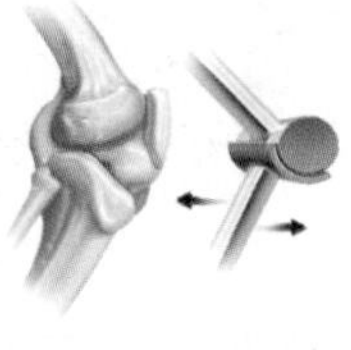
Ball-and-socket joint	shoulder, hips	rotational or circular	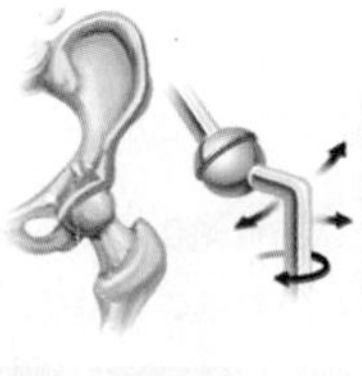

087 Muscular System

To allow movement, the bones and joints of the skeletal system must work with the muscular system. The **muscular system** includes three types of muscle.

Types of muscle

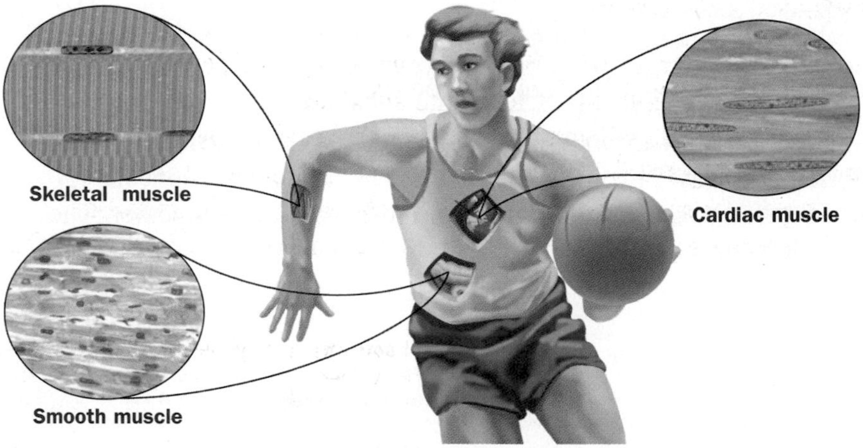

SEE ALSO
082 Tissues, Organs, and Systems

Skeletal Muscle Muscles that contract to move bones are called **skeletal muscles.** Tough cords of connective tissue called **tendons** attach skeletal muscle to bones. Because you control the movement of skeletal muscles, they are called **voluntary muscles.** Skeletal muscle is controlled by nerves that tell it when to contract or relax. Skeletal muscles often work in pairs to bend and straighten parts of your body. When one muscle contracts, the other relaxes, and vice versa.

SEE ALSO
095 Nervous System

Skeletal muscles work in pairs.

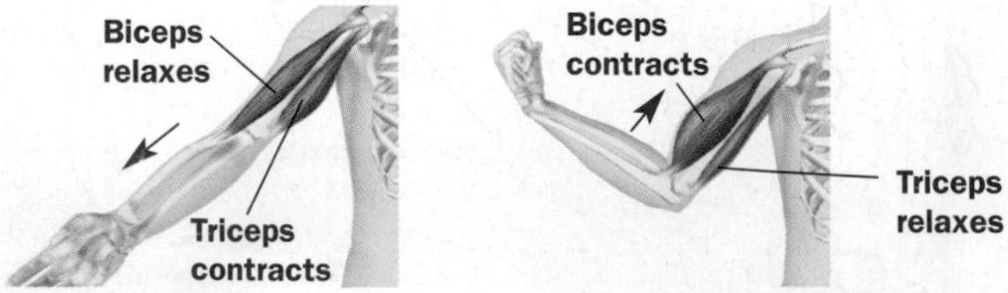

Smooth Muscle Your body also has **involuntary muscles**—muscles that are not under your conscious control. One type of involuntary muscle is **smooth muscle,** which is found in the walls of many organs. The rumbling you feel in your stomach before lunch is caused by contractions of smooth muscle in your stomach.

Cardiac Muscle The other type of involuntary muscle is called **cardiac muscle,** and it is found only in the heart. Cardiac muscle keeps your heart pumping throughout the day and night.

Digestive and Excretory Systems

088

The digestive and excretory systems work together to take in materials your body needs and get rid of wastes.

Digestive System

089

The energy and materials that keep your body working come from food. The breaking down of food into substances the body can use is the job of the **digestive system.** There are two kinds of digestion. **Mechanical digestion** breaks food into smaller pieces. **Chemical digestion** uses special proteins called **enzymes** to break up large food molecules into smaller molecules that can be taken in by cells.

SEE ALSO
079 Cell Processes

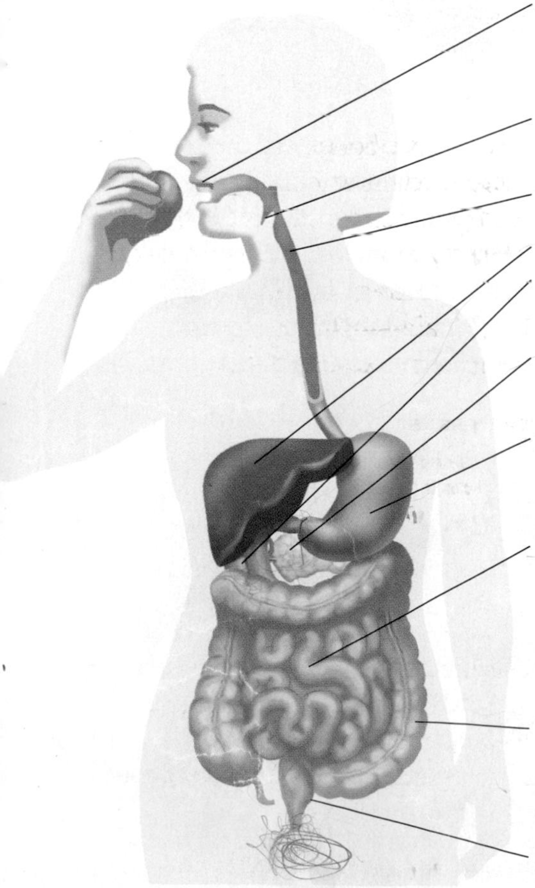

Mouth The teeth grind food into smaller pieces. Saliva begins to break down complex starches into smaller sugars.

Epiglottis This flap of tissue prevents swallowed food from entering the tube to your lungs.

Esophagus The esophagus carries food to the stomach.

Liver The liver produces bile, a liquid that is stored in the **gall bladder.** Bile is released into the small intestine, where it breaks up large fat molecules.

Pancreas Enzymes made here help break down carbohydrates and protein in the small intestine.

Stomach Muscles in the stomach grind food into smaller pieces. Gastric juice and hydrochloric acid made in the stomach break apart large protein molecules.

Small Intestine Liquid food moves from the stomach into the small intestine, where most chemical digestion occurs. Digested food is absorbed by tiny fingerlike structures called **villi** that line the small intestine. Blood vessels in the villi then absorb the nutrients. Once in the bloodstream, the nutrients are carried to cells throughout the body.

Large Intestine Materials that cannot be digested move into the large intestine. The large intestine absorbs much of the water still trapped in the food waste. The solid that remains is called **feces.**

Rectum and Anus Feces exit the large intestine through the rectum and move out of the body through the anus.

Digestive system

090 Excretory System

The job of the **excretory system** is to remove wastes produced by the activities of cells. Many of these wastes are eliminated as liquid urine. **Urine** is formed by the **urinary system,** which is made up of the kidneys, the urinary bladder, the ureters, and the urethra.

SEE ALSO
089 Digestive System
079 Cell Processes
093 Circulatory System

Science Alert!

Don't confuse the roles of the excretory system and the digestive system in eliminating wastes from the body. Feces are the unusable remains of food you eat. Urine is cellular waste that has been filtered from your bloodstream.

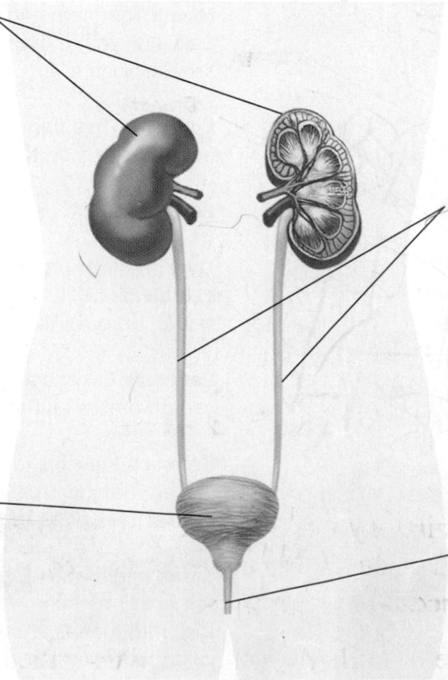

Kidneys Blood that enters the kidneys passes through millions of tiny filters called **nephrons**. Liquid waste carried in the blood collects in the filters and forms **urine.**

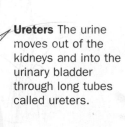

Ureters The urine moves out of the kidneys and into the urinary bladder through long tubes called ureters.

Urinary Bladder Urine is stored in the urinary bladder until it is eliminated from the body.

Urethra Urine leaves the body through the urethra.

Urinary system

Did You Know?

Your skin is the largest organ in your body. It serves as an organ of excretion when you get rid of water and salts through perspiration. Perspiring also helps cool your body.

Respiratory and Circulatory Systems

091

Your cells need oxygen to function. Taking in oxygen and transporting it to cells are jobs of the respiratory and circulatory systems.

Respiratory System

092

Each time you breathe, you take in oxygen. Getting oxygen into the body is one job of the **respiratory system.** The respiratory system also gets rid of the carbon dioxide that your cells produce as waste.

SEE ALSO
079 Cell Processes
105 Animal Physiology

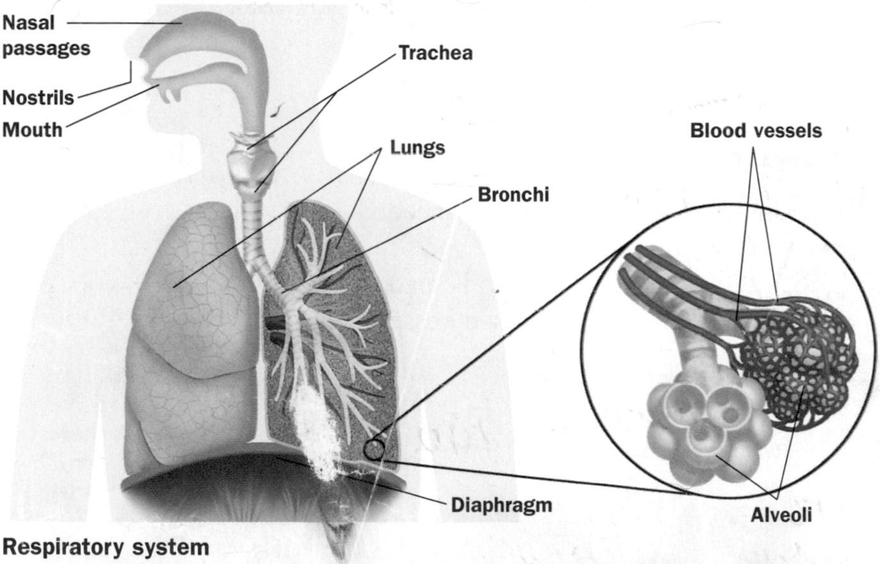

Respiratory system

Air enters your respiratory system through your **nostrils** or **mouth.** From there it moves through your **nasal passages,** into your **trachea,** and then into the **bronchi** of your **lungs.**

Lung tissue is made of millions of tiny air sacs called **alveoli.** Each alveolus is surrounded by tiny blood vessels. In the alveolus, oxygen moves through a thin membrane and into the blood vessels. Your blood carries this oxygen to the cells of your body. At the same time, carbon dioxide carried in the blood moves from the tiny blood vessels into the alveoli. This carbon dioxide moves up through your respiratory system, and is exhaled from your body.

SEE ALSO
093 Circulatory System

Word Watch!

Alveoli is the plural form of *alveolus*, a term meaning "pit," or "small cavity." Your lungs have about 700 million alveoli.

MORE ▶

Just below your rib cage is a large curved muscle called the **diaphragm.** The diaphragm moves up and down, expanding and contracting the rib cage and causing you to exhale or inhale.

Science Alert!

The terms *breathing* and *respiration* have different meanings in biology. Breathing is the mechanical process of taking air into and out of the body. Respiration is a chemical process that involves using oxygen to get energy from food.

SEE ALSO
079 Cell Processes

093 Circulatory System

Your **circulatory system** transports needed substances throughout your body and carries away wastes. This system is made up of your blood, heart, and blood vessels.

Blood cells

Red blood cells

White blood cells

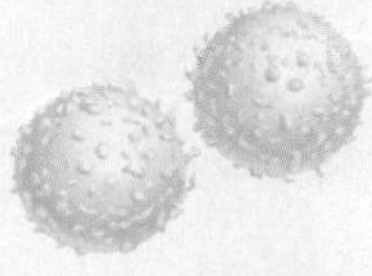

Platelets

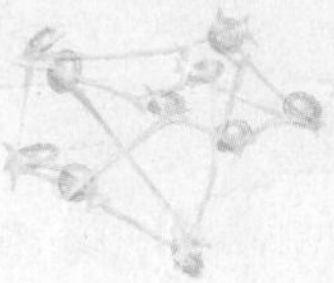

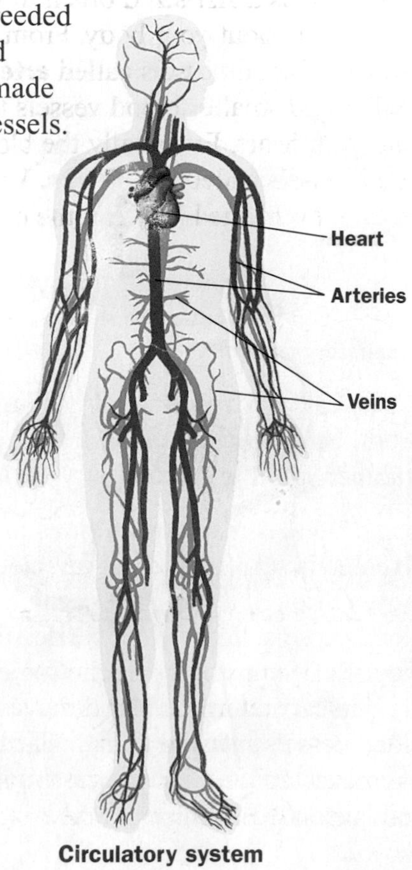

Circulatory system

Blood is a tissue made up of cells and cell parts that are carried in a liquid. **Red blood cells** are specialized to carry oxygen and carbon dioxide. **White blood cells** help you fight disease. Blood also contains platelets. **Platelets** are cell pieces that help your blood clot when you have an injury. The blood cells, platelets, and dissolved food and proteins are all carried in **plasma**—a pale yellow liquid.

SEE ALSO
082 Tissues, Organs, and Systems

Did You Know?

Certain proteins on the surface of red blood cells cause people to have different blood types. You can have A, B, AB, or O type blood.

Your **heart** is a fist-sized organ in your chest. The heart pumps blood throughout your body. From the heart, blood moves into large blood vessels called **arteries.** Arteries divide into smaller and smaller blood vessels that carry blood away from your heart. Eventually the blood is carried into tiny blood vessels called **capillaries.** Valuable nutrients in blood are then exchanged between the capillaries and your cells.

Arteries and *away* both start with *A*. Use this mnemonic to help remember that arteries carry blood away from the heart.

Blood cells moving through capillaries

Blood carrying wastes (including carbon dioxide) and depleted of oxygen then returns to the heart through a system of blood vessels called **veins.** From the heart, the blood is pumped to the lungs where it releases carbon dioxide waste and picks up more oxygen. This fresh blood then returns to the heart where it is again pumped out to the body.

SEE ALSO
079 Cell Processes
105 Animal Physiology
092 Respiratory System

Nervous and Endocrine Systems

094

Your body has not one, but two message centers—the nervous system and the endocrine system. These systems transmit information throughout your body in different ways.

Nervous System

095

SEE ALSO
096 The Five Senses

The **nervous system** controls and coordinates your body's activities and helps you sense and respond to changes in your environment. The nervous system is made up of the brain, the spinal cord, and the nerves that extend throughout your body. Your sense organs—eyes, ears, nose, tongue, and skin—are also part of your nervous system.

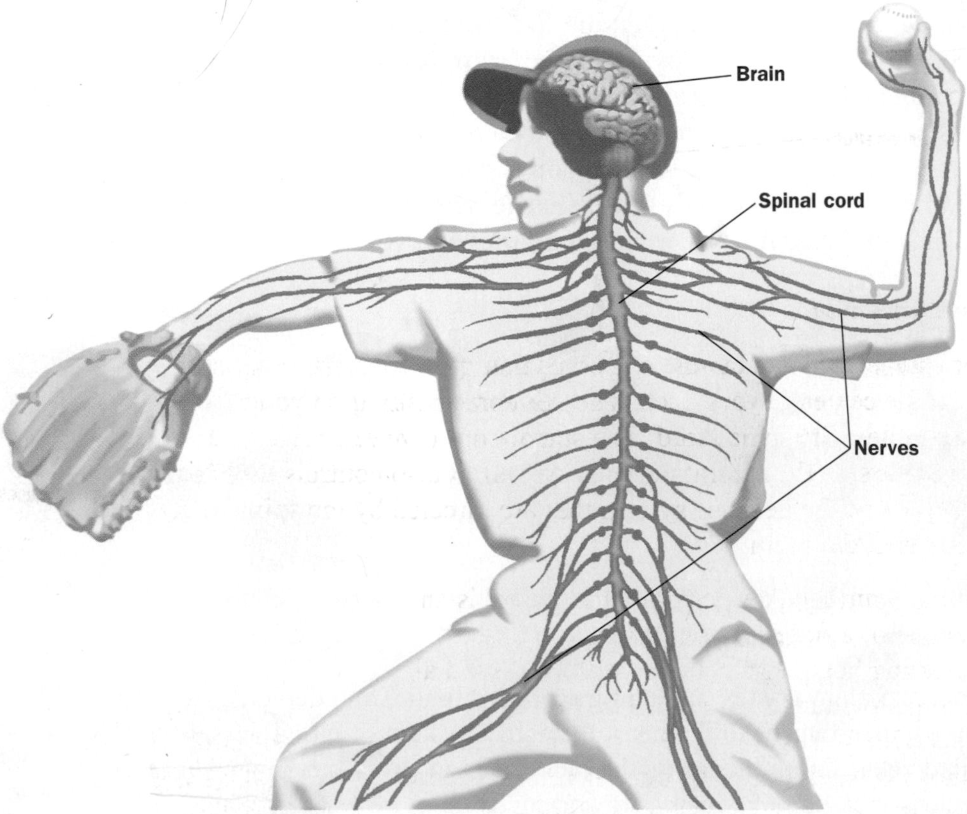

The nervous system

Your brain and spinal cord make up your **central nervous system.** The **brain** has three distinct parts. Each of these parts has a different function.

The **cerebrum** is the control center of your thoughts and voluntary actions. It is where you experience the sensations of touch, taste, sight, hearing, and smell. The cerebrum has two halves or **hemispheres.** In most people, the left hemisphere is specialized for language and logical thinking. The right hemisphere is specialized for activities that require imagination and creativity. It's also involved in recognizing patterns, such as individual faces.

SEE ALSO
096 The Five Senses

The **brain stem** is at the base of your brain. It controls vital and continual processes such as breathing, the beating of your heart, and digestion. The **cerebellum** helps with balance and coordination.

SEE ALSO
092 Respiratory System
093 Circulatory System
089 Digestive System

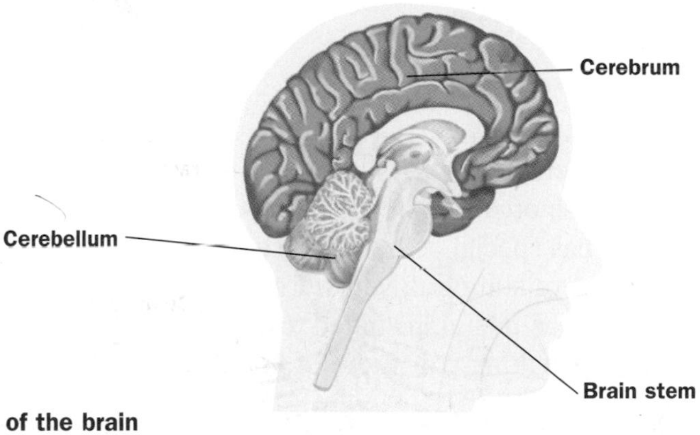

Parts of the brain

The **spinal cord** is a bundle of nerves that goes from the brain stem down the center of your back. The vertebrae making up your back-bone protect the spinal cord. The spinal cord connects with other nerves outside the central nervous system. It also controls **reflexes,** responses of the nervous system that are directed by the spinal cord, rather than the brain.

SEE ALSO
086 Skeletal System
161 Vertebrates and Invertebrates

Pulling your hand away from a hot object is an example of a reflex action. When you touch something hot, nerve cells in your hand send a message to your spinal cord. The spinal cord sends a reply message that tells your muscles to yank your hand away. The brain does not become aware of what happened until a split-second later.

MORE

SEE ALSO
077 Animal Cell

Nerve cells, or **neurons,** are very specialized cells. A typical neuron has a central cell body that contains cytoplasm and a nucleus. Branching away from this cell body is a long arm known as an **axon.** Nerve impulses travel from the axon of one nerve cell to the **dendrites** of another nerve cell.

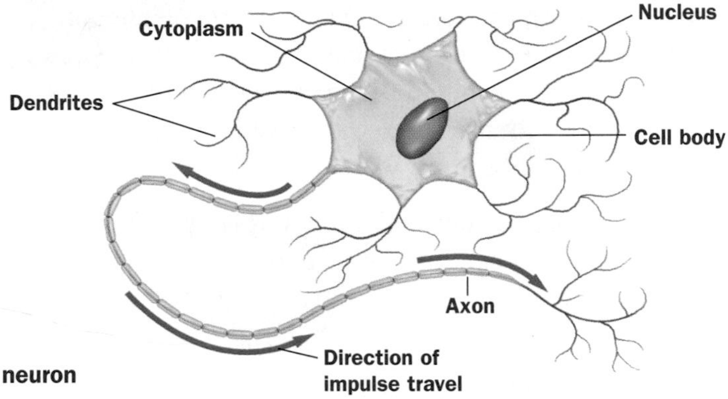

A neuron

096 The Five Senses

Information about your environment is taken into your body through **sense organs.** Your sense organs include your eyes, ears, skin, tongue, and nose. Each organ has special cells, called sensory cells, that respond to certain types of stimuli in your surroundings. Information taken in by sensory cells is then transmitted to your brain. Your brain interprets these signals, making you aware of your surroundings.

The Five Senses

Sense		Sense Organ
Sight		**Eyes:** Sensory cells are located in the retina at the back of the eye.
Hearing		**Ears:** Sensory cells are located inside the inner ear.
Smell		**Nose:** Sensory cells line the nose.
Taste		**Tongue:** Sensory cells for sweet, salty, sour, and bitter cover the surface of the tongue.
Touch		**Skin:** Sensory cells sensitive to temperature, pressure, pain, and texture are found just below the skin's surface.

Endocrine System

097

The **endocrine system** regulates body activities by producing chemical messengers in **glands.** The chemical messengers of the endocrine system are called **hormones.** Hormones are released directly into the bloodstream where they are carried to other parts of the body.

Word Watch!

Hormon means "to urge on." Hormones work to activate, or urge on, certain organs.

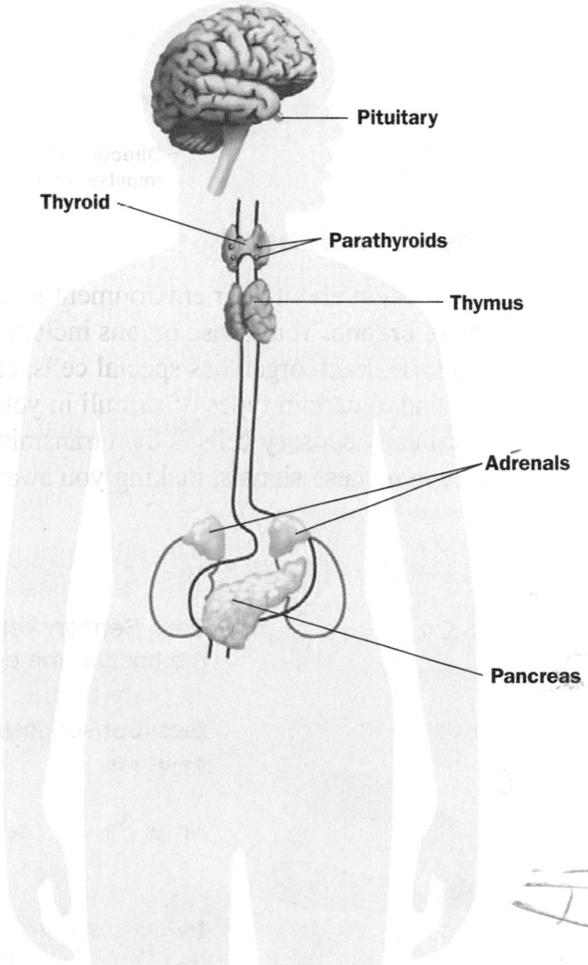

Pituitary
- releases hormones that control other glands
- releases growth hormone
- controls ovaries in females and testes in males

Thyroid
- regulates metabolism
- causes bones to store calcium

Parathyroids
- maintain calcium balance in blood

Thymus
- allows body to make white blood cells

Adrenals
- prepare body for emergencies
- regulate blood pressure
- regulate metabolism
- control salt and water balance

Pancreas
- regulates blood sugar levels

Glands of the Endocrine System

MORE

SEE ALSO
095 Nervous System

Growth hormone is released by the **pituitary gland,** a pea-sized gland located at the base of the brain. Growth hormone determines how tall you will get. It also controls your metabolism.

The **adrenal glands** produce **epinephrine** (ep-uh-NEF-rehn). Epinephrine is a hormone that is released when you are frightened or angry. This hormone makes your heart beat faster and your blood pressure go up. Epinephrine also tells your liver to release stored sugar, and so may give you a sudden surge of energy.

Did You Know?

Epinephrine is known as the "fight-or-flight" hormone, because it allows you to confront danger or flee from it.

SEE ALSO
079 Cell Processes

The adrenal glands also produce steroids. **Steroids** are hormones that affect food metabolism and stimulate protein production in tissue. Steroids affect your water balance, which in turn, affects your mental balance. Steroids are powerful and affect many body systems at once. That's why taking artificial steroids to build up muscle tissue without medical supervision is extremely dangerous.

In people with a condition called **diabetes,** the pancreas does not produce correct amounts of insulin. These people must control their condition with diet, and may also need insulin supplements.

The **pancreas** produces two hormones that work in opposite ways to balance your blood sugar levels. **Insulin** helps lower your blood sugar by controlling how this sugar is used in body tissues. When blood sugar levels get too low, **glucagon** causes blood sugar levels to rise.

Immune System

SEE ALSO
152 Kingdoms

Your body must constantly protect itself against microscopic invaders called **pathogens.** These bacteria, viruses, and fungi are all around you. Usually, your skin, tears, and saliva work to keep the pathogens from making their way into your body. But sometimes the invaders make it through this first line of defense.

SEE ALSO
093 Circulatory System

Once inside your body, pathogens face a fierce set of attackers known as **white blood cells.** One type of white blood cell, called a **macrophage,** surrounds and engulfs pathogens, destroying them in the process. Pieces of the destroyed pathogen remain on the outside of the macrophage. These pieces, called **antigens,** alert other white blood cells of the danger. The white blood cells either attack the pathogens directly, or produce **antibodies.** Antibodies bind to pathogens and help to destroy them.

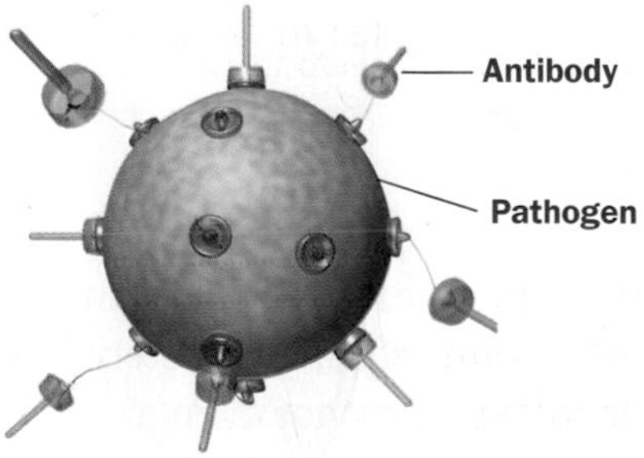

Antibodies attacking a pathogen

White blood cells also fight cancer cells — cells that grow at an uncontrollable rate.

Each antibody is designed to attack only one type of pathogen. So each type of pathogen requires its own type of antibody. The white blood cells that produce antibodies remember pathogens they have fought before. If a pathogen returns, the cells can quickly produce more antibodies to fight it.

Pathogens in the blood are removed at locations called **lymph nodes.** As blood passes through these small lumps of tissue, white blood cells attack any pathogens and filter them out. When you are sick, you might notice that your lymph nodes, like the ones found in your neck, become swollen and sore. This is because they are fighting an invader!

Did You Know?

Allergies are the body's overreaction to antigens that are not normally harmful, such as pollen or pet hair.

Infectious and Noninfectious Diseases

099

Think about the last time you were sick with a cold or strep throat. Chances are that, before you got sick, you were in contact with someone else who was sick. You were infected with pathogens from that person, and became ill. An **infectious disease** is caused by pathogens. Many common diseases are caused by pathogens that are spread from one person to another. Pathogens that can be spread from one organism to another include viruses, bacteria, and fungi. Infectious diseases affect many kinds of organisms. Colds and strep throat are examples of infectious diseases that affect humans.

Some diseases are not caused by pathogens. These **noninfectious diseases** cannot be spread from one organism to another. Noninfectious diseases can be caused by a person's environment, by their genetics, or by the way they live. The causes of some noninfectious diseases are unknown.

100 Viral Diseases

A **virus** is a tiny particle that has characteristics of both living and nonliving things. Even though a virus has some of the characteristics of a living thing, it is not a complete organism. It is not even a complete cell. A virus cannot reproduce by itself. Instead, a virus uses the living cells of an organism to reproduce. First, the virus attaches itself to a cell. Next, it injects the cell with instructions for making more viruses. When this happens, the cell has become infected with the virus. The cell stops going about its normal functions. Instead, the infected cell makes new viruses. Eventually the cell bursts open. The new viruses are released. Those viruses infect other cells, and the process continues.

When a virus uses your cells to make more viruses, you may end up with a viral disease. Colds and flu are two common categories of viral disease. Many different kinds of viruses cause these infectious diseases. Your immune system fights against these kinds of infections. So it is possible to have a disease-causing virus enter your body without becoming ill with an infectious disease.

Bacterial Diseases

101

Many kinds of disease are caused by bacteria. **Bacteria** are single-celled organisms that do not have a true nucleus. Not all bacteria cause disease. Those that do, cause disease in different ways. Some kinds of bacteria damage body cells directly. For example, in bacterial pneumonia, large numbers of bacteria reproduce rapidly and damage the cells in the lungs. In this case, the bacteria itself cause illness in the infected organism. Other kinds of bacteria produce powerful poisons, or toxins. In these cases the poisons, rather than the bacteria itself, cause illness in the infected organism. For example, *Salmonella* bacteria cause most cases of food poisoning. These bacteria have a toxin in their cell walls. *Salmonella* reproduces rapidly in foods such as egg salad, chicken, and milk that have been left unrefrigerated for several hours. Eating foods infected with *Salmonella* can cause cramps, vomiting, and diarrhea. Vomiting and diarrhea are ways that the body tries to rid itself of the toxins.

You can't "catch" food poisoning from another person, the way you can catch a cold or the flu. But food poisoning is still an infectious disease, because it is caused by a pathogen.

SEE ALSO
157 Archaebacteria and Eubacteria Kingdoms

Noninfectious Diseases

102

A **noninfectious disease** is not caused by pathogens. Some noninfectious diseases are inherited. An inherited disease is caused by the genes that a person received from his or her parents. Sickle cell disease is one example of a noninfectious disease that is inherited. Sickle cell disease causes red blood cells to be the wrong shape. This leads to problems with blood circulation.

SEE ALSO
116 Genes
121 Heredity

Other noninfectious diseases can be caused by the choices a person makes about how to live. Constantly high blood pressure, or hypertension, is an example. Hypertension can lead to heart attack or stroke, both of which can be fatal. To some extent, the tendency to have hypertension is inherited. But the choices a person makes about what to eat and how much to exercise also have an effect on blood pressure, no matter what genes that person inherited.

103

Physiology and Behavior

All organisms must carry out a series of daily activities. These include making use of resources, growing, reproducing, and maintaining internal conditions in an environment that is ever-changing and often hostile. How organisms go about these activities is the study of physiology and behavior.

An organism's **physiology** refers to its internal activities, like when a plant closes openings on the undersides of its leaves to conserve water on a warm day. **Behavior,** on the other hand, involves external activities, like when a spider spins a web to catch insects.

Physiology

104

Physiology is the study of all the physical and chemical processes that take place inside the body of an organism as it goes about its basic daily activities. These activities include processes going on inside cells, tissues, organs, and organ systems. Muscle contraction, actions of the nervous system, growth, and reproduction are just some of an organism's physiological activities.

Even sleeping animals are quite busy on the inside. Body systems are working to maintain balanced internal conditions, including temperature, pressure, and moisture.

An organism must regulate its internal body conditions in order to stay alive. It does this by constantly adjusting its physiological activities.

SEE ALSO
079 Cell Processes
082 Tissues, Organs, and Systems
085 Skeletal and Muscular Systems
113 Reproduction

SEE ALSO
074 Structure of Life
076 Cells
154 Animal Kingdom

The dog's internal body systems are quite active, even if the dog is not.

Animal Physiology

105

The earthworm and the elephant are both animals. You already know that these two animals have different body types. You can probably guess that their physiological activities would be different too. Even so, most animals share at least some basic physiology.

All the chemical processes that take place inside cells, tissues, and organs make up the **metabolism** of an organism. These activities include breaking down some chemical materials and building up others. Chemicals are broken down to release energy and to get rid of waste products. Chemicals are put together to form new cells or to create materials needed by the body.

MORE ▶

SEE ALSO
079 Cell Processes
105 Animal Physiology
259 Elements, Molecules, and Compounds

SEE ALSO
079 Cell Processes
267 Chemical Formulas
269 Chemical Reactions

Where does the energy to power all these physiological processes come from? All animals get the energy they need through a process called **cellular respiration.** In cellular respiration, oxygen (O_2) is combined with digested food (glucose) within a cell to release energy in the form of a molecule called **ATP.** Carbon dioxide (CO_2) and water (H_2O) are given off as waste products. This process can be summarized by the following equation:

$$\text{glucose (sugar)} + O_2 \rightarrow CO_2 + H_2O + \text{energy (as ATP)}$$

Carbon dioxide (CO_2) is given off as a waste product of cellular respiration. This gas must be eliminated from the animal's body. Humans do this by exhaling.

Word Watch!

Aerobic respiration refers to respiration that occurs with oxygen (O_2). *Anaerobic respiration* is respiration that occurs without oxygen. Certain body cells can use anaerobic respiration temporarily when oxygen is not available.

SEE ALSO
092 Respiratory System

All animals need oxygen in order to get energy from the food they eat. Different animals have different ways of getting oxygen. Many land animals, including humans, have lungs to breathe in air. Some insects have small openings (called spiracles) on the sides of their bodies to take in oxygen from the air. Fish and other water animals may have gills for getting oxygen that is dissolved in water. Other animals may take in oxygen through their moist skin.

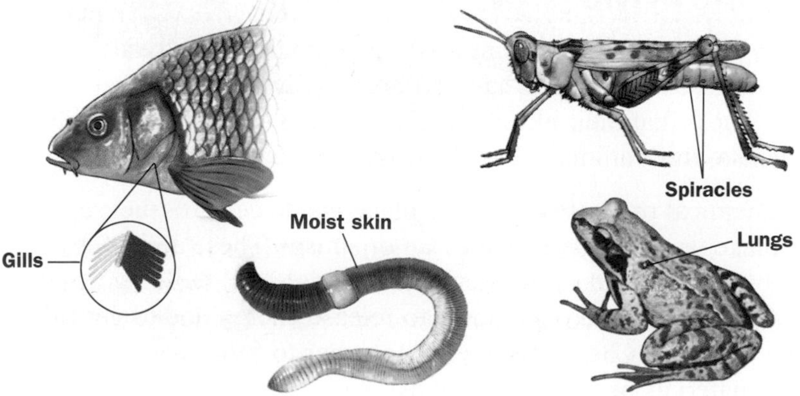

Ways animals get oxygen

Animal Life Cycles

Like all living things, animals **reproduce** to make more of their own kind. Once formed, a new animal usually grows in a predictable way. The stages in the life of the animal as it grows, develops, and matures to reproduce the next generation are known as its **life cycle.** Life cycles vary for different kinds of organisms.

Mammals

Horses, cows, dogs, and bats are all mammals. So are you! **Mammals** are animals that have some fur or hair covering their bodies, usually give birth to live young, and nurse their young with milk made by the mother. The young of most mammals develop inside the mother's body nourished by an organ called a **placenta.**

Word Watch!

Placenta comes from a Greek word meaning "flat cake." The placenta is a flattened organ that forms in the female's uterus. It transports food and wastes between the mother and the fetus.

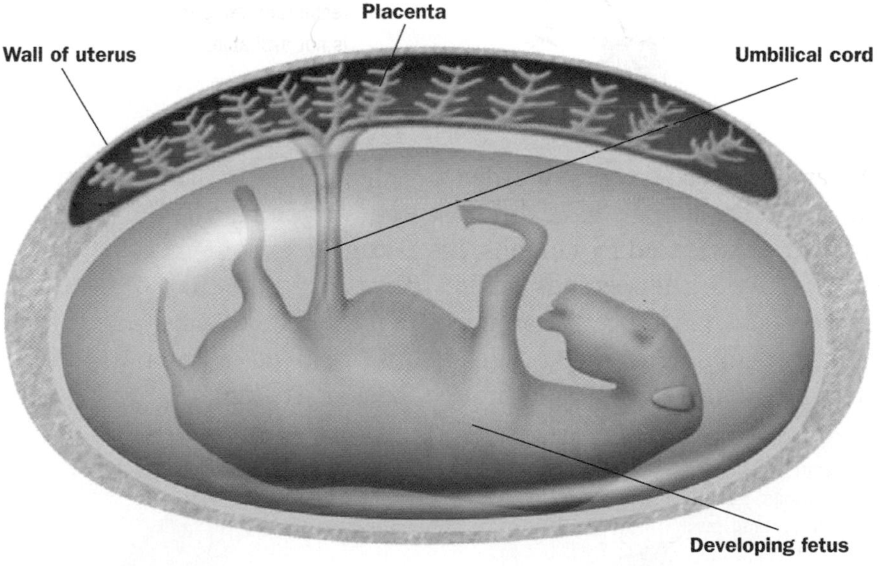

A developing mammal

Mammals are born looking much like small versions of the adults they will become. As they nurse on milk provided by their mothers, mammals grow and develop. Soon they are eating on their own. Eventually they become old enough to reproduce themselves.

SEE ALSO
113 Reproduction

MORE ▶

Insects

Some insects, including grasshoppers, produce young that look like tiny versions of the adult. The young grow and develop through time to become adult-size, but their outward body appearance does not change substantially. This sort of development is known as **incomplete metamorphosis.**

But many other insects, including butterflies and moths, undergo what is called **complete metamorphosis.** In complete metamorphosis, the body of an organism completely changes in shape and appearance at each stage of its life cycle. In butterflies and moths, complete metamorphosis includes four stages: egg, larva (caterpillar), pupa, and adult.

Word Watch!

***Metamorphosis* is made up of the prefix *meta-* meaning "change" and the root *morph* meaning "shape."**

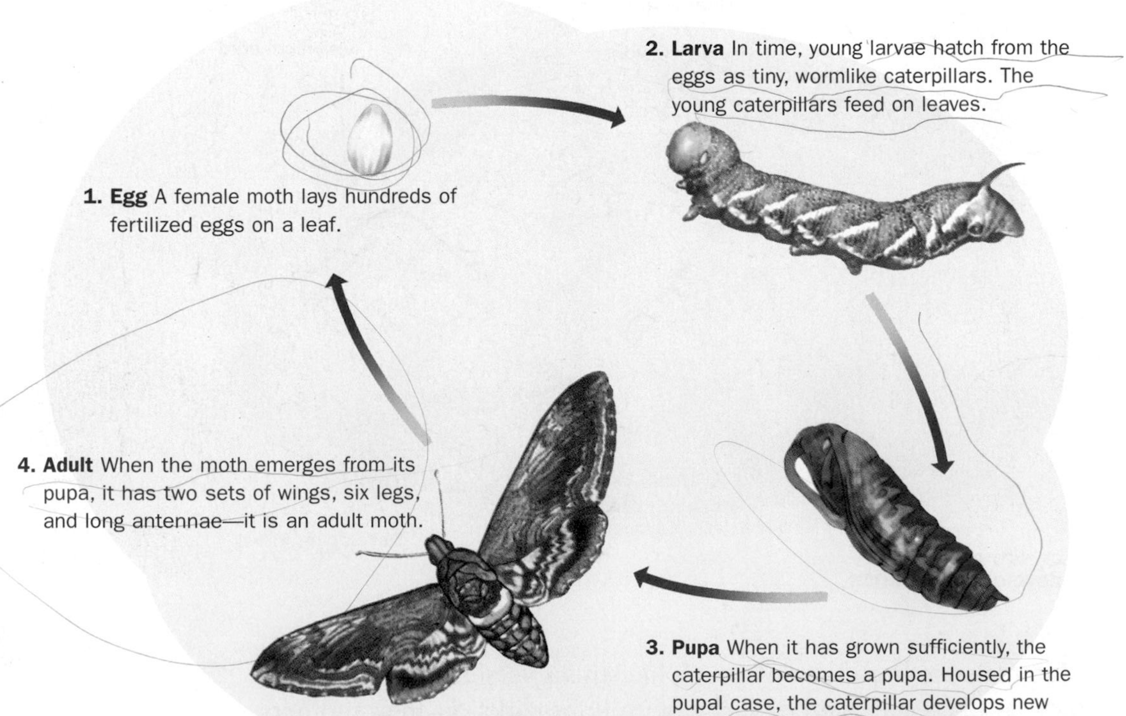

1. Egg A female moth lays hundreds of fertilized eggs on a leaf.
2. Larva In time, young larvae hatch from the eggs as tiny, wormlike caterpillars. The young caterpillars feed on leaves.
3. Pupa When it has grown sufficiently, the caterpillar becomes a pupa. Housed in the pupal case, the caterpillar develops new body parts and changes form.
4. Adult When the moth emerges from its pupa, it has two sets of wings, six legs, and long antennae—it is an adult moth.

Life cycle of the tomato hornworm moth

Amphibians

Frogs and toads are **amphibians,** animals that begin life in water (with gills), but breathe air and can live on land as adults. Like many insects, amphibians undergo metamorphosis during their life cycles.

Word Watch!

The word *amphibian* is formed from the Latin prefix *amphi-* meaning "both" and the Greek *bios* meaning "life." Amphibians live their lives both in water and on land.

1. Female frogs lay large masses of eggs in water. Males deposit sperm that fertilize the eggs.
2. Tiny tadpoles with long tails and no legs hatch from the fertilized eggs. They use gills to get oxygen from water.
3. The tadpole grows hind legs and begins developing lungs that will eventually be used to take in oxygen from the air.
4. The tadpole looks more froglike as it grows front legs and its tail gets smaller. Its lungs are fully functioning, so it must come to the surface to breathe.
5. The tail of the young frog continues to shrink as the body of the frog increases in size.
6. The adult frog has four legs and no tail. It breathes air with lungs, but must remain near water to keep its skin moist.

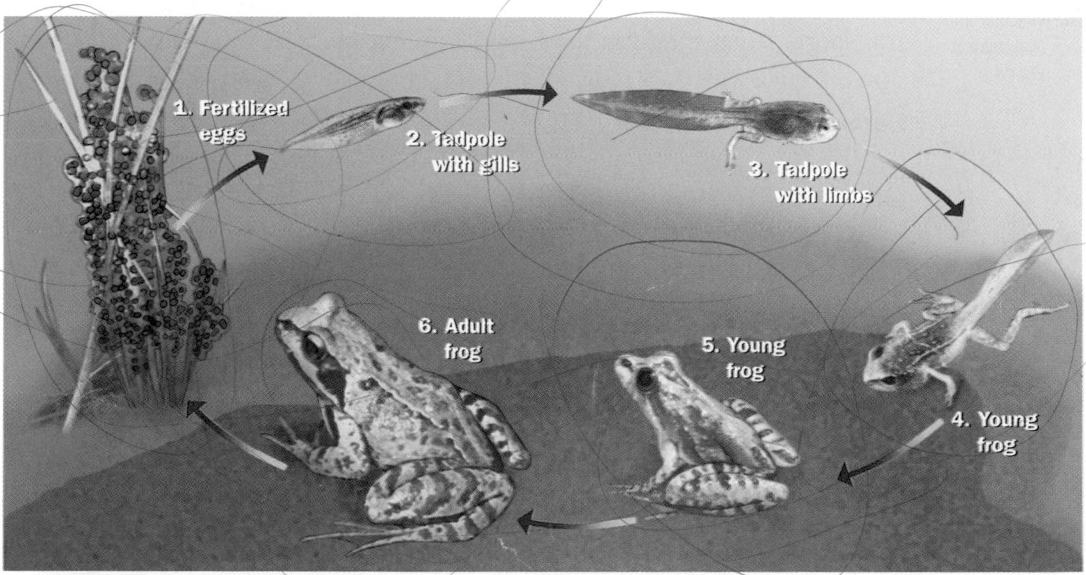

Frog life cycle

Did You Know?

Although both are amphibians, toads have rougher, drier skin than frogs, and cannot jump as high or as far.

107

Plant Physiology

SEE ALSO

079 Cell Processes
153 Plant Kingdom
267 Chemical Formulas
269 Chemical Reactions

Have you ever seen a plant that wasn't green? Probably not. That's because all plants contain the pigment **chlorophyll,** which gives them their green color. But chlorophyll does more than just make a plant green. It also allows the plant to make its own food through a process called **photosynthesis.** During photosynthesis, energy from the sun is used to fuel a chemical reaction between water and carbon dioxide. This reaction produces glucose (a simple sugar) and oxygen.

$$CO_2 + H_2O + \text{energy (sunlight)} \rightarrow \text{glucose (sugar)} + O_2$$

Plants take in carbon dioxide (CO_2) through tiny openings on the underside of their leaves. Oxygen (O_2) formed during photosynthesis is expelled through these same holes.

SEE ALSO

162 Vascular and Nonvascular Plants

Water (H_2O) needed for photosynthesis is taken in by the plant's roots and transported up to the leaves by a specialized tissue called **xylem** (ZY-lum). Another tissue, called **phloem** (FLOW-um), transports sugar made in the leaves to other parts of the plant.

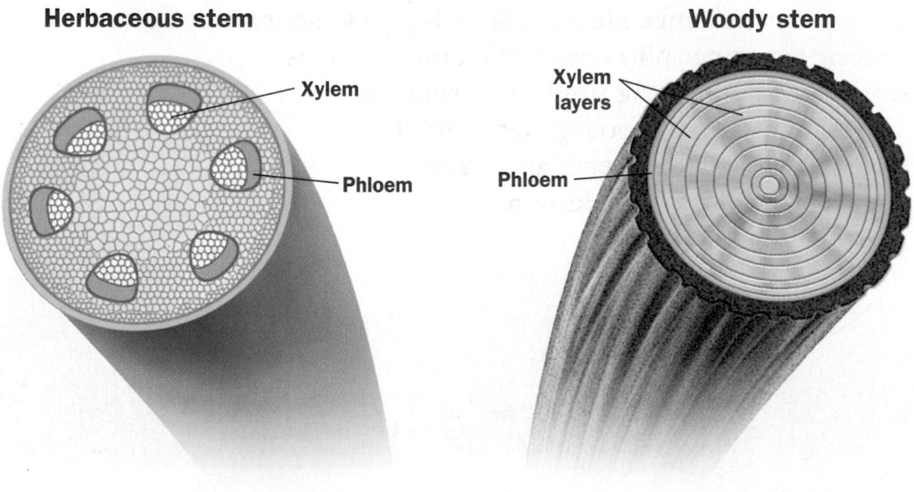

Location of xylem and phloem in herbaceous and woody stems

SEE ALSO

105 Animal Physiology

Like animals, plants get energy through **cellular respiration,** the chemical process where food is combined with oxygen to release energy. Unlike animals, plants produce their own food through photosynthesis, and do not consume other organisms for energy.

Plant Life Cycles

108

Like animals, plants too have life cycles. Let's look at the life cycle of flowering plants, those that produce flowers.

SEE ALSO
153 Plant Kingdom

Science Alert!

Not all plants reproduce using flowers. Some, like pine trees, use cones. The part of the potato plant used for food storage, the potato tuber, can sprout buds that can grow into new plants.

Flowering plants reproduce by forming seeds. A **seed** consists of a young plant and a food supply enclosed in a protective seed coat. Seeds are formed when the female part of a flower is **pollinated** by the male part.

SEE ALSO
114 Sexual Reproduction

A seed can **germinate,** or grow, if environmental conditions such as water and temperature are right. As it begins to germinate, the seed's protective coating splits open and a primary root is sent out from the young plant. Food stored in the seed nourishes the young plant until it can develop the roots, stems, and leaves that will allow it to make its own food.

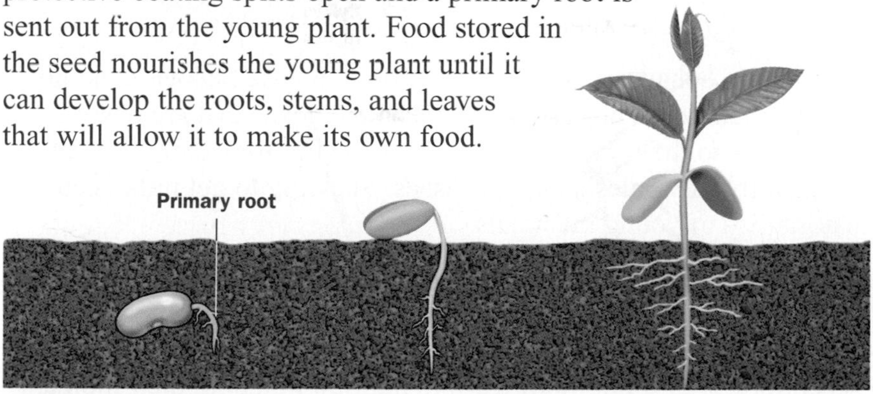

From seed to plant

The young plant develops new leaves as its stem grows up and its roots push deeper into the soil. In some plants, like corn and daisies, the stem grows thicker and stronger but remains green and fleshy, or **herbaceous.** Other plants, like oaks or maples, develop woody stems.

Eventually the plant develops into an adult capable of producing its own seeds. And so the life cycle continues.

Behavior

109

SEE ALSO
127 Natural Selection

A **behavior** is an activity or action that helps an organism survive in its environment, or surroundings. An organism's behavior evolves through adaptation to its environment.

A behavior comes in response to a stimulus. A **stimulus** is any change in the environment that affects the activity of an organism. Changes in light, temperature, sound, and odor are just some of the stimuli that can affect an organism's behavior.

Word Watch!
The plural of *stimulus* is *stimuli*.

110

Animal Behavior

Meerkats are small mammals of southern Africa that live in burrows dug into the soil. Each morning, meerkats emerge from their burrows and line up to take in the warmth of the sun. This behavior is a meerkat ritual.

SEE ALSO
116 Genes
121 Heredity
106 Animal Life Cycles
132 Relationships Between Populations

Many animal behaviors are innate or inborn. **Innate behaviors** do not need to be learned. They are coded for in the genes that are passed from parents to their young. The ability to swim, for example, is an innate ability of whales and most fishes. Suckling to get milk is an innate ability of young mammals.

Other animal behaviors are learned from observations or direct experience. Young animals often learn behaviors by watching their parents. For example, chimpanzees learn to use small sticks to dig insects from soil. Young lions learn to hunt by watching their mothers capture and kill other animals.

Some animals show cooperative behavior that helps them accomplish a task. For example, wolves hunt in packs because they are more likely to capture prey that way. Other animals show cooperative behaviors that help keep them safe from predators. Musk oxen, for example, form a circle when approached by a pack of wolves. By huddling together with their powerful horns facing outward, they protect their bodies from an attack by the wolves.

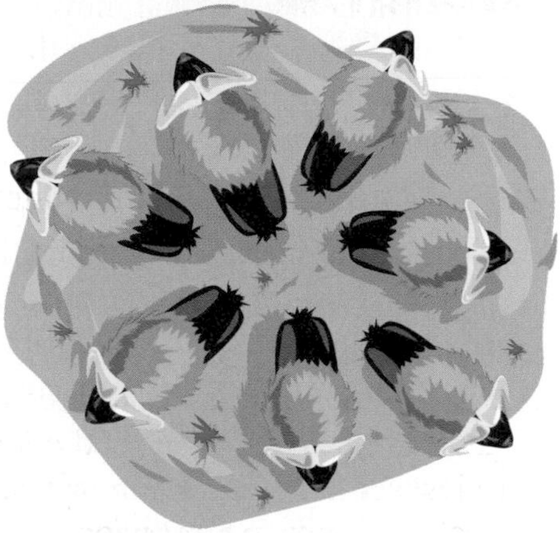

Musk oxen huddling for defense

Much animal behavior is centered on finding a mate. Many birds have elaborate courtship displays and mating dances. It's usually the male birds that have the most colorful plumage and impressive dances. The females are picky when it comes to choosing a mate.

SEE ALSO
113 Reproduction
114 Sexual Reproduction

Baboons and many other primates have complex facial expressions and threatening yawns that keep the social ranks in order. These expressions help other members of the troop to know "who's the boss." Baboons form troops in which the animals work together. This sort of societal living is itself a kind of behavior.

Baboons use facial expressions to show who's in charge.

MORE ▶

Migration is the seasonal movement of animals from one place to another. This behavior allows the animals to take advantage of resources (like food or water) in one location when they run low in another location.

Many birds go on long migrations to reach food or nesting sites. Scientists think that birds may use the position of the sun or Earth's magnetic field to find their way over long distances. The arctic tern holds the record for the longest migrations. Each year it travels from the Arctic to the Antarctic and back, a round trip of more than 35,000 kilometers (about 22,000 miles).

Migratory path of Arctic tern

Another complex behavior of some animals is **hibernation,** a resting state that helps animals survive the winter. During hibernation, a warm-blooded animal such as a ground squirrel slows down its heart rate and breathing rate, and its internal temperature drops to just above freezing in many cases. Only essential life activities take place as the animal goes into a deep sleep in an underground burrow or den. The animal may awake occasionally to move about before entering a hibernating state again. When temperatures rise in the spring, the animal wakes up and leaves the burrow.

SEE ALSO
234 Revolution and Seasons
104 Physiology
105 Animal Physiology

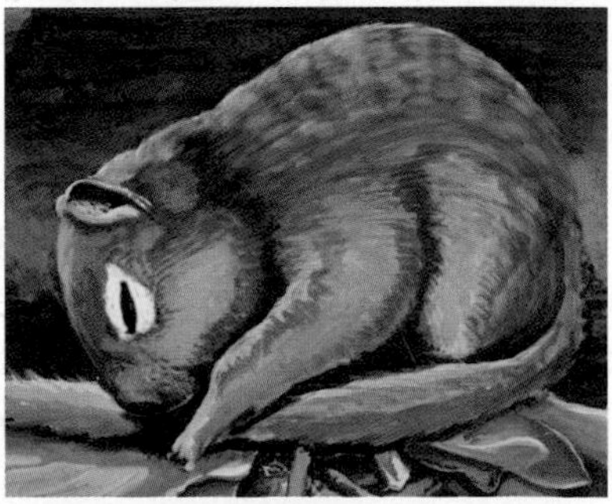
A hibernating squirrel

Science Alert!

Most bears are not *true* hibernators. Bears do enter a sleeplike state when temperatures drop, but their body temperatures do not drop as severely as true hibernators', and they only remain asleep for short periods of time.

Plant Behavior

111

Plants can't move like animals can, but they will still respond to a **stimulus,** or change in the environment. A plant growth in response to a stimulus is called a **tropism.** Plants respond to stimuli such as gravity, light, and touch.

When you drop a seed in soil, you don't have to worry about which direction the seed faces. Why? Because plant roots respond to gravity and so grow down toward Earth's center. Stems, on the other hand, grow upward, or away from the pull of gravity. Plant growth in response to gravity is called **gravitropism** (grav-ih-TROH-piz-um), or geotropism.

Gravitropism

SEE ALSO
276 Gravity

If you place a plant near a window, you will notice that, eventually, most of the leaves will be facing the sun. The leaves turn when cells on one side of the stem grow longer than cells on the other side. This change in the growth of a plant in response to light is called **phototropism.** Phototropism is important because plants need light to carry out photosynthesis.

Phototropism

SEE ALSO
107 Plant Physiology

Some plants respond to touch. For example, vines of beans, peas, and other plants will grab onto and grow upward along a vertical support to maximize the amount of sun they receive. The response of a plant to touch is called **thigmotropism** (thig-ma-TROH-piz-um).

Thigmotropism

Science Alert!

The hinged leaf of a Venus' flytrap plant will snap shut when an insect lands on it. This response is not a tropism, however, because it does not involve growth. The leaf can return to its original position within minutes.

112

Genes and Heredity

Living things reproduce to make more organisms like themselves. When organisms reproduce, many traits, or characteristics, of the parents are passed to the new organism.

113

Reproduction

The process of making more of one's own kind is called **reproduction.** Each **species,** or kind, of organism reproduces only its own kind. So, green mold makes only green mold, octopuses make only octopuses, and humans make only humans. Reproduction is essential for the survival of the species.

114

Sexual Reproduction

SEE ALSO
116 Genes
121 Heredity

Many organisms reproduce by combining cells from two different parents. This type of reproduction is called **sexual reproduction.** In sexual reproduction, the offspring receive genetic material from both parents.

Special cells, called **sperm** and **egg cells,** are used in sexual reproduction. These cells form by a type of cell division called **meiosis.** Cells formed through meiosis have only half the number of **chromosomes,** or genetic material, of the parent cell. For example, most cells of fruit flies have 8 chromosomes (arranged as four **homologous,** or similar, pairs). But the egg or sperm cells of a fruit fly have only 4 chromosomes.

SEE ALSO
077 Animal Cell
078 Plant Cell
116 Genes

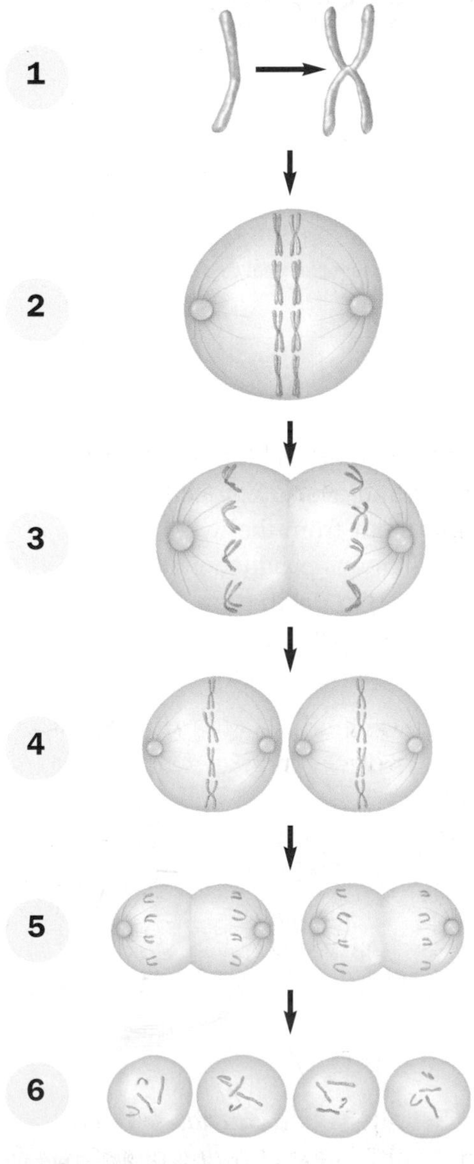

1. Before the cell divides, each chromosome copies itself. Held together at their centers, the copies form a sort of "X."
2. Each chromosome in a cell has a homologous, or similar, pair. These pairs now line up two-by-two in the center of the cell.
3. Each pair of homologous chromosomes separates from the other as they move to opposite sides of the cell. The cytoplasm splits and two new cells form. Each new cell has only one of each homologous pair of chromosomes, half the genetic material of the original cell.
4. The chromosomes again line up in the center of the cell, but this time single-file instead of in pairs.
5. The X-shaped chromosomes split and the copies separate. One copy is pulled to one side of the cell. The other copy is pulled to the other side of the cell.
6. Four new cells have formed from the original cell. Each of the four cells has only half the number of chromosomes that the original cell had, and therefore only half the amount of genetic material.

Stages of meiosis

MORE ▶

For reproduction to occur, the sperm and egg must join together in a process called **fertilization.** Once fertilized, the egg has a complete set of genetic material. This cell, which is now called a **zygote,** is a unique individual that has some traits of each parent.

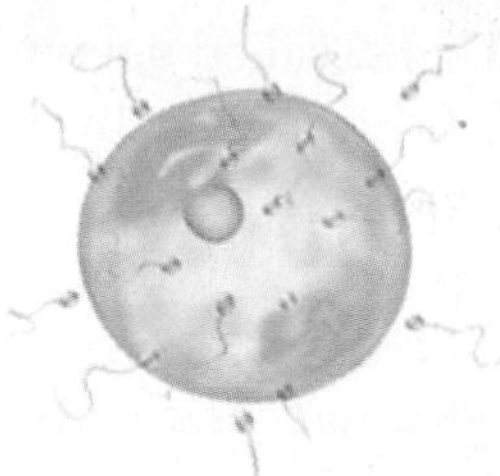

Fertilization occurs after a single sperm enters the egg cell.

Did You Know?

Reproduction without sperm and eggs is called **non-sexual reproduction** (or sometimes **asexual reproduction**). Non-sexual reproduction involves only one parent organism. Some single-celled living things reproduce through simple cell division. In this process, a cell divides, forming two new cells that are identical to the original cell.

SEE ALSO
080 Cell Division
081 Stages of Cell Division

Fertilization occurs in animals when the male's sperm is joined with the female's egg. Something similar occurs in flowering plants.

The female part of the flower is called the **ovary.** Egg cells form in the ovary. A long tube, or **pistil,** grows out from the ovary. Surrounding the pistil are **stamens.** Stamens produce **pollen,** a dust-like material that contains sperm cells. **Pollination,** the transfer of pollen from stamen to pistil, must occur in order for a new plant to form. When pollen lands on a pistil, sperm cells move down to the ovary, fertilizing the egg cells.

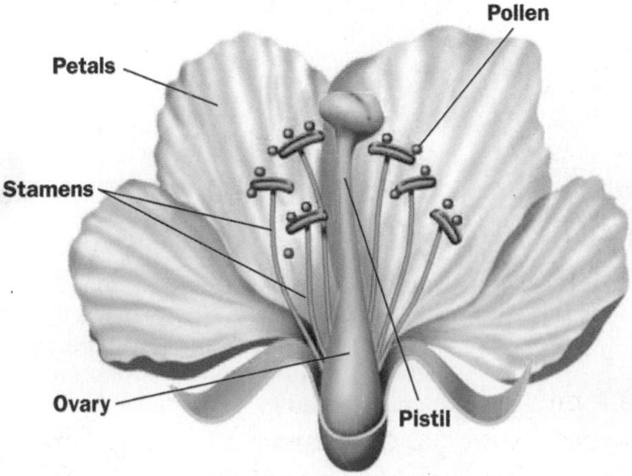

Parts of a flower

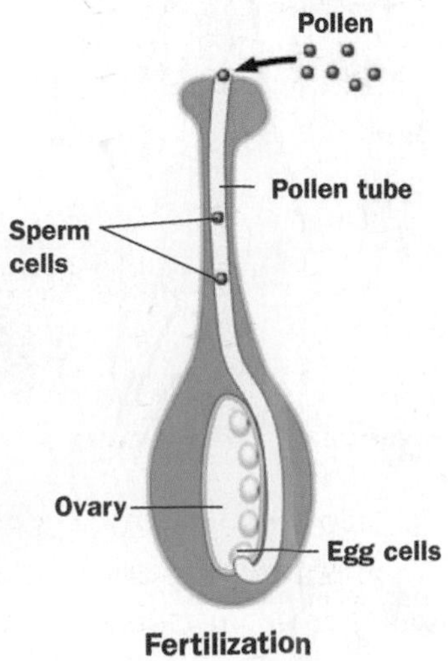

Fertilization

DNA

115

When organisms reproduce, traits are passed from parent to offspring. These traits are carried in **DNA,** the genetic material found in a cell's nucleus. DNA acts like a blueprint for the cells of an organism, instructing them how to put together materials to produce certain traits.

SEE ALSO
077 Animal Cell
078 Plant Cell

DNA is a very large molecule with a shape similar to a twisted ladder. The rungs of the ladder are made up of molecules called bases. The bases are adenine, thymine, guanine, and cytosine. These bases always pair up so that adenine is joined with thymine (A–T) and cytosine is joined with guanine (C–G). The sides of the ladder are made up of phosphate and sugar molecules.

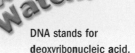

Word Watch! DNA stands for **deoxyribonucleic acid.**

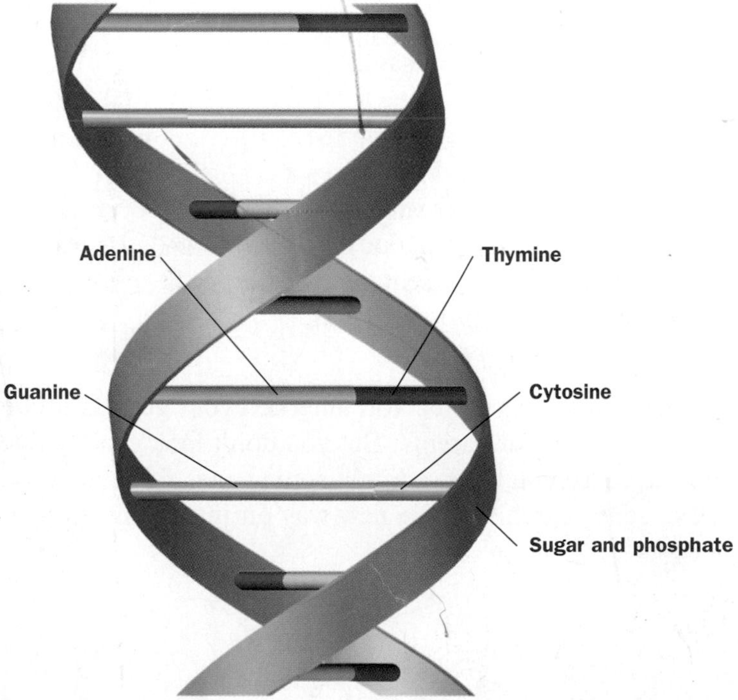

A model of DNA structure

A DNA molecule may contain millions of base pairs. It is the arrangement of these base pairs that determines whether the organism is a rose, a robin, a fish, or a fruit fly.

Genes

116

SEE ALSO

077 Animal Cell

115 DNA

A mother cat has a litter of kittens. Each kitten in the litter has different colors, markings, or other features. Why? Each kitten received a different combination of genes from its parents. **Genes** are segments of DNA that carry instructions for the traits of an organism from parent to offspring. Genes are located on **chromosomes** in the nuclei, or center, of cells. Each type of organism has a fixed number of chromosomes.

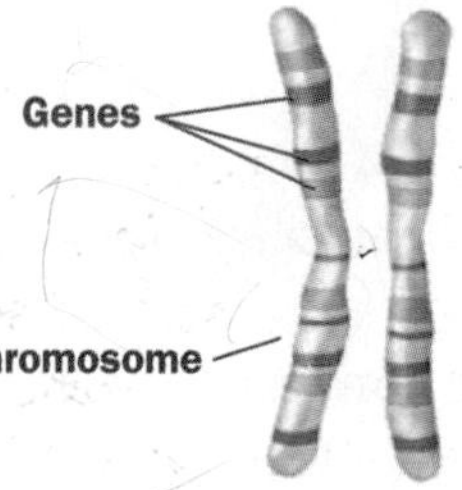

Genes are located on chromosomes.

A chromosome may contain thousands of genes. Genes control traits. Imagine a cat with black and white fur. The genes in the nuclei of this cat's cells direct the production of proteins that cause black or white fur to grow on certain parts of its body. The petals of a sunflower are bright yellow because its genes direct the production of proteins that specify a yellow color.

SEE ALSO

079 Cell Processes

114 Sexual Reproduction

Your genes determine your traits. You inherited your genes and the traits they carry from your parents. But you don't look exactly like either parent because you received only some genes from each parent. These genes combined in a new way during fertilization.

Science Alert!

Some genes control more than one trait, and some traits are controlled by more than one gene.

The Human Genome

117

Your genes determine your skin color, your hair texture, and whether or not you can roll your tongue into a U-shape. Each of these three traits is controlled by a segment of DNA called a **gene.** Humans have thousands of different genes. They are located on the 23 pairs of chromosomes in the nuclei of our body cells. Taken together, all these genes make up the human **genome.**

SEE ALSO
115 DNA
077 Animal Cell

Mom, Tommy's
rolling his tongue
at me again!

One pair of chromosomes is different from all the others in your cells. This chromosome pair decides if you are male or female. Females have two X chromosomes (written XX). Males have one X and one Y chromosome (written XY). The X and Y chromosomes are the only pair that doesn't match in size.

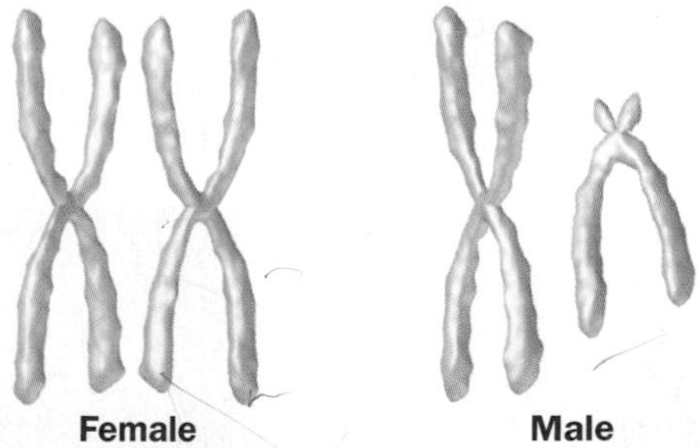

Female
(Two X chromosomes)

Male
(X and Y chromosomes)

The Human Genome Project

118

The DNA of the human genome is like a huge puzzle. Many scientists have spent years trying to find the meaning of all its pieces. Mapping the role of each of the genes located on 23 pairs of human chromosomes was the primary goal of the **Human Genome Project.** This project has shown that the human genome contains a sequence of more than three billion base pairs. Some of these bases form the 30,000 or so genes evidence suggests make up the human genome.

SEE ALSO
115 DNA

MORE ▶

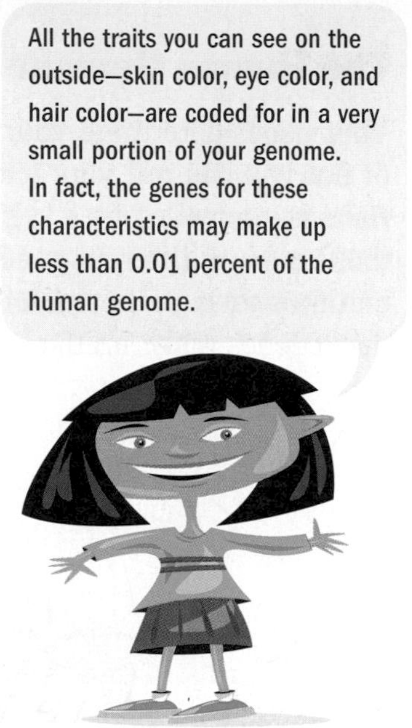

All the traits you can see on the outside—skin color, eye color, and hair color—are coded for in a very small portion of your genome. In fact, the genes for these characteristics may make up less than 0.01 percent of the human genome.

SEE ALSO
089 Digestive System
093 Circulatory System
115 DNA

By the summer of 2000, scientists announced that they had made a rough map of the human genome. And what they discovered was amazing: evidence they found suggests that 99.9 percent of the human genome is the same in everyone. For example, everyone has identical genes for making enzymes that digest food, or for making red blood cells. Scientists call these identical base pair sequences "workhorse" genes. Scientists have also identified what they call "junk DNA," long sequences of genetic material that don't seem to serve any purpose. Scientists may one day discover a function for these base pair sequences as well.

SEE ALSO
093 Circulatory System
092 Respiratory System

Because some health disorders are passed from parent to offspring, another goal of the Human Genome Project was to identify where genes that cause hereditary disorders are located on chromosomes. Examples of such disorders include hemophilia (a blood-clotting disorder) and cystic fibrosis (a respiratory disorder). Knowing exactly where these disorders occur in the genome can help scientists in their effort to combat them.

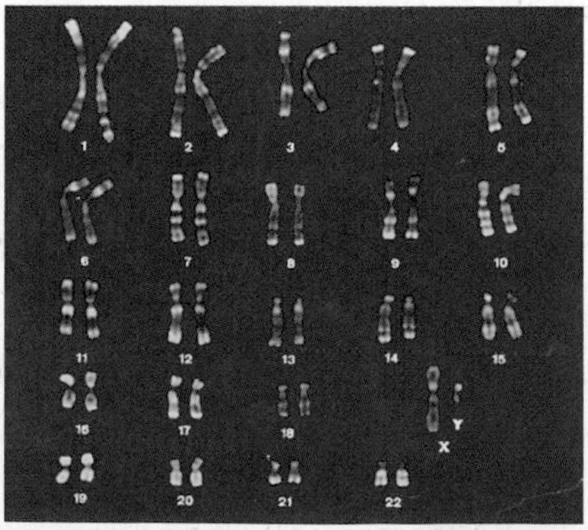

The gene responsible for cystic fibrosis is found on chromosome 7.

Knowing the exact sequence of base pairs in DNA is helping scientists learn a great deal about human traits. Scientists are also studying the genomes of many other animals and plants. Data from such projects may help scientists develop cures for diseases, and improve life for people and other organisms all over the world.

Twins

119

Your DNA is not exactly the same as that of your parents or your siblings—unless you have an identical twin. **Identical twins** are two individuals that formed from one egg fertilized by one sperm. Because identical twins form from the same egg and sperm, they have exactly the same genes. This is why identical twins are either both girls or both boys.

SEE ALSO
117 The Human Genome

Identical twins

Fraternal twins

Not all twins are identical. Sometimes a female releases two egg cells at the same time. Each egg cell can be fertilized by a different sperm and develop inside the mother at the same time. This results in **fraternal twins,** offspring formed when two different egg cells are fertilized by different sperm cells at the same time. Unlike identical twins, the fraternal twins are no more genetically similar than any other two children from the same parents. This is why fraternal twins can be of the opposite sex.

Cloning

120

A process called **cloning** can be used to produce offspring that are genetically identical to their parent. Cloning uses cells or tissues from the body of an organism to produce a new organism with identical traits. In recent years, scientists have developed ways of cloning animals and plants. For example, scientists in Scotland used cells from the body of a mature sheep to develop a genetically identical offspring. Cloning may someday be used to develop farm animals that have very specific traits.

Many people are concerned that the cloning of animals may lead to the cloning of people. **Scientific ethics** is the study of the impact of technology and science on human society.

SEE ALSO
361 Ethical Limits on Technology
116 Genes

SCILINKS NSTA
Keyword: Medical Ethics/Cloning
www.scilinks.org
Code: GSSM361

121 Heredity

Genes are segments of DNA that carry instructions for the traits of an organism. When organisms reproduce, genetic information from each parent is passed to the next generation. This passing of traits from parents to offspring is called **heredity.**

SEE ALSO
116 Genes
115 DNA
114 Sexual Reproduction

Did You Know?

The Austrian monk Gregor Mendel is often called the "Father of Genetics." Mendel did many early experiments with heredity, setting the stage for **genetics,** the study of heredity.

Human heredity is fascinating. Many easily observable traits are inherited, including hair and eye color, skin type, and height.

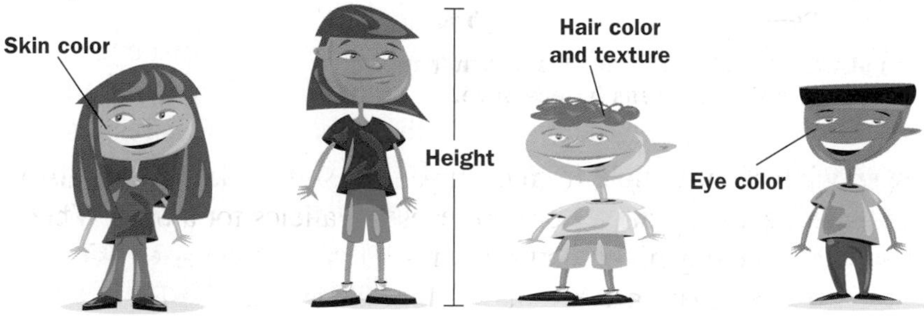

Some inheritable traits

Traits acquired during your lifetime, such as a dyed hair color or the shape of a nose that has been altered by surgery, cannot be inherited.

Traits for health conditions can also be inherited. Examples of such conditions include hemophilia (a blood-clotting disorder) and color-blindness (a disorder that makes a person unable to distinguish some colors).

Traits like height, weight, and the shape of your body and face are the kinds of traits that are inherited but are also greatly influenced by your environment. For example, your diet, state of health, and the amount of exercise you get can change your body size and appearance. Exposure to the sun can change the pigment in some people's skin, as happens when they tan. The genes you inherit give you the potential for many traits. But the person you become depends very much on your environment.

Dominant and Recessive Alleles

Every organism has a set of genes that determines its traits. These genes occur in pairs. Each gene in a pair is known as an **allele.** If one of the alleles masks the effect of the other allele, it is called a **dominant** allele. The allele that is masked by the dominant allele is called a **recessive** allele.

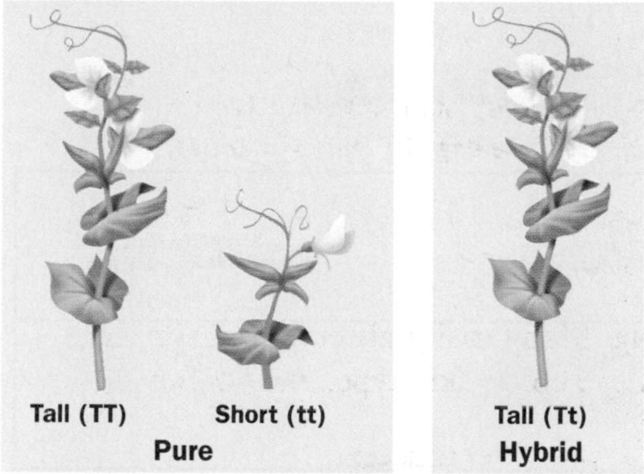

In pea plants, the allele for tallness is dominant while the allele for shortness is recessive.

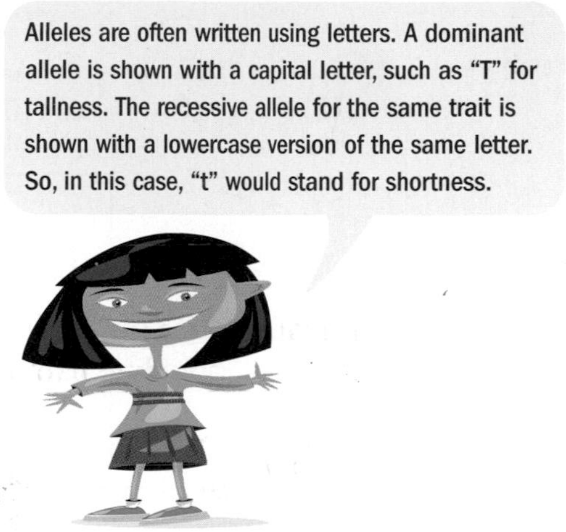

Alleles are often written using letters. A dominant allele is shown with a capital letter, such as "T" for tallness. The recessive allele for the same trait is shown with a lowercase version of the same letter. So, in this case, "t" would stand for shortness.

Offspring inherit one allele from each parent. Sometimes an organism inherits two dominant alleles or two recessive alleles for a trait. When this happens, the organism shows the trait carried by the allele. For example, if a pea plant has two alleles for tallness (the dominant trait), it will be tall. If, however, it has two alleles for shortness (the recessive trait), it will be short. An organism that carries two dominant or two recessive alleles for a given trait is said to be **pure** for that trait.

SEE ALSO
114 Sexual Reproduction

In other cases, organisms inherit two different alleles for a trait. For example, a pea plant may inherit an allele for tallness from one parent and an allele for shortness from the other. When this happens, the dominant allele hides the effect of the recessive allele. An organism that carries both a dominant allele and a recessive allele for a certain trait is called a **hybrid.**

DOMINANT AND RECESSIVE TRAITS

Dominant Form of Trait	Recessive Form of Trait
curly hair	straight hair
widow's peak	straight hairline
free ear lobe	attached ear lobe

123

Punnett Squares

SEE ALSO

122 Dominant and Recessive Alleles

A table called a **Punnett square** can be used to predict what traits offspring will have based on what traits the parents have. In a Punnett square, the top of the table shows the alleles contributed by the male. Along the side are the two alleles that the female contributes. The squares show the possibilities of allele pairs in the offspring.

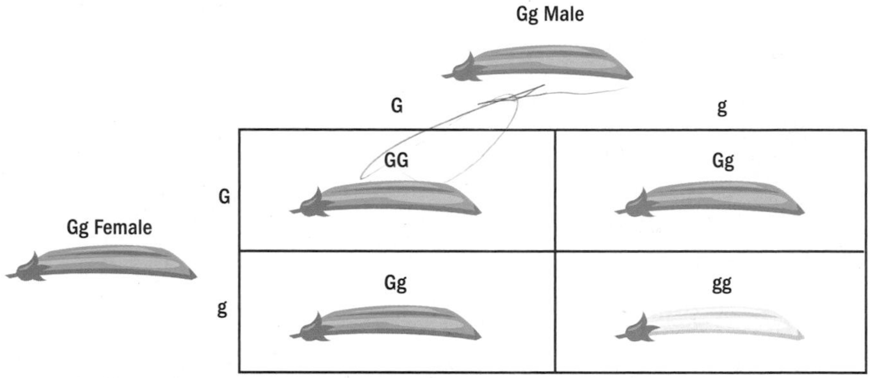

Punnett square showing results of Gg × Gg cross

In pea plants, green (G) is the dominant pod color. Yellow (g) is the recessive pod color. As the Punnett square above shows, GG, Gg, and gg are all the possible genotypes pea plant offspring can have for pod color. A **genotype** is the set of alleles an organism has for a trait. A **phenotype** is the appearance the trait takes on. In this example, the plants with gg genotype have a yellow phenotype. But, both the GG and Gg genotypes show a green phenotype because green is a dominant color in pea pods. Three of the squares show a green pod and only one shows a yellow pod. So it's likely that if these two plants (Gg male and Gg female) were crossed, the offspring would show about three times as many green pods as yellow.

SEE ALSO

116 Genes

It's sometimes difficult to predict traits—like hair and eye color—in people because you may have several different genes that control these traits. But tongue rolling is controlled by a single gene. You can either roll your tongue (R) or you can't (r). If a RR parent and a rr parent have offspring, all will be able to roll their tongue as all will be hybrids (Rr).

124

Change and Diversity of Life

Earth is home to millions of different organisms, some as large as whales, others as small as algae. This variety of life is known as **biodiversity.** But the organisms that share Earth today may not have shared it thousands of years ago. This is because the diversity of life on Earth is always changing.

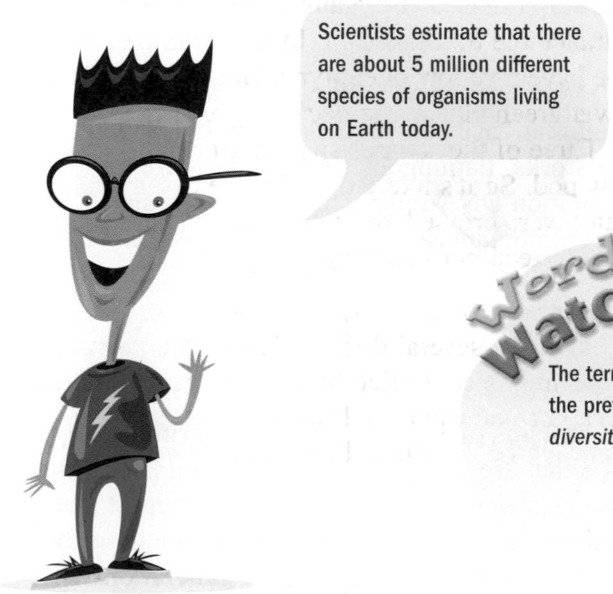

Scientists estimate that there are about 5 million different species of organisms living on Earth today.

Word Watch!

The term *biodiversity* is formed from the prefix *bio-* meaning "life," and *diversity* meaning "variety."

125

Recognizing Common Ancestors

SEE ALSO
130 Populations

Tigers from India, lions from Africa, and jaguars from South America are different species, or kinds, of animals. But these "big cats" are related to each other and to other animal species. In fact, scientists have found evidence suggesting that all organisms on Earth share a common ancestor.

Biologists look at physical structures to decide how closely related different species are. The bone in your upper arm, for example, is very similar to the upper bone of a whale's flipper, a bat's wing, or a horse's front leg. These similarities suggest that you and these other animals have a common ancestor.

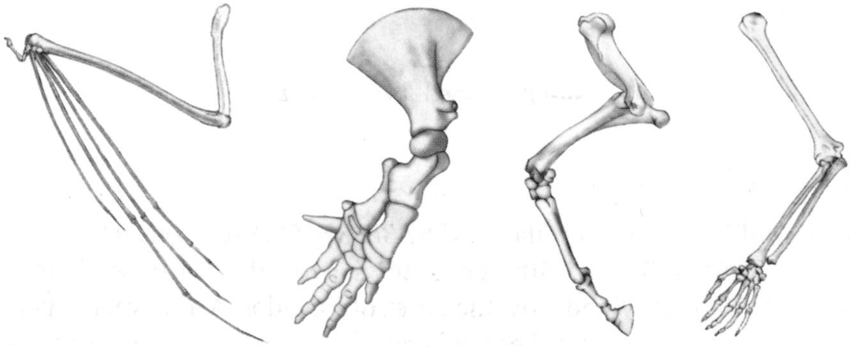

Similar bone structure in the upper arm suggests these animals have a common ancestor.

SEE ALSO
115 DNA

Other comparisons show that organisms with certain physical similarities often have similar base pair sequences on their DNA. Large wading birds like storks, flamingoes, and pelicans, for example, share many common DNA sequences. This suggests that these birds have a common ancestor.

126

The Theory of Evolution

SEE ALSO
198 Fossils
200 Geologic Time Scale

Fossils are the physical remains of organisms, or an imprint of the physical remains. Fossils that are millions of years old tell about life on Earth long before humans were around. Fossils also suggest that organisms have changed over time. The **theory of evolution** describes the slow change in organisms that occurs over many generations.

Many of today's ideas about evolution are based on the work of Charles Darwin. In the 1850s, Darwin described how organisms might change over time. Most of these ideas came from observations Darwin made during the five years he worked as a naturalist on the research ship H.M.S. *Beagle.*

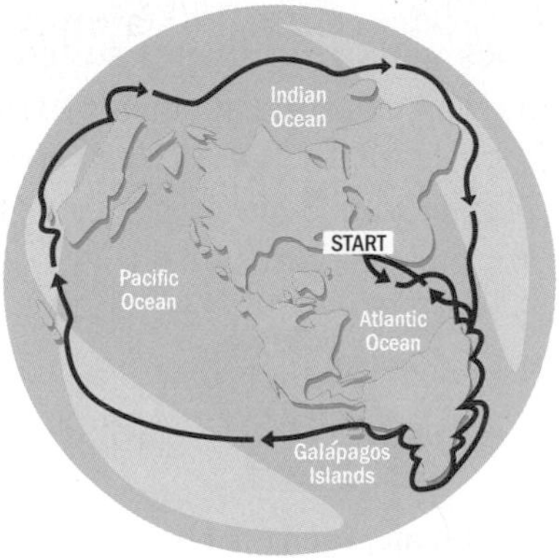

Voyage of the H.M.S. *Beagle*

Natural Selection

As part of his journey on the H.M.S. *Beagle,* Charles Darwin observed and studied 13 different species, or kinds, of finches living on the Galápagos Islands, off the coast of Ecuador. A few years later, Darwin proposed that all these different finches had evolved, through natural selection, from a single kind of finch found on mainland Ecuador. Darwin defined **natural selection** as the process by which organisms change over time, as those best suited to their environment survive to pass their traits to the next generation.

SEE ALSO
130 Populations
121 Heredity

Here are the main points of Darwin's ideas about natural selection:

1. Organisms produce many more offspring than can survive.
2. There is competition among offspring for food, space, and other resources.
3. There is natural variety (difference) among the offspring of an organism. These variations are caused mainly by genetic differences.
4. Individuals with certain traits are better suited to survive in their environment than those without the traits.
5. Organisms that survive and reproduce pass the genes for their useful traits on to the next generation.

SEE ALSO
113 Reproduction
131 Factors That Affect Populations
132 Relationships Between Populations
116 Genes
121 Heredity

MORE ▶

Darwin argued that natural differences in the beak shapes of some finches allowed them to eat food other finches could not. For example, finches with long, pointy beaks could pick insects from tree bark. Finches with harder, more rounded beaks could easily grind large seeds and fruits. Over time, the finches best able to get food had offspring with similar beak shapes. Over many generations, separate groups of finches with beak shapes suited to specific types of food emerged. In this way, a single species of finch evolved into many different species.

Large ground finch
Beak suited for grinding fruits

Small ground finch
Beak suited for eating tiny seeds

Warbler finch
Beak suited for picking insects from tree bark

SEE ALSO
147 Deserts
121 Heredity

Adaptation plays a major role in natural selection. An **adaptation** is a characteristic or trait that helps an organism survive in its environment. Spiny leaves are an adaptation of the cactus plant that reduces water loss and keeps the plant from being eaten. An adaptation makes an organism more suited to its environment, and therefore more likely to survive and pass on its traits to the next generation.

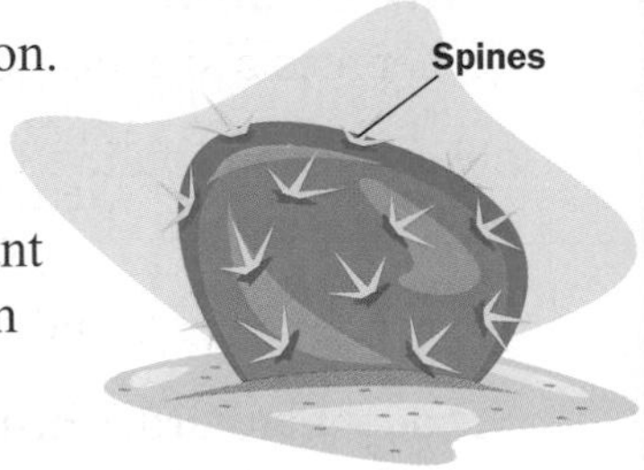

SEE ALSO
116 Genes
080 Cell Division
132 Relationships Between Populations

Adaptations can arise only if there is variety within the offspring of a species. Variety in offspring is the result of **genetic variation,** the normal differences that exist among individuals of the same species. Greater variation is caused by **mutations,** or random changes in genes. Sometimes mutations are harmful. For example, a mutation may cause an animal that usually has brown fur to be born with white fur. If the white color makes it hard for the animal to hide, it may be captured by a predator. Other mutations are helpful, such as a mutation that causes bright color patterns in flower petals—all the better to attract pollinating insects.

SEE ALSO
108 Plant Life Cycles

Extinction

When all the organisms of a species die, the species goes **extinct.** Today, about 5 million species live on Earth. But fossil evidence suggests that these are only a small fraction of all the species that have ever lived. Some species have evolved into new species. Other species have died out.

SEE ALSO
340 Wildlife Conservation

One important way scientists know that living things have changed over time is through evidence provided by fossils. **Fossils** are the remains or other evidence of organisms that lived in the past. Bones, seeds, leaves, flowers, shells, and even animal tracks can become fossils over time.

SEE ALSO
198 Fossils
200 Geologic Time Scale

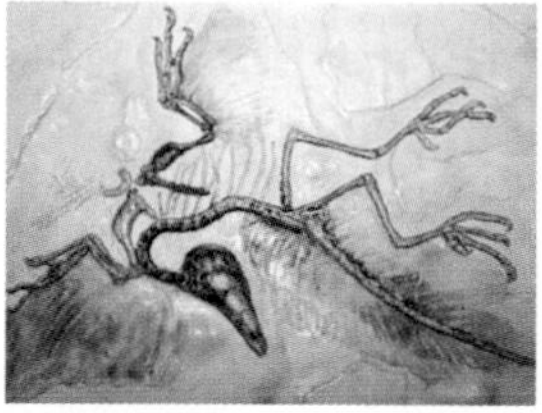

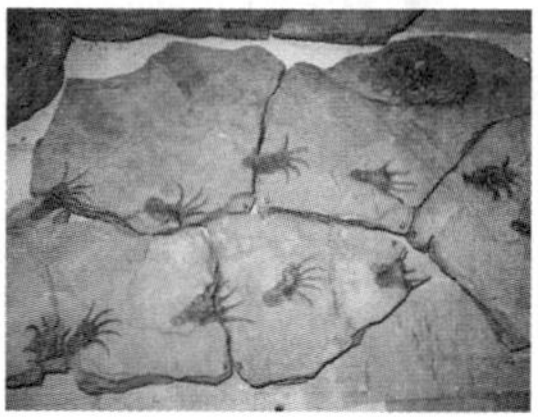

Sometimes a species goes extinct because its environment changes and the species cannot adapt to the change. For example, a species may go extinct if the temperature or rainfall in its environment changes and it cannot find a way to adapt. Or perhaps a main food source disappears and the species cannot find a substitute source.

SEE ALSO
131 Factors That Affect Populations

Throughout Earth's history, many instances of widespread extinction have occurred. **Mass extinctions** are periods when many species of organisms died out at the same time. These extinctions usually occurred when living things could not adapt to sudden and severe changes in their environment. Such changes may have included climatic changes, such as those that accompanied the ice ages, or geological changes, such as volcanic eruptions. Extinction is a natural part of the process of evolution.

SEE ALSO
194 Earth History

SEE ALSO
107 Plant Physiology

Did You Know?

Dinosaurs ruled the Earth during the Jurassic Period, approximately 180 million years ago. Evidence suggests that the dinosaurs died out 65 million years ago when an asteroid struck Earth, throwing ash and other particles up into the atmosphere and blocking out sunlight plants needed to grow. Without plants to eat, the dinosaurs soon died out.

129

Ecosystems

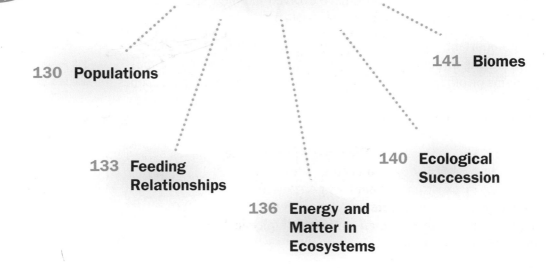

An **ecosystem** is all the organisms that live in an area together with the nonliving factors of the environment. The study of how organisms interact with each other and with their physical environment is the focus of **ecology.**

130

Populations

When you talk about a certain *kind* of organism, you're really talking about a certain *species* of organism. A **species** is a group of organisms that can mate and produce offspring that in turn can produce more offspring.

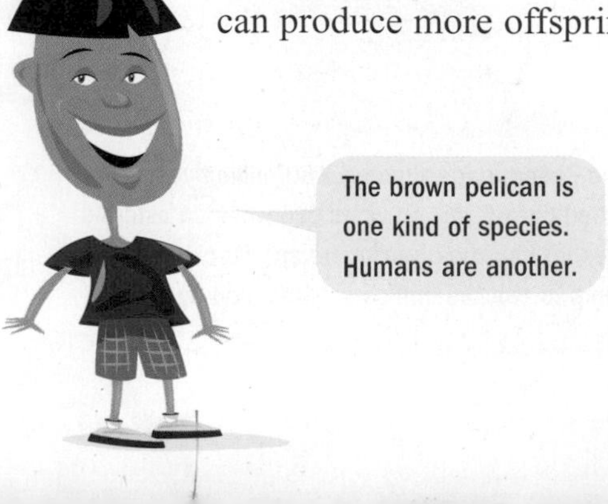

The brown pelican is one kind of species. Humans are another.

All the organisms of the same species that live in the same place at the same time make up a **population.** The mice living in a small meadow are an example of a population. All the pine trees in a forest are a different population.

Populations do not live alone. They share the environment with other populations to form a **community.** The pine trees in a forest, for example, may form a community with populations of deer, mice, raccoons, bacteria, mushrooms, and ferns.

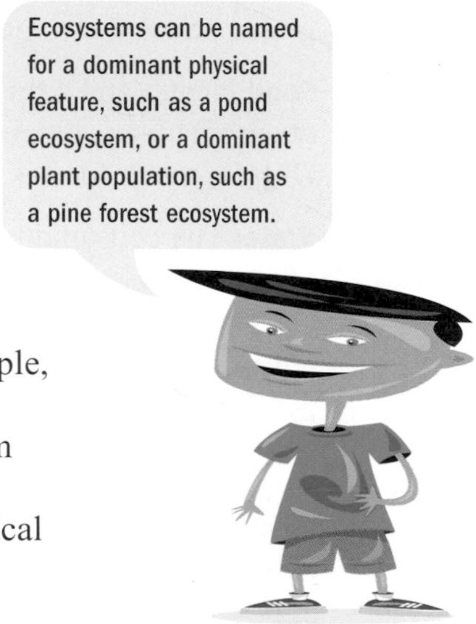

Ecosystems can be named for a dominant physical feature, such as a pond ecosystem, or a dominant plant population, such as a pine forest ecosystem.

Populations do not interact only with each other. They also interact with the nonliving factors of the environment. Pine trees, for example, need soil to grow. They also need air and water. Together, these living and nonliving factors form an ecosystem. An **ecosystem** includes all the populations that live in an area along with physical factors in the environment.

■ **Non-living factors** □ **Living factors**

A pine forest ecosystem

131 Factors That Affect Populations

For any population to thrive, there must be enough food, water, and living space. Such factors are called **limiting factors** because they limit how many organisms can live in an environment.

Listed below are some of the different kinds of limiting factors.

Food Plants (and a few other organisms) make their own food. All other organisms obtain food by eating plants or other organisms. Only so much food is available in an ecosystem.

Water The cells and tissues of animals and plants are made up mostly of water. All living things need water to move materials around in the cells and tissues of their bodies.

Light Plants and other organisms that make their own food need light to carry out photosynthesis. If light is limited, the growth of these organisms will also be limited.

Living space Organisms need enough room to live, obtain resources, and reproduce. The place where an organism lives is called its **habitat.**

One way organisms reduce competition for food and other resources is to occupy a specific niche within a habitat. A **niche** is the special role an organism plays within its habitat. Different species may share the same habitat, but no two can have exactly the same niche. For example, deer, rabbits, and squirrels may live in the same leafy forest, but because deer browse higher up on trees, rabbits graze on grasses, and squirrels eat acorns, each animal occupies a different niche.

SEE ALSO
156 Protist Kingdom
157 Archaebacteria and Eubacteria Kingdoms
077 Animal Cell
078 Plant Cell
082 Tissues, Organs, and Systems
079 Cell Processes
107 Plant Physiology
113 Reproduction

Animals with same habitat, but different niches

Relationships Between Populations

Different species, or kinds, of organisms living together interact with one another. The relationships they form can be divided into three main categories:

Competition occurs whenever more than one individual or population tries to make use of the same limited resource. Because resources such as food, water, and space are limited, there is not enough for every organism. Only those organisms able to get the resources they need will survive.

SEE ALSO
130 Populations
127 Natural Selection

Predation is a type of feeding relationship in which one animal captures and eats another animal for food. The animal that is eaten is the **prey.** The animal eating the prey is the **predator.** Predator-prey relationships help keep an ecosystem in balance by preventing any one population from getting too large.

SEE ALSO
133 Feeding Relationships
134 Food Chains
135 Food Webs
129 Ecosystems

Symbiosis is a close relationship between two species. There are several types of symbiosis. **Mutualism** is a relationship in which both species benefit. **Commensalism** is a type of symbiosis in which one species benefits while the other seems to be unaffected. **Parasitism** occurs when an organism called a parasite feeds on the cells, tissues, or fluids of another organism called the **host.** In this relationship, the parasite benefits by getting food; the host is usually weakened, but not killed.

SEE ALSO
076 Cells
082 Tissues, Organs, and Systems

Mistletoe is a parasite that gets its nutrients from other plants.

Word Watch!

Symbiosis comes from the Greek *symbioun,* meaning "to live together."

133

Feeding Relationships

SEE ALSO
159 Heterotrophs and Autotrophs
107 Plant Physiology

All organisms need energy to live. Organisms can be divided into three main groups—producers, consumers, and decomposers—based on how they get the energy they need to live.

Plants, algae, and bacteria that make their own food are **producers.** Most producers make their food using the energy of the sun and raw materials from the environment.

Any organism that gets its food by eating other organisms is a **consumer.** Consumers are classified into groups based on what they eat.

SEE ALSO
153 Plant Kingdom
154 Animal Kingdom
155 Fungi Kingdom
156 Protist Kingdom
157 Archaebacteria and Eubacteria Kingdoms
139 Nitrogen Cycle

- **Herbivores** are plant-eaters. They feed directly on producers. Animals that eat plants (such as rabbits) or those that eat plant products (such as squirrels eating acorns) are herbivores.
- **Carnivores** are meat-eaters. They get food by eating herbivores or other carnivores. Examples of carnivores include sharks, wolves, and eagles. **Scavengers,** on the other hand, eat the remains of organisms left behind by other animals. Examples of scavengers include hyenas and crabs.
- **Omnivores** are organisms that feed on both producers and other consumers. Raccoons, bears, people (except strict vegetarians), and skunks are omnivores.

Organisms that feed on the remains or wastes of other organisms are known as **decomposers.** Many bacteria and fungi are decomposers.

Producer

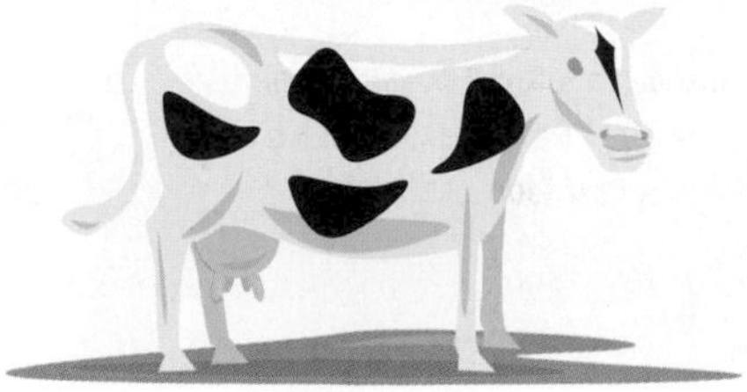

Consumer

Decomposer

Food Chains

134

Organisms get the energy they need from food. A **food chain** traces the path of energy as it moves from one organism to the next in an ecosystem. In most ecosystems, energy begins with the sun, so producers (organisms that use the sun's energy to make food) always form the base, or starting point, of a food chain. Arrows show the direction of energy movement in a food chain.

SEE ALSO
300 Forms of Energy
137 Energy

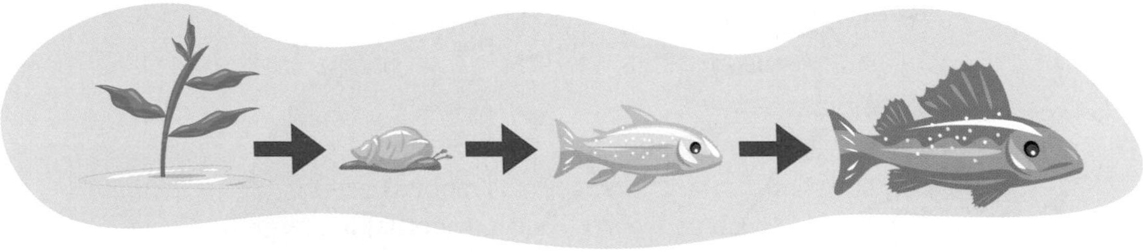

A food chain

In the food chain above, the pondweed is the producer. As shown by the arrow, energy moves from the pondweed to the snail that eats it. The snail is the **primary consumer** in this food chain because it is the first to feed. Energy next moves from the snail to the minnow. As the second consumer in the food chain, the minnow is a **secondary consumer.** When the perch eats the minnow, it takes in energy. The perch is the **tertiary consumer** in this food chain—the third feeder. The final link in a food chain is filled by the bacteria and fungi that act as decomposers. These organisms feed on and break down the remains of the perch when it dies.

SEE ALSO
133 Feeding Relationships
139 Nitrogen Cycle

Science Alert!

Decomposers are often left out of food chain diagrams. But remember that decomposers are always the final link in a food chain.

135 Food Webs

SEE ALSO
134 Food Chains
129 Ecosystems

A food chain shows only one energy path in an ecosystem. But most organisms are part of more than one food chain. Scientists often use a food web to show a more complete picture of the flow of energy in an ecosystem. A **food web** is a system of several overlapping food chains.

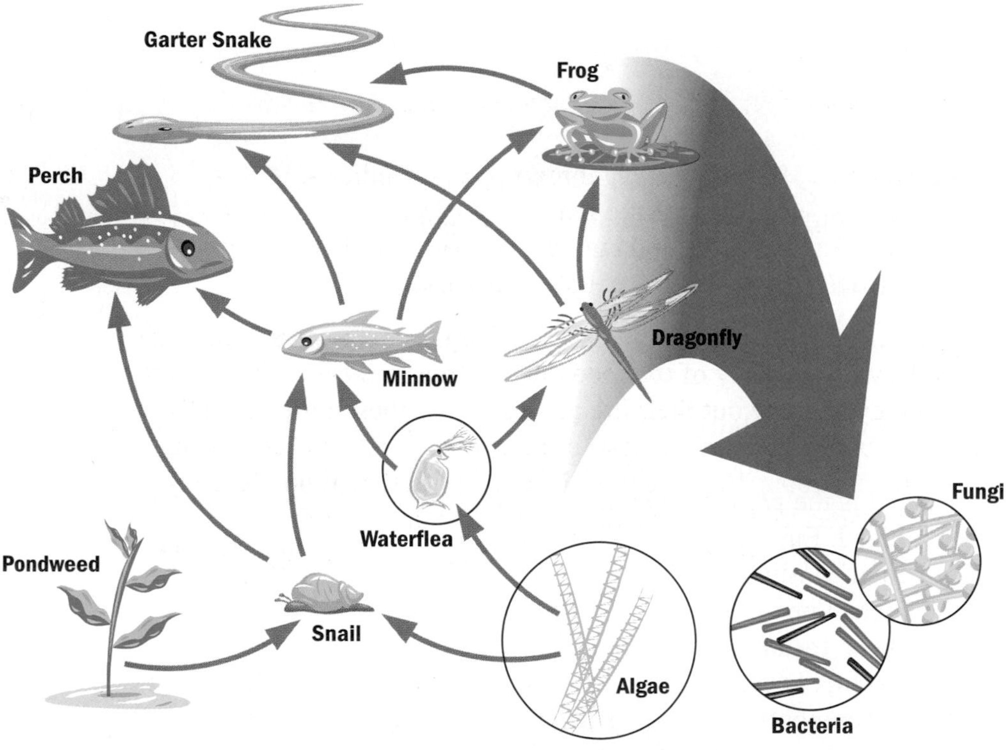

A food web

SEE ALSO
300 Forms of Energy
137 Energy
133 Feeding Relationships
139 Nitrogen Cycle

As with most ecosystems, the energy in a pond ecosystem starts with the sun. This energy is taken in by producers and converted to food energy. The energy in food then moves through different levels of consumers. The movement of energy ends with the many bacteria and fungi that live in the mud at the bottom of the pond. These decomposers feed on the wastes and remains of pond organisms. As they feed, they break down the organisms' tissues into valuable materials that are then returned to the ecosystem.

Energy and Matter in Ecosystems

136

Energy and matter are two factors present in every ecosystem. Most of the energy that enters an ecosystem comes from the sun. Some of this energy is converted into chemical energy that moves through the ecosystem by way of food chains. The matter in an ecosystem includes food, water, and air. This matter is constantly being changed in form and recycled through the environment.

SEE ALSO
250 Matter
300 Forms of Energy
134 Food Chains

Energy

137

The energy in most ecosystems begins with the sun. Plants and other organisms with chlorophyll in their cells can capture this energy and use it to make food through photosynthesis. In this process, light energy is used to make sugar from carbon dioxide and water. Energy from food may be used by an organism for its life activities, or stored in its cells and tissues.

SEE ALSO
107 Plant Physiology
076 Cells
082 Tissues, Organs, and Systems

Energy stored in the cells and tissues of organisms is passed through the ecosystem by way of the food chain. Organisms at each level use the energy to carry out their life processes. As these processes are carried out, some energy is lost to the environment as heat. For this reason, only about 10 percent of the energy present at one feeding level is passed to the next feeding level. The decrease in available energy at each level of a food chain is shown in an **energy pyramid.**

SEE ALSO
134 Food Chains

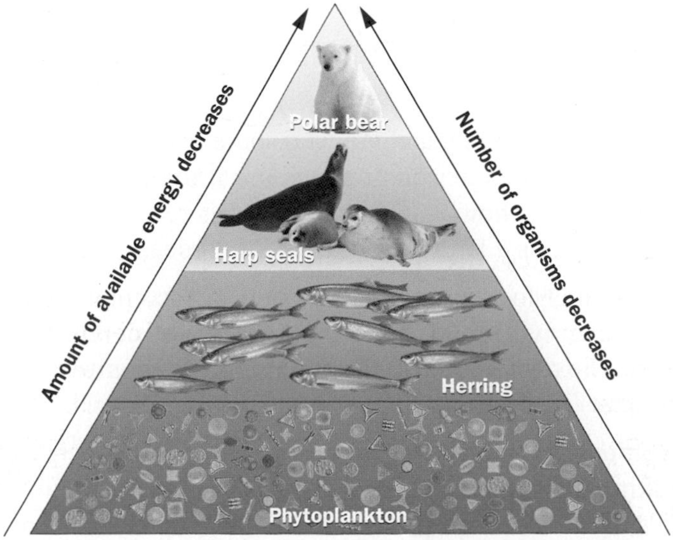

Energy pyramid

138 Carbon Dioxide-Oxygen Cycle

SEE ALSO
250 Matter

Matter moves in cycles through the environment, getting used over and over again. Carbon dioxide and oxygen are two important forms of matter that cycle through an ecosystem. The continual movement of carbon dioxide and oxygen between living things and the environment is known as the **carbon dioxide-oxygen cycle.**

SEE ALSO
079 Cell Processes
330 Renewable Material Resources

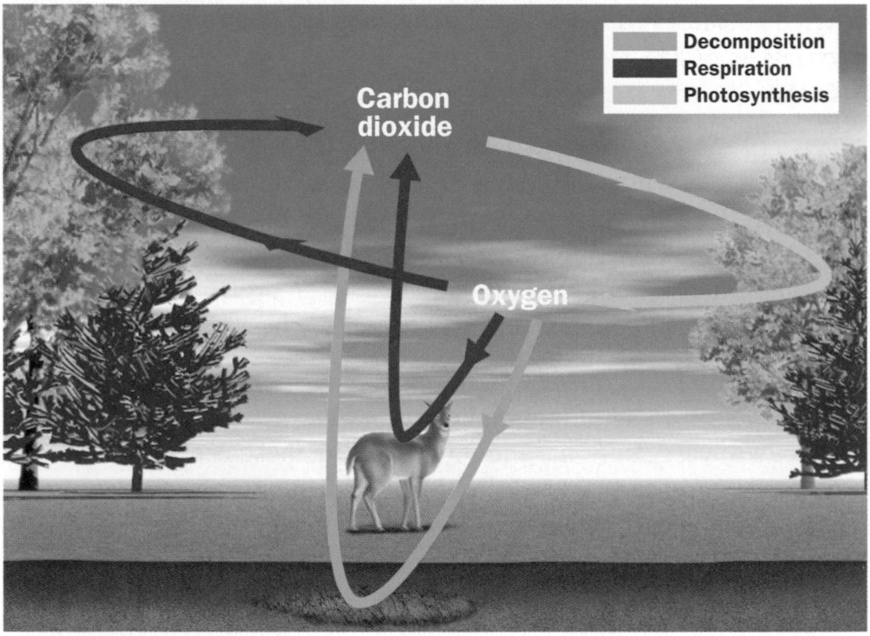

Carbon dioxide-oxygen cycle

Several important processes are part of the carbon dioxide-oxygen cycle.

SEE ALSO
107 Plant Physiology
105 Animal Physiology
133 Feeding Relationships

- **Photosynthesis** Plants, algae, and some bacteria take in carbon dioxide from the environment and use it to make food through the process of photosynthesis. Oxygen is released back to the environment as a waste product of this process.
- **Respiration** Most organisms get energy by combining oxygen from the air with food in a process known as cellular respiration. Carbon dioxide is released back into the environment as a waste product of respiration.
- **Decomposition** Fungi and some bacteria obtain energy by breaking down the wastes or remains of other living things into smaller molecules. Carbon dioxide is released back to the environment through this process.

Nitrogen Cycle

Nitrogen is one of the elements needed to build the proteins that make up the structures of living things. Almost 78 percent of Earth's atmosphere is made up of nitrogen gas. But most organisms cannot use this nitrogen until it is combined with other elements to form nitrogen compounds. At the same time, nitrogen compounds found in the bodies of dead organisms must be broken down in order to return nitrogen gas back to the air where it can be used again. The constant movement of nitrogen between living things and the environment is represented by the **nitrogen cycle.**

SEE ALSO
079 Cell Processes
214 Composition of the Atmosphere
133 Feeding Relationships

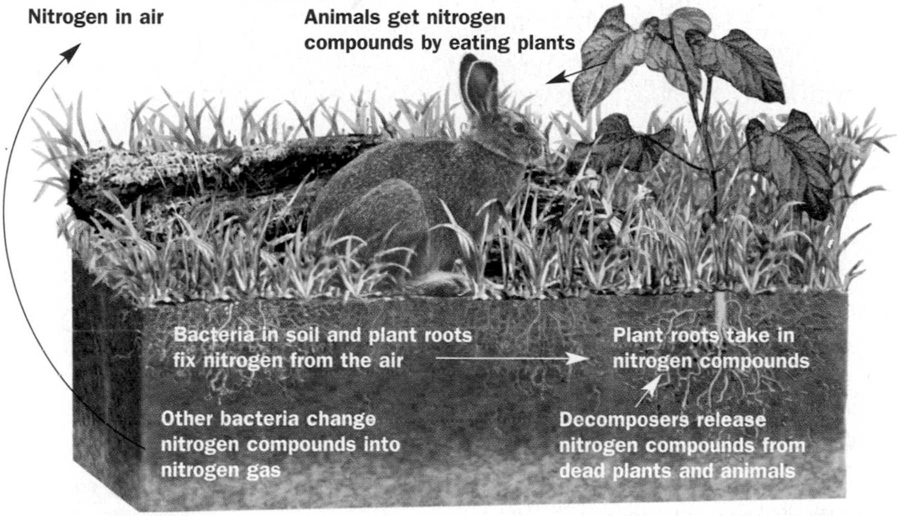
Nitrogen in air
Animals get nitrogen compounds by eating plants
Bacteria in soil and plant roots fix nitrogen from the air
Plant roots take in nitrogen compounds
Other bacteria change nitrogen compounds into nitrogen gas
Decomposers release nitrogen compounds from dead plants and animals

Nitrogen cycle

Nitrogen fixation is the changing of nitrogen gas from the air into nitrogen compounds plants can use. Bacteria that live in soil carry out most nitrogen fixation. After plants take in these compounds from soil, the compounds can be passed to animals through the food chain.

Plants and animals return nitrogen compounds, such as ammonia, to the environment in their wastes. Bacteria break down the nitrogen compounds and release nitrogen gas back into the atmosphere.

Peas, clover, alfalfa, and soybeans are all legumes, plants that house nitrogen-fixing bacteria in their roots. The bacteria get the energy they need from the plant, and nitrogen compounds fixed by the bacteria fertilize the plant. Both organisms benefit from this relationship.

SEE ALSO
132 Relationships Between Populations

140

Ecological Succession

The set of organisms that occupy an area is constantly changing. The natural process by which one community of organisms slowly replaces another in a certain area is called **ecological succession.**

SEE ALSO
144 Deciduous Forests

Let's look at the development of one kind of ecological community, a deciduous forest:

SEE ALSO
079 Cell Processes
107 Plant Physiology

The first organisms to live in an area are called **pioneer species.** Mosses and **lichens,** organisms made up of a photosynthetic alga (or a cyanobacterium) and a fungus that live in close association with each other, are common pioneer species. They are both able to grow on bare rock. As they grow, they release acids that break down the rock to form soil. In time, enough soil is formed to support the growth of larger plants such as ferns or grasses.

An example of ecological succession

SEE ALSO
153 Plant Kingdom
154 Animal Kingdom

As a plant colony is established, small animals that feed on the plants will move into the area. Larger animals that feed on the small animals can also move in. Wastes and remains from these organisms decay, helping the soil to become richer and deeper. This deeper, richer soil can support the growth of larger plants, such as shrubs. As the shrubs replace the grasses, some populations of grass-eating animals leave the area in search of another food source. New animals that use the shrubs as food move in to take their place.

SEE ALSO
191 Soil

Soil continues becoming richer and deeper as new wastes and remains break down. In time, trees such as oaks and hickories take root and replace the shrubs. Still later, maples and beeches grow and mature. Eventually, the community reaches a stable point where very few new plants can **colonize,** or move into, the area. This type of community is known as a **climax community.**

Biomes

141

Organisms live almost everywhere on Earth. The part of Earth that supports life is called the **biosphere.** The biosphere extends several kilometers up into the atmosphere (where microscopic organisms float on air currents) and deep down to the ocean floor (where unusual tubeworms live near hot water vents).

SEE ALSO
215 Earth's Atmosphere
207 Ocean Floor

Physical factors such as climate determine what ecosystems exist in different parts of the biosphere. **Climate** is the general weather of an area over a long period of time, including its seasonal changes. The climate of an area is largely determined by its location on Earth. Areas close to the equator receive more direct sunlight than areas near the poles, and so are warmer year-round. Areas nearer the poles experience warm summers but cold winters.

SEE ALSO
227 Climate
230 Pattern of World Climates

The climate of an area determines what plants can grow in that area. The plants, in turn, determine what animals and other organisms the area can support. A **biome** is a large region characterized as having a distinct climate and specific types of plant and animal life. Biomes exist both in the ocean and on land.

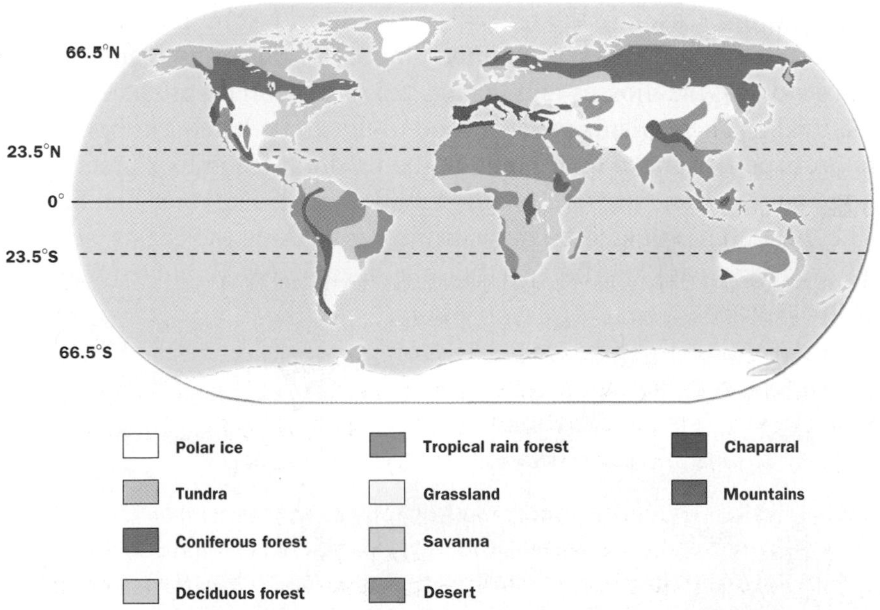

142 Tundra

The **tundra** is a cold, dry, mostly treeless land biome that encircles the Arctic Ocean. Temperatures in the tundra are well below freezing for much of the year. For this reason, most of the ground is covered by **permafrost,** soil that remains frozen to a depth of about 1 meter (about 3 ft). Only 20 to 50 cm (8 to 20 in.) of precipitation fall in the tundra each year. Most of this precipitation falls as snow or ice because of the cold temperatures.

Did You Know?

There is almost no tundra in the southern hemisphere because there is very little land at that latitude.

The average winter temperature in the tundra is about −26°C (about −15°F), although temperatures often drop much lower. In the summer, the area receives continuous daylight that allows temperatures to rise to an average of 12°C (about 54°F). The warming temperatures of summer melt surface ice, creating many small ponds and streams.

SEE ALSO
133 Feeding Relationships

The growing season in the tundra is very short, lasting for only about 60 days. During this time, a limited number of flowering plants come to life to join the mosses and lichens that are the main producers of the tundra. These plants provide food to the arctic hares, caribou, and musk oxen that make their home in the tundra. Mosquitoes breed in large numbers and provide food to small animals like mice and birds. The most common land predator is the wolf. Along the coasts, seals and walruses eat plentiful fish, but may themselves be preyed upon by polar bears.

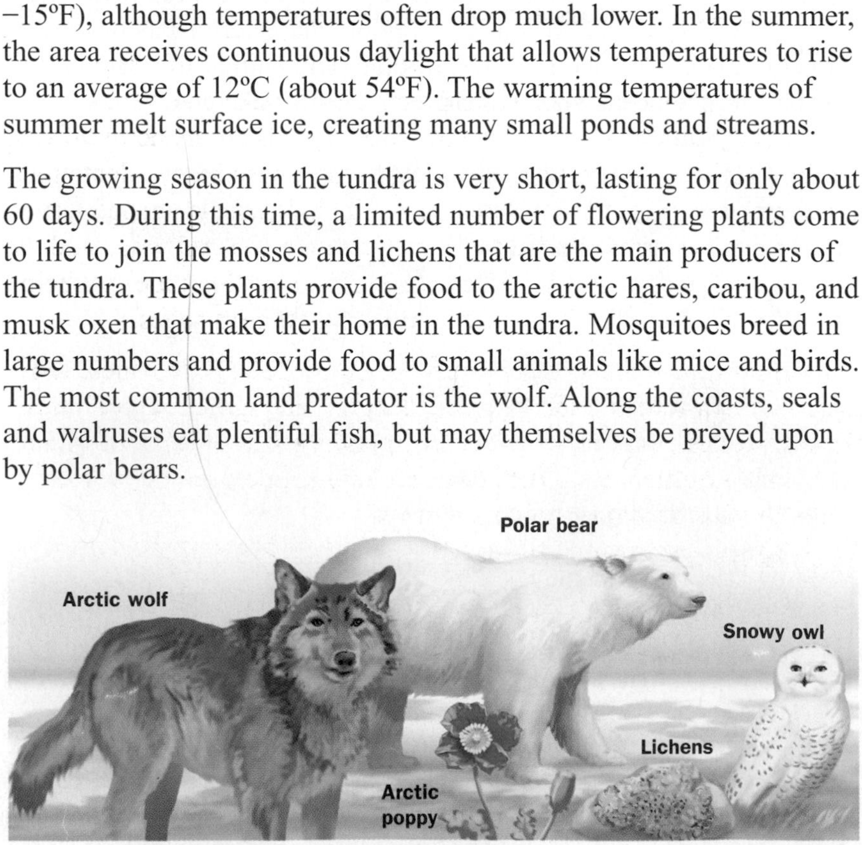

Tundra organisms

Coniferous Forests

Trees that remain green throughout the year, have needle-like leaves, and produce seeds in cones, are called **coniferous trees.** Many coniferous forests are found just south of the tundra in an area called the **taiga.** Much of Canada, Alaska, and the northern Rocky Mountains of the United States are taiga.

Science Alert!

Not all coniferous forests are in the taiga. Forests of white pine, red pine, spruce, and hemlock exist in many parts of the northern United States.

Winter temperatures in coniferous forests average about −10°C (about 14°F), while in summer they average about 14°C (about 57°F). The forests get about 50 cm (about 20 in.) of precipitation each year. This precipitation falls as snow during the winter and as rain during warmer seasons.

Warmer temperatures and regular precipitation make coniferous forests very suitable for tree growth. These forests are made up of firs, hemlocks, pines, and spruces. Coniferous trees have many adaptations to help them survive cold winters. These include needle-shaped leaves with a waxy covering that helps the tree retain water and withstand the cold. Many conifers also have flexible branches and a shape that helps keep snow from building up on and breaking their branches.

SEE ALSO
127 Natural Selection

In the coniferous forest, herbivores like moose, elk, porcupines, red squirrels, chipmunks, rabbits, mice, beavers, and geese are common. Wasps, beetles, and other insects are abundant. Many kinds of birds seek shelter in the trees. Carnivores include bobcats, foxes, wolves, and in the northernmost regions, lynxes.

SEE ALSO
133 Feeding Relationships

Coniferous forest organisms

144 Deciduous Forests

Many broadleaf trees, such as oaks, maples, and birches, drop their leaves in autumn. This adaptation helps the trees conserve water and energy during winter months. Trees that drop all their leaves each year are called **deciduous trees** and are the main plants of the deciduous forest biome. Deciduous forests are located in temperate climates. Such areas are found in the eastern United States, parts of central Europe, and parts of Asia.

SEE ALSO
127 Natural Selection
227 Climate

Word Watch!

Deciduous comes from the Latin *deciduus*, meaning "to fall off."

With a lot of rain, moderate temperatures, and a long growing season, deciduous forests are home to a wide variety of trees and other plants. Rainfall averages between 75 and 125 cm (about 30 to 49 in.) per year. Temperatures range from 6°C to 28°C (about 43°F to 82°F). Soil and climate determine which deciduous trees will form the climax community. In the eastern and southern United States, hickory trees are common. Beech and maple form the climax community in many northern forests. Other trees of the forest include oak, elm, and poplar. Smaller plants, such as mosses, ferns, and grasses, grow nearer the ground.

SEE ALSO
140 Ecological Succession

Deer are the most common browsing herbivore in many deciduous forests. Other plant-eaters include squirrels, chipmunks, mice, rabbits, turtles, and many birds. Raccoons, opossums, and black bears are omnivores found in many deciduous forests. Carnivores include foxes, coyotes, snakes, insect-eating birds such as woodpeckers, and birds of prey such as hawks, owls, and falcons.

SEE ALSO
133 Feeding Relationships

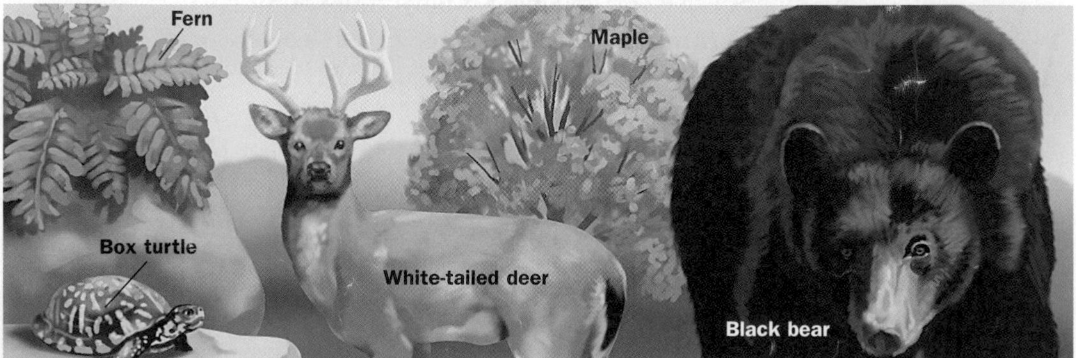

Deciduous forest organisms

Tropical Rain Forests

145

Near the equator, warm temperatures (around 25°C, or 77°F) and abundant rainfall (more than 150 cm, or 60 in., each year) allow tropical rainforests to flourish. These ecosystems are home to more species than any other ecosystem on Earth.

The rainforest is divided into many vertical layers. Organisms live on the ground, in the trees, or in the **canopy,** the uppermost layer of the forest. Because of the thick vegetation, little light is able to reach the forest floor, and relatively few small plants grow there.

SEE ALSO
107 Plant Physiology

The tall plants of the rainforest ecosystem include a great variety of hardwood trees. In South America, these trees provide a home to monkeys and jaguars. In Africa, they provide habitat for leopards. In any one rainforest tree there may be hundreds of different species of ants, beetles, termites, and other insects. The rainforest abounds with crickets and tree frogs, toucans and parrots.

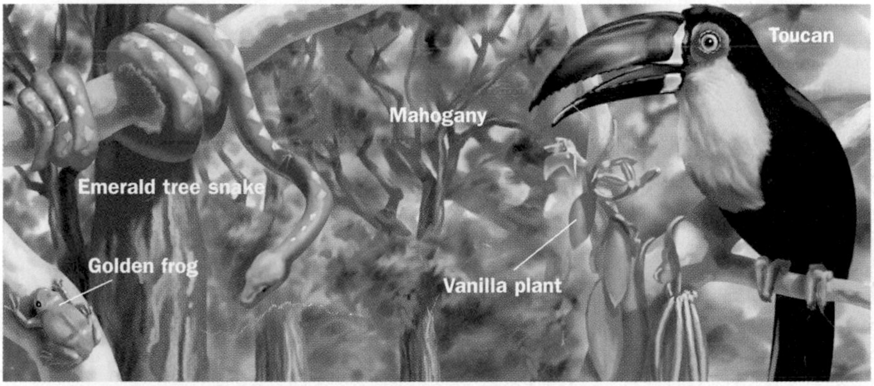

Tropical rainforest organisms

Did You Know?

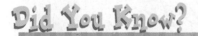

The Amazon rain forest in South America is the world's largest rain forest. But as development has occurred, some of the rain forest has been cleared to make room for roads or farms.

SEE ALSO
341 Habitat Loss

146 Grasslands

SEE ALSO

139 Nitrogen Cycle
191 Soil

Grasslands are biomes in which the main types of plants are grasses. Temperatures in the grassland are mild in summer (about 30ºC, or 86ºF) and cool to cold in winter (about 0ºC, or 32ºF). With only 25–75 cm (about 10–30 in.) of rainfall each year, the grassland is too dry to support the trees of a forest, but it is fertile and can support many species of grasses. This grass provides a source of food to grazing animals. The roots of grasses spread, helping to hold the soil in place. As grasses die and decay, rich soils are formed.

SEE ALSO

140 Ecological Succession
134 Food Chains
135 Food Webs

North America is home to the Great Plains and tall-grass prairie where huge, thunderous herds of bison once grazed. Today there is a new population of bison as well as pronghorn antelope. They share the ecosystem with many other grassland dwellers. Prairie dogs, rabbits, and pocket gophers build vast underground homes—sometimes like cities. These animals provide a food source to snakes, prairie hawks, weasels, and coyotes.

Grassland organisms

A **savanna** is a grassland with a few scattered trees. In Australia, large savannas provide a home to kangaroos and wombats. A savanna near the Serengeti Plain in Africa provides a home to giraffes and elephants that feed on the trees. South America also has large savanna areas called pampas.

SEE ALSO

110 Animal Behavior

The best-known grassland of Africa is the Serengeti Plain. This region is home to antelope, zebra, and lion, among others. Twice a year, hundreds of thousands of wildebeests migrate across this immense grassland.

Deserts

147

When you think of the desert, you might imagine the Sahara Desert of northern Africa. But there are many other deserts throughout the world. The huge Gobi Desert cuts a large path across central Asia. More local deserts include the Sonoran and Mohave Deserts of the American west.

Deserts are dry environments that generally receive less than 25 cm (about 10 in.) of rainfall each year. So desert organisms must be able to survive in dry regions. In a typical desert food web, cacti, mesquite bushes, small flowering plants, and thorny bushes are the producers. Animals that eat seeds and other parts of these plants include kangaroo rats, insects, lizards, rabbits, and armadillos. These animals serve as prey for snakes and vultures.

SEE ALSO
133 Feeding Relationships
135 Food Webs

A cactus is a plant with obvious adaptations to desert life. Spiny leaves help prevent water loss. Well-developed roots spread out near the ground's surface to quickly take in any water that falls.

SEE ALSO
127 Natural Selection

Desert temperatures can reach over 38°C (100°F). For many animals, it is a daily challenge to keep cool. To accomplish this, many animals burrow in the ground or take cover under rocks during hot, daylight hours. The animals come out to find food at night, when temperatures are much lower. Animals that are active mainly at night are **nocturnal.**

SEE ALSO
110 Animal Behavior

Desert organisms

Did You Know?

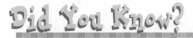

The kangaroo rat does not need to drink water. It gets the water it needs from the seeds and fruits it eats.

148

Freshwater Ecosystems

SEE ALSO

105 Animal Physiology

106 Animal Life Cycles

Freshwater ecosystems include lakes, ponds, swamps, streams, and rivers. Swift flowing rivers provide habitat to many fish species that need the high amount of oxygen that a fast-moving stream provides. These streams are also home to the larvae (young) of many kinds of insects.

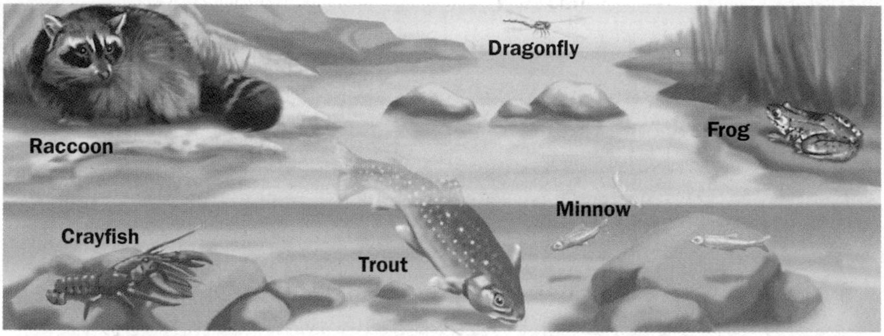

Freshwater organisms found in streams

Slower moving streams that meander through valleys usually have more plants growing on their banks. This growth provides a sheltered habitat to fish, aquatic birds, and insects. Rivers that empty into oceans may be home to saltwater fish species that come upriver to have their young. Areas where freshwater rivers flow into the ocean are known as **estuaries.** Estuaries are very rich in nutrients and provide a good environment for the young of many types of fish and shellfish.

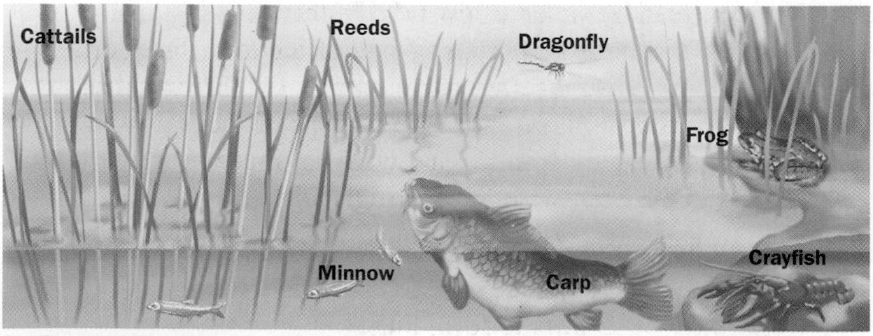

Freshwater organisms found in lakes

SEE ALSO

133 Feeding Relationships

Lake ecosystems are home to a wide variety of organisms. Plants may grow along the edges of the lake where water is shallow and the plants can take root in soil. Algae are also important lake producers. Many animal species live near the lake's edges, visiting only to get water and food. Different types of fish live in the lake's waters. Amphibians, such as frogs and newts, may also make their home near the water.

149

Saltwater Ecosystems

The ocean is divided into three zones of life. The largest of these areas is the **open-ocean zone.** Lack of mineral nutrients and sunlight prevent many organisms from living in this region. The main food source in this zone is **plankton,** one-celled algae, protists, and tiny animal larvae that float at or near the water's surface.

SEE ALSO
211 Open-Ocean Zone
156 Protist Kingdom

Ocean life zones

Intertidal zones are shoreline areas that are covered by water at high tide and not covered by water at low tide. In this zone live many shelled animals that have adaptations for clinging to surfaces or burrowing in sand to avoid being carried out to sea. Periwinkles, snails, and other species often live near the tops of rocks, where they are exposed to sunlight, salt spray, and wind for much of the time, only to be covered by salt water during high tide.

SEE ALSO
210 Neritic Zone
209 Intertidal Zone
127 Natural Selection

The **coral reef** is a type of marine ecosystem common in many tropical regions. Life in the coral reef centers on coral, a small animal that grows with others of its kind to form huge colonies. As these corals live and die, they build on the skeletons of others, expanding the reef structure. The crevices of a coral reef provide sheltered habitat to many types of animals, including sea stars, shrimps, lobsters, fish, sea anemones, and sponges.

SEE ALSO
131 Factors That Affect Populations

A coral reef

150

Classification

Do you collect baseball cards, coins, CDs, or rocks? If so, you probably organize the items to make them easy to find. Scientists have a system for keeping track of the millions of different organisms that live on Earth. They **classify,** or organize, the organisms into groups based on similar characteristics.

The Greek philosopher Aristotle was the first person known to classify living things scientifically. In his classification system, living things were classified as animals or plants. Aristotle later divided each of these large groups into smaller groups. For example, plants were divided into herbs, shrubs, or trees. Animals were classified according to where they lived—on land, in water, or in the air.

Aristotle's classification system

Nearly two thousand years later, the Swedish biologist Carolus Linnaeus created a different classification scheme. His idea was to group animals and plants based on similarities in their structures. For example, Linnaeus placed animals into groups based on whether or not they had a backbone.

SEE ALSO
161 Vertebrates and Invertebrates
113 Reproduction

Today's scientists still compare the structures of organisms to classify them. They also look at features such as how an organism moves, gets food, and produces more of its own kind.

Like Aristotle, Linnaeus divided living things into two large groups—plants or animals—called kingdoms. But tools and technology available to today's scientists have allowed them to study organisms more closely. Scientists now realize that some organisms don't quite fit into the plant or animal group. As a result, several other kingdoms of organisms are now recognized.

SEE ALSO
152 Kingdoms

151

Classification Hierarchy

The classification hierarchy is a system used to organize into groups the many different organisms found on Earth. Swedish biologist Carolus Linnaeus developed the first modern classification hierarchy. The system has changed since Linnaeus' time. It continues to change as scientists learn more about organisms. In the system used today, the groups that have the largest number of different organisms are called **domains.** There are three domains: archaea, bacteria, and eukarya. The next level in the hierarchy is **kingdom.** The domains archaea and bacteria have only one kingdom each. The domain eukarya has four kingdoms: plants, animals, fungi, and protists.

The kingdom level is broken down into six smaller levels. These include **phylum, class, order, family, genus,** and **species.** Each level contains fewer types of organisms than the level before. The species level includes only one type of organism. Organisms also become more closely related as you move from the kingdom to the species level.

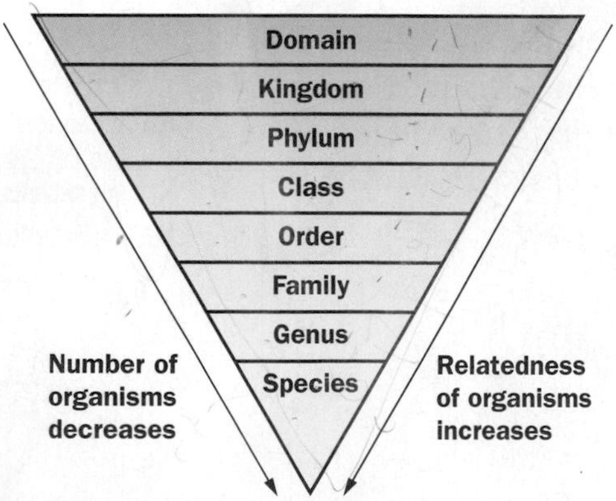

To remember the correct order of levels in the classification hierarchy, make up a sentence whose words begin with the first letters of each level, like **D**ear **K**ing **P**hilip **C**ame **O**ver **F**or **G**reat **S**paghetti.

SEE ALSO

130 Populations
113 Reproduction

Sometimes, there is great variety within a species. Some breeds of dog, for example, look very different from others. However, these different-looking dogs can still mate with one another to produce young. Different dog breeds are **varieties** of the same species.

Organisms are called by their **scientific name,** which consists of their genus and species names. For example, the domesticated dog is known as *Canis familiaris.*

SciLINKS NSTA Keyword: Classification Hierarchy
www.scilinks.org
Code: GSSM151

Kingdoms

152

When the earliest classification systems were developed, organisms were classified as either plants or animals. Since then, scientists have discovered that many organisms have traits that don't quite fit in with those of plants or animals. For this reason, six kingdoms of organisms are generally recognized—plants, animals, fungi, protists, eubacteria, and archaebacteria.

SEE ALSO
150 Classification

Plant Kingdom

153

From the mighty oak to common crabgrass, all members of the plant kingdom are made up of many cells that are surrounded by cell walls. All plants make their own food through photosynthesis. Some groups of plants are mosses, ferns, conifers, and flowering plants. Flowering plants produce seeds in flowers, while conifers make seeds in cones. Mosses and ferns reproduce by spores.

SEE ALSO
078 Plant Cell
107 Plant Physiology
108 Plant Life Cycles
162 Vascular and Nonvascular Plants

Animal Kingdom

154

Members of the animal kingdom are made up of many cells. All animals get their energy by eating other organisms. Animals are divided into two large groups: invertebrates (those without backbones) and vertebrates (those with backbones). Examples of invertebrates are sponges, jellies, coral, sea stars, insects, worms, and scorpions. Fish, frogs, lizards, peacocks, and kangaroos are all vertebrates.

SEE ALSO
077 Animal Cell
105 Animal Physiology
161 Vertebrates and Invertebrates

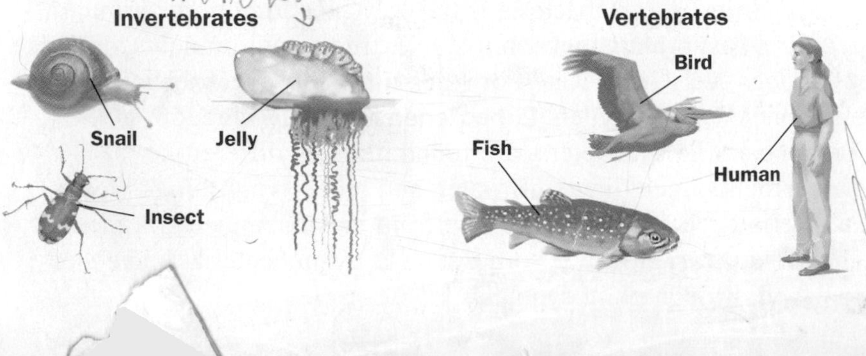

155 Fungi Kingdom

SEE ALSO
078 Plant Cell
107 Plant Physiology
133 Feeding Relationships
159 Heterotrophs and Autotrophs

Fungi are single or many-celled organisms that reproduce by spores. Like plants, the cells of fungi are surrounded by cell walls. However, these cell walls are made up of a material called chitin rather than cellulose. Examples of one-celled fungi include yeasts and some molds. Other fungi include mushrooms, bracket fungi, and puffballs. Unlike plants, fungi lack chlorophyll and so cannot photosynthesize. They get their energy by feeding on living or dead organisms.

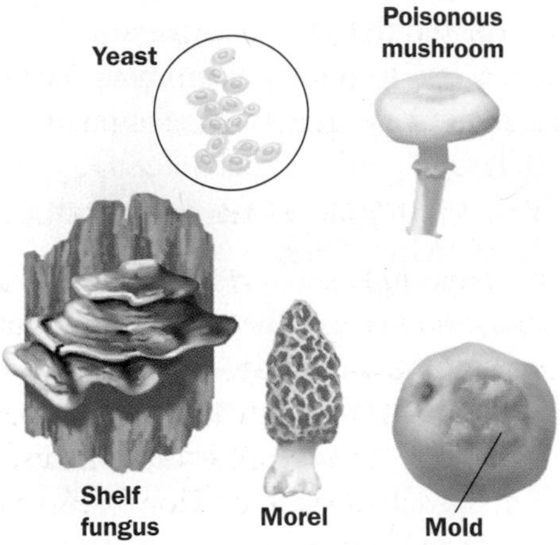

156 Protist Kingdom

SEE ALSO
077 Animal Cell
079 Cell Processes
160 Prokaryotes and Eukaryotes

The **protist** kingdom is made up of one-celled organisms and simple many-celled organisms. The nucleus of protist cells is enclosed in a nuclear membrane. Some protists, such as the one-celled amoeba and paramecium, feed on other organisms. Others, such as the one-celled euglena or many-celled algae, make their food through photosynthesis.

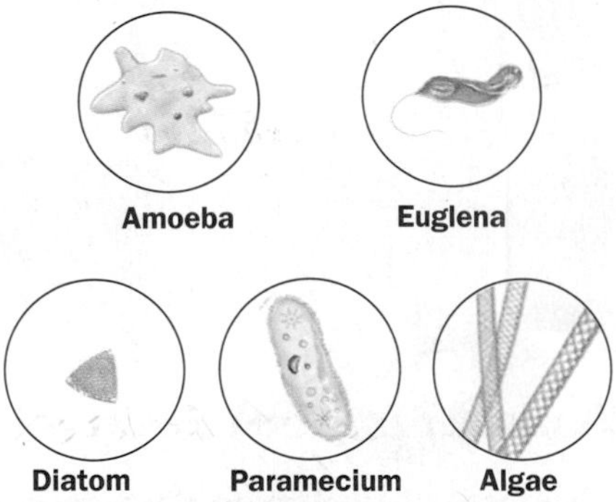

157 Archaebacteria and Eubacteria Kingdoms

SEE ALSO
160 Prokaryotes and Eukaryotes
159 Heterotrophs and Autotrophs
079 Cell Processes

Members of these two kingdoms are single-celled organisms that lack a true nucleus. Differences in the substances that make up these organisms have led scientists to classify them in different domains and kingdoms. Archaebacteria is the only kingdom in the domain archaea. Most **archaebacteria** live in extreme environments, such as hot springs, very salty water, or black mud. Most archaebacteria die in the presence of oxygen. **Eubacteria** is the only kingdom in the domain bacteria. Eubacteria are found in many different environments, including soil, water, and other living things. Some eubacteria need oxygen, others die from it. Most eubacteria feed off other organisms. However some, such as cyanobacteria, make their own food through photosynthesis.

Major Groupings of Organisms

158

One way to classify organisms is according to their place within the kingdoms. Scientists also find it helpful to look at how organisms can be grouped together according to other general characteristics. For example, we can create a group for all organisms that make their own food, and all organisms that cannot make their own food.

SEE ALSO
152 Kingdoms

Heterotrophs and Autotrophs

159

One way organisms are classified is according to how they get their food. Plants, algae, and some eubacteria make their own food through photosynthesis. Organisms that can make their own food are called **autotrophs,** a term meaning "self feeder." Like other animals, you must obtain food from other organisms. Any organism that uses another as its source of food is classified as a **heterotroph.**

SEE ALSO
133 Feeding Relationships

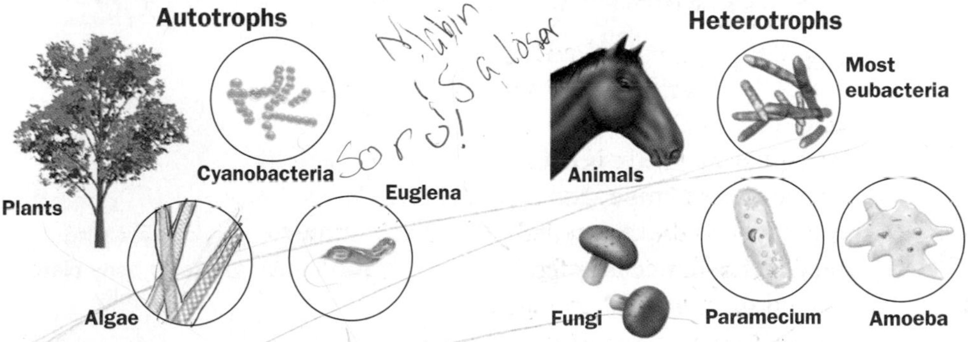

Prokaryotes and Eukaryotes

160

Organisms can be classified according to whether or not their cells contain distinct, membrane-bound structures. Single-celled organisms that do not have membrane-bound internal structures are called **prokaryotes** (PRO-care-ee-oats). All eubacteria and archaebacteria are prokaryotes. The cells of most other organisms contain membrane-bound structures known as **organelles.** Organisms made up of cells that have organelles are called **eukaryotes** (YOU-care-ee-oats). Eukaryotic cells tend to be much bigger than prokaryotic cells.

SEE ALSO
077 Animal Cell
078 Plant Cell
157 Archaebacteria and Eubacteria Kingdoms

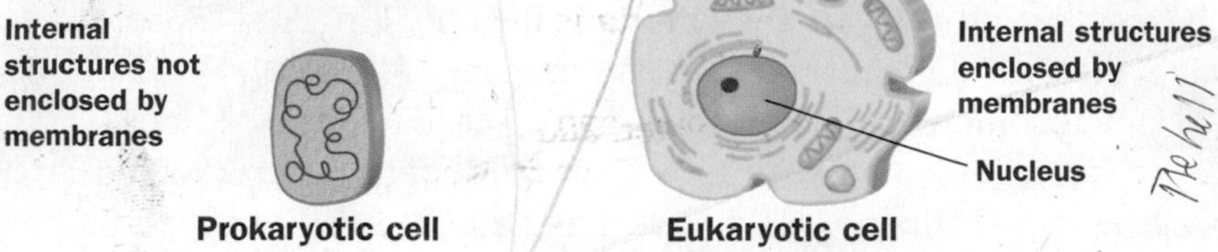

161 Vertebrates and Invertebrates

SEE ALSO
095 Nervous System
086 Skeletal System
082 Tissues, Organs, and Systems

Animals that have a backbone are classified as **vertebrates.** Vertebrates take their name from the bones called *vertebrae* that make up the backbone. These bones, which have a space at their center, surround and protect the spinal cord.

Mammals, fishes, amphibians, reptiles, and birds are all vertebrates. In addition to a backbone, these animals have other bones that aid in movement and protect important organs like the heart and brain.

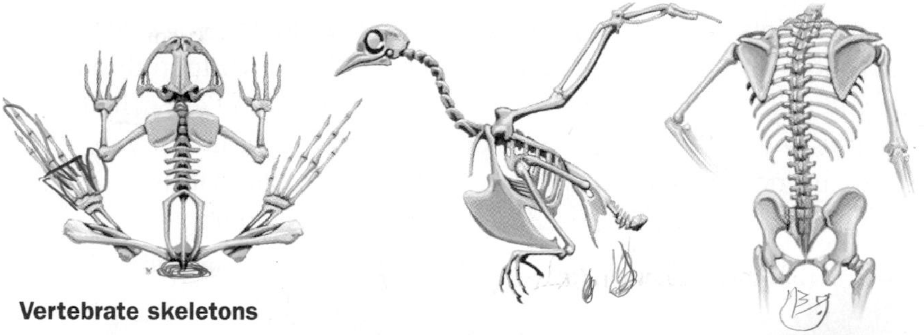

Vertebrate skeletons

Animals that do not have a backbone are classified as **invertebrates.** In general, invertebrates have simpler body plans than vertebrates. For example, a jelly has only one opening for taking in food and getting rid of wastes.

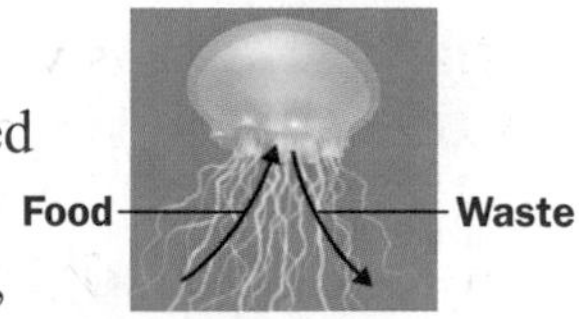

Basic body plan of the jelly

SEE ALSO
095 Nervous System
093 Circulatory System

Other invertebrates have more complex body plans. An earthworm takes in food through one opening and gets rid of wastes through another opening. Some invertebrates even have simple nervous and circulatory systems. The largest single group of invertebrates is the arthropods. **Arthropods** are animals with distinct body sections, jointed legs, and a hard body covering that forms an outer skeleton. Insects, spiders, and crustaceans (such as lobsters) are all arthropods.

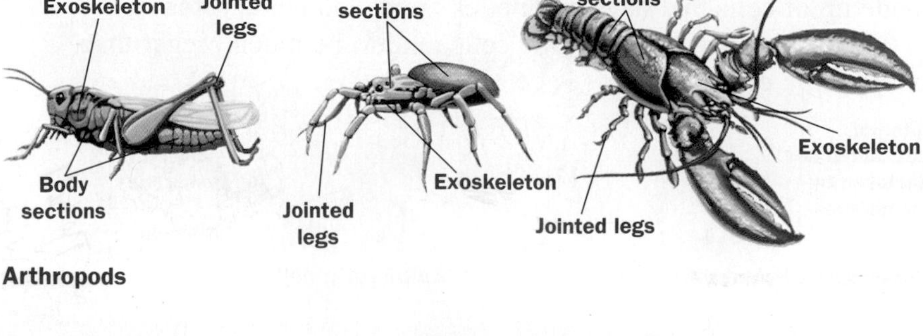

Arthropods

Vascular and Nonvascular Plants

162

Any plant that has tube-like structures for the internal transport of food and water is classified as a **vascular plant.** In a vascular plant, **xylem** (ZY-lum) tissue forms the structures that carry water throughout the plant. Food made in the leaves is carried to where it is needed in tissue called **phloem** (FLOW-um). All vascular plants have roots, stems, and leaves.

SEE ALSO
107 Plant Physiology

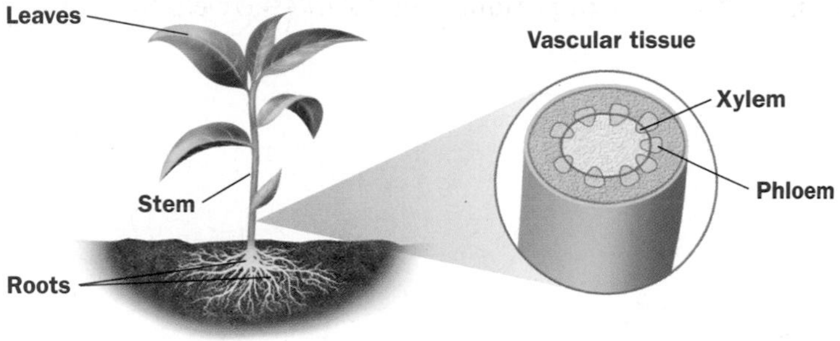

A typical herbaceous vascular plant

Most of the plants you are familiar with—trees, grasses, shrubs—are vascular plants. These plants are divided into two smaller groups based on the type of stems they have. For example, trees and many shrubs are classified as **woody** because their stems are made of wood. Grasses, tomato plants, dandelions, and other plants with green, fleshy stems are classified as **herbaceous.**

SEE ALSO
153 Plant Kingdom

Mosses, liverworts, and hornworts are small plants. One reason these plants are small is because they do not have vascular tissue to carry substances within the plant. Instead, materials are absorbed directly into the plant's cells through the cell membrane. Plants that do not have vascular tissue are classified as **nonvascular plants.** Unlike vascular plants, nonvascular plants do not have true roots, stems, or leaves.

SEE ALSO
078 Plant Cell

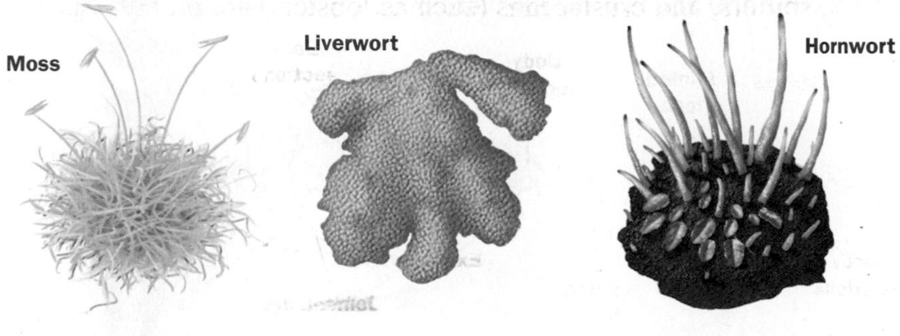

Nonvascular plants

Taxonomic Trees

163

SEE ALSO
125 Recognizing Common Ancestors

One goal of classification is to show what ancestors organisms have in common. Relationships between organisms can be shown in a taxonomic tree.

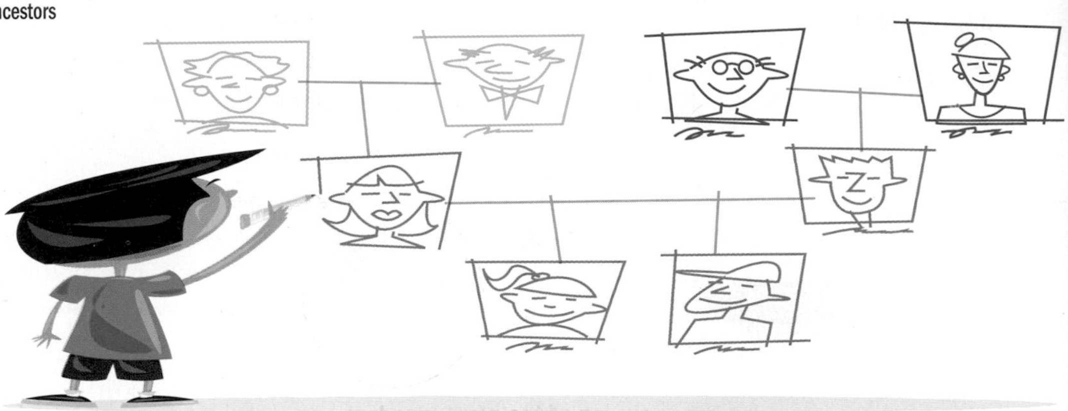

SEE ALSO
126 The Theory of Evolution

Have you ever created a family tree? The idea of a family tree is to show connections among family members and to trace the relationships back a few generations. Another type of tree, called a **taxonomic tree,** is used to show the evolutionary relationships among different groups of organisms. In a taxonomic tree, common branches show groups of organisms that are closely related in their evolutionary history. Organisms separated by many branches are less closely related.

SEE ALSO
153 Plant Kingdom
156 Protist Kingdom

The taxonomic tree on the next page shows the evolutionary relationships among the different divisions of plants making up the plant kingdom. Notice that all the plant groups are connected to green algae (a protist) by a common branch. This indicates that green algae are believed to be a common ancestor of all plants.

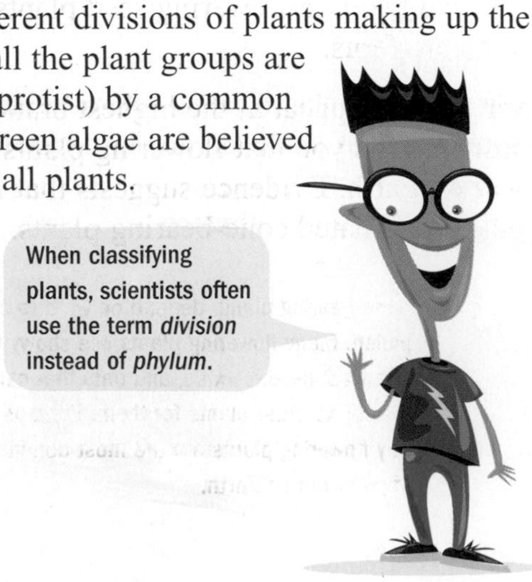
When classifying plants, scientists often use the term *division* instead of *phylum*.

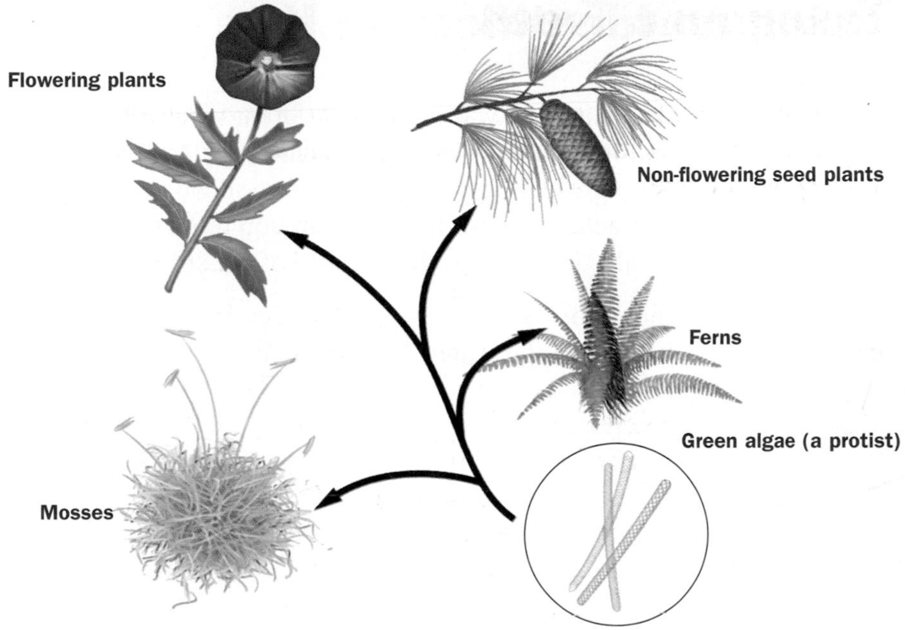

A taxonomic tree showing the evolution of the plant kingdom

Look again at the taxonomic tree. Notice that the branch containing mosses shoots off from the main branch at an earlier point than the branch containing the ferns. This tells you that mosses appeared on Earth at an earlier time than ferns. It also tells you that mosses are believed to be more closely related to algae than are ferns. The branch containing non-flowering seed plants (including cone-bearing plants), however, appears higher on the tree than ferns. This indicates that non-flowering seed plants appeared on Earth after the ferns. It also tells you that non-flowering seed plants are less closely related to algae than are ferns.

SEE ALSO
200 Geologic Time Scale
162 Vascular and Nonvascular Plants
153 Plant Kingdom

Flowering plants appear at the highest branch on the taxonomic tree. This position tells you that flowering plants are the most recent plants to appear on Earth. Evidence suggests that flowering plants evolved from insect-pollinated cone-bearing plants.

SEE ALSO
108 Plant Life Cycles

Cone-bearing plants depend on wind to carry their pollen. Many flowering plants use showy flowers to attract insects, birds, and bats that carry pollen directly to other plants for them. Perhaps this is why flowering plants are the most dominant form of plant life on Earth.

Using an Identification Key

164

An identification key can help you identify different types of organisms. A special key, called a **dichotomous key,** helps you identify organisms by presenting you with a series of choices. The choices describe characteristics of the organism you're identifying. Your choices eventually lead you to the identity of the species.

SEE ALSO
110 Animal Behavior

The following dichotomous key can be used to identify whale species based on their behaviors in the water. This key is based on observations experts made while watching whales along the Atlantic coast. Whale observers rarely see much of a whale's body unless it jumps above the water's surface in a behavior called breaching. But many whales show their tails, or flukes, when they are about to dive. They also produce a characteristic spray as they blow air through their blowholes. These features are used to identify different whale species.

Did You Know?

The largest animal in the world is the blue whale, which can grow up to 30 m (100 ft) in length.

Use this dichotomous key to identify the whales described on the facing page.*

1	a. Shows flukes when diving b. Raises flukes only slightly	*Go to 2* Blue Whale
2	a. Head seen when surfacing b. Head not reported to be seen when surfacing	*Go to 3* *Go to 4*
3	a. Blow bushy b. Blow not noticeable	Northern Bottlenose False Killer Whale
4	a. Breaching common b. Breaching rare	*Go to 5* Longfinned Pilot
5	a. Blow bushy b. Blow at 45 degree angle	*Go to 6* Sperm Whale
6	a. Dorsal fin prominent b. Dorsal fin small c. No dorsal fin	Killer Whale Humpback Whale Northern Right Whale

- Shows flukes when diving
- Head not seen when surfacing
- Breaching common; blow bushy
- Other characteristics: no dorsal fin

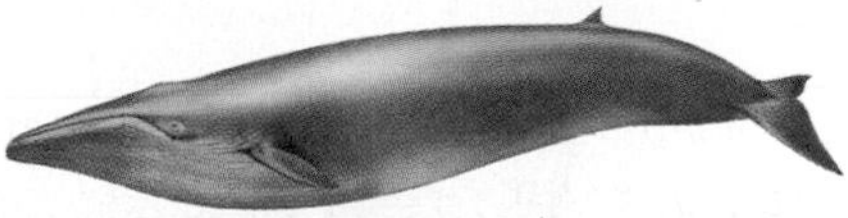

- Raises flukes only slightly when diving

- Shows flukes when diving
- Head not seen when surfacing
- Breaching common; blow bushy
- Other characteristics: small dorsal fin, long flippers

- Shows flukes when diving
- Head not seen when surfacing
- Breaching common; blows at 45 degree angle

- Shows flukes when diving
- Head seen when surfacing
- Blow bushy

- Shows flukes when diving
- Head not seen when surfacing
- Breaching common
- Blow bushy
- Other characteristics: prominent dorsal fin, striking black and white coloring

- Shows flukes when diving
- Head seen when surfacing
- Blow not noticeable

- Shows flukes when diving
- Head not seen when surfacing
- Breaching rare

* **Whales are not drawn to scale.**

EARTH SCIENCE

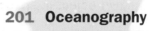

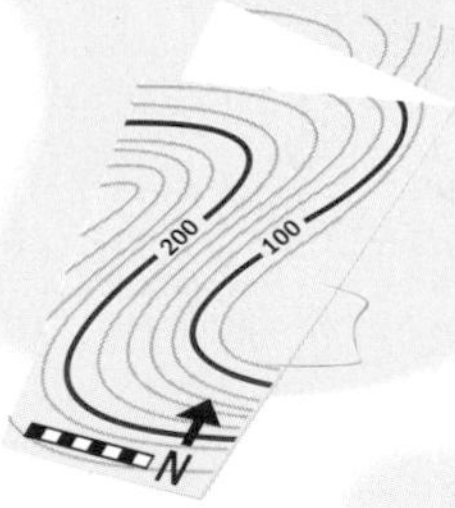

The Martian students always enjoyed their Earth science field trips.

How would you describe the area in which you live? Is it hilly or flat? Is it near an ocean or a large lake? Earth has more different features than any other known object in space. Its surface has mountains, hills, valleys, plains, and canyons. Liquid water collects in streams, lakes, and oceans. Weather of all kinds is created in its atmosphere. Earth is only one of many objects in space—a planet among other planets, moons, streaking comets, and fiery stars. The study of all these things is called Earth science.

166

Showing Earth on Maps

Imagine you are traveling to a place you have never visited. How do you choose the shortest and safest path? How do you keep from getting lost? If you think ahead, you will have answers to these questions folded in your pocket. These answers are found on a map. A **map** is a model that shows all or part of Earth's surface. A map can help you find the locations of places. It can also be used to find distances between places. Some maps show where roads, mountains, valleys, lakes, streams, and swamps are located.

167

Map Basics

Maps have many features that make them useful. But maps can be useful to you only if you know how to use all their features. It also helps to understand how a map is made in the first place. People who make maps are called **cartographers.**

168

Map Projections

No map of the world can accurately show the whole surface of Earth. Why? Earth is spherical—it's round, like a ball. A map is flat. How can you copy the surface of a ball onto a flat piece of paper? Mapmakers have tried to solve this problem by making different

projections, or flat pictures, of Earth's rounded surface. Each map projection shows some things correctly and others incorrectly. For example, some world maps are drawn as Mercator projections. A **Mercator projection** shows the shapes of landmasses correctly, but it shows their sizes incorrectly. Landmasses far from the equator look larger than they really are. For example, Greenland may look almost as big as the United States and Canada put together. Yet Greenland is only about one-ninth the size of these two countries put together.

SEE ALSO
169 Latitude and Longitude

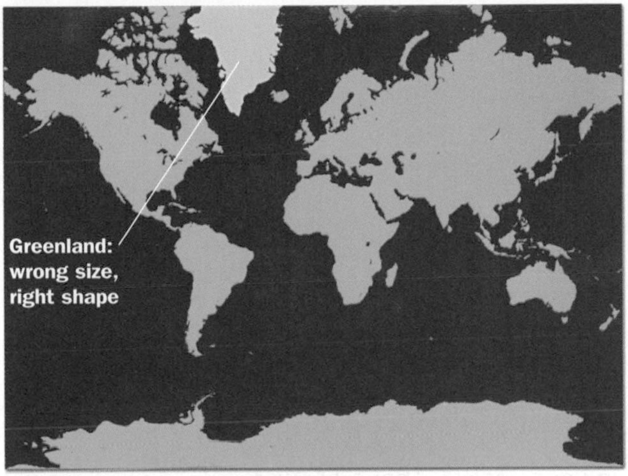

Mercator Projection

An **equal-area projection** produces an oval-shaped map. Its landmasses have the same proportions as they do on Earth, but the shapes are distorted. This kind of map is good for comparing landmass sizes, but not for navigating the oceans. Sailors use Mercator projections because they more accurately show the shapes of coastlines.

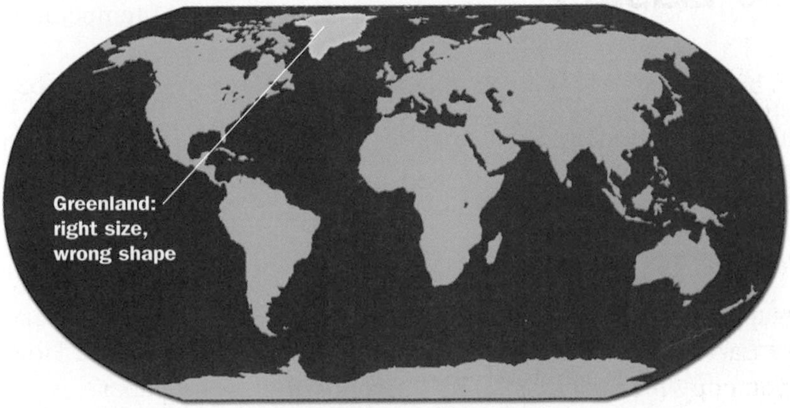

Equal-Area Projection

169 Latitude and Longitude

Mapmakers use a set of imaginary lines that cross each other to identify places on Earth. One set of lines, called lines of latitude, circle Earth in an east-west direction. The other set, called lines of longitude, circle Earth in a north-south direction.

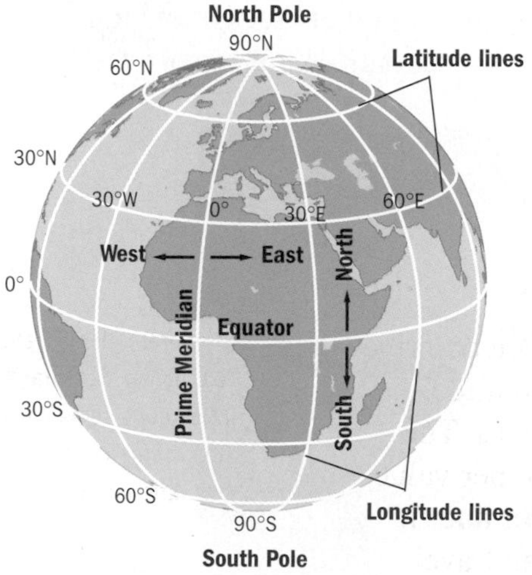

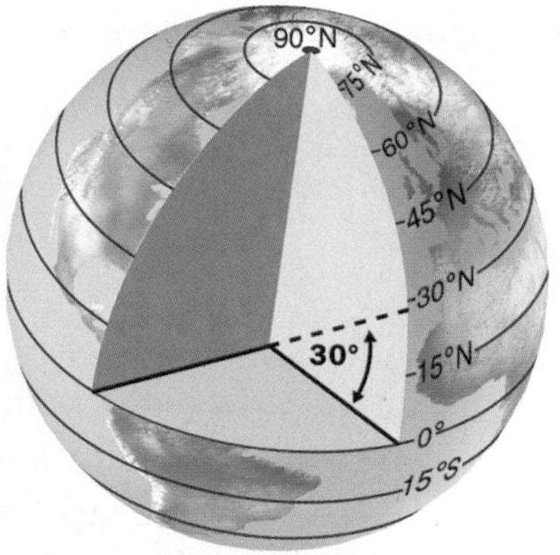

Latitude is the distance of a place north or south of the equator measured in degrees. Lines of latitude are called **parallels,** because they are always the same distance apart and never cross one another. They look like steps in a ladder going north and south of the equator. The central line of latitude, the **equator,** divides Earth into two halves—the northern and southern hemispheres. The equator and all other lines of latitude are numbered in degrees (°). The equator is 0° latitude. The highest latitudes are the North Pole (90°N) and the South Pole (90°S). (Both latitude and longitude are measured in degrees of a circle, 0°–360°. Do not confuse these with degrees of temperature, °C or °F.)

Many maps number lines of latitude every 15° north and south of the equator. The latitude of a place along the line that is 15° north of the equator is described as 15° north (15°N) latitude. A place on the line 30° south of the equator is located at 30°S latitude.

Did You Know?

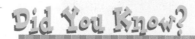

Time zones are based on lines of longitude. There are 24 major time zones, one for every 15° of longitude (and one for every hour in the day).

Longitude is the distance of a place east or west of the prime meridian measured in degrees. Lines of longitude, or **meridians,** run in a north-south direction around Earth and pass through both the North and South Poles. The **prime meridian** is the central line of longitude and represents 0° longitude. It runs through Western Europe and Africa to divide Earth into an eastern hemisphere and a western hemisphere.

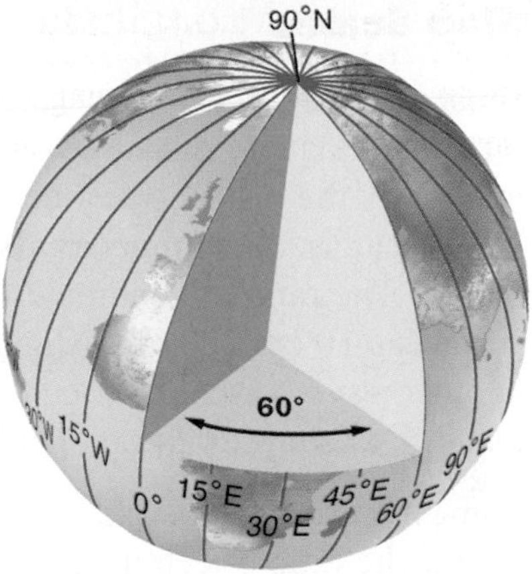

Locations east of the prime meridian are described as east longitudes, such as 15°E longitude. Locations to its west are west longitudes. The line of longitude with the highest number value, 180°E and W, is the **international date line**. It runs through the Pacific Ocean. If you travel across this line from west to east, it is suddenly one day earlier. If you cross the line from the opposite direction, it is suddenly one day later.

The international date line is crooked, not straight. This keeps some countries from being divided into two different days.

Many locations can share the same latitude. Reno, Nevada, and Denver, Colorado, for example, are both at about 39°N latitude. Other locations may share the same longitude. Reno, Nevada, and Fresno, California, both lay at about 119°W longitude. However, only one city, Reno, Nevada, is located at both 39°N latitude, 119°W longitude.

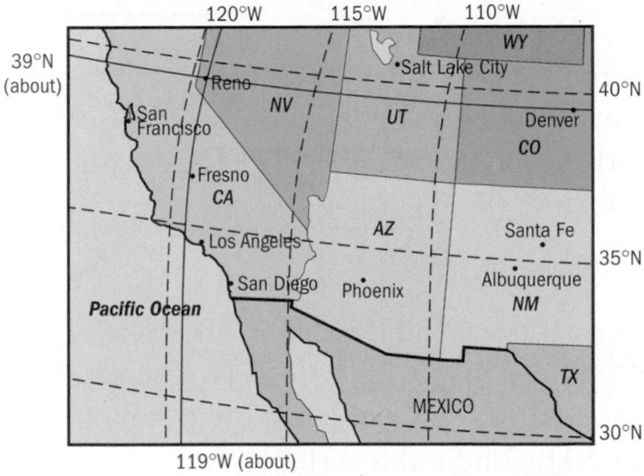

Dad, can you pick me up at 33° N and 112° W in an hour?
MAP
N

170 Map Scales

Most maps are drawn to a scale. A **map scale** shows how distances on a map relate to distances on Earth's surface. For example, a map may show the distance between Mobile, Alabama, and New Orleans, Louisiana, as 10 centimeters. The actual distance is about 200 kilometers. The ratio of centimeters on that map to kilometers on Earth's surface is 10 cm:200 km, which you can simplify to 1 cm:20 km. Put another way, the scale is 1 cm equals 20 km. The map uses 1 cm of distance to show 20 km of distance on Earth.

Some map scales look like a line with tick marks. You can use a ruler to find the ratio of centimeters (or inches) to kilometers (or miles). For example, if the ticks on the map scale run from 0 to 15 kilometers and you measure this line as 3 centimeters long, you divide the kilometers (15) from the scale by the number of centimeters (3) on your ruler to get 1 cm = 5 km. This means 1 cm on the map equals 5 km on Earth's surface. With this information, you can use a ruler to find the true distance between any two points on this map. Simply multiply the number of centimeters between the two points on the map by 5 to get the number of kilometers between the locations on Earth.

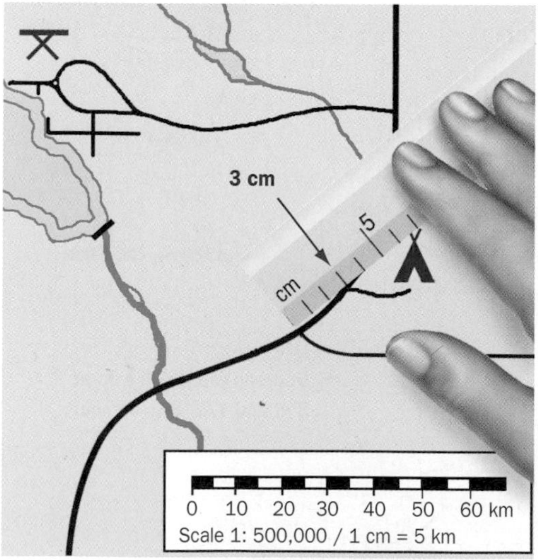

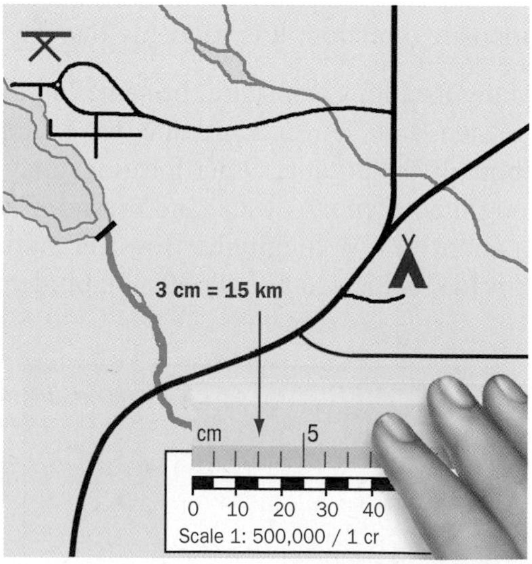

SEE ALSO
382 Ratios

A map scale may be written as a ratio such as 1:500,000. These numbers tell you that a distance on the map is $\frac{1}{500,000}$ (one five-hundred-thousandth) its actual distance on Earth's surface. Therefore, 1 cm on the map equals 500,000 cm, or 5 km, on Earth's surface.

A map scale tells you how detailed a map is. A map with a scale of 1:400,000 shows less detail than a map with a scale of 1:4000. Here's an example. On a map with a scale of 1:400,000, Lake Ponchartrain (just north of New Orleans) would be about 1.5 cm across. On a map whose scale is 1:40,000, Lake Ponchartrain would be 15 cm across. If you want to explore the coves around the lake, the map with the scale of 1:40,000 will be more helpful because it shows those coves in greater detail.

Map Legends 171

Features on a map may be shown with drawings called **map symbols.** A **map legend** lists the symbols used on a map and explains their meaning. Different maps use different symbols depending on the map's purpose. For example, a road map uses symbols to show different types of roads (interstate highways, state routes, and roads that are under construction), but it may not show schools or museums. A map of a tourist spot may use symbols to show mountains, parks, scenic views, beaches, or camping sites. A map showing the kinds of plants growing in your state would have very different symbols from the road or tourist map.

Word Watch!

A *map legend* is sometimes called a *map key.*

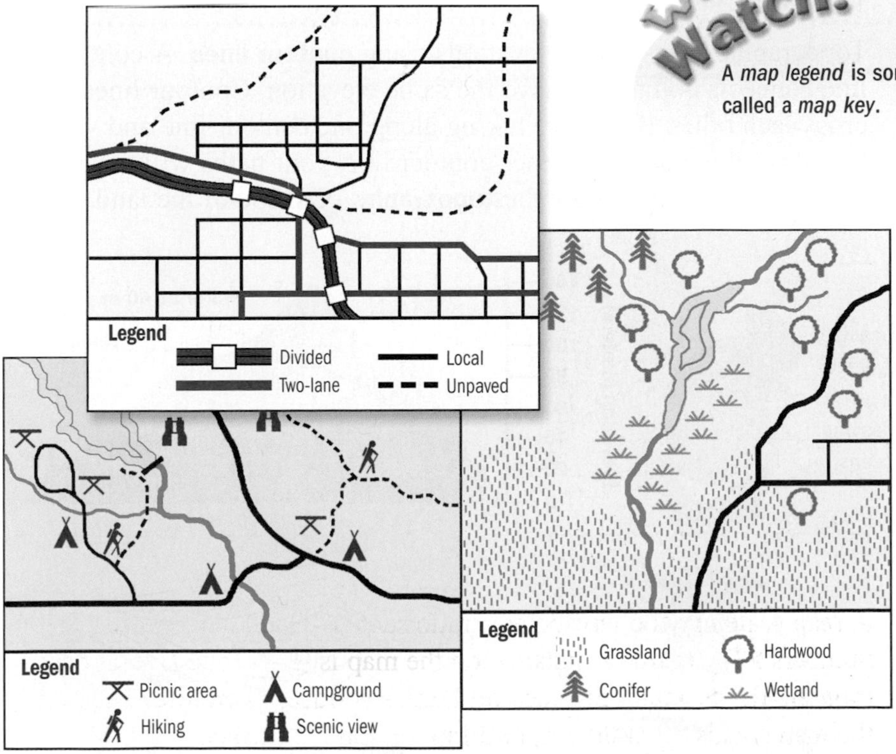

172

Topographic Maps

Most maps show information in two dimensions: east to west and north to south. They don't show how high or low an area is—a third dimension. A **topographic map** shows elevations, or high and low areas in land. **Elevation** is the height of land above or below sea level. Some maps give elevation in feet; others give it in meters. No matter what units are used, the elevation at sea level is always 0. You may be familiar with topographic maps if you go hiking. Topographic maps are also useful for planning roads and buildings. Like other maps, topographic maps are drawn to a certain scale. Many have a small scale and show changes in elevation over a small area. These maps give greater detail of the area than a map with a larger scale.

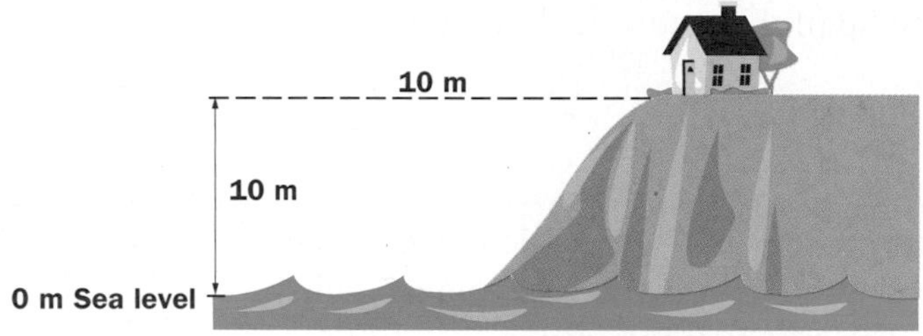

Elevation of house is 10 meters.

173

Contour Lines

Topographic maps show elevations using **contour lines.** A contour line connects points that have the same elevation. Contour lines never cross each other. If you are hiking along one contour line and your friend is hiking along another contour line, your paths will never cross. Contour lines show the **topography,** or shape of the land.

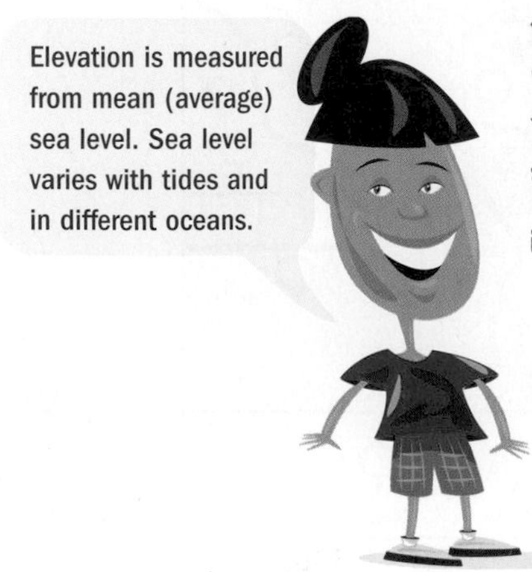
Elevation is measured from mean (average) sea level. Sea level varies with tides and in different oceans.

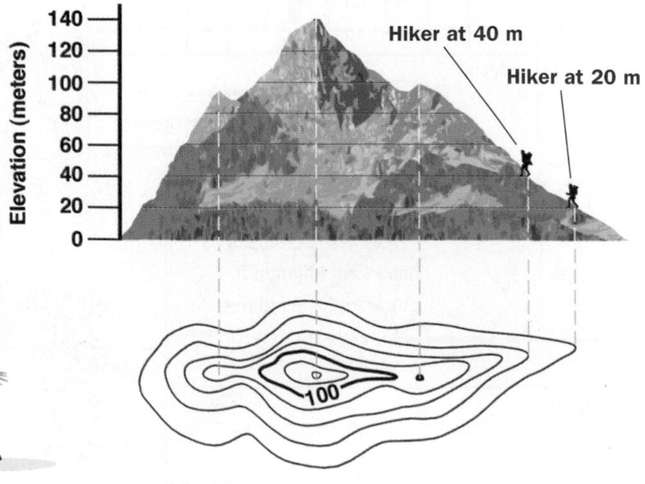

A **contour line** connects points on a map with the same elevation. Contour lines are brown on most maps.

The difference in elevation between two contour lines is the **contour interval.** To find the contour interval, see the example on the next page.

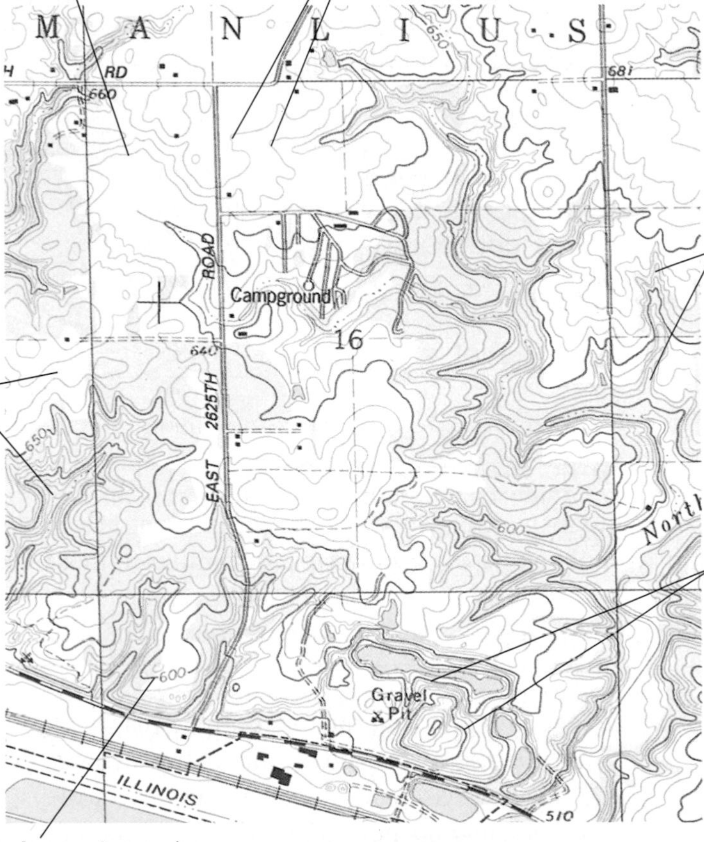

The distance between contour lines shows steepness of slope. Contour lines that are close together show a steep slope. A gentle slope is shown by contour lines that are far apart.

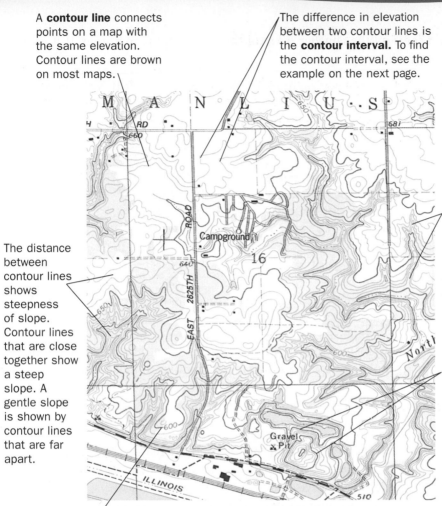

A V-shape in a contour line shows a valley. If a river (usually colored blue) flows through the valley, the V points upstream.

A series of closed, looped contour lines shows a hill, mountain, or a hollow or depression. The inside of a contour line that shows a hollow has little lines pointing inward.

Index contours show elevations and are darker than other contour lines.

Make sure you check contour intervals when you compare slopes on different maps. Two equally steep slopes can look different if their maps use different contour intervals.

MORE ▶

You can find the contour interval of a topographic map even if it isn't given in the map legend.

EXAMPLE: The elevation of one index contour is 100 ft. The elevation of the next index contour is 200 ft. There are 5 spaces, or intervals, between these index contours. What is the contour interval?

$$\text{Contour Interval} = \frac{\text{Elevation difference}}{\text{Number of spaces between index contours}}$$

$$\frac{(200 - 100)}{5} = \frac{100 \text{ ft.}}{5}$$

$$\text{Contour Interval} = 20 \text{ ft.}$$

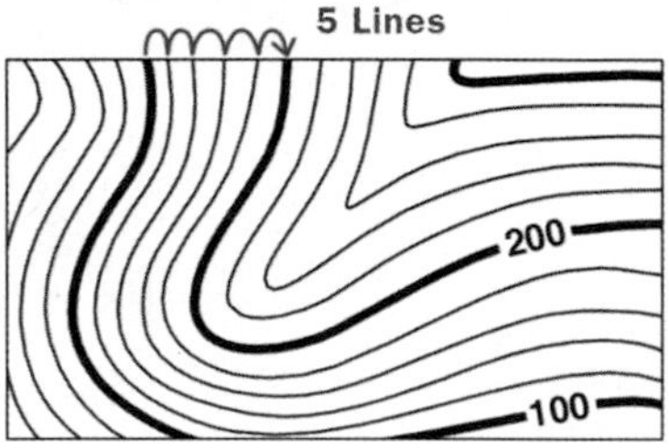

174 Topographic Map Symbols

Topographic maps use symbols to show different features on the land. Some symbols on topographic maps are similar to those used on other maps. Roads and railroad tracks look similar on road maps and topographic maps. Other symbols are unique to topographic maps, such as marsh and quarry symbols.

Look at the legend below and the topographic map on the page before this one. On the map, find all the features you can that have a symbol in the legend. Also see if you can find two valleys, two different index contours, and a steep slope.

SEE ALSO
173 Contour Lines

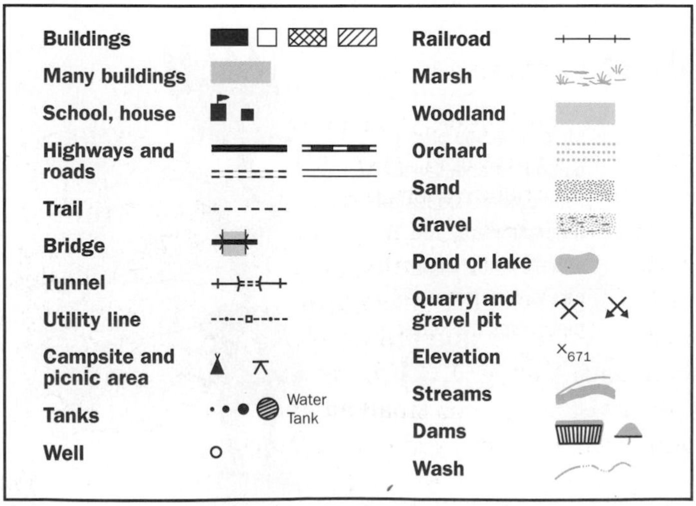

175

Geology

176 Earth Structure and Composition

181 Plate Tectonics and Mountain Building

188 Weathering, Soil, and Erosion

194 Earth History

You might think Earth is basically a giant ball of rock and soil. This description is partly correct. Earth is roughly spherical and has a rocky surface. But beneath this solid surface, Earth is very different.

Earth Structure and Composition

176

Research shows that Earth is made of several materials. The materials make up different layers.

Structure of Earth

177

Every time you walk outdoors, you are in contact with Earth's outermost layer, the **crust**. Based on your own experience, you know that some of Earth's crust is made up of soil. Beneath this soil is a thick layer of rock. Most rocks that make up Earth's crust are made up primarily of the elements silicon and oxygen. As shown in the chart, the crust also holds small amounts of aluminum, iron, calcium, and other elements.

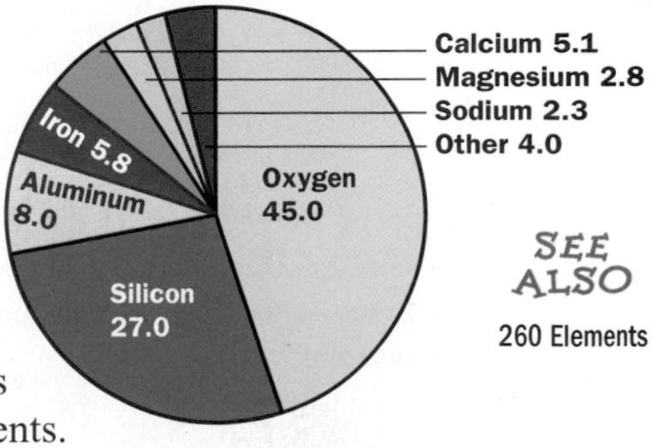

SEE ALSO
260 Elements

MORE

If you have ever planted a garden or dug a hole in the ground, you know that Earth's crust is made up of soil and rocks. But what would you find if you kept digging until you reached Earth's center? If you could dig a hole to the center of Earth, you would pass through four layers. From outside to inside, these layers are the **crust,** the **mantle,** the **outer core,** and the **inner core.** Each layer has its own characteristics.

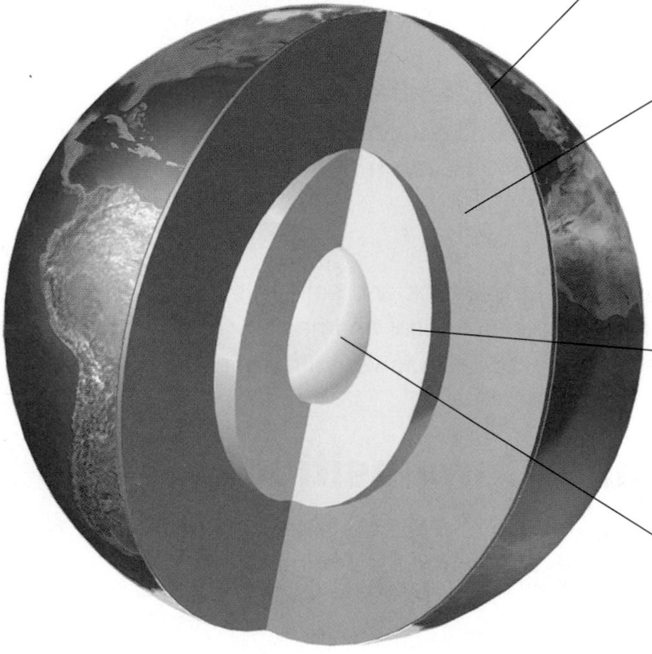
CRUST
Thickness: 5–10 km beneath the oceans; 20–70 km beneath the continents.
Other Features: Mostly solid rock
MANTLE
Thickness: About 2900 km
Other Features: High temperatures (2800–3200°C) in the upper part of the mantle melt rocks, forming a substance called magma. Magma flows like hot and thick oatmeal.
OUTER CORE
Thickness: About 2250 km
Other Features: Made up mostly of molten (melted) iron and nickel; Temperatures between 4000–5000°C
INNER CORE
Thickness: About 1280 km
Other Features: Solid iron and nickel; Temperature estimated at 6000°C; Although the inner core is very hot, it is kept solid due to the great pressure of the layers above it.

Did You Know?

If Earth were the size of an apple, the crust would be only as thick as the apple's skin.

Earth's Size and Shape

178

Earth is almost spherical, or ball-shaped, but its shape is not perfect. Earth is a little flattened at its poles and bulges a bit at its equator. For this reason, Earth's diameter from the North Pole to the South Pole is slightly smaller than its diameter from one point on the equator to an opposite point halfway around the equator.

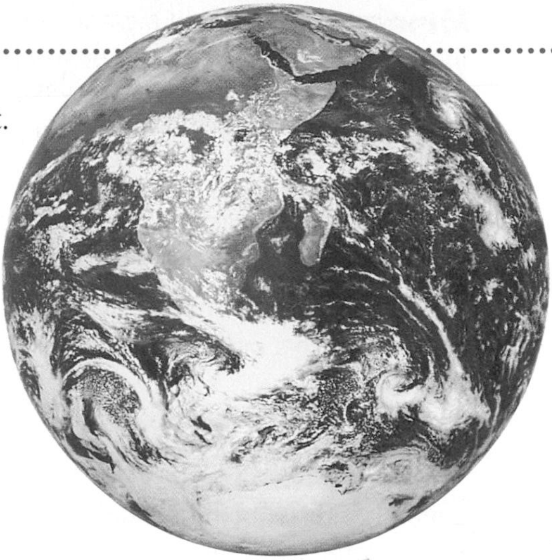

Word Watch!

The **diameter** of a sphere is the length of a line that passes through its center. The distance around the sphere is its **circumference**.

Earth Profile

Characteristic	Measurement
Diameter: North to South Pole	12,664 km
Diameter: Equator	12,756 km
Circumference: Around Poles	39,995 km
Circumference: Around Equator	40,064 km
Mass	5,882 sextillion metric tons
Volume	1,083 billion km^3
Total Surface Area	510 million km^2
Land Area	149 million km^2
Water Area	361 million km^2
Average Distance from Sun	149,573,900 km
Average Distance from Moon	384,400 km
Length of Day (one rotation on axis)	23 h, 56 min, 4.1 s
Length of Year (one revolution around sun)	365 days, 5 h, 48 min, 46 s
Axial Tilt (° tilted on axis from vertical)	23.5°

Source: Science Desk Reference, New York Public Library

179 Minerals

A **mineral** is a naturally formed solid substance with a crystal structure, which was not formed from living things. A **crystal structure** is a definite pattern in the way that particles in a substance are arranged. A mineral has a crystal structure even if it does not have a crystal shape that you can see.

Amethyst (quartz)

Each kind of mineral has certain properties that you can use to identify it. One property of minerals is hardness. **Hardness** is the ability of a mineral to resist being scratched. A harder mineral will always scratch a softer one. German scientist Friedrich Mohs developed a system for comparing the hardness of a mineral to 10 common minerals. These 10 minerals make up Mohs' Hardness Scale. The scale is based on familiar minerals, not on exact differences in hardness. The difference in hardness between minerals 3 and 4, for example, is much less than the difference in hardness between minerals 9 and 10. Even though the scale is not exact, it is still quite useful for identifying specimens.

Mohs' Hardness Scale for Minerals

Hardness	Mineral	Common Object
1	Talc	
2	Gypsum	Fingernail (2.5–3)
3	Calcite	Copper penny
4	Fluorite	
5	Apatite	Steel blade
6	Feldspar	Glass 5–6
7	Quartz	
8	Topaz	
9	Corundum	
10	Diamond	

To remember Mohs' Hardness Scale, make up a sentence with the first letters of each mineral, like The Giant Cat Found A Foolish Quail That Couldn't Dance.

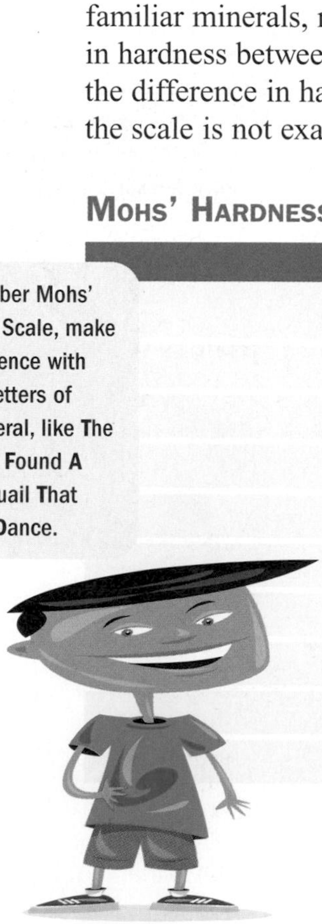

Other properties used to identify minerals include:

- **Color** A mineral may be one color or many colors. You cannot identify a mineral by color alone, but color is helpful along with other properties.
- **Luster** This property describes how a mineral reflects light from its surface. Some minerals are shiny like metal or glass (a glassy luster is called vitreous). Others have dull, waxy, or earthy lusters.
- **Streak** Streak is the color of a mineral in powder form. You can find out a mineral's streak by rubbing it across an unglazed porcelain streak plate. Each mineral makes a streak of a certain color. This color may differ from the color of the mineral.

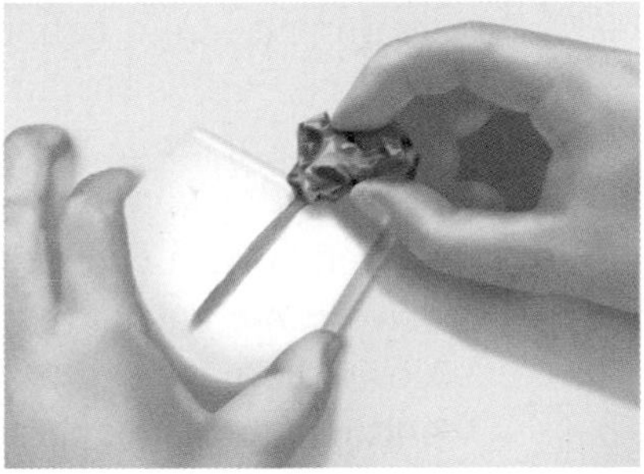

- **Crystal Shape** The atoms or ions of a mineral are arranged in a certain pattern. That pattern may result in a distinct crystal shape for the mineral. The pattern of the atoms in a mineral also affects its cleavage.
- **Cleavage and Fracture** Minerals break according to how their atoms are arranged. **Cleavage** is the tendency of a mineral to break along a flat surface where layers of atoms are attached weakly to each other. **Fracture** is the tendency of a mineral to break in a way that is not along a flat surface.

Halite

- **Specific Gravity** The specific gravity of a mineral is a comparison of its density to the density of an equal volume of water.

SEE ALSO
068 Finding Density

You can find mineral properties in a field guide. Using such guides along with observations and a few tests, you can find out if a yellow-colored mineral you find is gold or pyrite (fool's gold). A greenish-black streak tells you it is pyrite.

180 Rocks

Rocks are solid earth materials formed from a mixture of minerals and sometimes other materials. Rocks are classified into one of three groups based on how they formed. These groups are igneous rocks, sedimentary rocks, and metamorphic rocks.

SEE ALSO
177 Structure of Earth

Igneous Rocks High temperatures deep in Earth's crust cause rocks and minerals to melt, forming a liquid called **magma.** Magma that reaches Earth's surface is called **lava. Igneous rocks** form when magma or lava cools and becomes solid. Rocks that form from quickly cooled lava, such as rhyolite, are called **extrusive** or **volcanic** and have small mineral grains. Rocks that form from slowly cooled magma, such as granite, are called **intrusive** or **plutonic** and have large mineral grains.

Granite

SEE ALSO
272 Parts of a Solution

Sedimentary Rocks Pieces of rocks, minerals, remains of living things, and dissolved minerals that come out of water (such as lime) are all kinds of **sediment.** When sediment becomes solid material, it makes a **sedimentary rock.** Sediment is moved by wind and water and piles up on land and on riverbeds, lake bottoms, and the ocean floor. New layers of sediment build up over time, pressing down on older layers underneath. Dissolved minerals, such as calcite, come out of the water and cement the grains together. In time, the pressure and cementing form a **clastic** sedimentary rock, such as sandstone, shale, and many kinds of limestone. A **chemical** sedimentary rock, such as rock salt, forms when minerals come out of solution and settle on the ocean floor. An **organic** sedimentary rock, such as chalk, forms from the remains of once-living things.

Sandstone

Metamorphic Rocks Over time, heat and pressure inside Earth squeeze and melt existing rocks. This process changes the grain size and even the minerals that make up those rocks, forming a new type of rock, called a metamorphic rock. **Metamorphic rock** is rock that has been changed in form by pressure and heat. Gneiss and slate are examples of metamorphic rocks. Gneiss many form from granite. Slate forms from shale.

Gneiss

Throughout Earth's history, rocks of each type have been changed into other types by natural forces. They have been broken, heated, pressed, and pushed around over and over again. This constant changing in the form and structure of rocks is called the **rock cycle.**

The Rock Cycle

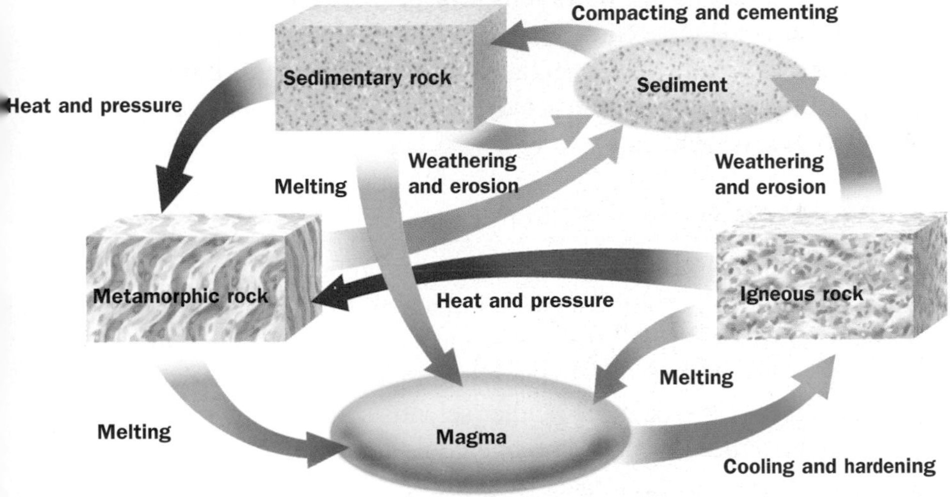

Melting	Hot temperatures deep inside Earth melt rocks, forming magma.
Cooling and Hardening	Magma that rises from deep inside Earth cools as it reaches the surface, hardening into rock. Magma also cools beneath the surface.
Weathering and Erosion	Weathering breaks apart existing rocks, forming sediment. Erosion moves sediment to new locations.
Compacting and Cementing	Pressure compacts sediments together. Water between particles evaporates, leaving minerals that cement sediments.
Heat and Pressure	Heat and pressure inside Earth melt and squeeze minerals in rocks. This changes the minerals themselves or their grain sizes.

SEE ALSO
188 Weathering, Soil, and Erosion
195 Geologic Principles

Science Alert!

The rock cycle shows many possible paths rocks can undergo to change from one form to another. A certain rock may go through all or only some stages in the rock cycle.

Plate Tectonics and Mountain Building

181

Based on your own observations, you may think of Earth as a rigid, unchanging planet. The TV news tells how parts of Earth can change suddenly from volcanoes, earthquakes, or floods. Earth is also changing slowly beneath your feet, even as you read these pages. Large parts of Earth are always on the move. Some parts move sideways, while others rise or sink.

182

Continental Drift

SEE ALSO
199 Earth's Continents through Time

In 1912, the German scientist Alfred Wegener proposed two ideas that are now known as the theory of continental drift. The **theory of continental drift** states that Earth's continents were once joined in a single large landmass that broke apart, and that the continents have drifted to their current locations. Other scientists at the time made fun of Wegener's ideas, because no one could imagine how continents could have moved. But geologists have found a lot of evidence to support the theory of continental drift, including rocks, fossils, measurements, and ocean-floor structures. Today's **theory of plate tectonics** is a more complete picture that includes all the evidence that the continents have moved and are still moving.

One piece of evidence is that the shapes of continents fit together like puzzle pieces. Compare the shapes of South America and Africa.

Continents 200 million years ago in age of dinosaurs

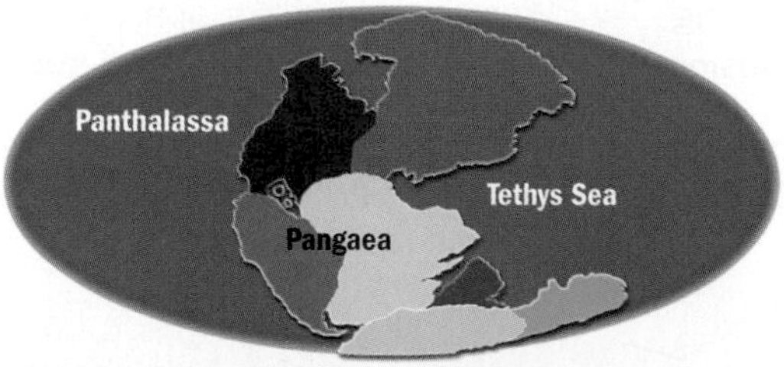

Continents today

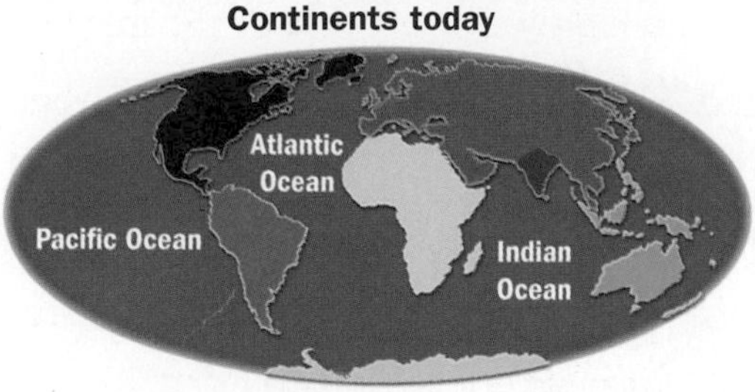

Lithospheric Plates

183

No one has been able to dig through Earth to see what it's like inside. Scientists must use indirect evidence, such as the way earthquake waves move through Earth, to form a model of Earth's interior. The best evidence supports this model: Earth's solid crust lies over a layer of solid but flexible material called the **mantle.** As material deep in the mantle is heated, it becomes less dense and rises. At the same time, material nearer Earth's surface spreads out, cools, and becomes denser. This denser material sinks below the hotter, less dense material. Uneven heating causes material in the mantle to constantly and slowly rise and fall in a **convection current.**

SEE ALSO
006 Forming a Hypothesis
177 Structure of Earth

Convection Current

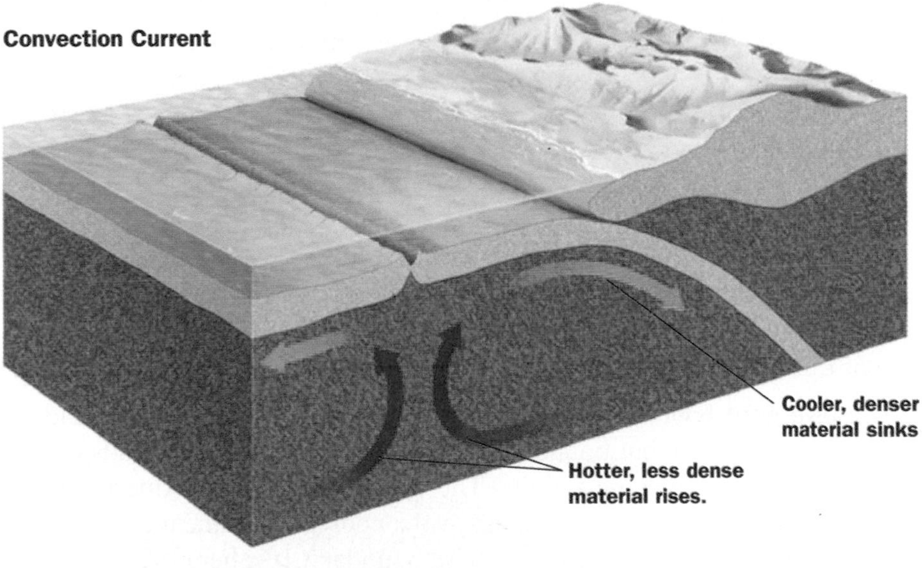
Cooler, denser material sinks below.
Hotter, less dense material rises.

The mantle material that is moved by the convection currents, together with the rocky crust that lies on the top of the mantle, make up the **lithospheric plates**. The **lithosphere** is the rocky outer shell of Earth, which is made up of the crust and the rigid upper part of the mantle.

Earth has two kinds of crust: **continental crust** and **oceanic crust.** Continents are made of continental crust, which is made up of rocks that are less dense than those of oceanic crust. Because it is less dense, continental crust rides higher on the mantle than oceanic crust.

Word Watch!

The prefix *litho-* comes from the Greek *lithos* meaning stone or rock. The root word *sphere* in this case means a layer in a ball shape.

SCILINKS NSTA
Keyword: Plate Tectonics
www.scilinks.org
Code: GSSM181

184 Plate Boundaries

Earth's crust is made up of seven major and several minor lithospheric plates. The plates are named for the surface features that lie on top of them. The seven major plates are the: Pacific, North American, South American, Eurasian, African, Indo-Australian, and Antarctic. The edges of most plates lie beneath the oceans. **Plate boundaries** occur where the edges of plates meet. The type of boundary depends on whether the plates forming them are moving toward each other, separating, or sliding past each other.

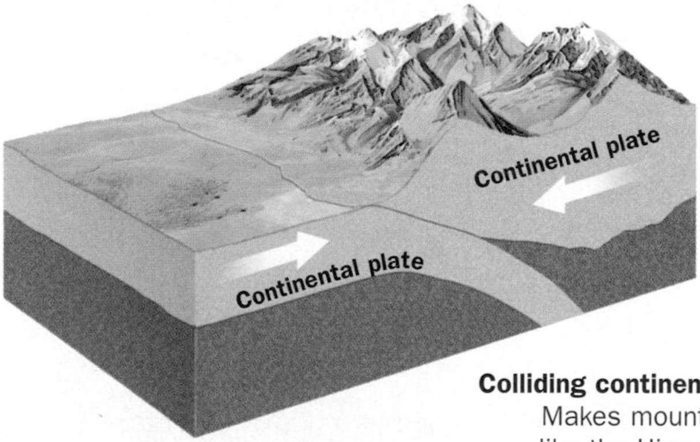

Colliding continental plates
Makes mountains like the Himalayas

A **convergent boundary** forms where plates collide. The pressure and violence at convergent boundaries produces mountains and bands of earthquake and volcanic activity. The west coast of South America with its towering Andes mountains, volcanoes, and frequent earthquakes is the location of a convergent boundary. It is here that the Nazca Plate crunches into the South American plate.

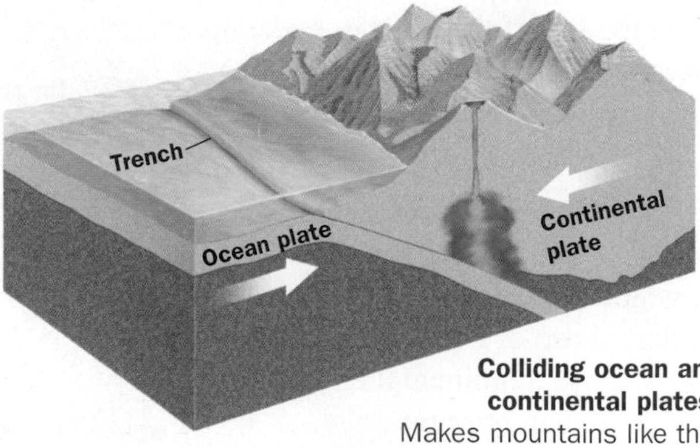

Colliding ocean and continental plates
Makes mountains like the Andes

The movement of one plate under another is called **subduction.** Subduction happens at converging plate boundaries. When a plate undergoes subduction, the rocks in that plate are pushed deep into Earth where they are heated and changed into molten material. This molten material, which is under great pressure, can escape through weak spots in Earth's crust as an erupting volcano.

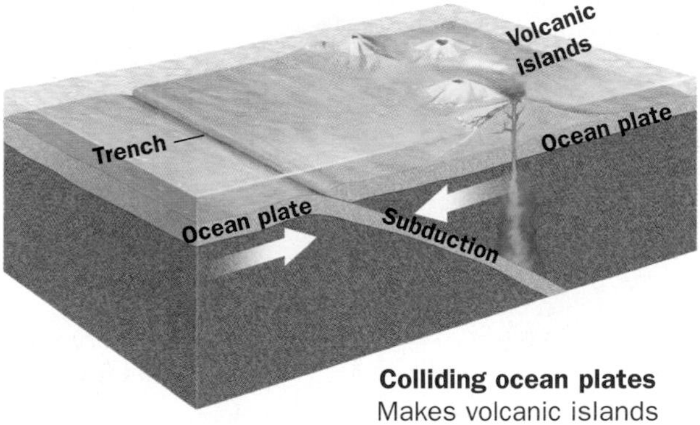

Colliding ocean plates
Makes volcanic islands like the Aleutians

A **divergent boundary** forms when two plates diverge, or move away from each other. Melted rock from the mantle can seep to the surface at divergent boundaries and form new crust. Most divergent boundaries are in the oceans. Here, they build undersea mountain ranges called **mid-ocean ridges.** The Great Rift Valley in Africa is at the edge of a divergent boundary on a continent.

As new crust forms at mid-ocean ridges, other crust is consumed at deep-sea trenches. So Earth's surface doesn't get any bigger.

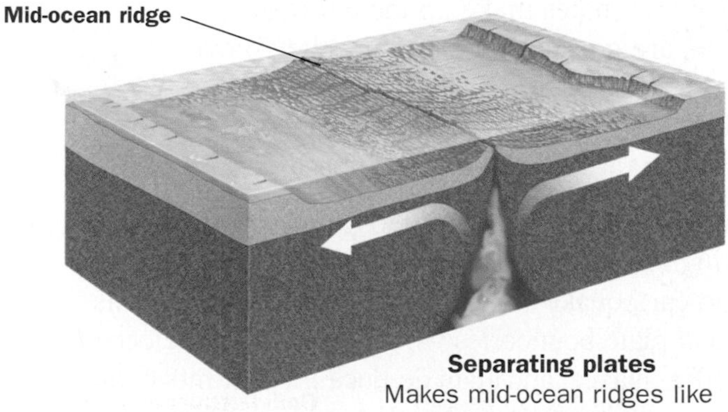

Separating plates
Makes mid-ocean ridges like Mid-Atlantic Ridge

MORE ▶

A **transform boundary** forms where two plates slide past each other. If you live on the west coast of the United States you may have felt the effects of a transform boundary. Here, the Pacific and North American plates slide past each other in a north-south direction. The sliding causes rocks along the boundary to grind against each other from time to time, causing jolts that you feel as earthquakes.

Transform Boundary

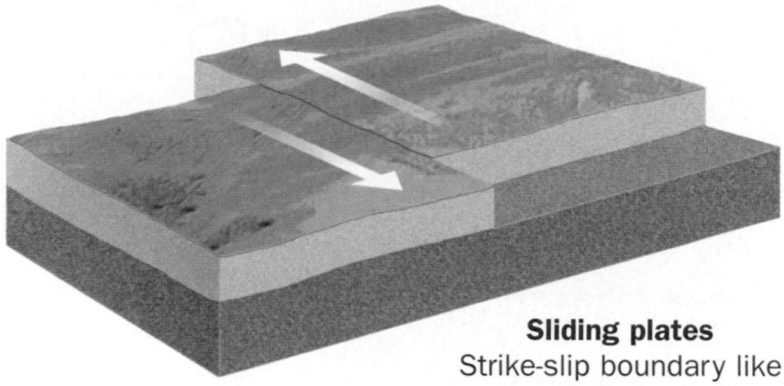

Sliding plates
Strike-slip boundary like San Andreas Fault

Did You Know?

The transform boundary between the Pacific and North American Plates is moving Los Àngeles north toward San Francisco at a rate of about 5 cm a year. At this rate, it would take the two cities about 11 million years to be side-by-side (but the rate is usually slower).

The Juan de Fuca plate is a small plate off the coast of the northwest United States. The movement of this small plate causes a lot of volcanic activity.

185

Map of Plate Boundaries

Earth's lithospheric plates make up the entire surface of Earth. Plates are constantly in motion; they move toward each other, away from each other, or slide past each other. Most earthquake and volcano activity takes place at the plate boundaries.

An interesting feature produced by lithospheric plate boundaries is the Ring of Fire. The **Ring of Fire** is a ring-shaped belt of volcano and earthquake activity in the Pacific Ocean. This belt is formed at plate boundaries where plates of dense oceanic crust (the Pacific, Nazca, and Juan de Fuca Plates), move under less dense continental plates (the North American, Eurasian, Indo-Australian, and South American Plates).

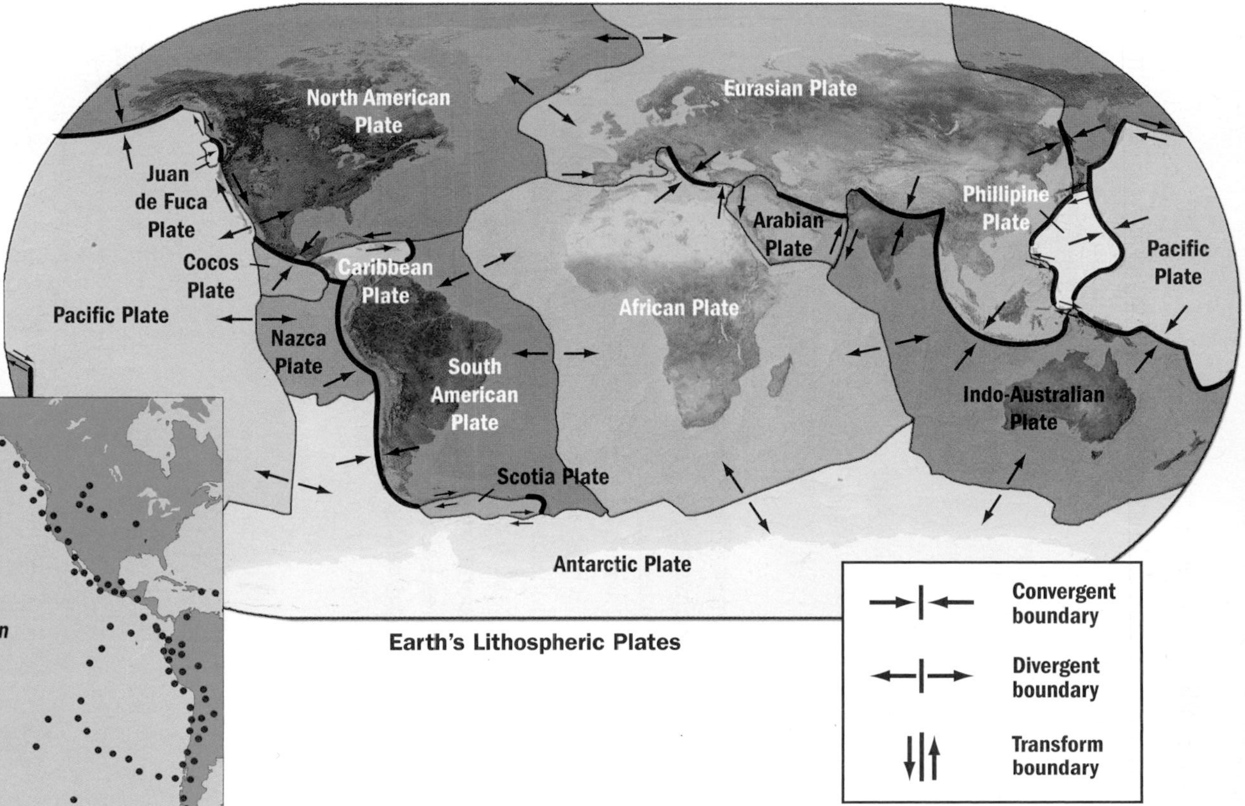

Earth's Lithospheric Plates

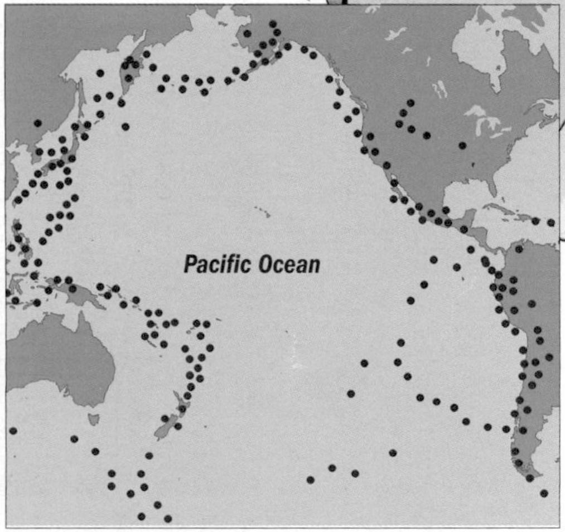

Ring of Fire: Dots show where earthquakes or volcanic activity are common.

SciLinks NSTA
Keyword: Plate Tectonics
www.scilinks.org
Code: GSSM181

186

Earthquakes

Press the palms of your hands flat together as hard as you can. While you are doing that, try to slide one hand past the other. Unless your hands are wet, they probably do not slide past each other smoothly. Most likely your hands stay in place until they suddenly slide a few centimeters, then stop. This is the way movement takes place in Earth's crust. Movement occurs along **faults,** which are large cracks in Earth's crust. Rocks on either side of a fault are under pressure and get locked together, just like your hands did. When too much pressure builds up, the rocks suddenly slide past each other and release the pressure. You feel the result as an **earthquake,** or violent shaking of Earth's crust.

The place in Earth's crust where the pressure was released is called the **focus.** Earthquake waves, or **seismic waves,** spread out in all directions from the focus like ripples through a pond. The focus can be many kilometers down in the crust, so usually people talk about an earthquake **epicenter,** which is the spot on Earth's surface directly above the focus. Earthquakes make three kinds of seismic waves. **Primary waves** (also called P-waves) stretch and compress land as they pass through. **Secondary waves** (also called S-waves) move land side to side. **Land waves** (also called L-waves) form when P- and S-waves combine. Land waves move land up and down, like ripples travelling through a pond.

SEE ALSO
307 Kinds of Waves

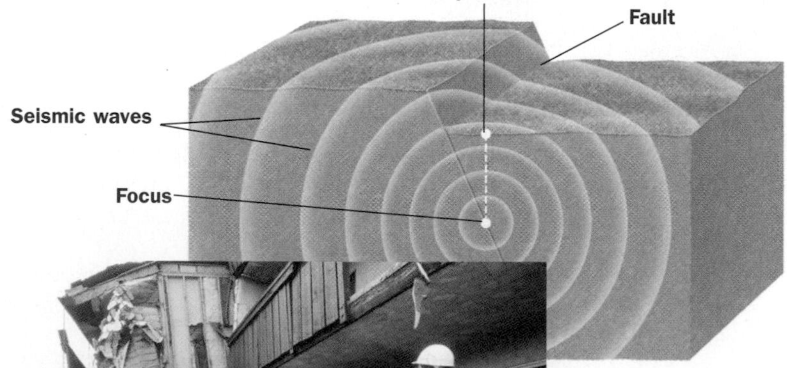

Earthquake damage

Another scale that is often used to measure earthquake magnitude is the Mercalli scale. This scale describes magnitude based on how much damage the earthquake causes.

Seismic waves provide evidence for the model of Earth's layers. P-waves travel through solids and liquids, but S-waves can travel only through solids. When an earthquake occurs, both P- and S- waves reach nearby seismographs, while only P-waves reach seismographs on the other side of Earth. So there must be a liquid layer stopping the S-waves. The P-waves do not come out where you would expect, so there must be a change in density causing the P-waves to bend. The strength, or **magnitude,** of an earthquake can be measured using a seismograph. A few different scales are used to measure earthquake magnitude. You will most often hear about the **Richter scale.** The Richter scale is named for the American scientist Charles F. Richter, who invented the scale in 1935. On the Richter scale earthquake magnitudes range from 1 through about 9. Each number on the scale stands for a ten-fold increase in the size of the earthquake wave. For example, a magnitude 5 earthquake has a wave that is ten times larger than a magnitude 4 earthquake.

Richter Scale

Magnitude	Earthquake Effects
1–3	Not felt; recorded on local seismographs
3–4	Felt by people; no damage
5	Felt by most people; causes slight damage near epicenter
6	Damage caused to poorly constructed buildings and other structures within about 10 km
7	Causes major damage to structures up to 100 km from epicenter
8	Very destructive; may cause loss of life over a distance of several hundred kilometers
9	Very rare; major damage to areas as much as 1000 km away

Source: Geological Survey of Canada

Did You Know?

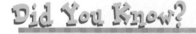

The strongest earthquake recorded in the United States struck Alaska in 1964 and measured 9.2 on the Richter scale.

187

Mountain Building and Volcanoes

SEE ALSO

183 Lithospheric Plates
184 Plate Boundaries

A major force shaping the land is **uplift,** the lifting of land by forces in Earth's crust. Moving plates uplift land, forming mountains. Three types of mountains are folded mountains, fault-block mountains, and volcanic mountains. Each forms by a different type of plate movement.

Place a sheet of paper flat on your desk. Place a hand on one edge of the paper. Push your other hand against the free edge of the paper. What happens? A fold, or bulge, forms in the paper. Earth's crust may experience the same effect when lithospheric plates collide. In this case, the "bulge" becomes a mountain range. Mountains formed in this way are called **folded mountains.** The Rocky Mountains of North America, the Andes of South America, the Alps of central Europe, and the Himalayas of Asia are examples of folded mountains.

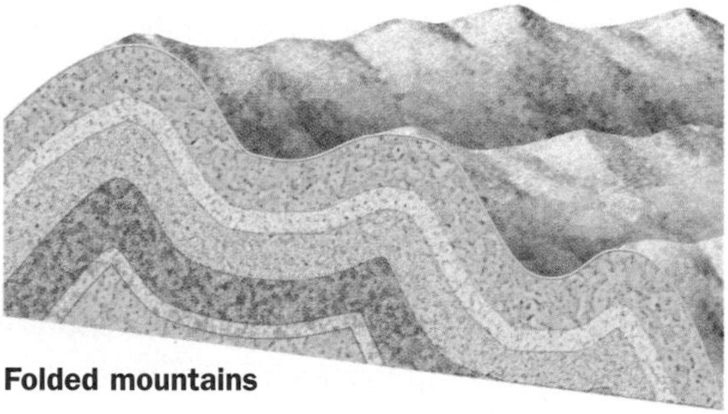

Folded mountains

Mountains can form when blocks of Earth's crust on either side of a fault are dropped below or pushed above the surrounding land. This happens where sections of crust are pulling apart or pushing together. At these places, large blocks of the crust are sliding up and down past each other. The taller blocks form **fault-block mountains.** Examples of fault-block mountains include the Sierra Nevadas of California, the Wasatch Range of Utah, and the Teton Range of Wyoming.

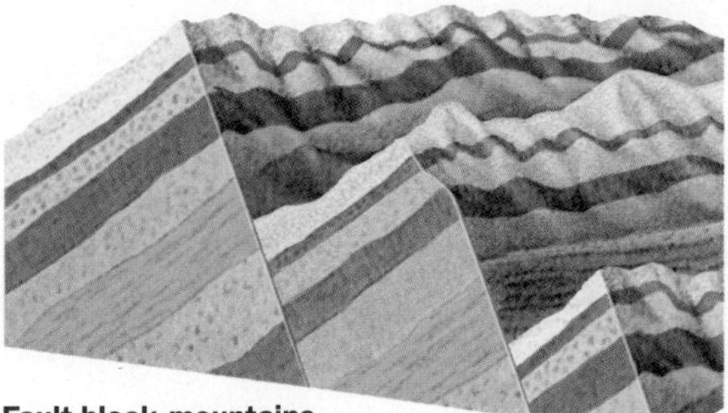

Fault-block mountains

Volcanoes, or volcanic mountains, form when material from inside Earth reaches the surface. Volcanic mountains are most common at plate boundaries. Within converging boundaries, heat and pressure melts rock into magma, which can rise through cracks in the crust. When magma is forced up onto Earth's surface, it becomes lava that hardens into rock. At diverging boundaries, where plates are pulling apart, magma rises through cracks and forms the mountains at mid-ocean ridges.

Volcanoes are classified into three types based on how they form.

Cinder cone volcano

- sudden, violent eruption
- formed from ash, cinders, dust
- cone-shaped mound
- Mount Paricutín, Mexico; Mount Isalco, El Salvador

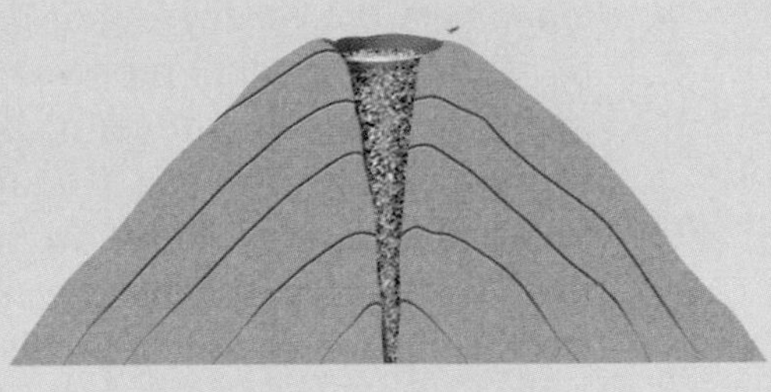

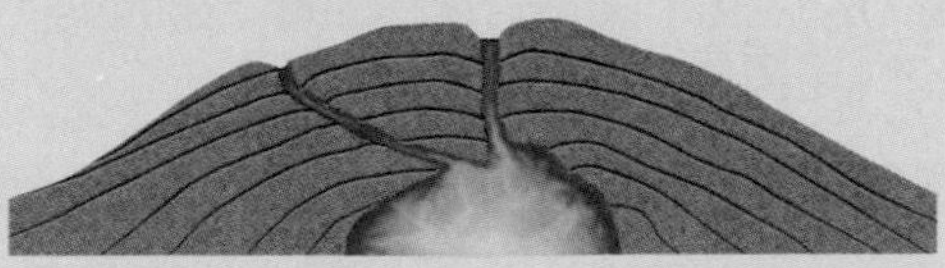

Shield volcano

- slow, gentle eruption
- formed from layers of cooled lava
- low, gently-sloped sides
- Mauna Loa, Mauna Kea in Hawaii

Composite cone volcano

- both violent and gentle eruptions
- formed from alternating layers of ash and lava
- cone-shaped mound, steep sides
- Mount Vesuvius, Italy; Mount St. Helen's in Washington State; Mount Egmont, New Zealand

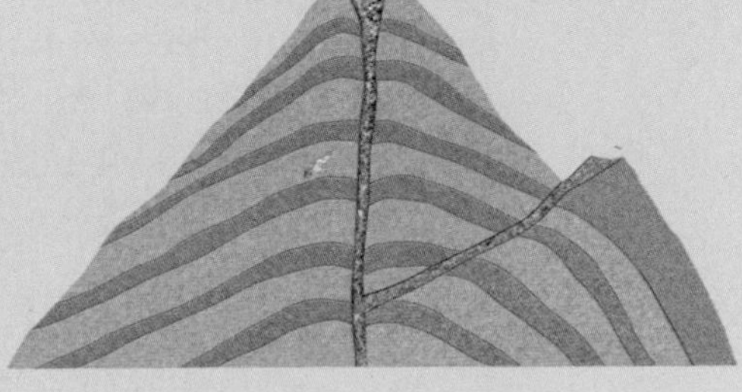

188

Weathering, Soil, and Erosion

Earth's surface is constantly changing. Movements at plate boundaries build up Earth's surface, forming mountains. At the same time, two other processes wear down Earth's surface. Weathering changes Earth by breaking rocks and other matter into smaller particles called sediment. Erosion sweeps these weathered particles away.

Weathering breaks up rock into smaller pieces, much like you might do using a hammer. Unlike using a hammer, the weathering of rock in nature is a gradual process. No matter how slowly, sooner or later, every rock that is in water or air will be weathered away. There are two main types of weathering: mechanical weathering and chemical weathering.

Word Watch!

Weathering means breaking rock apart by water, wind, and other agents. *Erosion* means the movement of those rock particles, often from a higher to a lower elevation.

189

Mechanical Weathering

Mechanical weathering, also called physical weathering, takes place when rocks are broken apart by a physical force.

- **Ice Wedging** When the temperature drops below the freezing point of water (0°C), water in cracks turns to ice. Water expands as it freezes, pushing apart the walls of the crack.
- **Release of Pressure** When a large mass of a rock such as granite reaches Earth's surface, the pressure on it is reduced. There is evidence that this release of pressure can cause pieces of the rock to flake off. As they start to flake, chemical weathering helps to speed the process.

SCILINKS NSTA
Keyword: Weathering/Erosion
www.scilinks.org
Code: GSSM188

- **Abrasion** Moving water and air (wind) can carry sand and other particles. When these particles strike rocks, they chip away the surface, much as you would if you rubbed a rock with sandpaper.

- **Plant Action** Plant roots can grow in cracks in rocks. As roots grow, they break apart the rock.

Chemical Weathering

Chemical weathering changes the chemical makeup of rocks and minerals. Chemical weathering can remove certain minerals from some rocks. It can also change the minerals into new substances. There are two main types of chemical weathering.

- **Oxidation** The red-brown crust called rust is iron oxide. It forms when oxygen joins chemically with iron. Oxidation is the joining of oxygen with other substances. Oxidation can weaken and crumble rocks as well as metal.

- **Dissolving by Acids** Water can dissolve minerals. Water that contains acid dissolves minerals more quickly than neutral water. One source of acid is acid rain. Acid rain can form when chemicals given off by factories, power plants, cars, and volcanoes join with water vapor in the air. This forms acids that return to Earth in precipitation such as rain and snow. Some plants and fungi also make acids as they carry out their life processes.

SEE ALSO
180 Rocks
351 Acid Rain

Carbon dioxide that mixes with water forms carbonic acid. This acid dissolves calcium carbonate in rocks such as limestone. As water containing calcium carbonate drips from cavern ceilings and dries, it leaves behind stalactites, icicle-shaped spikes of rock hanging from the ceilings. Other spikes called stalagmites form when water drips from the stalactites onto the floor and then evaporates, leaving solid minerals behind.

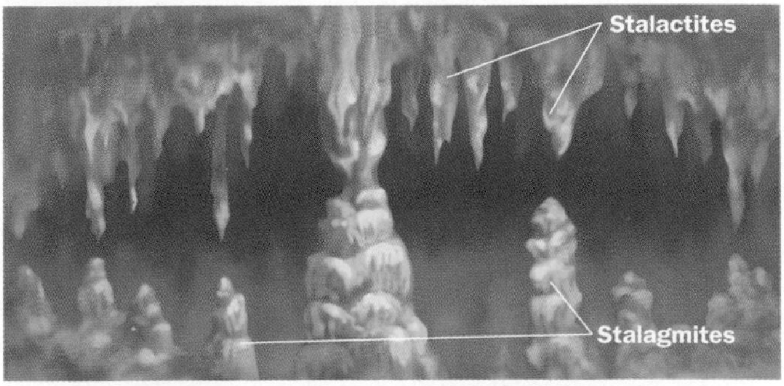

191 Soil

Soil is a mixture of rock, mineral particles, and organic matter. Weathering forms the rock and mineral particles of soil. These particles are inorganic parts of soil. Other inorganic parts of soil are the water and air that fill the spaces between soil particles.

In life and earth sciences, **inorganic** substances are those that were not formed from living things. **Organic** substances are those formed by living things.

Most organic material in soil, called **humus**, comes from decaying animals and plants. Living things, such as bacteria and fungi, break down plant and animal remains and form humus.

Soil is made up of layers called **horizons.** It takes thousands of years for a soil to mature. Mature soils have four horizons. Less mature soils have fewer horizons.

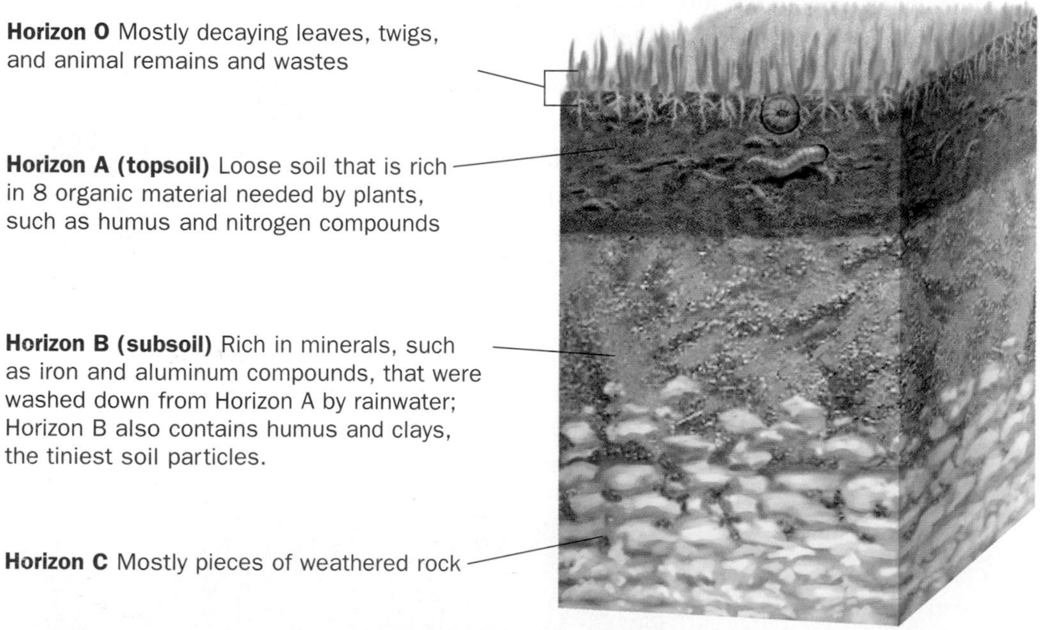

Horizon A (topsoil) Loose soil that is rich in 8 organic material needed by plants, such as humus and nitrogen compounds
Horizon B (subsoil) Rich in minerals, such as iron and aluminum compounds, that were washed down from Horizon A by rainwater; Horizon B also contains humus and clays, the tiniest soil particles.
Horizon C Mostly pieces of weathered rock

Soil horizons are home to a variety of living things. These include burrowing animals such as groundhogs and moles, and smaller animals such as snails, worms, ants, spiders, and centipedes. Many plants, fungi of all sizes, and microscopic bacteria and protists also live in soil.

SEE ALSO
156 Protist Kingdom

Erosion and Deposition

Weathering breaks rocks into smaller pieces. These pieces can be swept away through **erosion.** Erosion takes away land in one place and builds land in another. When moving water, ice, wind, or gravity drops a load of Earth materials in a new place, it is called **deposition**.

Streams are called by many names, such as creek, brook, and river. Scientists just use the term *stream*.

Moving Water Rainwater running off land carries away sediment, leaving behind an eroded path called a gully. Over time, as water keeps flowing in the gully, it widens and deepens to form a stream or river. Great rivers, such as the Mississippi River, deposit the sediment they carry where they enter the ocean, forming a **delta**. Moving water affects sediment at the shore, too. Ocean waves and currents carry sand off one beach, and deposit it later on another beach somewhere else.

A gully forms where moving water erodes sediment.

Rivers slow down where they enter an ocean. The slower-moving water deposits sediments, forming a delta.

SCILINKS NSTA
Keyword: Weathering/Erosion
www.scilinks.org
Code: GSSM188

MORE ▶

Ice Rivers and sheets of year-round ice called **glaciers** slowly move over land. As they travel, glaciers can move boulders the size of houses, as well as smaller sediments. Over time, the rocks and sediment carried by moving glaciers can carve or deepen valleys.

Wind Fast-moving wind can carry sand and dust that scour and weather the surfaces they strike. Wind erosion is greatest in dry areas, such as deserts, where there is little water to hold soil particles together or trees to block the wind's path. When the wind slows, it drops its load. This is how sand dunes are built.

Gravity Gravity is the underlying force of erosion and deposition. It causes water and glaciers to move downhill, and particles carried by water and wind to settle to a stream or lake bed and to the ground. Gravity can also directly cause erosion in the form of landslides and mudflows.

193

Divides and Drainage Basins

A **divide** is any line of high land where rainwater or snowmelt runs down one side or the other. A divide might cross a small hill or an entire mountain range.

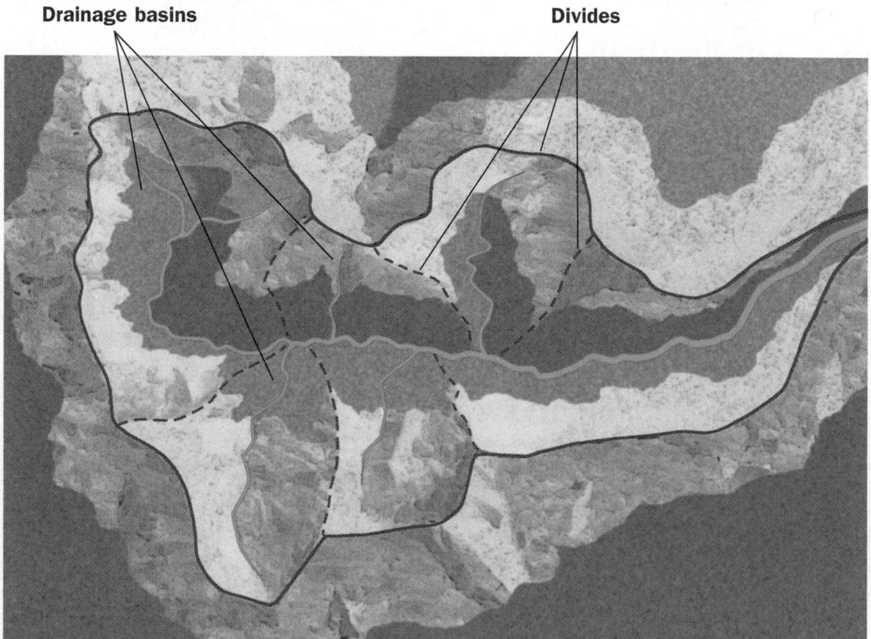

This large drainage basin is made up of six smaller ones.

Water that runs down each side of a divide forms small streams that join together into larger streams, and finally rivers. Together these bodies of flowing water form a drainage system that drains water away from a divide. All of the land where the water collects and flows toward a river is called a **drainage basin**. Large drainage basins are made up of many smaller drainage basins.

The largest drainage basin in the United States is the land between the Rocky Mountains and the Appalachian Mountains. The Great Continental Divide of North America runs through the Rocky Mountains. The Rocky Mountains run north to south through the United States and Canada. From the western slopes of these mountains, water runs toward the Pacific Ocean. From the eastern slopes, it runs toward the Gulf of Mexico. A lesser continental divide to the east is in the Appalachian Mountain range. Water that runs down the western slopes of the Appalachians flows into the Gulf of Mexico. Water that runs down the eastern slopes flows into the Atlantic Ocean.

Word Watch!

The terms *drainage basin* and *watershed* mean the same thing.

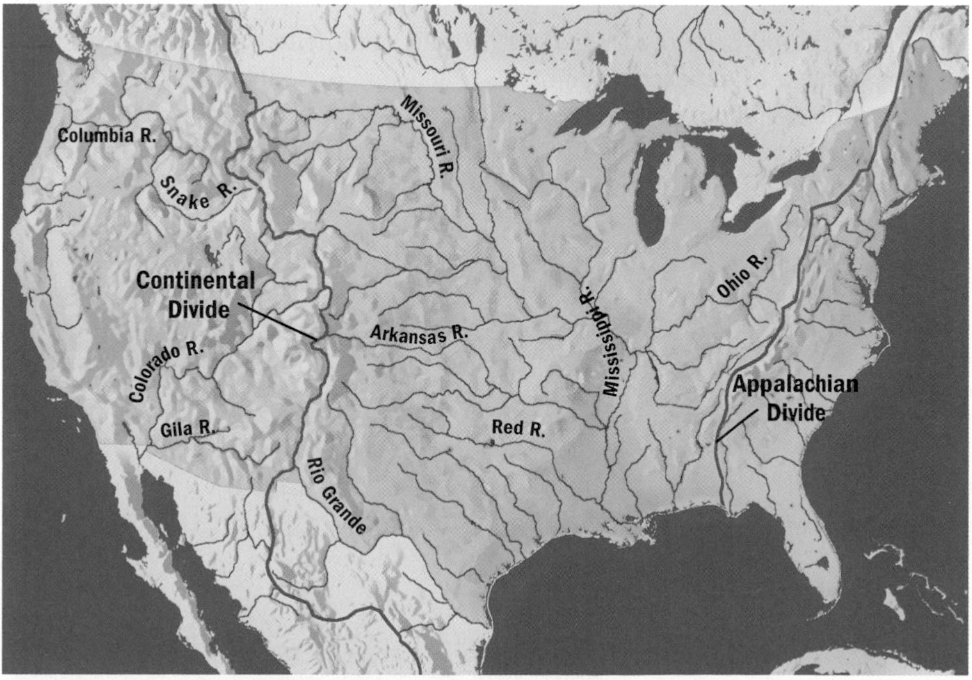

The map shows the two major divides that cross the United States.

Earth History

194

Evidence suggests that Earth formed about 4.6 billion years ago. If you had a time machine to visit Earth back then, you would not recognize it. The Earth of 4.6 billion years ago was very hot. No water flowed on its surface. No wind blew over its land and no living things lived here. In time, all these characteristics changed, forming the Earth you know today. During the past few hundred years, scientists have learned much about the changes that have occurred and have come up with theories to explain how the changes happened.

195

Geologic Principles

SEE ALSO
187 Mountain Building and Volcanoes
188 Weathering, Soil, and Erosion

In 1795, the Scottish geologist James Hutton published a book called *Theory of the Earth*. In this book, Hutton described the idea of the principle of uniformitarianism. The **principle of uniformitarianism** states that the processes we see changing Earth's surface today are the same as those that changed its surface in the past, even when we were not around to see it happen. These processes include uplift (mountain building) and wearing down (weathering, erosion, and deposition).

Weathered earth materials, shells, and bone fragments settle in layers at the bottoms of bodies of water. Over time, these materials are compacted and cemented together, forming sedimentary rock layers. The **principle of superposition** states that layers of sedimentary rock nearer the surface are younger than layers of rock deeper down, unless something has disturbed the layers. Thus, each layer is older than the one above it and younger than the one below it.

Word Watch!

Uniform means "same." Super means "above." Position means "where something is."

Geologic Cross-Sections

196

Molten rock, called magma, can move up through cracks and cut through layers of sedimentary rock. The **principle of cross-cutting relationships** states that such features are younger than all the layers they cut through.

After rock layers are formed, uplift can raise them to Earth's surface, where erosion wears them away. An **unconformity** is a place where rock layers are missing. Rock layers often occur above an unconformity, but they are not the kind of rock that would have formed in the same way as the rock layers beneath the unconformity.

SEE ALSO
192 Erosion and Deposition

A geologic cross-section is a cutaway view of the rocks in a certain place. Sometimes you can see cross-sections at road cuts. You can use geologic principles to "read" the story in a geologic cross-section.

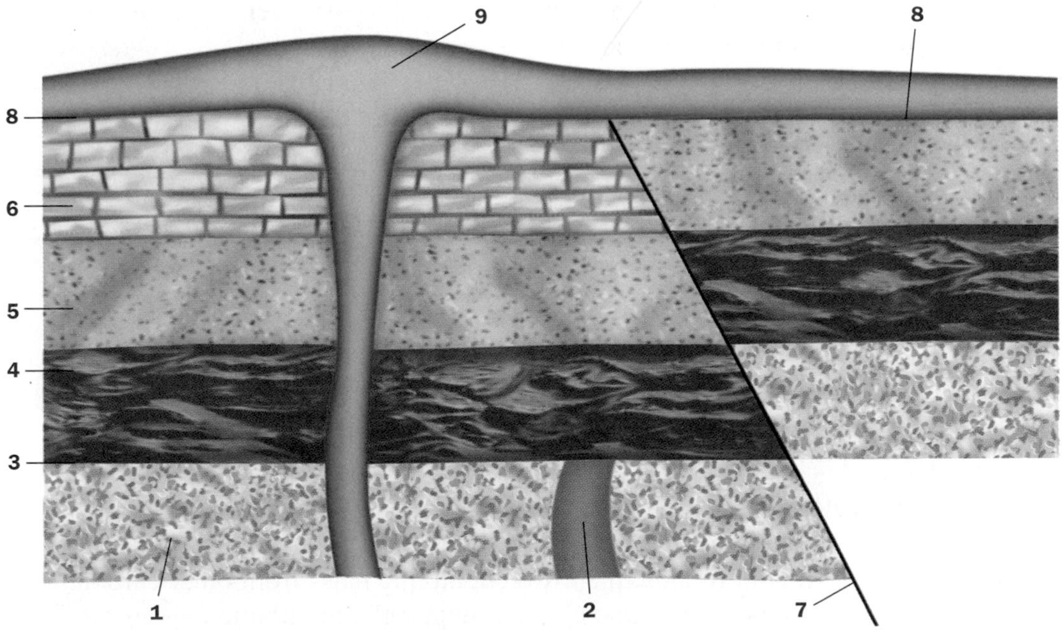

1. Rock layer 1 forms.
2. Magma squeezes into crack in rock layer 1, forming igneous rock.
3. Weathering and erosion cause unconformity over layer 1.
4, 5, 6. Rock layers form, in that order.
7. Movement along fault displaces rock layers.
8. Weathering and erosion remove layer 6 and part of layer 5 from one side of fault.
9. Lava flow cuts across layers and flows over top of formation.

197 Relative and Absolute Age Dating

The principle of superposition can be used to estimate ages of rocks and other objects compared with other rocks and objects. **Relative age dating** is a way to describe the age of one object or event compared to another object or event. Relative age dating is based on comparisons of the ages of objects. Thus, this method of dating objects always includes words such as *before, after, earlier, later, older,* and *younger*. For example, if you find a stone ax head in one sedimentary rock layer and an animal skull in a lower layer, you can use the law of superposition to conclude that the skull is older than the ax head.

Word Watch!

In this case, *relative* means "compared with something else" and *dating* means "finding out how old something is." *Absolute* means "compared to a standard measurement."

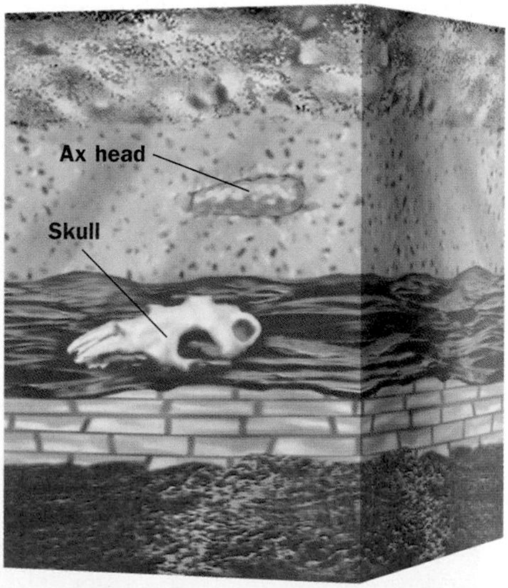

Absolute age describes the actual age of an object or event. The absolute ages of objects from long ago are found by analyzing the chemicals in the objects or the rock layers in which they were found. An example is carbon-14 dating.

SEE ALSO
256 Atomic Structure

Most atoms of carbon contain 12 neutrons in their nuclei, or cores. A very few carbon atoms have a different number of neutrons in their nuclei, which gives them a different atomic mass from other carbon atoms. Atoms of the same element with different atomic masses are called **isotopes** of that element.

The isotope carbon-14, or C-14, has fourteen neutrons in its nucleus. The carbon-14 atom is **radioactive**—that is, it tends to give off particles from its nucleus. When this happens, the C-14 atom changes into an atom of a different element. This change is called radioactive decay.

Scientists have figured out that it takes about 5730 years for half of the C-14 in a sample to change into a different element. In another 5730 years, another half of the C-14 has changed. The time it takes for half of the C-14 to change is called the **half-life** of carbon-14.

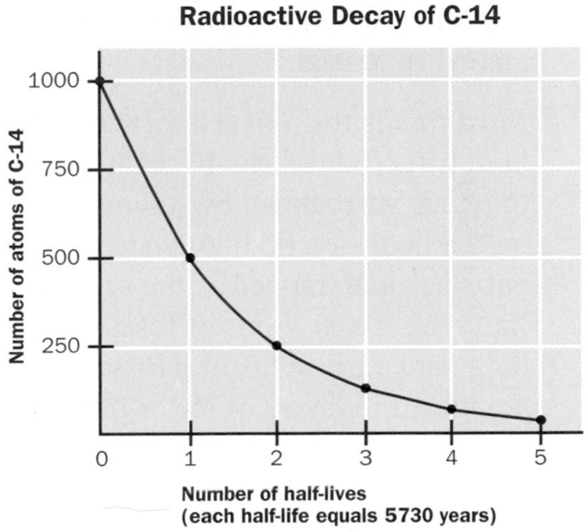

All living things contain the element carbon. While an organism is alive, the amount of C-14 it contains, compared to other kinds of carbon, stays pretty much the same. After the organism dies, no more carbon is coming into it, but the C-14 starts to change into another element. Imagine a piece of wood found at the site of an ancient village. In a laboratory, scientists can count the number of C-14 atoms in a sample of the wood and compare it to the number that was probably in the wood when it was cut (in other words, when the tree died). This tells them how much of the C-14 has changed (for example, half, more than half, less than half). Because they know how many years it takes for half of the C-14 to change, they can figure out about how many years ago the tree was cut or died. That information tells them about how long ago people were living in the village.

Carbon-14 dating does not work for most rock layers because the half-life of carbon-14 is too short compared to the ages of rocks. But other radioactive isotopes, such as uranium-235, potassium-40, and thorium-232, have longer half-lives. These isotopes are useful for figuring out the absolute ages of some rocks and fossils.

Should we try C-14 dating on that candy before we eat it?
Candy

198 Fossils

Scientific evidence suggests that different kinds of living things have existed on Earth for at least 3.5 billion years. Remains or evidence of those organisms in layers of rock are called **fossils.**

Most fossils form in sedimentary rock. The hard parts (bones, shells, teeth) of a living thing are surrounded by sediments that collect on the floor of a body of water. These hard parts become trapped as the sediments harden into rock. Other kinds of fossils form when both hard parts and soft parts of living things are buried in layers of ice or trapped in tree sap that later hardens.

Insects in amber

A **petrified fossil** forms when minerals replace the bone, shell, or other hard part that was trapped, turning it into rock. Most dinosaur bones are petrified fossils.

Petrified wood

Trace fossils include the footprints, tracks, trails, and burrows made by living things. There are trace fossils of human ancestors who walked on two feet.

Dinosaur footprints

A **cast** is a model in the shape of a living thing or its remains. A cast forms when minerals or rock particles fill the space in a mold.

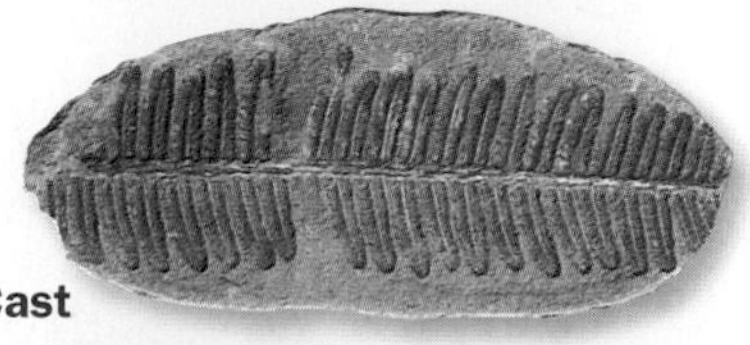
Cast

A **mold** is a space in a rock that has the shape of the remains of a living thing that once occupied that space.

Mold

Fish imprints

Coprolites are the petrified remains of animal dung. Coprolites can reveal what an animal ate, which also shows what other living things shared the animal's environment.

Imprints are impressions of parts of organisms left in soil or sediment before it hardens. Thin objects, such as leaves, fish, and feathers, form imprints.

Earth's Continents through Time

Evidence suggests that the continents were not always in the places they now occupy. This idea was first stated in the theory of continental drift. According to this theory, Earth's continents were once joined in a single large landmass that broke apart. The continents then drifted to their current locations.

SEE ALSO
182 Continental Drift

1. About 245 million years ago, the continents were joined in a single landmass, known as Pangaea. (Triassic Period, beginning of Mesozoic Era)

2. About 180 million years ago, North America, Europe, and Asia, separated from South America and Africa; Antartica, Australia, and India also separated. (Jurassic Period, middle of Mesozoic Era)

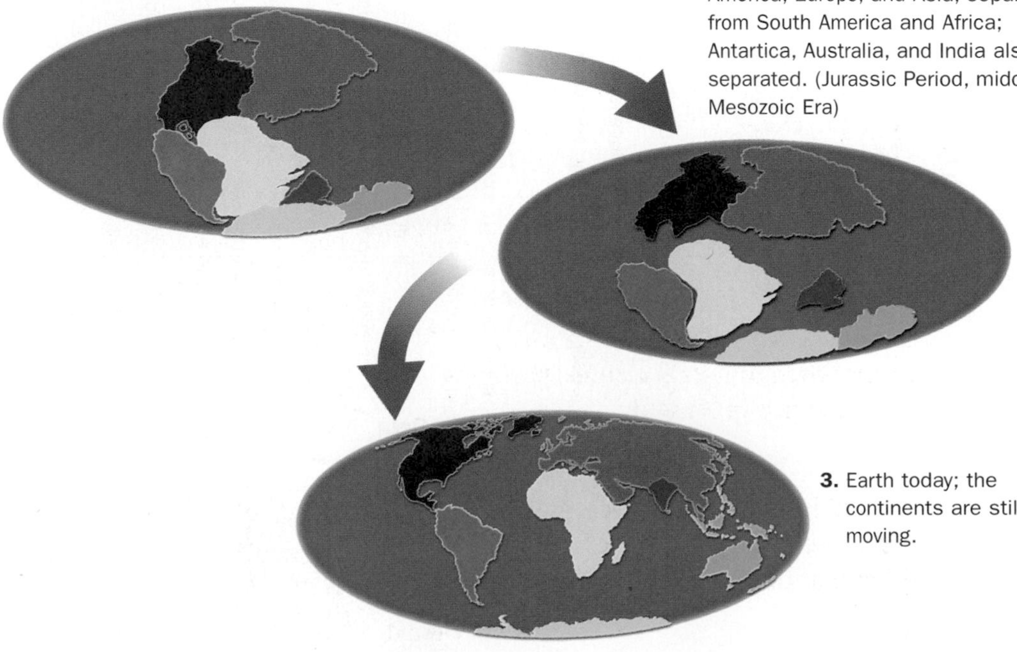

3. Earth today; the continents are still moving.

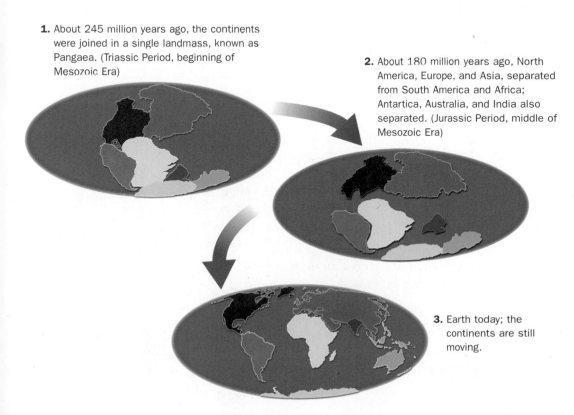

			245		
Paleozoic	Permian			Ural Mountains of Russia and Appalachians form; reptiles spread over Earth; ends with mass extinctions, many species	
			286		
	Pennsylvanian			Great ice age engulfs large areas of Earth; huge coal-forming swamps form in North America; amphibians dominate Earth; early reptiles evolve; seed plants evolve; forests spread over Earth	
			320		
	Mississippian			Large areas of continents flooded by the sea; insects and amphibians develop	
			360		
	Devonian			Acadian mountains of New York rise; erosion of land masses deposits sediments in seas; amphibians and insects evolve	
			408		
	Silurian			Caledonian Mountains of Scandinavia rise; first land plants and land invertebrates evolve	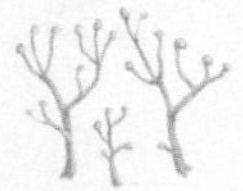
			438		
	Ordovician			Green Mountains of the northeastern United States form; plants evolve; animals with backbones evolve	
			505		
	Cambrian			Shallow seas cover large parts of land masses; animals evolve	
			570		
Proterozoic	Also called the Precambrian Era (8/9 of all time)	Upper		Multicellular organisms evolve	
			900		
		Middle		Cells with nuclei evolve	
			1600		
		Lower		Cells without nuclei float on Earth's seas	
			2500		
Archean				Oldest known rocks; life evolves as cells without nuclei	
			3800		
Hadean				Earth cools; seas and atmosphere form	
			4300		

Source: USGS

200

Geologic Time Scale

Note: Sizes of eons, eras, periods, and epochs do not match how long these time ranges lasted.

Eon	Era	Period	Epoch	Millions of Years Ago	Event	
Phanerozoic (1/9 of all time)	Cenozoic	Quaternary	Recent		Earth's climate becomes cooler and drier; Great Lakes of North America form; evolution of cities	
				0.01 (10,000 years ago)		
			Pleistocene		Most recent ice age; modern humans	
				1.6		
		Tertiary	Pliocene		North America and South America join; early human ancestors, mammals and birds dominate life on Earth	
				5.3		
			Miocene		Many volcanoes erupt in northwest United States; bony fishes spread through oceans	
				23.7		
			Oligocene		Himalayas and Alps form; modern mammals, including apes, evolve	
				36.6		
			Eocene		Coal forms in western United States; flowering plants dominate plant kingdom	
				57.8		
			Paleocene		Uplift of land in western United States continues; early mammals, birds and insects that pollinate plants spread over Earth	
				65		
	Mesozoic	Cretaceous			Flowering plants evolve; ends with mass extinctions, including dinosaurs	
				144		
		Jurassic			Warm, wet climate dominates Earth; Rocky Mountains begin to rise; age of dinosaurs; first birds evolve	
				206		
		Triassic			Palisades of New Jersey form; cone-bearing plants evolve	

201 Oceanography

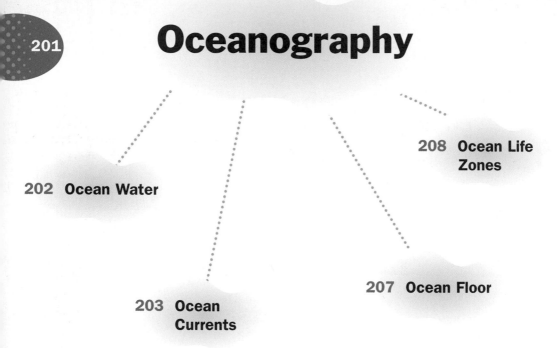

You can travel completely around the world on water. This is true because the world's oceans are linked to one another. This one huge ocean surrounds the large landmasses known as continents as well as smaller islands.

The world's oceans cover almost 71 percent of Earth's surface. Although all the oceans are connected, different parts have names: the Atlantic Ocean, the Pacific Ocean, the Indian Ocean, and the Arctic Ocean. The Pacific Ocean is the largest, with a surface area of 165.25 million square kilometers. Size is just one way that oceans are different from each other. Depth, temperature, currents, and other physical properties vary from ocean to ocean. By analyzing the properties of a sample of ocean water, scientists often can figure out which ocean the sample was taken from. These physical properties affect the climates of land areas near oceans.

SEE ALSO
227 Climate

SCILINKS NSTA
Keyword: Oceans
www.scilinks.org
Code: GSSM201

Ocean Water

The **salinity** or saltiness of ocean water comes from the variety of salts dissolved in the water. Ocean water has a salinity of about 3.5 percent. Salinity is often described in parts per thousand (ppt) instead of percent. Thus, in every liter of ocean water, there are on average 35 grams of salt per 1,000 grams of water.

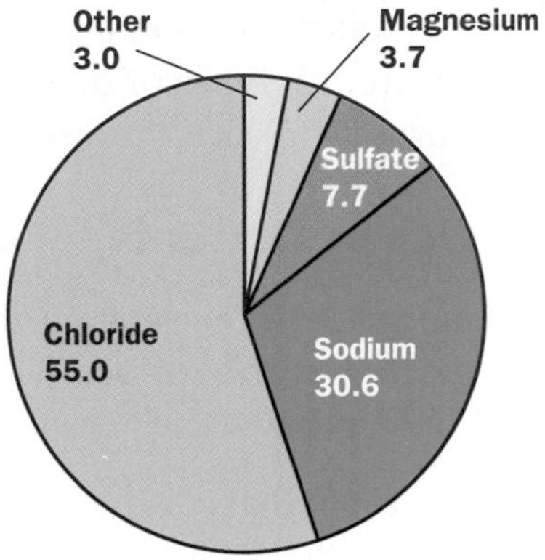

The term *salt* describes many substances, not just table salt. The most common salt in the ocean is, however, sodium chloride—table salt.

Density is a measure of the mass of a substance per unit volume. Because ocean water holds dissolved salts, it is denser than fresh water. The average density of seawater is about 1.035 g/cm^3, while that of fresh water is 1.000 g/cm^3. Objects float more easily on denser liquids than on less dense liquids.

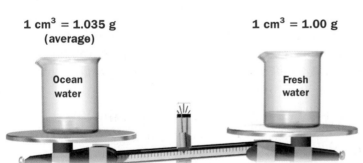

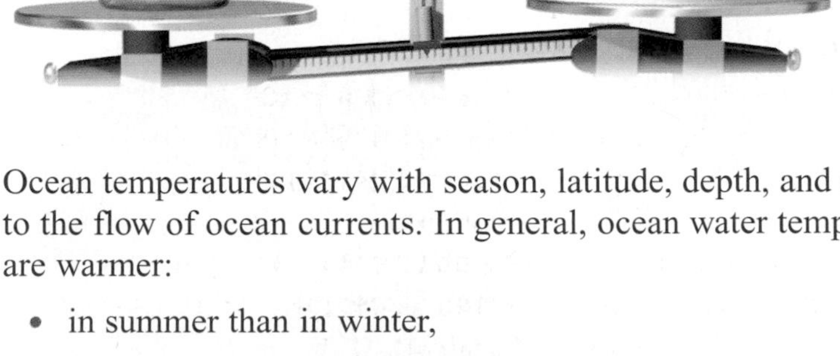

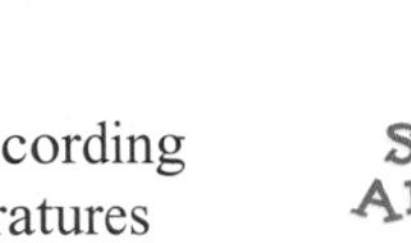

1 cm^3 = space taken up by a cube that is 1 cm on every edge

Ocean temperatures vary with season, latitude, depth, and according to the flow of ocean currents. In general, ocean water temperatures are warmer:

- in summer than in winter,
- at lower latitudes (those nearer the equator),
- nearer the surface than at the ocean bottom,
- in currents flowing from the equator than in currents flowing from the poles.

SEE ALSO
272 Parts of a Solution
068 Finding Density

203

Ocean Currents

Great rivers of water, called **ocean currents,** flow through the world's oceans. There are two types of ocean currents: surface currents and subsurface currents (or deep currents).

204

Surface Ocean Currents

As their name suggests, **surface currents** are rivers of water that move through the ocean's surface. The paths of the currents are determined by winds and the Coriolis effect.

Moving air, or **wind,** that steadily blows over the ocean's surface is made up of gas particles that rub against the ocean's surface. These rubbing particles drag water molecules in their direction of travel, producing a current of seawater.

Surface currents are classified into two groups—cold currents and warm currents. Cold currents tend to move from Earth's polar regions toward the equator. Warm currents move from tropical latitudes toward the poles.

205

Coriolis Effect

The paths of winds and ocean currents curve because of Earth's shape and rotation. Imagine a wind blowing from the North Pole toward the equator. As the wind blows, Earth turns beneath it, turning the wind toward the west. The wind drives an ocean current beneath it, so the current also turns. When the current bumps into a continent, it turns north and then east until it bumps into another. The current ends up making a huge circle, turning clockwise, in the ocean north of the equator. The same thing happens south of the equator, but counterclockwise. The effect of Earth's rotation on winds and currents is called the **Coriolis effect.**

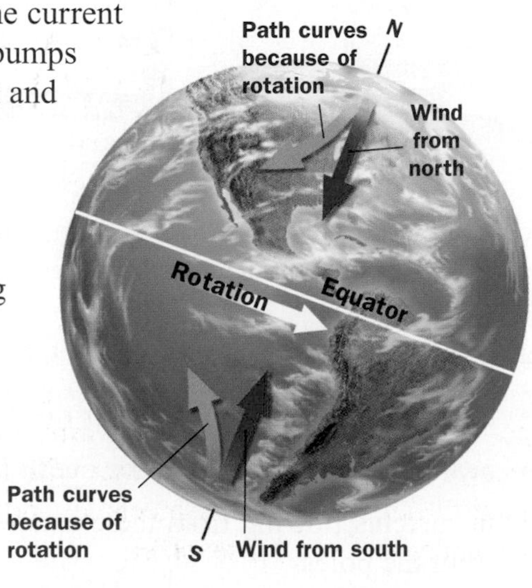

Major currents in Earth's oceans

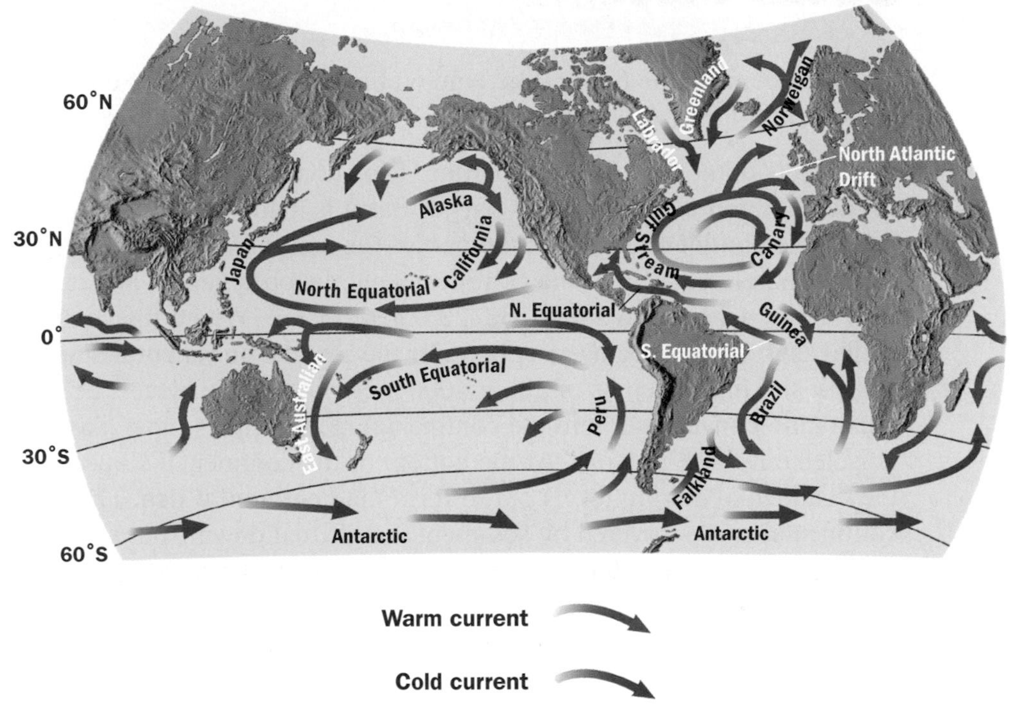

Science Alert!

The Coriolis effect only works over huge areas, such as whole oceans. It isn't strong enough to affect water in a sink. Try pulling out a sink plug first with one hand, then with the other (make sure the water is still first). Watch the sink drain each time. You will see that the water swirls both ways even though the hemisphere is the same.

Subsurface Currents

206

Subsurface currents in oceans happen because of differences in density. Density differences result from temperature and salinity differences. Cold water is denser than warm water, and water with many dissolved salts is denser than water with few dissolved salts. When colder, saltier, denser water meets less dense water, the denser water dives under the less dense water.

SEE ALSO
068 Finding Density

207 Ocean Floor

The land beneath the ocean, like land on the continents, is not the same in all places. A variety of features exist on the ocean floor.

Continents do not end at the shoreline. They continue under the sea as the **continental margin.** This part of Earth is made up of the three parts. The **continental shelf** is the part of the continental margin nearest the shoreline. Land of the continental shelf slopes gently, and is covered by water up to about 150–200 meters deep. Where the continental shelf starts to slope steeply under the sea, the **continental slope** begins, sinking to depths of about 4000 meters. In some places, deep **submarine canyons** cut into the continental slope. Rivers most likely chiseled out these canyons. At the bottom of the continental slope, the continental margin levels out to form the **continental rise.** The continental rise is covered by sediment that drifted down from the continental shelf and slope. At the bottom of the continental rise, the deep **abyssal plain** begins.

Continental margins have two basic shapes. A **passive margin,** such as the east coast of North America, does not have any plate boundaries near it. Passive margins have wide continental shelves that reach 100 kilometers or more out into the ocean before dropping off at the continental slope.

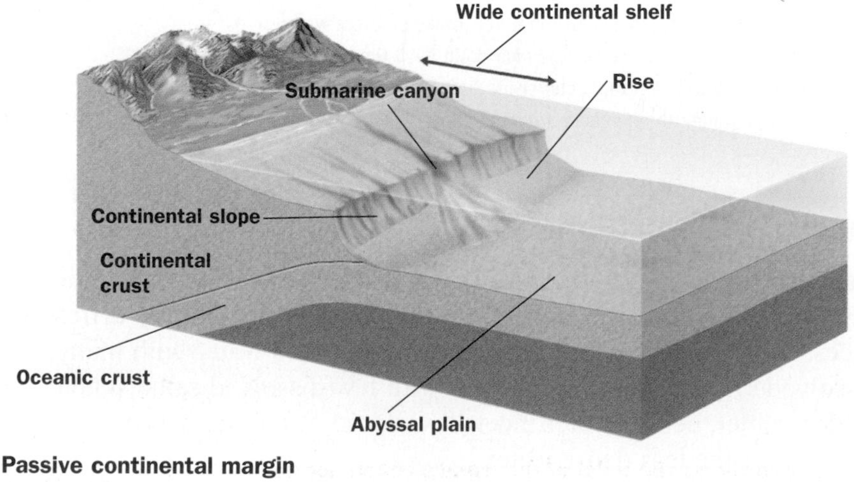

Passive continental margin

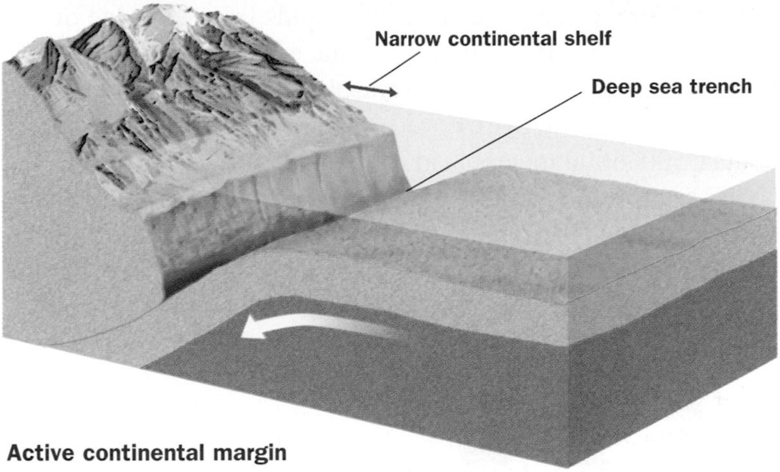

Active continental margin

SEE ALSO
184 Plate Boundaries
185 Map of Plate Boundaries

An **active margin,** such as the west coast of North America, has plate boundaries near it. Continental shelves near active margins are narrow. They extend only about 50 kilometers or less out into the ocean before dropping off at the continental slope. Active margins often have **deep-sea trenches** near them. Deep-sea trenches are the lowest places on Earth. Deep-sea trenches form at convergent plate boundaries where denser ocean crust is diving under continental crust. Volcanoes and earthquakes are common on the continent near an active margin.

Long mountain chains, called **mid-ocean ridges,** snake through Earth's oceans. They form Earth's longest continuous mountain range, stretching about 60,000 kilometers. These ridges form at the divergent boundaries of lithospheric plates.

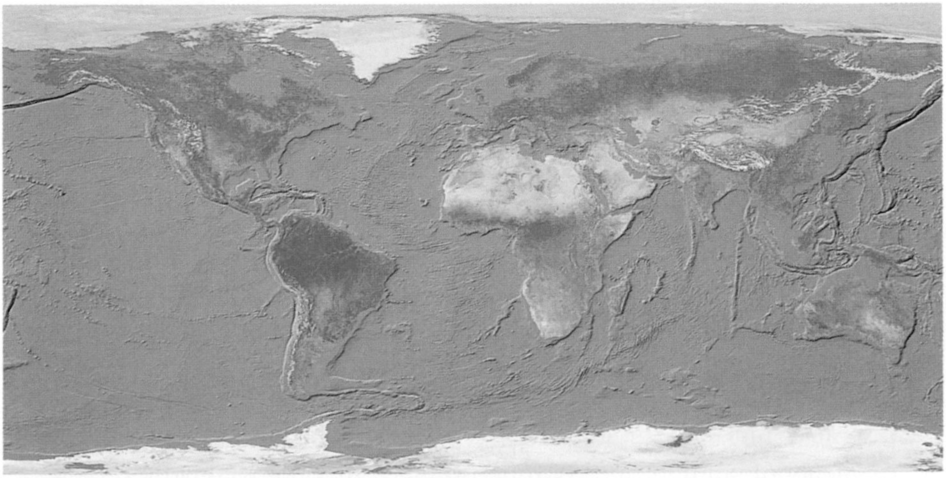

This image shows the relief of the world's ocean floors.

MORE ▶

The **deep-ocean floor,** or deep-ocean basin, extends from the edge of a continental rise on one side of an ocean to the edge of a continental rise on the opposite side of the ocean. **Abyssal plains** are the flattest sections of the ocean floor and are covered by sediment. Abyssal plains are from about 3500–6000 meters below the ocean surface. Abyssal hills can be narrow (100 m) or wide (100 km) and usually rise less than 1,000 meters from the abyssal plain. More than 10,000 volcanoes, called seamounts, lie beneath the ocean's surface. Oceanographers think flat-topped seamounts, called guyots (GEE-ohs), formed as their tops were eroded by waves.

208

Ocean Life Zones

Scientists describe the oceans as having three main life zones. Water temperature, pressure, and sunlight can be different in each of these zones. These conditions affect what organisms can live in each zone.

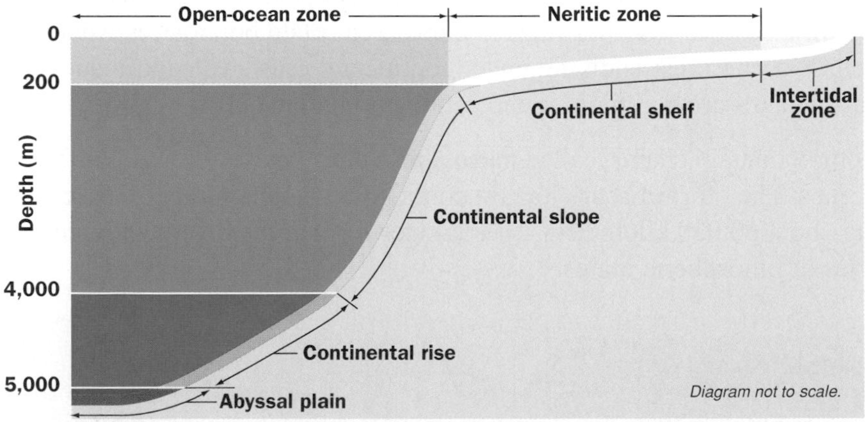

209

Intertidal Zone

SEE ALSO
237 Tides

The **intertidal zone** is the part of the shore that is between the high and low tide lines. This zone is covered by water at high tide and open to the air at low tide. Most living things in this zone have ways to survive both drying during low tides and flooding at high tides. These organisms must also attach themselves firmly to rocks or burrow into the sand—otherwise they might be carried out to sea. There is plenty of sunlight in this zone, so there are photosynthetic organisms such as sea plants and algae, and many organisms that eat them.

Neritic Zone

210

The **neritic zone** extends out from the intertidal zone across the continental shelf. Water depth is between a few meters and 200 meters. Sunlight is plentiful, so plants and algae grow here. Water temperature is about the same from top to bottom. Water pressure builds with depth, but does not get too great. Three groups of living things are in this zone: plankton, nekton, and benthos. **Plankton** are organisms that float at or near the surface, such as algae and some young animals. **Nekton** are free-swimming organisms, such as fish, that live at all water depths. **Benthos** are organisms that live on the ocean floor. Benthos include algae and plants and animals such as clams, lobsters, and sponges.

Nekton

Benthos

Open-Ocean Zone

211

The **open-ocean zone** is the part of the ocean above the continental slope and above deep ocean basins. The open-ocean zone is the largest zone. But, fewer organisms live here than in other zones because conditions are harsh in much of this zone. The ocean floor may be as much as 6000 meters below the surface. Sunlight can reach only about 150–200 meters into the water, so algae and plants, and most life forms that depend on them, are at or near the surface of this zone. Temperatures in the deepest parts of this ocean life zone are just above freezing. Water pressure increases greatly with depth. For example, the water pressure in a deep-sea trench, at 10,000 meters below the surface, is 1,000 times greater than at the surface. Some organisms that do not need sunlight live here.

SEE ALSO
295 Forces in Fluids

212 # Meteorology

Meteorology is the study of the atmosphere—the blanket of gases that surrounds Earth, which you could not live without.

213 ## Earth's Atmosphere

The **atmosphere**—the mixture of gases that surrounds Earth—extends from Earth's surface to more than 600 kilometers into space. Many of the gases of the atmosphere are vital to living things.

214 ### Composition of the Atmosphere

Evidence from rocks suggests that Earth's atmosphere has changed greatly through Earth's history. The early atmosphere would have been poisonous to you. Today, most gases in Earth's atmosphere support, protect, or do no harm to living things. Both oxygen and carbon dioxide support life. Certain bacteria change nitrogen from the atmosphere into substances plants can use to build proteins. High in the atmosphere, a form of oxygen called **ozone** shields living things from much of the harmful radiation given off by the sun.

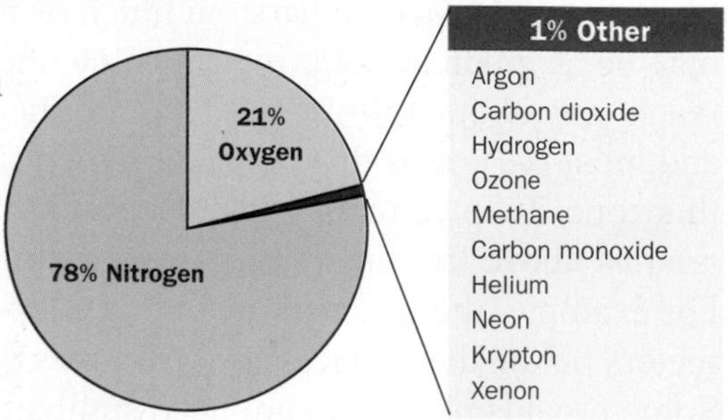

Layers of the Atmosphere

215

Earth's atmosphere is not uniform; its properties change with altitude. Two properties that change with altitude are air temperature and air pressure. Scientists use these properties to describe a model of the atmosphere that has five layers.

Exosphere (300 km– >600 km)

- Outermost layer of the atmosphere
- Temperature goes up with altitude
- Satellites orbit in this layer

Thermosphere (90 km–300 km)

- Temperature goes up with altitude; this is the hottest layer of the atmosphere
- Curtains of light called **auroras** occur in this layer

Mesosphere (50 km–90 km)

- Temperatures drop with altitude; this is the coldest layer of the atmosphere
- Meteors burn up in this layer
- Radio waves reflected to Earth in this layer

Stratosphere (16 km–50 km)

- Temperature goes up with altitude
- Most jets fly here
- Protective ozone layer at top of stratosphere

Troposphere (0–16 km)

- Layer nearest Earth
- All weather happens here
- More than half of air in total atmosphere in this layer
- Temperature drops as altitude increases

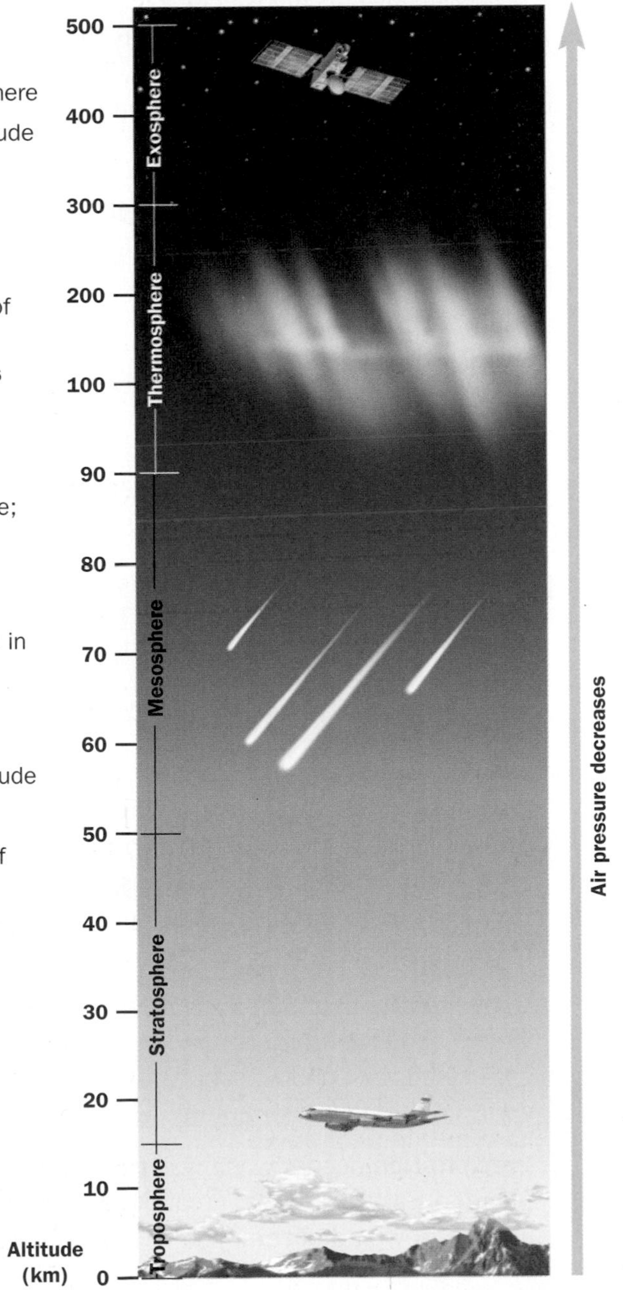

216

Water Cycle

A heavy rainfall may leave many puddles on your street today. Tomorrow, the puddles may slowly shrink and vanish under a warm, sunny sky. Several days later, clouds may again gather in the sky and produce rain that creates new puddles. These events illustrate the process known as the water cycle. The **water cycle,** also called the **hydrologic cycle,** is the continuous movement of water between the surface of Earth and the troposphere. The water cycle happens because of three repeating processes: evaporation, condensation, and precipitation.

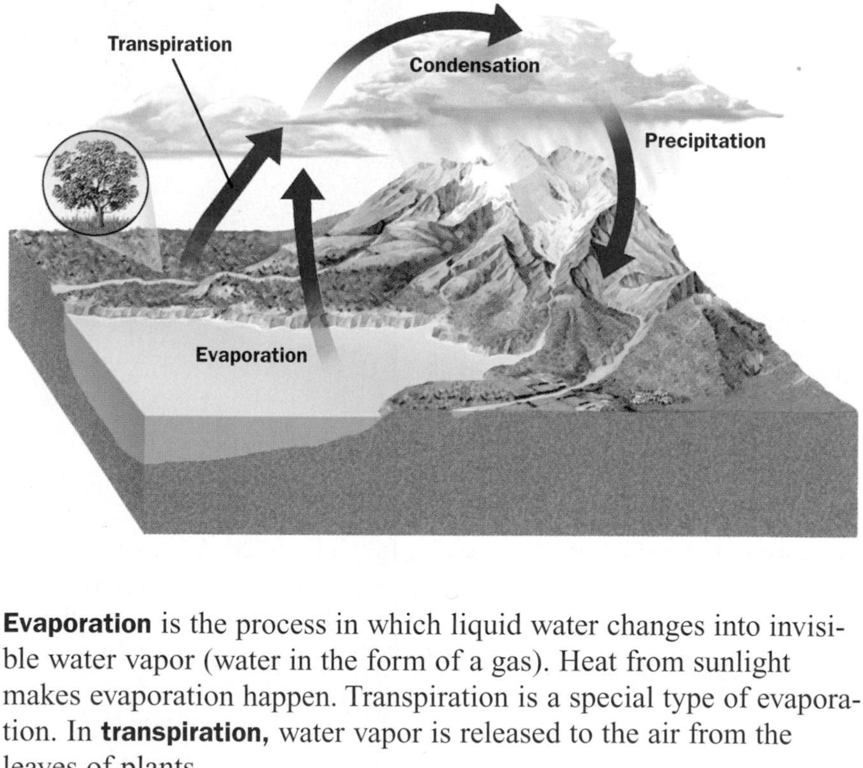

Evaporation is the process in which liquid water changes into invisible water vapor (water in the form of a gas). Heat from sunlight makes evaporation happen. Transpiration is a special type of evaporation. In **transpiration,** water vapor is released to the air from the leaves of plants.

Condensation is the process in which water vapor changes into liquid water. Condensation occurs as air with water vapor in it cools. Clouds are evidence of condensation. Clouds are formed when water vapor cools and condenses into tiny liquid water droplets.

Precipitation occurs when water or a form of ice falls from the atmosphere to Earth's surface. Precipitation forms when water droplets in clouds grow and become too heavy to stay in the atmosphere.

Global Winds and Jet Stream

Global winds blow steadily across Earth in paths that are thousands of kilometers long. Some of these winds blow in the lower parts of Earth's atmosphere, while others blow far above it. Global winds often steer weather in certain directions. Earth's low-altitude winds start out moving in north-south or south-north directions. This movement occurs as heated air near the equator rises and moves toward Earth's poles, while cooled air at the poles falls and moves toward the equator. Their straight paths curve, however, because of the **Coriolis effect.** In the Northern Hemisphere, the Coriolis effect causes global low-altitude winds to curve to the right. In the Southern Hemisphere, the winds curve to the left.

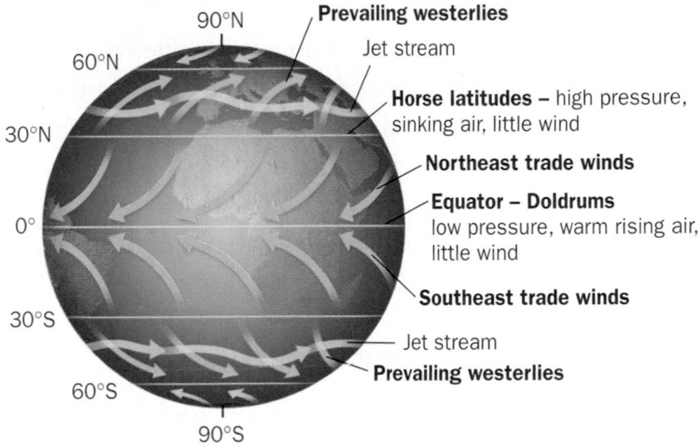

The **jet stream** is a global high-altitude wind that blows at speeds up to 350 kilometers per hour between 6,000–12,000 meters above Earth's surface. The jet stream races from west to east in one or more bands that snake across the northern and southern mid-latitudes. Over North America, the jet stream is around 40°N latitude, although it can dip as far south as 20°N latitude. The location of the jet stream can affect the weather where you live because it can steer the weather systems. Jets flying from west to east get a boost in speed from the winds of the jet stream. Jets flying in the opposite direction are slowed by these same winds.

SEE ALSO
225 Wind
205 Coriolis Effect

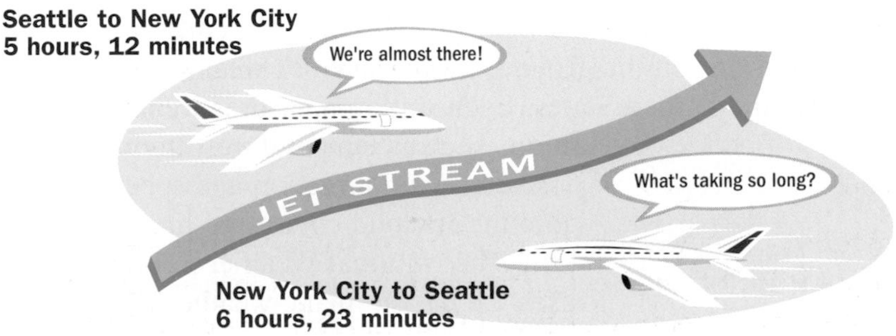

218 Weather

The conditions of the atmosphere at a particular time and place are called **weather**. Is weather important in your life? It affects what clothes you wear and your choices of activities. It may even affect your mood.

The weather of an area is due to four atmospheric factors: heat energy, air pressure, winds, and moisture. Changes in these factors determine the kind of weather you experience, from the fierce winds of a hurricane or tornado, to the blinding snow of a blizzard, to the calm of a warm summer day.

219 Collecting Weather Data

To make weather maps and forecast weather, weather data must be collected from Earth's surface and atmosphere. Scientists analyze the weather maps and the data they hold to forecast the weather. These data are collected in a number of ways.

- Weather satellites orbiting high above Earth's surface make images of clouds and storms and can track their movement. You often see such images on television weather broadcasts.
- **Radar** is a useful tool for gathering data. Radar, which stands for *ra*dio *d*etecting *a*nd *r*anging, sends out radio signals that are reflected from objects such as clouds and rain. Computers turn the reflections into images. Radar on ground level is used to identify areas of heavy, medium, or low precipitation. You have probably seen radar images on television. They usually appear in different colors to show different amounts of precipitation.
- Data that are used to make weather maps are also collected at weather stations on the ground. More than 400 weather stations dot the United States. Each station measures weather conditions such as temperature, atmospheric pressure, wind direction and speed, amount of cloud cover, and precipitation. The National Weather Service uses the data to make weather maps.

Word Watch!

The word *data* is plural. The singular is *datum*.

The diagram shows how data from a weather station may appear on a weather map. This kind of diagram is called a **station model.**

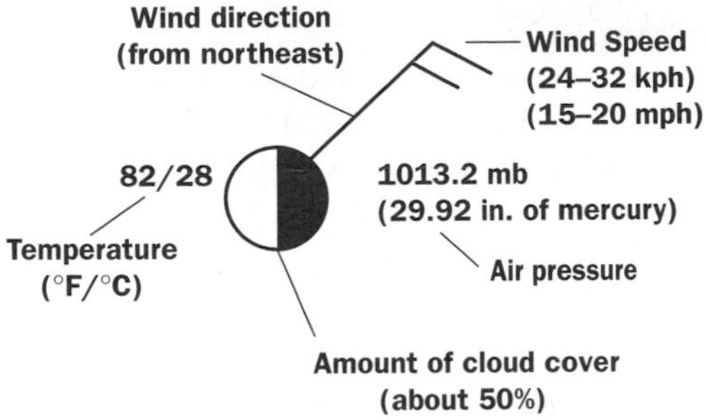

SEE ALSO
225 Wind
223 Clouds

Weather Maps and Symbols

220

Flip through the pages of your local newspaper and you are sure to come upon a weather map. At first, the many lines and symbols on the map may be difficult to understand. Yet with a little practice you will not only recognize what weather is happening at a particular place, but also what kind of weather is coming to that place.

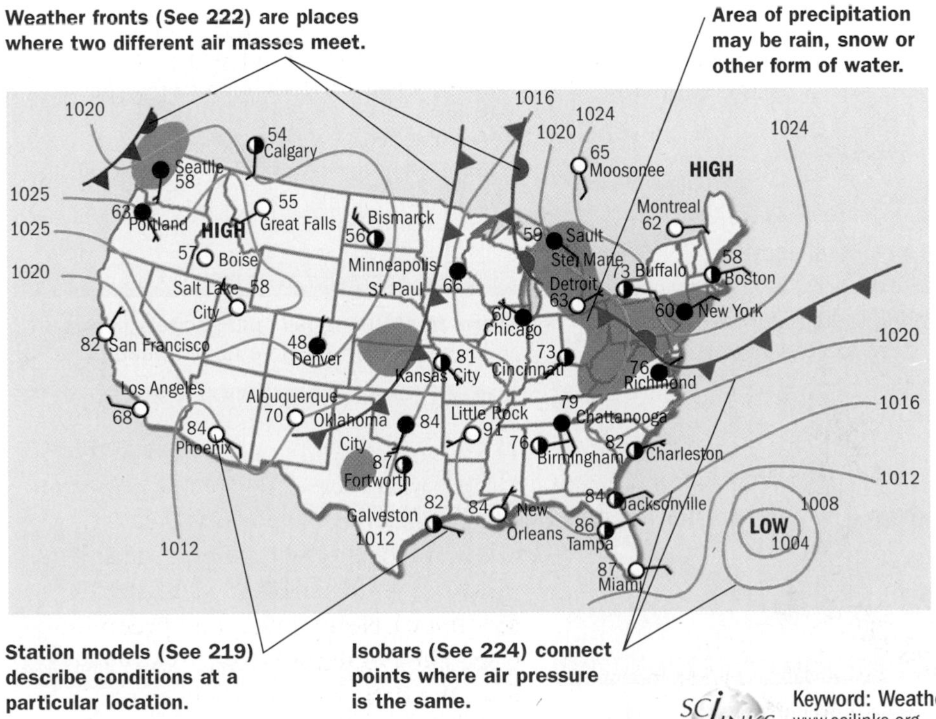

221 Air Masses

Your weather changes when a new air mass moves over your area. An **air mass** is a large body of air that has a certain temperature and amount of moisture. Four kinds of air masses affect weather in most of the United States.

- A **maritime tropical** air mass forms over the ocean near the equator and is made of warm, moist air.
- A **maritime polar** air mass forms over ocean waters north of the United States. It is made of cool, moist air.
- A **continental tropical** air mass is made of hot, dry air. It forms over Mexico and moves north in summer.
- A **continental polar** air mass is made of cold, dry air. It moves into the United States from Canada in winter.

222 Weather Fronts

The leading edge of an air mass is called a **front.** There are four types of fronts. Each type of front brings a different type of weather.

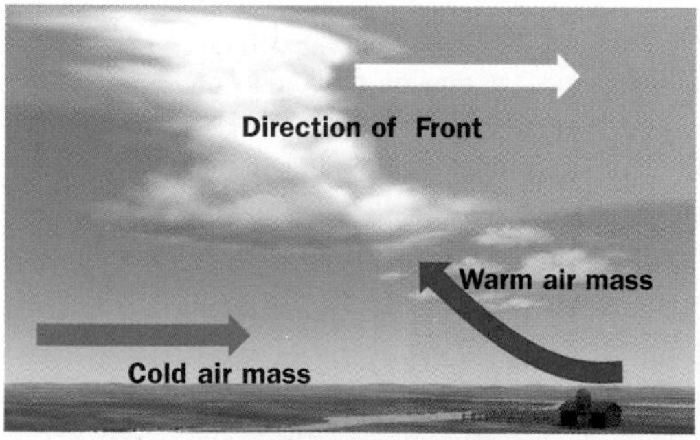

Cold fronts bring violent storms that are followed by fair, cooler weather.

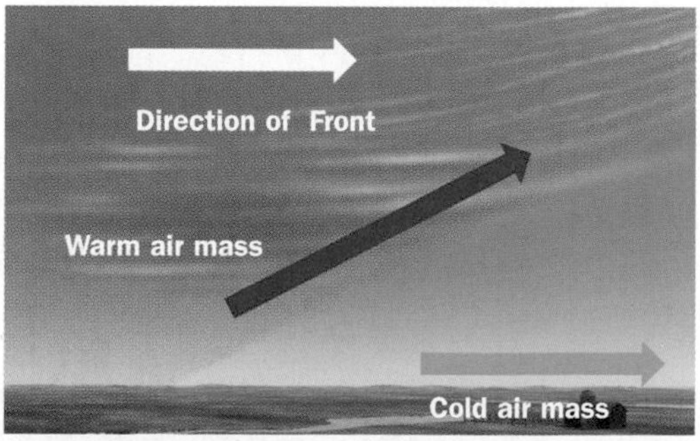

Warm fronts bring rain and showers followed by warmer, more humid weather.

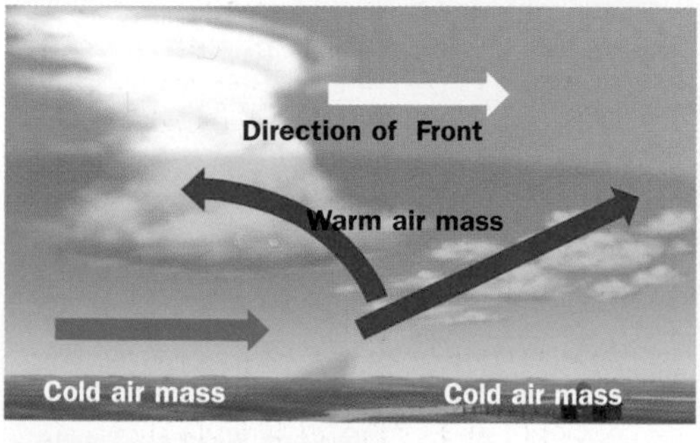

Occluded fronts usually produce light rain or other precipitation.

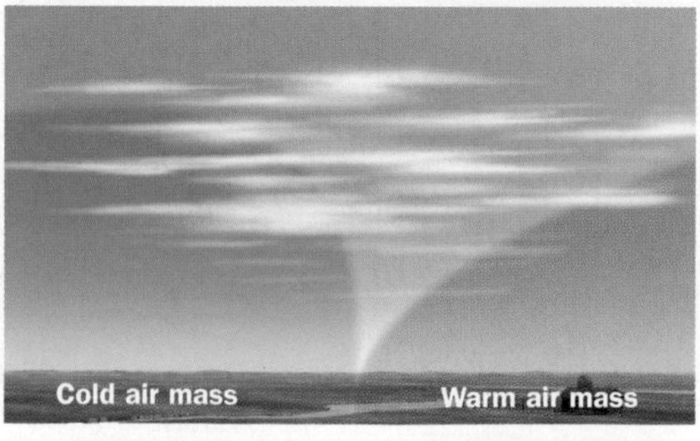

Stationary fronts often bring many days of almost continuous precipitation.

Clouds

223

It's almost impossible to talk about the weather without pointing out clouds. **Clouds** are masses of water droplets or ice crystals that hang in the troposphere over Earth. Clouds form when rising air cools to its dew point, making the water in the air condense into droplets. Most cloud droplets form around dust particles in the air. Clouds that are higher in the troposphere are made of ice crystals.

SEE ALSO
215 Layers of the Atmosphere
226 Humidity and Dew Point

Science Alert!

Clouds are made of tiny droplets of liquid water or tiny ice crystals. Clouds are not made of water vapor. Water vapor is invisible.

When you see the bottom of a cloud, you are seeing the height above Earth where the air has cooled to its dew point.

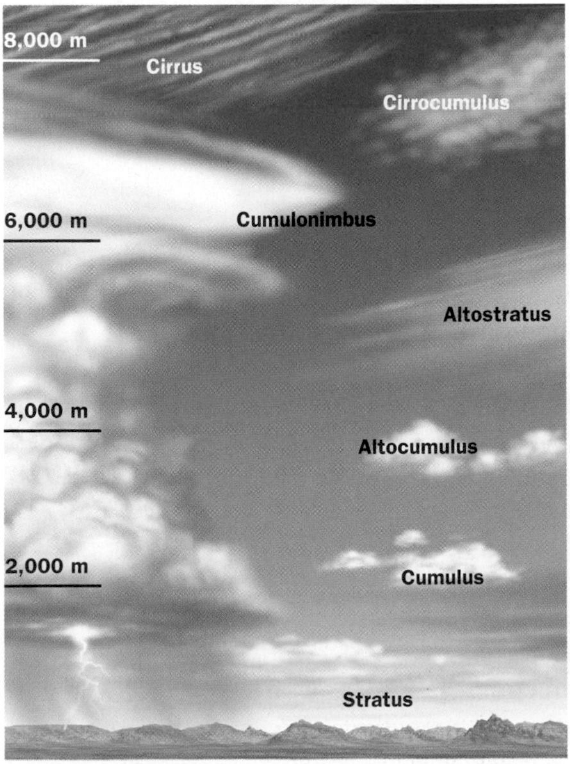

Cirrus or **cirro-** (prefix) wispy, feathery clouds made of ice crystals, usually high-altitude (above 6000 m); often seen at the leading edge of a warm front

Cumulus or **cumulo-** (prefix) puffy clouds, usually middle-altitude (between 2000–6000 m); "Fair-weather" clouds that often condense (form) and evaporate (disappear) quickly

Nimbo- (prefix) and **-nimbus** (suffix) added to a cloud name, means a rain cloud (for example, *nimbostratus*, a low, gray rain cloud, or *cumulonimbus,* a thundercloud)

Alto- a prefix meaning "middle altitude" (for example, altocumulus)

Stratus sheet-like clouds, usually low-altitude (below 2000 m); Stratus clouds are what you see on an overcast day.

224 Air Pressure

Have you ever heard a weather forecaster mention that the air pressure is rising, falling, or is steady? **Air pressure** or **barometric pressure** is a measure of the weight of air pressing down on a given area of Earth's surface. Changes in air pressure tell you that changes in weather are on the way. Generally, falling air pressure means that stormy weather is coming. When air pressure rises, fair weather is coming. If air pressure is steady, the weather you are having is likely to continue.

Weather maps usually show air pressure in units called **millibars** (mb). Weather forecasters may also report air pressure in *millimeters of mercury* (mm Hg) or *inches of mercury* (in. Hg). Normal, or standard, air pressure at sea level is: 1013.2 mb, 760 mm Hg, or 29.92 in. Hg. On weather maps, points where the air pressure is the same are connected with lines called isobars. Areas with the highest air pressure are called **highs** and are marked with an **H.** Areas with the lowest air pressure are called **lows** and are marked with an **L.**

SEE ALSO
220 Weather Maps and Symbols

225 Wind

Differences in air pressure cause **wind,** or moving air. Air moves from areas of high pressure to areas of low pressure. The greater the difference in air pressure, the faster the wind blows. Local winds that are part of the weather may blow over small areas that are no more than a few kilometers or over areas that are thousands of kilometers wide. Global winds circle the Earth in wide belts.

Wind conditions are an important part of weather forecasts and are shown on weather maps, using certain symbols. Wind conditions include two types of measurements: wind direction and wind speed. Wind direction, or the direction from which a wind blows, can be determined using a wind vane (sometimes called a weather vane). A wind vane has a wide end that catches the wind, changing its direction. The narrow end of a wind vane points in the direction from which the wind blows.

SEE ALSO
217 Global Winds and Jet Stream

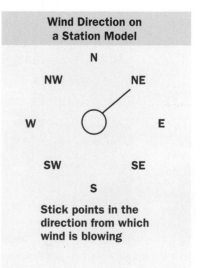

Wind Direction on a Station Model

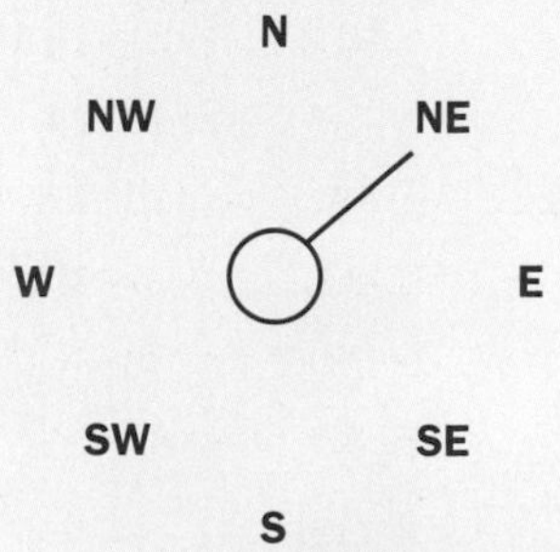

Stick points in the direction from which wind is blowing

Meteorologists use an instrument called an **anemometer** to measure wind speed. You can estimate wind speed by observing your surroundings and consulting the Beaufort wind scale. The **Beaufort wind scale** relates common observations to wind speeds. The scale describes wind speeds in kilometers per hour (kph) and in miles per hour (mph).

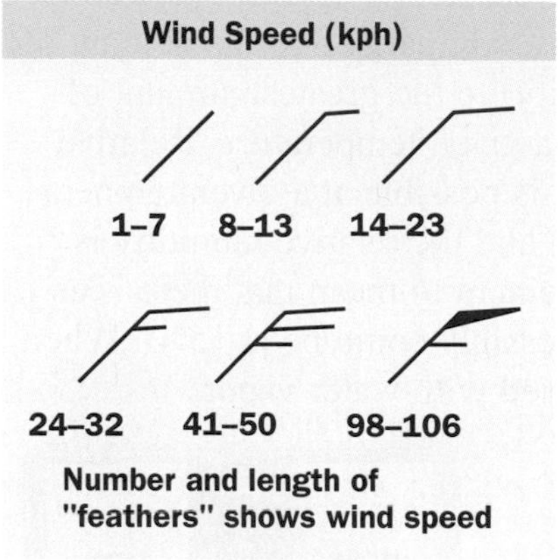

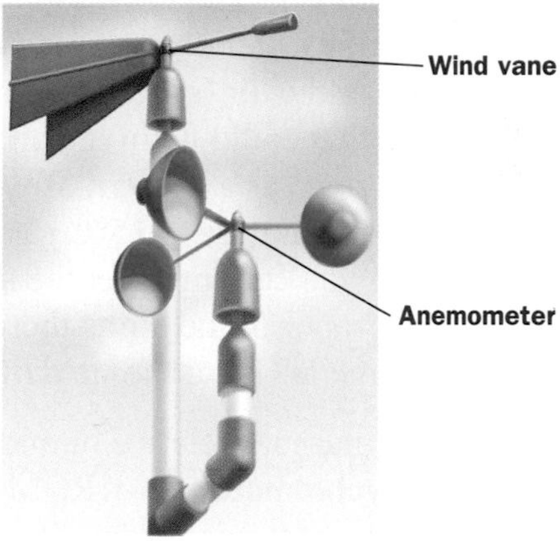

BEAUFORT WIND SCALE

Beaufort Number	Kilometers per hour	Miles per hour	Wind Effects on Land
0	1	1	smoke rises straight up
1	1–5	1–3	smoke drifts slowly
2	6–11	4–7	leaves rustle
3	12–20	8–12	leaves, twigs in motion
4	21–29	13–18	raises dust; small branches move
5	30–39	19–24	small trees sway
6	40–50	25–31	large branches move; overhead wires whistle
7	51–61	32–38	whole trees in motion
8	62–74	39–46	twigs break off trees
9	75–87	47–54	tiles blown off roofs; some damage to structures
10	88–101	55–63	small trees pulled up; moderate damage to structures
11	102–119	64–74	widespread damage
12	120	74	hurricane winds; great widespread damage

226

Humidity and Dew Point

When fog or mist swirls in the air, you don't have to be told that the airs holds moisture. You can feel it on your skin and see it with your eyes. However, even on a clear day the air around you holds invisible water vapor.

Humidity is moisture in air. Weather forecasters most often talk about relative humidity. **Relative humidity** is a comparison of the amount of water vapor in the air (specific humidity) to the greatest amount of water vapor that could be in the air at a given temperature. Relative humidity is given as a percent of what is possible at a given temperature. If the temperature is 15°C (59°F) and the relative humidity is 100 percent, you can interpret the statement to mean that there is as much water vapor in the air as there possibly could be at 15°C. When this is true, the air is said to be **saturated** with water vapor.

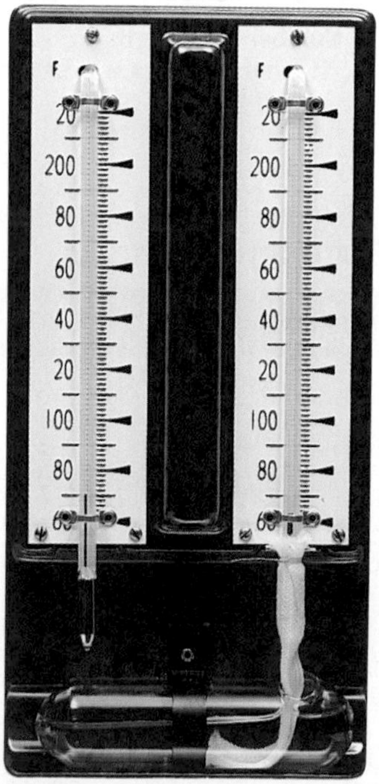

One way to measure relative humidity is with a **psychrometer** (sy-KROM-uh-ter). A psychrometer is made of two thermometers: a wet-bulb thermometer and a dry-bulb thermometer. The bulb of the wet-bulb thermometer is wrapped in a water-soaked cloth. The bulb of the dry-bulb thermometer is not covered, and is dry.

To use a psychrometer, fan the thermometers to evaporate the water from the wet bulb. Then record the temperature on each thermometer. Unless the air is saturated, the wet-bulb temperature is lower than the dry-bulb temperature. Water evaporating from the wet cloth makes the wet-bulb temperature lower. Find the difference between the two readings. Then use the table to find the relative humidity. Find the dry-bulb temperature on the left. Find the difference between the two readings at the top. The relative humidity is where the two meet.

EXAMPLE:

	Dry-bulb	**20°C**	
	− Wet-bulb	**−17°C**	
	Difference	**3°C**	**Relative humidity = 74%**

Relative Humidity (%)

Dry-bulb temperature (°C)	Difference between wet-bulb and dry-bulb temperatures (°C)																			
	1	2	3	4	5	6	7	8	9	10	11	12	13	14	15	16	17	18	19	20
0	81	64	45	29	13															
2	84	68	52	37	22	7														
4	85	71	57	43	29	16														
6	86	73	60	48	35	24	11													
8	87	75	63	51	40	29	19	8												
10	88	77	66	55	44	34	24	15	6											
12	89	78	68	58	48	39	29	21	12											
14	90	79	70	60	51	42	34	26	18	10										
16	90	81	71	63	54	46	38	30	23	15	8									
18	91	82	73	65	57	49	41	34	27	20	14	7								
20	91	83	74	66	59	51	44	37	31	24	18	12	6							
22	92	83	76	68	61	54	47	40	34	28	22	17	11	6						
24	92	84	77	69	62	56	49	43	37	31	26	20	15	10	5					
26	92	85	78	71	64	58	51	46	40	34	29	24	19	14	10	5				
28	93	85	78	72	65	59	53	48	42	37	32	27	22	18	13	9	5			
30	93	86	79	73	67	61	55	50	44	39	35	30	25	21	17	13	9	5		
32	93	86	80	74	68	62	57	51	46	41	37	32	28	24	20	16	12	9	5	
34	93	87	81	75	69	63	58	53	48	43	39	35	30	28	23	19	15	12	8	5

On some mornings, you may observe droplets of water, called dew, on blades of grass. **Dew** is water vapor that has condensed on a surface into liquid water. Dew forms when the temperature of a surface falls to a point where the air near that surface is saturated, and more water vapor is condensing than evaporating. This temperature is known as the **dew point** of the air.

Dew formation depends on two factors: the amount of water vapor in the air and the temperature of the air near the surface that the dew forms on. For example, as much as 11 grams of water vapor can be in 1 kilogram of air at 15°C. One kilogram of air at 10°C can have only 8 grams of water vapor. If the air at 15°C has 8 grams of water vapor per kilogram, and the temperature stays above 15°C, no dew forms. But if the temperature falls below 10°C, the dew point, then liquid water condenses (dew forms).

Dew drops on violets

227

Climate

How would you describe the climate of your area? It may generally be warm and dry. Maybe it's cool and wet or warm and wet. You may live in an area that has different conditions, depending on the season. Each area generally has its own climate. **Climate** is the general weather of an area over a long period of time, and includes seasonal changes in weather.

228

Factors Affecting Climate

Several factors affect the climate of an area.

SEE ALSO
169 Latitude and Longitude
217 Global Winds and Jet Stream

- **Latitude,** or the distance of a place north or south of the equator, affects the temperatures that commonly occur in an area. Temperatures generally are lower as you get farther from the equator (in other words, at higher latitudes).
- **Elevation,** or the distance of a place above sea level, affects an area's temperature. Temperatures generally decrease as elevation increases—about 6.5°C cooler for every kilometer you climb. As a result, areas at high elevations, such as tall mountains, are generally cooler than places closer to sea level.

Word Watch!

Elevation is also called *altitude.* Do not confuse altitude with latitude.

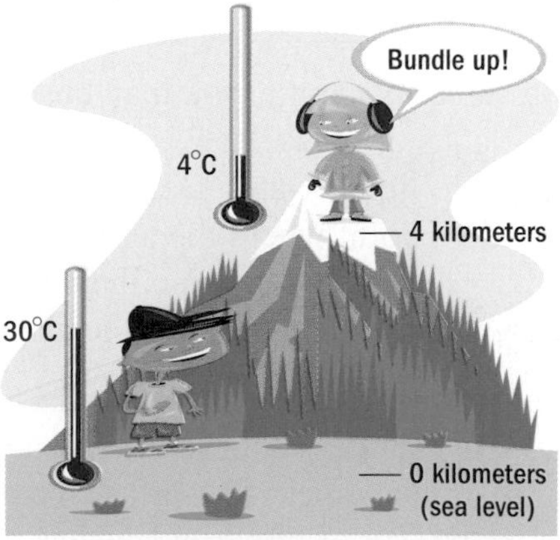

SEE ALSO
226 Humidity and Dew Point
223 Clouds

- **Topography,** or the shape of the land, can affect the amount of precipitation (rain, snow, sleet, hail) an area receives. The Pacific Northwest is a good example. When warm, moist air from the sea rises over mountains, it expands and cools. This causes moisture in the air to condense and fall as precipitation. As the air flows down the other side of the mountain, it is now dry. The climate on the downward slope of the mountain tends to be dry. This dryness is sometimes called the rain shadow effect.

Rain shadow effect in Washington State

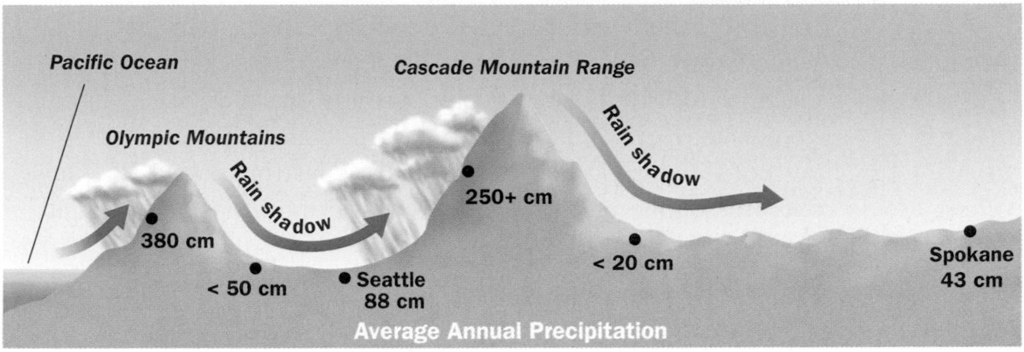

Source: Encyclopedia Britannica

- **Distance from Water** affects climate. Water temperature rises and falls much more slowly than land or air temperatures. This is why air at a shore in summer is generally cooler than air over the land. In winter, the water is generally warmer than the air over the land. The water helps to keep air temperatures from changing a lot over land that is near the ocean. This makes for relatively mild climates in shore areas. Areas farther inland generally have greater differences in temperature from summer to winter.

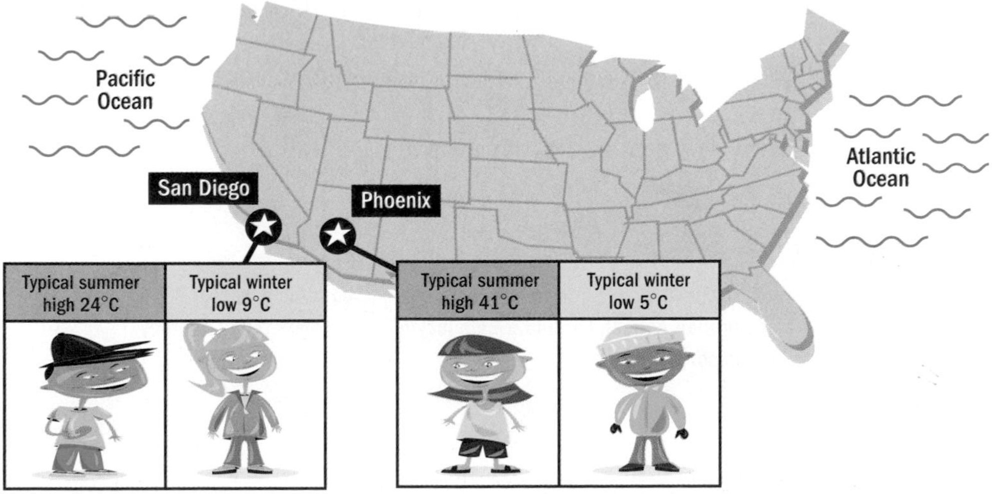

San Diego is on the shore of the Pacific ocean. It has a more moderate climate than Phoenix, which is inland.

- **Global Winds,** or winds that blow steadily in a specific direction, can affect the temperature and amount of moisture an area receives. For example, winds that blow onto land from a warm sea carry warm air and moisture over the land.

MORE ▶

SEE ALSO
203 Ocean Currents

- **Ocean Currents** affect the temperature of landmasses they pass by. Cold ocean currents have a cooling effect on nearby land, while warm ocean currents make nearby land warmer. An example of the effect of ocean currents on land is seen in San Francisco. Here, a cool ocean current called the California current flows past the San Francisco coastline. Wind flowing over this cool water toward the coast brings cool breezes onto the shore.

229 El Niño

Changes in winds and ocean currents in one part of the world can affect conditions in other areas. A common example is **El Niño,** an unusual warming of ocean water off the coast of Peru that takes place every few years. Evidence suggests that El Niño events begin with changes in the trade winds and air pressure over the South Pacific. Normally, strong trade winds push away a layer of warm surface water, allowing cold water from deeper in the ocean to reach the surface. The cold water contains many nutrients that support ocean life. During an El Niño event, weaker trade winds leave a thicker layer of warm water at the surface, which keeps cold water from bringing nutrients to the surface. Fish and other ocean life move away, and people cannot find or catch fish. El Niño events also affect rainfall in other areas, causing droughts in some areas and floods in others. Effects from El Niño have been noted in North and Central America and as far away as Australia.

Did You Know?

La Niña events occur when ocean water temperatures in this same part of the Pacific are cooler than normal. La Niña events may follow El Niño events, but they do not always do so.

230 Pattern of World Climates

SEE ALSO
234 Revolution and Seasons
141 Biomes

Different parts of Earth have very different climates. These climates can be classified according to their characteristics. Scientists do not all agree on one way to classify Earth's climates, but most base their classifications on average temperatures in an area and on how much and what type of precipitation an area receives.

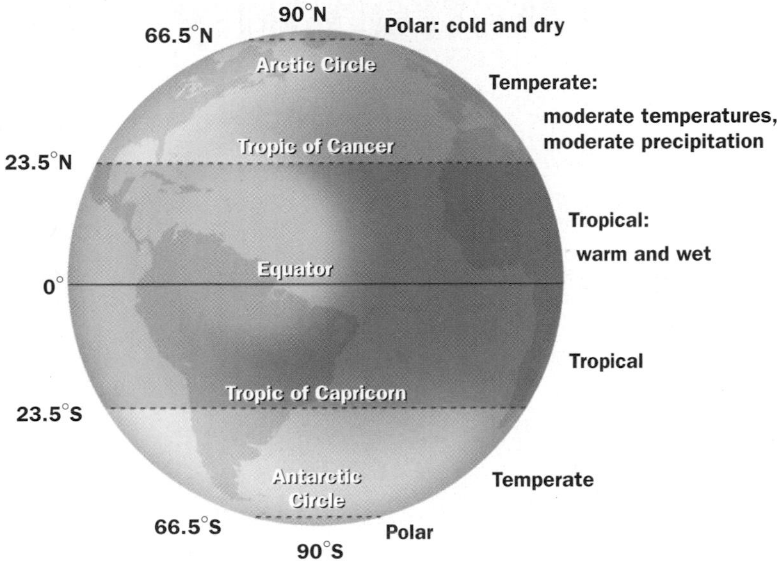

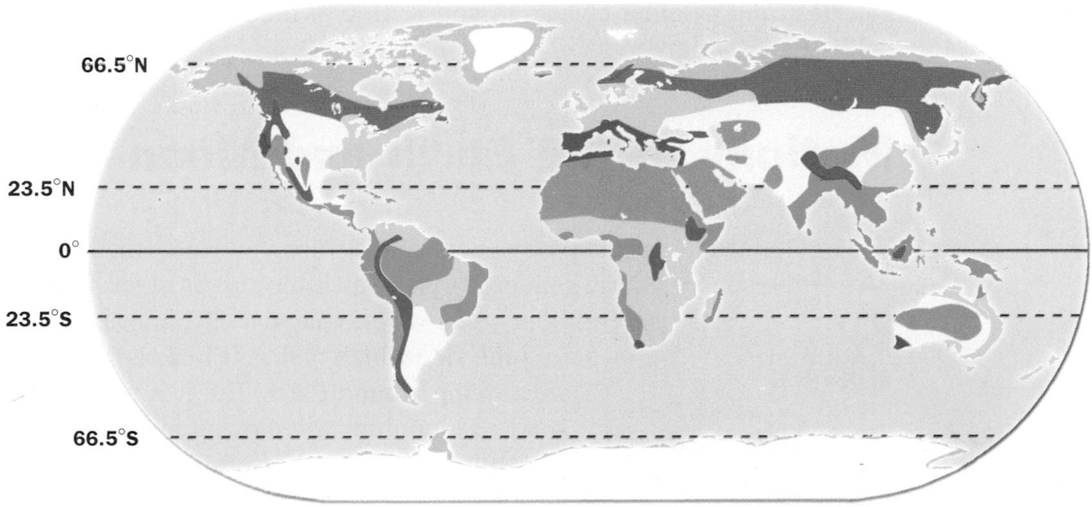

SCILINKS NSTA
Keyword: Weather/Climate
www.scilinks.org
Code: GSSM218

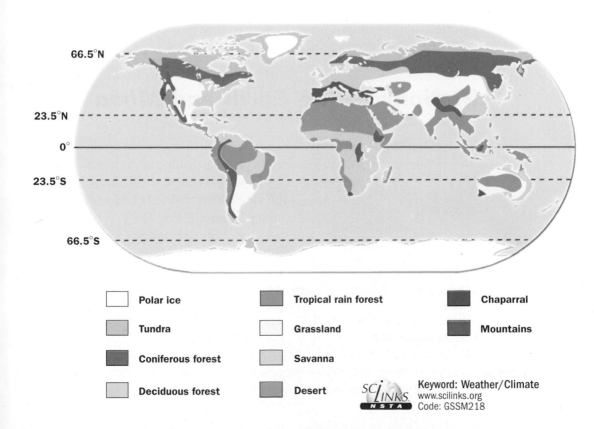

231

Astronomy

As a field of study, **astronomy** includes a study of the planets, stars, galaxies, and all other objects in space. One of these objects—the planet Earth—is the planet you call home.

232

Motions of the Earth and Moon

You've noticed at least two objects in space since you were small—the sun and Earth's moon. If you watch the sun or moon for several hours, you will notice that each moves across the sky, which makes it look as if they are moving around Earth. But it is not the sun and moon that are moving in such a short time—it is Earth itself. You may also have noticed that the shape of the moon appears to change, and that the lengths of daylight and darkness change throughout the year. All of these changes are caused by motions of Earth and its moon.

Word Watch!

Do not confuse astronomy with astrology. Astronomy is the scientific investigation of objects in space. Astrology is the attempt to predict human events based on star and planet positions, and it is not considered to be science.

Rotation

233

A **globe** is a three-dimensional model of Earth. If you look at a globe, you will notice that Earth spins, or rotates, around its axis. Earth spins from west to east. Earth's **axis** is an imaginary line that runs from its North Pole, through its center, to its South Pole. Each complete spin around the axis, or **rotation,** takes about 24 hours, which marks the length of a **day** on Earth. As Earth rotates from west to east, you change position compared to the sun. However, as you stay in place on a moving Earth, it looks as if the sun is moving across the sky.

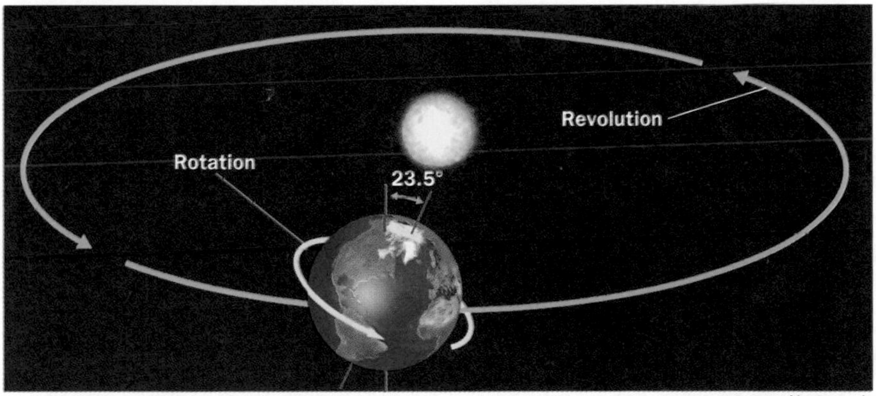

Not to scale

Another feature of a globe is that it is tilted at an angle of about 23.5°. A globe is tilted this way because the planet Earth is tilted at an angle of 23.5°.

Have you ever noticed that the lengths of day and night change throughout the year? This happens because Earth is tilted on its axis compared to its orbital plane. The **orbital plane** is an imaginary surface that contains Earth's orbit, or its path around the sun. Think of Earth's orbital plane as a flat plate with the sun near the center and Earth revolving around the edge.

Word Watch!

Rotation is Earth's spin, once each day. **Revolution** is Earth moving around the sun, once each year.

MORE ▶

Because Earth is tilted on its axis, its northern hemisphere tilts toward the sun during summer. This results in longer periods of daylight. In winter, the reverse is true. If Earth did not have a tilted axis, night and day would always have equal lengths—about 12 hours each all year long. In areas near the equator, the length of day and night are pretty close all year. Near the poles, the length of day and night changes from 0–24 hours.

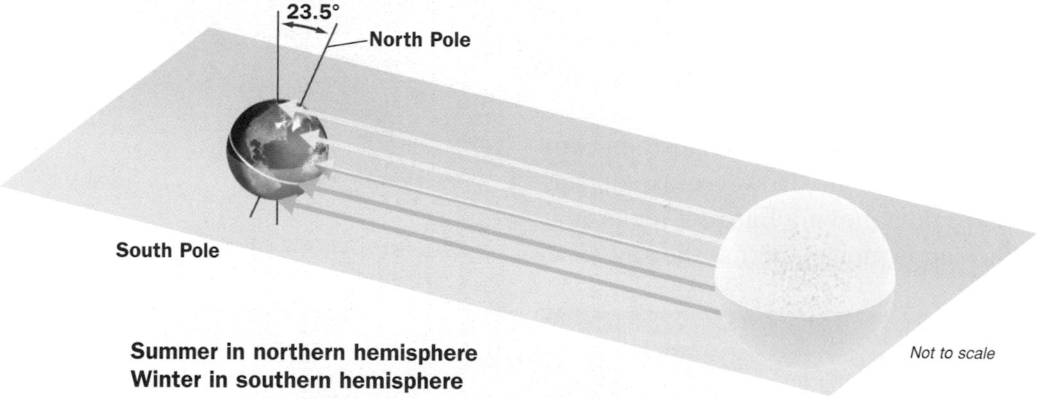

234 Revolution and Seasons

Earth has two major movements. Rotation on its axis is one. Earth revolves, or circles, around the sun. The path a moon or planet follows as it moves around the sun is called its **orbit.** The time it takes Earth to make one revolution around the sun is 365 days, 5 hours, 48 minutes, and 46 seconds. This equals one Earth **year.**

The combination of Earth's tilted axis and its revolution around the sun produces Earth's seasons. At different times of the year, Earth's tilt and revolution cause areas north and south of the equator to be tilted toward the sun, away from the sun, or neither toward nor away from the sun. The days when Earth is most tilted toward the sun, June 21 and December 21, are called **solstices.** The days when Earth is not tilted toward the sun are called **equinoxes.**

Word Watch!

The **equator** is the center (0°) latitude of Earth. The area north of the equator is called the **northern hemisphere.** The area south of the equator is called the **southern hemisphere.**

About June 21, Earth's northern hemisphere is tilted toward the sun. Sunlight strikes this part of Earth at a greater angle. Days become longer and warmer as summer begins. This point in Earth's orbit when summer begins is the **summer solstice** for the northern hemisphere.

About March 21, Earth reaches a point where the tilt is not toward or away from the sun, and the lengths of day and night are the same all over Earth. The **vernal equinox** marks the beginning of spring in the northern hemisphere.

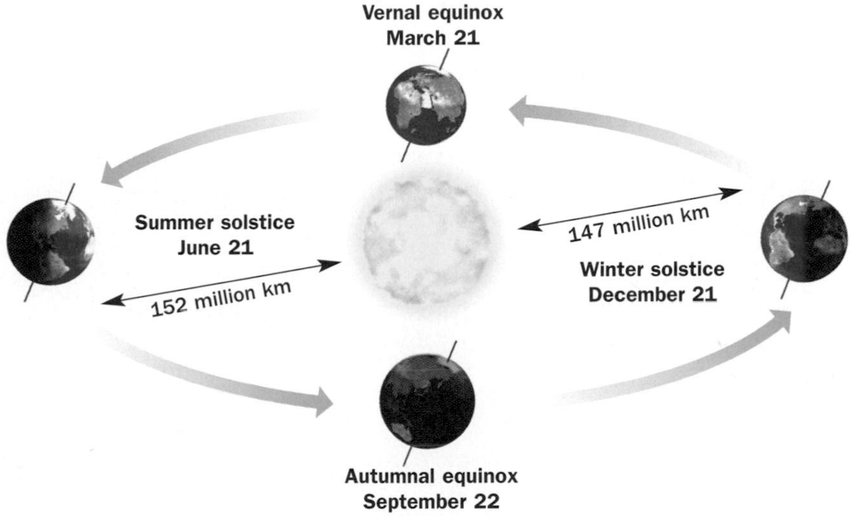

Earth reaches a point where the tilt is not toward or away from the sun, and the lengths of day and night are the same all over Earth. This occurs about September 22. Autumn begins in the northern hemisphere on this day, which is called the **autumnal equinox**.

About December 21, Earth reaches a point when the northern hemisphere is tilted away from the sun and the hours of daylight are shortest. The **winter solstice** marks the beginning of winter in the northern hemisphere.

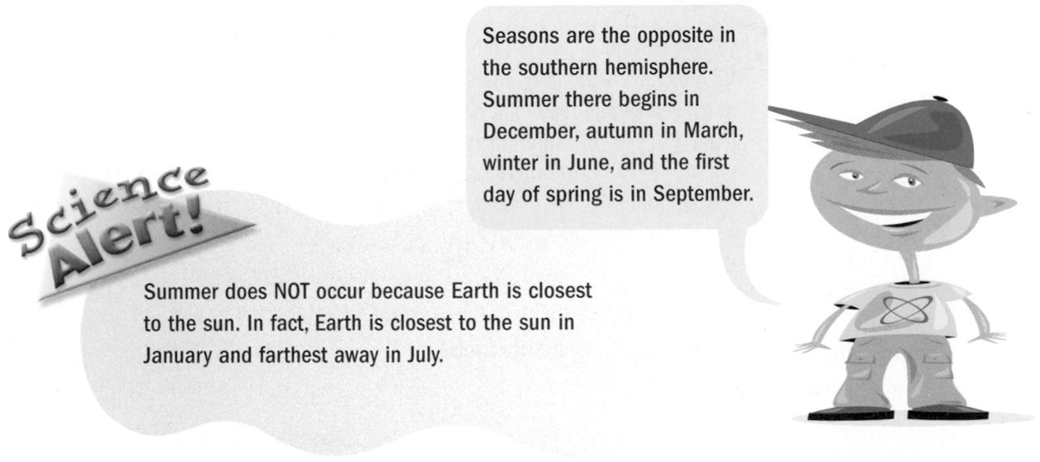

Seasons are the opposite in the southern hemisphere. Summer there begins in December, autumn in March, winter in June, and the first day of spring is in September.
Science Alert!
Summer does NOT occur because Earth is closest to the sun. In fact, Earth is closest to the sun in January and farthest away in July.

235 Moon Phases

The moon is lit by sunlight bouncing off it. That light reaches Earth as moonlight. Look for the moon in the sky each day for one month. You will see that the moon's shape appears to change, and that the time of night or day that you can see the moon also changes. The different shapes that the moon appears to have are called the moon's **phases.** The moon goes through eight phases as it revolves around Earth once every 27.3 days. The phase that you see depends on how much of the sunlit part of the moon you can see. The lit part you can see depends on the positions of Earth, moon, and sun.

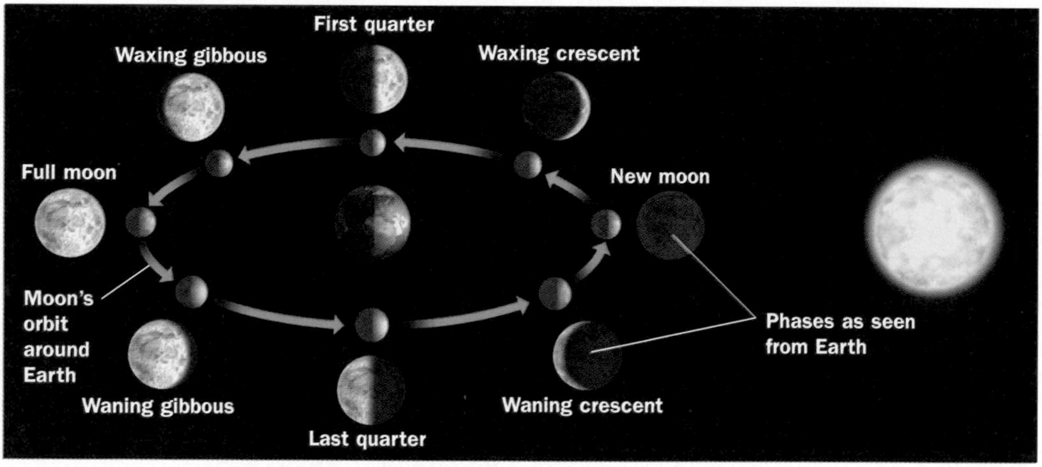

Not to scale

Science Alert!

No matter what phase the moon is in, one-half of the moon is always lit by the sun. During a full moon, you see all the sunlit half. During a new moon, you see (or rather don't see) all the dark half. During a quarter moon, you see one-half of the sunlit half.

Eclipses

The moon revolves around Earth once every 27.3 days. As it travels in its orbit, it sometimes moves between Earth and the sun, casting a shadow, and it sometimes moves into Earth's shadow, so that no sunlight falls on it. These events are called eclipses. An **eclipse** occurs when one object in space casts a shadow on another.

Place your hand between your eyes and a lighted bulb. Your hand will cast a shadow on your face and block the bulb from your view. This is similar to what happens when the moon moves directly between Earth and the sun. In this case, the moon casts a shadow on Earth, causing a **solar eclipse.** During a solar eclipse, people on Earth who are in the moon's shadow can't see the sun for a few minutes. Solar eclipses are visible only along a short path for a period of minutes.

There are two types of solar eclipses. A total solar eclipse occurs when the moon blocks the whole sun from view. If the moon blocks only part of the sun, the event is called a partial solar eclipse. A solar eclipse can occur only during the new moon phase.

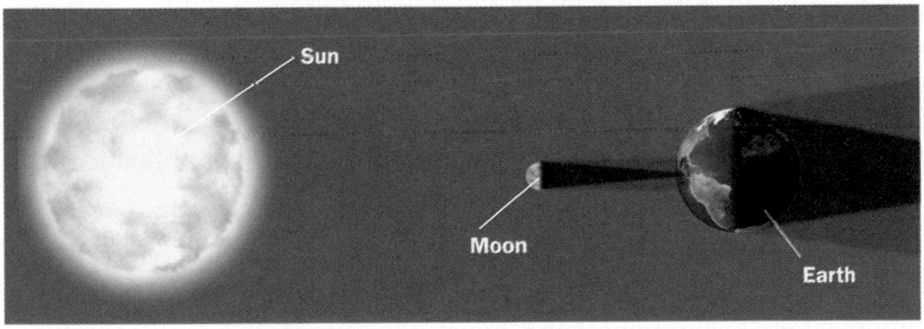

Solar eclipse

Not to scale

Did You Know?

The moon's orbit is tilted 5° compared to Earth's, so the moon's shadow usually falls in space. If it were not for the tilt, eclipses would happen every month.

MORE ▶

A **lunar eclipse** occurs when Earth casts a shadow on the moon. This happens when the sun, Earth, and moon are exactly lined up with Earth in the middle. Lunar eclipses can occur only when the moon is full. Lunar eclipses are visible over the whole nighttime side of Earth for many hours.

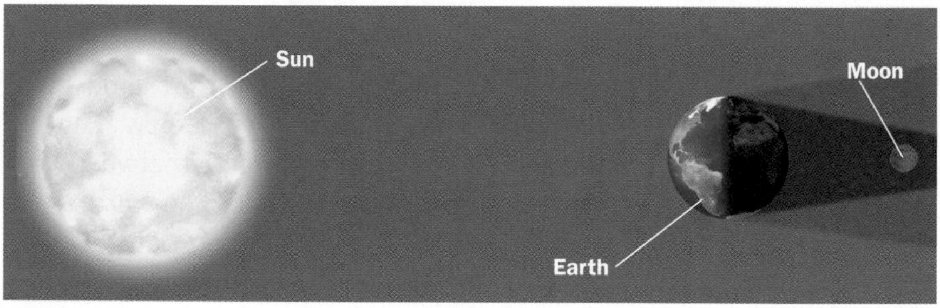

Lunar eclipse *Not to scale*

237 Tides

Tides are changes in ocean water levels that take place in a regular pattern. Tides are controlled mostly by the pull of gravity between the moon and Earth. The force of gravity due to the moon pulls ocean water away from Earth's surface. As Earth rotates, water is pulled up onto the shore at parts of Earth that face directly toward or away from the moon, causing high tides. At the same time, ocean water is pulled away from the shorelines of points on Earth that are not pulled by the moon at that moment. These areas experience low tides.

Tides usually change four times each day, as Earth rotates beneath the pull of the moon. An area having a high tide has a low tide about 6 hours later. In about another 6 hours, the same area has a second high tide, followed about 6 hours later by yet another low tide.

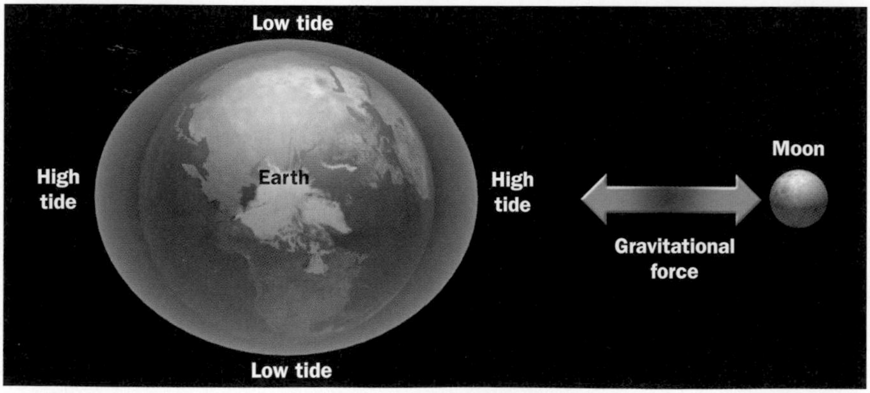

Not to scale

SEE ALSO
233 Rotation
208 Ocean Life Zones

Solar System Objects

Look into the sky on a dark night. Almost everything you can see with your eyes alone is part of our solar system. The **solar system** includes the sun and all objects in space that are affected by the sun's gravity.

The solar system is huge and contains many different objects. These objects range in size from tiny particles of dust to the sun, which is the star at the center of our solar system. The sun, with a diameter of 1,390,180 kilometers, is the largest object in our solar system. The diagram presents scale models of the sizes and distances of objects in the solar system.

Above: Scale model of the sizes of the planets.
Below: Scale model of the distances of the planets.

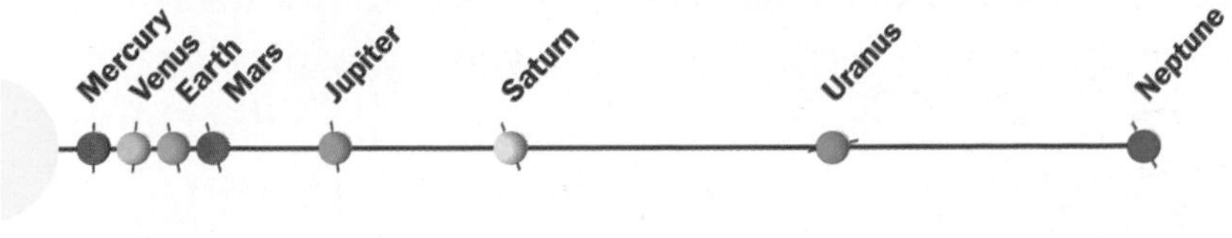

Keyword: Solar System
www.scilinks.org
Code: GSSM238

Did You Know?

If the sun were the size of a basketball at one end of a school basketball court, Earth would be the size of a sesame seed at the opposite end of the court. Jupiter would be the size of a cherry, outside the gym.

239 Earth's Moon

One of the most visible objects in space is Earth's moon. A **moon** is a natural satellite of a planet. A **satellite** is an object that stays in an orbit around a planet. The average distance between Earth and its moon is about 384,400 kilometers. The diameter of Earth's moon is 3,476 kilometers, slightly more than one-quarter the diameter of Earth. The moon revolves around Earth every 27.3 days.

Did You Know?

The same side of the moon always faces Earth, no matter what phase the moon is in. There are photos of the side that faces away from Earth, taken by probes, but only the *Apollo* astronauts have seen the far side. The *Apollo* missions took place between 1969 and 1972.

SEE ALSO
235 Moon Phases
236 Eclipses
237 Tides

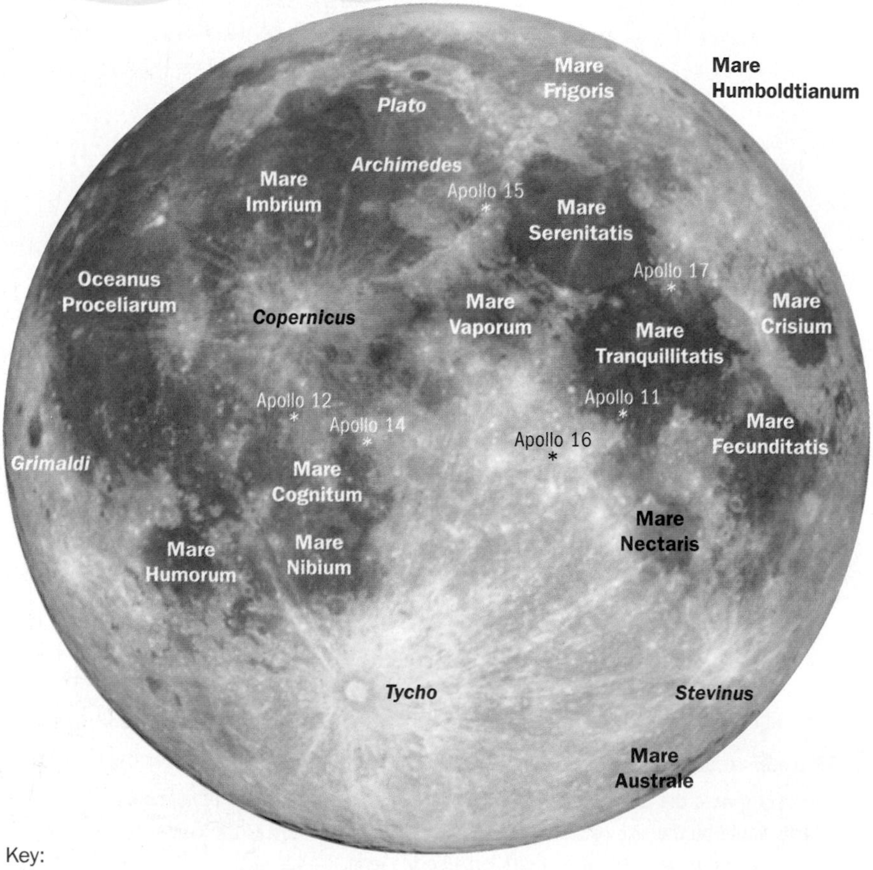

Key:

Mare Crisium	Lunar "sea"
Tycho	Major crater
*Apollo 11	Apollo landing site

Closeup of the lunar surface

The moon's surface is thick with dust and dotted with rocks of various sizes. Astronauts brought samples of moon rocks back to Earth for study. The side of the moon that faces Earth is covered by vast, dark plains. Galileo, the first person known to look at the moon with a telescope, thought he was looking at oceans. He named these plains **maria** (MAHR-ee-uh), Latin for seas. The singular of maria is **mare** (MAHR-ay). Actually, maria are made of basalt, a volcanic rock. The basalt is evidence that the moon once had magma near the surface. Other surface features include lunar mountains and **craters,** which are dish-shaped pits formed when objects from space struck the surface. Large craters, such as Tycho, have rays of dust around them that splashed out when the crater was formed. You can tell which craters are youngest by looking for the ones that have the most complete dust rays around them.

There is no water on the moon's surface. There is also no atmosphere. Because there is no air or water, temperatures vary from −172°C to 114°C, which is 14°C greater than the boiling point of water. The moon's smaller size and lower mass gives it lower gravity—one-sixth of Earth's gravity. For this reason, your weight on the moon would be one-sixth your weight on Earth.

SEE ALSO
276 Gravity

240 Planets

Eight planets—Mercury, Venus, Earth, Mars, Jupiter, Saturn, Uranus, and Neptune—revolve around the sun. These planets stay in orbit because of the gravitational force between each planet and the sun.

The planets are generally classified as terrestrial planets (or inner planets) and gas giants (or outer planets). Terrestrial means Earth-like. **Terrestrial planets** are those having rocky surfaces and cores (centers) made of iron, as Earth does. The terrestrial, or inner, planets include the four planets nearest the sun: Mercury, Venus, Earth, and Mars. Craters are common on the surfaces of most of the terrestrial planets. The craters formed when rocky objects from space crashed into the surfaces of these planets. Evidence suggests that Earth has been hit by objects too, but weathering, erosion, and uplift have erased most craters from Earth's surface. Also, most objects burn in Earth's atmosphere before reaching the ground.

Jupiter, Saturn, Uranus, and Neptune are the gas giants, sometimes called the outer planets. The **gas giants** are planets that have surfaces made of a kind of slush that forms from their gaseous atmospheres. Although their surfaces are not solid, there is evidence that the gas giants have solid cores made up at least partly of iron. The gas giants earned the name "giants" because of their large sizes compared to the terrestrial planets.

Not to scale

Dwarf planets revolve around the sun, are large enough for the force of gravity to pull them into a nearly round shape, but are not large enough to capture nearby objects. Pluto is the best-known dwarf planet. Until 2006, Pluto was known as the ninth planet in our solar system. However, Pluto is not a terrestrial planet or a gas giant. Pluto appears to be made of gases frozen into ice. Pluto and its one moon, Charon, are so close in size that they revolve around each other. Usually a moon revolves around its planet. Scientists had disagreed for years about whether Pluto qualified as a planet. Then, in 2005, an astronomer discovered an object that is larger and more distant than Pluto. Astronomers had to decide whether this new object would be called a planet. They decided it wouldn't. Instead, the International Astronomical Union (IAU) made a new category, dwarf planet. The IAU named three objects as dwarf planets: Pluto, the new object (now officially named Eris), and Ceres, an object in the asteroid belt. The IAU expects to rename more objects as dwarf planets. But the issue is not settled yet. Some scientists are unhappy that Pluto is no longer a planet. They are arguing for the dwarf planet definition to be changed.

To remember the names of the planets in order, try inventing a sentence whose words begin with the same letters as the planets. Here's an example: **My Very Eager Mother Just Served Us Nachos.**

SEE ALSO
241 Asteroids

Planetary Data

Planet	Diameter at Equator (km)	Distance from the Sun (million km)	Period of Rotation (Earth time)	Period of Revolution (Earth time)	Number of Known Moons
Mercury	4,878	57.9	58.64 days	88 days	0
Venus	12,104	108.1	243.0 days	224.7 days	0
Earth	12,756	149.6	23.9 hours	365.25 days (1 year)	1
Mars	6,786	227.9	24.6 hours	687 days (1.88 yrs)	2
Jupiter	142,984	778.3	9.84 hours	4,333 days (11.86 yrs)	62
Saturn	120,536	1427.0	10.2 hours	10,759 days (29.46 yrs)	56
Uranus	51,108	2869.6	17.9 hours	30,688 days (84.02 yrs)	27
Neptune	49,538	4496.6	19.1 hours	60,181 days (164.8 yrs)	13

Sources: New York Public Library Science Desk Reference, Encyclopedia of the Solar System; The Cambridge Atlas of Astronomy; Science News; NASA/ JPL Solar System Dynamics web site; NASA Solar System Exploration web site

241 Asteroids

The sun, the nine planets, and their moons are not the only objects in our solar system. After moons, the next largest objects in the solar system are large rocks called **asteroids.** A few asteroids are larger than the smallest moons of the solar system, but they are too small to be planets. Large asteroids are sometimes called "minor planets." Asteroids exist in all parts of the solar system, but most are concentrated in a belt that lies between the orbits of Mars and Jupiter. One explanation for these millions of stony and metallic bodies is that they are bits and pieces of a planet that never formed when the solar system took shape between 4 and 5 billion years ago.

Asteroids occur in many sizes and shapes, although none is larger than 940 kilometers across. Asteroids are irregularly shaped. Some resemble lumpy potatoes, while others are shaped like the rocks you might find in any field. No asteroids appear to have a round shape like the planets.

Did You Know?

Most scientists now accept the theory that an asteroid hitting Earth 65 million years ago caused a dust cloud that blocked the light of the sun, causing the death of many plants and possibly the extinction of the dinosaurs and other animal species.

242 Comets

A **comet** is a mixture of frozen gases (including water) and tiny particles of dust. Sometimes called a "dirty snowball," the core of a comet is usually no more than a few kilometers across, although its mass may be more than 1000 billion metric tons. A cloud of dust and gases called a **coma** surrounds the core. Together, the core and the coma form the comet's head. The heads of most comets are generally smaller than asteroids; however the tail of a comet (gases and dust given off by a moving comet) may extend millions of kilometers into space.

Like other objects in the solar system, comets follow an orbit around the sun. Some comets make many revolutions of the sun. The most famous returning comet is Halley's comet, which revolves around the sun once every 76 years. Halley's comet last visited the neighborhood of Earth in 1986 and will return again in 2061. Other comets make a single orbit before vanishing forever into outer space.

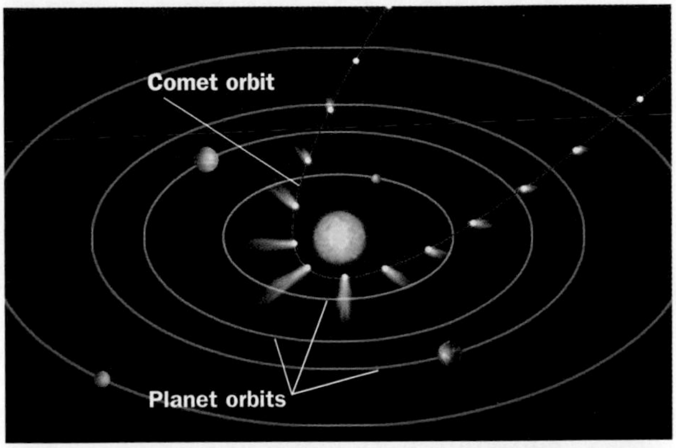

As a comet approaches the sun, particles from the sun—called the **solar wind**—rub away the head of the comet, to produce a long, glowing tail. Because the tail of a comet is blown outward by the solar wind, the tail always points away from the sun. As the comet moves away from the sun, its tail grows smaller again.

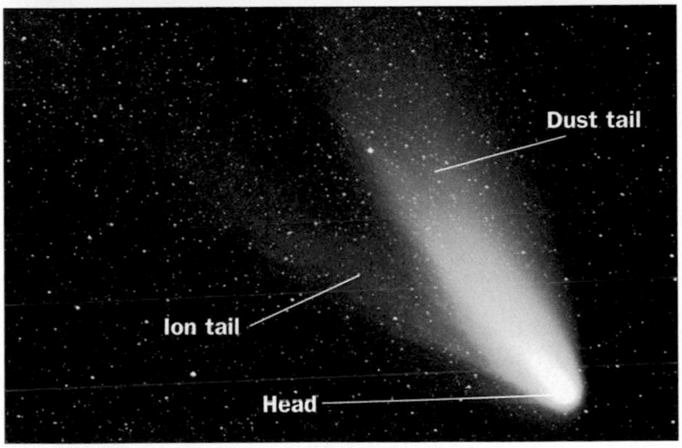

Meteors

Have you ever seen a "shooting star" flash across the sky? If so, you have observed a meteor. A **meteor** is a streak of light formed by a space rock burning up as it plunges into Earth's atmosphere. Most meteors are no larger than a grain of sand, but some can be many meters in diameter. If the rock strikes Earth's surface, it is called a **meteorite.** Meteorites can leave behind large craters. For example, a 45-meter-wide meteorite produced the 1.2-kilometer, 170-meter deep crater known as Meteor Crater in Arizona.

On any clear, dark night, you can see about six meteors per hour. During **meteor showers** as many as 60 meteors might be seen each hour. A meteor shower occurs when Earth passes through the tail of a comet or a cloud of dust left behind by a broken-up asteroid. Some meteor showers occur on a regular schedule each year as Earth's orbit takes it through these dust clouds. Listen for announcements of meteor showers on weather forecasts.

244

Stars, Galaxies, and Constellations

Space is filled with trillions of stars and groups of stars called galaxies. Throughout history, people have been fascinated by stars. Many have imagined that the stars form pictures in the sky. These pictures, called constellations, are made by "connecting the dots" formed by visible stars.

Wow, look at all those stars.
Yeah, I wonder what they're made of.

245

Stars

Stars are objects in space, made of gases, which produce their own light and heat. Earth's nearest star is the sun, which is about 149,600,000 kilometers away. The next nearest star, Proxima Centauri, is 4.24 light years away. A **light year** is a measurement equal to 9.5 trillion kilometers—the distance light travels in 1 year. Since Proxima Centauri is 4.24 light years away, the distance between Earth and Proxima Centauri is about 40 trillion kilometers.

The light and heat of stars comes from nuclear fusion reactions taking place inside the star. **Nuclear fusion** reactions occur when hydrogen atoms combine to form helium atoms. As this happens, great amounts of light and heat energy are given off. Except for a few laboratories on Earth, nuclear fusion takes place only in stars.

SEE ALSO
247 Galaxies
256 Atomic Structure

Different stars produce different amounts of energy. The amount of energy produced by a star determines the star's color and surface temperature. The relationship of star color to surface temperature is shown in the diagram on the next page.

Stars differ in composition, age, and size. Young stars are rich in hydrogen, with helium being the next most common substance. As a star ages, hydrogen is used up as more helium is made. With the passage of more time, the star also makes other elements such as carbon and oxygen.

Hertzsprung-Russell Diagram

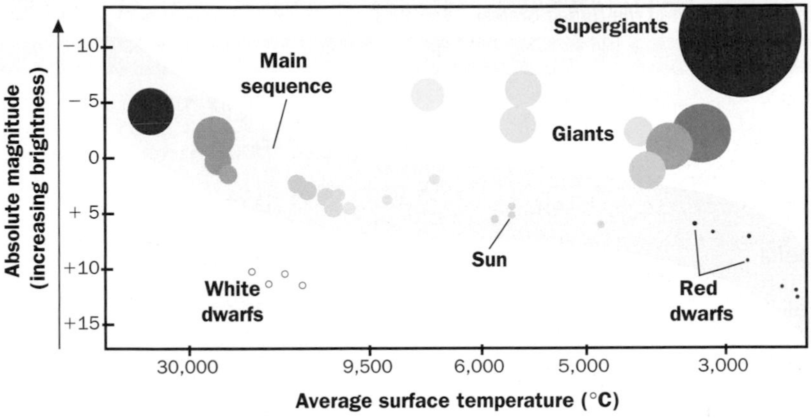

Star ages are related to their starting masses. In general, stars with the smallest starting mass—such as white dwarfs—last for the longest time, up to about 100 billion years. Stars that start with average masses—such as the sun—last about 10 billion years, or a little more than twice the age of the sun today. Stars with the largest masses may last only a few billion years.

The sizes of stars also vary greatly. For example, the sun, with a diameter of about 1,392,000 kilometers, is a medium-sized star. The smallest stars have diameters between about 10–30 kilometers. The largest have diameters as much as 640,000,000 kilometers.

Absolute and Apparent Magnitude 246

A sky full of stars greets your eye on a clear night. Some stars appear brighter than others, but they may not truly be brighter. Why is this so? The brightness of a star depends partly on its size and partly on its distance from Earth. Larger stars *are* brighter, but closer stars *look* brighter. The brightness of a star's light is called its magnitude. There are two kinds of magnitude: apparent magnitude and absolute magnitude. **Apparent magnitude** is a measure of how bright a star appears to be when you see it from Earth. **Absolute magnitude** is a measure of how bright the star really is, if all stars were the same distance from Earth.

Star magnitude is indicated with a number. A lower number means a brighter star. A star with a magnitude of 1 (first-magnitude star, such as Antares) is brighter than a star with a magnitude of 2 (a second-magnitude star, such as Polaris). A star with a magnitude of 3.2 is brighter than a star with a magnitude of 4.6. Stars and planets with negative magnitudes, such as Sirius, are brighter than stars having positive numbers.

The Ten Brightest Stars*

**Visible from much of the United States*

Star	Apparent Magnitude	Constellation
Sirius	−1.4	Canis major
Arcturus	−0.1	Boötes
Vega	0.0	Lyra
Capella	0.1	Auriga
Rigel	0.1	Orion
Procyon	0.4	Canis minor
Altair	0.8	Aquila
Betelgeuse	0.8	Orion
Aldebaran	0.8	Taurus
Antares	1.0	Scorpius

SEE ALSO
248 Constellations

You can use a table of apparent magnitudes, such as the one on this page, to help identify stars. The dimmest stars you can see with the unaided eye have an apparent magnitude of 6. The brightest star, other than the sun, is Sirius (−1.4). When you go stargazing, the brightest object you see may be a planet. Check a sky map for the month and year that you are observing to be sure.

247 Galaxies

If you look into a clear sky at night, away from a city or highway lights, you will see a thick band of stars across the sky. What you are really seeing is the side view of a family of stars called a **galaxy,** in this case the Milky Way Galaxy. The Milky Way Galaxy is a group of about 200 billion stars that includes the sun and almost all the other stars you can see in the night sky.

Space contains at least a billion galaxies beyond our own Milky Way Galaxy. The shapes of these galaxies fall into three major classes: spiral galaxies, elliptical galaxies, and irregular galaxies.

- **Spiral Galaxy** The Milky Way is a spiral galaxy. A spiral galaxy is disk-shaped with a bulge in the middle and arms that spiral out from the bulge. The arms rotate around the galaxy's center.

- **Elliptical Galaxy** An elliptical galaxy is shaped like a flattened or partially deflated football. Such galaxies contain trillions of stars. These galaxies either do not rotate at all or rotate much more slowly than spiral galaxies.

- **Irregular Galaxy** As its name suggests, an irregular galaxy does not have a distinct shape. Irregular galaxies are the least common type of galaxy. However, two of the closest galaxies to our own galaxy—the Large and Small Magellanic Clouds—are irregular galaxies.

Did You Know?

You can sometimes see the Andromeda Galaxy with your unaided eye. It is visible in the autumn and winter skies in the northern hemisphere.

Constellations

248

Since the beginning of human history, people have imagined that groups of stars form pictures in the night sky. Such imaginary star pictures are called **constellations.** Many constellations are named for animals or mythological characters.

Astronomers recognize a total of 88 constellations. Because of Earth's revolution, different constellations are visible in the night sky at different times of the year. The constellations you see change during the night, too, because stars rise and set due to Earth's rotation, just as the sun does. In addition, the constellations you can see from the southern hemisphere are different from those that you see from the northern hemisphere.

Knowing the constellations was very important to travelers long ago. For example, the star Polaris (or the North Star), in the constellation *Ursa Minor* (the little bear), is almost directly above Earth's North Pole. You may know *Ursa Minor* as the Little Dipper. Polaris is the last star in the handle of the Little Dipper. By finding Polaris, travelers could know in which direction north lies. You can also measure your latitude in degrees north, using Polaris. Many sailors have used this method to navigate their way across the ocean.

There's Polaris!
Our latitude is 12° north.
We are on course!

Did You Know?

Different cultures of the world call the constellations by many different names. The names used by astronomers for northern hemisphere constellations are mostly based on those described by the ancient Greeks.

Astronomers use constellations as a kind of map in the sky. For example, if an astronomer wants to describe where Jupiter is on a particular night, the astronomer would name the constellation in which Jupiter appears in the sky.

The maps on the facing page show constellations that you can see in the northern hemisphere sky in winter and in summer. To use the maps, stand outdoors facing south on a clear night. Hold the open book upside down over your head. Compare the stars that you see with the map. (Remember that there will be no lines connecting the stars in the sky!) The positions of the constellations change through the night, and from season to season, so the maps may not exactly match your view of the sky.

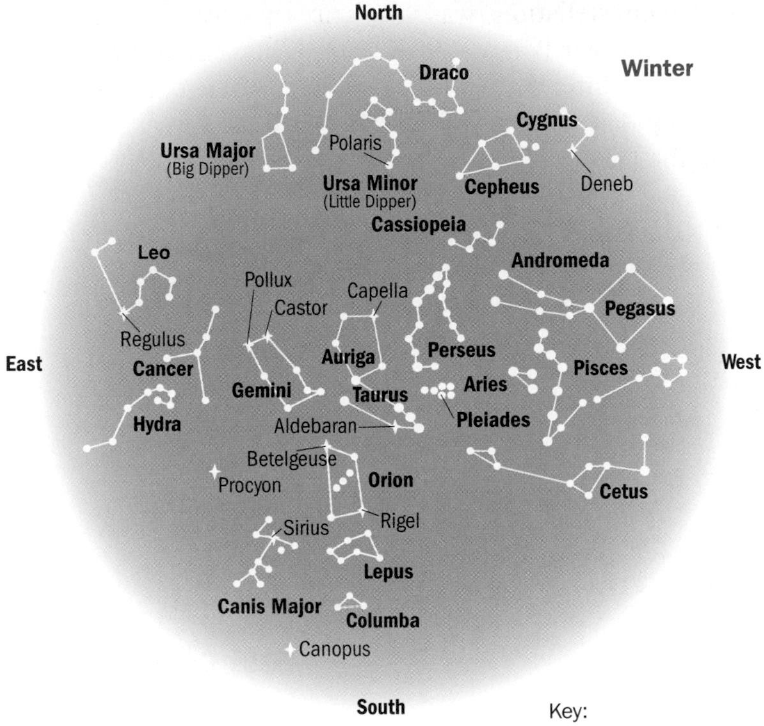

Key:
Star magnitude 1.5 or brighter
Constellation names boldface
Star names regular type

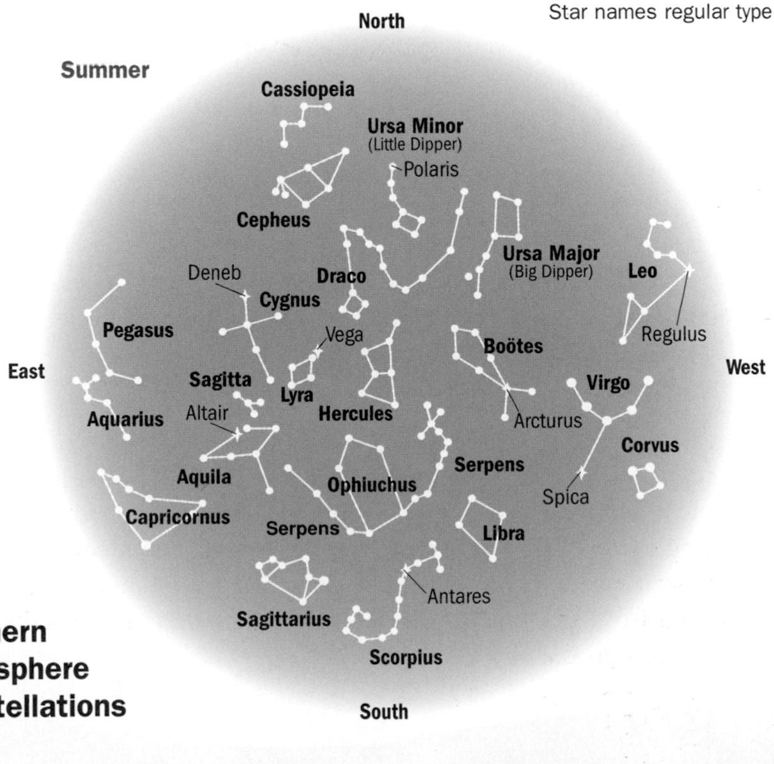

Northern Hemisphere Constellations

PHYSICAL SCIENCE

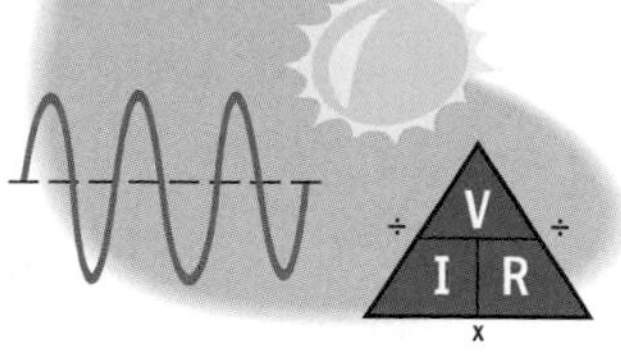

What are things made of? What holds things together? What makes things move? The branch of science that answers questions like these is called physical science. **Physical science** is the study of matter and energy. This section describes the properties and structure of matter, the different forms of energy, and how energy affects matter.

250

Matter

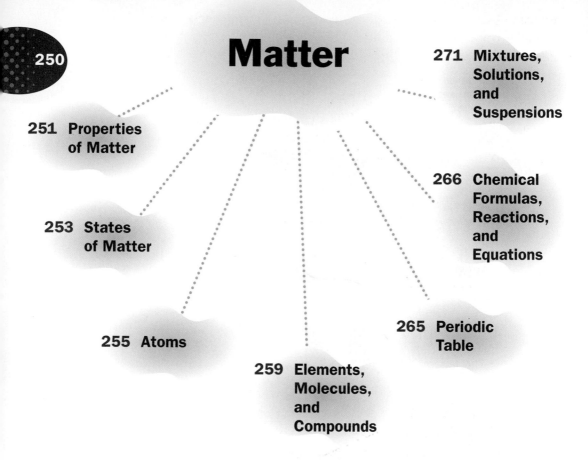

Matter is the "stuff" that all objects and substances in the universe are made of. Because all matter takes up space (has **volume**) and contains a certain amount of material (has **mass**), all matter can be detected and measured.

You can observe some types of matter easily with your senses. For example, you can see or feel things like rocks, trees, bicycles, and different kinds of animals. And you can see and smell things like smoke from a fire.

Other types of matter are a little more difficult to observe. The dust mites that live in your upholstered furniture and rugs are an example of matter that is too small to see with the naked eye. They can be observed only with special instruments, like a microscope.

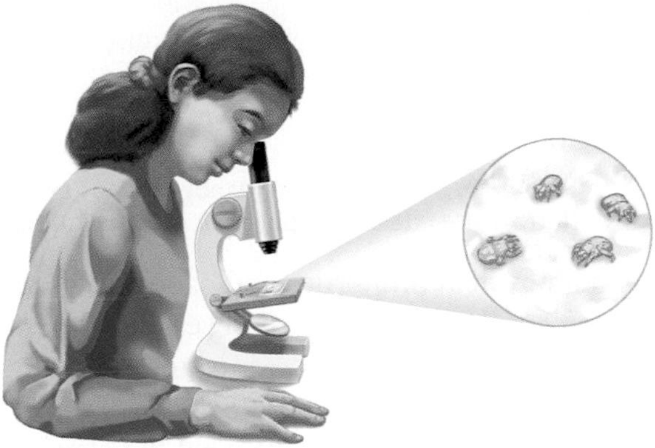

Another example of matter that's hard to detect is air, the invisible gas that surrounds you. How do you know it's there? You can't see it or smell it, but you know it exists because you can feel it when the wind blows and see it bend the branches of trees.

Word Watch!

The word *matter* comes from the Latin word *materia*, meaning "material" or "stuff."

Properties of Matter

251

You know that a piece of cork is different from a piece of clay. Cork will break if you squeeze it hard, but clay will flatten or bend into a new shape. If you had a scale handy, you would find that a piece of cork weighs less than a piece of clay the same size. If you dropped both objects in water, you would see that the cork floats but the clay sinks. Characteristics like these, that help us identify or classify matter, are called **properties.**

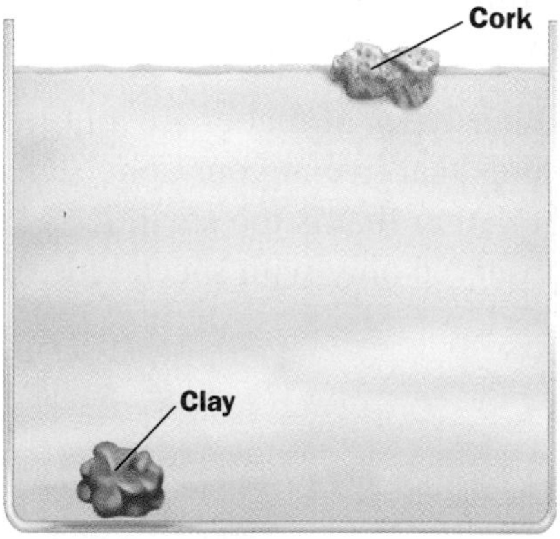

Tendency to float or sink is a physical property of matter.

All matter has both physical properties and chemical properties. **Physical properties** are those that can be observed without changing the make-up, or identity, of the matter. For example, clay is malleable, which means it will bend or flatten when squeezed. Squeezing changes the shape of the clay but does not change what the clay is made of. Malleability is an example of a physical property. The chart below lists some common physical properties of matter.

Physical Property	What It Means
Density	The amount of matter in a given volume (mass per unit volume)
Ductility	The ability to be pulled into a thin strand, like a wire
Malleability	The ability to be pressed or pounded into a thin sheet
Boiling point	The temperature at which a substance changes from a liquid to a gas
Melting point	The temperature at which a substance changes from a solid to a liquid
Electrical conductivity	How well a substance allows electricity to flow through it
Solubility	The ability to dissolve in another substance

Chemical properties describe matter based on its ability to change into a new kind of matter with different properties. For example, paper is flammable: it is capable of burning in the presence of oxygen. Flammability is a chemical property of paper. A chemical property of iron is its tendency to rust. Rusting occurs when iron reacts with oxygen to produce iron oxide. Reactivity to acid and to water are two more examples of chemical properties.

SEE ALSO
265 Periodic Table
269 Chemical Reactions

Physical and Chemical Changes

252

If you fold a sheet of paper into thirds, you're left with a piece of paper one-third the size of the original. But the newly folded paper is still paper. Two physical properties of the paper—its size and shape—have changed, but not its chemical properties. Such a change is called a **physical change.**

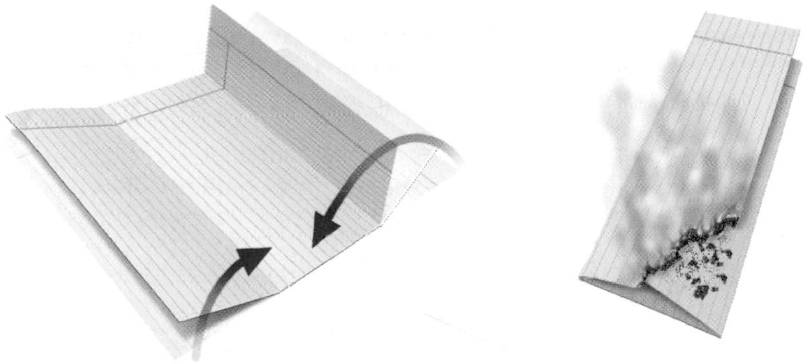

If you hold a lit match to the paper, the paper will burn. What you're left with—ash, gases, and smoke—is no longer paper. The chemical properties of the paper have changed, producing new substances. This kind of change is called a **chemical change.**

SEE ALSO
269 Chemical Reactions

Many physical changes can be reversed. For example, you can unfold the piece of paper to return it to its original size and shape. Most chemical changes, on the other hand, cannot easily be undone. For example, you can't "unburn" a charred piece of paper.

253

States of Matter

Think about the differences between, for example, a rock, milk, and air. The shape of a rock does not change unless you cut or smash it. Milk takes on the shape of its container, and if you pour it on the floor it will spread out to form a puddle. Air spreads out even more than milk does. And it keeps spreading out in all directions.

Rocks, milk, and air represent different physical forms in which a substance can exist: a rock is a **solid,** milk is a **liquid,** and air is a **gas.** Solids, liquids, and gases are three **states of matter.** The chart below lists the defining features of each state.

Word Watch!

The three **states of matter** are also known as the **phases of matter.**

SEE ALSO
254 Changing States of Matter

State of Matter	Defining Features
Solid	• keeps its shape and volume
Liquid	• takes on the shape of its container • keeps the same volume, in a container or not • can flow
Gas	• takes on the shape and volume of its container • can flow (through a room, for example)

Did You Know?

A fourth state of matter is called a plasma. Like a gas, a plasma does not have a definite shape or volume. Plasmas only exist at very high temperatures. Stars, including the sun, are made of matter in a plasma state.

SEE ALSO
255 Atoms
259 Elements, Molecules, and Compounds

But why are solids solid, liquids liquidy, and gases gassy? To answer this question, you first need to understand three things:

- All matter is made up of tiny particles called atoms and molecules.
- These particles attract each other; the greater the attraction, the closer the particles get.
- These particles are constantly in motion and bumping into each other. The temperature of a substance is related to the speed at which its particles move.

The state of a substance depends on how fast its particles move and how strong the attraction is between the particles.

Solid The particles of a substance in its solid state vibrate in place, but the vibration isn't great enough to overcome the attraction between the particles and cause them to separate. As a result, the forces between the particles cause them to lock together.

Liquid The particles of a substance move even faster when the substance is in a liquid state. As a result, the particles in a liquid can overcome some of the attraction between them. So, unlike the particles in a solid, which are locked together, the particles in a liquid can flow around and over each other. If you spill a glass of water on the floor, for example, the water molecules stick together enough to make a puddle, but not enough to keep the shape the water had when it was in the glass.

Gas The particles of a substance move fastest when the substance is in a gaseous state—so fast that they are able to overcome the attraction between them and separate from each other entirely. That's why a gas will spread out in all directions, filling up a balloon, a room, or the atmosphere.

SEE ALSO
213 Earth's Atmosphere

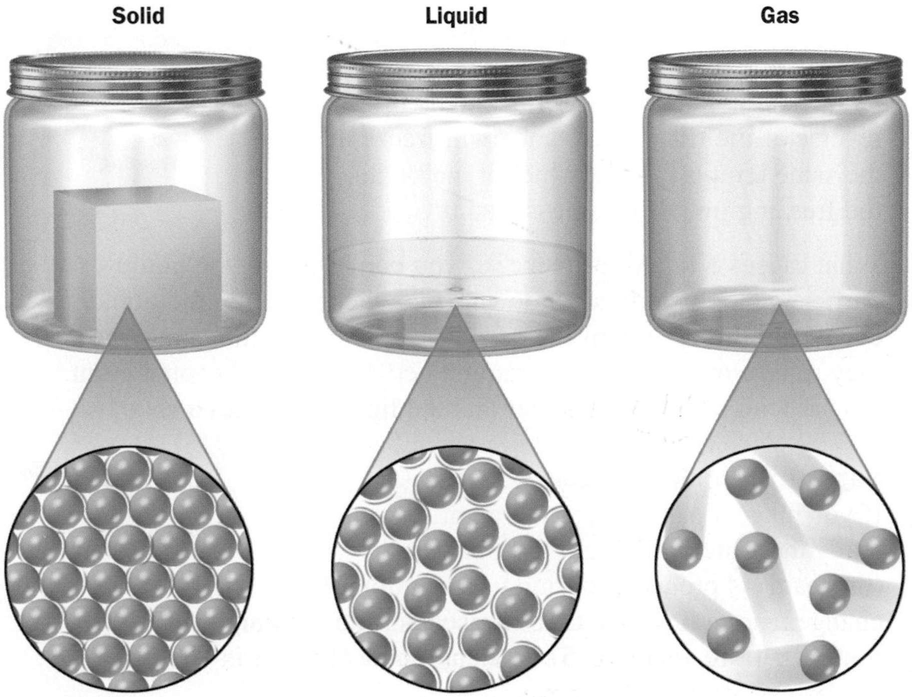

254 Changing States of Matter

Water is a substance that can be found in three states: solid ice, liquid water, and water vapor (a gas). You know from experience that water can change from one state to another. The same is true of most other substances as well.

Melting: From Solid to Liquid

Melting

If you put an ice cube in a cup and set it on the counter, the ice will melt. **Melting** is the change from a solid state to a liquid state. The temperature at which a solid melts is called its **melting point.** The melting point of ice is 0°C.

SEE ALSO
253 States of Matter

What causes a solid to melt? If you heat a solid, the particles in that solid will begin to move faster. If you keep heating the solid, eventually the motion of the particles will become great enough to overcome the attraction that locks the particles together. When that happens, the solid becomes a liquid.

Freezing: From Liquid to Solid

Freezing

If you place a cup of water in the freezer, the water will turn to solid ice. **Freezing** is the change from a liquid state to a solid state. The temperature at which a liquid freezes is called its **freezing point.** Because freezing is the reverse of melting, a substance will freeze at the same temperature at which it melts. So, the freezing point of water is also 0°C.

What causes a liquid to freeze? If you cool a liquid, the liquid's particles will begin to slow down. If you keep cooling the liquid, eventually the motion of the particles will slow to the point where they cannot overcome the attraction between them. At some point, the particles will lock together and the liquid becomes a solid.

Vaporization: From Liquid to Gas

Boiling

If you place a pan of water on a hot stove, eventually the water will begin to boil. Water vapor (or steam) is produced during **vaporization,** the change from a liquid state to a gaseous state. Boiling causes the liquid water to vaporize. The **boiling point** of water is 100°C.

The same process that causes a solid to melt causes a liquid to vaporize. As a substance is heated, its particles begin to move faster and faster. During vaporization, the fastest particles are able to overcome the attraction of the particles around them and break free completely. These escaped particles become a gas—water vapor.

A pan of water left on the counter top will evaporate over several days. **Evaporation** is vaporization that occurs at the surface of a liquid. Evaporation can take place at temperatures below the liquid's boiling point.

Condensation: From Gas to Liquid

Condensation is the change from a gaseous state to a liquid state. The temperature at which a gas condenses is called its **condensation point.** At sea level, the condensation point of water vapor is 100°C—the same as the boiling point of water. That is because condensation is the reverse of vaporization. Water vapor can exist in the air at temperatures below 100°C. If you pour cold juice into a glass on a humid summer day, you will begin to notice beads of water forming on the outside of the glass. What you observe is water vapor from the air around the glass that has condensed on the glass.

Condensation

SEE ALSO

226 Humidity and Dew Point

The same process that causes a liquid to freeze causes a vapor to condense. As a vapor cools, its particles begin to slow down. Condensation takes place when the particles slow down so much that they cannot overcome the attraction of the particles around them. When this happens, they clump together to form a liquid.

SEE ALSO

253 States of Matter

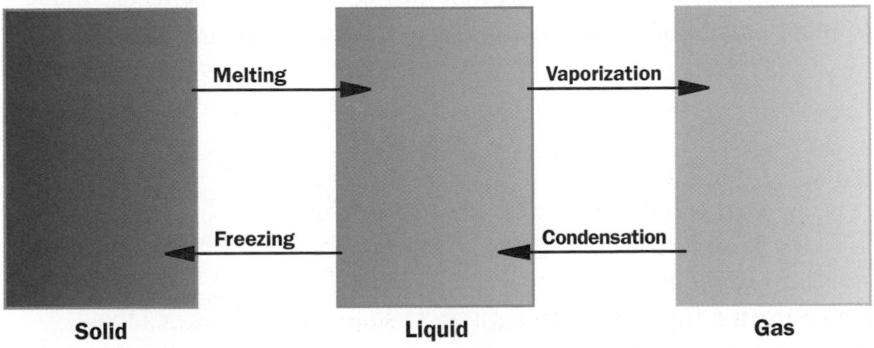

Atoms

255

Imagine finding a gold nugget while panning for gold in Colorado. You decide to share your prize with family and friends by having it cut into smaller pieces. Using a special tool, you cut the nugget in half, then in half again, over and over. Eventually you end up with a piece of gold that is too small to cut with your tool!

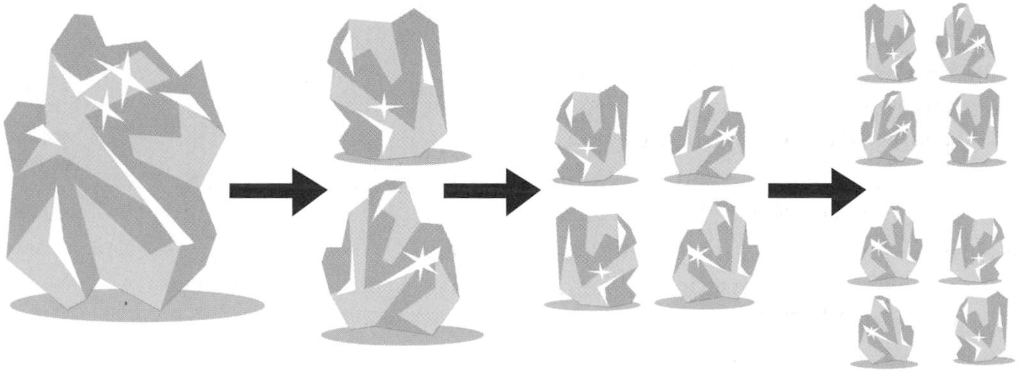

But you've got a lot of family and friends, so suppose you were able to keep cutting the gold into smaller and smaller pieces. Would you be able to keep cutting forever? The answer is no! At some point you would end up with a piece that could not be divided. That smallest piece would be an atom.

An **atom** is the smallest particle into which an element (such as gold) can be divided and still maintain the properties of that element. Because all matter is made up of elements, and all elements are made up of atoms, atoms are considered the building blocks of matter.

SEE ALSO
259 Elements, Molecules, and Compounds
265 Periodic Table

Word Watch!

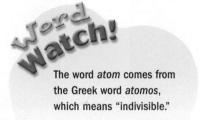

The word *atom* comes from the Greek word *atomos*, which means "indivisible."

SCILINKS NSTA
Keyword: Atomic Models
www.scilinks.org
Code: GSSM255

Atomic Structure

Atoms are made up of even smaller particles called protons, neutrons, and electrons. Protons and neutrons stick together to form an atom's **nucleus,** which is at the center of the atom. Electrons are found in regions surrounding the nucleus.

Current model of the atom

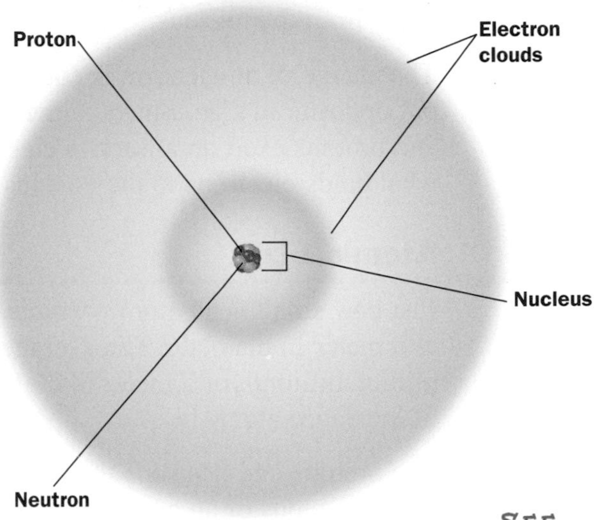

Protons are the positively charged particles located in the nucleus of an atom. All protons are identical. An atom is identified by the number of protons in its nucleus. For example, an atom with one proton is called hydrogen; an atom with eight protons is called oxygen. All atoms of the same element have the same number of protons.

SEE ALSO
265 Periodic Table

Neutrons are also located in the nucleus. As their name suggests, neutrons are electrically neutral. That is, they have no electric charge. All neutrons are identical. Sometimes, atoms of the same element can have different numbers of neutrons. Because neutrons have no charge, the overall charge of the atom is not changed by the extra neutrons. **Isotopes** are atoms of the same element that have different numbers of neutrons.

Electrons are the negatively charged particles found outside the nucleus of an atom. All electrons are identical. The number and arrangement of the electrons in an atom determine its chemical properties.

SEE ALSO
251 Properties of Matter
268 Electron-Dot Diagrams
258 The Evolution of Atomic Theory

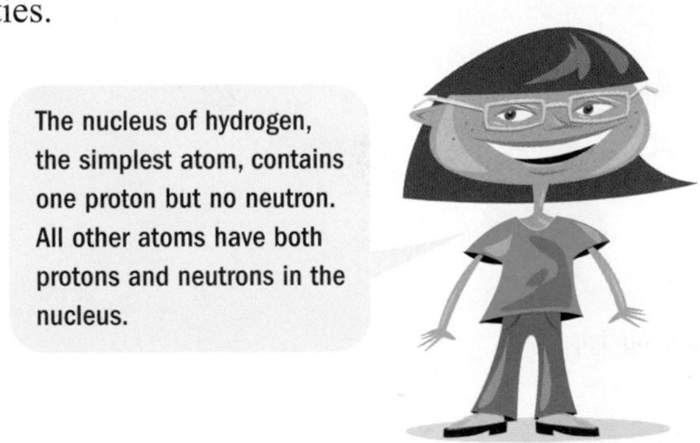

The nucleus of hydrogen, the simplest atom, contains one proton but no neutron. All other atoms have both protons and neutrons in the nucleus.

MORE ▶

SEE ALSO
240 Planets

Scientists used to think that electrons orbited the nucleus in fixed paths, the way the planets orbit the sun. Now they theorize that electrons travel in random paths in areas around the nucleus called **electron clouds**. An electron's **energy level** determines its average distance from the nucleus.

SEE ALSO
315 The Law of Electric Charges

The charge of an electron is equal in size to the charge of a proton, but opposite in sign. Since unlike charges attract each other, electrons and protons exert an attractive electrical force on each other. That's what holds electrons to the nucleus.

257 Atomic Size

Just how small is an atom? A typical atom is about one ten-billionth of a meter in diameter. The average nucleus of an atom is about one million billionth of a meter in diameter—a tiny fraction of the size of the entire atom.

SEE ALSO
250 Matter

The protons and neutrons that make up the nucleus of an atom have about the same mass. Electrons have a much smaller mass—about one two-thousandth the mass of protons or neutrons. That means most of the mass of an atom is in the nucleus.

Word Watch!

Mass is a measure of the amount of "stuff" in an object.

The particles that make up an atom are like tiny specks compared to the size of the atom as a whole. So the majority of an atom's volume consists of empty space. And since all objects are made of atoms, you could argue that objects are also mostly empty space!

There are more than a million million billion atoms in a single drop of water!

SCI LINKS NSTA
Keyword: Atomic Models
www.scilinks.org
Code: GSSM255

The Evolution of Atomic Theory

258

Atomic theory has changed quite a bit since the Greek philosopher Democritus proposed the existence of atoms in 440 B.C. By the early 1800s, British chemist John Dalton had come up with a theory that he based on observations from experiments. Dalton proposed that all substances were made of atoms—small, hard, dense spheres that could not be created, destroyed, or altered.

Dalton's model of the atom

SEE ALSO
440 History of Science Time Line

Then, in 1898, British scientist J. J. Thomson proposed that atoms themselves were made up of smaller particles. He discovered that atoms contain negatively charged particles, but he did not know the location of these particles. He theorized that they were spread evenly throughout positively charged material. His model of the atom was called the plum-pudding model.

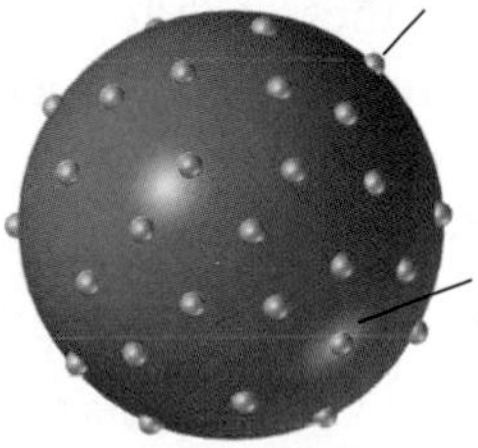

Thomson's model of the atom

In 1911, Ernest Rutherford, a former student of Thomson's, proposed that atoms had a dense, positively charged nucleus surrounded by electrons. Then, two years later, in 1913, Danish scientist Niels Bohr modified this model even further. He said that electrons revolved around the nucleus in circular paths, called orbits, and that electrons could only exist in certain orbits and at certain energy levels.

SEE ALSO
450 Famous Scientists

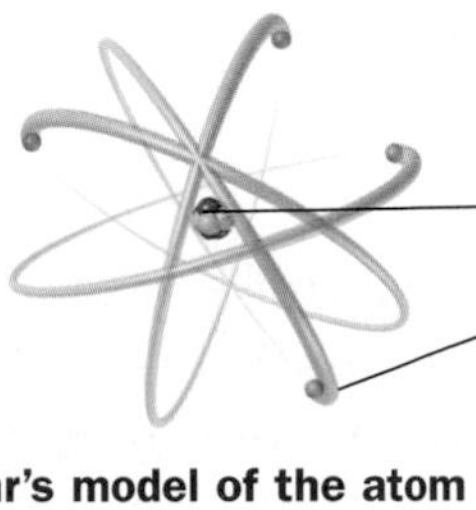

Bohr's model of the atom

Bohr's model was an important stepping stone to today's model of the atom, which was developed in the 1920s. According to the current model, called the **electron cloud model,** electrons surround the nucleus, traveling not in prescribed paths but in regions of various thicknesses, called clouds.

SEE ALSO
256 Atomic Structure

Elements, Molecules, and Compounds

259

SEE ALSO

255 Atoms

All matter is made up of atoms. But think about all the different kinds of matter there are in the universe. What makes one kind of matter different from another? Different kinds of atoms! Different kinds of atoms are called **elements.** Two or more elements that have combined are called a **compound.** Elements and compounds of elements make up all the different kinds of matter in the universe.

260

Elements

SEE ALSO

265 Periodic Table
177 Structure of Earth

An **element** is considered the simplest form of matter. It cannot be broken down into simpler substances under normal laboratory conditions. There are about 110 known elements in the universe. Ninety-two of these are found naturally on Earth or in the atmosphere. The rest are synthetic, or made in the laboratory.

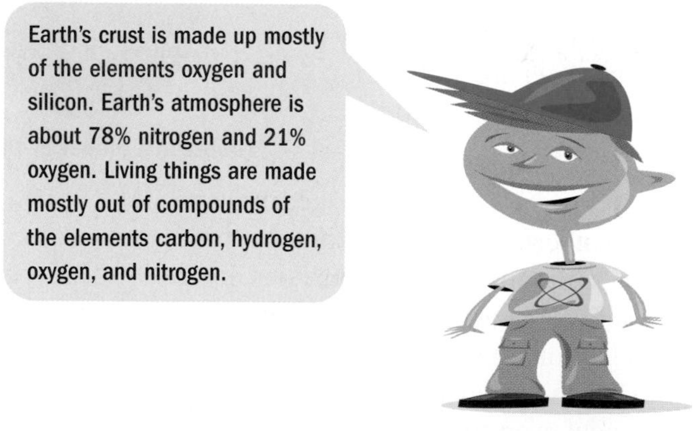

Earth's crust is made up mostly of the elements oxygen and silicon. Earth's atmosphere is about 78% nitrogen and 21% oxygen. Living things are made mostly out of compounds of the elements carbon, hydrogen, oxygen, and nitrogen.

Each element is made of atoms of the same type. For example, the element oxygen is made out of oxygen atoms. The element carbon is made out of carbon atoms. Each element is considered a pure substance because it contains only one kind of atom.

SEE ALSO

251 Properties of Matter

Each element has a unique set of physical and chemical properties that distinguish it from all other elements. These properties can be used to identify different elements. They can also be used to separate combinations of elements into pure substances.

Molecules

261

When two or more atoms combine, they form a **molecule.** Just as an atom is the smallest particle of an element with the same properties of that element, a molecule is the smallest particle of a substance with the same properties of that substance.

SEE ALSO
255 Atoms

The simplest molecules contain only two atoms. These are called **diatomic molecules** (the prefix *di-* means "two"). For example, an oxygen molecule (O_2) is a diatomic molecule. It is made up of two oxygen atoms (O) that have joined together. A hydrogen molecule (H_2) is also diatomic: it consists of two hydrogen atoms (H).

SEE ALSO
265 Periodic Table

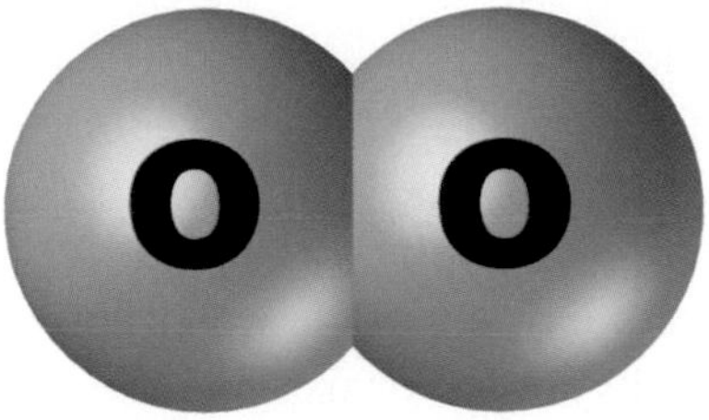

Oxygen molecule (O_2)

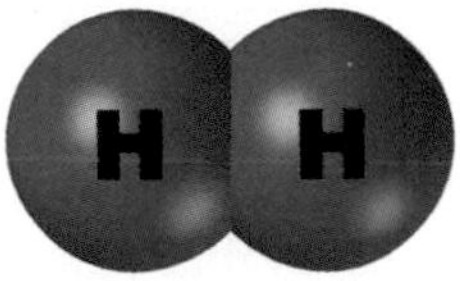

Hydrogen molecule (H_2)

Most molecules are made out of two or more atoms of different kinds (different elements). For example, a water molecule (H_2O) is made of two hydrogen atoms (H) and one oxygen atom (O). Each molecule of water behaves like water. If the molecules are divided into separate hydrogen and oxygen atoms, however, the particles no longer behave like water.

SEE ALSO
267 Chemical Formulas

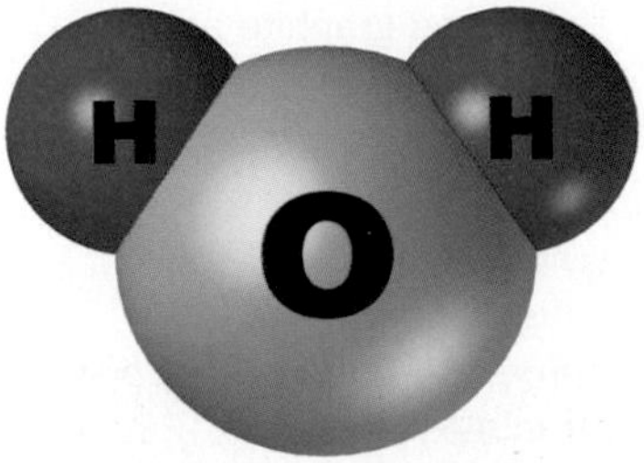

Water molecule (H_2O)

262 Compounds

Most elements are found in combination with other elements—that is, in chemical **compounds.** The elements in any given compound have a fixed ratio. For example, the compound water (H_2O) always has two parts of the element hydrogen to one part of the element oxygen.

SEE ALSO
261 Molecules

Science Alert!

What's the difference between a compound and a molecule? The term *compound* is used to describe the chemical substance in general, while the term *molecule* refers to the smallest particle of the substance that has the same properties of the substance.

The properties of compounds are different from the properties of elements that make up the compounds. For example, water has properties that are different from either hydrogen or oxygen, the elements that make up water.

Compound Name and Formula	Contains These Elements	Properties of Each Element	Properties of Compound
Table salt: sodium chloride ($NaCl$)	**sodium,** Na **chlorine,** Cl	**sodium**—a soft, extremely malleable metal; silver-white in color; reacts explosively with water **chlorine**—a poisonous, highly irritating greenish-yellow gas	colorless crystals are cubic; many crystals together look white; salty taste
Table sugar: sucrose ($C_{12}H_{22}O_{11}$)	**carbon,** C **hydrogen,** H **oxygen,** O	**carbon**—crystalline form includes graphite and diamonds; noncrystalline form includes charcoal and coal **hydrogen**—colorless, highly flammable gas **oxygen**—colorless, odorless, tasteless gas	clear crystals or white powder; sweet taste
Baking soda: sodium bicarbonate ($NaHCO_3$)	**sodium,** Na **hydrogen,** H **carbon,** C **oxygen,** O	see properties of each element above	white crystalline powder or lumps

Chemical Bonds

263

The atoms in a molecule are held together by chemical bonds. A **chemical bond** is the force of attraction between atoms. Chemical bonds occur when atoms either transfer or share electrons.

An **ionic bond** is a type of bond in which one or more electrons from one atom are transferred to another atom. The atom that loses electrons ends up with a positive charge (remember, electrons have a negative charge). An atom with a positive charge is called a positive ion. (An **ion** is simply an atom with a charge.) The atom that gains electrons ends up with a negative charge. An atom with a negative charge is called a negative ion. These two ions, having unlike charges, attract each other and form a bond.

SEE ALSO
264 Families of Chemical Compounds
315 The Law of Electric Charges

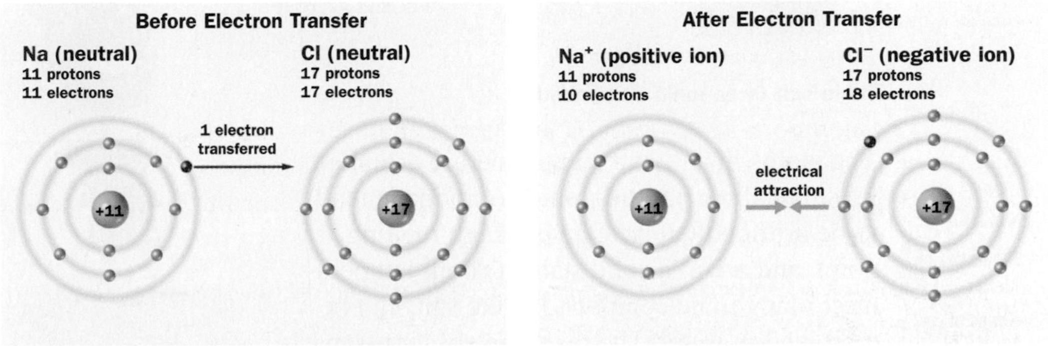

Example of ionic bonding (salt, NaCl)

A **covalent bond** is a type of bond in which atoms share one or more electrons. The shared electrons spend more time between the two atoms than anywhere else. These electrons, because of their negative charge, attract the positive nuclei of the atoms. This attraction holds the atoms together.

SEE ALSO
261 Molecules

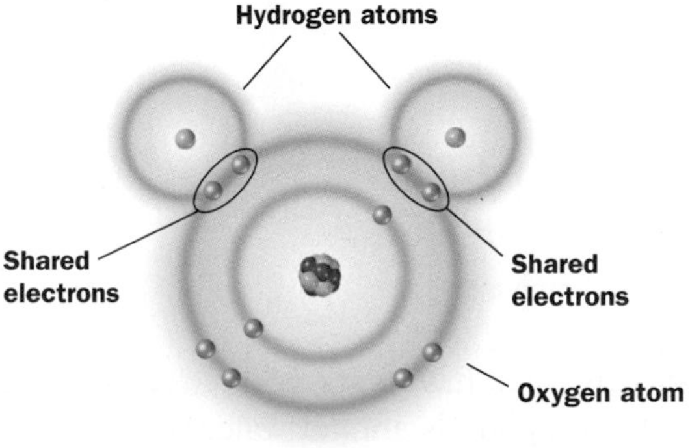

Example of covalent bonding (water, H_2O)

Word Watch!

Ionic bonds get their name from the ions that form as the bond is created. Covalent bonds get their name from the root *co-*, meaning "together" or "jointly," and the word *valence*, which refers to the capacity of an atom to join with other atoms.

264 Families of Chemical Compounds

There are millions of chemical compounds in the world. Scientists classify compounds by the similarities in their properties.

SEE ALSO
263 Chemical Bonds
261 Molecules

Ionic and Covalent Compounds

One way to classify compounds is by the type of bond they contain. **Ionic compounds** are compounds formed with ionic bonds. Ordinary table salt (sodium chloride, NaCl) is an example of an ionic compound.

Table salt is an ionic compound.

There aren't really individual molecules of ionic compounds. Instead, the ions form a crystal structure.

SEE ALSO
251 Properties of Matter
253 States of Matter
272 Parts of a Solution
317 Current Electricity

The atoms in an ionic compound are arranged in a crystalline pattern. Ionic compounds tend to be brittle, often have a very high melting point, and are in a solid state at room temperature. Many ionic compounds, like salt, can be dissolved in water. The resulting solution can conduct electric current.

Covalent compounds are compounds formed with covalent bonds. Water (H_2O) is an example of a covalent compound. So are butter and wax.

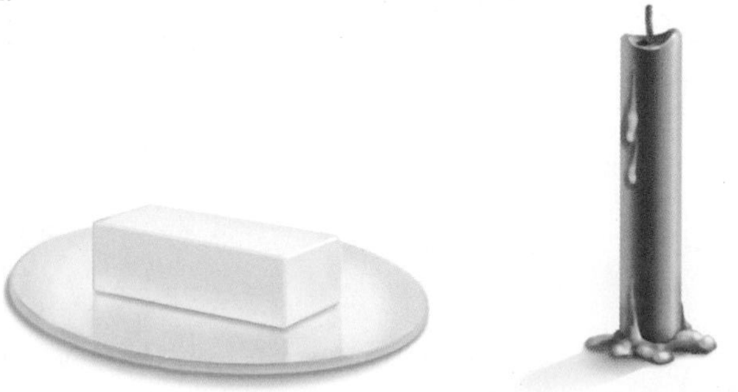

Butter and wax are both covalent compounds.

In general, covalent compounds often have a lower melting point than ionic compounds. Many such compounds are not water soluble, and those that are, such as sugar, usually do not conduct electricity.

Acids and Bases

Litmus paper is an **indicator,** a substance that changes color when it comes in contact with an acid or a base.

An **acid** is any compound that produces hydrogen ions (H^+) in water. (An **ion** is simply an atom that has gained or lost electrons and therefore has a positive or negative charge.) The greater the concentration of hydrogen ions produced, the stronger the acid. Acids taste sour, change blue litmus paper red, and react with metals to produce hydrogen gas. Acidic solutions also conduct electricity.

A **base** is any compound that produces hydroxide ions (OH^-) in water. The greater the concentration of hydroxide ions produced, the stronger the base. Bases taste bitter, change red litmus paper blue, feel slippery, and dissolve oils and fats. Bases also conduct electricity.

SEE ALSO
256 Atomic Structure
269 Chemical Reactions
317 Current Electricity

Indicators like litmus paper are used to tell if a substance is acidic or basic. The **pH scale** is used to tell *how* acidic or basic a substance is. Simply put, the pH of a solution is a measure of the hydrogen ion (H^+) concentration in the solution on a scale of 0 to 14. A solution with a pH of less than 7 is considered acidic. The lower the pH, the more acidic the solution. Likewise, a solution with a pH of more than 7 is considered basic. The greater the pH, the more basic the solution. A solution with a pH of 7 is considered neutral—neither acidic nor basic.

Word Watch!

pH comes from the French "pouvoir hydrogène," meaning "hydrogen power."

pH Scale with Values of Some Common Substances

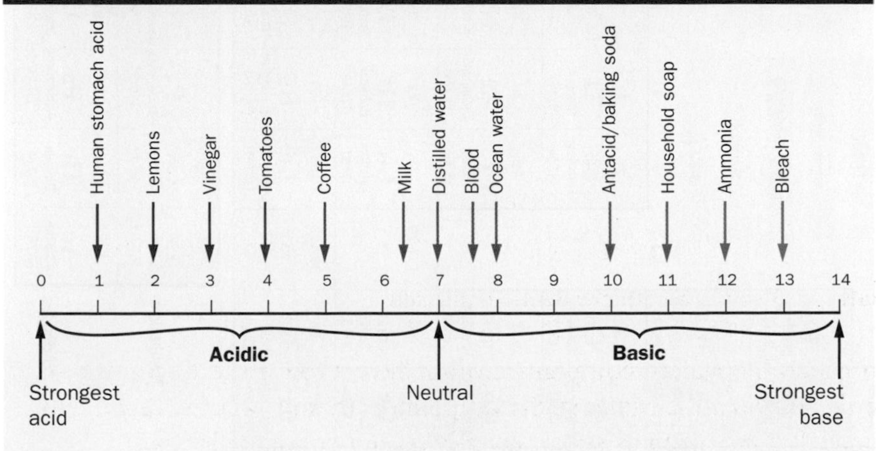

Periodic Table of Elements

- Alkali metals
- Alkaline earth metals
- Transition metals
- Lanthanide series
- Actinide series
- Other metals
- Nonmetals
- Noble gases

Key	
Atomic Number	6
Chemical Symbol	C
Element Name	Carbon
Atomic Mass	12.011

1	2		3	4	5	6	7	8	9	10	11	12	13	14	15	16	17	18
1 **H** Hydrogen 1.0079																		2 **He** Helium 4.0026
3 **Li** Lithium 6.941	4 **Be** Beryllium 9.0122												5 **B** Boron 10.811	6 **C** Carbon 12.011	7 **N** Nitrogen 14.007	8 **O** Oxygen 15.999	9 **F** Fluorine 18.998	10 **Ne** Neon 20.180
11 **Na** Sodium 22.990	12 **Mg** Magnesium 24.305												13 **Al** Aluminum 26.982	14 **Si** Silicon 28.086	15 **P** Phosphorus 30.974	16 **S** Sulfur 32.066	17 **Cl** Chlorine 35.453	18 **Ar** Argon 39.948
19 **K** Potassium 39.098	20 **Ca** Calcium 40.078		21 **Sc** Scandium 44.956	22 **Ti** Titanium 47.867	23 **V** Vanadium 50.942	24 **Cr** Chromium 51.996	25 **Mn** Manganese 54.938	26 **Fe** Iron 55.845	27 **Co** Cobalt 58.933	28 **Ni** Nickel 58.693	29 **Cu** Copper 63.546	30 **Zn** Zinc 65.41	31 **Ga** Gallium 69.723	32 **Ge** Germanium 72.64	33 **As** Arsenic 74.922	34 **Se** Selenium 78.96	35 **Br** Bromine 79.904	36 **Kr** Krypton 83.80
37 **Rb** Rubidium 85.468	38 **Sr** Strontium 87.62		39 **Y** Yttrium 88.906	40 **Zr** Zirconium 91.224	41 **Nb** Niobium 92.906	42 **Mo** Molybdenum 95.94	43 **Tc** Technetium (97.907)	44 **Ru** Ruthenium 101.07	45 **Rh** Rhodium 102.91	46 **Pd** Palladium 106.42	47 **Ag** Silver 107.87	48 **Cd** Cadmium 112.41	49 **In** Indium 114.82	50 **Sn** Tin 118.71	51 **Sb** Antimony 121.76	52 **Te** Tellurium 127.60	53 **I** Iodine 126.90	54 **Xe** Xenon 131.29
55 **Cs** Cesium 132.91	56 **Ba** Barium 137.33	57-70 *	71 **Lu** Lutetium 174.97	72 **Hf** Hafnium 178.49	73 **Ta** Tantalum 180.95	74 **W** Tungsten 183.84	75 **Re** Rhenium 186.21	76 **Os** Osmium 190.23	77 **Ir** Iridium 192.22	78 **Pt** Platinum 195.08	79 **Au** Gold 196.97	80 **Hg** Mercury 200.59	81 **Tl** Thallium 204.38	82 **Pb** Lead 207.2	83 **Bi** Bismuth 208.98	84 **Po** Polonium (208.98)	85 **At** Astatine (209.99)	86 **Rn** Radon (222.02)
87 **Fr** Francium (223.02)	88 **Ra** Radium (226.03)	89-102 **	103 **Lr** Lawrencium (262.11)	104 **Rf** Rutherfordium (261.11)	105 **Db** Dubnium (262.11)	106 **Sg** Seaborgium (266.12)	107 **Bh** Bohrium (264.12)	108 **Hs** Hassium (277)	109 **Mt** Meitnerium (268.14)	110 **Ds** Darmstadtium (271)	111 **Rg** Roentgenium (272)	112† **Uub** Ununbium (277)	113† **Uut** Ununtrium (284)	114† **Uuq** Ununquadium (289)	115 † **Uup** Urunpentium (288)	116† **Uuh** Ununhexium (289)		

*Lanthanides	57 **La** Lanthanum 138.91	58 **Ce** Cerium 140.12	59 **Pr** Praseodymium 140.91	60 **Nd** Neodymium 144.24	61 **Pm** Promethium (144.91)	62 **Sm** Samarium 150.36	63 **Eu** Europium 151.96	64 **Gd** Gadolinium 157.25	65 **Tb** Terbium 158.93	66 **Dy** Dysprosium 162.50	67 **Ho** Holmium 164.93	68 **Er** Erbium 167.26	69 **Tm** Thulium 168.93	70 **Yb** Ytterbium 173.04
**Actinides	89 **Ac** Actinium (227.03)	90 **Th** Thorium 232.04	91 **Pa** Protactinium 231.04	92 **U** Uranium 238.03	93 **Np** Neptunium (237.05)	94 **Pu** Plutonium (244.06)	95 **Am** Americium (243.06)	96 **Cm** Curium (247.07)	97 **Bk** Berkelium (247.07)	98 **Cf** Californium (251.08)	99 **Es** Einsteinium (252.08)	100 **Fm** Fermium (257.10)	101 **Md** Mendelevium (258.10)	102 **No** Nobelium (259.10)

†Scientists have discovered elements 112, 113, 114, 115, and 116, but other scientists have to repeat their experiments to make these elements official.

Periodic Table

265

Back in 1869, Russian chemist Dmitri Mendeléev organized all the known elements into a chart according to their properties. Today that chart is known as the **periodic table of elements.**

SEE ALSO
440 History of Science Time Line
450 Famous Scientists

The periodic table is made up of horizontal rows and vertical columns of boxes. Each box contains specific information about a single element. This information includes the element's name, the chemical symbol for the element, the element's atomic number, and the element's atomic mass.

The **chemical symbol** is one or two letters used to represent the element's name. The first letter is always capitalized; the second letter, if there is one, is always lowercase. The **atomic mass** is the average mass of an atom of that element. Atomic mass is measured in atomic mass units (amu). The **atomic number** is the number of protons in an atom of that element.

Word Watch!

Many of the chemical symbols used in the periodic table come from the Latin words for those elements. For example, *Fe* is the symbol for the element iron. The Latin word for iron is *ferrum*.

Each row of elements in the periodic table is called a **period.** If you read the elements in each period from left to right, you will see that they are arranged in order by their atomic number.

Each column in the periodic table is called a **group** or **family.** The elements in each group share similar physical and chemical properties.

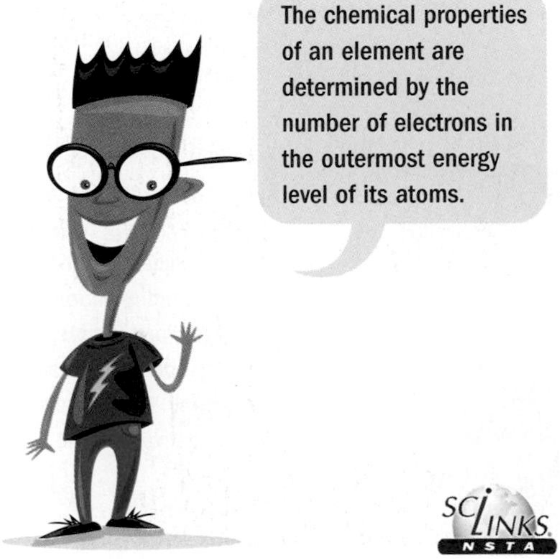

The chemical properties of an element are determined by the number of electrons in the outermost energy level of its atoms.

SEE ALSO
251 Properties of Matter
256 Atomic Structure

SciLinks NSTA
Keyword: Periodic Table
www.scilinks.org
Code: GSSM265

266 Chemical Formulas, Reactions, and Equations

"A water molecule contains two atoms of hydrogen and one atom of oxygen." If you had to describe each chemical compound like this, you'd spend all day writing! To simplify how we talk about chemicals, scientists came up with a form of shorthand in which symbols and numbers take the place of words.

267 Chemical Formulas

Just as each individual element in the periodic table is represented by a chemical symbol, so are molecules and compounds represented by combinations of chemical symbols and numbers. A **chemical formula** is a shorthand way of describing a chemical compound.

SEE ALSO
265 Periodic Table
255 Atoms
261 Molecules
262 Compounds

For example, H_2 is the chemical formula for a molecule of hydrogen. The small number 2 in the subscript, or lowered, position indicates that the hydrogen molecule contains two hydrogen atoms bonded together. $3H_2$ is the chemical formula for three hydrogen molecules, each of which contains two hydrogen atoms. The large number 3 in front of the H is called a **coefficient.**

CO_2 is the chemical formula for the compound carbon dioxide. A molecule of carbon dioxide contains one atom of carbon (C) bonded to two atoms of oxygen (O_2). The formula $Ca(NO_3)_2$ represents a compound whose molecules consist of one calcium atom bonded to two groups each of one nitrogen atom and three oxygen atoms. That makes a total of one calcium atom, two nitrogen atoms, and six oxygen atoms in each molecule of the compound.

Adding a plus or minus sign in the superscript, or raised, position following a chemical symbol indicates that the atom or compound is an ion—it has a charge. For example, Na^+ is the symbol for a positive sodium ion. Cl^- is the symbol for a negative chlorine ion.

Electron-Dot Diagrams

Another way to represent molecules and compounds is with **electron-dot diagrams.** In these diagrams, electrons in the outermost energy level of an atom are represented as dots around an element's symbol. Here are the electron-dot diagrams for some common elements.

Remember, the number of electrons in the outermost energy level of an atom determines the chemical properties of that element.

SEE ALSO
256 Atomic Structure

Word Watch!

The electrons in the outermost energy level of an atom are often called *valence electrons.*

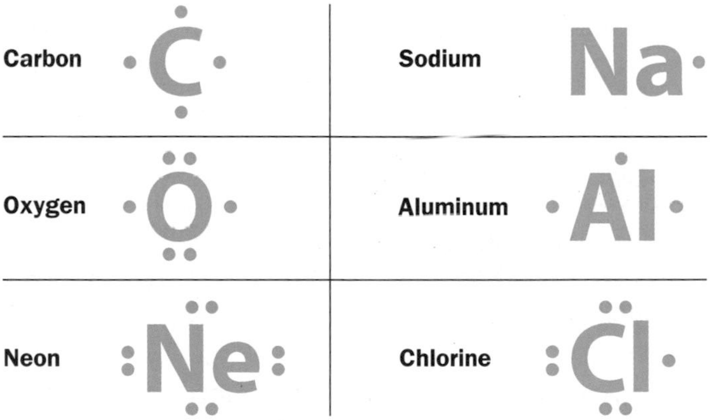
Carbon
C
Sodium
Na
Oxygen
O
Aluminum
Al
Neon
Ne
Chlorine
Cl

Electron-dot diagrams can be used to show how two elements share electrons in covalent bonding.

SEE ALSO
263 Chemical Bonds

H_2O—A molecule of water

One oxygen atom shares a pair of electrons with each of two hydrogen atoms.

269 Chemical Reactions

Have you ever added vinegar to baking soda? When these two substances are mixed together, they begin to bubble and fizz. That's because carbon dioxide gas is produced when the vinegar reacts chemically with the baking soda.

A **chemical reaction** takes place when one or more substances change to form one or more new substances. The substances that undergo the change are called the **reactants.** The substances that result from this change are called the **products.** In the example above, vinegar and baking soda are the reactants, and carbon dioxide gas is one of the products.

The products of a chemical reaction can include compounds that did not exist before the reaction. However, chemical reactions never produce compounds with elements not found in the reactants. Chemical reactions can only rearrange elements in the reactants to produce new compounds.

270 Chemical Equations

SEE ALSO
267 Chemical Formulas

How could you describe a chemical reaction to someone without using words? You could write a chemical equation. A **chemical equation** is a way of describing a chemical reaction using chemical formulas.

For example, hydrogen and oxygen atoms react chemically to produce water. The chemical equation that represents this is as follows:

$$2H_2 + O_2 \rightarrow 2H_2O$$

The reactants in a chemical equation are always on the left side of the equation, and the products are always on the right.

In any chemical reaction, the number and kinds of atoms in the reactants must equal the number and kinds of atoms in the products. In other words, the equation must be balanced. This rule obeys the **law of conservation of mass,** which states that matter can be neither created nor destroyed.

Let's look again at the equation

$$2H_2 + O_2 \rightarrow 2H_2O$$

Four hydrogen atoms ($2 \times H_2$) combine with two oxygen atoms (O_2) to form two molecules of water ($2 \times H_2O$):

$$2H_2 \quad + \quad O_2 \quad \rightarrow \quad 2H_2O$$

4 hydrogen atoms + 2 oxygen atoms → 4 hydrogen atoms and 2 oxygen atoms combined as 2 molecules of water

Note that the coefficient "2" is needed before each "H_2" in order for the equation to be balanced.

You can also use electron-dot diagrams in an equation to represent a chemical reaction.

SEE ALSO 268 Electron-Dot Diagrams

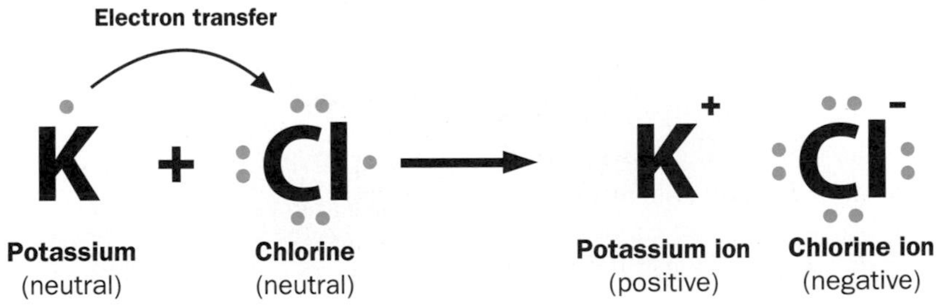

Potassium and chlorine combine to form potassium chloride.

Mixtures, Solutions, and Suspensions

271

SEE ALSO
262 Compounds

A compound is a substance made of two or more elements that are combined chemically. The ratio of the elements that form a particular compound is always the same. The properties of a compound are different from the properties of the elements from which it is made. A compound can be separated only by chemical means. Table salt (NaCl, or sodium chloride) is an example of a compound.

A **mixture** is a combination of two or more substances that have *not* combined chemically. A mixture can contain elements, compounds, or both, and in any amounts. Because the substances in a mixture are not combined chemically, they keep their unique properties and can be separated by physical means. Fruit salad is an example of a mixture.

Let's say you want to cook a pot of rice. First you add a pinch of salt to the water and stir. You notice the salt crystals seem to disappear. Where did they go? They dissolved and spread out evenly in the pot of water. This kind of mixture is called a solution. A **solution** is a mixture that looks like a single substance and has the same properties throughout.

Once the salted water begins to boil, you add the rice and stir. The rice grains swirl around in the pot of water. When you stop stirring, they settle to the bottom. This kind of mixture, in which the components are dispersed but large enough to see and to settle out, is called a **suspension.**

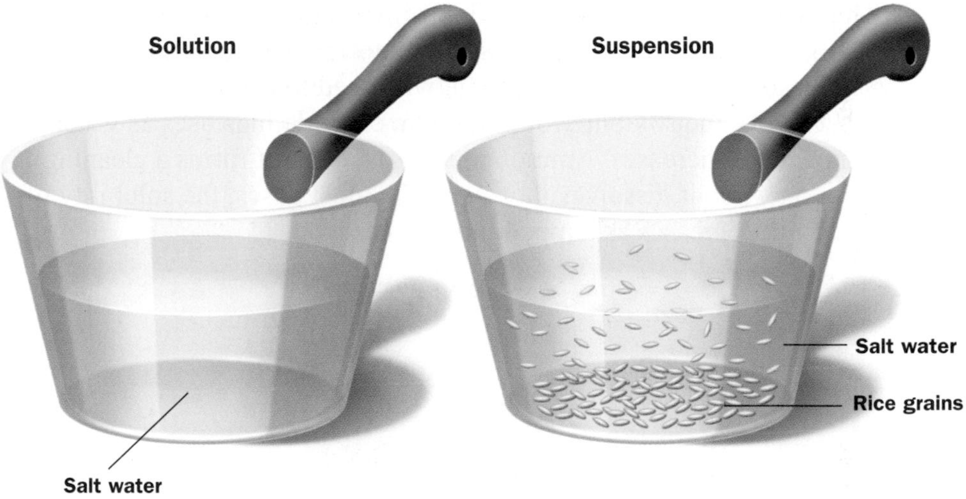

Parts of a Solution

272

Within a solution, one substance is dissolved in another substance. The substance that dissolves is called a **solute.** The substance into which a solute dissolves is called a **solvent.** In the example of salt water, the salt is the solute and the water is the solvent.

Solutions are not always in liquid form, however. Some gases and solids are also considered solutions. For example, the air you breathe contains oxygen dissolved in nitrogen. Bronze is a solution of the metals copper and tin.

Many substances dissolve in water. For this reason, water is considered a "universal" solvent.

273 Solubility and Temperature

SEE ALSO

271 Mixtures, Solutions, and Suspensions
272 Parts of a Solution

Hot tea will dissolve more sugar than cold tea. But cold soda will dissolve more carbon dioxide gas than warm soda. Temperature has an effect on solubility. **Solubility** is the ability of a substance to dissolve in another substance.

The graph shows how the solubility of two substances in water changes with temperature. Potassium chloride, KCl, is a solid. It is used instead of table salt by people who need to avoid sodium. Like most solids, the solubility of potassium chloride increases as water temperature increases. Ammonia, NH_3, is a gas. It forms a cleaning solution when it dissolves in water. Like most gases, the solubility of ammonia decreases as temperature increases.

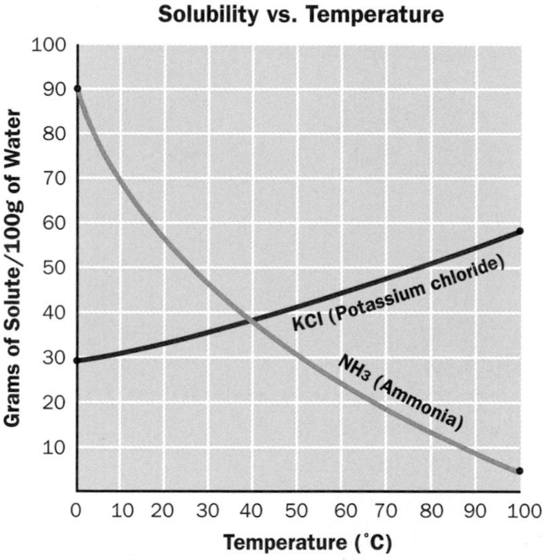

Temperature is not the only factor that affects solubility. Solubility of gases is also greatly affected by changes in pressure. Have you noticed what happens when you open a can of soda? Carbon dioxide dissolved in the liquid escapes rapidly from the bottle, sometimes more rapidly than you would like! Carbon dioxide gas is more soluble at higher pressures. When you open the can, you decrease the pressure on the gas, and it comes out of solution.

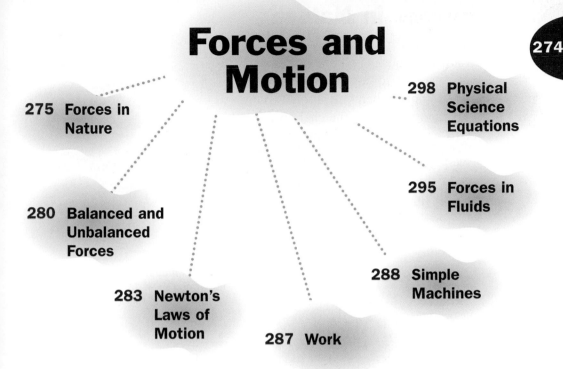

Forces and Motion

274

Forces are acting all around you. Objects, including you, are being pushed and pulled in different directions. Sometimes these forces cause motion, like when you slide a chair across the floor or throw a ball into the air. But did you know that even stationary objects have forces acting on them?

Forces are acting on the juggler as well as on the bean bags he is juggling.

Forces in Nature

275

SEE ALSO
280 Balanced and Unbalanced Forces
283 Newton's Laws of Motion

A **force** is a push or a pull on an object. Objects exert forces on each other. For example, when you sit on a chair, you exert a force on the chair and the chair exerts a force back on you.

Every force has a certain strength, or magnitude. It also has a direction. For example, as you stand on the ground, you exert a force on the ground equal to your weight and in a downward direction.

Force is measured in units called newtons (N). It takes about 45 N of force to lift the average cat.

Did You Know?

SEE ALSO
450 Famous Scientists

Newtons are named for the English scientist who came up with the set of laws that describe forces and motion—Sir Isaac Newton.

Forces can affect objects in several ways. For example, forces acting on a stationary object can set the object in motion. Or they can change a moving object's speed and/or the direction it's moving in. A force can also affect an object without making it move. Forces acting on a stationary object can change the object's shape, like when you sit on an inner tube and the sides bulge out.

SEE ALSO
281 Balanced Forces

Gravity

What happens when you hold up an apple and then let go of it? It falls to the ground. Why? Because the apple and Earth are attracted to each other. **Gravity** is the force of attraction between objects that have mass. Since all objects have mass, gravity acts between all objects, even apples and planets!

The strength of gravity between two objects depends on two things: the mass of the objects and the distance between them.

Mass is a measure of the amount of "stuff" in an object. The greater the mass of either object, the stronger the gravity between them. The force of gravity between Earth and the apple is stronger than the force of gravity between you and the apple because Earth has much more mass than you do. That explains why the apple falls to the ground when you let go of it, instead of sticking to your hand.

SEE ALSO
285 Newton's Second Law of Motion
286 Newton's Third Law of Motion

Science Alert!

Don't confuse mass with weight. Mass is a property of an object and does not depend on the object's location. Weight is a measure of the force of gravity acting on an object, and therefore can vary depending on the object's location. For example, your body has the same mass on Earth as it does on the moon, but you weigh about six times more on Earth than you would on the moon.

The strength of gravity between two objects also depends on the distance between the two objects. The closer together the objects, the stronger the gravitational force. The farther apart the objects, the weaker the force.

277 Electric and Magnetic Forces

SEE ALSO
256 Atomic Structure
320 Magnetism
314 Electricity and Magnetism

Electric force and **magnetic force** are closely related. This is because both are caused by negative and positive charges in matter. Atoms, which make up all matter, contain a positively charged nucleus and a negatively charged cloud of electrons. When charges from one piece of matter interact with those of another piece of matter, they produce both electric and magnetic forces. These forces can be attractive (pulling the objects together) or repulsive (pushing the objects apart).

Electric forces are those associated with unmoving charges. For example, when you rub a glass rod with silk, it becomes positively charged. When you then hang the rod close to another rod that has been rubbed with silk the same way, the two rods will repel one another. This is because both rods are positively charged, and like charges repel each other.

SEE ALSO
316 Static Electricity

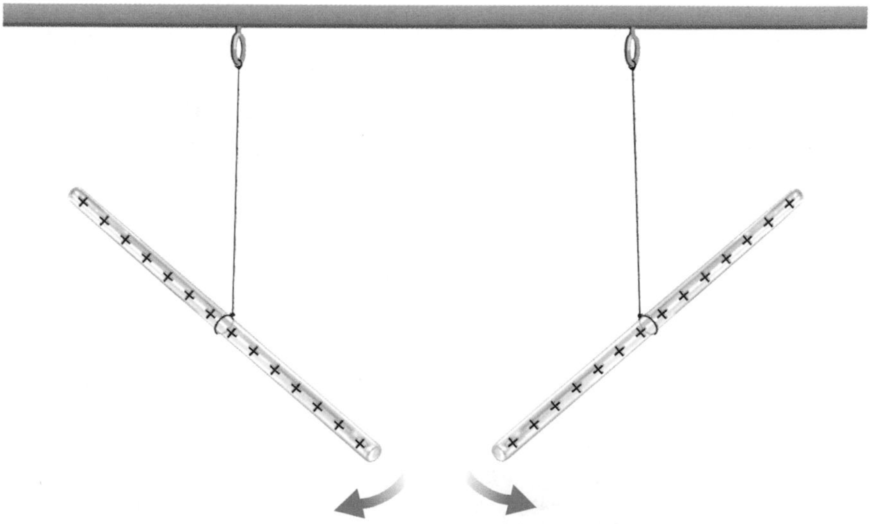

SEE ALSO
265 Periodic Table
320 Magnetism
321 Electro-magnetism

Magnetic forces, on the other hand, are created by moving electric charges. A **magnet** is any material that attracts iron, a metallic element. A magnetic force exists between a magnet and the piece of iron it is attracted to.

Did You Know?

While magnets provide the most visible evidence of magnetism, weak magnetic forces exist within all objects.

Much like gravitational force, electric and magnetic forces decrease when the distance between the interacting objects increases. In other words, as two objects move farther apart, the electric and magnetic forces between them, whether attraction or repulsion, decrease.

SEE ALSO
276 Gravity

Magnetic force decreases with distance.

Centripetal Force

278

Centripetal force is the force that causes objects to move in a circular path. The moon, for example, constantly **revolves** around, or circles, Earth. Gravity between Earth and the moon provides the centripetal force that pulls the moon towards the center of Earth, keeping it in orbit.

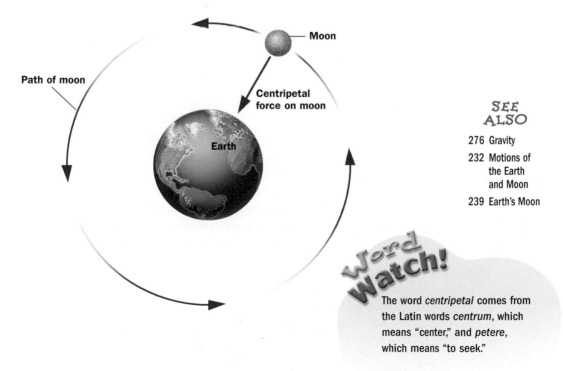

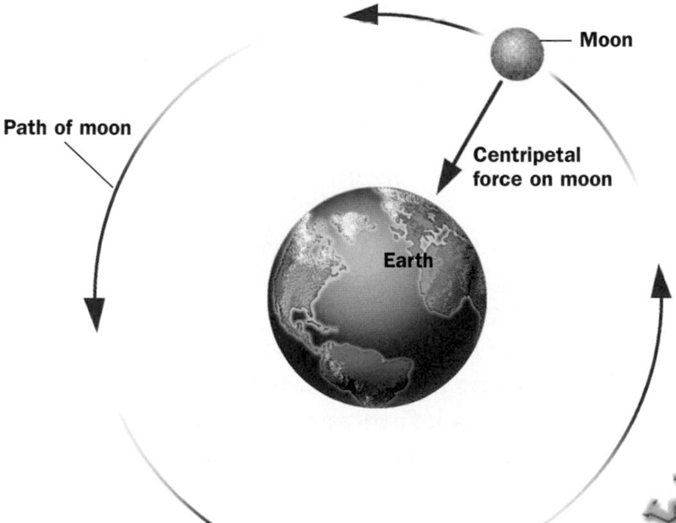

SEE ALSO
276 Gravity
232 Motions of the Earth and Moon
239 Earth's Moon

Word Watch!

The word *centripetal* comes from the Latin words *centrum*, which means "center," and *petere*, which means "to seek."

279 **Friction**

Friction is the force that opposes motion between two surfaces that are in contact with each other. Friction might prevent motion from starting, or it might oppose motion in progress. Friction between two solid surfaces sliding against each other is known as **sliding friction.**

Other types of friction include rolling friction, static friction, and fluid friction, or drag.

Let's say you slide the salt shaker to your best friend across the table, and the shaker stops just short of her plate. Perfect! Friction between the tabletop and the base of the salt shaker opposes the sliding motion of the salt shaker, making it slow down and stop moving.

The amount of friction between two surfaces depends on two things: what the two surfaces are made of and how hard they are pressing against each other. Obviously, two pieces of ice will slide past each other more easily than two pieces of sandpaper. Likewise, it's easier to drag a piece of sandpaper lightly over a surface than it is to press down on it firmly as you push or pull it.

Did You Know?

Sometimes friction is helpful. People often sprinkle sand on icy walkways. There is more friction between your shoes and the sandy ice than there is between your shoes and plain ice. As a result, you are less likely to slip and slide!

Balanced and Unbalanced Forces

Remember that the unit for force is *newtons*, abbreviated "N."

More than one force can—and usually does—act on an object at the same time. Sometimes these forces are applied in the same direction, like when you and your brother work together to move a heavy box. Sometimes the forces are applied in different directions, like when you and your brother both pull on the TV remote control. The **net force** on an object is the combination of all the forces acting on it.

To find the net force of forces that are acting in the same direction, simply add them together. For example, if you pull on a box with a force of 30 N while your brother pushes with a force of 20 N in the same direction, the total amount of force applied to the box in that direction is 50 N.

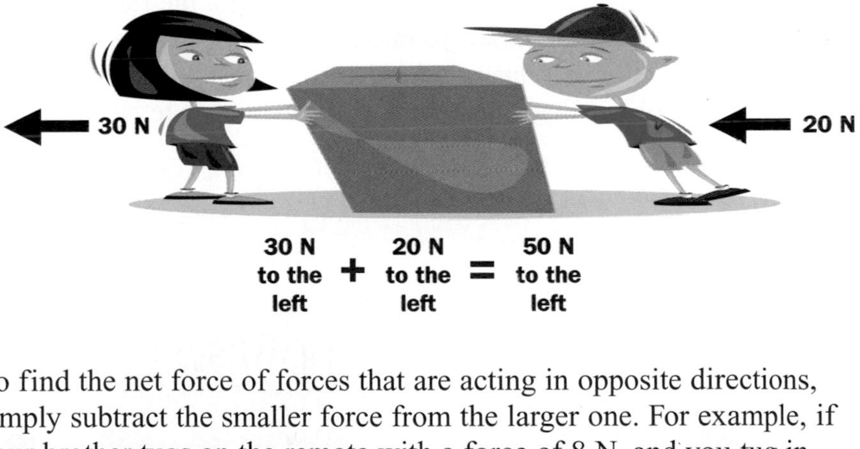

30 N to the left + 20 N to the left = 50 N to the left

To find the net force of forces that are acting in opposite directions, simply subtract the smaller force from the larger one. For example, if your brother tugs on the remote with a force of 8 N, and you tug in the opposite direction with a force of 10 N, the net force applied to the remote is 2 N in your direction. You win!

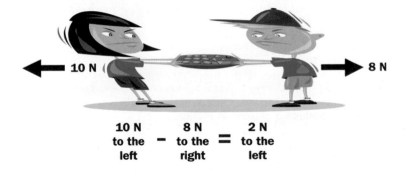

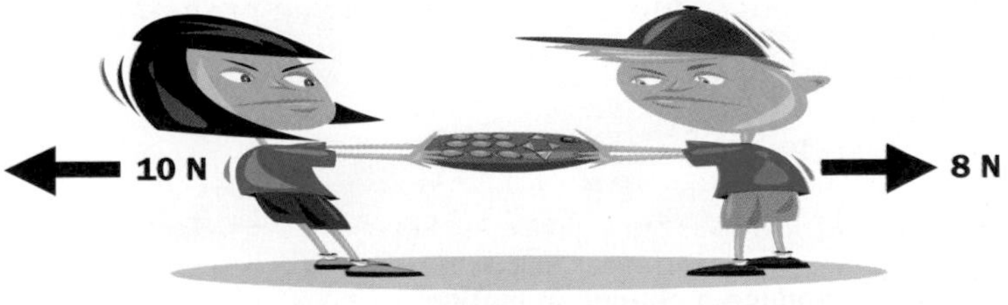

10 N to the left - 8 N to the right = 2 N to the left

281 Balanced Forces

When the net force on an object is zero, the forces are said to be balanced. **Balanced forces** produce no change in the motion of an object. That means an object that is not moving will stay motionless, while an object that is moving will maintain its speed and direction.

This does not mean, however, that balanced forces have no effect on an object. Balanced forces can crush an object. That's what happens, for example, when you squeeze a rubber ball. The object's physical properties may be affected, even if its motion does not change.

282 Unbalanced Forces

When the net force on an object is greater than zero, the forces are said to be unbalanced. **Unbalanced forces** produce a change in the motion of an object. That means a motionless object will begin to move, while an object that is already moving will change its speed and/or direction.

SEE ALSO
284 Newton's First Law of Motion

Unbalanced forces produce a change in motion.

Newton's Laws of Motion 283

Sir Isaac Newton

In 1687, English physicist and mathematician Isaac Newton published *Philosophiae Naturalis Principia Mathematica (Mathematical Principles in Natural History)*. In this book he explained the relationship between force and motion. His three **laws of motion** can be used to explain the movement of all objects in the universe.

Newton's First Law of Motion 284

An object at rest will stay at rest unless acted on by an unbalanced force. An object in motion will stay in motion at the same speed and in the same direction unless acted on by an unbalanced force.

According to Newton's first law, an object will keep doing whatever it's doing, whether sitting still or moving, unless the forces acting on it become unbalanced—in other words, unless it has a net force greater than zero acting on it.

For example, if you leave your skateboard lying in the driveway, it will stay there until someone moves it. That's the first part of the law. If you've ever toppled over the front of your skateboard after hitting a curb, you've experienced the second part of the law. The board stops short but you keep moving—until something stops *you*.

Word Watch!

Speed is the distance traveled by an object in a given amount of time. **Velocity** is an object's speed *and* direction at a given instant. **Acceleration** is the change in an object's velocity over time.

SciLinks NSTA
Keyword: Newton's Laws
www.scilinks.org
Code: GSSM283

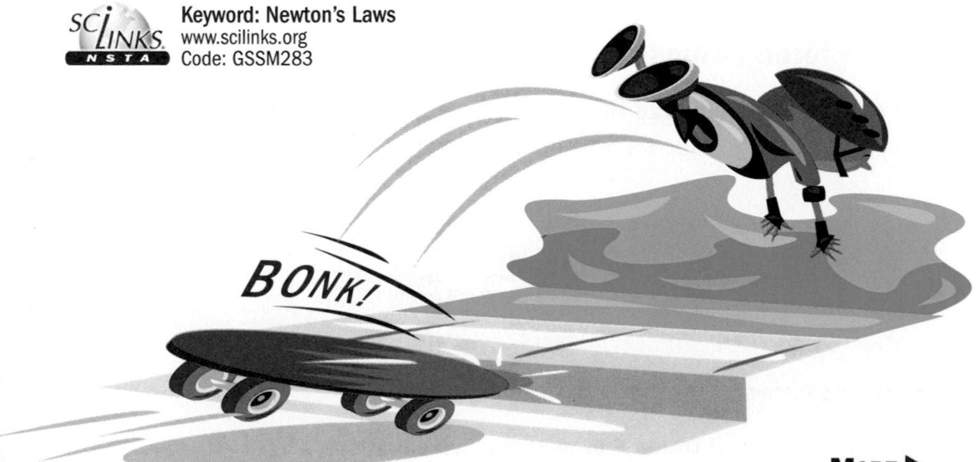

MORE ▶

Newton's first law of motion is also called the law of inertia. **Inertia** is an object's tendency to resist a change in motion. All objects have inertia. The greater an object's mass, the greater its inertia and the larger the force needed to overcome the inertia.

285 Newton's Second Law of Motion

The acceleration of an object by a force is inversely proportional to the mass of the object and directly proportional to the force.

To say that two quantities are *inversely proportional* means that as one increases, the other decrease by the same ratio. To say that two quantities are *directly proportional* means that as one increases, the other increases by the same ratio; and as one decreases, so does the other by the same ratio.

Newton's second law sounds trickier than it is. Let's break it down into two parts:

The first part states that the smaller the mass of an object, the greater its acceleration when a certain force is applied to the object. For example, if you apply the same force to an object with a small mass, like a marble, and an object with a large mass, like a bowling ball, the object with the small mass will accelerate more than the object with the large mass.

The second part states that the greater the force applied to an object, the greater the object's acceleration. For example, if you apply a large force and a small force to objects of equal mass, the object acted on by the larger force will accelerate more.

SEE ALSO
298 Physical Science Equations

The relationship between acceleration, mass, and force can be written mathematically, as follows:

force = mass × acceleration, or F = m × a

You could also rearrange this equation to find acceleration or mass. A formula triangle shows you how to do this:

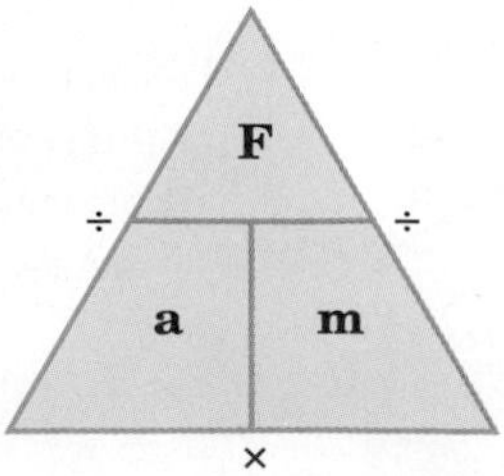

Divide *F* by *m* to find acceleration.
Divide *F* by *a* to find mass.

Newton's second law also explains why a heavy object and a light object dropped from the same height will hit the ground at the same time: they both accelerate at the same rate. Look at the diagram of the falling marble and bowling ball. Because the marble has less mass, the force of gravity on it is smaller. The bowling ball has more mass and so has a greater force of gravity acting on it.

SEE ALSO
276 Gravity

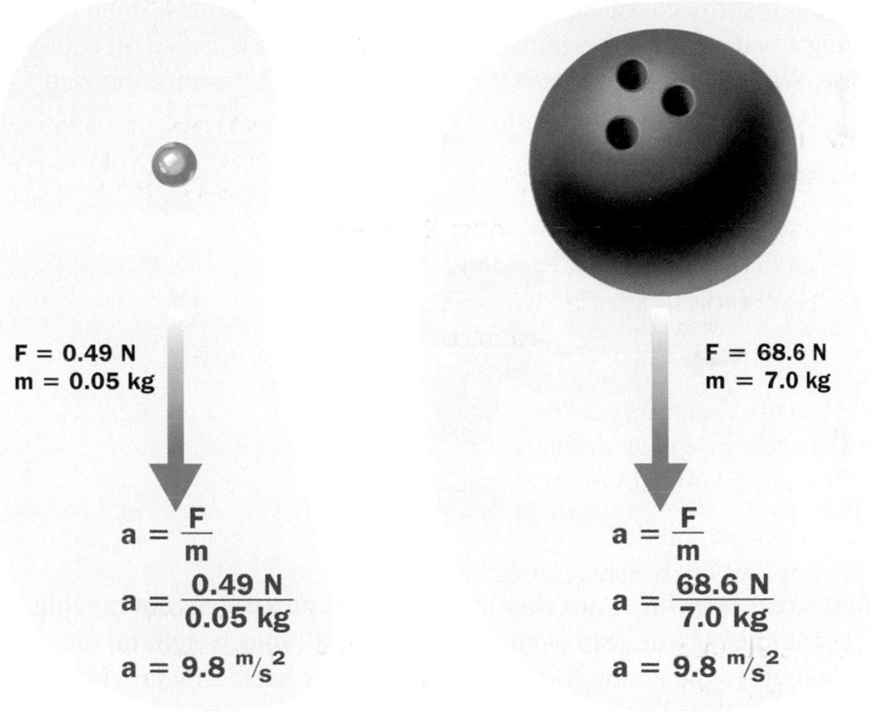

Falling objects don't accelerate through their whole fall. Eventually, the force of air resistance pushing up against the object equals the force of gravity pulling down on the object. When that happens, the net force on the falling object becomes zero, and so the object stops accelerating. This final speed is called **terminal speed.**

Raindrops reach terminal speed as they fall. That's why they don't hurt you. Their terminal speed is too low to cause injury.

SCILINKS NSTA
Keyword: Newton's Laws
www.scilinks.org
Code: GSSM283

286

Newton's Third Law of Motion

For every action, there is an equal but opposite reaction.

Newton's third law says that when one object exerts a force on a second object, the second object exerts a force back that is equal in size but opposite in direction. In other words, all forces act in pairs.

You can test the claim easily. Put on a pair of roller skates, stand facing a wall, and push against the wall. Your push is called an action force. What happens? You move backwards. Why? Because the wall pushes back on you. That's called a reaction force.

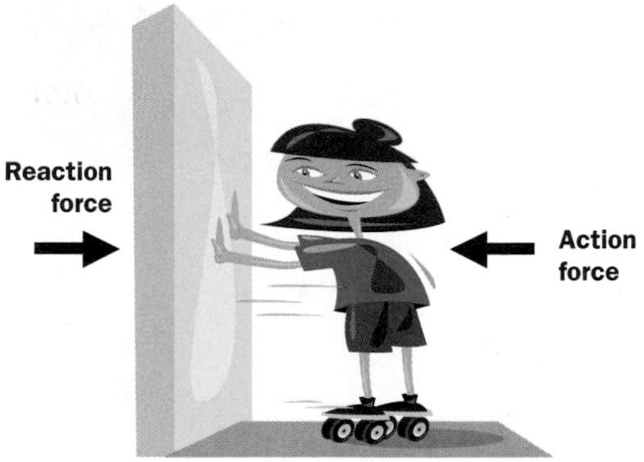

Action/reaction forces are at work even when objects are not moving. For example, as you lean against a wall to rest (your weight on the wall provides the action force), the wall pushes back on you with the same force (the reaction force). So, neither of you move.

SCILINKS NSTA Keyword: Newton's Laws
www.scilinks.org
Code: GSSM283

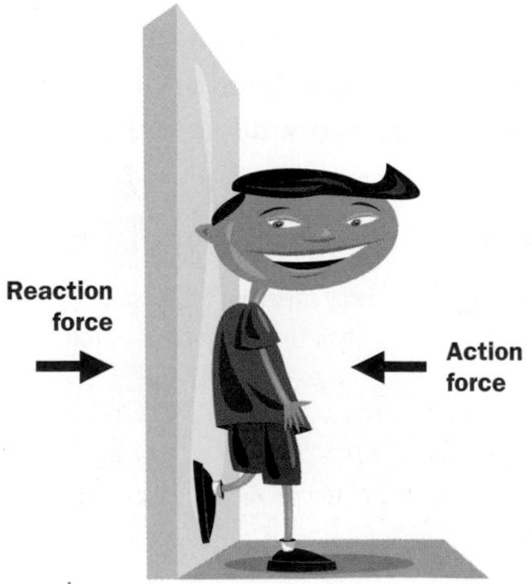

Work

What do you consider work? You might think that reading a science book is hard work. But scientists wouldn't consider that work at all. Scientists have something very specific in mind when they use the term *work*.

In the world of science, **work** is accomplished when force is applied to an object and the object moves a distance. Work is measured in newton-meters, more commonly called **joules (J).** If you want to find out how much work is being done, you can use this formula:

SEE ALSO
298 Physical Science Equations

work = force × distance, or W = F × d

For example, imagine that you push a large box with a force of 10 newtons. But because the box is so heavy, it doesn't budge. How much work have you done?

Solution: W = F × d
W = 10 newtons × 0 meters
W = 0 joules

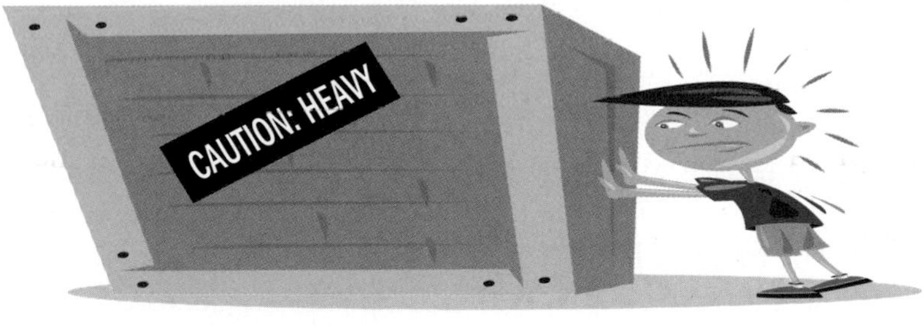

Next, imagine that you push the box with a force of 30 newtons over a distance of 2 meters. How much work have you done?

Solution: W = F × d
W = 30 newtons × 2 meters
W = 60 joules

How much work would you do if you pushed the same box 3 meters using 20 newtons of force? Again 60 joules!

288

Simple Machines

A **simple machine** is a device that makes work easier. There are six types of simple machines: the inclined plane, the wedge, the screw, the lever, the wheel and axle, and the pulley.

All simple machines transfer force. Some change the direction of force, while others change the magnitude, or strength, of force. Still others change both the direction *and* the magnitude of force.

Most simple machines make work easier by allowing you to use less force to move an object. The catch, however, is that the force must be applied over a greater distance. But some machines make work easier by allowing you to move things farther and/or faster. In these machines, a larger force is required, but over a shorter distance.

SEE ALSO
298 Physical Science Equations

The **mechanical advantage** of a simple machine can be calculated by dividing the output force (F_{out}) by the input force (F_{in}).

$$MA = \frac{F_{out}}{F_{in}}$$

SCILINKS NSTA
Keyword: Simple Machines
www.scilinks.org
Code: GSSM288

289

Inclined Plane

An **inclined plane** is really just a ramp, a flat surface that slopes. This type of simple machine is the only one that does not move. Instead, objects are moved over it in order to raise them. It takes less force to move an object up an inclined plane than it does to lift the object straight up. The tradeoff is that the object must be moved a greater distance—the entire length of the inclined plane—to achieve the same height.

Did You Know?

The pyramids in Egypt were built thousands of years ago using inclined planes.

Wedge 290

A **wedge** is an inclined plane that moves. Wedges are used to split or lift objects. Force is applied to the wide end of the wedge and gets transferred to the sides. In the process, the object either splits apart or gets lifted. It takes less force to drive a wedge into or under an object than it does to separate or lift the object yourself. However, the wedge must be driven a long distance (the length of the wedge) in order to move the object a short distance (the width of the wedge). Cutting tools (axes, scissor blades, saw blades), nail points, and plows are all examples of wedges.

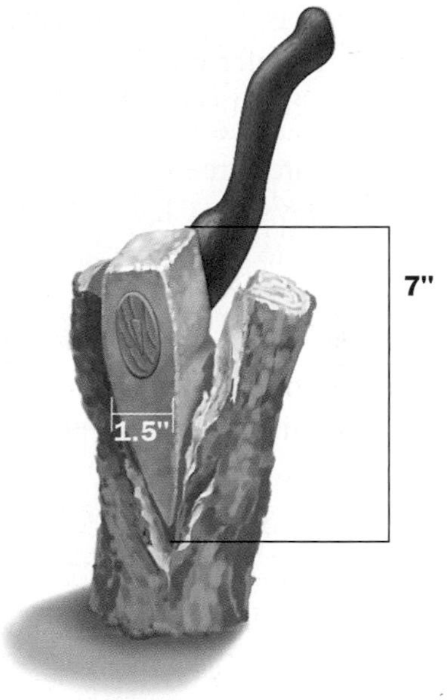

Screw 291

A **screw** is an inclined plane wrapped around a cylinder. The spiral ridges around the shaft of the screw are called threads. As the screw is turned, the threads pull the object up the shaft. It takes less force to turn a screw than to pound a nail the same size. However, the screw must be turned many times, while a nail can be driven in just a few blows of a hammer.

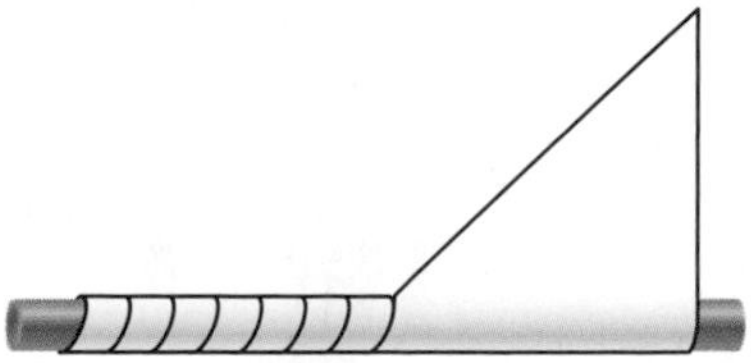

The more threads there are on a screw, the longer the inclined plane, and the easier it is to turn.

292 Lever

A **lever** is a long rigid bar that rests on and pivots around a support, called a **fulcrum.** Applying a force (called the **effort**) to one part of the lever causes the **load** at another place on the lever to move.

There are three types of levers: **first-class, second-class,** and **third-class levers.** A lever is classified by the location of its fulcrum in relation to the effort and load.

Type of Lever		Common Example
First-class	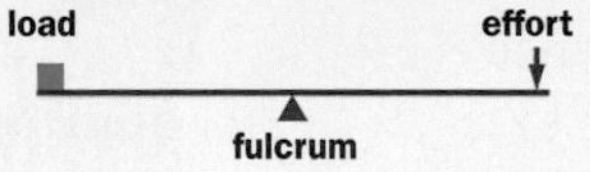	
Second-class	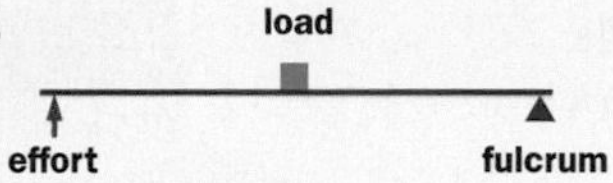	
Third-class	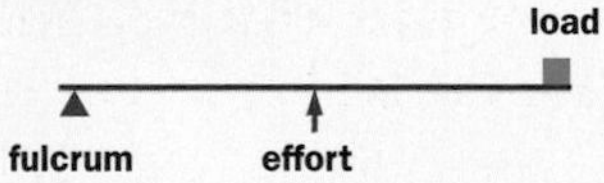	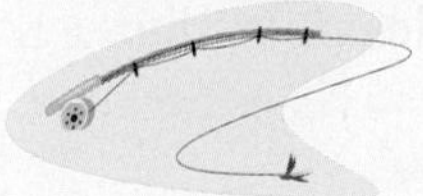

293 Wheel and Axle

A **wheel and axle** is a simple machine that consists of a shaft, called the axle, inserted through the middle of a wheel. Any force that gets applied to the wheel gets transferred to the axle, and vice versa.

When force is applied to the wheel, the difference in size between the wheel and its axle causes the force to get magnified as it is transferred to the axle. A screwdriver is an example of this. When force is applied to the axle, however, distance gets magnified. A bicycle wheel is an example of this.

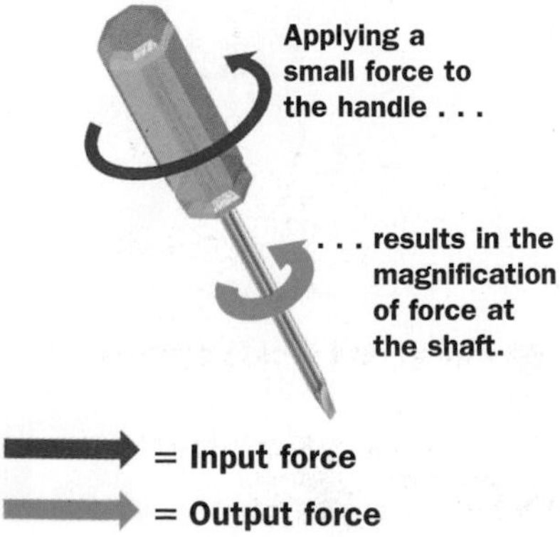

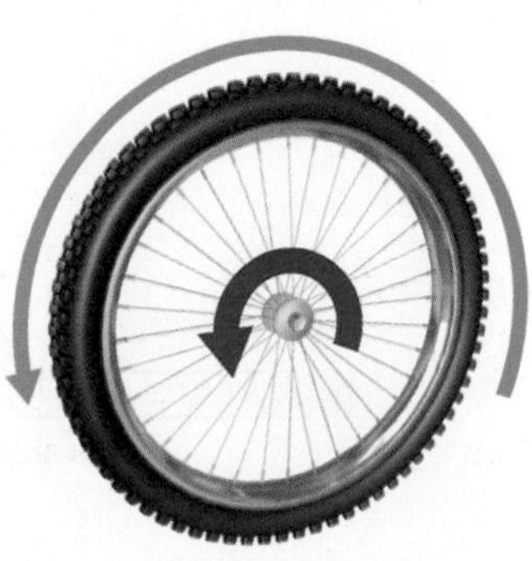

Applying a large force to the axle makes the wheel move farther (spin faster).

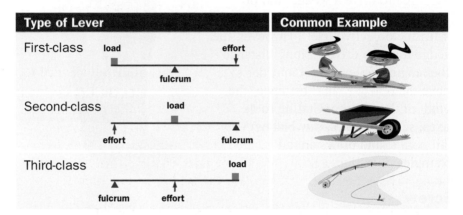

Pulley

294

A **pulley** is a wheel with a rope (or chain) wrapped around it. The wheel rotates around a fixed axle. The rope rides in a groove in the wheel. When the rope is pulled, the wheel turns.

There are two kinds of pulleys: fixed and movable. A **fixed pulley** is one that does not move. This type of pulley is often used to lift something. One end of the rope is attached to a load. When the other end of the rope is pulled down, the load gets lifted. A fixed pulley changes the direction of force, but does not reduce the amount of force needed to lift the load.

A **movable pulley** is a pulley that moves. One end of the rope is tied to a stationary object and the other is free for you to pull on. The load is attached directly to the pulley. The pulley moves along the rope as the free end of the rope is pulled. Because half of the weight of the load is supported by the stationary object and half is supported by you, it takes only half as much force to lift the load. However, you must pull the rope twice as far in order to move the load half the distance.

A **block and tackle** is a system of pulleys. Using more than one movable pulley reduces the amount of force needed to lift the load. The more pulleys that are used, the smaller the applied force but the farther the rope must be pulled to move the load a certain distance.

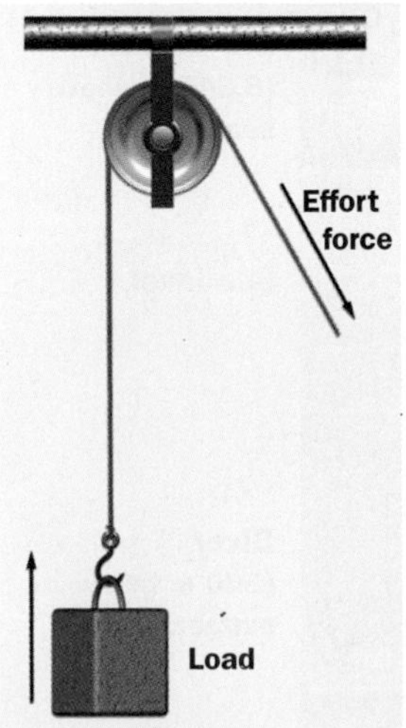

Fixed pulley

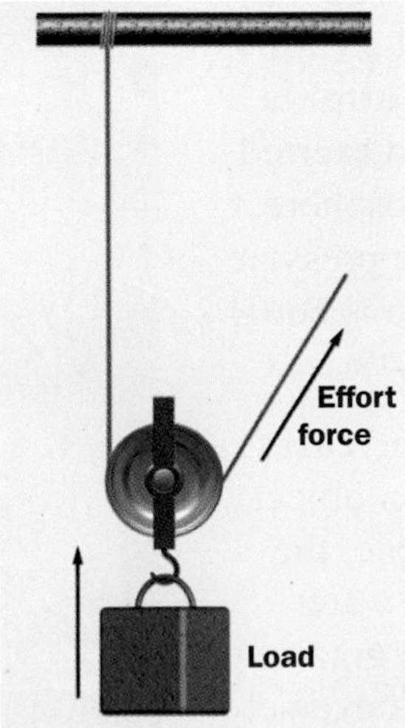

Movable pulley

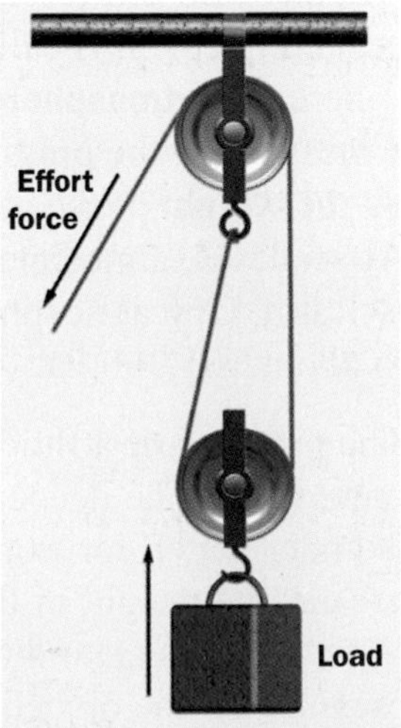

Block and tackle system

Keyword: Simple Machines
www.scilinks.org
Code: GSSM288

Forces in Fluids

295

SEE ALSO
253 States of Matter
261 Molecules
298 Physical Science Equations

A **fluid** is any material, either liquid or gas, that can flow. All fluids exert pressure as their molecules move around and bump into the surfaces of other matter. **Pressure** is the amount of force exerted by these molecules on a given area. You can find the pressure of a fluid if you divide the force it exerts by the area over which the force is exerted. The mathematical equation for this is as follows:

$$\textbf{pressure} = \frac{\textbf{force}}{\textbf{area}} \quad \textbf{or} \quad p = \frac{F}{A}$$

Did You Know?

Fluids flow from regions of higher pressure to regions of lower pressure. Air moving from areas of higher pressure to areas of lower pressure is known as wind!

SEE ALSO
224 Air Pressure
213 Earth's Atmosphere

The SI, or metric, unit of measurement for pressure is the **pascal (Pa).** One pascal is equal to the force of one newton acting over one square meter (1 Pa = 1 N/m^2). Another unit of pressure you may be familiar with is called an atmosphere. An **atmosphere (atm)** is a measure of the pressure exerted by the weight of the atmosphere. At sea level, atmospheric pressure is 1 atm. One atmosphere is equal to about 101,300 Pa.

The pressure of a fluid increases with depth. The deeper an object is under water, for example, the greater the weight of the water above the object, and the greater the pressure on the object. Conversely, the higher up in the atmosphere an object is, the less the weight of the air above the object, and the less the pressure on the object.

Airplane (12,000 m above sea level)

Mt. Everest (8,847 m above sea level)

Sea level

Diver (500 m below surface)

Viper fish (8,000 m below surface)

Buoyancy

296

Have you ever tried to hold an inflatable toy, like a beach ball, under water? It's not easy. As you push the toy under water, it seems to push right back at you. If you let go, it pops back up to the surface. This push that you feel is called buoyant force. **Buoyant force** is the upward force exerted on an object that is immersed in a fluid. Buoyant force is caused by differences in pressure within the fluid.

All fluids, both liquid and gas, exert a buoyant force. As long as the buoyant force exerted on an object is less than the weight of the object, the object will sink. But if the buoyant force is equal to the weight of the object, the object will float—neither sink nor rise in the fluid. And if the buoyant force is greater than the weight of the object—as is the case with a beach ball in water—the object will be buoyed up (rise). **Buoyancy** is the tendency of certain objects to float or rise in a fluid.

Archimedes, a mathematician in ancient Greece, was the first to explain buoyant force. One day, as he climbed into a full bath, some water spilled over the edge. He reasoned that his body had displaced, or pushed aside, the water.

SEE ALSO
450 Famous Scientists

After some more experiments and calculations, he concluded that the buoyant force of a fluid on an object was equal to the weight of the fluid displaced by the object. This is known as **Archimedes' principle.**

Did You Know?

Heavy steel ships are able to float because the shape of a ship's hull causes it to displace (push aside) an enormous amount of water. The weight of this displaced water is equal to the weight of the ship, so the ship floats.

297 Lift

Swiss mathematician Daniel Bernoulli was the first to describe a unique property of moving fluids. According to **Bernoulli's principle,** the pressure exerted on surfaces by a moving fluid decreases the faster the fluid flows. This principle can be used to help explain how heavier-than-air objects like planes can fly.

Airplane wings are shaped like an airfoil—relatively flat on the bottom and curved on top. Because of this unique shape, air flowing over the top of the wing moves faster than air flowing under the wing. According to Bernoulli's principle, as the wing moves through the air, the pressure under the wing becomes greater than the pressure above the wing, resulting in an upward push on the wing. This upward force due to differences in air pressure is called **lift.** When the lift is greater than the weight of the object, the object will rise.

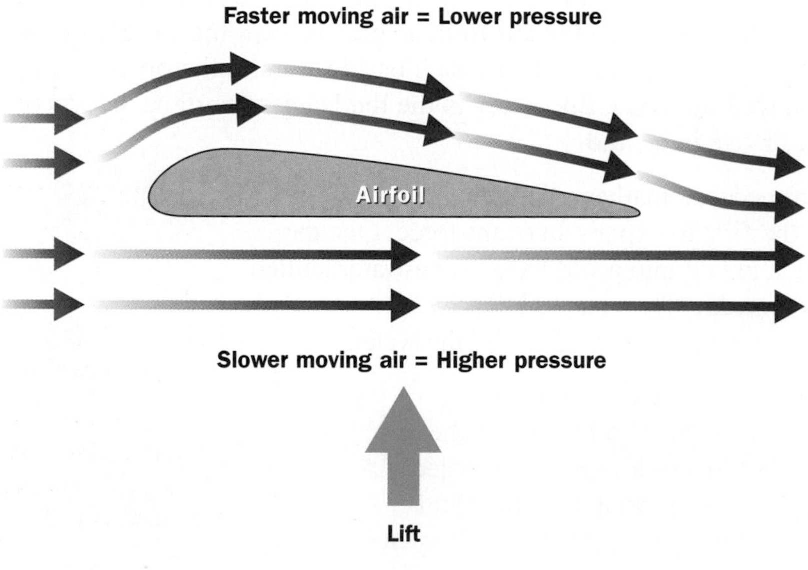

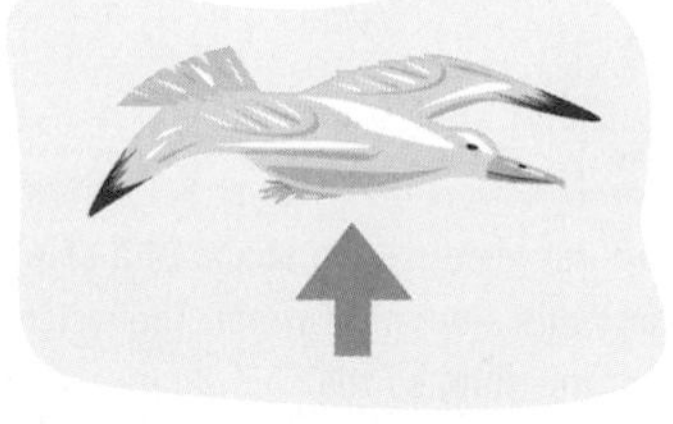

Lift also plays a role in helping birds to fly.

Physical Science Equations

298

Equation in Words	Equation Using Symbols	SI Units of Measurement
Weight = mass × acceleration due to gravity	$W = m \times g$	• newtons, N (weight) • kilograms, kg (mass) • meters per second squared, m/s^2 (acceleration)
Force = mass × acceleration	$F = m \times a$	• newtons, N (force) • kilograms, kg (mass) • meters per second squared, m/s^2 (acceleration)
Velocity = distance ÷ time	$v = \frac{d}{t}$	• meters per second, m/s (velocity) • meters, m (distance) • seconds, s (time)
Momentum = mass × velocity	$M = m \times v$	• kilogram-meters per second, kg•m/s (momentum) • kilograms, kg (mass) • meters per second, m/s (velocity)
Work = force × distance	$W = F \times d$	• joules, J (work) • newtons, N (force) • meters, m (distance)
Mechanical advantage = output force ÷ input force	$MA = \frac{F_{out}}{F_{in}}$	• no units—just a number (mechanical advantage) • newtons, N (output force) • newtons, N (input force)
Pressure = force ÷ area	$p = \frac{F}{A}$	• pascals, Pa (pressure) • newtons, N (force) • square meters, m^2 (area)
Current = voltage ÷ resistance (Ohm's law)	$I = \frac{V}{R}$	• amperes, A (current) • volts, V (voltage) • ohms, Ω (resistance)
Power = voltage × current	$P = V \times I$	• watts, W (power) • volts, V (voltage) • amperes, A (current)

299 Energy

It's sometimes easier to describe what energy does than what energy is. That's because, unlike matter, energy is not something you can see or touch. **Energy** is a property of matter, and all matter has it. Whenever a light bulb is lit, a turkey is roasted, an orchestra plays, a fan spins, a book falls off the shelf, or a fire burns, you can be sure that energy—in one form or another—made it happen.

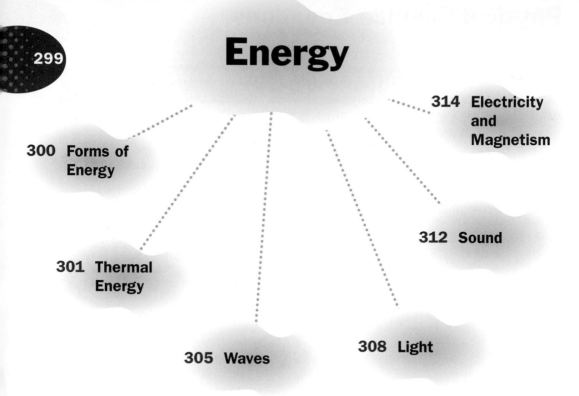

Forms of Energy

300

Energy comes in many different forms. While it can be transferred from one object or system to another, energy cannot be created or destroyed. This rule is known as the **law of conservation of energy.**

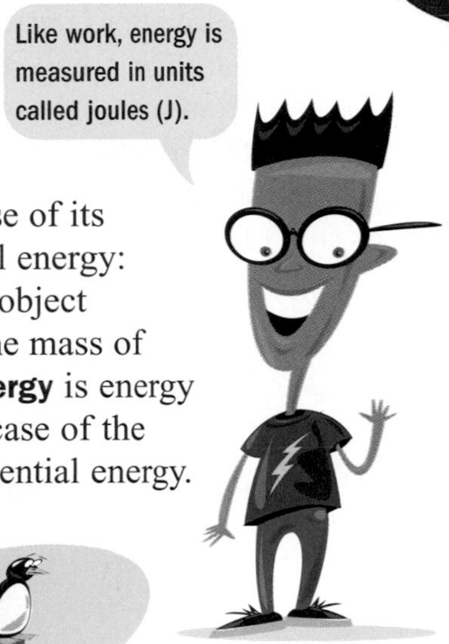
Like work, energy is measured in units called joules (J).

Mechanical energy is the energy an object has because of its motion or position. There are two kinds of mechanical energy: kinetic and potential. **Kinetic energy** is the energy an object has because it is moving. The greater the speed and the mass of the object, the greater its kinetic energy. **Potential energy** is energy an object has because of its position or shape. In the case of the penguin below, the higher up he is, the greater his potential energy.

The bigger cat has more kinetic energy than the smaller cat because he has more mass.

This penguin has potential energy because of his mass and his height above the water.

Other forms of energy include the following:

- **Thermal energy** (sometimes called heat energy) is the energy related to the temperature of a substance.
- **Light energy** is the energy carried by light and other kinds of electromagnetic waves.
- **Sound energy** is the energy carried by sound waves.
- **Electrical energy** is the energy produced by electric charges.
- **Chemical energy** is the energy stored in chemical bonds.
- **Nuclear energy** is the energy contained in the nuclei of atoms.

SEE ALSO
301 Thermal Energy
308 Light
312 Sound
315 The Law of Electric Charges
105 Animal Physiology
256 Atomic Structure

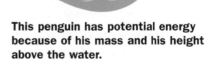

Thermal Energy

301

SEE ALSO

255 Atoms

261 Molecules

300 Forms of Energy

All matter is made of particles called atoms and molecules. These particles are in constant motion. They vibrate, rotate, or move from one place to another in a random manner. Some move faster than others. Since these particles are in motion, they have kinetic energy. Kinetic energy is the energy an object or substance has due to its motion.

Word Watch!

The prefix *therm-* means "heat."

Molecules of water have kinetic energy.

Thermal energy is the total amount of kinetic energy contained in all the particles of a substance. The greater the kinetic energy of the particles in the substance, the more thermal energy the substance has. But thermal energy also depends on the number of particles in a substance. The more particles a substance contains, the greater its thermal energy.

SEE ALSO

202 Ocean Water

302 Temperature versus Heat

Science Alert!

More thermal energy does not necessarily mean a higher temperature. For example, the ocean, because it is so massive, has far more thermal energy than a pot of boiling water.

Temperature versus Heat

302

When you think of temperature, you probably think "hot" or "cold." To scientists, **temperature** is a measure of the *average* kinetic energy of the particles in a substance. The more kinetic energy the particles have, the higher the temperature of the substance. Unlike thermal energy, however, temperature is not affected by the number of particles the substance contains.

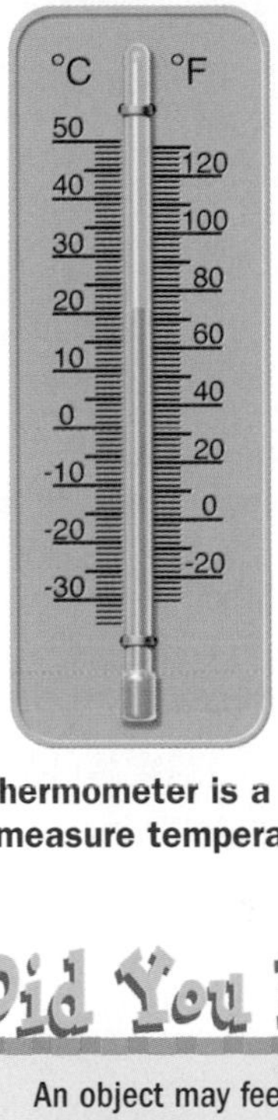

Two common units of temperature are degrees Celsius (˚C) and degrees Fahrenheit (˚F).

A thermometer is a device used to measure temperature.

SEE ALSO
072 Taking Temperature Readings

Did You Know?

An object may feel hot or cold, but you can't tell its temperature just by touching it. That's because your skin can only detect *differences* in temperature, not temperature itself. For example, if your hands are very cold, even a cool object will feel warm.

So if thermal energy is the total kinetic energy of the particles of a substance, and temperature is the average kinetic energy of the particles, what is heat? **Heat** is the transfer of thermal energy between substances that are at different temperatures. The energy is always transferred from the warmer substance (the one with the higher temperature) to the cooler substance (the one with the lower temperature). The term *heat* is also commonly used in place of the term *thermal energy*.

SEE ALSO
303 Equalization of Temperatures
304 Methods of Heat Transfer

303 Equalization of Temperatures

Whenever two objects come in contact with each other, heat will transfer (flow) from the object with the higher temperature to the object with the lower temperature. The heat will continue to flow until the temperature of the two objects has equalized, or reached the same temperature.

For example, suppose you place an ice cube in a glass of water. Because the water is warmer than the ice, heat flows from the water to the ice until the two reach the same temperature. Heat does not flow from the ice to the water.

Heat flows from the warmer substance to the cooler substance.

304 Methods of Heat Transfer

There are three methods of heat transfer: conduction, convection, and radiation.

Conduction is the transfer of heat from a warmer substance to a cooler substance through direct contact. When two substances come into contact, their particles collide. The energy from the faster-moving particles is transferred to the slower-moving particles, until the particles in both substances are moving at the same speed and their temperature has equalized. Conduction is what causes the handle of a spoon placed in a cup of hot tea to warm up.

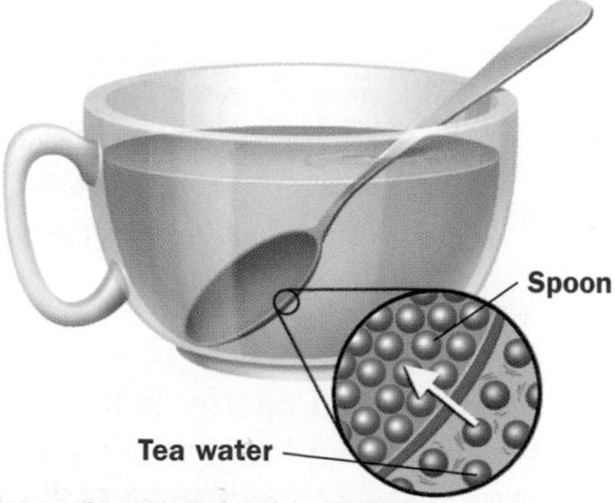

Transfer of thermal energy by conduction

SEE ALSO
317 Current Electricity

Did You Know?

A **conductor** is a substance that conducts thermal energy (and other forms of energy) well. Metals tend to be better heat conductors than other solids.

Convection is the transfer of heat in a fluid through currents. Suppose you place a pot of cold water on a hot stove. As the water at the bottom of the pot heats up, it becomes less dense (its particles spread out and become less compact). Because the warm water is less dense than the cold water above it, the warm water rises and displaces the cold water. The cold water, in turn, sinks. The movement of water that results is called a **convection current.** The convection current transfers thermal energy throughout the water in the pot.

Transfer of thermal energy by convection

Radiation is the transfer of energy as electromagnetic waves. Unlike conduction and convection, which involve the collision or movement of particles, radiation can occur through empty space. The sun heats Earth through the process of radiation.

SEE ALSO
309 Electromagnetic Spectrum
305 Waves

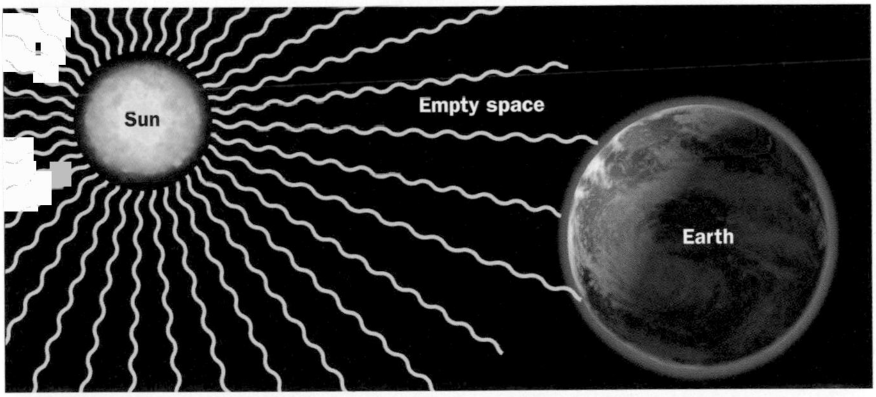

Transfer of energy by radiation

Waves

305

One way that energy is transported is through waves. A **wave** is an oscillation (a back-and-forth or up-and-down motion) that travels from one place to another with a certain velocity (speed and direction.) Some waves, like sound waves and water waves, travel through matter. Waves that travel through matter are called **mechanical waves.** Other waves, like visible light, microwaves, X-rays, and radio waves, travel through empty space (as well as through matter). Waves that can travel through empty space are called **electromagnetic waves.**

SEE ALSO
308 Light
312 Sound
186 Earthquakes

306 Characteristics of a Wave

All waves have the following four characteristics:

The **amplitude** of a wave is the distance a wave oscillates from its resting position. The larger the amplitude, the more energy carried by the wave.

Wavelength is the distance from any point on one wave to a corresponding point on an adjacent wave.

SEE ALSO
313 Properties of Sound

Frequency is the number of oscillations produced in a certain amount of time. The greater the number of oscillations per second, the higher the frequency. The higher the frequency, the more energy carried by the wave. Frequency is measured in **hertz (Hz).** One hertz is equal to one wave per second.

Wave speed is the distance a wave travels in a given amount of time. Waves move faster through some mediums than through others.

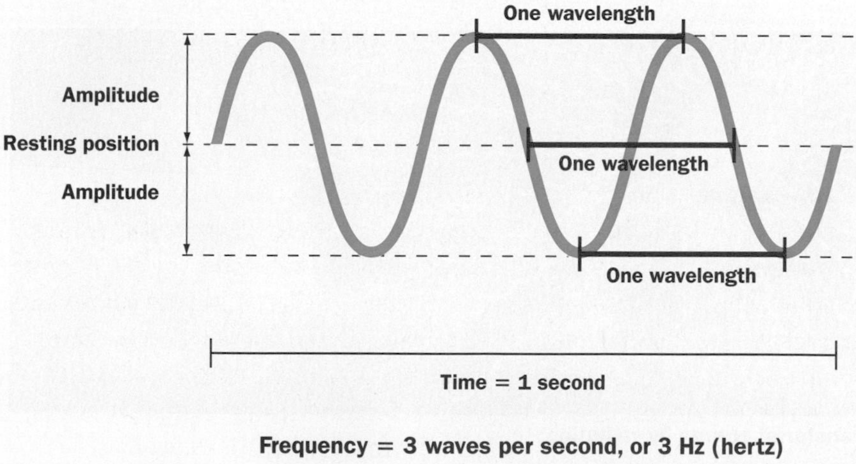

Create your own waves by tying one end of a rope to a doorknob and moving the other end up and down.

Kinds of Waves

307

When the oscillation (back-and-forth or up-and-down motion) of a wave is perpendicular to the direction in which the wave travels, the wave is called a **transverse wave.**

Look at the figure of the transverse wave. The peak, or highest point, of a transverse wave is the **crest.** The valley, or lowest point, between two crests is the **trough.** Some examples of transverse waves include electromagnetic (light) waves and a type of seismic wave (a wave that occurs during earthquakes) called a secondary wave (S-wave).

SEE ALSO
186 Earthquakes

Transverse Wave

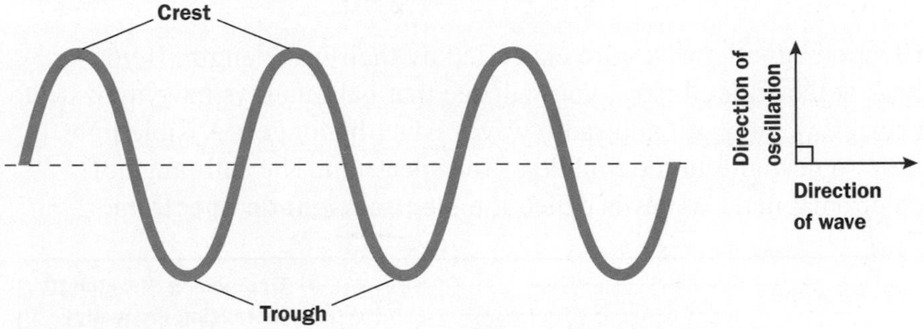

A **longitudinal wave** is a wave whose oscillation is parallel to the direction in which the wave travels. For example, if you set a spring on your desk and push the end of the spring over and over, you create regions where the coils are closer together (called **compressions**) and regions where the coils are farther apart (called **rarefactions**). The compressions and rarefactions move in the same direction in which the wave travels. Examples of longitudinal waves are sound waves and a type of seismic wave called a primary wave (P-wave).

Longitudinal Wave

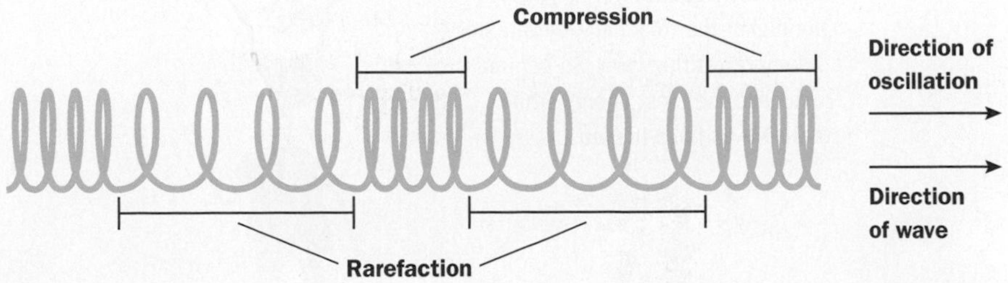

Light

308

Look around you. What do you see? You might say books, pencils, desks, and chairs. But what you really see is light bouncing off books, pencils, desks, and chairs. You can see objects only if they reflect light or produce it themselves. **Light** is a type of energy produced by the vibration of electrically charged particles.

309

Electromagnetic Spectrum

Light travels in the form of electromagnetic waves. There are many different types of electromagnetic waves, most of which cannot be detected by the human eye.

SEE ALSO
306 Characteristics of a Wave

Electromagnetic waves are classified by their wavelength. If you look at the figure below, you will see that gamma rays have the shortest wavelength and radio waves have the longest. Visible light falls somewhere in the middle of the spectrum. The full range of electromagnetic waves is called the **electromagnetic spectrum.**

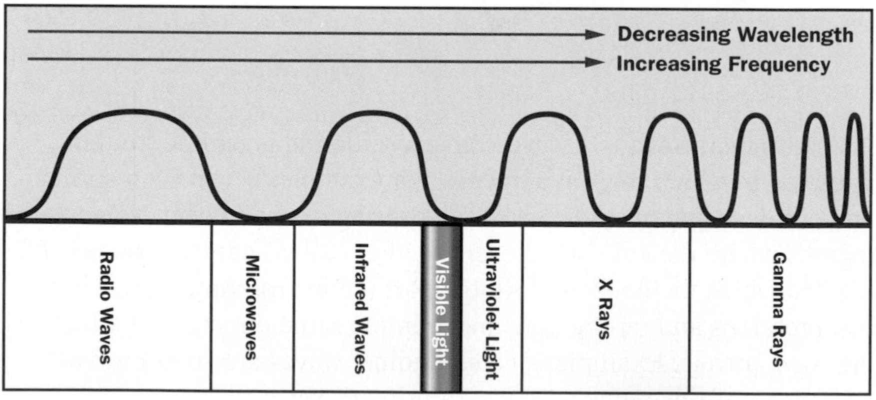

The shorter the wavelength, the higher the frequency of the wave. The higher the frequency, the greater the energy of the wave. So gamma rays have the most energy, while radio waves have the least.

The only part of the electromagnetic spectrum that you can see with your eyes is visible light. Visible light includes all the colors of the rainbow: red, orange, yellow, green, blue, indigo, and violet. Red light has the longest wavelength; violet light has the shortest. When all the different colors of light are combined, you see them as white light.

SEE ALSO
306 Characteristics of a Wave

You can remember the order of the colors in the visible light spectrum with the help of my good friend, Roy G. Biv.

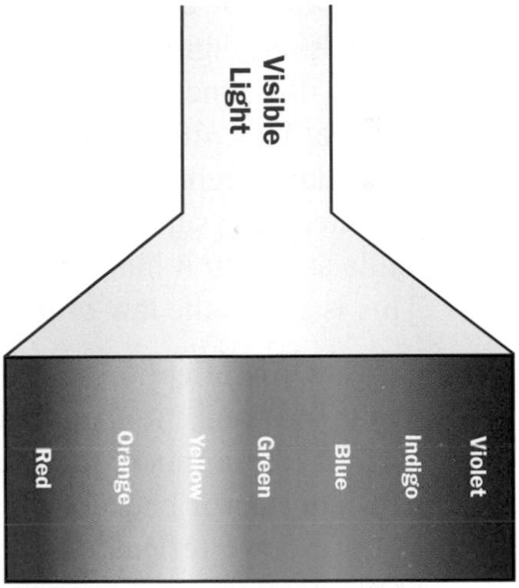

Properties of Light 310

How would you describe the properties of light? One way is to describe how light travels.

- **Light spreads out in all directions from its source.**
- **Light travels in straight lines called rays.**
- **Light travels "at the speed of light"** (about 186,282 miles per second, or 299,792 kilometers per second).
- **Light can travel in a vacuum.** A vacuum is empty space. Like all electromagnetic waves, light can travel through empty space as well as through matter.

These same properties apply to all types of electromagnetic waves, not just light.

311 Light at a Surface

Three things can happen to light when it hits the surface of matter. The light can be reflected by the matter, it can pass through the matter, or it can be absorbed by the matter.

Reflection of Light

If you shine light on a surface, some of that light will bounce off, or be reflected by, the surface. This process is called **reflection.** Light will always be reflected by a surface at the same angle at which it hits the surface. This is called the **law of reflection.**

The **angle of incidence** is the angle at which light hits a surface. The **angle of reflection** is the angle at which light is reflected by a surface. The angle of incidence always equals the angle of reflection.

The law of reflection is evident when you look into a smooth, shiny surface like a mirror. You see yourself in a mirror because all the light rays are reflected at the same angle. Reflection from a smooth surface is called **specular reflection.**

But the law of reflection is at work even on rough surfaces. Think of a rough surface as being made of many small smooth surfaces positioned at different angles. So, when light shines on a rough surface, such as a brick wall, the light rays get reflected at many different angles. You cannot use such a surface as a mirror. Reflection of light from a rough surface is called **diffuse reflection.**

Specular Reflection

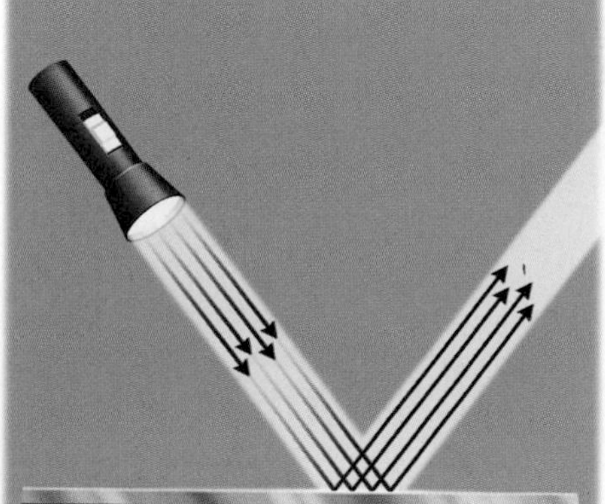

Mirror

Diffuse Reflection

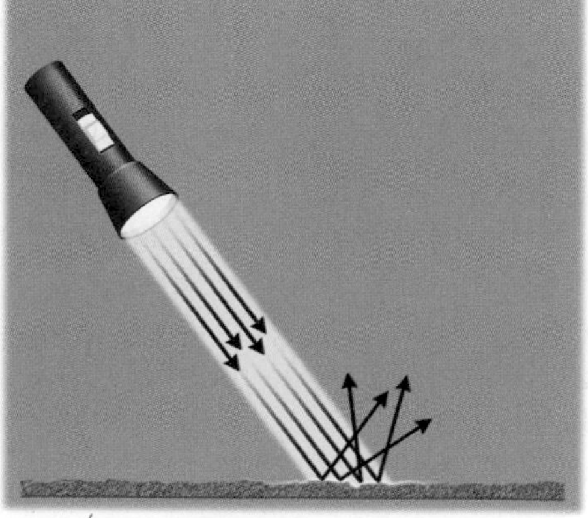

Rough Surface

Transmission of Light

Sometimes light passes through matter. This is called **transmission.** Light passes through some materials more easily than others. For example, light passes through water, air, and glass very easily. These materials are said to be **transparent.** You can see through transparent matter because light passes through it.

Translucent matter transmits some but not all of the light that hits it. An example of translucent matter is a sheet of waxed paper. **Opaque** matter does not transmit any light. You cannot see through it because light does not pass through it. Your desk is an example of opaque matter. So is this book.

Light always travels in straight lines. But when it passes from one medium to another (from air to water, for example), light changes direction slightly. This is called **refraction.** You can see this phenomenon when you put a spoon in a glass of water. Refraction occurs because light travels at different speeds through different materials. In the case of the spoon and glass of water, the light rays bend as they pass from the water to the air because light travels faster through air than through water.

Refraction

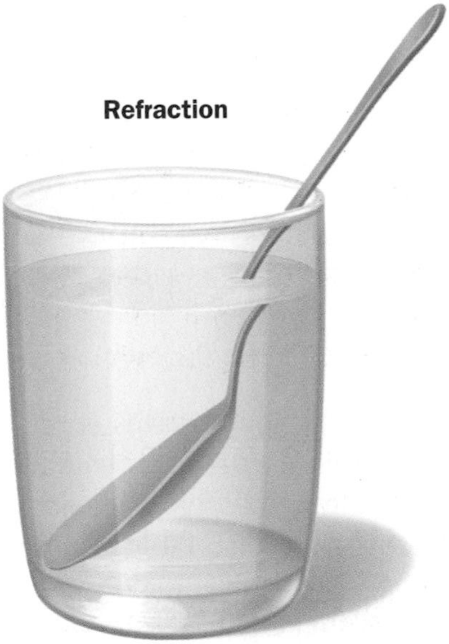

SEE ALSO
306 Characteristics of a Wave

Absorption of Light

The atoms in matter can also absorb light. Absorbed light energy is converted into some other form, such as thermal energy.

SEE ALSO
301 Thermal Energy

Objects get their color from selective absorption. For example, an apple looks red because it absorbs all the colors of light except red. Red light gets reflected to your eyes. A white object looks white because it reflects all colors of light and absorbs none. A black object looks black because it absorbs all colors of light and reflects none.

Remember that all the colors of light seen together appear to us as white light.

Sound

312

Did you hear that? Sound is all around you: clocks ticking, horns blowing, feet shuffling, babies crying.

Sound is produced when an object vibrates. The vibrating object pushes the particles of matter next to it and causes them to compress (squeeze together). That compressed matter, in turn, compresses the matter next to it. The compression travels through the matter as a wave of energy. Sound waves travel in all directions away from their source. Sound waves are longitudinal waves.

SEE ALSO
307 Kinds of Waves

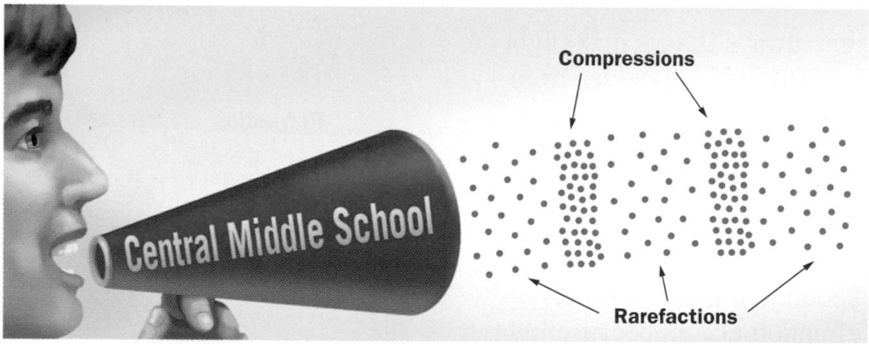

Unlike light, sound waves need a medium (matter) to travel through. Sound cannot exist in a vacuum. Like light, sound travels at different speeds through different materials. In general, sound travels faster through solids than through liquids, and faster through liquids than through gases. Sound waves also travel faster through a warmer medium than through a cooler medium.

SEE ALSO
310 Properties of Light

Material	Speed of Sound (m/s)
Steel	5200
Glass	4540
Oak wood	3850
Silver	3650
Water	1520
Cork	500
Air	330

Sound travels much more slowly than light. That's why you often see a flash of lightning before you hear the rumble of thunder. The thunder is produced by the lightning, but it takes sound much longer to reach your ears than it takes light to reach your eyes.

Properties of Sound

313

How would you describe a sound? Is it loud or soft? High or low? Soothing or jarring? The properties of sound depend in large part on the amplitude and frequency of the sound waves.

Amplitude and Loudness

Amplitude is the distance a wave oscillates from its resting position. The greater the amplitude of the sound wave, the louder the sound. Loudness is measured in units called **decibels (dB).** The softest sound that can be heard by the human ear is assigned a decibel level of 0. The average human can hear sounds between 0 and 120 decibels. Beyond that, the energy of the sound waves is so great that it can injure your ears.

SEE ALSO
306 Characteristics of a Wave

Sound	Decibel (dB) Level
Rustling leaves	10
Whisper	30
Normal conversation	65
Vacuum cleaner	75
Lawn mower	100
Rock concert	120
Jet engine at takeoff	150

Frequency and Pitch

Frequency is the number of waves produced in a given time. The frequency of a sound wave determines its pitch, or how high or low the sound is. The higher the frequency of a sound wave, the higher the pitch. Most humans can perceive sound waves within a frequency range of 20 to 20,000 Hz, or waves per second.

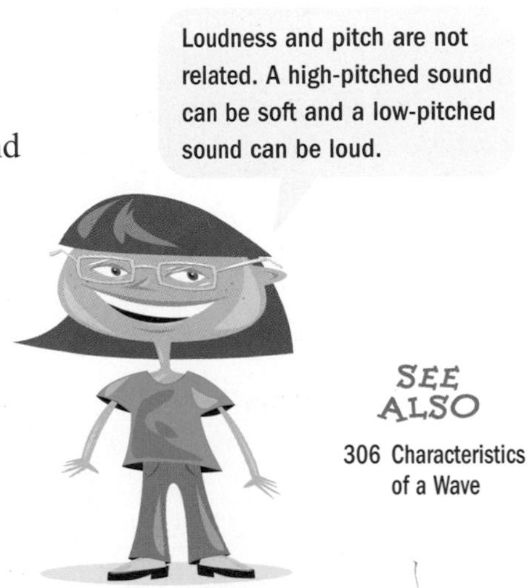

Loudness and pitch are not related. A high-pitched sound can be soft and a low-pitched sound can be loud.

SEE ALSO
306 Characteristics of a Wave

Electricity and Magnetism

314

SEE ALSO
277 Electric and Magnetic Forces

Electricity and magnetism are closely related. This is because both are caused by negative and positive charges in matter. When charges from one piece of matter interact with those from another piece of matter, they produce both electric and magnetic forces. Electricity can produce magnetism, and magnetism can create electricity.

The Law of Electric Charges

315

SEE ALSO
256 Atomic Structure

Electricity is the interaction of electric charges. An **electric charge** is a physical property of protons and electrons, particles that make up every atom. There are two kinds of electric charges: positive and negative. Protons have a positive charge, and electrons have a negative charge.

Most atoms contain an equal number of electrons and protons. If the number of electrons in an atom equals the number of protons, then the atom has no charge and is said to be neutral. However, an atom can gain or lose electrons. If an atom ends up with more electrons than protons, it has a net negative charge. If an atom ends up with more protons than electrons, it has a net positive charge. An object becomes charged when its atoms gain or lose electrons.

According to the **law of electric charges,** like charges repel and unlike charges attract. The attractive or repulsive force between charged objects is called **electric force.** The strength of the electric force between charged objects depends on the size of the charges and the distance between them. The greater the charges and the closer together they are, the greater the electric force between the objects.

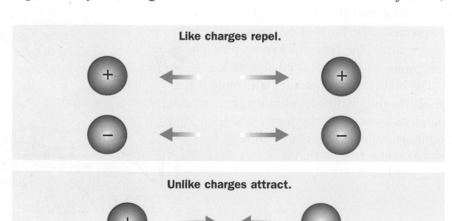

Like charges repel.

Unlike charges attract.

Static Electricity

316

The buildup of electric charges on an object is called **static electricity.** One way static electricity is created is through rubbing. For example, if you rub a balloon against your head (both of which start out neutral), electrons from the atoms that make up your hair get transferred to the balloon. Your hair becomes positively charged due to the loss of electrons. The balloon becomes negatively charged due to the gain of electrons. If you then hold the balloon several centimeters from your head, your hair will stand on end. Your hair and the balloon are attracted to each other because unlike charges attract.

Word Watch!

The word *static* means "not moving." Static electricity is the electric energy that resides on an object.

Electrons are transferred to the balloon from your hair.

Your positively charged hair is attracted to the negatively charged balloon.

Eventually the charges that build up on an object move off the object. This sudden and brief flow of electrons is called **electric discharge** (or **static discharge**). The small shock you get when you touch a metal doorknob after shuffling your feet on carpeting is an example of electric discharge on a small scale. Lightning is an example of electric discharge on a grand scale.

Lightning is a form of static discharge.

317 Current Electricity

SEE ALSO
318 Electric Circuits

Unlike static electricity, which does not move except when discharged, **current electricity** is a continuous flow of electric charge. More specifically, **electric current** is the amount of charge that moves past a certain point each second. The SI unit of measurement for current is the **ampere**, or **amp (A).** In an equation, the symbol for current is "I."

SEE ALSO
256 Atomic Structure

Water is also a good conductor of current. That is why it's so dangerous to use electric appliances near water.

Certain materials are especially good at carrying electric current because of the structure of their atoms. These materials are called **conductors.** Metals such as copper and aluminum are good conductors. Other materials, though, are not good at carrying current. These materials are called **insulators.** Rubber, wood, glass, and air are examples of good insulators.

Direct Current vs. Alternating Current

There are two kinds of current: direct current and alternating current. **Direct current (DC)** is current in which the electric charges move in one direction. Batteries produce direct current.

Alternating current (AC) is current in which the electric charges flow in one direction, then in the reverse direction, over and over again. The electric current supplied by your local power company to your home is alternating current.

Direct Current (DC)

Electric charges move in one direction only.

Alternating Current (AC)

Electric charges move in one direction, then in the reverse direction.

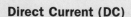

Electric Circuits

318

Electric current flows through a path called a **circuit.** You can think of a circuit as a big loop. In order for the current to flow through the loop, the path must have no breaks; in other words, it must be closed. A **closed circuit** has no breaks in it. An **open circuit** has a break.

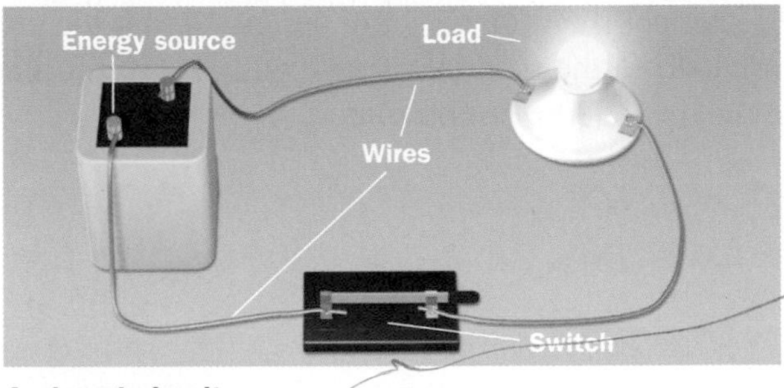

A closed circuit

Parts of a Circuit

There are four main parts of a circuit: the energy source, the load, the wires, and the switch.

1. **Energy source** Something has to push electric charges through a closed circuit. A battery has a positively charged terminal and a negatively charged terminal. In a closed circuit, electric charges are repelled by one terminal and attracted to the other terminal. This attraction and repulsion provides the push that keeps the electric charges moving.

   One way to describe the pushing effect of a battery is to measure the potential energy difference between its positive and negative terminals. This potential difference is called **voltage.** The greater the voltage, the greater the electric force driving the charges in the circuit. Potential difference is measured in **volts (V).**

2. **Load** Circuits deliver electrical energy to a device. The device, in this case a light bulb, is called the **load.** A light bulb contains a wire called a filament. When current passes through the filament, electrical energy is converted into thermal energy. The filament gets so hot that it starts to glow, giving off light.

SEE ALSO
301 Thermal Energy

3. **Wires** Wires connect the energy source to the load. Wires are often made of copper because copper is a good conductor. Plastic insulation around the wires keeps the current from flowing into other conductors—your fingers, for example.

MORE ▶

4. **Switch** A switch opens and closes a circuit by bringing together or separating two pieces of metal. When the metal pieces touch, the circuit closes. When the metal pieces separate, the circuit opens.

Types of Circuits

There are different ways of connecting multiple loads in a circuit. One way is to connect them in a line, or series, so that the current flows from one load to the next in a single path. A circuit that is arranged like this is called a **series circuit.**

Another way to connect multiple loads is to divide the current among the different devices. This type of circuit is called a **parallel circuit.**

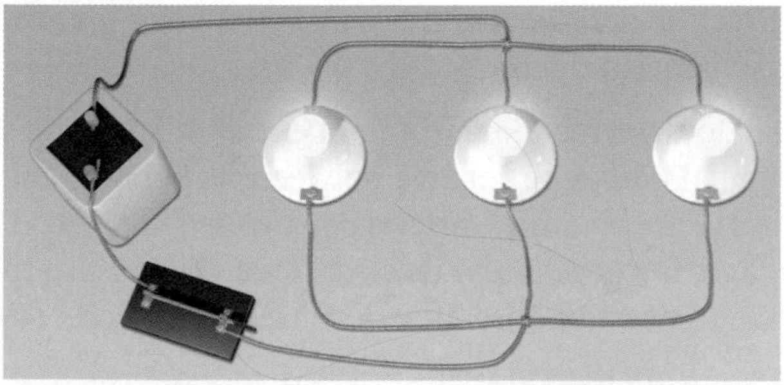

The advantage of a parallel circuit over a series circuit is that the parallel circuit is not broken by a faulty load device. Each load makes its own closed circuit with the energy source. So, for example, if one light bulb goes out, the others stay lit.

Ohm's Law

Resistance is a measure of how much a material opposes the flow of electric current through it. A substance that is a good conductor, like copper wire, has low resistance. A substance that is a poor conductor, like the plastic insulation that covers the wire, has high resistance.

SEE ALSO
317 Current Electricity
318 Electric Circuits

The SI unit of measurement for resistance is the **ohm** (Ω), named after the German physicist (Georg Ohm) who came up with an equation that describes the relationship between current, voltage, and resistance. This equation, called **Ohm's law,** is as follows:

SEE ALSO
298 Physical Science Equations

$$\text{current} = \frac{\text{voltage}}{\text{resistance}} \quad \text{or} \quad I = \frac{V}{R}$$

According to Ohm's law, the greater the voltage across a device with resistance, the greater the current through the device. For example, imagine that a 1.5-volt battery is connected to a small light bulb. If the resistance of the filament in the light bulb is 3 Ω, then what is the current flowing through the circuit?

$$I = \frac{1.5\ \text{V}}{3\ \Omega}$$

$$I = 0.5\ \text{A}$$

Remember, the unit of measurement for current is amperes, or amps (A).

You can also use Ohm's law to find voltage or resistance. Just rearrange the equation as follows:

$$\text{voltage} = \text{current} \times \text{resistance, or } V = IR$$

$$\text{resistance} = \frac{\text{voltage}}{\text{current}} \quad \text{or} \quad R = \frac{V}{I}$$

A formula triangle can help you remember these equations.

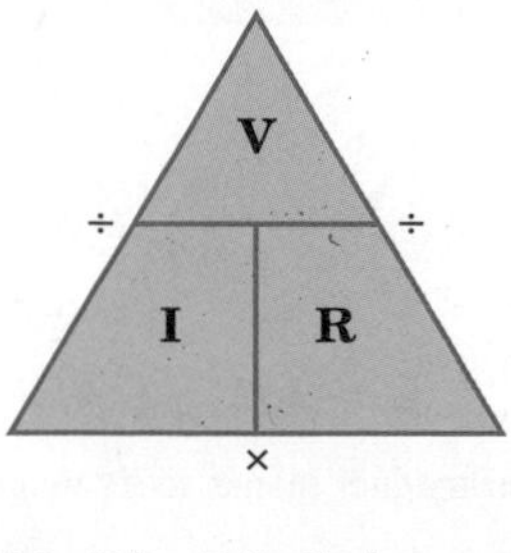

Divide *V* by *R* to find current.
Divide *V* by *I* to find resistance.

320 Magnetism

Even if you cut a magnet in half, each half will have a north pole and a south pole!

A **magnet** is any material that attracts iron. All magnets have certain properties in common. For example, they all have two poles—a negative pole and a positive pole. The **poles** are regions in a magnet where the magnetic force is strongest.

SEE ALSO
277 Electric and Magnetic Forces

When you bring two magnets together, the north pole of one magnet is attracted to the south pole of the other magnet. But when you try to join like poles together, they repel each other. The attractive or repulsive force between the poles of magnets is called **magnetic force.**

Like poles repel.

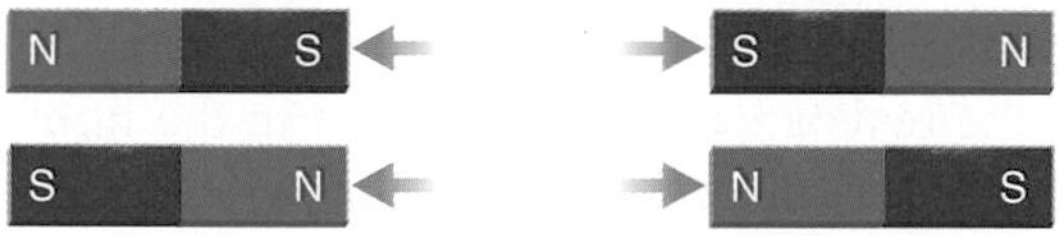

Opposite poles attract.

SEE ALSO
176 Earth Structure and Composition

A **magnetic field** is the region around a magnet that is affected by magnetic forces. You can represent the magnetic field of a magnet by drawing **field lines** between the north and south poles. The field lines are drawn closer together around the poles to indicate that is where the magnetic field is strongest.

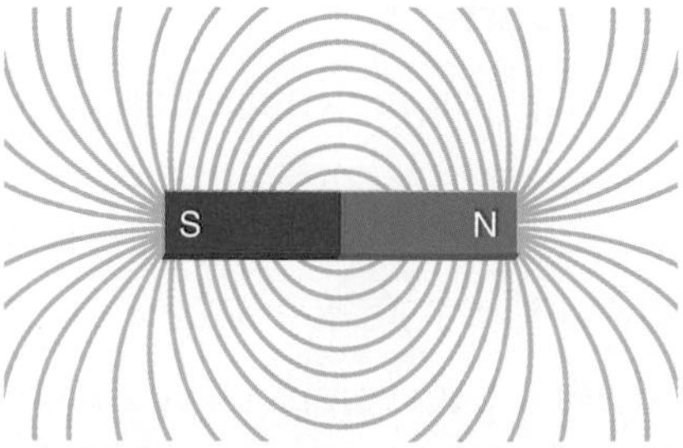

Did You Know?

Even the Earth itself acts as a giant magnet thanks to its magnetic core.

Electromagnetism

321

Electromagnetism is magnetism resulting from electric charge in motion. Danish physicist Hans Christian Oersted was the first to discover that electric current produces a magnetic field around a wire.

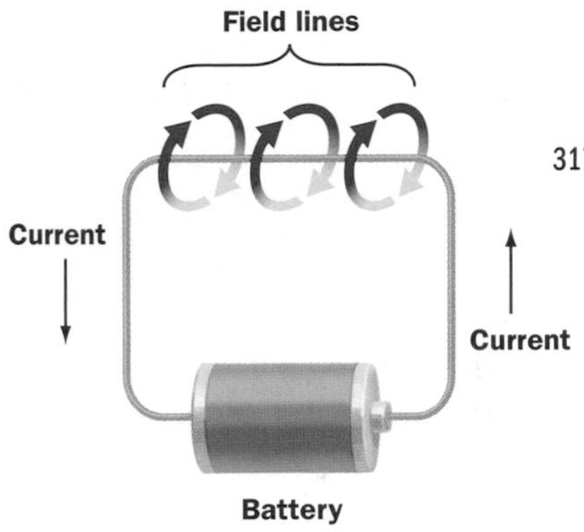

SEE ALSO
317 Current Electricity

You can increase the strength of the magnetic field around a wire with current in it by wrapping the wire into a coil. The more loops in the coil, the stronger the magnetic field. The coil acts like a permanent magnet.

To produce an even stronger magnetic field, you can wrap the coils of wire around an iron rod. Current passing through the coils of wire magnetize the rod, producing a powerful magnet. This device is called an **electromagnet.**

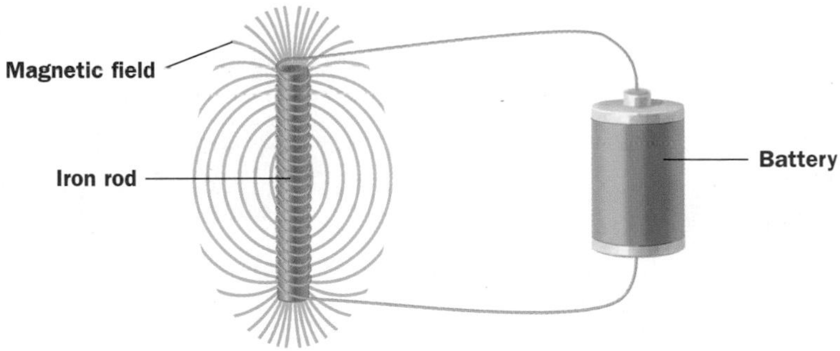

Electromagnets are used in electric motors and in many other devices, from loudspeakers and television sets to doorbells and automatic doors. Electromagnets are used to lift heavy pieces of metal in junkyards. They are also used in *maglev* trains, which are trains that "hover" above the tracks as they move forward.

If current moving through a wire can produce a magnetic field, can a magnet moving past a wire produce a current in the wire? In 1831, British physicist Michael Faraday proved it could. Using wires and magnets to create electric current is called **electromagnetic induction.** Today almost all of the electricity supplied to our homes is produced by electromagnetic induction.

NATURAL RESOURCES AND THE ENVIRONMENT

322

Being environmentally conscientious, Frankenstein's monster was quite pleased to find out that he was made entirely from recycled parts.

Earth contains a vast array of natural treasures. Air, water, soil, mountains, plants, and animals cover its surface. You get all the things you need to survive from the natural resources in the environment, including food, energy, and shelter. Unfortunately, some human activities damage the environment. People must protect Earth's natural resources to make sure they will be available for future generations.

323 Earth's Natural Resources

Look around you. Many things you see were once something else. The paper in your notebook and the wood in your pencil were once trees. The plastic in your CD case was once oil. Many things you use each day began as part of the **environment**. Materials from the environment that are used by people are called **natural resources**.

Natural resources can be divided into two main groups:

SEE ALSO
300 Forms of Energy

- **Energy Resources** Natural resources that provide people with energy are called **energy resources.** Sunlight is an energy resource that provides light and heat. The energy of sunlight can also be changed into electricity. Other energy resources include wind (moving air), moving water, and fuels such as wood, coal, gasoline, and oil.
- **Material Resources** Minerals, water, plants, animals, rocks, and soil are all **material resources.** Some of these things can be used to make different products. For example, sand is used to make glass, and wheat kernels are ground up to make flour.

Land and water areas used for recreation, and areas of natural beauty or historical value, are also considered natural resources.

Natural resources are not all alike. Some can be used over and over again. Others can be used only once.

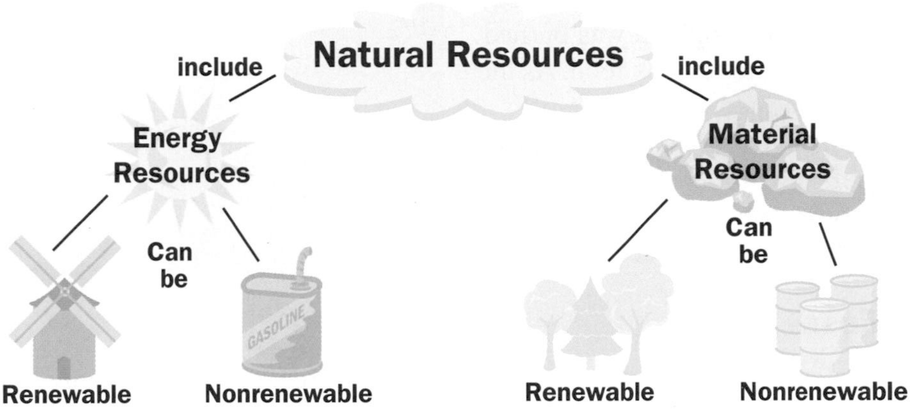

Renewable resources are those that are regularly replaced or replenished by nature. Plants, animals, and water are all renewable resources. Plants and animals reproduce to make more of their own kind. Thus when some plants are harvested, new plants can be grown to take their place. Water is replaced through the water cycle: water that evaporates from Earth is later returned as precipitation.

SEE ALSO
113 Reproduction
216 Water Cycle

Some natural resources are forever lost when used. Others take many years to be replaced by natural processes. **Nonrenewable resources** are those that can be used only once, or those that are not replaced by nature nearly as quickly as they are used. Oil, coal, and natural gas are considered nonrenewable resources because it takes millions of years for them to form. Minerals, including metals, are also considered nonrenewable resources.

SEE ALSO
325 Fossil Fuels
331 Nonrenewable Material Resources

All natural resources must be used with care. Nonrenewable resources can be used up, making them unavailable to people in the future. Even renewable resources can be polluted or destroyed if not treated carefully.

324 Energy Resources

Wood was once the main energy source for people. It was burned for heat and to cook food. As the wood burned, it also gave off light, allowing people to find their way in the dark. Today, people obtain energy from many other resources.

325 Fossil Fuels

The sun is Earth's most important energy source. Plants use energy from sunlight to make food. Animals depend on the food in plants for energy.

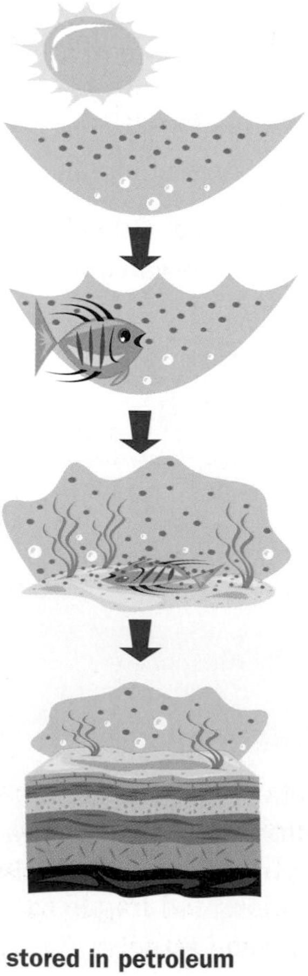
Plants use sun's energy to make food
Animals take in sun's energy when they eat plants
When living things die, the sun's energy is trapped in their remains
Over millions of years, buried remains change to form petroleum

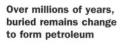

How the sun's energy is stored in petroleum

When plants and animals die, some energy is still stored in the tissues of their bodies. Over millions of years, as layers of dead plant and animal material build up at the bottom of swamps, lakes, and oceans, this energy becomes concentrated into energy-rich materials such as oil. Oil (or petroleum), coal, and natural gas are considered **fossil fuels** because their energy comes from the fossil remains of organisms.

The fossil fuels that formed millions of years ago are the energy source most commonly used by people today. These fuels are burned to provide energy for heating, cooking, and transportation. They can also be used to generate electricity.

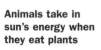

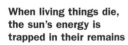

Petroleum, or crude oil, is a liquid fossil fuel. It varies in form from a thin clear liquid to a thick tar-like black goo. Like most fossil fuels, petroleum is found deep below Earth's surface. Giant machines known as drill rigs must be used to pump it up from underground reservoirs.

Before being used, petroleum is separated into different substances in a process called **refining.** Refined petroleum produces fuels such as gasoline and home heating oil. Many other useful byproducts are also made from the petroleum refining process.

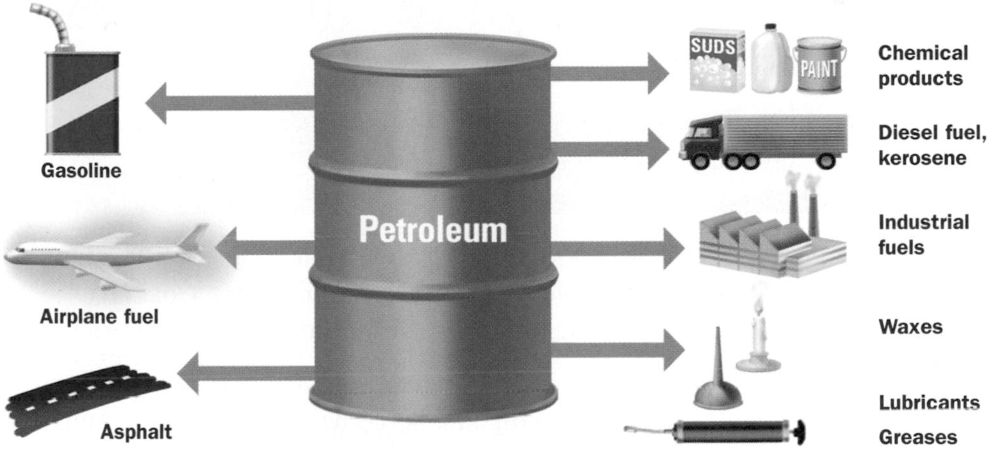

Products from Petroleum

Although petroleum can be found all around the world, it seems to be more plentiful in some places than in others.

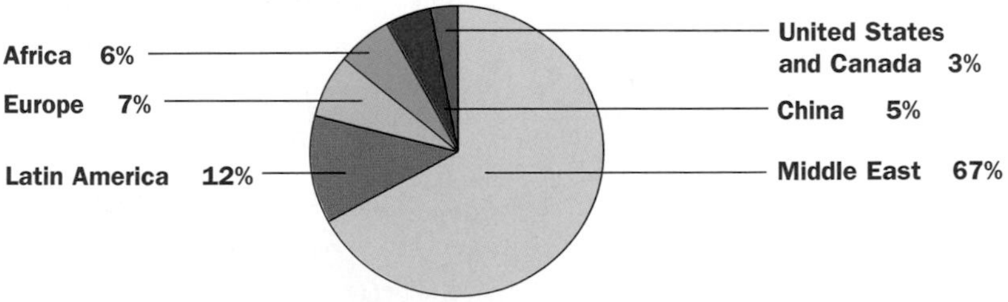

Locations of World Petroleum Reserves

Humans are always looking for new petroleum **reserves,** or sources of petroleum. New sources may lie beneath the ocean floor. Some areas in the Arctic also have untapped petroleum reserves. But, the locations of these reserves make them costly to explore and use. Also, many people feel the Arctic is a precious and fragile natural resource that should not be disturbed by human activity.

SEE ALSO
207 Ocean Floor

MORE ▶

Natural gas is a fossil fuel that often forms on top of petroleum. Natural gas is collected by drilling wells into Earth and letting the gas flow up through pipes into collecting tanks. Most natural gas is used for heating and to generate electricity. It can also be changed into a liquid and used as fuel for automobiles.

Coal is a solid fossil fuel formed from dead plant material. It is both more available than petroleum, and easier to transport. Coal is removed from Earth through **mining,** or digging down into Earth.

Like other fossil fuels, coal is burned to release its energy. In some places, coal is used for cooking and home heating. Most coal mined today is burned in power plants to generate electricity.

All fossil fuels are nonrenewable sources of energy. That means once used, they are gone forever —or at least for another several million years! That's why people must be careful about how much fossil fuel they use.

Coal is used to produce about 50 percent of the world's electricity and about 20 percent of the energy used in the United States.

Source: DOE, Fossil Energy Education, FAQs.

SCILINKS NSTA
Keyword: Nonrenewable Resources
www.scilinks.org
Code: GSSM325

Geothermal Energy

326

Heat energy from within Earth is called **geothermal energy.** In some places, hot water and steam from inside Earth escape to the surface through vents or geysers. This heated water and steam can be used to generate electricity in a geothermal power plant.

SEE ALSO
177 Struture of Earth
328 Renewable Energy Resources

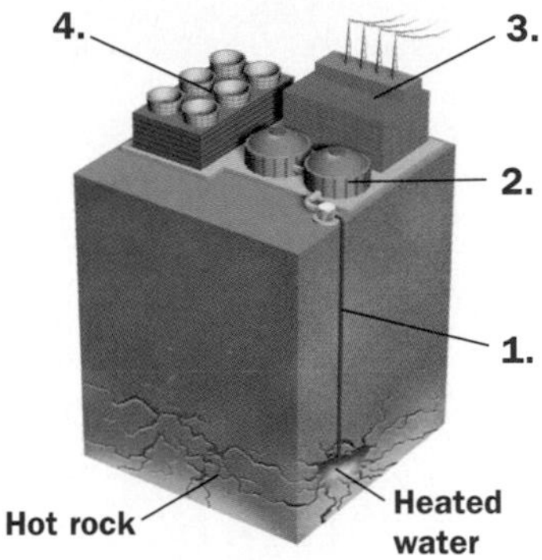

1. A well dug into Earth captures steam.
2. Steam is directed at turbines that drive electric generators.
3. Electricity produced by the generators is sent out along power lines.
4. Vents in power plant release excess steam to the air.

Electricity production in a geothermal power plant

Geothermal energy is one of the cheapest energy sources as it uses heat that is already made naturally inside Earth. Unfortunately, geothermal vents are found only in a few areas around the world, usually areas with high volcanic activity.

Word Watch!

The word *geothermal* is formed from the Greek words *geo*, meaning "Earth," and *thermo*, meaning "heat."

Nuclear Energy

327

Nuclear energy is energy that comes from the nuclei, or centers, of atoms. One kind of nuclear energy, called **fission,** results when the nucleus of an atom is split apart. In this process, the nucleus produces new elements, free neutrons, and a great deal of energy. Most often, the element used for nuclear fission is the **radioactive** element uranium. Uranium is found in rocks that can be mined like coal.

SEE ALSO
256 Atomic Structure
265 Periodic Table
347 Toxic Waste

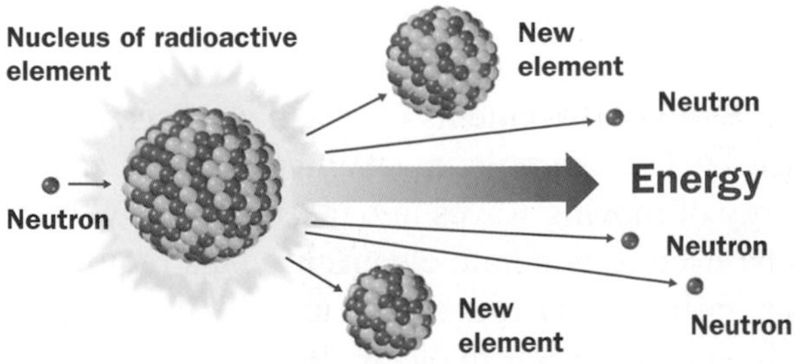

Fission produces energy.

328 Renewable Energy Resources

Renewable energy resources are good alternatives to nonrenewable resources like fossil fuels. Their supply is not limited, and many are cleaner to use than nonrenewable resources.

SEE ALSO

225 Wind
326 Geothermal Energy

Wind Energy Moving air, or wind, contains energy. For centuries, this energy has turned windmills used to pump water or grind grain. Today, wind turbines are used to generate electricity. A **turbine** is an engine that uses a **generator** to convert the **mechanical energy** of moving wind, water, or steam into **electrical energy.**

A wind farm

SEE ALSO

341 Habitat Loss

Hydroelectric Energy Moving water has energy. Hydroelectric power plants use turbines and generators to convert the energy of moving water into electricity. Most hydroelectric power plants are part of dams built across rivers. Falling water causes turbines at the base of the dam to turn. Generators then convert the energy of the moving water into electricity.

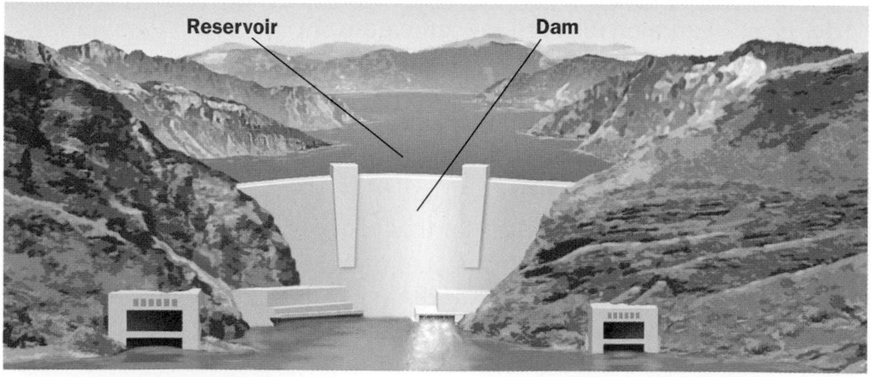

A hydroelectric power plant

SEE ALSO

237 Tides

Wave and Tidal Energy Movements of ocean water can also be used to generate electricity. For example, mechanical devices can be built to change the energy of moving waves into electricity. The energy of ocean tides can also be used to generate electricity. This requires building a barrier across a harbor or narrow inlet. Turbines in the barrier change the energy of the moving water to electricity as the tide rolls in and out.

Solar Energy Energy from the sun is called **solar energy.** Many homes, especially those in cold climates, are built so that sunlight can enter windows directly during the day, supplying the house with heat and light. Sunlight can also be converted into other forms of energy. For example, **photovoltaic (PV) cells** are devices that use the energy of sunlight to generate electricity. Small PV cells are often used to power watches and calculators. Many larger PV cells can be mounted on buildings to change the sun's energy into electricity for use in homes.

Solar energy in use

Biomass Matter formed from plants and animals that contains stored energy is called **biomass.** Several types of biomass are used as energy resources.

- **Wood** is a type of biomass that comes from trees. People in many parts of the world use wood as their main source of energy. In these places, wood is burned mostly to produce heat for homes and for cooking.
- **Peat** is a type of biomass that forms as swamp plants begin to break down and decay. Peat can be burned to produce heat.
- Dried animal waste, or **dung,** is a type of biomass that can be burned for heat.
- Many kinds of plants can be used to make **alcohol.** Some alcohols are burned directly as fuel. Others are mixed with gasoline to make a fuel called **gasohol.**
- As biomass decays, it gives off a gas called **methane**. Methane gas can be collected and burned as a fuel.

SCiLINKS NSTA Keyword: Renewable Resources
www.scilinks.org
Code: GSSM328

Did You Know?

Only 5 percent of the people in the world live in the United States, yet in the year 2000 it used 23.3 percent of the world's energy. In the same year, India used 3.2 percent of the world's energy to meet the needs of 15 percent of the world's population.
Source: Energy Information Administration, Annual Energy Outlook.

329

Material Resources

Earth provides many natural resources in the form of materials. You need some of these resources, such as air, water, and food, to live. Other natural resources, such as rocks, minerals, and trees, are used in products that make your life more comfortable.

330

Renewable Material Resources

Many of the natural resources around you have been on Earth for millions of years in one form or another. The oxygen you breathe today is the same as that inhaled by dinosaurs 70 million years ago. A glass of water you drink before bed could have fallen as raindrops in a tropical rainforest thousands of years before there were people on Earth. Air and water are both renewable natural resources, meaning they do not get "used up."

SEE ALSO
105 Animal Physiology
107 Plant Physiology
138 Carbon Dioxide-Oxygen Cycle

Air is a renewable natural resource that is needed by most living things. You, and other organisms, use oxygen from the air for **cellular respiration,** the process in which food is broken down to get energy. Carbon dioxide is released back into the air as a waste product of respiration. Plants use carbon dioxide from the air to make food by **photosynthesis.** During this process, oxygen is released back into the air as a waste product. Together, the processes of respiration and photosynthesis continually cycle oxygen and carbon dioxide through the environment.

SEE ALSO
216 Water Cycle

All living things need a regular supply of clean water to survive. Water is a renewable resource that constantly cycles through the environment, moving from land to air and back again.

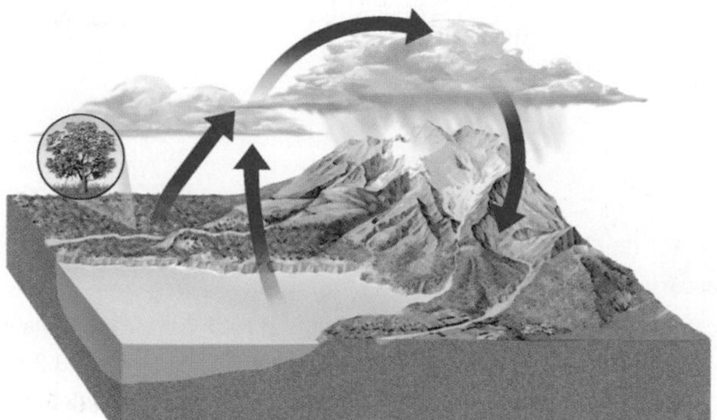

The water cycle

Many products you use each day come from living things. For this reason, plants, animals, and other living things can be thought of as natural resources.

Organisms are considered renewable resources because they can reproduce to make more living things like themselves.

Plants Many of the products you use each day come from plants. These products include the fruits, vegetables, seeds, and breads you use as food. Plants are also a source of many types of cloth, including cotton, used in the making of clothing and other textiles. Trees supply wood for houses, furniture, and paper. Other plants produce chemicals that are used to make medicines, varnishes, rubber, fertilizers, and paints.

Animals All of the foods you consider meats come from animals. Animals also provide you with food products such as milk and eggs. Like plants, animals provide people with materials used to make clothing, such as wool, leather, and fur. Animals also provide chemicals used in the making of medicines, glues, and shampoos.

Other organisms Fungi, protists, and bacteria also provide people with useful products. For example, mushrooms (a fungus) and algae (a protist) are both used as food. The fungi known as yeasts are used in the making of bread, and bacteria in the making of cheese, yogurt, and sauerkraut. Chemicals from bacteria, fungi, and protists are also used to make medicines.

Did You Know?

The antibiotic penicillin was originally made from a mold. Antibiotics kill bacteria and are used as medicines.

Keyword: Renewable Resources
www.scilinks.org
Code: GSSM328

331 Nonrenewable Material Resources

For thousands of years, humans have been trying to find steady supplies of nonrenewable material resources. Because these resources are limited, they often have special value. For example, at one time in history, salt and other spices were so rare they were considered as valuable as gold. Gold itself costs so much partly because there isn't that much of it available on the planet. As a general rule, the scarcer the resource, the more it's worth.

Did you know that rocks are considered natural resources? Rocks such as granite, marble, and slate have long been used as building materials for homes. Granite, for example, may form the outside walls of a home or be used in the construction of fireplaces. Marble and slate are often used to make countertops and flooring. These same rocks may also be used to make monuments or sculptures.

SEE ALSO

179 Minerals

180 Rocks

Minerals are among the most commonly used natural resources. More than 3000 different minerals are found in Earth's crust. Minerals are used in a variety of ways. For example, quartz is used to help keep time in watches and clocks. Rock salt is used in winter to melt snow and ice from sidewalks and roadways. Graphite is the dark-colored mineral found in pencils. The greasy texture of graphite makes this mineral useful as a writing tool. Gypsum is a chalk-like mineral that is used to make the plaster and sheet rock used in buildings. Minerals are considered nonrenewable natural resources because most take millions of years to form.

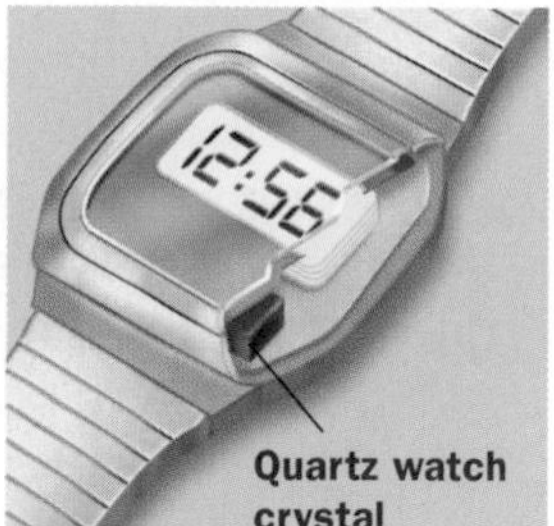

Quartz watch crystal

One group of especially useful minerals is **metals.** Gold, silver, copper, aluminum, and iron are examples of metals. Sometimes metals are found in a pure form, but more often they are combined with other minerals in rocks. Most metals can be easily formed into shapes or drawn into wire. Another property of metals that makes them useful is that they are usually good conductors of heat and electricity.

SEE ALSO
265 Periodic Table
317 Current Electricity

Did You Know?

Eighty percent of the known elements are metals. The rest are nonmetals, most of which are gases.

How many of the products you use each day are made of plastics? Pens, garbage bags, food wrappers, beverage bottles, and your bicycle helmet are just a few of the many products made from plastics. **Plastics** are chemical compounds that are easily molded into different shapes. Plastics are not natural resources. But, most plastics are made from petroleum. **Petroleum** is a liquid that forms from the fossil remains of organisms deep below Earth's surface. The processes that form petroleum take millions of years to occur, so petroleum is considered a nonrenewable natural resource.

SEE ALSO
325 Fossil Fuels

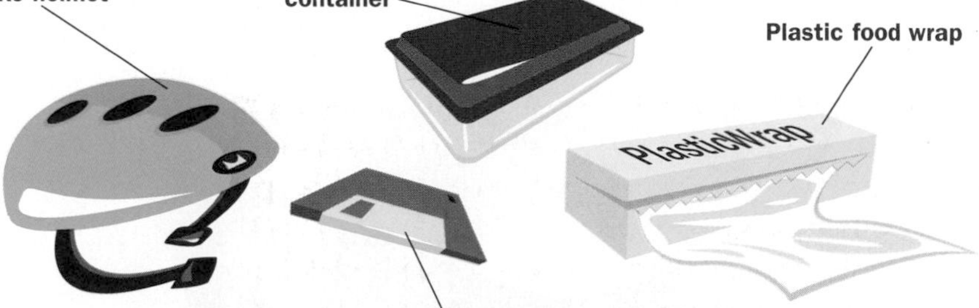

Products made from plastics

As human populations continue growing, the demand for many nonrenewable natural resources will increase. One challenge for the future is to find alternatives to nonrenewable resources in order to slow the rate at which they are used up.

332

Resource Conservation

When the first settlers from Europe came to the Americas, they often remarked that they had found a land with an endless supply of resources: limitless space, clear running water, and an abundance of plants and animals.

Today, computer models show that many of Earth's resources are in danger of being used up or becoming too polluted to use. So, people must find ways to conserve natural resources to make sure they will be available in the future. **Conservation** is the wise use of natural resources. As human populations continue to grow, so will the demand for these resources. Without conservation efforts, reserves of these resources will quickly dwindle.

Conservation of Energy

333

Most of the energy people use to carry out their daily activities comes from fossil fuels, a nonrenewable energy source. There is only a limited supply of nonrenewable energy resources. Nothing but nature and millions of years can make coal or oil.

SEE ALSO
325 Fossil Fuels

Limiting Consumption

334

The first step in conserving resources is to reduce **consumption.** This means using less of a resource in the first place.

SEE ALSO
325 Fossil Fuels

One way to reduce the amount of resources used is to decrease the demand for products that use these resources. For example, if people use public transportation more often instead of driving their cars, not as much oil will need to be pumped from the ground. Driving cars that use less fuel also helps reduce the amount of gasoline people consume.

Another way to reduce energy consumption is to reduce energy waste. Most homes and other buildings in colder climates are lined with insulation to help reduce heat loss. As a result, less energy needs to be used for heating. Buildings in warmer climates, on the other hand, are insulated to keep heat out and cold in. This helps reduce the amount of energy used for air conditioning.

Adobe house in a hot climate

335 Alternative Energy Sources

SEE ALSO
328 Renewable Energy Sources
325 Fossil Fuels

One way to protect limited energy resources is to find alternatives that do the same job. Solar energy, geothermal energy (energy from the heat of the Earth), biomass (the energy of plant and animal material), wind energy, and the energy of moving water are all examples of energy sources that are not in limited supply. Today, most people are dependent on fossil fuels for their energy needs. But scientists and engineers around the world are trying to develop ways of making alternative fuel use more efficient and affordable.

336 Conservation of Material Resources

SEE ALSO
346 Solid Waste

Earth's supply of natural material resources is limited. So people must make sure to conserve as much as possible so that future generations will be able to make use of the same resources. By reducing, reusing, and recycling natural resources, fewer new resources need to be taken from Earth.

Using fewer resources also reduces the amount of waste that ends up in landfills.

Percentage of Students Taking Steps to Improve the Environment

Turn off lights to save energy

Source: Hazardous Substances & Public Health, vol. 5, no. 1, winter 1995.

Reduce

If it's your job to take the trash out in your house, you know that less waste is better. There are many ways to reduce material waste. Rethinking the design of products is one way. Take packaging for example.

Packaging keeps foods clean and prevents them from becoming damaged or spoiled. But most packaging, including plastic wrap, cardboard, paper, and foam food containers, is used only once. This is not a very good use of a resource.

Today, many consumers look for items that have less packaging. They also look for packaging made from recycled or biodegradable materials. **Biodegradable** materials are those that break down easily when exposed to sun, water, and other elements of nature. Many consumers have shown they will pay more for these so-called "green" products (those that show an effort to conserve resources or protect the environment). Some consumers bring their own reusable containers and packaging to avoid using those provided by the store.

Here are some guidelines for how to shop with an eye to reducing waste.

- Try to buy unpackaged goods.
- Bring your own cloth bag or basket to collect unpackaged goods. Reuse paper or plastic bags from earlier store visits.
- Look for glass bottles that can be recycled or refilled.
- Choose beverages in cans that are recyclable.
- Look for plastic products that can be recycled.

Did You Know?

In Germany, stores that sell packaging for beverages, soaps, paints, and other items must collect the packaging after it's been used and recycle it. By law, all containers for liquids must be refillable.
Source: Garbage And Other Pollution (Information Plus), 2000.

MORE ▶

Here are some suggestions for other ways you can reduce waste.

- Consider buying used products rather than new ones.
- Repair broken items (when possible) instead of replacing them.
- Rent tools, furniture, or appliances that you need to use only a few times, instead of buying them.
- Share newspapers, magazines, and clothing with others.
- Donate items you no longer use to those who might be able to use them.
- Clean packaging containers and find other uses for them.

Did You Know?

The plastics industry has reduced the thickness of plastic containers while keeping them just as strong. Forty years ago, a 3.8-liter (1-gallon) milk container had a mass of about 120 grams. Today, a 65-gram plastic container does the same job. *Source: American Plastics Council.*

338

Reuse

Reusing material resources involves recovering items that would have been thrown away and finding another use for them.

Many containers and bags can be used more than once. Before you throw something away, try to see if you can find another use for it. Perhaps you could use a shoebox to organize supplies in your room. Bags from the supermarket can be used a number of times before being placed in the recycle bin.

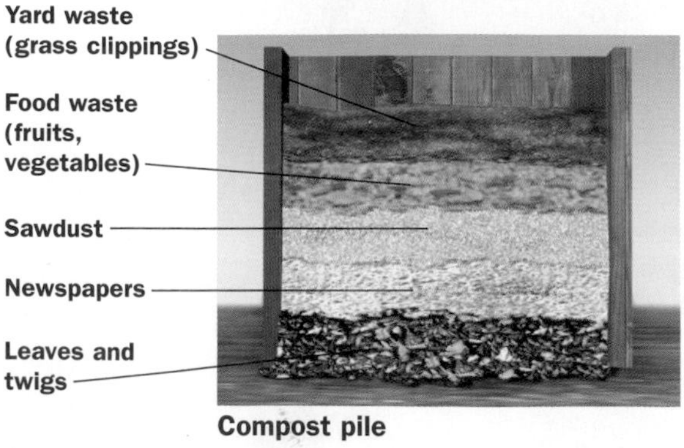

Compost pile

Another great way to reuse materials is to create a compost pile. A compost pile is made up of discarded fruit and vegetable material, yard waste, and other plant materials. As the materials break down over time, they produce fertilizer that is great for plants.

Recycle

339

Many types of wastes are recyclable. Materials you should recycle instead of throwing away include the following:

- batteries
- yard trimmings (grass, leaves, etc.)
- tires
- used motor oil
- glass
- paper (including newspaper)
- aluminum
- plastic containers and other forms of recyclable plastic

A better way to dispose of garbage

Recyclable materials you leave outside your house or bring to a collection center are usually then taken to a Materials Recovery Facility. These facilities sort recyclables that have been all mixed together, preparing them for recycling. Various belts move trash along where it is usually sorted by hand. More high-tech equipment uses magnets, electric sensors, and shakers to separate the items.

Word Watch!

The term *precycling* is used to describe products made to be easily recycled or reused. These products last longer and use less throwaway packaging.

Methods of Resource Recovery

Item	How Recycled	Becomes
Scrap Steel 	melted down in furnace	support beams, steel plates, reinforcement bars 
Aluminum 	shredded, washed, melted	sheet aluminum, then cans 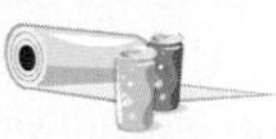
Newspapers 	soaked in water, screened, more wood pulp added	newsprint, paper; ink used as fuel or as new ink 
Plastics 	sorted by type, shredded, melted, remixed	new containers, industrial uses 

340

Wildlife Conservation

Almost 40 percent of medicines come from plants or animals.

SEE ALSO
124 Change and Diversity of Life
128 Extinction

More than 1 million different **species**, or kinds of living things, live on Earth today. Many other species that once lived on Earth no longer exist. The dying out of all members of a species is called **extinction.** Extinction is a natural process. But the extinctions of some species are related to the activities of people.

A number of factors affect how an organism is able to survive in its environment. Habitat loss, pollution, and over hunting are some of the biggest factors affecting wildlife survival today.

341

Habitat Loss

An organism's **habitat** is the area where it lives. Organisms get everything they need to survive within their habitats. If an organism's habitat is destroyed, the organism must find a new habitat to live in or else it will die.

SEE ALSO
187 Mountain Building and Volcanoes

Habitats can be harmed by a variety of factors. Volcanic eruptions and forest fires are two natural activities that can destroy habitats. But human activities are more commonly at fault.

As humans expand into areas where wild plants and animals live, habitats are lost. Where roads, houses, and businesses move in, animals and plants must move out. The harvesting of natural resources is another problem. As people cut down trees for wood, the natural habitats of birds, insects, rodents, and other organisms are lost.

Logging destroys habitats.

Other human activities destroy natural habitats as well. Dams built across rivers to produce power cause water to rise on one side of the dam and slow to a trickle on the other side. This action often destroys the habitats of wildlife on both sides of the dam.

SEE ALSO
328 Renewable Energy Resources

Pollution

342

Many habitats are threatened by pollution. One type of air pollution, acid rain, damages forests and makes them unsuitable for plants and animals. Water pollution from acid rain, waste disposal, and industrial processes has damaged some lakes, rivers, and streams to the point where they are no longer good habitats for organisms.

Wildlife harmed by oil spill

SEE ALSO
351 Acid Rain
352 Water Pollution

Perhaps the most visible form of water pollution is an oil spill. Oil spills from offshore oil drilling and shipwrecks kill many different kinds of marine life, from the very tiny to the very big.

SEE ALSO
325 Fossil Fuels

Water pollution caused by dumping waste at sea is thought to be at least partly responsible for the death of many coral reefs. These shallow breeding and feeding grounds are considered the rainforests of the sea because of the wide variety of plants and animals that live among the reefs.

A coral reef

SEE ALSO
149 Saltwater Ecosystems

343 Over Hunting

Humans have hunted wild animals for thousands of years. But as human populations grow in size, so does their demand for food. As a result, some wildlife populations have been hurt by over hunting.

SEE ALSO
113 Reproduction

Fish are a good example. Today's commercial fishing boats can catch many more fish that those of fifty years ago, thanks to improvements in boats, fishing nets, and other technology. Often the boats take so many fish that not enough are left to reproduce. And it's not just the fish being taken. Nets often kill animals that fishers are not hunting, such as dolphins, whales, and sea turtles.

Did You Know?

Many fishing fleets once used driftnets as much as 64 kilometers long. The United States banned use of these nets in 1992 to protect ocean mammals.

Animals that have been hunted to extinction by humans include the passenger pigeon and the great auk, which went extinct around 1900. Other animals have been hunted to near extinction. Among them are the humpback whale, the African black rhinoceros, and the sea otter. Today, laws make it illegal to hunt these animals.

Passenger pigeon

Plants too are in danger of being over hunted. Some plants are collected for their extraordinary beauty. For example, many species of cacti and orchids are nearly extinct in the wild because people remove them to display in their homes or to sell.

Orchid

Protecting Wildlife

344

All around the world, laws have been passed to help save plants and animals from extinction. In the United States, the Endangered Species Act of 1973 set up a way to identify plants and animals that need help. Today, the California condor is considered an **endangered species.** Endangered species are in immediate danger of becoming extinct unless actions are taken to protect them. Eastern Cougars are considered a **threatened species.** This means they may become endangered if their numbers continue to shrink.

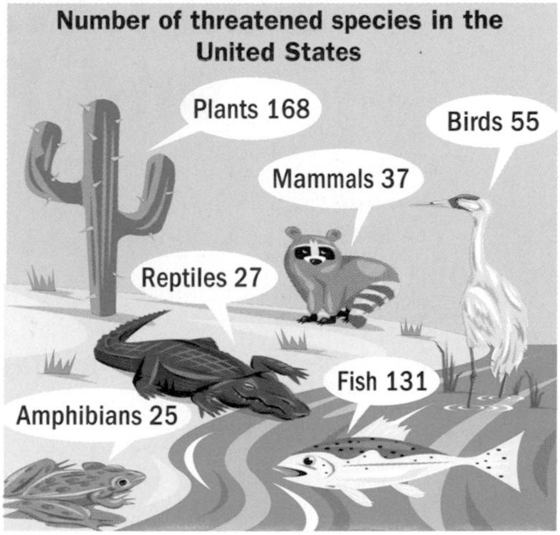

Source: The International Union for Conservation of Nature and Natural Resources.

Sometimes land is set aside for endangered plants or animals to live away from humans. Such a place is called a **sanctuary** or a **wildlife preserve.** Usually such places take the form of a park or safety zone where the endangered animal will not be disturbed by human activity.

In some extreme cases, scientists will actually raise young endangered animals themselves. Zoos and wildlife organizations make sure to raise the young in such a way that they will be able to survive as adults in the wild. This technique, called **captive breeding,** was successful in saving the whooping crane and the peregrine falcon.

Did You Know?

Scientists and ultralight aircraft pilots have teamed up to teach sandhill cranes how to migrate. Conservationists hope to use the same methods to teach endangered whooping cranes raised by people how to migrate south for the winter.

345

Solid Waste and Pollution

The human **population**, or number of people living on Earth, grew to more than 6 billion in the year 2000. As the population grows, so does its use of natural resources. Unfortunately, natural resource use sometimes creates environmental problems, including the production of solid waste and pollution.

Did You Know?

Between 1990 and 2000, Earth's population grew by 900 million people. It is expected to increase by another 2.3 billion people by the year 2025.
Source: The United Nations.

Human Population Growth (2000 B.C. to 2000 A.D.)

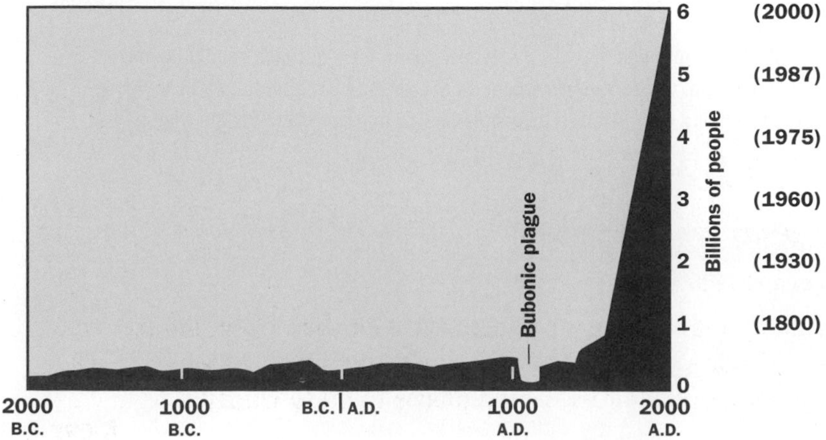

Solid Waste

What happens to your garbage after a truck hauls it away? Most likely, it's buried underground in areas called **landfills.** In some areas, garbage is burned in an **incinerator.** But this practice has been stopped in many places because it causes air pollution. Some items in garbage are also recycled.

SEE ALSO
337 Reduce
338 Reuse
339 Recycle

57% Landfill | 6% Burned | 27% Recycled

What happens to garbage that is thrown away

Before people started building landfills, garbage was often disposed of in open dumps. Besides being ugly to look at, dumps smelled bad and were home to unwanted pests such as rats and cockroaches. Oftentimes, dumps leaked poisonous materials into the environment. Today, open dumps are illegal in most places.

Sanitary landfills, on the other hand, are lined with natural and synthetic materials that prevent pollutants from leaking out. Garbage is then spread out between thin layers of clean soil, compacted, and finally planted with grass or other vegetation.

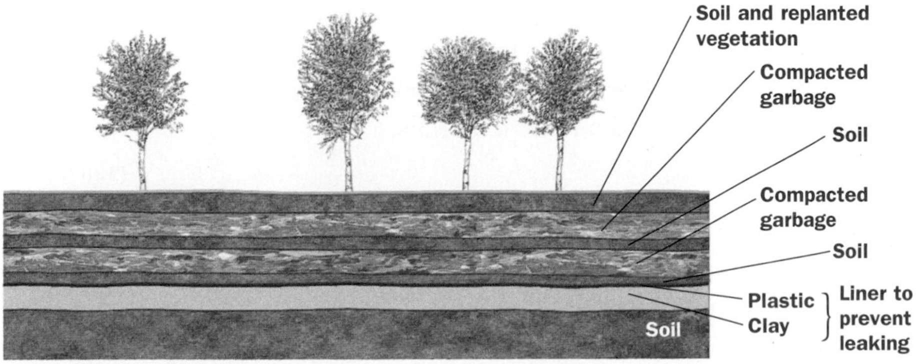

Parts of a landfill

Even though landfills are cleaner and safer than open dumps, most people still don't want them in their communities. As a result, it's getting harder and harder to find places to build landfills.

MORE

Some people use incineration, or burning, to get rid of garbage. Incineration is most often used in places where there is no space for landfills. The heat given off by the burning of garbage can also be used to heat buildings or generate electricity. But burning creates its own problems too. This practice releases smoke and pollutants into the air. It also leaves behind ashes that must be gotten rid of.

SEE ALSO
348 Air Pollution
339 Recycle

The best way to get rid of wastes is to recycle them. Recycled wastes are made into new products that people can use.

347 Toxic Waste

You may think your brother's toothbrush is toxic waste, but the real thing is far scarier. **Toxic wastes** are substances that can damage living things. Some contain poisonous metals or other destructive ingredients. Others can explode or burn spontaneously. For the most part, toxic wastes are the byproducts of industrial processes. That is, they are created not on purpose, but simply in the process of making another product.

An expensive and complex series of steps must be taken to handle toxic wastes before they can be disposed of. In many cases, they are treated to make them less dangerous. Then they are disposed of in the safest possible way. Many are sealed in containers that are designed not to leak. These containers are then placed in waste sites designed to handle toxic materials.

SEE ALSO
327 Nuclear Energy

The production of nuclear energy creates materials that are considered toxic wastes.

Air Pollution

348

Anything in the environment that is harmful to living things is called **pollution.** Smoke, ash, and dust released into the air by forest fires and volcanic eruptions are forms of **air pollution** caused by natural events. Most air pollution, however, is caused by the activities of people.

The burning of fossil fuels, like oil and coal, causes most air pollution today. When these fuels are burned to produce the energy needed to power cars and heat homes, gases and dust particles are released into the air.

SEE ALSO
325 Fossil Fuels

Sources of air pollution

Volcanoes

Factories

Cars

One air pollution problem common in cities is smog. Cars and factories release large amounts of chemical pollutants into the air. Smog forms when sunlight reacts with these chemicals. You might see smog as a haze in the air over polluted areas. The chemicals in smog can irritate your eyes, nose, and throat.

Strict laws have helped to lower the amounts of some pollutants in the air. Power plants and factories must remove some chemicals from their waste smoke. Cars are designed to burn fuel more cleanly. Scientists are also working on cars that run on electricity instead of gasoline. Still, there is plenty more work to be done.

349

Greenhouse Effect

One form of air pollution that some scientists are very worried about is the production of too much carbon dioxide and other so-called greenhouse gases.

SEE ALSO
213 Earth's Atmosphere

Greenhouse gases trap heat in the atmosphere, the layer of air above Earth's surface. This action, which is like the trapping of heat inside a greenhouse, produces what is called the **greenhouse effect.** The greenhouse effect helps keep Earth at a temperature that supports life. But human activities are increasing the amounts of some greenhouse gases in the atmosphere. Many people believe this increase in greenhouse gases is causing **global warming,** an increase in temperatures around the world.

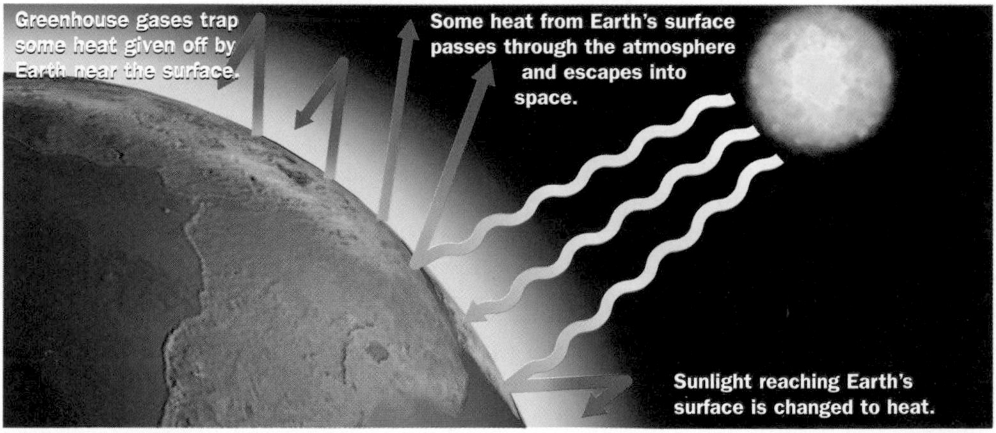

Greenhouse gases trap some heat given off by Earth near the surface.
Some heat from Earth's surface passes through the atmosphere and escapes into space.
Sunlight reaching Earth's surface is changed to heat.

How the greenhouse effect works

SEE ALSO
325 Fossil Fuels

When fossil fuels are burned in power plants and automobiles, carbon dioxide is released into the air. When trees are burned to clear forests, more carbon dioxide is released. Concern over carbon dioxide production has led to new manufacturing methods that reduce the amount of carbon dioxide produced. In addition, laws and international treaties have been written in an effort to reduce the output of greenhouse gases around the world.

Global temperatures have risen and fallen many times during Earth's history, and many scientists suspect that some global warming may be natural. But human activities are also changing the amounts of different gases in the atmosphere. Taking action to reduce the amounts of these gases produced by people seems like a smart idea.

Ozone Depletion

High up in Earth's atmosphere is a layer of gas known as the **ozone layer.** The ozone layer is vital to life on Earth because it keeps most of the **ultraviolet (UV) radiation** from the sun from reaching Earth's surface. Too much UV radiation harms living things by damaging or destroying cells.

SEE ALSO
214 Composition of the Atmosphere
076 Cells

CAUTION: Too much UV radiation can cause sunburn and skin cancer. Always wear sunscreen when you spend time outdoors. Protect your eyes by wearing a hat and sunglasses on sunny days.

About 25 years ago, scientists studying the ozone layer observed that it was becoming thinner. In some places, the thinning was so great that a hole formed in the ozone layer. Thinning of the ozone layer occurs partly from natural processes. But air pollution is also a cause.

Use of **chlorofluorocarbons,** or **CFCs,** is believed to cause thinning of the ozone layer. CFCs are compounds of the chemicals chlorine, fluorine, and carbon. These chemicals were once used as coolants in refrigerators and air conditioners. They were also used in aerosol spray cans.

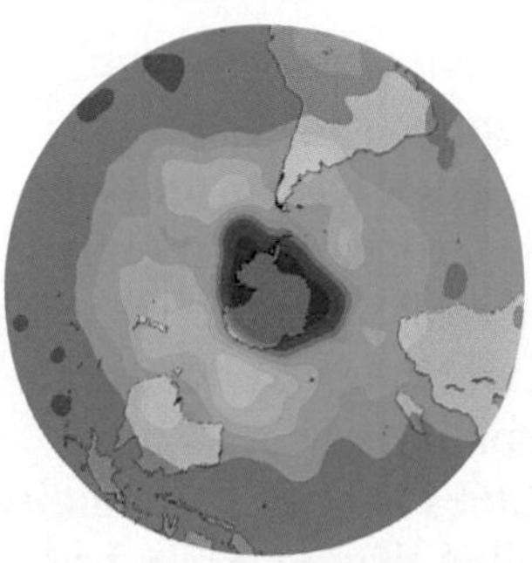

The ozone hole over the South Pole

SEE ALSO
259 Elements, Molecules, and Compounds
265 Periodic Table

Not all scientists agree that CFCs cause holes in the ozone layer. But most countries have stopped using CFCs in their products to be safe. Scientists continue to measure changes in the ozone layer to see whether stopping CFC use has any effect.

351

Acid Rain

SEE ALSO

325 Fossil Fuels
253 States of Matter
216 Water Cycle
264 Families of Chemical Compounds

Your electricity is probably provided by a power plant. Most power plants burn fossil fuels to generate electricity. As these fuels burn, they release smoke and chemicals into the air. Some of these chemicals combine with water vapor (water in the gas phase) in the air to form acids that return to Earth as **acid rain.**

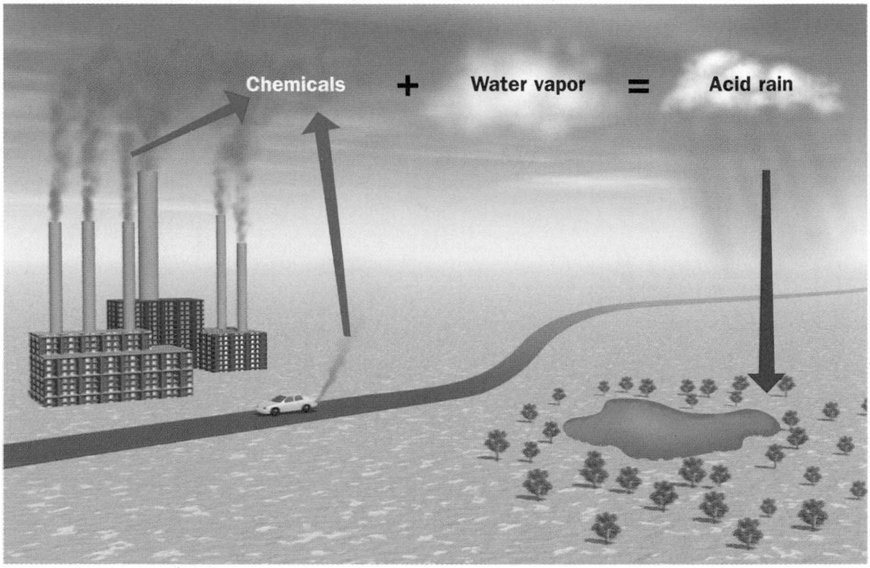

How acid rain forms

SEE ALSO

179 Minerals
180 Rocks
190 Chemical Weathering

Acid rain can react with and change things it lands on. For example, acids react with some minerals in rocks, causing the rocks to break apart. Many acids corrode, or "eat away," metals. If you look closely at stone or metal statues in your community, you may see that acid rain has caused such changes.

Word Watch!

Acid rain is sometimes called *acid precipitation* because acids can be carried in rain, snow, drizzle, sleet, or fog.

SEE ALSO

216 Water Cycle
191 Soil

Living things can also be harmed by acid rain. When such rain falls into lakes or streams, it makes the water acidic. This may harm some of the small plants and animals. In time, the water may become so acidic that few organisms can live there. Acid rain can also harm plants by damaging leaves or making the soil too acidic to grow in.

Water Pollution

352

People once dumped almost all their wastes into lakes, rivers, or oceans. As bodies of water became polluted, people looked for other ways to get rid of wastes. Today, sources of water pollution are not as obvious, but water pollution is still a problem.

Surface and Groundwater Contamination

353

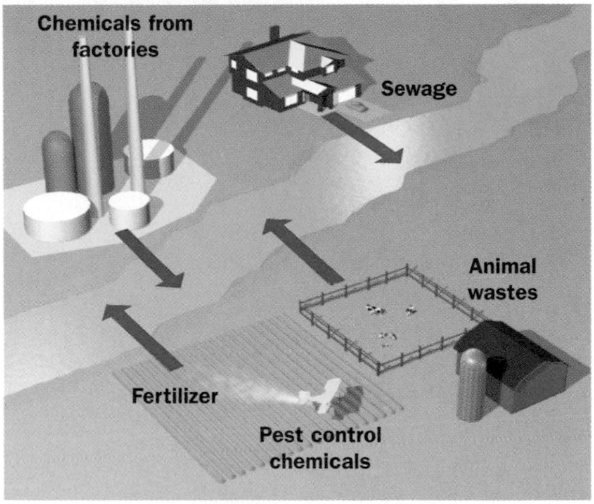

Some sources of water pollution

Factories, homes, and farms are all sources of water pollution. As factories make products, they also make many chemical wastes, some of which are harmful to living things. Pollution from homes is mostly sewage and dirty wash water. If not disposed of carefully, wastes from factories and homes can be carried into lakes and streams. Water pollution from farms and some lawns is usually in the form of fertilizers or chemicals used to control insects. These chemicals can be carried into rivers and lakes by rain or irrigation water. Fluids that leak from cars, such as motor oil and antifreeze, can also be washed off roads and carried into streams by rainwater.

Pollution of surface water is only one problem. Pollutants that make their way into **groundwater**—water that collects in cracks below Earth's surface—can end up in our drinking water.

Many laws have been passed to help control the amount of wastes that are allowed to enter oceans, lakes, and rivers. Rather than simply dumping wastes somewhere, people and businesses must now deal with the pollutants they create.

Fertilizers are chemical nutrients for plants. In streams and lakes, these chemicals encourage algae to grow. But too many algae can lower the oxygen level in water, making it hard for fish and other organisms to live there.

SCIENCE, TECHNOLOGY, AND SOCIETY

354

While Tom was having his brainstorm, Ann was having her energy efficient, compact fluorescent brainstorm.

People often look for ways to do tasks more easily and make their lives more comfortable. Technology helps to do this. **Technology** is the use of scientific knowledge and processes to solve problems and carry out tasks. Technology can help solve many problems. But technology may not help everyone in the same way. Some products are too costly for many people to use. Other products may harm the environment. In this section, you will think about the benefits and drawbacks of different types of technology. You also will look at some limits on technology.

Word Watch!

Technology is sometimes called *applied science.*

355

Science and Technology

People have been inventing and using technology for a very long time. Much of human survival has depended on the use of technology. For example, very early people found that putting a sharpened stone on the tip of a wooden spear made the spear a better hunting tool. This new technology became common practice and helped ancient people survive in their environment.

356

Search for Solutions

SEE ALSO
002 Scientific Inquiry

Some advances in technology occur by accident. This may have been true when native people of the Amazon rain forest discovered that a substance from a certain plant could paralyze living things. Hunters began to coat darts with the substance. They shot the poison darts through blowguns at their prey. A deer struck by a dart was paralyzed and easily caught. Poison dart technology made hunting easier for these ancient people of the Amazon rain forest.

Ancient people in other lands struggled with other problems of survival: What kind of soil is best for growing wheat? How can we measure time, so we know when to plant crops? How can we build better roads so we can move food to market? New technology results from answers to such questions. For example, about 2000 years ago Roman engineers wanted to find a stronger material to build roads and other structures. This search led to the recipe for concrete—a building material that we still use today.

Technology also can be an idea, such as a calendar. About 3000 years ago, the Babylonians used their knowledge of events in the sky to create a calendar. Their year was made up of 12 cycles of the moon. Each cycle, from one full moon to the next full moon, formed a lunar month. The 12 lunar months make up a year of only 354 days. The Babylonians knew that a solar year is 365.25 days, so they added an extra month every now and then. In another part of the world, the Mayan people of Central America came up with one of the most accurate calendars ever created. The Mayan calendar was based on overlapping cycles that caused days to repeat in a pattern every 20 days, 360 days, and at longer intervals. Other calendars from the same part of the world, such as the Aztec, were based on similar cycles.

Aztec calendar stone

Ancient Romans also had a calendar, which was used for centuries. However, it became so inaccurate over several centuries that the first day of spring on the calendar was 11 days different from the actual day. By using careful observations of the sun and seasonal changes, a more-accurate calendar was developed in Europe around 1582. This calendar, called the Gregorian calendar, is the most widely-used calendar today. Every fourth year, leap year, an extra day is added to February to keep the calendar in step with Earth's revolution. Even leap-seconds are added to Universal time when needed, to keep the calendar accurate.

Did You Know?

The Gregorian calendar is named for Pope Gregory XIII, who first ordered its use.

Older knowledge may be used to develop new technology in many fields. For example, curare—the poison discovered by Amazon peoples—is sometimes used to relax the muscles of patients while broken bones are reset. The curare stops the muscles from contracting and pulling on the bones while the surgeon works. The amount of curare is carefully controlled so the patient is not paralyzed permanently.

357 Steps in Technology Design

Some advances in technology occur by accident. But most new technology is developed using time-tested steps. Technology advances when people make careful observations, ask questions, do research, conduct experiments and tests, and draw conclusions.

1. A need or problem is identified.
2. Research is done to find out what is already known about the problem, and about any limits on possible solutions.
3. A product or solution is designed to meet the need or solve the problem.
4. The technology is built, tested, and the design is changed and retested.
5. The final product is tested and evaluated.
6. The technological design is accepted or redesigned.

Redesign

Here is an example of how technology design can happen.

SEE ALSO
358 Limits on Technology Design

In the middle 1800s, city streets, buildings, and homes were lit using gas lamps. The gas in the lamps was poisonous and costly. It was a common cause of accidental fires, and it formed a sticky, black soot when burned. People wanted a less costly, safer, and cleaner way to light their homes and streets.

1. The wish for a new light source led people to wonder if electricity could produce light. American inventor Thomas Alva Edison tackled this challenge in the 1870s.
2. Edison did research and found out all he could about heat, light, and electricity. He knew that heat energy could be changed into light energy—that is, if something is heated enough, it also gives off light. Edison also knew that electricity heats some substances as it passes through them. Edison hypothesized that electricity could be used to heat a substance enough to make the substance produce light. But he had to find a way to produce light without burning up the substance.

3. Substances burn only in the presence of oxygen. So Edison designed a product—a glass light bulb—that had the air sucked out of it. Edison's design also contained a fine wire, or filament, made of platinum. When electricity passed through the platinum filament, the filament would heat up and glow without burning.

4. Edison built his light bulb, and it worked. But platinum is very expensive. Thus, this light bulb design was too costly for most people to buy. Edison needed to change his original design to make a working light bulb that was more practical.

5. Edison searched for a material to replace the platinum filament. One of many substances he tried was an inexpensive strip of carbon made from bamboo fiber. He then tested the new bulb. The new light bulb design worked well.

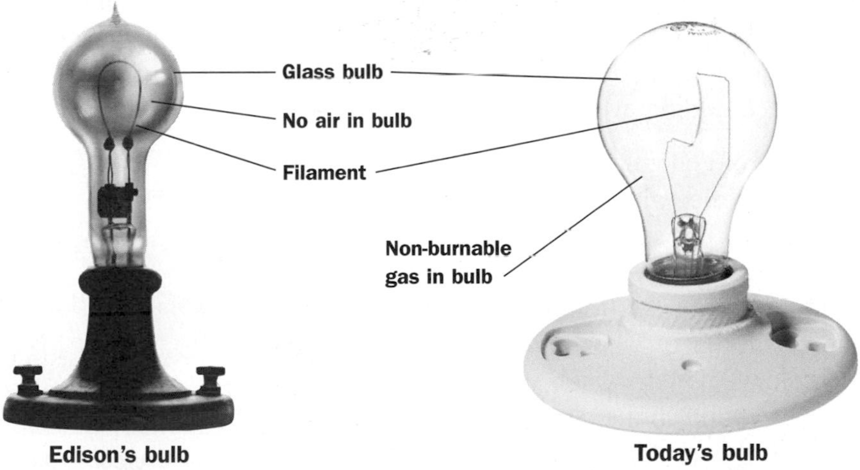

6. Edison's new design for producing light from electricity was cost-effective, cleaner, and safer than gas light. Many people accepted the design, and started using light bulbs. But this new technology has continued to change. For example, filaments made of the metal tungsten—still used in light bulbs—replaced the carbon filaments. Instead of a vacuum, gases that did not support burning, such as nitrogen and argon, were put inside the bulbs. All of these advances improved the light bulb by making it perform better and cost less.

SCILINKS NSTA Keyword: Thomas Edison
www.scilinks.org
Code: GSSM357

358

Limits on Technology Design

A limit is a factor that keeps something from happening. For example, you cannot drive a car until you are tall enough to reach the pedals—a natural limit. You also cannot drive a car until you are of legal driving age and pass a test—a societal limit. Nature, cost, and **ethics,** or people's beliefs about issues, also limit the development of technology. Inventors and designers of technology must understand these limits and make adjustments for them.

359

Natural Limits on Technology

SEE ALSO
287 Work
251 Properties of Matter

Weight is the measure of the force of gravity on an object. Weight is an example of a natural limit on technology. The heavier an object is, the more energy and power needed to move it. For example, a larger, heavier car needs more energy and a more powerful engine to move it than a smaller, lighter car. A more powerful engine, in turn, uses more fuel, adding even more weight to the car!

Physical and chemical properties of substances also place natural limits on technology. For example, pure water freezes at 0°C. For this reason, you can't use pure water to cool hot car engines in places where temperatures dip below 0°C. The water would freeze, expand, and crack engine parts. To solve this problem, antifreeze is added to the water in a car's radiator. Antifreeze lowers the freezing point and increases the boiling point of the water in the radiator.

Antifreeze helps overcome the natural limit of temperature.

360

Economic Limits on Technology

SEE ALSO
371 Risk-Benefit Analysis

How much things cost, or economic limits, affect technology. The cost of making something has to be balanced against whether people can or will buy it. The cost of a product is decided partly by labor costs (money paid to workers) and partly by the cost of raw materials. If a manufacturer spends too much on labor or raw materials, then not enough people will be able to buy the finished product. If the manufacturer does not spend enough on labor and materials, then the item may have poor workmanship and the materials may wear out quickly.

Ethical Limits on Technology

361

Technology answers "can we?" questions. Can we build, create, or do something, using technology? Ethics involves "should we?" questions. **Ethics** are people's beliefs about what is right and good for themselves, other people, other living things, and the environment. Ethical beliefs limit the development of some technologies.

One example of ethics affecting technology is testing new medicines. At one time, many medicines were tested on people without their knowledge or understanding. Now, most people believe it is wrong to test a medicine on a person without first getting their informed consent. **Informed consent** means first telling a patient the purpose of an experiment, how it will be conducted, and how it may affect them, then asking for their permission (or consent) to include them in the experiment. If the patient consents, then he or she signs a paper giving the scientists or doctors permission to perform the experiment. Informed consent is an ethical way to research medical technology. But if not enough patients consent to an experiment, then the development of the technology may be slowed or stopped.

Another technology that may be slowed (or stopped) by ethics is cloning. **Cloning** is growing an exact copy of a living thing by transplanting its genetic material into an egg cell. Scientists have successfully cloned some animals, such as sheep. Some people disapprove of all cloning. Others believe cloning of animals is acceptable, but cloning of humans should not be allowed. Most people who oppose cloning do so for ethical reasons. Cloning may go against their religious and personal beliefs about birth, life, and individuality. They may be concerned that humans would be cloned to provide organ transplants for other humans. Other people believe cloning can have benefits. For example, cloning of tissues, rather than whole humans, could provide perfect matches for transplants. Cloning of rare or endangered animals could lessen the chances of extinction for that species.

Dolly, the first large mammal cloned from another animal

SCILINKS NSTA
Keyword: Cloning
www.scilinks.org
Code: GSSM361

362

Science and Society

Throughout history, scientific study has been limited by the technology available to scientists. Likewise, scientific knowledge advances when new technologies are available. That knowledge can affect how people live in a society. At the same time, society can affect what scientists study and how they study it.

363 Technology and Discovery

Technological advances can lead to scientific discoveries. For example, when people discovered that a curved piece of glass magnifies the image of an object, lenses were invented. The new technology, lenses, was used to build microscopes. Using microscopes, scientists discovered microscopic organisms. Later, other scientists showed that some of these organisms, often called germs, cause disease. Knowledge of germs later led to food being sterilized as a way to help keep people from becoming sick. Food sterilization, along with hand-washing and other methods used to fight germs, has benefited people around the world.

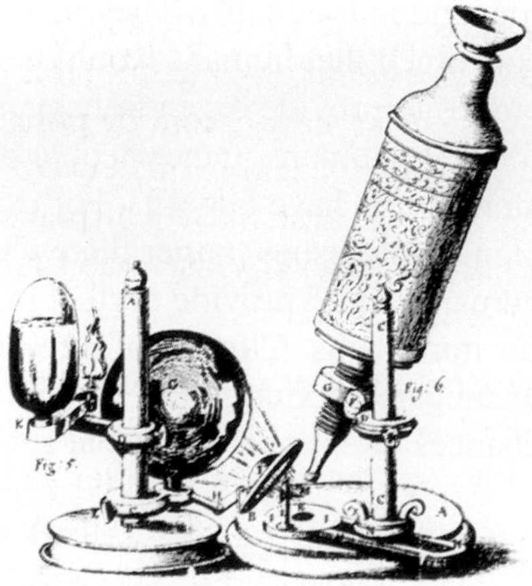

Early microscope

Society and Research

364

Scientific research is not only affected by the technology available to scientists. Is it also affected by the society in which a scientist lives. A society can discourage and encourage different areas of scientific research, depending on its values and needs.

Society's Values

365

Society's needs, wants, and values or ethics can affect how scientific research is done. The physician Vesalius lived in the 1500s. Vesalius studied anatomy by cutting apart the bodies of people who had died. He did this in secret because in his society, at that time in history, most people thought it was wrong to study the body in this way. Medical knowledge could not have advanced without scientists first learning what is inside the body. After Vesalius' time, some societies decided that the benefits of understanding the body outweigh the ethical concerns about using bodies in this way.

Military and Space Technology

366

It is a sad fact that throughout history, nations have gone to war with each other. During wars, the soldiers with better equipment and weapons have an advantage. This is why many countries spend large amounts of money to develop and improve equipment used in the military.

Some technology that was developed for military use benefits society in peacetime. Radar systems are an example. Today, radar is used not only by the military, but also by pilots for navigation, by police tracking speeding cars, and by meteorologists tracking weather systems. Jet airplanes are another technology that was first developed for military use.

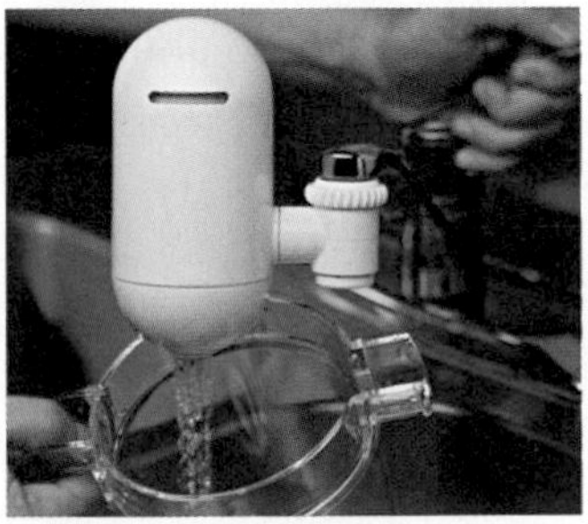

Home water filter

Technology that was developed for use in space also finds its way into life on the ground. Water filters commonly used in homes today were first developed to filter water for reuse in spacesuits. Scratch-resistant coatings on eyeglasses also started out as a solution to a problem in space—in this case, protecting expensive equipment from harsh conditions.

367 Research Priorities

SEE ALSO
324 Energy Resources

It costs money to do scientific research. Funding for research comes from governments and from private companies. Often, the problems that society considers most important, or the solutions that seem most promising, are the ones that get the most funding. For example, many people want scientists to find and develop clean and renewable energy sources. They want better computer models for more accurate predictions of hurricanes, tornadoes, and blizzards—predictions that can save lives. Researchers also receive funding to develop medical instruments, machines, materials, and drugs that will save and improve lives. Each year, billions of dollars are spent on scientific research to solve these and other pressing problems.

368 Research Bias

SEE ALSO
013 Drawing Conclusions

To be useful, scientific research must be based on data that are gathered using controlled studies and experiments. But **bias,** or the influence of a person's beliefs or wishes, can lead to false or misleading conclusions from data. Bias can occur when the people doing the research, or paying for it, want the results to support a certain hypothesis. This desire can affect how people interpret the results. For example, during the 1960s and 1970s, tobacco companies paid for scientific research about cigarette smoking. The tobacco companies wanted to show that cigarette smoking was not harmful to people's health. The results from much of their research seemed to support the hypothesis that cigarette smoking was not harmful. But other research about cigarettes was paid for by groups that did not sell tobacco. Most of that research showed that smoking is a serious danger to health.

SURGEON GENERAL'S WARNING
Smoking Causes Lung Cancer, Heart Disease, Emphysema, And May Complicate Pregnancy

Always ask who paid for research, and think about whether that group might wish for a certain result. This can help you decide how much you can trust the results.

Tradeoffs

Often a new product of technology has both good and bad effects. This forces people to consider the value of the good effects against those of the bad effects. They then decide whether the good effects outweigh the bad ones. Accepting the drawbacks of a technology because of its benefits is called a **tradeoff.** In a tradeoff, people "trade" something bad for something good. Most people would prefer to make use of a technology that has only good effects. But few products of technology are like that. Oil drilling and pipeline laying are a good example of a technology tradeoff.

Oil, or petroleum, is used to provide the energy that runs most cars, trucks, buses, trains, and ships. Oil forms naturally deep underground. To use this oil, it must be pumped out of the ground and then carried by ship or through pipelines to where it is refined into gasoline and other products.

Deposits of oil lie under the frozen ground, or **tundra,** of Alaska. Scientists and engineers have the technology needed to get this oil out of the ground and move it across the state through pipelines. Some people support drilling for Alaska's oil and moving it over the land in pipes. Other people fear that digging into the tundra will be harmful to the environment. They also fear that above-ground pipelines and spilled oil may harm the plants and animals in the region. People who are opposed to drilling in Alaska don't want to take the benefits of having more oil with the potential bad effects on the environment. Other people feel that this tradeoff is worth the benefits it will give to the community, or to the country as a whole. Still others say new technology should be developed to reduce the dangers to the environment before drilling is allowed.

SEE ALSO
340 Wildlife Conservation
342 Pollution

Oil pipelines may disrupt the migration patterns of some animals.

370 Community Decision-Making

Community health and safety needs are sometimes placed over individual needs. For example, most cars run on gasoline. Gasoline gives off air pollutants such as carbon monoxide, nitrous oxides, and soot, when it is burned. Air pollutants are harmful to the health of people and other organisms.

Reducing the amount of air pollution is a community health issue. By law, cars in some states must pass yearly emissions tests. These tests measure the amount of pollutants in a car's exhaust. Cars that pollute too much have to be repaired or taken off the road. These laws are meant to improve air quality for the community. But they can be a hardship for anyone who cannot afford to repair or replace a car that is needed to get to work or school.

SEE ALSO
325 Fossil Fuels

Other laws require the use of special technologies. For example, one law in California requires a certain percentage of new cars to give off no pollution at all. Car makers have designed electric cars to meet this need. Since electric cars don't burn fossil fuels, they don't pollute the air around them. They are also quieter than gasoline-powered cars. However, electric cars are also smaller and less safe in an accident. Electric cars have to be recharged more often than regular cars have to be refilled. Much of the electricity that would be used to recharge electric cars comes from power plants that burn oil or coal, and thus produce pollutants. For example, a coal-fired power plant in Utah sends power to southern California. Some people argue that electric cars do not pollute less—they just move the pollution somewhere else. Engineers are looking for ways to solve the problems of both gasoline and electric cars. Hybrid cars, which use both gasoline and electricity, combine some of the benefits of both kinds of vehicle.

Should one community have more pollution so that another community may have more power?

Risk-Benefit Analysis 371

The use of most technology has both benefits and drawbacks. Cancer, for example, may be treated with chemicals, radiation, surgery, or combinations of these. Each of these technologies has both benefits and risks. So which should be used to treat a particular kind of cancer?

Acceptable Risk Analysis 372

Society sets the level of risk it is willing to accept from a technology. In the United States, this may be done by government agencies such as the Food and Drug Administration (FDA). Before the FDA approves a new medicine it does a **risk-benefit analysis.** In this process, scientists identify the risks and benefits of the medication. The risks and benefits are then compared. If the benefits outweigh the risks, the medication may be approved for use. If the reverse is true, the medication will probably not be approved and will not be available to doctors or patients.

During a risk-benefit analysis for a new medicine, it is studied to see how well it works at treating an illness (the medicine's benefit). The medicine is also studied to find out what side effects it may cause (its risks). A **side effect** is an unwanted response caused by the medicine. Side effects can range from those that are mild, such as a rash or stomachache, to those that are life-threatening, such as a stroke.

WARNINGS/SIDE EFFECTS Use of this product may cause one or more of the following: drowsiness, excitability, headache, joint aches, dry mouth, difficulty in breathing, rash, or irritability. Discontinue use if you experience one or more of these problems.

Not all members of society agree on what's an acceptable level of risk. For example, a person dying of cancer may be willing to take a medicine that may poison the body. But a person with a head cold might not want to take a medicine that has a risk of a slight rash. To address such issues, an organization such as the FDA often decides for society what risks are acceptable. In some cases, the FDA may approve a drug for use in very sick people, but not for less sick people.

373

Reasonable People Disagree

Agreeing on how much risk is acceptable for a technology is not always as easy as adding up risks and benefits. People can honestly disagree on the level of risk that they—or even the whole community—should accept.

Many kinds of technology have been developed to make riding in a car safer. These technologies include seat belts, air bags, head rests, and movable bumpers that absorb some of the shock of a crash. But not all people like to use some of these technologies. For example, many cars have air bags to protect the driver and front-seat passenger in case of a crash. Yet children and small adults may be injured by some air bags. For this reason, some people do not think an air bag is an acceptable risk, if they are already using seat belts. They would like the option of buying a car without air bags. Other people think all cars should have air bags, because air bags provide more benefits than risks for society as a whole. They worry that people whose lives might be saved by air bags would buy cars without air bags if given a choice.

Car safety raises other questions about acceptable risk. Many people like to drive large cars or trucks. The large size of these vehicles may offer better protection to passengers in an accident. But when large cars hit smaller cars, the people in smaller cars are at greater risk of injury. Should society do anything about this risk? Should large cars be outlawed? Should small cars be outlawed? Should people continue to be free to buy and drive their own choice of car? Questions such as these come up all the time as new technologies are invented. In order to decide what to do about a new technology, you must first find out as much as you can about the risks and benefits of that technology. Only then can you make an informed decision.

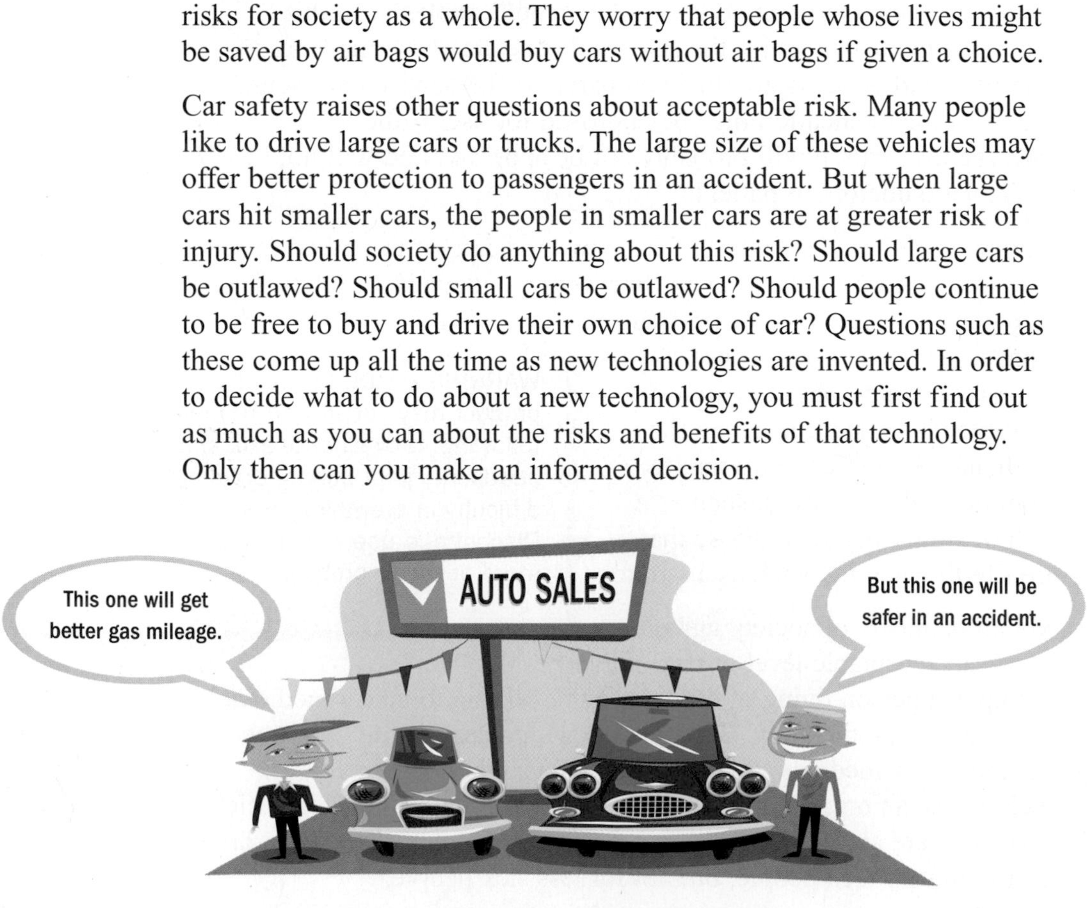

374

ALMANAC

375

Scientific Numbers

In science, you will use a wide variety of numbers and units to describe objects, dimensions, and events in the universe.

376

Extreme Numbers

Because some objects and events in the universe are both extraordinarily large and extraordinarily small, scientists have had to invent new ways of using numbers in order to describe them. For example, the mass of the universe equals about a thousand trillion trillion trillion trillion kilograms, or the numeral 1 followed by 51 zeros! Atomic particles lie at the other end of the mass scale. For example, the mass of an electron—a tiny part of an atom—is about one hundred thousand trillion trillionths of a kilogram. Imagine trying to add, subtract, multiply, or divide these numbers! Reporting data would take a lot of paper and the data would be very difficult to understand. Scientific notation was invented to solve these problems.

How many electrons would it take to equal the mass of the universe? A billion trillion trillion trillion trillion trillion trillion electrons, or the number 1 followed by 81 zeros. It would take three lines on this page just to write the number!

Scientific Notation

377

Scientific notation expresses numbers in powers of ten using exponents. In the table below, count the number of places following the "1" in each number greater than one. Compare it with the exponent in the last column for that number. You will find that the number of places after the one equals the value of the exponent. Now count the number of places after the decimal point for each number less than one. The number of places after the decimal point equals the absolute value of the negative exponent.

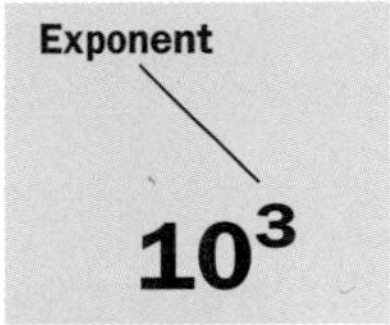

SCIENTIFIC NOTATION

Name	Decimal	Equivalent Fraction	Scientific Notation
Trillion	1,000,000,000,000	$\frac{1,000,000,000,000}{1}$	10^{12}
Billion	1,000,000,000	$\frac{1,000,000,000}{1}$	10^{9}
Million	1,000,000	$\frac{1,000,000}{1}$	10^{6}
Hundred thousand	100,000	$\frac{100,000}{1}$	10^{5}
Ten thousand	10,000	$\frac{10,000}{1}$	10^{4}
Thousand	1,000	$\frac{1,000}{1}$	10^{3}
Hundred	100	$\frac{100}{1}$	10^{2}
Ten	10	$\frac{10}{1}$	10^{1}
One	1	$\frac{1}{1}$	10^{0}
Tenth	0.1	$\frac{1}{10}$	10^{-1}
Hundredth	0.01	$\frac{1}{100}$	10^{-2}
Thousandth	0.001	$\frac{1}{1,000}$	10^{-3}
Ten thousandth	0.0001	$\frac{1}{10,000}$	10^{-4}
Hundred thousandth	0.00001	$\frac{1}{100,000}$	10^{-5}
Millionth	0.000001	$\frac{1}{1,000,000}$	10^{-6}
Billionth	0.000000001	$\frac{1}{1,000,000,000}$	10^{-9}
Trillionth	0.000000000001	$\frac{1}{1,000,000,000,000}$	10^{-12}

MORE ▶

Any number in scientific notation is expressed as the product of a number between 1 and 10 and a power of ten. For example, a distance of 1,000 km would be written as 1.0×10^3 km. A distance of 1,500 km would be 1.5×10^3 km. The exponent "3" tells you that the decimal point is really three spaces to the right of where it is shown. A negative exponent tells you that the decimal point is really that number of spaces to the left, for example,

2.0×10^{-2} dollars equals \$0.02 (or 2 cents).

(\$ 0 0 2.0×10^{-2} = \$0.02)

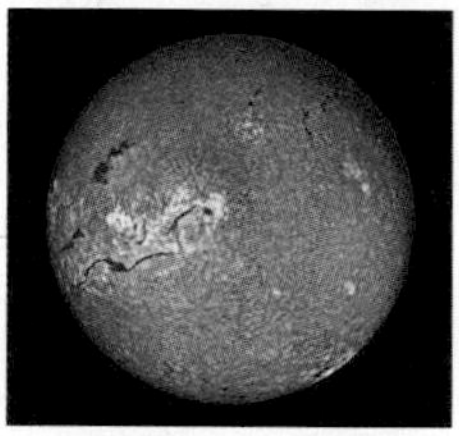

Mass of sun
1.989×10^{30} kg

Deepest known dive of a sperm whale
2.000×10^{3} m

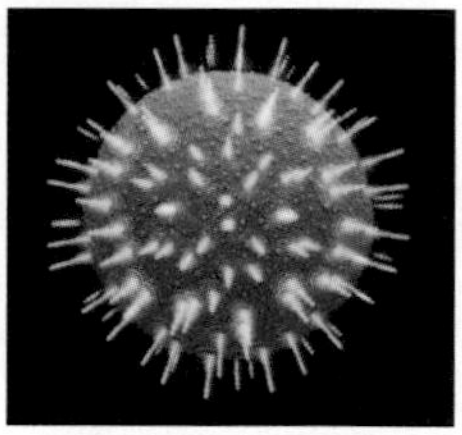

Diameter of HIV (AIDS) virus
1.1×10^{-11} m

378
Decimals

The decimal system is a way of counting or measuring using units that are powers of ten such as thousands, hundreds, tens, ones, tenths, hundredths, or thousandths. Whole numbers are written to the left of the decimal point. Fractions are written to the right of the decimal point.

Word Watch!

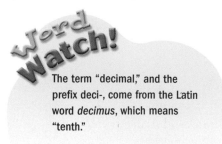

The term "decimal," and the prefix deci-, come from the Latin word *decimus*, which means "tenth."

EXAMPLE

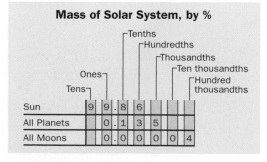

Mass of Solar System, by %

	Tens	Ones	.	Tenths	Hundredths	Thousandths	Ten thousandths	Hundred thousandths
Sun	9	9	.	8	6			
All Planets		0	.	1	3	5		
All Moons		0	.	0	0	0	0	4

379
Rules for Rounding Decimals

When rounding a decimal, look to the right of the place to which you want to round. If the digit to the right of that place is 5 or greater than 5, round up. If the digit to the right is 4 or less than 4, do not change the number in the place you are rounding to.

Amount of the rarest element in Earth's crust (astatine):

hundredths — digit to right is > 5, so round up

0.15876 gram

Rounded to the hundredths place, this value is 0.16 gram.

Weight of the fruit of the flowering duckweed plant:

ten thousandths — digit to right is < 5, so do not change

0.0007087 gram

Rounded to the ten thousandths place, this value is 0.0007 gram.

Source: The Guiness Book of World Records 1998, Guiness Media, Inc. 1997

Comparing Numbers

380

Scientists often compare numbers in order to describe and analyze data. You already do this in everyday life. For example, you compare numbers representing distance (kilometers, or km) and time (hour, or h) so you can talk about speed (kilometers per hour, or km/h).

Rates

381

Rates involve comparing a measurement to a period of time. A rate is always expressed as a fraction. A unit of time is in the denominator. A unit of another quantity, such as distance, is in the numerator.

Speed limit: $\frac{\text{100 kilometers}}{\text{hour}}$ — Numerator (100 kilometers); per (fraction bar); Denominator (hour)

Any unit of time may be used in the denominator—years, months, weeks, days, hours, minutes, seconds, or fractions of seconds. Almost any kind of unit may be used in the numerator—dollars, meters, heart beats, homework assignments. Read the fraction bar as the word "per", such as $5 *per* hour for babysitting, or 20 miles *per* hour speed limit.

Alligator—normal heart rate 38 beats per minute

Cold medicine 1 tablet per 4 hours

Escape velocity from Earth 11 kilometers per second (11 km/s)

382 Ratios

A ratio is a comparison between two quantities that do not involve time. Ratios can be expressed a couple of different ways. A ratio can be stated in a sentence, such as: For each hand there are 5 digits (4 fingers and 1 thumb). This sentence describes a comparison between the quantity of hands (1) to the quantity of digits (5). You can write this comparison as the proportion 1:5, or as the fraction $\frac{1}{5}$.

Examples of Ratios

Statement	Proportion	Fraction
Forty-six out of 100 people are likely to have blood type O.	46:100	$\frac{46}{100}$
In every molecule of iron III oxide (Fe_2O_3), or rust, there are two atoms of iron and three atoms of oxygen.	2:3	$\frac{2}{3}$
Every centimeter on a map represents 40,000 cm on land.	1:40,000	$\frac{1}{40,000}$

383 Percent, Per Thousand, Per Million

Scientists often compare quantities as parts per hundred, or percent (%), parts per thousand (ppt), or parts per million (ppm).

Follow the steps to find these values (an example is done for you):

1. Write the relationship of the numbers as a fraction.

   There are about 3.5 grams of salt in every 100 grams of sea water.

   $\frac{3.5}{100}$

2. Divide the numerator by the denominator to get a decimal.

   $\frac{3.5}{100} = 0.035$

3. Multiply the decimal by 100 to get percent.

   $0.035 \times 100 = 3.5\%$

   Multiply by 1000 to get parts per thousand

   $0.035 \times 1{,}000 = 35$ ppt

   Multiply by 1,000,000 to get parts per million

   $0.035 \times 1{,}000{,}000 = 0.035000 = 35{,}000$ ppm

Average

Suppose you want to analyze rainfall patterns in a city you might move to. One way to analyze data is to figure out averages. There are three kinds of averages:

- Mean: sum of data divided by number of data measurements, or values
- Median: middle value, or average of the two middle values, of a set of data when you arrange it in order from smallest to largest
- Mode: value, or values, that occur most often in a set of data

You may also analyze a set of data for two other characteristics.

- Frequency: number of times a value occurs in a set of data
- Range: difference between largest and smallest values in a set of data

Typical Yearly Precipitation in Reno, Nevada, in Inches

Jan.	Feb.	March	April	May	June	July	Aug.	Sept.	Oct.	Nov.	Dec.
1.1	1.0	0.7	0.4	0.7	0.5	0.3	0.3	0.4	0.4	0.9	1.0

Source: World Almanac and Book of Facts, based on data for a 30-year period, 1961-1990

- **Mean** precipitation per month: 7.7 in. (sum of data) ÷ 12 months (number of data) = 0.64 inches per month
- **Median** (inches of precipitation):

  0.3, 0.3, 0.4, 0.4, 0.4, **0.5, 0.7,** 0.7, 0.9, 1.0, 1.0, 1.1

  (0.5 + 0.7) ÷ 2 = 0.6 inches per month
- **Mode:** 0.4 inches (occurred three times)
- **Frequency:** 0.4 (three times); 0.3 (two times); 0.7 (two times), 1.0 (two times), 0.5 (one time); 0.9 (one time); 1.1 (one time)
- **Range:** 1.1 – 0.3 = 0.8 inches of precipitation

What do these data tell you? Well, compare these values with the data analysis for another city. You might choose to live in Reno if sunshine is important to you. Seattle, Washington, with heavier rainfall, would be a better choice if you like lush, green forests: *Mean:* 3.17 in.; *Median:* 2.9 in.; *Mode:* none; *Frequency:* each value occurs once; Range: 6.0 (December) – 0.9 (July) = 5.1 in.

385

Using Data Tables and Graphs

Data tables are used to organize and present observations and measurements, so that they are easier to analyze and interpret. Because ideas in science must be based on data, it is extremely important to make sure that your data are recorded accurately. Not long ago, a scientist was accused of making up data for the results of an experiment. It turned out that the data were real, but the scientist had recorded them in such a sloppy way that many other scientists had thought the data were not real. Accuracy in science is important.

A **graph** is a kind of picture used to present quantitative data. Graphs allow you to understand data at a glance, to find trends in a set of data, or to compare different sets of data. In science, you will make your own graphs, as well as read them.

Word Watch!

Data are facts, figures, or other kinds of information that can be analyzed to reach conclusions. *Data* is the plural of *datum*.

Organizing Data Tables 386

The best time to create a data table is before you record data. A well-planned data table lets you record data neatly and quickly while doing your experiment. In your science work, you will collect two main kinds of data. **Quantitative data** are numbers, usually measurements with units. Temperature in degrees Celsius, length in centimeters, and mass in grams are examples of quantitative data. **Qualitative data** are recorded as descriptions. The color of a flower, the movements of an insect, and the patterns in a rock are examples of qualitative data. Each kind of data needs a certain kind of data table.

Tables for Quantitative Data 387

A **data table** is organized in columns and rows. The first column of a data table usually describes the contents of each row. All the other columns need headings, so you know the quantity and unit of the data in that column. When you plan how to organize a data table, consider the following:

- The purpose of the table: what you want other people to learn from the table
- The kind and number of items that will be in the table: the number of values for the independent variable, dependent variable, units for each value, total number of trials, and averages of those trials
- The clearest way to set up the table so that recording data and reading it back are quick and easy

SEE ALSO
009 Gathering Data
384 Average

The example shows a table you might make for an experiment involving the temperature of ice water.

Example

Temperature of a Cup of Water with Ice

Time (s)	Temperature (°C)			Average (Mean)
	Trial 1	Trial 2	Trial 3	
0 (ice added)				
30				
60				
90				

Running more than one trial for your experiment makes your data more reliable.

388 Tables for Qualitative Observations

Imagine you are planning to observe the behavior of African mountain gorillas in the wild for the next two months. Most of your data will be qualitative, or descriptive, and you'll need a way to keep it organized for a long time. If you plan in advance, you can record and keep track of your observations quite easily (even if you're just observing a plant growing over a period of two weeks).

- Keep your observation table in a bound notebook, so loose pages don't get lost.
- Record the date and time of the observation every time you make an observation.
- Leave enough space so you can write down all of your observations.
- Think up some shortcuts for noting observations that you make over and over again, and keep a record of what those shortcuts mean (in the example, M means male, F means female, and each individual gorilla has a code number, such as "A-2")

Example

Gorilla Behavior and Populations in the Virunga Area of Central Africa

Date/Time	Gorillas Seen	Observations
2/15 7:31 a.m.	5 total: A-1, A-2, B-3, C-4, C-5	Small troop: 2 F. w/2 infants (< 3 months old) led by old silver back M. about 1.7 m tall; adults ate leaves, buds, stalks, berries; infants clung to mother's fur and nursed.
2/16 11:02 a.m.	4 total: A-3, B-2, B-4, C-1	Small troop: 1 adult M., 2 F., 1 young M.; animals resting after morning meal; saw me but not frightened.
2/17 8:45 p.m.	5 total: A-1, A-2, B-3, C-4, C-5	Same troop seen on 2/15; they have made nests of twigs and leaves; all are asleep, infants next to their mothers.

Source: Based on Whitfield, Philip, The Simon and Schuster Encyclopedia of Animals.

Recording Data Electronically

389

You can collect data electronically in the laboratory or on field trips. Electronic instruments that do this have sensors, also called probes, that measure certain kinds of data. Many electronic instruments measure more quickly and more precisely than other kinds of equipment. Some electronic instruments can collect data over a long time, even when you are not there. So if an experiment runs through the night, you don't have to be there to collect and record data. You can also use electronic sensors to collect data over very short periods of time, such as every few seconds. Ordinarily you would not be able to make and record measurements in such a short time period.

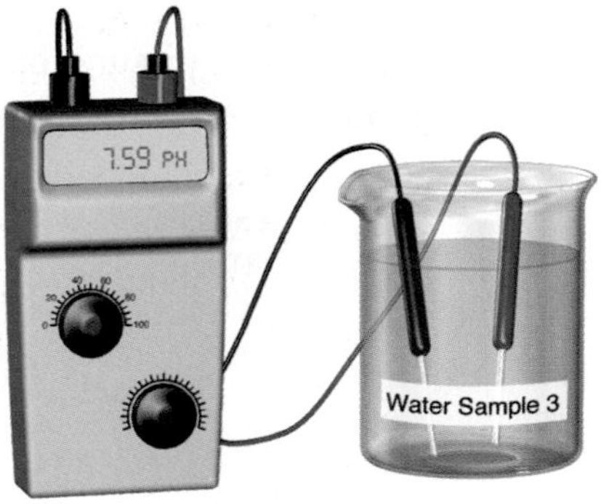

Many electronic instruments come with software and cables that link the instrument to your computer. You can load the data into a computer to store it, analyze it, and make graphs. Some electronic data collecting instruments can also be connected to a graphing calculator that instantly produces graphs of your data.

Not every piece of electronic equipment collects data. Some just displays data, and you have to record it somewhere else. Check the instructions for the equipment you are using.

SEE ALSO

401 Using a Graphing Calculator

Data that can be Collected Electronically	
air pressure	DC electric current
magnetic field	heart rate
oxygen dissolved in water	sound level (dB)
relative humidity	pH of a solution
distance between objects	light intensity
motion	pressure
substances dissolved in water	temperature

390 Kinds of Graphs

A **graph** is a picture that helps you and others understand data at a glance. Most kinds of graphs have the same basic parts.

SEE ALSO
395 Making a Line Graph

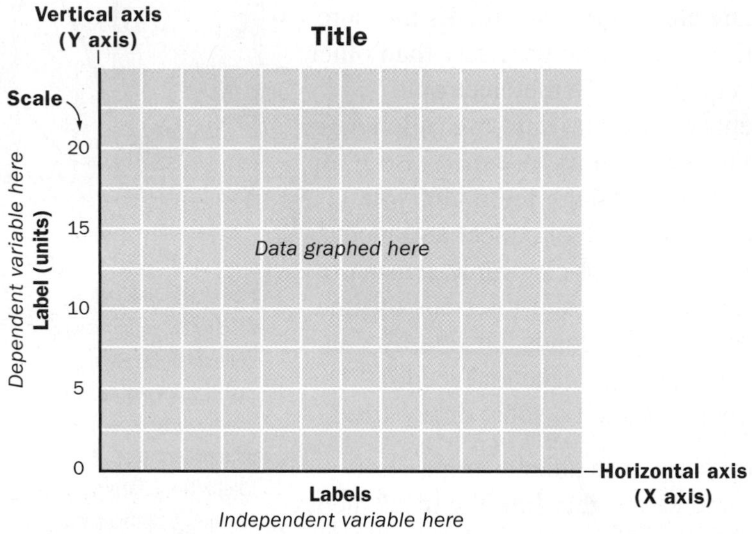

For a line graph, horizontal axis will also have a scale and units.

You can use different kinds of graphs to present data. Choose the kind of graph that will most clearly present the data you have collected.

391 Bar Graphs

Bar graphs are used to compare quantitative data (numbers) and qualitative data (places or things). The qualitative data are labeled along the horizontal axis. The quantitative data are marked on the vertical axis. Each quality (place or thing) has a vertical bar.

The example at the top of the next page compares the fatty acid content of various foods. Notice that fatty acid content is the quantitative data and goes on the vertical axis. The foods being compared, the qualitative data, are on the horizontal axis. The height of each bar shows the measurement for that food.

Fatty Acid Content of Foods

Food	Fatty Acids (%)
Swiss cheese	27.6
turkey (white meat)	2.6
peanuts	49.7
eggs	11.3
olive oil	100.0
shrimp	1.2
butter	80.1

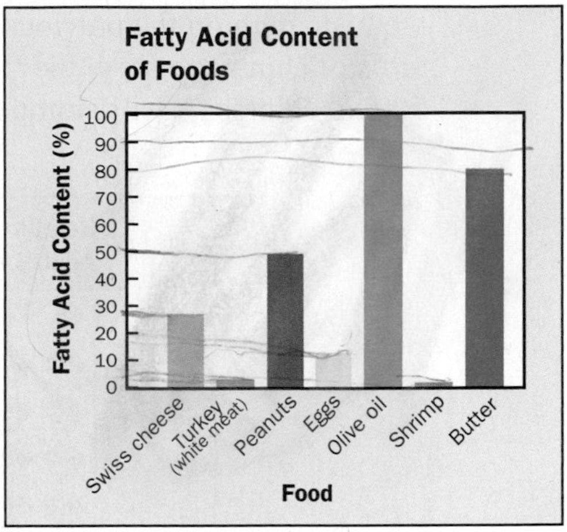

Source: Home Facts, World Book, Inc.

Histograms and Pictograms 392

Histograms are graphs used to present large quantities of numerical data. Usually, data in a histogram are first organized into a frequency table. For example, the frequency table below contains 990 pieces of data. The same data are displayed in a histogram next to the table.

Heights of 990 Adult Chimpanzees

Height (cm)	Frequency (number of chimps)
68–71	29
72–75	75
76–79	240
80–83	280
84–87	266
88–91	68
92–95	32

Source: Based on Whitfield, Philip, The Simon and Schuster Encyclopedia of Animals.

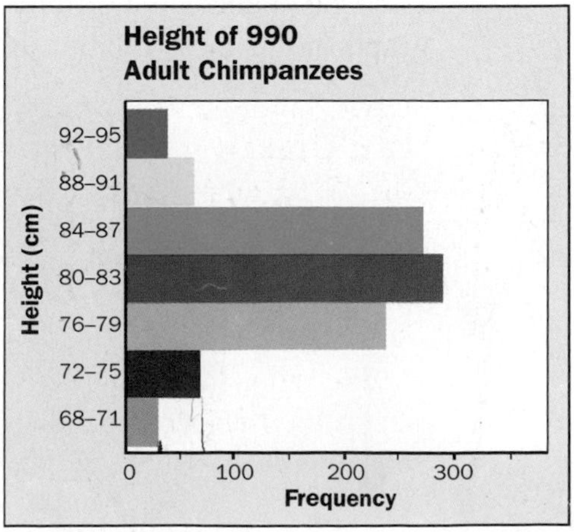

MORE ▶

Pictograms show data using pictures of objects. For example, to turn the histogram on the previous page into a pictogram, you can use pictures of chimps to show the frequencies. Each full chimp represents 50 real chimps. A half chimp represents 25 real chimps.

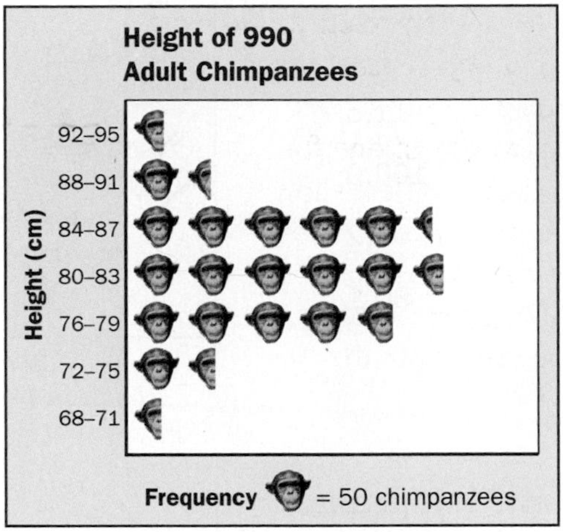

393

Pie Charts

Circle graphs, sometimes called **pie charts,** are used to give a quick view of the relationships among parts of a whole. The values in a circle graph always add up to 100%. For example, the whole (100%) of Earth's atmosphere is made up of different gases. Each gas makes up a different percent of the atmosphere. The circle graph shows these relationships at a glance.

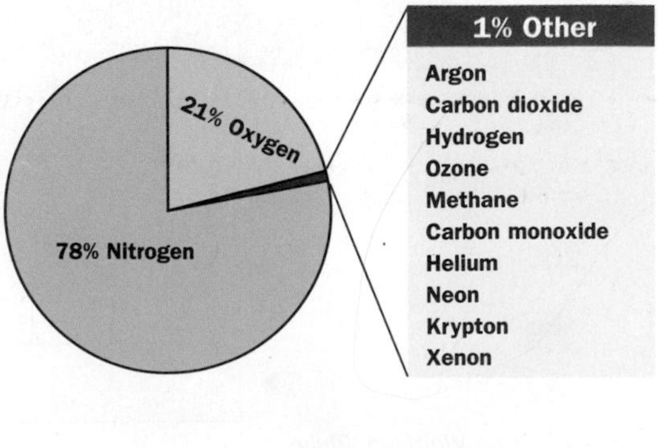

Line Graphs

Line graphs show the relationship between two quantities as those quantities are changing. Both axes of a line graph show quantitative data. The example shows how a person's heart rate changes during 9 minutes of exercise. A graph for one person would have one line. A graph for more than one person would have multiple lines, with a key or label identifying each line. The example shows such a graph, with two lines: one for an athlete, one for a non-athlete. The graph shows that during a workout, heart rate at first increases, then levels off, and that the athlete has a lower heart rate overall than the non-athlete.

The plural of *axis* is *axes* (pronounced AX-eez).

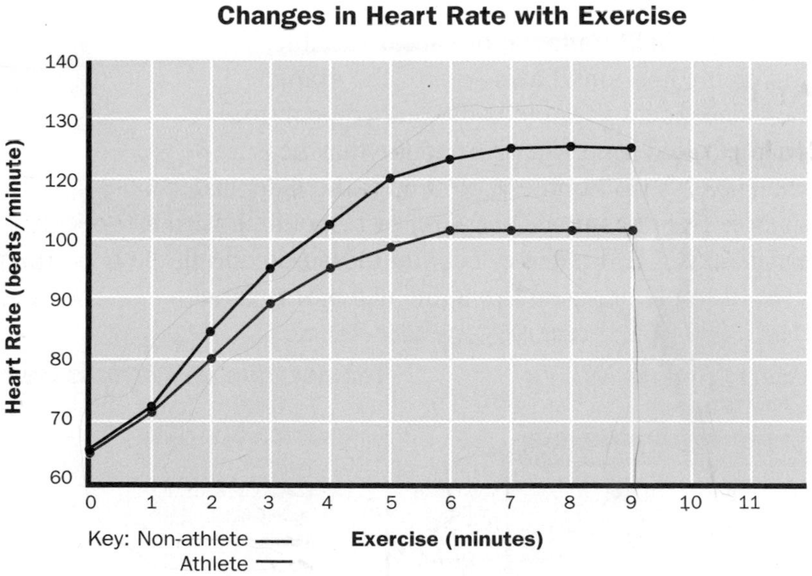

395 Making a Line Graph

Line graphs are the best choice when you are comparing two sets of quantitative data (values) where changes in one value cause changes in the other value.

396 Drawing and Labeling the Axes

Let's say you need to show how the temperature of a beaker of water changed as you heated the water for 10 minutes. In other words, you need to show the relationship between time and temperature. You've collected your data in a table and are ready to start your graph.

Make sure the labels on your graph axes are the same as the headings on your data table. The titles of the table and the graph should match, too.

First, you have to decide which axis of the graph will represent time and which will represent temperature. There is a guideline for choosing which is which.

The **independent variable,** or causal variable, goes on the horizontal axis (↔) of the graph. The independent variable is the one you control. You controlled time when you took your measurements (every two minutes), so time is the independent variable. The **dependent variable,** or responding variable, goes on the vertical axis (↕). It is the effect you measured during the experiment. In the example, temperature is the dependent variable.

Temperature as Water Is Heated

Time (min.)	Temp. (°C)
0	18
2	28
4	45
6	67
8	84
10	96

Temperature as Water is Heated

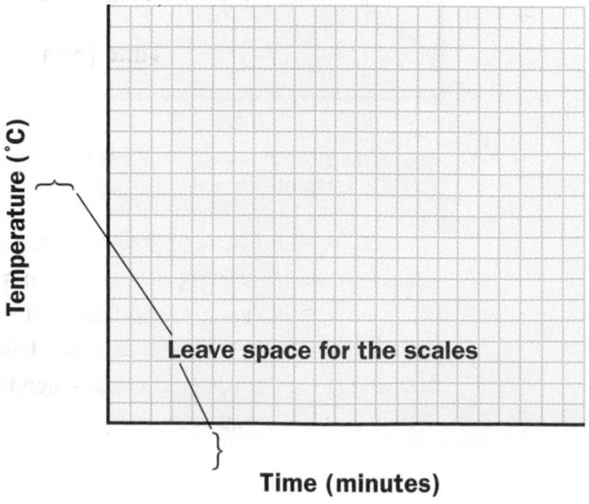

Once you have figured out which variable goes on which axis, label each axis with a value and a unit. In the example, label the horizontal axis *Time (minutes)* and the vertical axis *Temperature (°C)*.

Next, you need to mark the axes with scales. A **scale** is a series of equally-spaced marks. The marks stand for equal intervals in a measurement. Choose graph scales so that the line of your graph is neither too long nor too short. Also choose an interval that is easy to read, such as 2, 5, 10, 50, or 100. In the example, measurements were taken every 2 minutes over a range of 0–10 minutes. A good scale for the horizontal axis has five or more equally-spaced marks, one mark for each 2-minute interval. For the vertical axis, temperature ranges from 18°–96°C, with most measurements falling in the middle of a ten-degree span (28, 45). A good scale for that axis is 0°–100°C with a 5° interval. In the example, notice that the interval for each mark is 5°, even though the labels are every 10°. In this case, labeling every other interval mark makes the scale easier to read.

Temperature as Water is Heated

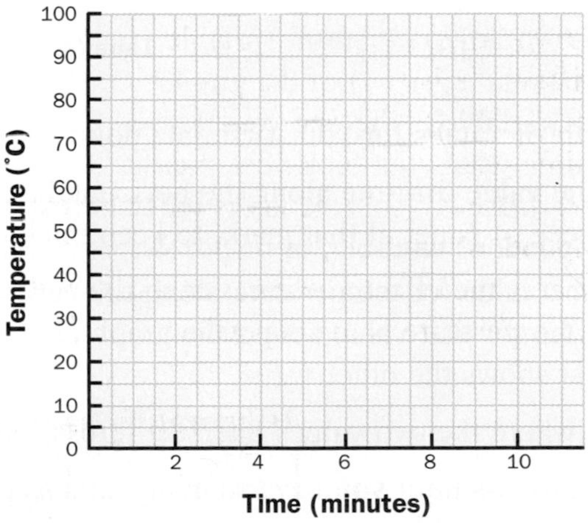

Science Alert!

Choose scales that make sense with your data. For example, there is no sense starting your vertical axis scale at 0°C if you have ten temperature readings ranging from 50°C–90°C. Better to start with a number at or just below the starting temperature of the water. End with a number a little greater than the ending temperature.

397 Plotting Points

Your graph is set up and you're ready to plot data points. In a line graph, each data point has two values: one for the horizontal axis and one for the vertical axis. A well-organized data table will make it clear which values belong together.

Temperature as Water Is Heated

Time (min.)	Temp. (°C)
0	18
2	28
4	45
6	67
8	84
10	96

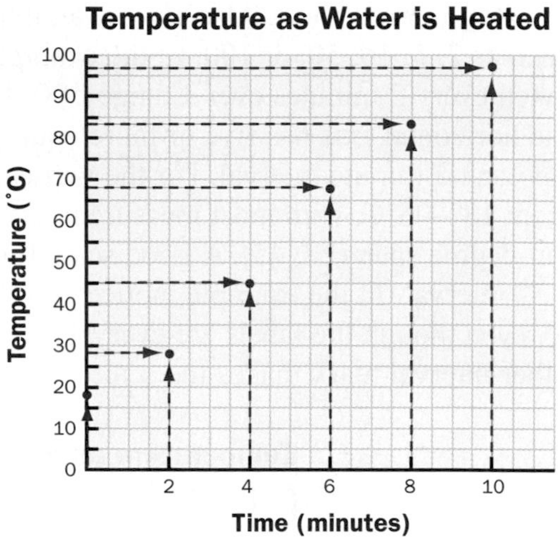

Start with the pair of values for your first data point.

1. First, find the value for time along the horizontal axis. Place the edge of a piece of paper at that mark, to keep track of it.
2. Next, find the value for temperature along the vertical axis. Follow the line for that value across the graph until you reach the mark that shows the other value.
3. Make a dot where the two values intersect (cross) on your graph.
4. Repeat this process until you have as many dots as pairs of values in your data table.

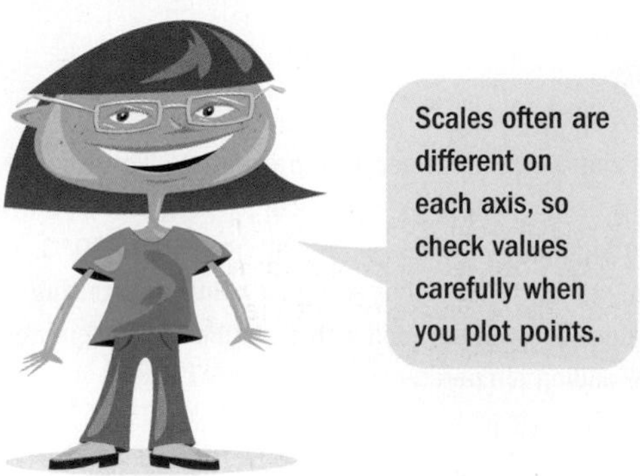

Scales often are different on each axis, so check values carefully when you plot points.

Drawing a Graph Line

398

Your points are plotted and it's time to look for trends in your data. You can construct a graph line by simply connecting points. However, it's often easier to spot general trends if you construct a **best-fit line.** Look at the graph below. Notice that although the points are somewhat scattered, they do represent a trend: the temperature of the water rises the longer the water is heated. To show this trend, the graph line has been drawn through some data points and between other points.

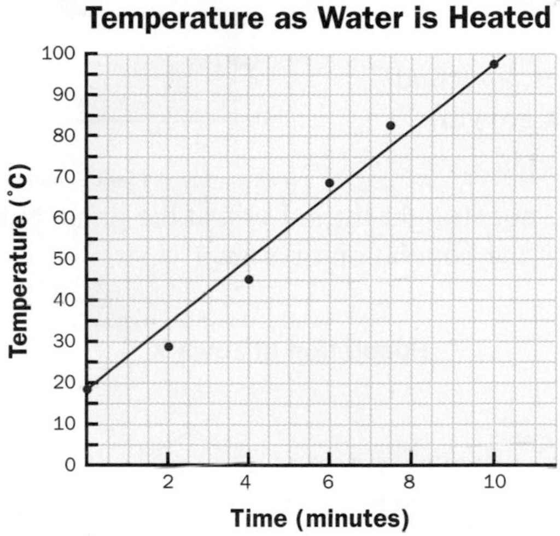

To draw a best-fit line, lay a ruler on the graph. Move the ruler back and forth until the edge of the ruler comes closest to as many data points as possible. (A ruler that you can see through is helpful.) Your best-fit line may pass through some points but not others. It may not pass through any points at all. As long as it passes near most points, it will show the general trend.

Science Alert!

Some graph lines clearly show more than one trend—they rise, fall, or plateau (level out). In these cases, draw a best-fit line for each clear trend in the data.

399

Interpreting Graph Lines

Graphs are useful for interpreting data. In the graph shown, a good interpretation is "As hours of light per day for a plant increase, plant growth also increases". Another way to say this is "Plants that get more hours of light each day grow more." As one set of data (exposure to light) increases, a second set of data (plant growth) also increases.

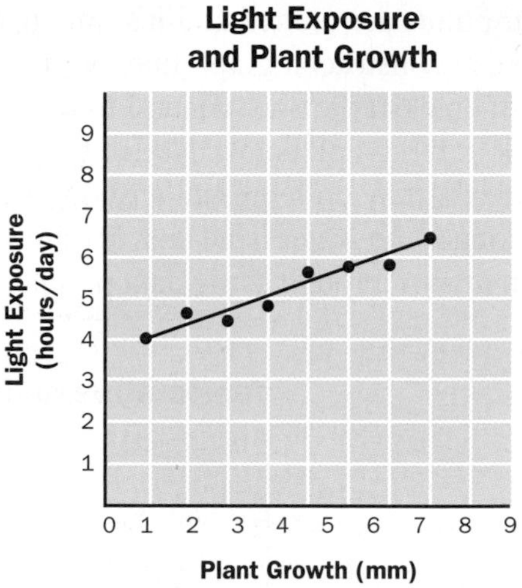

Some graphs are not straight lines. Look at the graph below, which shows changes in the population of a town.

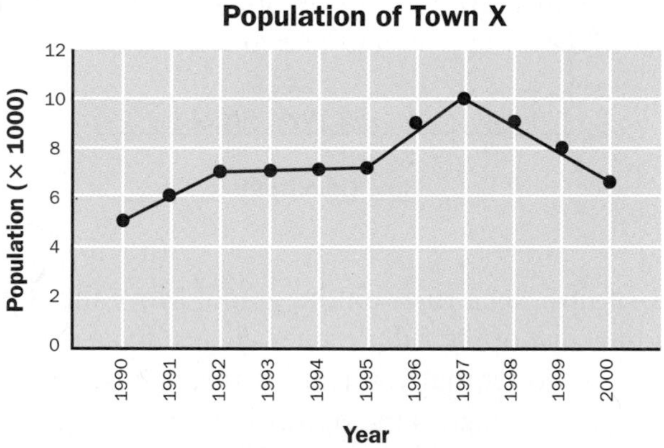

- 1990–1992: The line slopes upward from left to right. This is an increasing slope, which means that population increased during these years.
- 1992–1995: The line is flat, that is, it neither slopes upward or downward. This is called a **plateau,** or a period of no change.
- 1995–1997: The line rises again, indicating another increase in population.
- 1997–2000: The line slopes downward from left to right. This is a decreasing slope, which means that population decreased during this period.

Extrapolating and Interpolating

Graph lines can let you predict values between data points and beyond data points, that is, beyond the end of the graph line. Predicting values between points is called **interpolation.** Predicting values beyond points is called **extrapolation.** Extrapolation and interpolation are most accurate when graph lines have clear trends and many points.

Study the graph below, which shows changes in the percent of adult Americans (over 18) who smoked from 1978–1990. The best-fit line for the data shows a clear downward trend, a decrease, in the number of smokers. Note that data points do not appear for all years. Even though there is no data point for 1985, the clear trend allows you to interpolate a value for 1985. To do this, follow the vertical line for 1985 until it intersects the graph line. Then read across to the vertical axis to find the estimated percentage of smokers for that year. The value you would find is about 29.9%. You may also extrapolate a value for dates after 1990. Extend the graph line and read the value where it intersects with 1990, for a value of 24%. You can predict that the total number of smokers will continue to decrease.

U.S. Adults (over age 18) Who Smoke, %

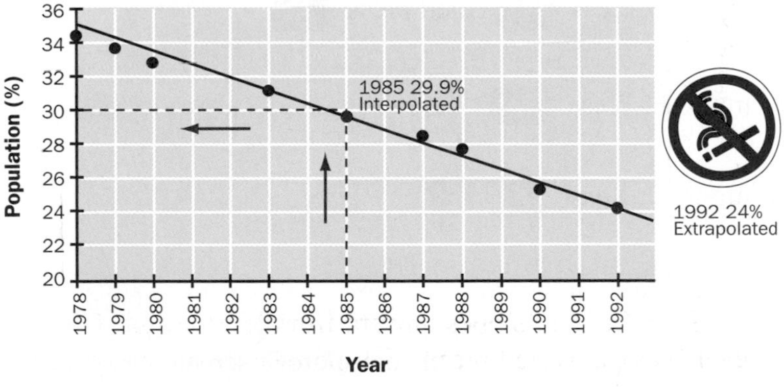

Science Alert!

Let common sense guide you when extrapolating data. Suppose the daily high temperature for a five-day period in early January has risen by 2°C each day, from 0°C to 10°C (32°F to 50°F). Extrapolating a graph of these data suggest that by the end of January, the high for the day will be 50°C (122°F). Common sense tells you that this can't be right. The temperature is likely to rise, fall, or plateau many times during the month.

401 Using a Graphing Calculator

Graphing calculators create and display histograms, line graphs, data tables, and related pictures from data. Some models can be connected to your home computer so you can print out your graphs or send them to other people.

Example

Graph the equation for converting temperature from Fahrenheit to Celsius. The equation is $F = \frac{9}{5}C + 32$. This is a linear equation with the form $y = mx + b$. Note which part of the temperature conversion equation corresponds with each part of the linear equation form.

$$\begin{array}{ccccccc} F & = & \frac{9}{5} & C & + & 32 \\ | & & | & | & & | \\ y & = & m & x & + & b \end{array}$$

To input the equation into the calculator,

1. To input F: Press Y=
2. To input $\frac{9}{5}$: Press 9 ÷ 5
3. To input C: Press ALPHA then press x
4. To input +: Press +
5. To input 32: Press 3 2
6. Press GRAPH

The graph will be displayed on the calculator's screen.

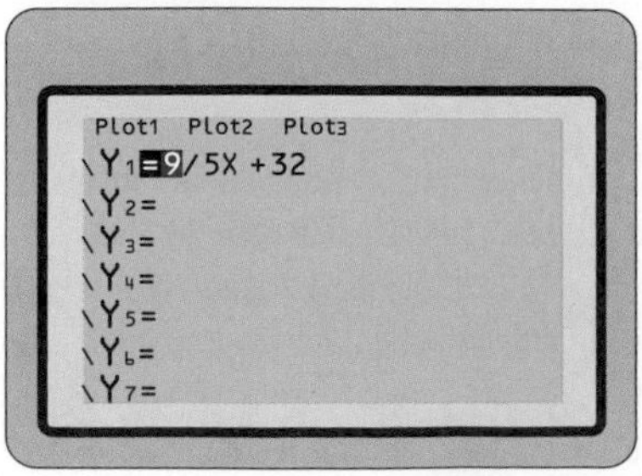

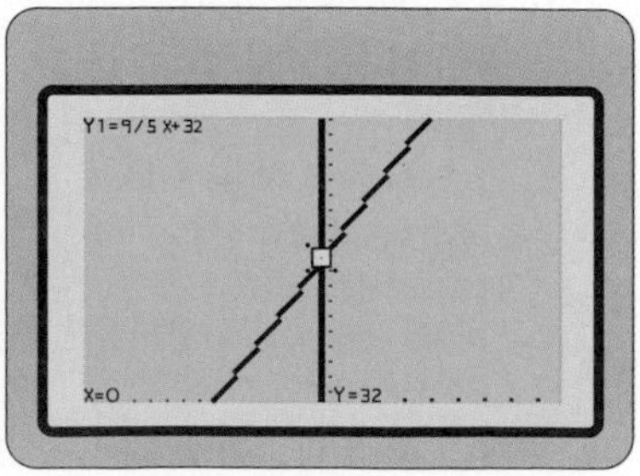

402

Solving Math Problems in Science

A tsunami (soo-NAH-me) is a giant ocean wave, usually caused by an earthquake, that can sweep away houses, cars, and people in an instant. If you heard that a tsunami is heading toward your beach-front home, you might ask yourself a few questions such as: How far away is the wave? How fast is it moving? When will it reach my beach? Each of these questions states a scientific problem. Each problem can be solved by collecting data and using them in mathematical equations.

Solving for an Unknown

403

There are many equations for solving math problems that use scientific data. There are also different ways to use each equation. Before you jump into solving any problem, it's important to know what you are trying to find out, and what data you have to work with. Following a series of steps helps to make sure you'll find the right answer.

Steps in Solving a Math Problem in Science

1. Identify what you know and what you need to know.
2. Choose the correct equation.
3. Set up the problem.
4. Solve for the unknown.
5. Check your work.

404 Identifying the Problem

Let's say you've just heard that a tsunami is heading toward your beach. The first step you must take in solving any problem is to figure out what it is you want to know, and what data you have to work with. In this case, you want to know how much time you have to get out of the area with family, friends, and as many precious possessions as you can carry. The report says that the tsunami is 2470 km away, and that it's traveling at a speed of 760 kilometers per hour. You have data for distance (2470 km) and for speed (760 km/h). You want to solve for time (hours).

405 Choosing the Correct Equation

You've identified the problem of when the tsunami will arrive as a speed, time, and distance problem. Your next step is to find the equation that describes the relationship among these values. You can find equations in textbooks and other references. You look in a science reference book and find the equation for speed. It is written in words, and in symbols.

$\text{speed} = \frac{\text{distance}}{\text{time}}$ or $s = \frac{d}{t}$

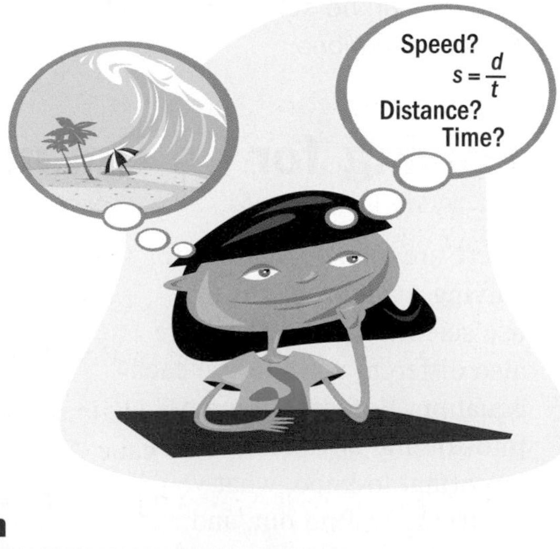

In words, this reads: speed equals distanced divided by time. Notice that the symbols are set in italic, or slanted, type. This helps you to keep track of which symbols stand for the variable (such as distance, *d*), and which stand for the units used for that variable (such as kilometers, km).

406 Setting Up the Problem

As long as you know two of the values in an equation, you can calculate the third, unknown value. To do this, the unknown value needs to be at the left of the equals sign. To find out when the tsunami will arrive, you need to solve for time. Rewrite the equation to put the unknown value, time, at the left.

EXAMPLE: Rewrite the speed, distance, time equation to put time on the left side of the equals sign.

$$\text{speed} = \frac{\text{distance}}{\text{time}} \text{ or } s = \frac{d}{t}$$

Multiply both sides of the equation by time, *t*. This cancels time out of the right side of the equation.

$$t \times s = \frac{d}{\cancel{t}} \times \cancel{t}$$

This gives you: $s \times t = d$

Now divide both sides of the equation by speed. This cancels speed out of the left side of the equation.

$$\frac{\cancel{s} \times t}{\cancel{s}} = \frac{d}{s}$$

This gives you $t = \frac{d}{s}$, or "time equals distance divided by speed."

You now have an equation that will solve for time, the unknown that you want to find out. Substitute the data for distance and speed for the symbols in the equation.

$$t = \frac{2470 \text{ km}}{760 \text{ km/h}}$$

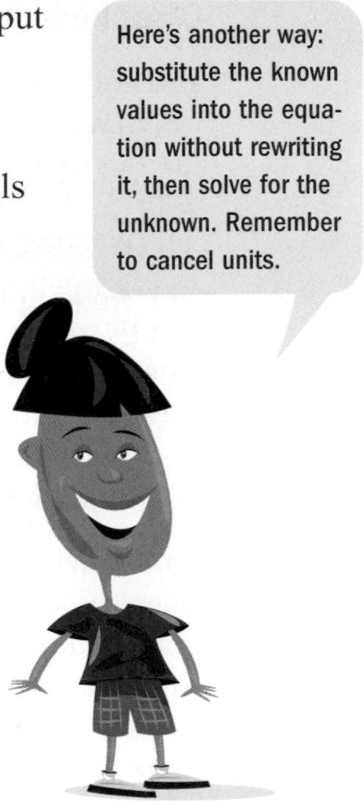

Here's another way: substitute the known values into the equation without rewriting it, then solve for the unknown. Remember to cancel units.

Solving for the Unknown

407

After all the work you've done to identify the problem and set it up, solving for the unknown is fairly simple. You might call this part "doing the math."

EXAMPLE: The problem you set up to solve for time is:

$$t = \frac{2470 \text{ km}}{760 \text{ km/h}}; \text{ Do the math: } 2470 \div 760 = 3.25$$

But what does 3.25 stand for? Kilometers? Kilometers per hour? Hours? Watch how the units cancel.

$$t = \frac{2470 \cancel{\text{km}}}{760 \cancel{\text{km}}/\text{h}}; \; t = 3.25 \frac{1}{1/\text{h}}; \; \frac{1}{1/\text{h}} = \frac{\text{h}}{1} = \text{h}$$

Kilometers divided by kilometers equals one, so kilometers is out of the answer. The reciprocal of 1 divided by hours equals hours divided by 1, or hours. You are left with 3.25 hours.

There is one more step you need to do: checking your work.

408 Checking Your Work

You are not really finished solving an equation until you check your work. Ways to check your work include:

- Checking your arithmetic
- Working the problem another way
- Working the problem backward
- Estimating an answer using rounded numbers
- Seeing whether the units of your answer make sense (for example, if you were solving for time, you have a unit of time for your answer)

By the way, 3.25 hours equals 3 hours and 15 minutes, so you would have that long before the tsunami struck to gather your things and head inland to higher elevations. But don't hang around long—there will certainly be traffic jams.

409 Problem-Solving with Your Data

When you solve problems out of a book, usually you are given two out of the three values. You already have a good idea which equation to use, because it's in the book near the problem. You solve for the unknown and get tidy values that end after two decimal places.

SEE ALSO
017 Designing Your Own Investigations

When you work with real, live data from your own experiments, problem-solving is a little messier, but it's the same process. You need to identify the problem. You need to figure out which values you can collect yourself, and which value is the unknown. The data you collect may at first glance seemed jumbled or confusing. Whether you can trust your conclusions depends on how carefully you follow the problem-solving process when you solve for the unknown.

Example

What will be the ratio of red eyes to white eyes in the third generation of a fruit fly population? The first generation (grandparents) included a pure white-eyed male and a pure red-eyed female. The second generation (parents) all have red eyes.

You know the eye color of the first- and second-generation flies. This information can help you make a prediction, or hypothesis, about the problem. However, to solve this problem by experiment, you need to get and observe third-generation fruit flies. In order to have reliable data, you set up three trials—in this case, three breeding containers. All three containers have males and females from the second generation. Two weeks later you have new flies to count. The data table shows the results.

THIRD-GENERATION FRUIT FLIES (RATIOS ROUNDED TO 0.1)

Trial	Red Eyes	White Eyes	$\frac{\text{Red}}{\text{White}}$	Ratio
1	83	31	$\frac{83}{31} = 2.7$	2.7:1
2	116	27	$\frac{116}{27} = 4.3$	4.3:1
3	97	34	$\frac{97}{34} = 2.9$	2.9:1
Mean	98.7	30.7		3.3:1

Notice that if you used only data from Trial 2, you would have reached a much different conclusion. That's why it's important to have more than one trial.

To analyze your results, you first identify that you need to find means and ratios. You look up how to find means and ratios, then you do the math and record your results. The last column shows the ratios of red-eyed flies to white-eyed flies for each trial, and the mean of the three ratios. Notice that the ratios are not whole numbers, even though the flies are all whole flies.

By rounding the mean ratio from 3.3:1 to 3:1, you can conclude that for every 4 fruit flies in the third generation, there are likely to be 3 red-eyed fruit flies and 1 white-eyed fruit fly.

Now you need to check your work. For these data, you can check your ratio value by solving the problem another way. Use the mean number of red-eyed fruit flies (98.7) and white-eyed fruit flies (30.7) for all three trials, then find the ratio of those means ($98.7 \div 30.7 = 3.2$). Notice that the two values are slightly different. That's okay—remember, real data are messy. The values are close enough that they round to the same whole number, so you know you solved the problem correctly.

SEE ALSO
121 Heredity
382 Ratios
384 Average

410

Classroom and Research Skills

411

Managing Your Time

Like other courses you have, some of your science work takes place during class, while other work takes place as homework. It's important to plan your time well both inside and outside of class.

412

Planning Your Classroom Time

When you enter science class, settle down promptly. Get out the materials you need before class begins. Look and listen for instructions posted on the board or spoken by your teacher. During class, make use of any time your teacher gives you to get started on assignments. That way, if you have a question, you can get help right away, rather than finding out later that you aren't sure what to do.

SEE ALSO
419 Laboratory Partners and Groups

During science class you will sometimes work with a group to do experiments. While it is fun to work with friends, this time is not just social. It is a cooperative effort. It is important to get started right away and to stay on task. You also must allow at least five minutes at the end of class to clean up. Have one group member keep track of the time.

Planning for Long-Term Projects

413

In science class you will have some assignments that take a week or several weeks to finish. A successful long-term project requires special planning, whether it is an experiment or a research project.

Steps for Completing a Long-Term Project

1. Read assignment carefully.
2. List any materials you need to gather.
3. List tasks to be done and the time each task will take. Decide which parts of the project are most important.
4. Decide whom you need to ask for help.
5. Make a calendar showing what tasks you need to do each day or each week in order to finish the project on time.

Let's look at an example.

Project: Woodland Terrarium

Purpose: To construct and observe a terrarium containing local woodland plants and animals.

A **terrarium** is a miniature ecosystem containing soil, plants, and animals. It is a closed system that has everything it needs except sunlight. Your assignment is to create a terrarium of the local forest floor ecosystem and observe it for two weeks: one week with plants only, the second week with small animals added. You have three weeks to complete this assignment. Create your terrarium in a 2-liter bottle, using plants, small animals (such as insects and worms), and soil from the local woods. Put sand or gravel in the bottom of the bottle, charcoal on top of the sand or gravel, and soil on top of the charcoal. Get permission from the landowner and from your parents before you collect any materials. Take a buddy with you.

MORE

The first item on the checklist is to read the assignment carefully. Look up any words you don't know, such as ecosystem or landowner. Ask questions about anything you're not sure of. When you are sure you understand the assignment, make a list of materials you'll need. Decide what's the most important thing to do first. For the terrarium, you must first find a place to collect materials and get permission to do so. Otherwise, you cannot do the assignment.

Make a calendar or a timeline for what you need to do each day. A project schedule will help you plan around personal events, too.

Assignment—Woodland terrarium

Purpose—To construct and observe a terrarium containing local woodland plants and animals.

Materials needed—2 liter bottle, scissors to cut it, tape to seal it, sand or gravel, soil, small plants and animals from woods. Borrow small shovel.

Activity	Days to complete
Week 1	
Read assignment and plan	Monday
Gather bottle, shovel, sand, scissors, tape, ask Jo's parents if we can dig in their woods	Tuesday–Thursday

Activity	Days to complete
Big game on Friday so no project time.	
Collect soil and plants, make terrarium, write up data table, start observations	Saturday–Sunday
Week 2	
Observe and record plants and soil	Monday–Saturday
Add snail, pillbugs, and worm	Sunday

414 Asking Questions

Asking questions is at the heart of all science, whether you are a student or a working scientist. Questions lead to investigation, which leads to understanding.

415 Questions for Understanding

Ask yourself silent questions while you listen, read, and study. Self-questioning helps you think actively and understand completely. For example, if you ask yourself, "What are the most important points of this paragraph?" then you'll be more likely to focus on the main point. Other helpful self-questions include: "What do I know so far?", "What do I need to know?," and "How can I figure out what I need to know?" Another way to test your understanding is to ask "if-then" questions, such as "If temperature decreases as elevation increases, then my cousin's house in Denver should be cooler than my house in Los Angeles." All these questions help you fill in gaps in your knowledge.

416

Questions for Investigation

Ask yourself questions about objects and experiments while you are observing them. Good questions help you to notice details, and details make your observations more complete. Good questions are also the starting point for good investigations.

Don't be shy about asking questions in class. Even if you worry that a question might be "dumb," ask it. If you don't ask, you won't know. Other students usually need the answer, too.

Details:
How many petals? What shape are the petals?

Investigation:
How might petal shape affect pollination?

Details:
Is there a pattern in the grains? What is the pattern? Are the grains all the same size or different? Are they pointing the same way?

Investigation:
What forces might cause the grains to all point the same way?

Details:
Which claw is larger, right or left? How many crabs have a larger right claw? How many have a larger left?

Investigation:
How are crabs using claws? What purpose does the larger claw have?

Most science investigations begin with testable questions. **Testable questions** can be answered by investigating and collecting data. A question like "Which ball bounces better?" is hard to test because the word "better" is not clear. A testable question is "Which ball bounces higher?" This question can be tested by investigation.

SEE ALSO
003 Asking Scientific Questions

417 # Working with Others

Working in small groups is a valuable skill in school and in life. Most jobs require people to work well with others.

418 ## Basic Group Skills

Science classes often include labs and other activities that are done in small groups. Group work can make learning more productive and more fun. For group work to be successful, group members must be able to work well together. Any problems that come up have to be worked out among all the group members. Each person in the group has the job of helping the whole group succeed. Effective group work begins with respect for each other. Here are some pointers for successfully working in any group.

Be an active listener.
Listening is more than hearing with your ears. To be an active listener, think about what the other person is saying (not about what you're going to say when it's your turn). Show that you are listening. Look at the person, nod to show you hear the message. Think about what the person said. Summarize the person's ideas to show you understood, and ask for more information or for an example if you need one. Of course, everyone appreciates a sincere compliment as well.

Encourage everyone's contributions.
It is important to find out what everyone thinks. More points of view help to make sure that the group's work is done well. A good way to encourage others to share their ideas is to ask them politely, such as "Cam, what do you think?", then give them time to answer.

Be polite and respectful.

You won't always like everybody's ideas, but you can be respectful while you disagree. Avoid putting down another person's idea. Instead, politely restate the other person's idea first. Then, say why you disagree. For example, "Susan, you seem to think our project should be about how the DNA of space aliens differs from our own. I'm worried that we'll have trouble finding information on that topic. Maybe we should consider Chantelle's idea instead…."

CHECK IT OUT…DOES YOUR GROUP WORK EFFECTIVELY?

An effective group….	If your group doesn't…
Stays on task	Ask for clarification of what the task is and when it is to be done.
Takes turns with roles	Suggest that roles change for each class or each project.
Finishes work on time	Ask members for ideas for how the group can finish on time. Make a list of what needs to be done and who will do it.
Shares the work equally	Review what each person is supposed to contribute and how important each job is.
Respects each other	Show respect to others by being an active listener. Ask everyone to listen to each other and disagree politely.

In an effective group, each member has a specific role.

419 Laboratory Partners and Groups

You will almost certainly work with a partner or small group when you perform lab activities. By working with others, you can share limited lab equipment and work space. Also, for many investigations two or more people are needed just to handle the materials.

You may get to choose your lab partner or you may be assigned to a partner or group. Either way, you need to make your best effort to work with your group. Stay with the task at hand. Share the jobs with others so you finish on time. When each member of the group makes a contribution, the whole group benefits. If a group member gets off task, the whole group misses out. For most lab activities, the jobs include:

- reading and understanding the activity
- setting up materials
- performing the activity
- recording measurements and observations
- keeping track of time
- cleaning up materials

It is important that each lab partner or group member takes turns doing every job. If you find yourself always being the one who records data, or the one who "does the experiment" (handles the materials), or you usually do most of the cleanup, then speak up for yourself. Ask to do the other jobs. Doing different jobs helps you to think about your work from different points of view. This, in turn, will make your understanding of your work more complete.

You will learn even more about working with others if you can switch lab partners or groups every month or two. The experience you have working with many different people will help you both inside and outside of school.

Researching Information

420 Finding published information is an important skill in any subject. In science, you may need to find information as part of preparing for an investigation. You may need to find information for a research report on a certain science topic, such as Kodiak bears. Your school or public library has many resources to help locate science information. The Internet is a great source, too.

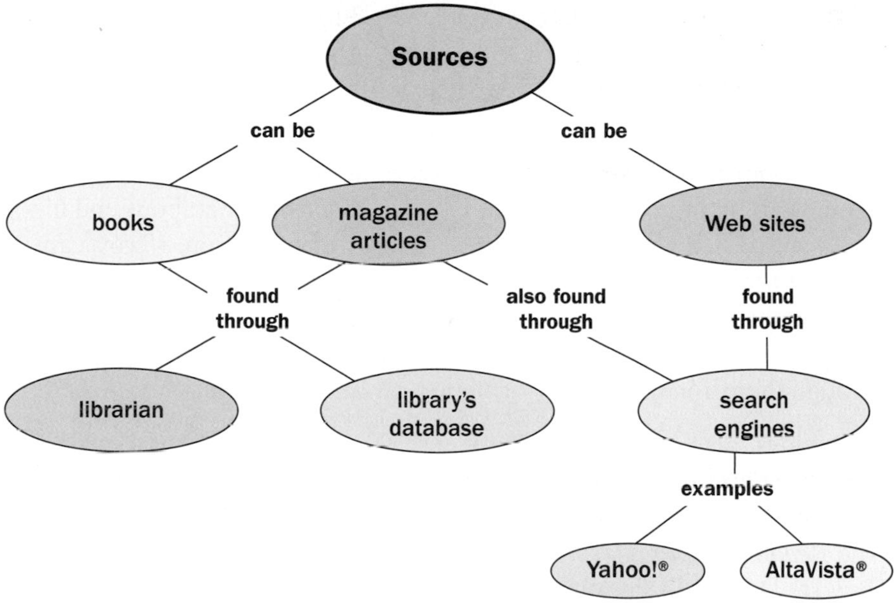

Finding Books and Magazine Articles

421 Most libraries have their collections catalogued in a computer database. The computer terminals are easy to use and allow you to search by Author, Title, or Subject. Let's say you are looking for information on Kodiak bears. When you search a library's catalog, you will turn up more items if you start with a general subject, such as "Bears," rather than a specific subject, such as "Kodiak bears." For a broad subject, such as bears, you may get a second listing of categories before you get to book listings.

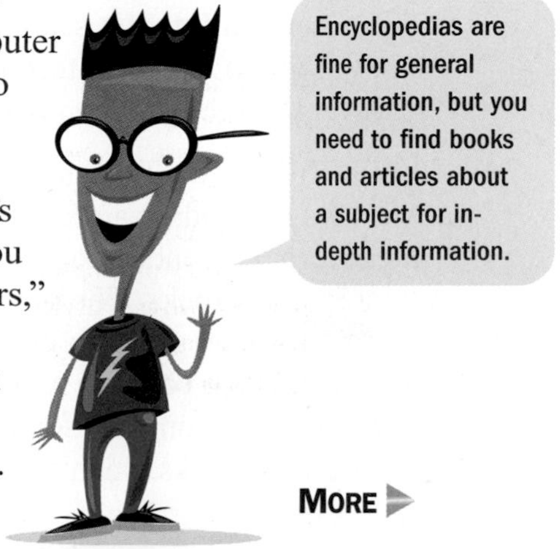

Encyclopedias are fine for general information, but you need to find books and articles about a subject for in-depth information.

MORE ▶

EXAMPLE

For your purpose, categories 3 and 4 are the best bets. Click on these items for a listing of nonfiction books about bears, and about endangered species (including bears) in the library's collection. If you can, find out how to limit your search to just your local library's collection. Books labeled "interlibrary loan" have to come from another library, and this can take weeks. When you find the books, scan through them for specific information on Kodiak bears.

SEE ALSO
425 Using Sources

Magazines, also called **periodicals,** are other sources of good information. The *Reader's Guide to Periodical Literature* lists all articles that have been printed over many years in 240 different periodicals. The *Reader's Guide* is available to libraries as a book, a CD-ROM, or as a site license for an on-line database. Ask your librarian how to access the *Reader's Guide* from your library.

422 Searching the Web

Conducting an Internet search, or Web search, can be a fun and productive way to collect information. There is information available on nearly any topic you can imagine.

To search the web, first go to a search engine's web site. There are two ways to conduct a search. Some search engines let you **browse** by category, from general to specific. Let's say you need to find out about igneous rocks. The picture of a computer screen shows what you might see at a search engine site that lets you browse by category. "Science" is the obvious choice to start your igneous rock search. When you click on the "science" link, you'll see a set of more specific topic links, such as "astronomy, botany, chemistry, geology,

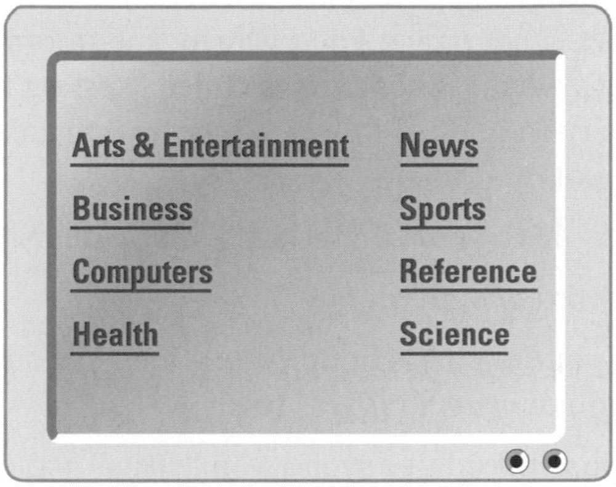

A **link** is any colored text on a web page (often blue and underlined) that takes you to another web page. Follow the link by moving the cursor over it, then clicking or double-clicking on it. You will get a new screen of information with new links.

meteorology, physics, zoology." The "geology" link will give you another set of choices. Continue through the series of screens until you reach links for web sites related to igneous rocks.

Most search engines also let you search by keyword. A **keyword** is simply the term you are searching for, or a term that is related to it. You're usually better off to choose keywords that are more specific, rather than more general. For example, the keyword "rock" may get you over 6 million sites, with sites 1-10 devoted to rock music, but not geology. When you use the keywords "igneous rock," 6000 sites come up, with 19 of the first 20 sites clearly on target.

Tips for Searching by Keyword

- Choose specific terms as keywords.
- Put quotation marks around phrases, for example, "Kodiak bear." This tells the search engine to find only those sites that contain all words in the phrase.
- Usually, the first 15–20 sites on the list will be most useful.
- Sites that end in *.edu* (educational institution), *.gov* (government agency), and *.org* (nonprofit institution) are usually the most reliable sources for science information.
- Institutional websites often include sites written for students. Try NASA, USGS, NOAA, and EPA.
- If you're having trouble, try a different keyword on the same subject. In the igneous rock example, you could also search using the keywords "magma" or "volcano."

423

On-Line Guidelines

Searching the Internet is not only a good way to find information. It can also be fun. That's why it is sometimes called "surfing the web." There are some important rules to follow whenever you are surfing on-line, either at school or at home.

- Follow the rules—both your school's and your parents.'
- Keep your password private.
- Remember that your e-mail is not private. Don't say anything in it that you would not want strangers to know.
- Report to a responsible adult anyone who "chats" about inappropriate topics on-line.
- Never give your full name, address, or phone number over the Internet. If you must, use only your first name and the school address.
- Use appropriate language—no swear words or put-downs!
- Never plagiarize from the web—give credit for the source.

SEE ALSO

426 Citing Sources

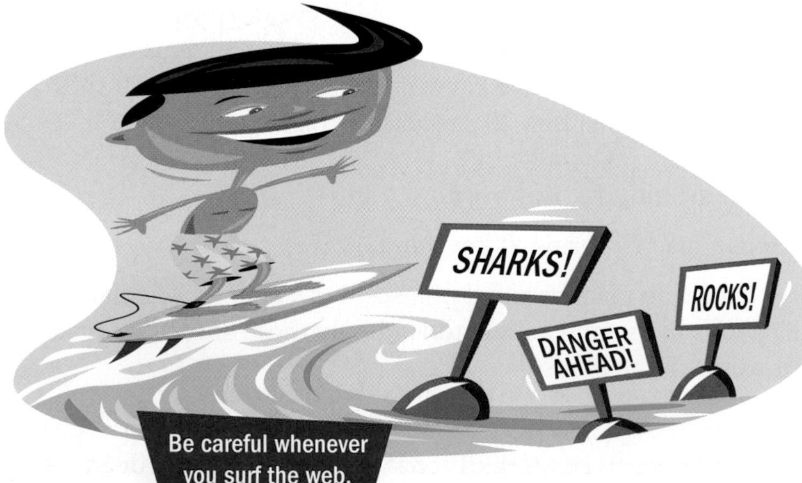

Be careful whenever you surf the web.

Did You Know?

School network computers keep copies of all e-mail, as well as lists of websites that each computer visits. Many school networks also use filters to block student access to inappropriate web sites.

Evaluating Sources

Once you've found sources, you need to figure out which are useful and which are not worth your time. You'll turn up more information that you can't use on the Internet than in a library, because a librarian has already evaluated the library's collection.

When was this written? For some science topics, information more than a few years old may be outdated. Check the publication dates of books, usually on the back of the title page. On the Web, check when a site was last updated.

Who wrote this? What does the author know about the subject? Check the front or back of a book for author information. On a web site, click on the link for the author's name. Books written by a team of people may not give author information. In that case, check the publisher.

WHO said this?
THE WORLD IS FLAT!

What is its purpose? Use only sources that are meant for factual research. For example, some science fiction novels have science facts in them, but the main purpose of fiction is to entertain. A dot-com web site offering fossils to collectors may have facts, but its main purpose is to sell you something.

Who is meant to read it? Look for sources that are pitched at your needs. A professional geologist's scientific paper will be too specific and have too many technical terms. A guide for preschool teachers introducing 3-year-olds to rocks will be too general.

MORE

Do sources agree? If three reliable sources say the same thing, you probably have accurate information. For measured data, such as the elevation of Mount Everest or the world population, reliable sources should be close, but do not have to match exactly.

425

Using Sources

You will save a lot of time if you learn how to find the information you need without reading the whole source. Before you read, make sure the source has the information you need. Check the index and table of contents for your topic. If an article has a summary or conclusion, read that first. While you are reading, ignore information that is not useful. Read actively by thinking of the headings on the page as questions. Take notes by briefly writing down the most important ideas in your own words.

426

Citing Sources

As you take notes, write down the source of the information. List the author, title of the book or name of the article, publication date, page number, and publishing company. For a web site, list the web address and the group that posted it, instead of the page number and publisher. Check with your teacher for the way to organize this information in your report.

Copying and turning in somebody else's work as if it is your own is called plagiarism (PLAY juh riz um). It is dishonest and illegal.

Test-Taking Skills

427

Test-taking is a skill, just like basketball, skateboarding, or playing an instrument. You can improve your test performance by preparing and practicing, by thinking about what you're doing during the test, and by reviewing your performance afterward.

Preparing for the Test

428

Doing well on tests has a lot to do with being prepared for them. Good preparation takes time. Here are helpful tips to get ready.

Stay on top of things.

- Get any notes or assignments you might have missed as soon as you can. Ask reliable classmates or your teacher for the information.
- Find a regular place and time to study. You need room to lay out your notes, good lighting, and quiet. If your home is noisy, then ear plugs may be helpful.
- Review your notes every day or two. Ask about anything you don't understand the next time your class meets.

MORE ▶

Plan and organize your studying.

- Find out what material will be on the test.
- Make the most of in-class review. Study for the test the night before the review. Jot down questions. Bring the questions to class on the day of the review—not the day of the test!
- As you study, review the assigned reading, your notes, and your homework. Circle or highlight key concepts in your notes. Use a different color for each key concept.
- Facts are easier to remember if you make up words or phrases that use their first initials. For example, to remember the Great Lakes, use HOMES: ***H***uron, ***O***ntario, ***M***ichigan, ***E***rie, ***S***uperior.
- Make up a set of index cards with key concepts and information. Carry them with you to study whenever you have a moment.
- Connect and organize ideas. In science, tests often require you to think and problem-solve, not just repeat facts. One way to connect ideas is to make a concept map.
- Talk to yourself. If you explain concepts out loud, your brain stores the information from both seeing and hearing it.
- Form a study group. After you have reviewed on your own, meet with other students to review questions and discuss key concepts.

Take care of yourself.

- The day of the test starts the night before. Get enough sleep. Sleep helps you remember what you've learned, and if you are tired it will be hard to concentrate during the test.
- Eat a good breakfast. Your brain needs energy to function.

429 Concept Mapping

Concept mapping is a method of showing how ideas are related to each other. Concept maps are used in books to help show relationships among ideas. You can also make your own concept maps to help organize ideas while studying for a test.

When you make your own concept map, you are making a picture of how you understand scientific ideas and their relationships. Because each person understands things a little differently, there is no one "right way" to draw a concept map. However, you will sometimes discover that your understanding of a concept is incorrect, once you put it into a concept map. Making a concept map several days before a test, and sharing it with others in a study group, will help you to recognize your misconceptions and to correct them.

Steps for Making a Concept Map

1. List the important concepts of the topic you are mapping. Often, you can start with a vocabulary list.
2. Write the main concept at the top of the map. The main concept is the one that includes most of the other concepts. Circle it.
3. Write other concepts beneath the main concept. Draw lines to connect related concepts. (These lines are sometimes called *links.*)
4. On or next to each connecting link, write words that describe how those concepts are related.
5. Add other concepts until you have added all the concepts on your list. Add more concepts if you want to.
6. Look over your map. Make your map stronger by adding more links to show more connections among concepts. In the example, these links are shown in red.

Concept List

Cells
Cell wall
Cell membrane
Nucleus
Chromosomes
Cell division
Plants
Animals

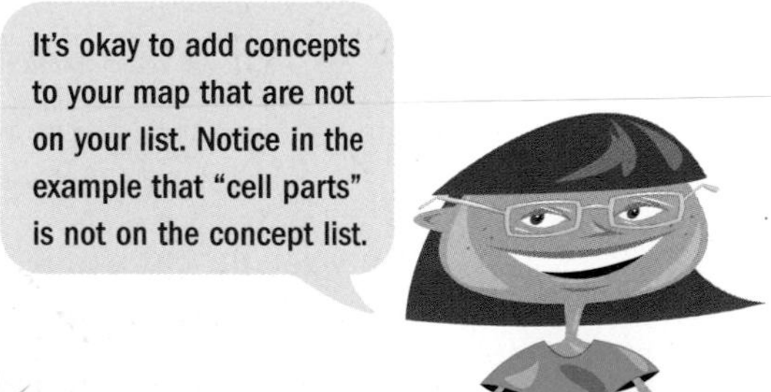

It's okay to add concepts to your map that are not on your list. Notice in the example that "cell parts" is not on the concept list.

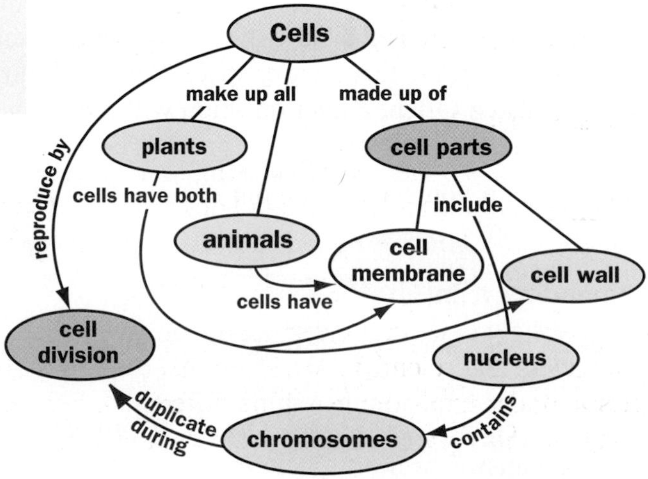

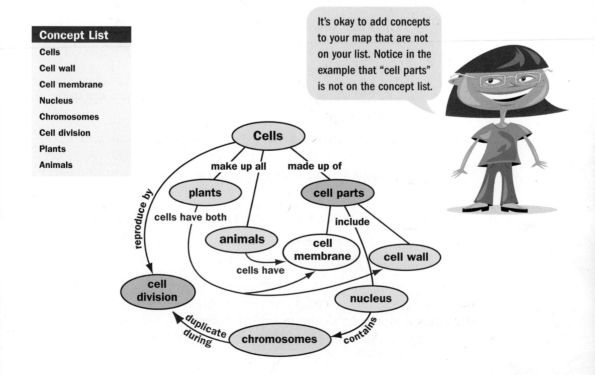

Taking the Test

430

The tips in this section are great for standardized achievement tests, as well as for regular tests your science teacher gives.

Right before the test...

- Review once more if you have the chance.
- Ask about the rules for this test. How much time do you have? May you use a calculator? Are you allowed to use notes?
- Check that you have all the materials you need.
- Relax.

As soon as you get the test...

- Quickly survey the whole test. Get a general idea of its length and the kinds of questions in it.
- Speak up right away if a page seems to be missing or if the test is hard to read.
- Read all the directions carefully. Ask about any unclear directions before you get started.

While you take the test...

- Follow the tips for each type of test question, which begin on the next page of this handbook.
- Answer the questions that go quickly right away. Save the questions that take more thought for later.
- Answer the questions that you are sure of first. If you get stuck on a question, leave that answer space blank and move on. Come back to it later. Often, a later question will remind you of the answer to an earlier item.
- Don't panic if you start to run out of time. Relax and complete what you can.

Before handing it in...

- Check to make sure you have answered all items. Make sure your handwriting is clear.
- Beware of changing your first answer. When you are unsure, your first answer is more likely to be correct.

Tips for Multiple-Choice Tests

On multiple-choice tests, you sometimes need to "read between the lines" to evaluate choices. Here are tips for multiple-choice items.

- Read all the directions and all the choices for each item.
- Notice key words that can change an item's meaning: *not, best, most likely, greatest, all, alike* or *same, different, cause, effect.*
- There is usually only one correct answer. Try to eliminate one or two choices right away by using common sense and your science background.
- Concentrate on what you know. Don't be fooled by long choices with big, unfamiliar words.

Sometimes the correct answer is "D—All of the above," so make sure you read **all** choices before answering.

Example

An *environmental impact statement* is a report about how a project might affect the environment. Which information would most likely be included in an environmental impact statement about a waste incinerator planned near a large city?

A. number of new jobs that would be created

B. expected savings to the average person per ton of trash burned

C. amount and kind of substances that would be released into the air from the incinerator

D. possible ways the city might change the direction that the wind blows so smoke from the incinerator would not manifest itself over the city, causing trauma to citizens

You can cross off choice A, because creating new jobs isn't what an environmental impact statement is about. Cross off choice B for the same reason. Choice C seems to makes sense because it talks about the air. Air is part of the environment. For choice D, go with what you know about science and use common sense. A city probably can't change the wind direction. You can cross off choice D even if you don't understand every word in it. Item C has to be the best choice.

432 Tips for Short-Answer, Fill-In, and True/False Tests

- Read directions carefully and follow them exactly.
- Read the questions carefully, paying attention to details. Ask yourself what each question means.
- Examine pictures, charts, and diagrams. Notice the labels and keys and what they refer to.
- Write clearly. For true-false items, write out the whole word instead of T/F.
- Write a short answer that fits in the space provided.
- Don't read too much into true/false items. Think about what is generally true. You will just confuse yourself if you start thinking about rare cases where things may be different.

433 Tips for "Analyze the Science" Tests

Science involves problem solving so it is likely you will be asked to think through science situations on tests. Often these types of test questions ask you to write a short essay to explain your thinking. Sometimes a diagram is included, which you need to analyze or explain.

- Start with what you know. Look for science concepts you've studied. Use your common sense as well as science knowledge.
- Notice key phrases in the directions. Ask what they mean if you are unsure: *argue, analyze, compare, contrast, define, describe, explain, demonstrate, give examples, discuss, list.*
- Look for the parts of an experiment in a description: *hypothesis, variable, control, data, trial, analysis, conclusion.*
- Take a moment to outline or map out your writing before you start to answer. Make sure you answer what's being asked. Give specific examples when you are asked to. If the item asks for a specific number of examples, make sure to give that many.

EXAMPLE: Explain how cutting down all the trees above point A might affect the land, the lake, and the town. Give examples of how each site might be affected.

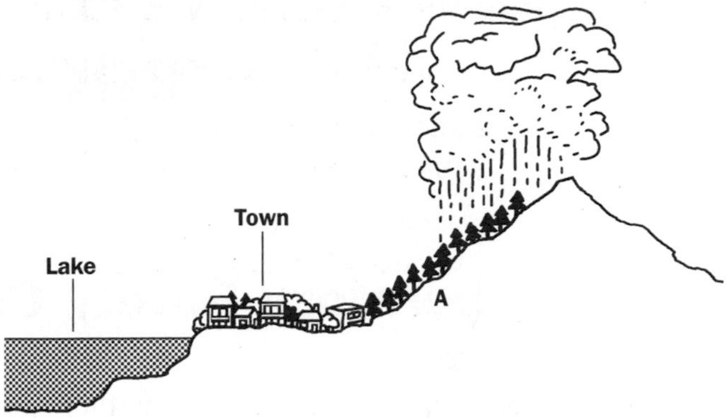

Source: Adapted from an Ohio Proficiency Practice Test

The key words are "affect," "explain," and "examples." You must think about what might happen and draw your own conclusions based on your science knowledge. For example, once the mountain slope no longer has trees to hold the soil, erosion and mudslides could occur. The town could be hit by the mudslides or by avalanches of snow. The lake could silt up from all the soil that would wash down the mountain. A change in the lake might cause fish and other animals to die. Losing wildlife might cause the town to lose money, if they depend on fishing for food or for tourism.

After the Test

434

You can learn about how to prepare for—and take—the next test if you take time to go over the one you just finished.

When you get your test back...

- Check to make sure the score was added correctly. If you have a question, ask to speak with the teacher privately.
- Questions you missed may come up again on later tests. Look up the answers in your notes or your book. Ask about anything you still don't understand.
- Notice the types of questions you did well on and the ones you had trouble with. Decide whether you need to work on writing better long answers, or at taking more time with multiple choice.
- Think about how you prepared. If you did well, use those same study strategies for the next test. If you didn't do as well as you would like, think about how you can prepare differently next time.

435

References

436

Laboratory Safety Contract

Read, understand, and agree to these guidelines before you work in a science laboratory.

General Behavior

- Never work in a lab unless a teacher or another responsible adult is present.
- Follow all directions, including written directions that come with lab equipment.
- Show respect for the lab. Never run, throw things, or play around in lab.
- Never eat or drink in the lab or from lab containers.

Dress Code and Cleanliness

- Wear protective clothing—goggles, aprons, gloves—as appropriate.
- Wear shoes that completely cover your feet.
- Tie back long hair.
- Wash your hands after doing a lab investigation in which you handle chemicals, living things, or once-living things.
- Keep the lab clean and picked up. A clean lab reduces accidents.

Waste Disposal

- Learn the proper way to dispose of each type of waste. Dispose of each type of waste only in the proper way.
- Leave hazardous waste for a waste collection specialist to handle.
- NEVER pour a hazardous waste down the drain or onto the ground.
- Do not put hazardous waste into the trash can.

Working with Heat

- Understand how a heat source (Bunsen burner, hot plate) works before you use it.
- Avoid lighting matches if anyone in the lab is sensitive to sulfur.
- Don't walk away from a heat source that is in use.
- Heat materials only in heat-resistant containers.
- Never heat a closed container.
- Wear goggles and use mitts or tongs when handling hot materials.

Working with Chemicals

- Always know what chemical you are handling.
- Label containers before adding chemicals to them. Never take a substance out of an unlabeled container.
- Do not smell chemicals directly. Observe chemical odors by wafting, or fanning, fumes toward your nose.
- Know how to properly store each chemical.
- Wash hands with soap and water after handling chemicals.

Working with Live or Once-Living Materials

- Only work with the approval of a responsible adult.
- Wear gloves and goggles (wear non-latex gloves if sensitive to latex).
- Do not touch face or skin while handling materials.
- Use sealed containers for mold and bacteria.
- Wash hands with soap and water after handling living or once-living materials.

Working with Electricity

- Make sure outlets within 6 feet of a water source are ground fault circuit protected (GFCI).
- NEVER submerge an electrical appliance in water.
- Position power cords so you don't trip over them.
- Position electrical appliances so they are not knocked over easily.

Working with Sharp Instruments

- Handle sharp instruments (knives, scalpels, and scissors) with care.
- Always cut in a direction away from yourself and others.

Handling Emergencies

- Be prepared. Know the location of all safety equipment in the lab *before* any emergencies happen.
- In any emergency, immediately alert the adult in charge. Move away from the site of the emergency.
- Always have fire extinguishers and fire blankets handy.
- If your clothes catch fire, stop, drop, and roll. Do not run.
- Always have on hand and know how to use a first aid kit.

I, ___Student Name___, agree that the guidelines in this contract make sense, and I agree to follow them. (Do not write in this book.)

SEE ALSO
021-045 Laboratory Safety

Physical Maps

437

Map of World

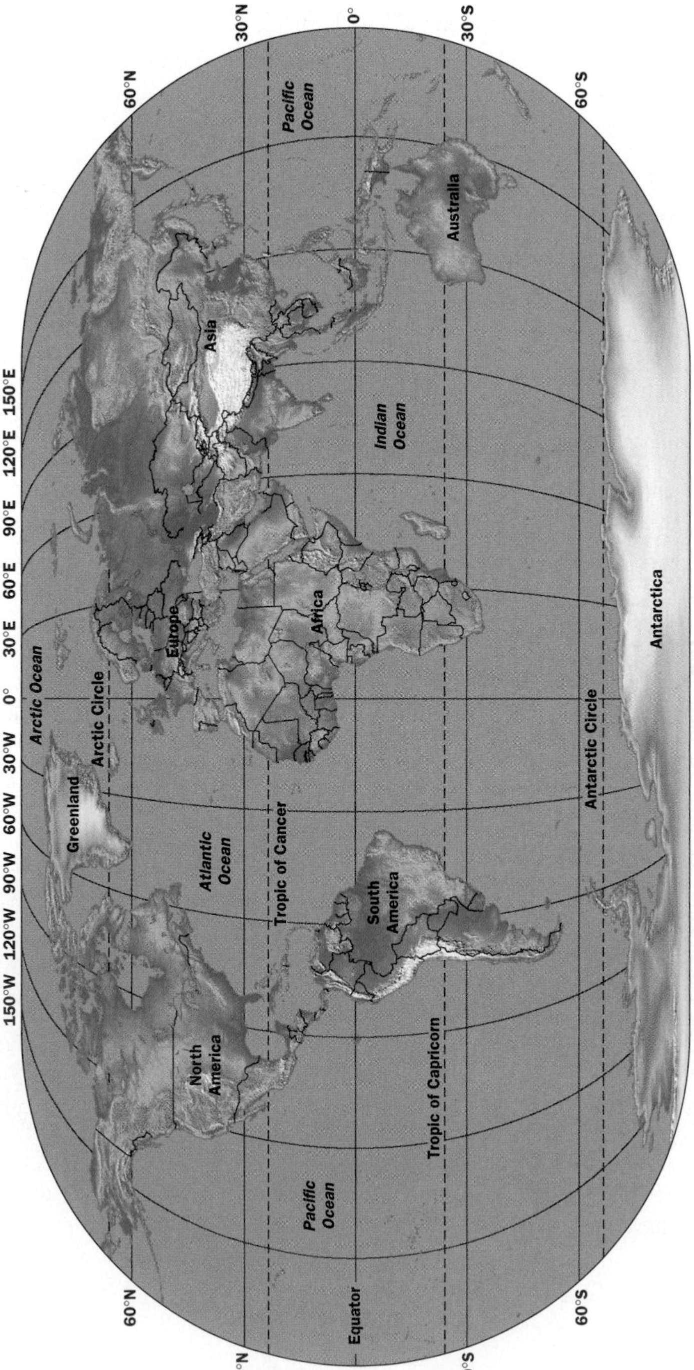

Europe and Asia are sometimes called Eurasia because they are one continuous land mass

Map of North America

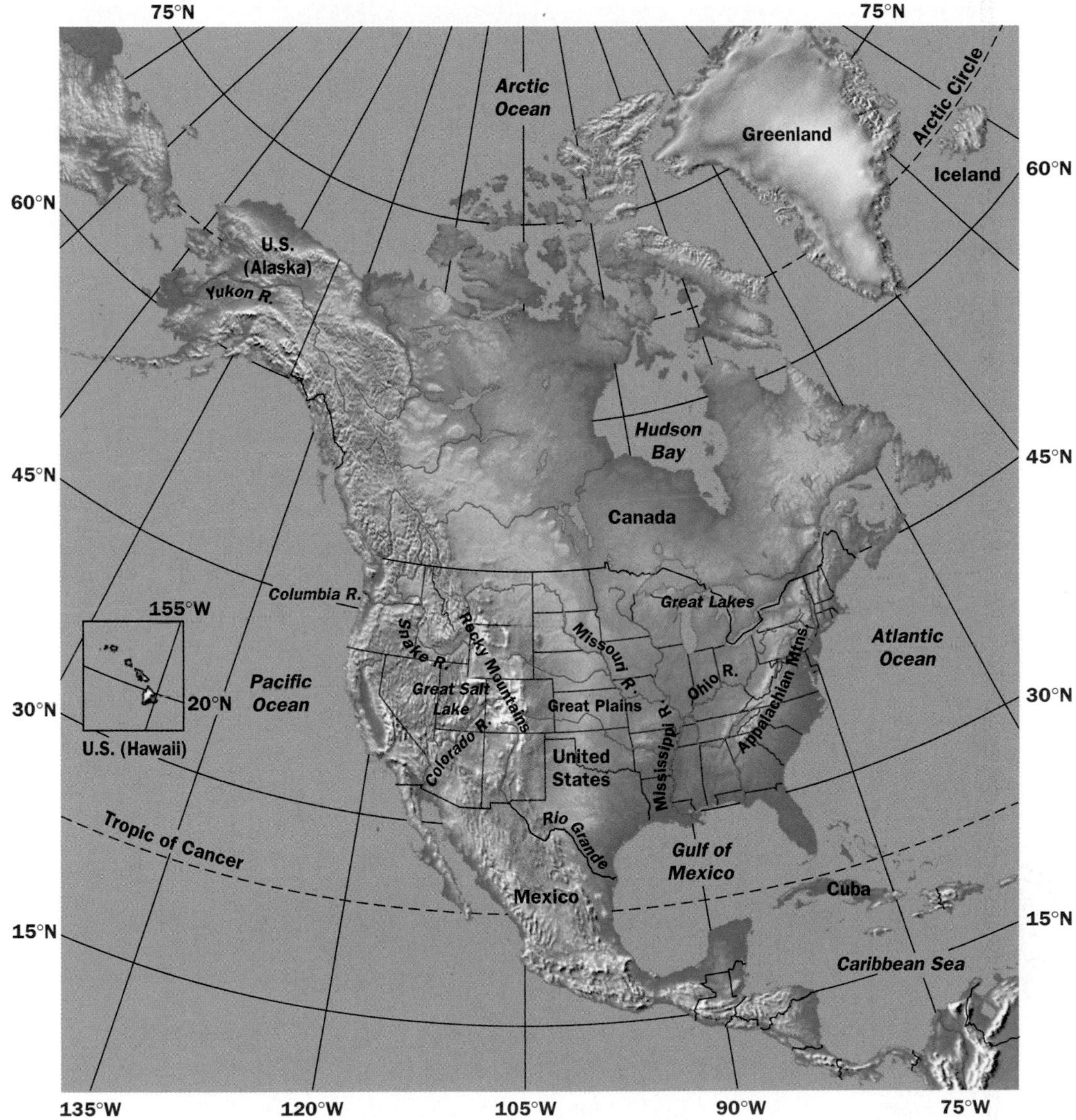

Conversion Tables

438

Length (*SI*: centimeter, meter, kilometer; *English*: inch, foot, mile)

Read units across →	centimeter (cm)	meter (m)	kilometer (km)	inch (in.)	foot (ft)	mile (mi)
1 centimeter (cm) =	1	0.01	0.00001	0.3937	0.03281	0.000006214
1 meter (m) =	100	1	0.001	39.37	3.281	0.0006214
1 kilometer (km) =	100,000	1,000	1	39,370	3,281	0.6214
1 inch (in.) =	2.540	0.0254	0.00002540	1	0.08333	0.00001578
1 foot (ft) =	30.48	0.3048	0.0003048	12	1	0.0001894
1 mile (mi) =	160,900	1,609	1.609	63,360	5,280	1

Volume (*SI*: liter, cubic centimeter or milliliter; *English*: fluid ounce, quart)

Read units across →	cubic centimeter (cm^3) or milliliter (mL)	liter (L)	fluid ounce (fl oz)	quart (qt)
1 cubic centimeter (cm^3) or 1 milliliter (mL) =	1	0.001	0.034	0.00104
1 liter (L) =	1,000	1	33.8	1.057
1 fluid ounce (fl oz) =	30	0.03	1	0.03125
1 quart (qt) =	950	0.95	32	1

Mass to Equivalent Weight (*SI*: kilogram, gram; *English*: ounce, pound)

Read units across →	grams (g)	kilograms (kg)	ounces (oz)	pounds (lb)
1 gram (g)=	1	0.001	0.0353	0.00221
1 kilogram (kg) =	1000	1	35.27	2.2
1 ounce (oz) =	28.3	0.0283	1	0.0625
1 pound (lb) =	0.00045	0.45	16	1

Yellow Pages

The History of Science

One of the greatest scientists of all time, Sir Isaac Newton, once declared that "If I have seen further it is by standing on the shoulders of giants." What Newton meant was that the discoveries of scientists that came before him allowed him to make his own discoveries. And that is true of all scientific discoveries. Each scientist uncovers information that scientists who follow build on.

The History of Science Time Line shows some of the important scientific discoveries and technological inventions that have occurred over the past 600 years. Why start with 1400? There certainly were scientists before that year. But the age of modern science, with its careful observations and structured experiments, began near that time. So this is where you will begin your journey.

The work of a small number of scientists is looked at in the Famous Scientists section. Keep in mind that this list includes mainly people from the Western, as opposed to Eastern, world. Scientists working in Asia, Africa, and Central and South America have also made great contributions to their areas of study.

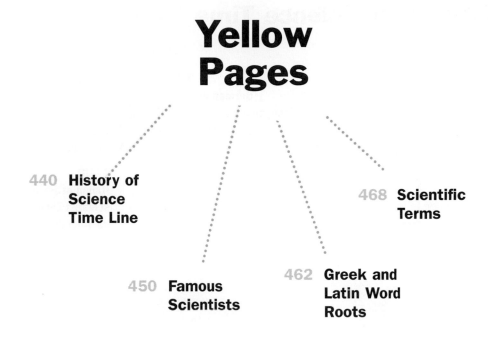

History of Science Time Line

Science and Technology

1400
Chinese determine length of solar year to be 365.25 days.

1408
Windmill used in Holland to move water from land to sea.

1440
German scholar Nicholas of Cusa proposes that Earth revolves around the sun.

1450
Johann Gutenberg develops the printing press.

1472
German astronomer Regiomontanus is the first to scientifically observe and describe a comet.

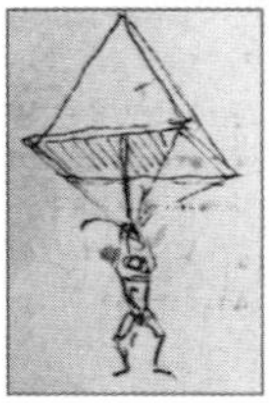

1480
Italian artist and scientist Leonardo da Vinci draws a design of the first parachute.

1492
Christopher Columbus discovers that a compass needle points in different directions as a ship moves from east to west.

1497
Polish astronomer Nicolas Copernicus observes and records the moon passing in front of a star.

1400	1410	1420	1430	1440	1450	1460	1470	1480	1490

Politics and Society

1429
Joan of Arc leads French to victory against the English in Battle of Orléans.

1438
Inca empire founded in South America.

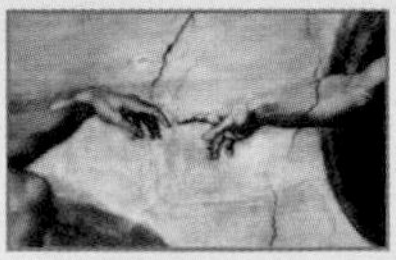

1473
Michelangelo paints ceiling of the Sistine Chapel in Rome.

1492
Christopher Columbus discovers the West Indies.

1498
Vasco da Gama makes first voyage around Africa's Cape of Good Hope to reach India.

Approximate World Population in 1400: **390,000,000 (estimate)**

•1502
German inventor Peter Henlein makes first pocket watch.

•1568
Flemish geographer Gerardus Mercator invents a map of the world that allows sailors to more precisely navigate Earth's oceans.

•1540
German astronomer Peter Apian is first European to note that the tail of a comet always points away from the sun.

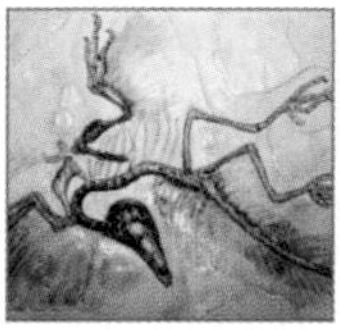

•1517
Italian physician Girolamo Fracastoro states that fossils are the remains of once-living things.

•1572
Danish astronomer Tycho Brahe discovers an exploding star, which he calls a "nova."

1543•
Flemish anatomist Andreas Vesalius publishes first accurate book on human anatomy based on dissections of dead bodies.

1590•
Dutch spectacle maker Zacherais Janssen is thought to make the first compound microscope.

1543•
Nicolas Copernicus publishes a book in which he presents mathematical evidence that the sun, not Earth, is at the center of the "universe."

1596•
Chinese scholar Li Shih-Chen describes 8000 medical uses for more than 1000 plants and 1000 animals.

1500 | 1510 | 1520 | 1530 | 1540 | 1550 | 1560 | 1570 | 1580 | 1590

•1519
Ferdinand Magellan starts voyage around the world; one of his ships will complete the voyage.

•1558
Elizabeth I becomes Queen of England.

•1582
The modern Gregorian calendar is introduced.

AUGUST

S	M	T	W	T	F	S
			1	2	3	4
5	6	7	8	9	10	11
12	13	14	15	16	17	18
19	20	21	22	23	24	25
26	27	28	29	30	31	

1532•
Francisco Pizzaro begins conquest that will destroy the Inca civilization of Peru.

•1564
William Shakespeare born in England.

Approximate World Population in 1500: **460,000,000**

Science and Technology

1600
William Gilbert suggests Earth is a huge magnet.

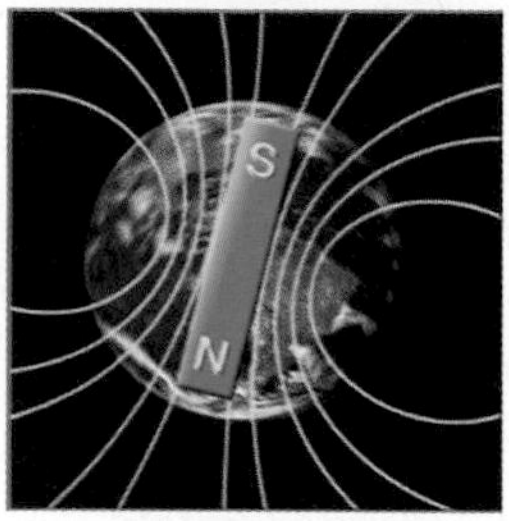

1608
Dutch scientist Hans Lippershey invents the refracting telescope.

1609
German astronomer Johann Kepler describes elliptical orbits of planets.

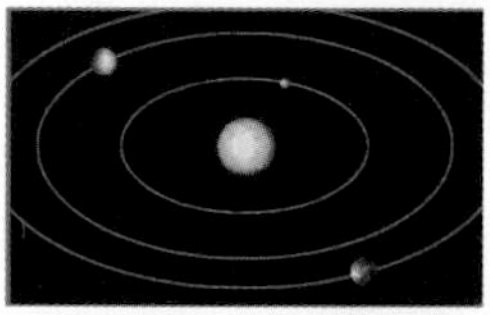

1643
Italian physicist Evangelista Torricelli invents the barometer.

1665
English physicist Robert Hooke describes cells for the first time.

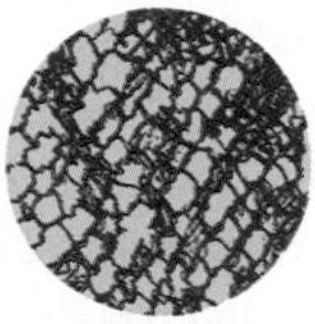

1668
Newton invents the reflecting telescope.

1677
Dutch biologist Anton van Leeuwenhoek discovers microscopic organisms (protozoa).

1687
Newton describes his three laws of motion and the law of universal gravitation.

1600	1610	1620	1630	1640	1650	1660	1670	1680	1690

Politics and Society

1607
First English settlement in America is established at Jamestown in Virginia.

1620
Pilgrims land at Plymouth Rock.

1642
Start of the English Civil War.

1665
Great Plague kills 75,000 people in London.

1682
William Penn founds Pennsylvania.

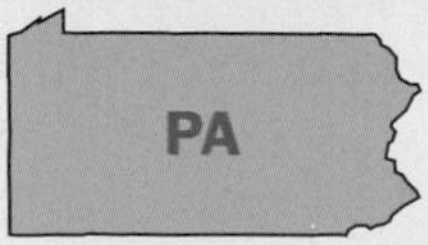

Approximate World Population in 1600: 550,000,000

1714
Gabriel Fahrenheit builds a mercury thermometer and a temperature scale that will later be named after him.

1760
English geologist John Michell proposes that the destructive force of earthquakes is caused by waves in the ground.

1765
Scottish engineer James Watt invents the steam engine.

1735
Swedish botanist Carolus Linnaeus invents a classification system for living things.

1742
Anders Celsius invents the Celsius scale of temperature.

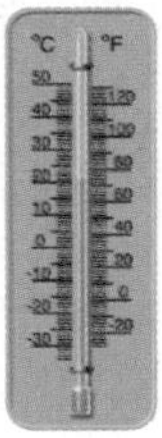

1774
German geologist Abraham Gottlob Werner introduces a classification system for minerals.

1796
English physician Edward Jenner performs first vaccination against smallpox using the cowpox virus.

1752
Benjamin Franklin demonstrates that lightning is a form of electricity.

1799
Italian physicist Alessandro Volta invents the electric battery.

1700 | 1710 | 1720 | 1730 | 1740 | 1750 | 1760 | 1770 | 1780 | 1790

1709
Italian instrument maker Bartolomeo Cristofori invents the pianoforte, later called the piano.

1773
American colonists protesting English taxes on imported tea dump tea from English ships into Boston harbor.

1789
The French Revolution begins on July 14.

1776
U.S. Declaration of Independence adopted on July 4.

Approximate World Population in 1700: 650,000,000

Science and Technology

1803
English chemist John Dalton proposes his atomic theory.

1807
American inventor Robert Fulton builds the first commercial steamboat.

1816
French physician René Laënnec invents the stethoscope.

1819
Danish physicist Hans Christian Oersted demonstrates that electricity can produce magnetism.

1831
English physicist and chemist Michael Faraday reports that magnetism can produce electricity.

1837
American inventor Samuel Morse patents his telegraph.

1846
German astronomer Johann Galle discovers the planet Neptune.

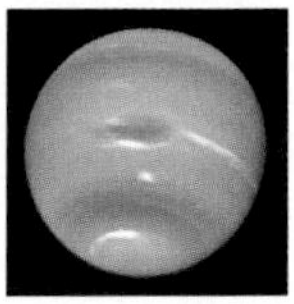

1800 | 1810 | 1820 | 1830 | 1840

Politics and Society

1804
Native American woman Sacajawea helps guide Lewis and Clark expedition across America.

1815
French emperor Napoleon suffers final defeat at Waterloo, Belgium.

1818
English novelist Mary Shelley writes *Frankenstein.*

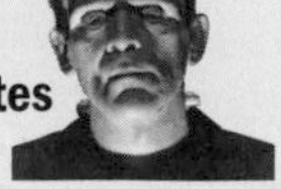

1831
African-American slave Nat Turner leads slave revolt in Virginia.

1848
Gold discovered in California.

Approximate World Population in 1800: **1,000,000,000**

•1869
Russian chemist Dmitri Mendeléev organizes elements into a Periodic Table.

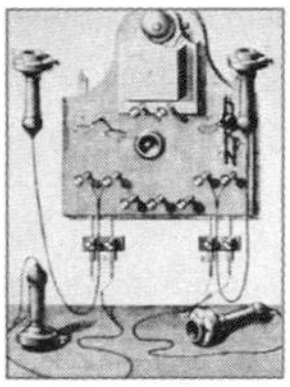

•1876
Scottish-American inventor Alexander Graham Bell patents the telephone.

TT tt

•1857
Austrian botanist Gregor Mendel launches the science of genetics.

•1879
American inventor Thomas Alva Edison invents first practical light bulb.

•1880
French physician Louis Pasteur develops germ theory of disease.

1859•
English naturalist Charles Darwin publishes *On the Origin of Species,* which describes the theory of evolution.

1880•
English geologist John Milne invents the seismograph, which detects and measures earthquakes.

1898•
Polish-French chemist Marie Curie discovers polonium and radium.

1850 | 1860 | 1870 | 1880 | 1890

1861•
U.S. Civil War begins.

•1850
Harriet Tubman begins her crusade to guide southern slaves to freedom in the north.

•1863
Abraham Lincoln's Emancipation Proclamation frees slaves.

•1865
U.S. Civil War ends.

•1876
Dakota and North Cheyenne Native Americans defend their territory and defeat U.S. troops led by George Custer at the Battle of the Little Bighorn.

•1886
Statue of Liberty unveiled in New York Harbor.

Approximate World Population in 1900: **1,650,000,000**

Science and Technology

1903
American inventors Wilbur and Orville Wright launch their airplane.

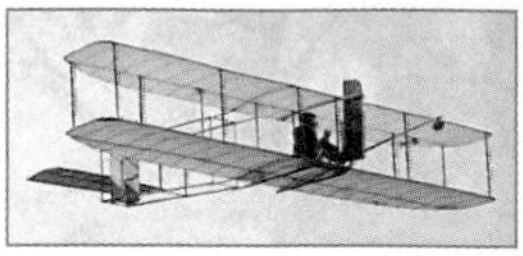

1905
$E = mc^2$

German-Swiss physicist Albert Einstein publishes his theory of relativity, which includes the equation $E = mc^2$.

1915
The first transatlantic telephone conversation takes place between the United States and France.

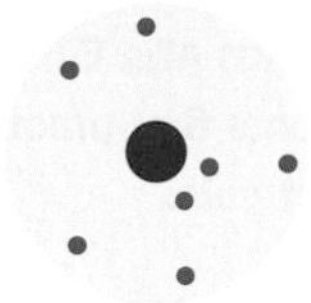

1911
British physicist Ernest Rutherford proposes that an atom has a positive nucleus surrounded by negative electrons.

1912
German geologist Alfred Wegener presents evidence that Earth's continents were once part of a single land mass that broke apart.

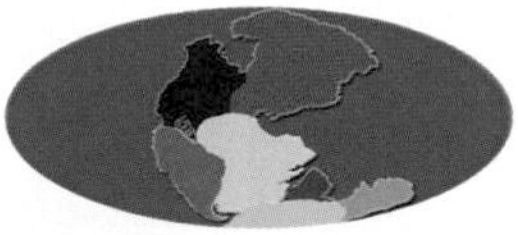

1920
Commercial radio broadcasting begins.

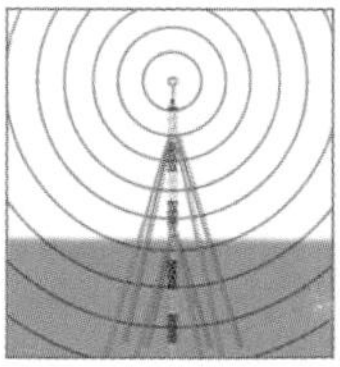

1913
Automobile-maker Henry Ford introduces the assembly line.

1900 | 1905 | 1910 | 1915 | 1920

Politics and Society

1906
An earthquake of magnitude 8.3 on the Richter scale strikes San Francisco.

1910
Boy Scouts of America founded.

1914
World War I begins.

1918
World War I ends.

1912
Girls Scouts of America founded.

1909
American explorers Robert Peary and Matthew Hensen are first to reach North Pole.

1920
Nineteenth Amendment to the U.S. Constitution gives women the right to vote.

Approximate World Population in 1930: 2,000,000,000

1926
Robert Goddard launches first liquid-fueled rocket.

1942
Italian-American physicist Enrico Fermi creates first controlled nuclear reaction.

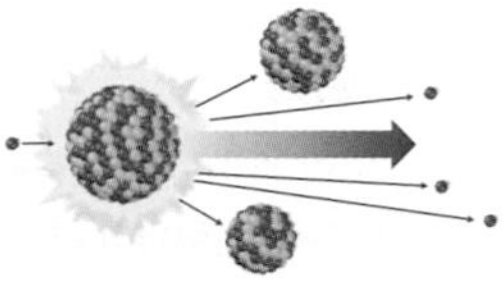

1928
Scottish bacteriologist Alexander Fleming accidentally discovers the antibiotic properties of penicillin.

1942
First electronic computer built.

1930
American astronomer Clyde Tombaugh discovers the planet Pluto.

1933
First electron microscope built; magnifies objects 12,000 times.

1948
Transistor invented at the Bell Telephone Laboratories.

1935
Radar developed by British scientists.

1937
First jet engine built.

1948
Swiss engineer George deMestral invents Velcro.

1925 | 1930 | 1935 | 1940 | 1945

1927
First television broadcast.

1927
American aviator Charles Lindbergh makes first nonstop solo flight across the Atlantic Ocean.

1929
Stock market crashes leading to Great Depression.

1933
Hitler rises to power in Germany.

1941
Japanese bomb Pearl Harbor in Hawaii, bringing the United States into World War II.

1945
World War II ends.

1947
Jackie Robinson becomes first African-American in major league baseball.

Approximate World Population in 1950: 2,400,000,000

Science and Technology

1952
American microbiologist Jonas Salk develops the polio vaccine.

1953
American biochemist James Watson and English biophysicist Francis Crick discover the structure of DNA.

1967
South African physician Christiaan Barnard performs first human heart transplant.

1969
American astronaut Neil Armstrong is first human to walk on the moon.

1957
First artificial satellite, *Sputnik 1,* is launched by Soviet Union.

1971
British engineer Godfrey Hounsfield invents the CAT scan, which shows 3-D images of the brain.

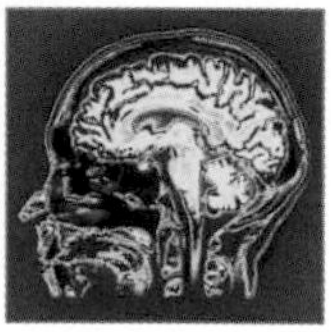

1959
First silicon microchip produced.

1961
Soviet cosmonaut Yury Gagarin becomes first human to orbit Earth.

1962
American biologist Rachel Carson writes *Silent Spring,* warning of dangers to the environment by human activity.

1974
American scientists warn that hole in ozone layer above Earth may be caused by gases used in spray cans and refrigerators.

1950 | 1955 | 1960 | 1965 | 1970

Politics and Society

1953
African-American Rosa Parks sparks civil rights movement by not giving up her seat at front of bus.

1953
Edmund Hillary of New Zealand and Tenzing Norgay of Nepal are first to reach top of Mt. Everest.

1959
Alaska and Hawaii become 49th and 50th states.

1963
U.S. President John F. Kennedy assassinated.

1968
Civil rights leader Martin Luther King, Jr. assassinated.

1974
U.S. President Richard Nixon is forced to resign because of Watergate scandal.

Approximate World Population in 1970: 3,900,000,000

1977
First personal computer, the Apple II, goes on sale.

1978
First human baby conceived in a test tube is born in England.

1981
U.S. Space Shuttle goes into operation.

1984
HIV, virus that causes AIDS, discovered.

1986
Worst nuclear accident ever occurs in Chernobyl, Ukraine.

1990
Hubble Space Telescope launched.

1991
World Wide Web created.

1997
Scottish scientists Ian Wilmut and Keith Campbell produce first cloned mammal, a sheep.

2000
American researchers Francis Collins and J. Craig Venter decipher human genetic code.

1975	1980	1985	1990	1995

1976
The United States celebrates its 200th birthday.

1981
Sandra Day O'Connor becomes first woman Supreme Court justice.

1989
Berlin Wall is torn down.

1991
Soviet Union breaks up.

1994
Nelson Mandela becomes President of South Africa.

Approximate World Population in 2000: **6,250,000,000**

Famous Scientists

Alvarez, Luis
(1911–1988), American physicist. In 1981, Louis Alvarez and his son, American geologist Walter Alvarez, proposed an explanation for why the dinosaurs (and many other forms of life) went extinct 65 million years ago. Evidence the scientists had gathered suggested that a large object from space, such as an asteroid or a comet, had struck the surface of Earth. Such a collision, the Alvarezes pointed out, might have produced great clouds of dust that blotted out sunlight for many months. Green plants that needed sunlight to grow would have died. Animals that fed on green plants, or on the animals that ate the plants, would also have died. Recent evidence suggests that such an impact occurred about 65 million years ago on the northern edge of Mexico's Yucatan Peninsula.

Archimedes
(287 B.C.–212 B.C.), Greek mathematician and engineer. Archimedes is famous for discovering that an object placed in water displaces a volume of water equal to its own volume, and that the weight of the displaced fluid was equal to the buoyant force acting on the object. Archimedes also discovered the principle that explained how a lever allowed a person to lift a weight that the person could not lift with bare hands. With regard to this discovery, Archimedes is supposed to have said, "Give me a place to stand on and I can move the world!" All he would have needed was an extremely long and unbending lever.

Banting, Sir Frederick
(1891–1941), Canadian physician and physiologist. In the early part of the 20th century, Banting became interested in diabetes, which was then a killer disease. He knew that diabetes occurred when an organ in the body called the pancreas was either destroyed or did not function well. Scientists had guessed that the pancreas produced a hormone, named insulin, that prevented diabetes, but no one had been able to isolate insulin. In 1921, at the University of Toronto, Banting (working with a few other scientists) isolated insulin. Today insulin is used to treat people with diabetes.

Bell Burnell, Jocelyn
(1943–), British astronomer. From an early age, Bell Burnell was interested in radio astronomy, the kind that involves listening for signals from space rather than looking for objects through telescopes. After graduating from college with a degree in physics, she began working towards her Ph.D. in astronomy. Part of her research involved scanning charts for radio

signals. One day, she noticed something strange on the charts—a "ragged and scruffy" signal that appeared at regular intervals. Bell Burnell and her colleagues didn't know where the signal was coming from. Some even suggested maybe aliens were trying to contact them! After more research, however, Bell Burnell and her supervisor identified the signals as coming from pulsars—small, dense neutron stars that spin very quickly and release radio waves. No one had ever identified a pulsar before.

Boyle, Robert (1627–1691), Irish-British physicist and chemist. Working with air, Boyle first discovered that a gas was compressible, meaning it could be squeezed into a smaller volume. But more importantly, in 1662 Boyle found that a decrease in the volume of a gas was proportional to an increase in its pressure. If pressure was doubled, the volume of the gas was reduced by half. If pressure was tripled, the volume of the gas decreased to one third of its original volume. Today, scientists refer to this relationship as "Boyle's law."

Brahe, Tycho (1546–1601), Danish astronomer. In 1572, Brahe described the appearance of a new star that became brighter than any other object in the night sky except the moon. After about 18 months the star faded, but the Latin name given it—*nova*—is still used to describe an exploding star. Brahe's greatest contributions to astronomy were his measurements, which were more accurate than any made before. Brahe stressed the collection of systematic, regular measurements. These measurements revealed patterns that allowed Brahe to propose explanations based on evidence.

Brown, Rachel Fuller (1898–1980), American biochemist. Together with American microbiologist Elizabeth Hazen, Brown searched for, and in the late 1940s found, an antibiotic that could safely attack fungi that caused diseases in humans. The substance, called nystatin, was produced by a species of soil bacteria. Today, nystatin is not only used to treat fungal infections in people, it is also used to treat fungal plant diseases, such as Dutch elm disease.

Cannon, Annie Jump (1863–1941), American astronomer. There are various ways to classify stars, and Annie Jump Cannon discovered one that is still in use today. Cannon studied the spectra, or patterns of light, given off by different stars. As it turns out, each star, or family of stars, has a characteristic spectrum, which you can think of as a fingerprint of light. Using such "light fingerprints," Cannon was able to contribute to the cataloging of 225,300 stars.

Carson, Rachel Louise (1907–1964), American biologist and author. Carson had been interested in wildlife since she was a young girl. She began her career by studying the animals that lived in the sea and eventually became concerned with the fate of all living things on

Earth. This led her to focus on the effects of human activities on living things, including the use of pesticides on the land and the pollution of air and water by industrial wastes. Carson concluded that these activities threatened the existence of many living things and warned of the danger in her famous book *Silent Spring,* which was published in 1962. Many believe that Carson's work led to the establishment of the United States Environmental Protection Agency (EPA).

Carver, George Washington (1864–1943), American agricultural chemist. Born into slavery, Carver eventually went north and graduated at the top of his class at the Iowa State Agricultural College. By the mid 1890s, farmland all over the southern United States had lost much of its natural nutrients thanks to the constant planting of cotton and tobacco. Southern farmers faced economic disaster. While they knew that the soil could be made rich again by planting it with such crops as sweet potatoes and peanuts, they could not sell these crops to anyone. Carver developed hundreds of industrial uses for sweet potatoes and peanuts so it became worthwhile for farmers to plant them.

Celsius, Anders (1701–1744), Swedish astronomer. Although an astronomer, Celsius's claim to fame lies in his invention in 1742 of a temperature scale that bears his name. The scale divided the difference between the freezing temperature of water and the boiling temperature of water into 100 equal units, or degrees. The freezing point of water was given the value of 0°C and its boiling point 100°C. Today, the Celsius scale is used to make all scientific measurements of temperature, and in many countries it is also used to describe temperatures in everyday life.

Charles, Jacques (1746–1823), French physicist. In 1662, Robert Boyle had discovered how the volume and pressure of a gas were related (see Boyle, Robert). More than a hundred years passed until Charles found a relationship between the volume of a gas and its temperature. The relationship, which came to be called Charles's law, was that for every increase or decrease in 1°C, the volume of a gas increased or decreased by $\frac{1}{273}$. In other words, the volume and temperature of a gas were directly proportional. As one went up, the other went up. As one went down, the other went down.

Collins, Francis (1950–), American physician-geneticist (see Venter, J. Craig).

Copernicus, Nicolas (1473–1543), Polish astronomer. Considered the founder of modern astronomy. In 1512, Copernicus began using mathematics to study the motions and positions of the planets. Up until this time, most people believed the planets revolved around the Earth, while Earth itself stood still. But the mathematics of Copernicus suggested that the planets, and even Earth, revolved around the sun. Some scientists believed that Copernicus's idea made sense. However, two powerful forces, the

Roman Catholic Church and the leader of the Protestants, Martin Luther, strongly opposed the idea. It was not until the discovery of the telescope in the next century that evidence was found to support Copernicus's idea (see Galilei, Galileo).

Crick, Francis
(1916–), English biochemist. By 1953, scientists had discovered that a substance in living cells was responsible for passing on inherited characteristics from one generation of living things to the next. The substance was deoxyribonucleic acid, or DNA for short. The first step in understanding how DNA worked lay in the discovery of its structure. In 1953, Crick, together with American biochemist James Watson, discovered that structure. It was a double helix, which resembled a spiral staircase (see Franklin, Rosalind). That discovery eventually led to the unraveling of the human genetic code in 2000 (see Venter, J. Craig).

Curie, Marie
(1867–1934), Polish-French chemist. Along with her husband, Pierre Curie, Marie Curie performed groundbreaking research in the field of radioactive elements. She discovered the elements polonium and radium, and invented the term "radioactivity." Much of what is known today about atoms is based on the Curies' work. Marie was also the first woman to win the Nobel Prize—she actually won two Nobel Prizes—and the first woman to teach at the Sorbonne, France's greatest university.

Darwin, Charles
(1809–1882), English naturalist. On a voyage to the remote Galápagos Islands in the Pacific Ocean, 650 miles west of the coast of Ecuador, Darwin observed that finches (a kind of bird) that lived on different islands had slightly different beaks and other body parts. Darwin suggested that these different kinds of finches had all descended from an original kind of finch. Darwin proposed that over long periods of time, the Galápagos finches had developed different characteristics that allowed them to survive on their particular islands. These observations eventually led Darwin to develop his theory of natural selection, which accounted for the great variety of living things on Earth.

Einstein, Albert
(1879–1955). German-Swiss-American physicist. In 1905, Einstein developed "The Special Theory of Relativity." Among other things, this theory contained the equation $E = mc^2$, where E is energy, m is mass, and c is the speed of light. Since the speed of light is a huge number, the equation suggested that great amounts of energy could be obtained from very small amounts of mass. This was demonstrated 40 years later when a very small amount of uranium was used to produce an explosion equivalent to that produced by 20,000 tons of dynamite. In 1915, Einstein developed another theory, called "The General Theory of Relativity." This theory included the prediction that gravity could bend light. In 1919, observations of a solar eclipse made by other scientists confirmed Einstein's prediction.

Elion, Gertrude Belle (1918–1999), American pharmacologist. Elion, together with George Hitchings, developed drugs to treat a variety of diseases, including leukemia, rheumatoid arthritis, gout, malaria, urinary and respiratory infections, and herpes. Elion and Hitchings based their work on studies of the differences between diseased cells (such as cancer cells) and normal cells, as well as on the differences between disease-causing organisms (such as bacteria) and normal cells. This research allowed them to design drugs that would attack the "bad cells" while leaving the "good cells" alone.

Ewing, William Maurice (1906–1974), American geologist. Ewing used sonar, instruments that measured the force of gravity, and devices that drilled cores from the ocean bottom to explore the ocean floor. In 1956, Ewing discovered that the mid-Atlantic Ridge, an underwater mountain chain, formed a huge belt that wound under all Earth's oceans. This ridge turned out to be the place where the ocean floor was spreading apart.

Faraday, Michael (1791–1867), English physicist and chemist. Intrigued by Oersted's experiment, which showed that magnetism could be produced by electricity (see Oersted, Hans Christian), Faraday wondered whether the reverse was possible: could magnetism be used to produce electricity? In an early experiment, Faraday produced pulses of electricity in a wire coil by moving a magnet into and out of the coil. In 1831, Faraday built a device that produced a continuous flow of electricity. He had invented the electric generator. Today, generators provide the electricity used by billions of people around the world.

Fermi, Enrico (1901–1954), Italian-American physicist. In 1942, Fermi produced the first controlled nuclear fission chain reaction, a process that produces a continuous flow of atomic energy. This feat ushered in the "atomic age," which led to the development of atomic bombs—two of which helped end World War II—and nuclear power plants, which generate electricity for people all over the world.

Fleming, Sir Alexander (1881–1955), Scottish bacteriologist. In 1928, Fleming observed a green mold in a lab dish in which he was growing bacteria. Fleming noticed that no bacteria were growing near the mold. Instead of throwing away the moldy dish, Fleming decided to investigate the antibacterial properties of the mold, a species called *Penicillium notatum.* In this way, Alexander Fleming accidentally discovered the properties of a "miracle drug" that would become known as penicillin, the first antibiotic.

Franklin, Rosalind (1920–1958), British physical chemist. Franklin was the first to photograph the DNA molecule using a technique she developed herself. The images clearly showed the double-helix shape of the DNA molecule. Franklin's research was given to biochemists Francis Crick and James

Watson without her permission. A few months later, Crick and Watson published a paper describing the structure of DNA. The two men were awarded the Nobel Prize for their work in 1962, four years after Franklin's death. Whether or not Franklin would have shared in the prize had she lived is still a matter of great controversy.

Galilei, Galileo
(1564–1642), Italian astronomer and physicist. Galileo defied the Roman Catholic church's teachings that all objects in the universe revolved around Earth. In 1610, using a telescope, Galileo discovered Jupiter's four largest moons. Since these moons revolved around Jupiter, not Earth, Galileo proved that all objects did not revolve around Earth. Galileo wrote and published his conclusions, and for doing so was accused of heresy by the Roman Catholic church. Heresy is the crime of opposing the beliefs of a religion. The punishment for heresy included death by burning at the stake. Galileo avoided this fate by publicly admitting he had been wrong (which he hadn't been) and promising never again to express his ideas. He was also sentenced to house arrest, and spent the last eight years of his life confined to his home.

Gilbert, William
(1544–1603), English physician and physicist. By observing the behavior of compass needles, Gilbert reached a number of conclusions. He observed that the magnetized needle of a compass pointed approximately north and south and slightly downward. This led Gilbert to propose that Earth itself acted as if it were a huge magnet, a concept that turned out to be true.

Goddard, Robert
(1882–1945), American physicist. Although the Chinese had invented rockets centuries before the 1900s, they had been solid-fuel rockets that were propelled by gunpowder, which limited their flight. In 1923, Goddard built and tested a liquid-fueled rocket engine, which burned gasoline in liquid oxygen. Two years later, Goddard placed the engine in a four-foot-tall rocket, and successfully launched it into the air. A little more than 40 years later, similar rockets would carry people into space.

Goodall, Jane
(1934–), British ethologist (specialist in the behavior of animals). Goodall has spent much of her life studying chimpanzees in Africa. She discovered that chimps were not vegetarians, as had been previously thought, but fed on both plants and animals. Goodall also found that chimps could make and use tools, and led complex family and group lives. Goodall's work revolutionized the study of animal behavior.

Halley, Edmund
(1656–1742), English astronomer. Halley is best known for the comet that bears his name. However, Halley did not discover the comet. (Its existence had been known for hundreds of years.) What Halley did was determine its period, the time it took to revisit the neighborhood of the sun, and predict its next approach to the sun. Halley found that the

comet's period was 75–76 years, and in 1705 he predicted its return in 1758, 76 years after its last appearance in 1682. The comet reappeared right on Halley's schedule. It last appeared in the winter of 1985–86.

Hooke, Robert
(1635–1703), English physicist. Although trained as a physicist, Hooke had many scientific interests and made his most famous discovery in the field of biology. He had been studying various objects through the lenses of a microscope. One day, he happened to look at thin sections of cork, part of the bark of a tree. He saw what reminded him of the tiny *cells,* or rooms, of a monastery. Later, scientists discovered that the cell is the basic unit of all living things.

Hubble, Edwin
(1889–1953), American astronomer. In 1924, looking out into the night sky through the most powerful telescope of his time, Hubble discovered galaxies—families of stars—that lay outside of our own galaxy, the Milky Way Galaxy. Hubble also discovered that objects in the universe were speeding away from one another, that is, that the universe was expanding. Hubble said it had been doing so since its creation 10–20 billion years ago.

Humboldt, Friedrich
(1769–1859), German naturalist. Humboldt had a tremendous natural curiosity, which led him to travel all over the world and explore many of Earth's features. He studied ocean currents that moved off the west coast of South America, and had one—the Humboldt Current—named after him. He mapped the positions of American volcanoes and noted that they formed a more or less straight line as if they were resting on a deep crack in the Earth, which was very close to the truth. He discovered that Earth's magnetism seemed to drop off as the distance from Earth's poles increased. And he found that, in general, the temperature of air decreased as altitude increased.

Hutton, James
(1726–1797), Scottish geologist. Considered the founder of geology, Hutton developed the "principle of uniformitarianism," which stated that Earth's surface was slowly and continuously changing and always had been changing. His observations of the slow processes of erosion and rock building led him to conclude that the Earth was extremely old.

Kepler, Johannes
(1571–1630), German astronomer. Kepler studied the motions of the planets, especially Mars. In 1609, he declared that the orbits of the planets were not circles, as people believed, but ellipses. This idea became known as Kepler's first law. Kepler was also able to show that a planet's speed increased as it neared the sun, and decreased as it became more distant from the sun. This was part of Kepler's second law.

Koch, Robert
(1843–1910), German bacteriologist. Koch's greatest contributions were in identifying the bacteria that caused various diseases and in describing how diseases were

transmitted. He identified the bacteria that caused tuberculosis and cholera. He also discovered that bubonic plague was transmitted to humans through the bite of fleas that lived on rats, and that African sleeping sickness was spread from person to person by infected tsetse flies.

Lavoisier, Antoine (1743–1794), French chemist. Considered the founder of modern chemistry. In 1774, Lavoisier performed experiments that showed that when an object burned or rusted, it actually combined with something in air. He also identified two gases in air. The one that combined with objects that burned or rusted he called oxygen (see Priestley, Joseph). The other gas, which was not involved in burning or rusting, he called azote. Today, we know this gas as nitrogen.

Leakey, Mary (1913–1996), English archaeologist and paleontologist. Mary Leakey, along with her husband Louis, spent 30 years searching in Africa for clues to the history of human beings. In 1948, Mary found the skull of a 2.5-million-year-old creature that seemed to be an ancestor of both apes and humans. In 1978, at a place called Laetoli in Africa, Mary found two sets of footprints preserved in volcanic ash that was 3.5 million years old. By analyzing the footprints, Mary concluded that they were made by ancestors of humans that walked on two legs. Before Mary's discovery, scientists had thought that humans had not developed the ability to walk upright until a much later date.

Leeuwenhoek, Anton van (1632–1723), Dutch biologist. Using a simple microscope made of only a single lens, Leeuwenhoek examined almost anything he could get his hands on—muscle tissue, skin, hair, scrapings from his teeth, and red blood cells, to name a few. But perhaps his greatest discovery came when he peeked into a drop of pond water, for it was there that he found a world of microscopic living things, which today are known as protozoa.

Linnaeus, Carolus (1707–1778), Swedish botanist. Classifying the millions of different species of living things is the work of taxonomists, and Linnaeus was the first great taxonomist. He developed the binomial system of classification whereby a species is given two names, a group name (genus) and a specific name (species). For example, Linnaeus gave modern humans the name *Homo sapiens,* which is Latin for "man wise."

Maury, Matthew (1806–1873), American oceanographer. Maury began his career as a U.S. Navy sailor, but a stagecoach accident cut that dream short. Nevertheless, Maury's love of the sea led him to explore its mysteries, and he became one of the founders of the science of oceanography. Maury was the first to describe ocean currents, the Gulf Stream in particular, as "...a river in the ocean." Based on Maury's research on these "rivers," sea captains chose routes that allowed their ships to ride the currents rather than fight against them. Maury also made a map of depths across the Atlantic Ocean and in doing so accidentally discovered what would later be identified as the mid-Atlantic Ridge (see Ewing, William Maurice).

McClintock, Barbara (1902–1992), American geneticist. McClintock specialized in the study of plant genetics. In particular, she investigated variations in the color of corn kernels from one generation of corn plants to the next. Her observations and experiments led McClintock to conclude that genes can switch their positions on chromosomes. McClintock's work contributed greatly to our understanding of how genes produce the characteristics of organisms. Although her early work was largely criticized, she was finally recognized with a Nobel Prize in 1983.

Meitner, Lise (1878–1968), Austrian-Swedish physicist. Meitner made great contributions in the field of nuclear physics. Among other things, her research led to the discovery of uranium fission, the process by which the nucleus of a uranium atom splits apart, yielding huge amounts of energy. These accomplishments were made despite great obstacles. Early in her career in Germany, Meitner was banned from working in labs occupied by men. That was one of the prejudices she faced. The other was her Jewish ancestry. In 1938 she was forced to leave Germany, where the persecution of Jews had become intolerable.

Mendel, Gregor (1822–1884), Austrian botanist. Mendel, a Roman Catholic monk, eventually earned the unofficial title of "father of genetics" by studying the inherited traits of pea plants. Beginning in 1857, Mendel bred pea plants with different traits, such as tallness and shortness. He kept careful count of how many offspring were tall, short, or had other traits. He discovered patterns of inheritance that eventually came to be known as Mendel's laws of heredity. It was not until 1900, 16 years after his death, that scientists recognized the importance of Mendel's discoveries.

Mendeléev, Dmitri (1834–1907), Russian chemist. In the 1860s, while examining the properties of the 63 elements known at the time, Mendeléev discovered a pattern that allowed him to organize the elements in a table of rows and columns. Critics, however, pointed out that there were "holes" in his table that were not occupied by any elements. Mendeléev countered by predicting that one day the missing elements would be discovered and that they would fit neatly into those holes. What's more, Mendeléev predicted the properties of the missing elements. Mendeléev lived to see each of these elements discovered, and each of their properties were close to what he had predicted. Today we know Mendeléev's table as the Periodic Table of Elements.

Mercator, Gerardus
(1512–1594), Flemish geographer. Among other things, Mercator was a cartographer, or a map maker. A challenge that faced Mercator, and all map makers in his time and ours, was how to produce a flat map that accurately represented a spherical world. No one has completely succeeded in doing this. However, Mercator was able to produce a map that, although it had major distortions in size, was able to safely guide sailors in their voyages. This map has come to be called a Mercator projection.

Molina, Mario
(1943–), Mexican-American chemist. Together with American chemist F. Sherwood Rowland, Molina discovered that certain substances were destroying the ozone layer in Earth's atmosphere. (The ozone layer blocks harmful ultraviolet rays from the sun from reaching Earth's surface.) These substances, which have been used in refrigerators, air conditioners, and aerosol cans, belong to a family of chemicals called chlorofluorocarbons (CFCs). Because of the work of Molina and Rowland, most uses of CFCs were banned in the United States in 1978. Other countries joined the ban later.

Newton, Sir Isaac
(1642–1727), English scientist and mathematician. Newton made many great discoveries. He discovered that white light was actually made of all the colors of the rainbow. He was the first person to describe the "law of universal gravitation," which explained that every object in space and on Earth was affected by the force of gravity. Newton also studied the motions of objects, which led to his famous three laws of motion. And if that wasn't enough, he also developed a new branch of mathematics called calculus.

Oersted, Hans Christian
(1777–1851), Danish physicist. In 1819, Oersted brought a magnetic compass near a wire through which an electric current was passing. The needle suddenly changed position, coming to rest at a right angle to the wire. This simple experiment demonstrated that electricity and magnetism were related. Moreover, it showed that electricity could be converted into magnetism (see Faraday, Michael). This was the beginning of the science of electromagnetism. Today, electromagnets are used in such diverse products as telephones, refrigerators, washing machines, doorbells, and electric can openers.

Pasteur, Louis
(1822–1895), French chemist. Although trained as a chemist, Pasteur made great achievements in the fields of biology and medicine. In experiments, he disproved once and for all the long-held idea that living things could be born from non-living things. He developed the "germ theory of disease," which stated that infections could be caused and spread by microorganisms. He also developed vaccines for deadly diseases of farm animals and humans: anthrax in the cases of farm animals, and rabies in the case of humans. Pasteur also invented a process of slow heating to kill microorganisms found in milk

and other beverages, thus helping to keep them from spoiling. Today this process is known as "pasteurization."

Pavlov, Ivan
(1849–1936), Russian physiologist. Pavlov's early scientific work focused on the processes of the digestive system. However, he later turned to the investigation of processes that affected learning and behavior. He knew that certain behaviors, such as a dog salivating at the sight or smell of food, were automatic, or not learned. These were called unconditioned reflexes. However, Pavlov showed that the same behavior could be caused by an event that was completely unrelated to food. These were called conditioned responses. For example, Pavlov trained dogs to salivate at the sound of a bell, which he had rung when the dogs were fed. But later, when he rang the bell when no food was nearby, the dogs salivated anyway.

Priestley, Joseph
(1733–1804), English chemist. In addition to inventing soda pop, or seltzer, by dissolving carbon dioxide in water, Priestley was famous for making a far more important discovery. In 1774, Priestley heated a compound of mercury, which produced pure mercury and a strange new gas. Priestley found that the gas made objects burn more brightly than they did in air, and that he felt light-headed when he breathed it. He had discovered a new element, which was later given the name oxygen by French chemist Antoine Lavoisier (see Lavoisier, Antoine).

Ptolemy
(about 100 A.D.–about 170 A.D.), Greek astronomer. Ptolemy (pronounced TAHL-uhm-ee) was among the first astronomers who tried to make sense of their observations of the planets and Earth's moon. The Ptolemaic system, as Ptolemy's ideas came to be called, had Earth at the center of the universe with the planets, Earth's moon, and the sun orbiting Earth. Fourteen centuries would pass before Ptolemy's ideas were seriously challenged (see Brahe, Copernicus, and Galileo).

Roentgen, Wilhelm
(1845–1923), German physicist. In 1895, Roentgen discovered a kind of radiation that was at the same time invisible but penetrating, meaning it could pass through certain materials such as sheets of paper and thin sheets of metal. Roentgen called this mysterious radiation "X rays." Today, pictures produced by X rays passing through objects and striking photographic film are used in many applications, especially medicine. Roentgen was the recipient of the first Noble Prize in physics. He won the award in 1901.

Rutherford, Ernest
(1871–1937), New Zealand-British physicist. In the early 1900s, Rutherford performed an experiment in which he "fired" atomic particles at very thin sheets of gold. Rutherford observed that while most of the particles passed through the sheet, some were scattered by it as if they had struck solid objects. This led Rutherford to suggest that atoms of

atoms—were made mostly of space surrounding a tiny nucleus. This model of the atom is the one accepted by scientists today.

Sabin, Albert
(1906–1993), Polish-American microbiologist. In the late 1950s, Sabin developed a polio vaccine made of live, but weak, viruses. This vaccine provided a longer period of immunity than the polio vaccine developed by Jonas Salk a few years earlier (see Salk, Jonas). By the 1960s, the Sabin vaccine had replaced the Salk vaccine. Result? By 1995, poliomyelitis had been wiped out in the Americas.

Salk, Jonas
(1914–1995), American physician and microbiologist. In 1952, a disease called poliomyelitis (polio) infected 58,000 people in the United States alone. Many were children. Three thousand people died of the disease and many more became paralyzed. In 1947, Salk had begun work to develop a vaccine that would prevent the poliomyelitis virus from infecting people. By 1952, Salk had produced a vaccine made of dead viruses. In 1954, 1.8 million U.S. school children were injected with the vaccine. The vaccine worked, but for a fairly limited amount of time. (See Sabin, Albert.)

Tonegawa, Susumu
(1939–), Japanese molecular biologist. In 1971, Tonegawa began to probe the mysteries the body's immune system, especially how the body produces antibodies, which are substances that attack invading organisms such as bacteria and viruses. Tonegawa knew that antibodies were produced by white blood cells called B lymphocytes, or simply B cells. What puzzled him was that these cells only had about 1000 gene segments but could turn out one billion different antibodies instead of just 1000. Tonegawa discovered that the 1000 gene segments could rearrange themselves to form an enormous number of different combinations, each producing a different antibody.

Venter, J. Craig
(1946–), American biochemist. In the year 2000, two scientists, Venter and American biochemist Francis Collins, independently decoded most of the human genome, the detailed sequence of genes that determine the characteristics of human beings. Armed with this knowledge, scientists hope one day to find ways to cure or prevent many diseases or conditions that are now incurable.

Watson, James
(1928–), American biochemist (see Crick, Francis).

Wegener, Alfred
(1880–1930), German meteorologist and geologist. Noticing that the coasts of South America and Africa fit together like pieces of a jigsaw puzzle, Wegener proposed in 1912 that all of Earth's continents had once been joined as a single giant continent (which Wegener called Pangaea or "All-earth"), but had then drifted to their present locations. Considered a crazy idea by scientists of the time, evidence has since been uncovered that strongly supports Wegener's concept of "continental drift."

Scientific Terms

Greek and Latin Word Roots

Many words we use today have Latin or Greek **roots.** This means that part of the word—a root—started out in the language of ancient Greece (Greek) or Rome (Latin). Such word roots are often in the form of **prefixes,** at the beginning of a word, and **suffixes,** at the end of a word, as well as in the middle of a word. Greek and Latin roots are especially common in science terms. Knowing the meanings of roots can help you figure out words that are new to you.

EXAMPLE: baro • meter

bar- means *pressure* *-meter* means *measure*

The roots of the word *barometer* tell you that it has something to do with measuring pressure, which is correct: a barometer is an instrument used to measure air pressure.

Refer to the following table to find the meanings of new words that you read.

Root, Prefix, or Suffix	Meaning	Example	Origin
a-	not	atypical	Latin, Greek
-act-	act	reaction	Latin
alt-, alto-	high	altitude	Latin
amphi-	both	amphibian	Greek
ann-, anno-	year	annual	Latin
anthrop-	human	anthropologist	Greek
anti-	against	anticline	Greek
arthro-	joint	arthropod	Greek
astr-, astro-	star	astronomy	Latin, Greek
auto-	self	autotroph	Greek
bar-, baro-	pressure, heavy, weight	barometer	Greek
bi-	two	bipedal	Latin
bio-	life	biology	Greek
cardi-	heart	cardiac	Greek
cent-, centi-	hundred	century	Latin
centr-, centri-	middle	centripetal	Greek
chrono-	time	chronology	Greek
circum-	around	circumference	Latin
co-, com-, con-	with	covalent	Latin, Greek
curr-	run	current	Latin
cycl-, cyclo-	circle	cycle, cyclone	Greek
de-	down	decomposer	Latin
deci-	ten, tenth	decimal	Latin
-derm-	skin	epidermis	Greek
di-	two	diatomic	Greek
dia-	across, through	diameter	Greek

MORE

Root, Prefix, or Suffix	Meaning	Example	Origin
-dict-	say, speak	prediction	Latin
-dorm-	sleep	dormant	Latin
end-, endo-	within	endoplasmic	Greek
epi-	on top	epicenter	Greek
equ-	equal	equation	Latin
ex-	out of, out from	excretion	Greek
exo-	outside	exoskeleton	Greek
extra-	outside, beyond	extraterrestrial	Latin
-fin-	end	final, infinite	Latin
-flex-	bend	flexor, flexible	Latin
form	shape	transform boundary	Latin
-fract-	break	fracture	Latin
gen-	begin, birth	generate	Greek
-geo-	earth	geology	Greek
-graph	write	seismograph	Greek
gravi-	heavy	gravity	Latin
hemi-	half	hemisphere	Greek
hetero-	different	heterotroph	Greek
hex-	six	hexagon	Greek
homeo-, homo-	same	homeostasis	Greek
hydr-, hydro-	water	hydroelectric	Greek
hyper-	over	hyperactive	Greek
hypo-	under	hypodermic	Greek
ign-	fire	igneous	Latin
in-	not	inorganic	Latin
inter-	between	interstellar	Latin

Root, Prefix, or Suffix	Meaning	Example	Origin
intra-	inside	intracellular	Latin
iso-	equal	isotope	Greek
-ject	throw	reject	Latin
-lev-	raise	elevation	Latin
-lithic, litho-	stone	lithosphere	Greek
-logy	word, study	geology	Greek
luna-	moon	lunar	Latin
macr-, macro-	long, large	macrophage	Greek
magn-	great	magnify	Latin
mari-	sea	maritime	Latin
mechan-	machine	mechanical	Greek
meta-	change, after	metaphase	Latin, Greek
-meter	measure	kilometer	Greek
micro-	small	microscope	Greek
-morph-	shape, form	metamorphosis	Greek
mort-	death	mortality	Latin
multi-	many	multicellular	Latin
mut-	change	mutation	Latin
neo-	new	Neolithic	Latin
noct-, -nox	night	nocturnal, equinox	Latin
non-	not	nonrenewable	Latin
nova	new	nova	Greek
nucl-	kernel, nut	nucleus	Latin
oct-	eight	octopus	Greek
omni-	all	omnivore	Latin
oph-, opt-	eye	optical	Greek
ov, ova-	egg	ovary	Latin

MORE

Root, Prefix, or Suffix	Meaning	Example	Origin
paleo-	ancient	paleontology	Greek
pan-	every	Pangaea	Greek
para-	beside	parallel	Greek
-ped-, -pod-	foot	tripod	Latin
pend-	hang	pendulum	Latin
pent-	five	pentagon	Greek
per-	through	percolate	Latin
peri-	around	perimeter	Greek
petr-	rock	petrified	Greek
-phag-	eat	esophagus	Greek
-phil-	love	hydrophilic	Greek
-phob-	fear	hydrophobic	Greek
-phon-	sound	telephone	Greek
photo-	light	photograph	Greek
phys-	natural world	physics	Latin, Greek
pict-	to paint	pictogram	Latin
poly-	many	polymer	Greek
-port-	carry	report	Latin
post-	after	posterior	Latin
pre-, pro-	before, forward	prophase	Latin, Greek
prim-	first	primitive	Latin
pyr-	fire	pyroclastic	Greek
quad-	four, fourth	quadruped	Latin
rad-	ray	radiation	Latin
re-	again	reproduce	Latin
-rupt-	break	erupt	Latin
-saur	lizard	dinosaur	Greek

Root, Prefix, or Suffix	Meaning	Example	Origin
sci-	know	science	Latin
-scope	look at	microscope	Greek
-sect-	cut	cross-section	Latin
-sed-	settle, sit	sedimentary	Latin
semi-	half	semitropical	Greek
sequ-	follow	sequence	Latin
solu-, -solv-	loosen	dissolve	Latin
-spect-	look	inspect	Latin
-sphere-	ball, globe	biosphere	Greek
-stella-	star	interstellar	Latin
strat-	sheet, spread	stratus	Latin
sub-	under	submerge	Latin
super-	above, over	superposition	Latin
-syn-	put together	photosynthesis	Greek
tele-	distant	telescope	Greek
termin-	end	terminate	Latin
terra-	land	terrain	Latin
-therm-	heat	thermometer	Greek
trans-	across	transform boundary	Latin
tri-	three	tripod	Greek
trop-, tropo-	turn	phototropic	Greek
un-	not	unbalanced force	Latin, Greek
uni-	one	uniform	Latin
voc-	call	vocal	Latin
-vor-	devour, eat	herbivore	Latin
-volv-	turn, roll	revolve	Latin

Source: Webster's Ninth New Collegiate Dictionary

Glossary of Scientific Terms

A

abrasion: wearing away by scraping or rubbing; often refers to a kind of weathering **(189)**

absolute age: age in years of a geologic event, fossil, or rock, usually found by radioactive tests **(197)**

absolute magnitude: brightness that a star would have if it were 32.6 light-years from Earth **(246)**

abyssal hill: small hill rising from part of the deep ocean floor **(207)**

abyssal plain: flat area on deep ocean floor made up of thick layer of sediments **(207)**

acceleration: change in an object's speed or direction (its velocity) over time **(285)**

acid: any compound that produces hydrogen ions (H^+) in water, and reduces its pH to below 7 **(264)**

acid rain: rain that has a lower pH (is more acidic) than normal; caused by chemical air pollutants combining with water vapor in air; the most common pollutants are sulfur dioxide (SO_2) and nitrogen oxides (NO_x) **(351)**

active margin: a continental margin with plate boundaries near it **(207)**

adaptation: structure, behavior, or other trait in an organism that helps it to survive in its environment **(127)**

adrenal glands: glands that lie above the kidneys, and secrete a hormone (epinephrine) that helps the body to prepare itself for emergencies **(097)**

adrenaline: *See epinephrine* **(097)**

adult: an organism that is fully developed and (usually) is able to reproduce **(106)**

air mass: a large body of air that has about the same temperature and humidity throughout it **(221)**

air pollution: contamination of the air with substances that can be harmful to living things **(348)**

air pressure: a measure of the weight of the atmosphere per unit of area on Earth's surface; also called **barometric pressure (224)**

alcohol: any of several colorless, flammable liquids used as a fuel source; often made from plants **(328)**

algae: protists that are able to make their own food **(156)**

allele: one of a pair of genes that determine a specific trait **(122)**

alternating current (AC): flow of electricity in a conductor, in which electric charges change direction many times per second **(317)**

altitude: Astronomy: angular height of an object above the horizon; Geology: height above average sea level; *See diagram at elevation* **(172)**

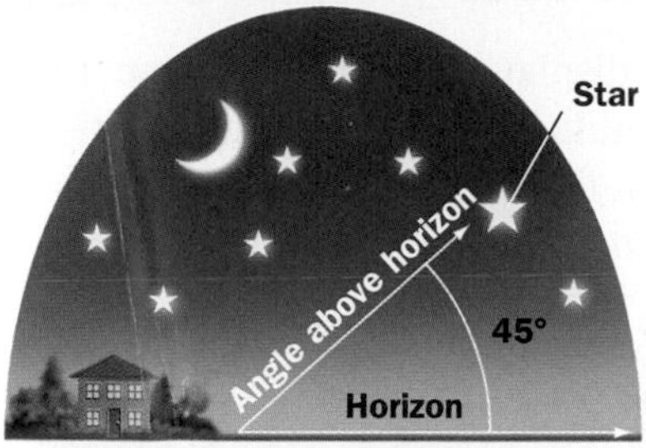

Altitude of an object in sky

alveoli: tiny air sacs in the lungs where gases are exchanged; *See diagram at respiratory system* **(092)**

amino acids: compounds that are the building blocks of proteins **(079)**

ampere (A): unit of measurement for electric current **(317)**

amphibian: animal that lives both on land and in water; Amphibians begin life in water with gills, but have lungs and breathe air as adults. **(106)**

amplitude: total distance a wave moves (oscillates) from its resting position **(306, 313)**

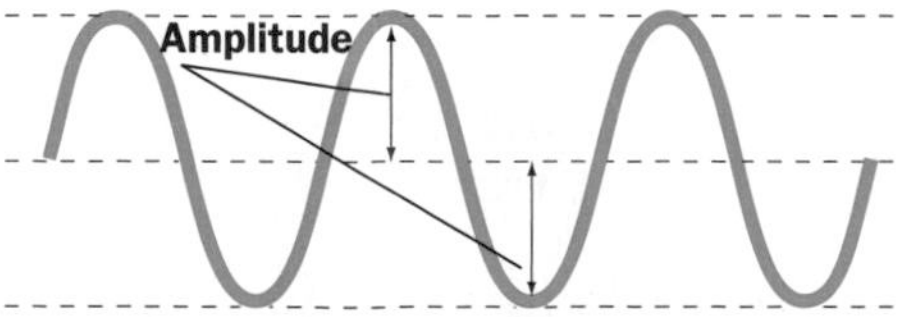

Amplitude of a transverse wave

anaphase: stage of cell division during which the chromosome copies begin to separate **(081)**

anemometer: instrument used to measure wind speed **(225)**

antibody: protein made by the body that fights against a certain disease-causing substance **(098)**

antigen: pieces of destroyed pathogens; Antigens alert white blood cells to an invader's presence. **(098)**

anus: the opening at the end of the digestive system, where wastes are released **(089)**

apparent magnitude: brightness of a star, planet, or other object, as it appears from Earth **(246)**

archaebacteria: kingdom of single-celled organisms that lack a nucleus and contain some unusual compounds. Most live in extreme environments, such as hot springs. **(157)**

Archimedes' principle: states that the buoyant force of a fluid on an object is equal to the weight of the fluid displaced by the object **(296)**

artery: a vessel in the circulatory system that carries blood away from the heart; *See diagram at circulatory system* **(093)**

arthropod: a phylum of invertebrates that have hard segmented body coverings (exoskeletons) and jointed legs, such as insects **(161)**

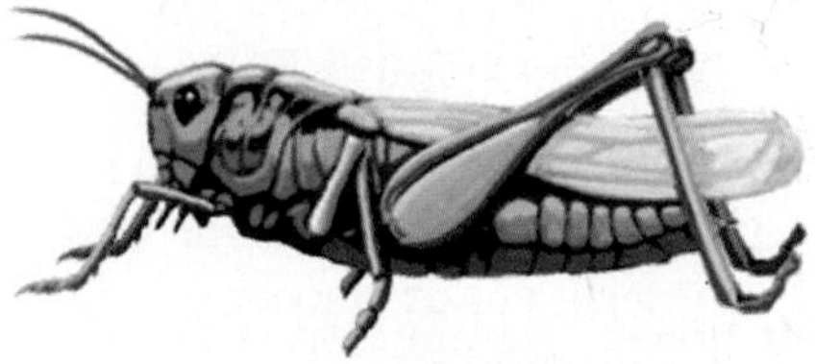

asexual reproduction: reproduction involving only one parent organism; also called **non-sexual reproduction** **(114)**

asteroids: objects of rock, metal, and ice that are smaller than planets and revolve around the Sun **(241)**

asthenosphere: layer in the upper part of Earth's mantle that is made of material that can be reshaped and deformed, and on which the continents move

astrolabe: instrument used to measure the angle of an object in the sky, above the horizon (its altitude)

astronomy: study of space, including stars, planets, and other objects in space, and their origins **(231)**

atmosphere: layers of air surrounding Earth **(213);** also, a measure of pressure exerted by the weight of Earth's atmosphere at sea level **(295)**

atom: smallest particle into which an element can be divided and still have the properties of that element **(255)**

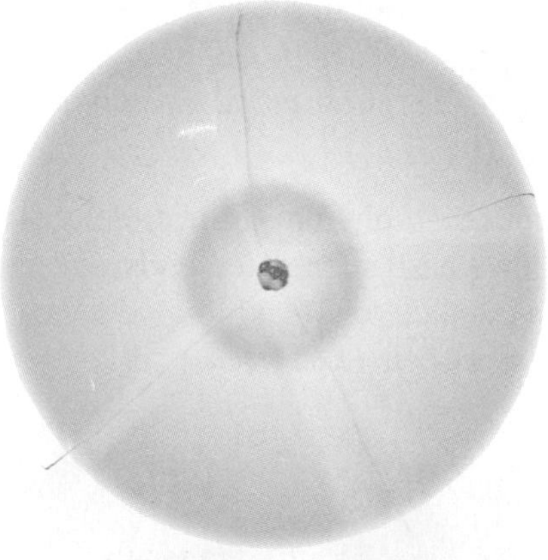

Model of an atom

atomic mass: average mass of one atom of an element **(265)**

atomic number: number of protons in the nucleus of one atom of an element **(265)**

ATP: adenosine triphosphate, the major energy-carrying molecule of the cell **(079)**

aurora: display of light in sky, usually at high latitudes; formed where particles from the sun enter Earth's atmosphere and magnetic field **(215)**

autotroph: an organism, such as a plant, that makes its own food **(159)**

autumnal equinox: *See equinox* **(234)**

axis: Earth Science: imaginary line passing through the center of a planet (such as Earth), that the planet spins around **(233)** Graphing: line on which a scale is drawn to show values for a variable **(390)**

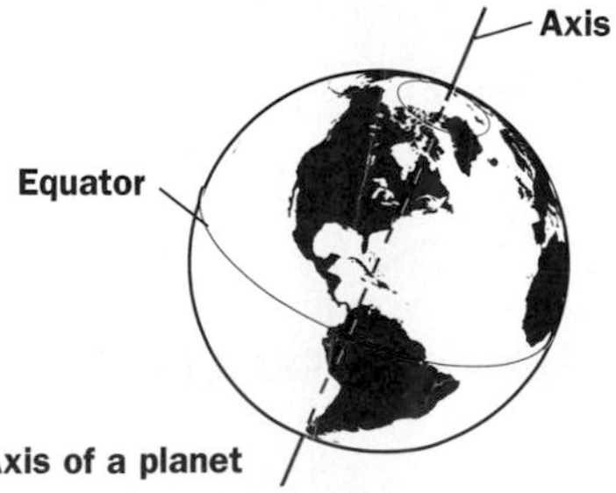

Axis of a planet

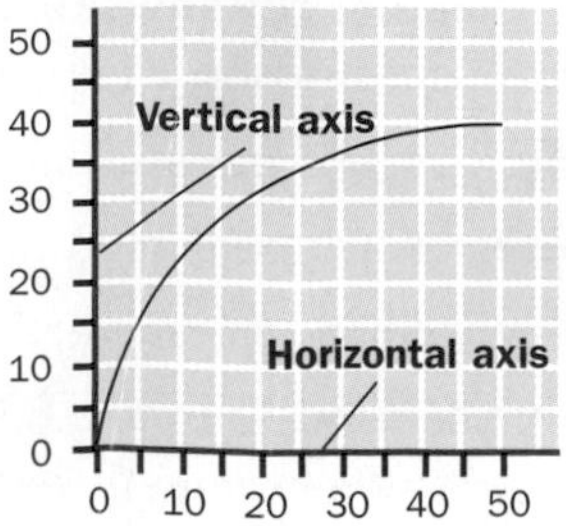

Graph axis

axon: long fiber branching from the central cell body of a nerve cell; *See diagram at neuron* **(095)**

B

bacteria: domain of single-celled organisms that lack a nucleus; The term also refers to organisms in the kingdom eubacteria. **(101, 157)**

balanced forces: occur when the total of all forces on an object equals zero and the object's motion does not change; *See also unbalanced forces* **(281)**

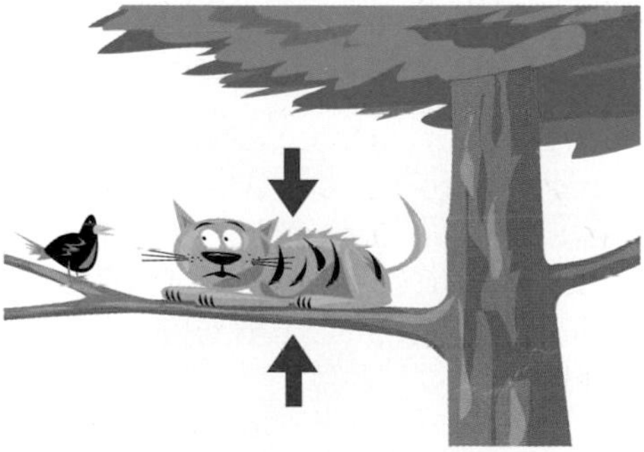

Forces on the cat are balanced.

bar graph: graph that uses bars of different lengths to compare data **(391)**

barometric pressure: *See air pressure* **(224)**

base: Chemistry: any compound that produces hydroxide ions (OH^-) in water and raises its pH above 7 **(264)** Genetics: one of four molecules making up a strand of DNA **(115)**

beaker: a container, usually made of heat-resistant glass, that has a spout for pouring and marks for measurement **(047)**

Beaufort wind scale: a system for estimating wind speed based on observations **(225)**

bedrock: solid rock that lies under layers of soil and sediment

behavior: an activity or action that generally helps an organism survive in its environment **(109)**

benthos: organisms living on the floor of a body of water **(210)**

Bernoulli's principle: states that the pressure that a moving fluid puts on a surface decreases the faster the fluid flows **(297)**

best-fit line: line on a graph that most closely fits a set of data points that share a trend **(398)**

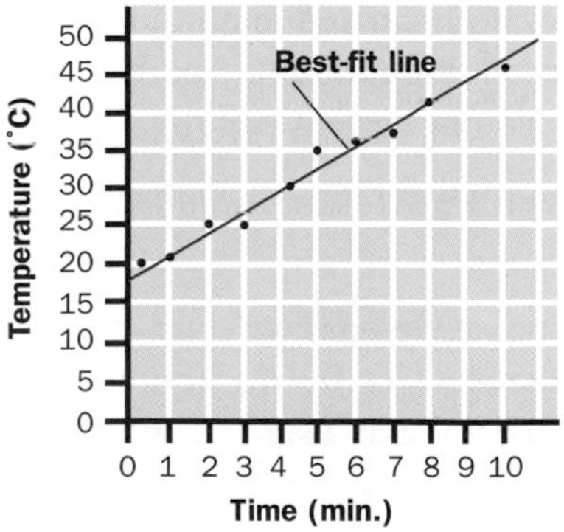

bias: the influence of a person's beliefs or wishes on their opinions and interpretations **(368)**

bile: substance made by the liver that breaks down large fat molecules **(089)**

biodegradable: substance that will break down into simpler compounds when buried or exposed to sun, water, and air **(337)**

biodiversity: the variety of organisms in a specific environment, or on Earth as a whole **(124)**

biology: study of living things **(073)**

biomass: Ecology: total mass of living organisms in a certain area; Resources: matter formed by plants or animals that is used as a fuel, such as wood or dung **(328)**

biome: a large region of land with a distinct climate and certain types of plant and animal life **(141)**

biosphere: the part of the Earth that is able to support life **(141)**

bladder: *See gall bladder* **(089)** *or urinary bladder* **(090)**

blood: a tissue made up of cells and pieces of cells carried in a liquid; transported throughout the body by the circulatory system **(093)**

blue-green algae: *See cyanobacteria* **(157)**

boiling point: temperature at which a substance changes from a liquid state to a gaseous (vapor) state; same as condensation point for that substance **(254)**

brain: organ that is the control center for actions, thoughts, and emotions **(095)**

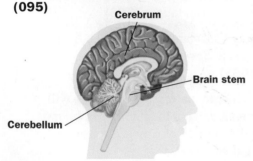

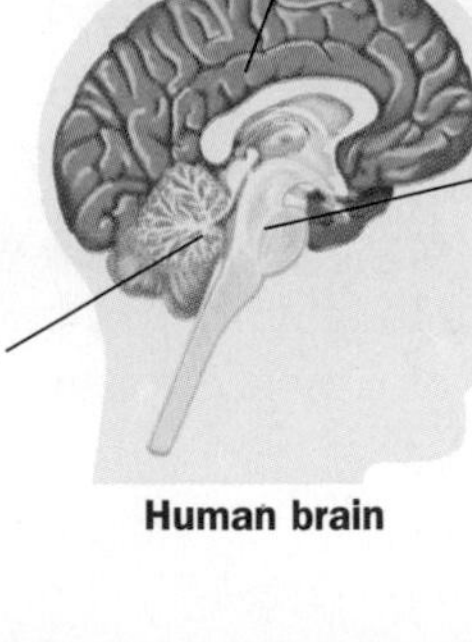

Human brain

brain stem: structure of the brain that controls internal organs and basic body functions **(095)**

bronchi: two large tubes that branch off the trachea into the lungs; *See diagram at respiratory system* **(092)**

Bunsen burner: laboratory heat source that burns natural gas **(033)**

buoyancy: tendency of an object to float or rise in a fluid that is more dense than the object is **(296)**

buoyant force: upward force exerted on an object by a fluid, when the object is placed in the fluid **(296)**

C

calorie (cal): unit of thermal energy equal to amount of energy needed to raise the temperature of 1 g water (1 cm^3 or 1 mL) by 1°C; Kilocalorie (kcal or Cal) = 1000 calories, the unit used to measure energy stored in food; SI system uses joule (J) (1 cal = 4.184 joules)

canopy: the uppermost layer of a forest, at the tops of the trees **(145)**

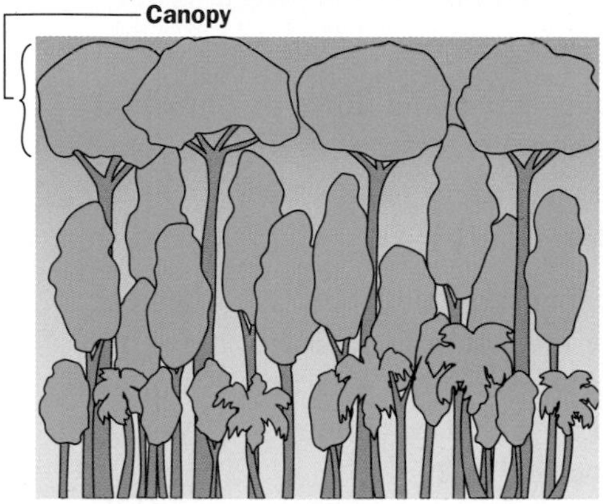

capacity: amount that can be held by a container; for example, a 2-L bottle has a capacity of 2 liters **(059)**

capillary: smallest vessel in the circulatory system; site of nutrient and gas exchange between blood and body cells **(093)**

captive breeding: breeding of wild animals in a zoo, in such a way that the animals may be released into the wild and help prevent extinction of the species **(344)**

carbohydrate: molecule made up of carbon, hydrogen, and oxygen, which is the product of photosynthesis; sugars and starches are examples

carbon dioxide-oxygen cycle: the continual transfer of carbon dioxide and oxygen between living things and the environment **(138)**

cardiac muscle: heart muscle; It is involuntary (not consciously controlled), and keeps the heart beating. **(087)**

carnivore: an animal that feeds on other animals, such as a wolf **(133)**

cartilage: firm, flexible tissue that is part of the skeletal system; The nose and ears contain cartilage. **(086)**

cartographer: person who makes maps **(167)**

cast: kind of fossil formed when sediments fill a hole left by an organism; *See diagram at mold* **(198)**

catalyst: substance that helps start or speed up a reaction between two other substances, without being changed by the reaction

caterpillar: the larval stage in the life cycle of certain insects **(106)**

cell: basic unit of structure and function in living things **(076)**

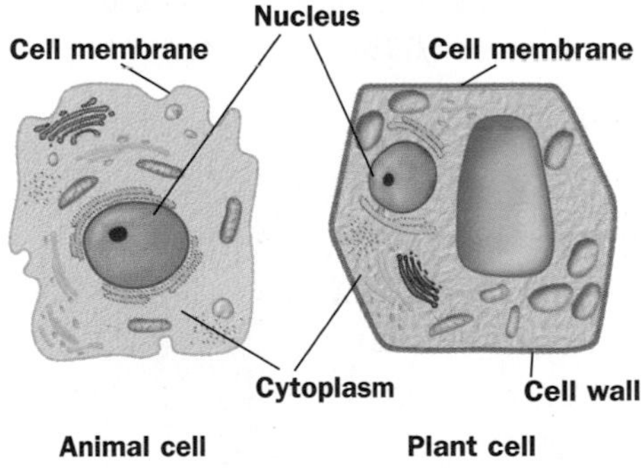

cell division: process by which cells divide to form new cells **(080)**

cell membrane: structure that surrounds the cytoplasm of the cell **(077, 078)**

cell wall: stiff outer barrier of a plant cell, outside the cell membrane, which is made mostly of cellulose **(078)**

cellular respiration: process in cells by which oxygen is chemically combined with food molecules and energy is released **(079, 105)**

$$C_6H_{12}O_6 + 6O_2 \longrightarrow 6CO_2 + 6H_2O + ATP$$

glucose (sugar) + oxygen ⟶ carbon dioxide + water + energy

Cellular respiration

Celsius (C): temperature scale in which the freezing point of water is 0° and the boiling point of water is 100° **(071)**

cementation: process that turns sediments into hard rock when a binding material, often calcite, filters into the sediment **(180)**

central nervous system: message system made up of the brain and spinal cord **(095)**

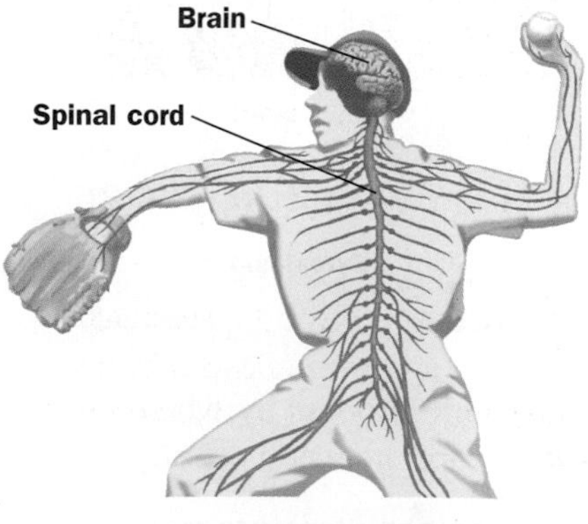

centripetal force: force that is directed toward the center of a circle, which keeps an object moving in a circle instead of flying away **(278)**

cerebellum: part of the brain that helps coordinate body movements; *See diagram at brain* **(095)**

cerebrum: part of the brain that is the control center of thoughts and voluntary actions; *See diagram at brain* **(095)**

chemical bond: force of attraction that holds together atoms in a compound; ionic and covalent bonds are examples **(263)**

chemical change: occurs when one or more substances are changed into new substances with different properties; cannot be undone by physical means **(252)**

chemical digestion: process that breaks large food molecules into smaller molecules that can be taken in by cells **(089)**

chemical energy: energy stored in chemical bonds **(300)**

chemical equation: a way of writing changes in the arrangement of atoms during a chemical reaction, using chemical symbols **(270)**

$$2H_2 + O_2 \longrightarrow 2H_2O$$

Reactant + Reactant $\xrightarrow{\text{Yields}}$ Product

Chemical equation

chemical family: *See group* **(265)**

chemical formula: a way of describing the number of atoms that make up one molecule of a compound **(267)**

H_2O	CO_2
Water	Carbon dioxide

Chemical formulas

chemical property: characteristics of a substance that describe its tendency to combine with other substances and forms new ones; for example, iron changing to rust by combining with oxygen **(251)**

chemical reaction: change that takes place when two or more substances (reactants) interact to form new substances (products); *See also chemical equation* **(269)**

chemical sedimentary rock: rock formed when a body of mineral-rich water evaporates and the dissolved minerals crystallize and fall to the bottom **(180)**

chemical symbol: one- or two-letter code that stands for an element; Many symbols are abbreviations of the element's name, which may be English, Latin, or Greek in origin. **(265)**

He	C	Pb
Helium	Carbon	Lead

Chemical symbols

chemical weathering: wearing away of rocks by chemical processes, such as oxidation or dissolving **(190)**

chemistry: the study of the structure, properties, and interactions of matter

chlorofluorocarbons (CFCs): substances that were formerly used in spray cans, refrigerators, and air conditioners; Evidence suggests that CFCs cause a loss of ozone in the upper atmosphere. **(350)**

chlorophyll: green pigment in plants that captures the energy of sunlight for use in photosynthesis **(079, 107)**

chloroplast: a structure in a plant cell that contains chlorophyll; Sugar molecules are made in chloroplasts through the process of photosynthesis. **(078)**

chromosome: a structure located in the nucleus of a cell, made of DNA, that contains the genetic information needed to carry out cell functions and make new cells **(116)**

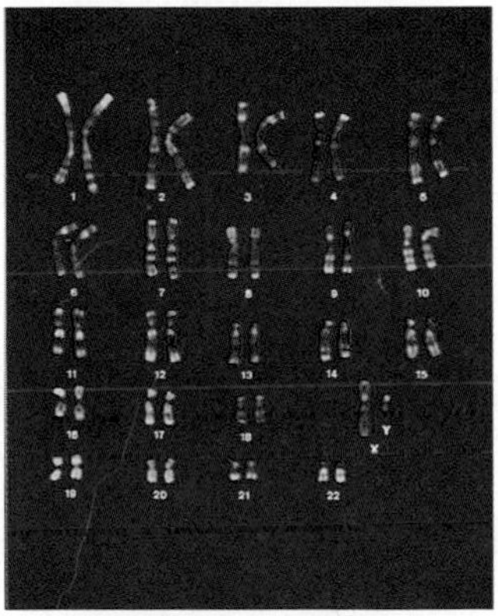

Chromosomes

circle graph: *See pie chart* **(393)**

circuit: path that electric current flows through; a closed circuit has no breaks; an open circuit has a break and current cannot flow through it. **(318)**

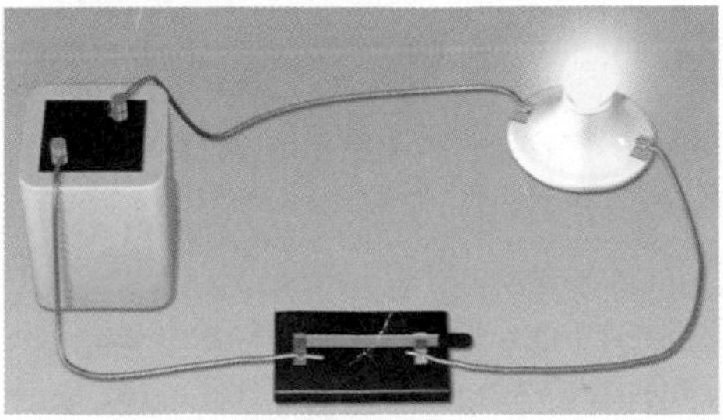

Circuit

circulatory system: organ system that transports needed substances throughout the body and carries away wastes **(093)**

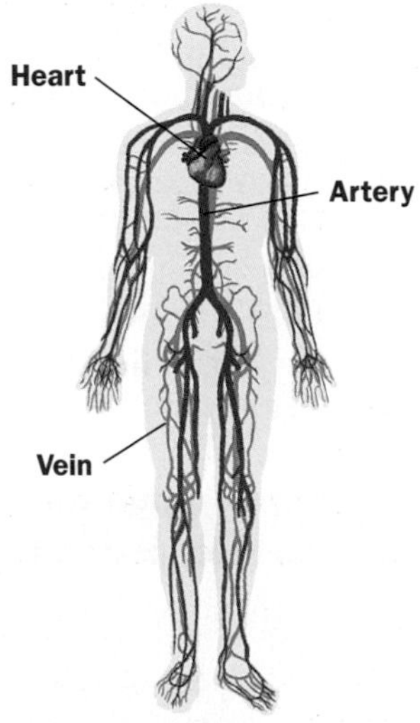

circumference: distance around a circle or sphere

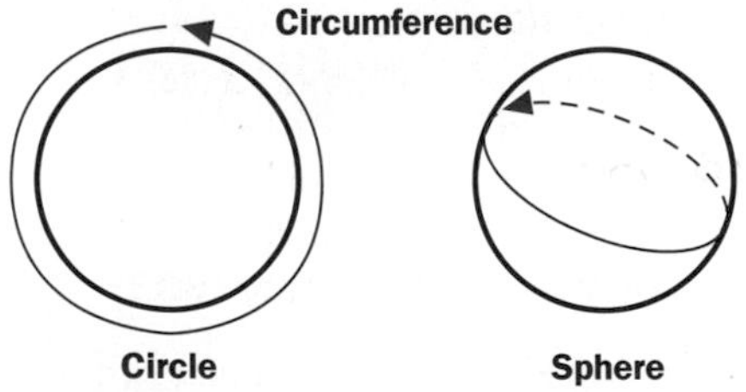

cirro-, cirrus: very high wispy clouds made of ice crystals **(223)**

class: division of organism classification below phylum and above order, as in the class *Insecta* (insects) **(151)**

classify: to organize into groups based on similar characteristics **(150)**

clastic sedimentary rock: rock formed from rock particles that are cemented and pushed together, for example sandstone and shale **(180)**

cleavage: Biology: division of a fertilized egg into additional cells; Geology: splitting of minerals along flat surfaces where bonds between atoms are weak **(179)**

climate: the general pattern of weather in a particular part of the world over a long period of time **(141, 227)**

climax community: dominant community of plants and animals that come to live in an area; *See ecological succession* **(140)**

cloning: process of using a cell or tissue from an organism to produce a new organism with an identical genotype; done in a laboratory **(120)**

cloud: group of tiny liquid water droplets hanging in the air **(223)**

coal: solid fossil fuel, formed deep within Earth over millions of years **(325)**

coefficient: in a chemical equation, the number placed in front of a chemical formula to balance the equation **(267)**

cold front: leading edge of a cold air mass that is pushing a warm air mass **(222)**

colloid: mixture in which small clumps of molecules of one substance are evenly spread throughout another substance and do not settle out

colonize: migration of a species into a new area; *See ecological succession* **(140)**

color: light of various wavelengths; The eyes see each wavelength of light as a different color. **(309, 311)**

coma: Astronomy: mass of cloud-like material around the center of a comet **(242)**

combustion: rapid oxidation; also called **burning**

comet: solar system object made mostly of ice, which follows a long, narrow orbit around the sun; A comet comes near the sun only occasionally. **(242)**

Comet

commensalism: relationship between species in which one species is helped and the other is unaffected **(132)**

community: all of the populations sharing a specific area or region; for example, all the organisms in a lake **(130)**

compaction: process by which sediments are reduced in size or volume by pressure of rock or soil lying above them **(180)**

competition: in an ecosystem, occurs when more than one individual or population tries to make use of the same limited resource **(132)**

complete metamorphosis: describes the life cycle of an organism whose form changes substantially at each stage of its life cycle **(106)**

compound: matter made of two or more elements; The elements in a compound are chemically bonded, cannot be separated by physical means, and a compound has properties that are different from the elements that make it up. **(262)**

compression: *See longitudinal wave* **(307)**

condensation: process in which matter changes from a gaseous state (vapor) to a liquid state; also, matter (especially water) that has condensed on a cold surface, such as water on the outside of a cold glass **(216)**

condensation point: temperature at which a substance changes from a gaseous (vapor) state to a liquid state; same as boiling point for that substance **(254)**

conduction: transfer of heat from a warmer substance to a cooler substance through direct contact **(304)**

conductor: substance that conducts heat readily; also a substance that allows an electric current to pass through it **(317)**

conifer, coniferous tree: tree that produces seeds in cones and has needle-like leaves **(143)**

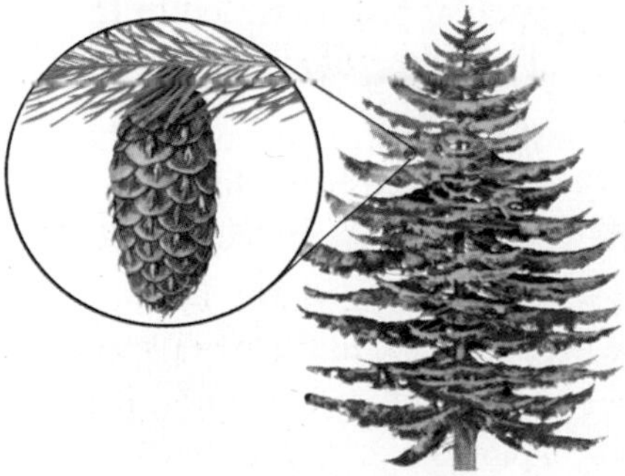

conservation: the wise use and protection of natural resources **(332)**

constellation: an apparent pattern of stars in the sky, such as the Little Dipper (Ursa minor) **(248)**

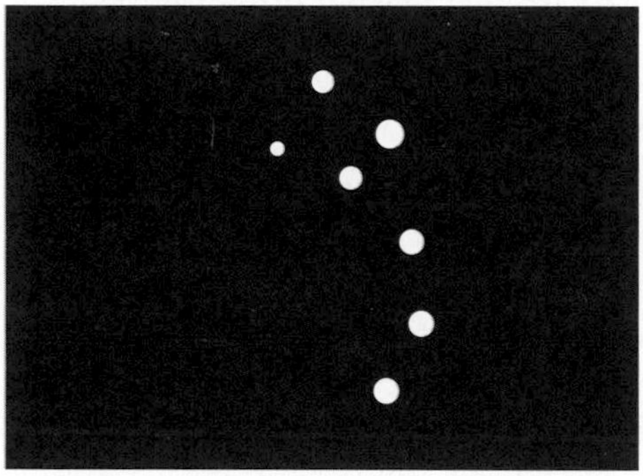

consumer: an organism that feeds on other organisms **(133)**

consumption: the use of a resource **(334)**

continent: any of Earth's seven large land masses

continental crust: rocky material that makes up continents; It is less dense and contains a greater amount of lighter-colored minerals than oceanic crust. **(183)**

continental drift: hypothesis that continents were once part of a single landmass that broke apart and moved to their present positions; led to the theory of plate tectonics **(182)**

continental margin: portion of the seafloor extending from the shoreline to the edge of the deep ocean **(207)**

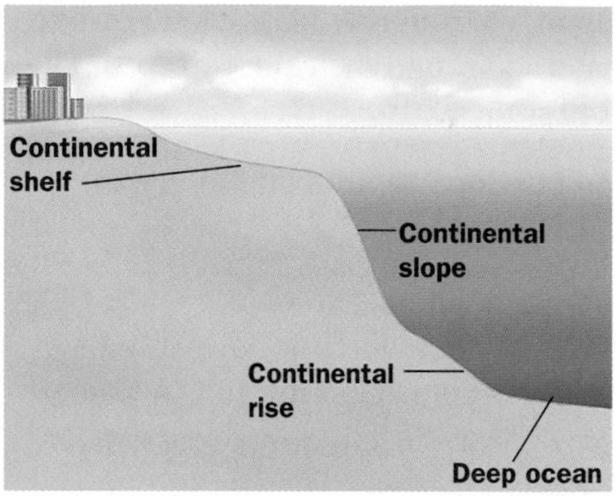

Continental margin

continental polar: cold, dry air mass that forms over Canada and moves south **(221)**

continental tropical: hot, dry air mass that forms over Mexico and moves north **(221)**

contour interval: difference in elevation between any two contour lines on a topographic map **(173)**

contour line: on a map, line that connects points of equal elevation above sea level **(173)**

Countour interval 25 feet

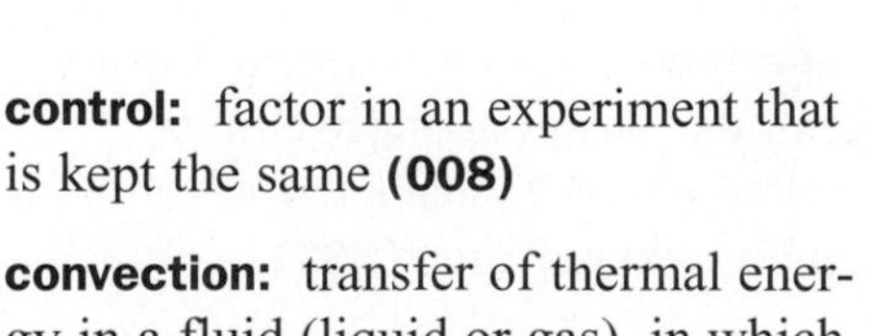

Contour lines

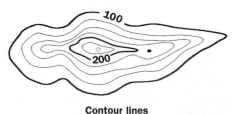

control: factor in an experiment that is kept the same **(008)**

convection: transfer of thermal energy in a fluid (liquid or gas), in which warmer fluid rises and cooler fluid sinks in a **convection current (304)**

convergent boundary: formed where two sections of Earth's crust are colliding **(184)**

coprolite: fossilized animal dung **(198)**

coral reef: warm ocean ecosystem based on tiny animals called coral, which build a rock-like structure (reef) that shelters other organisms **(149)**

Coriolis effect: effect that Earth's rotation has on the path of air and water moving at or above its surface, causing the fluid's path to curve **(205)**

covalent bond: chemical bond in which atoms share one or more electrons; compounds formed this way are called **covalent compounds (263, 264)**

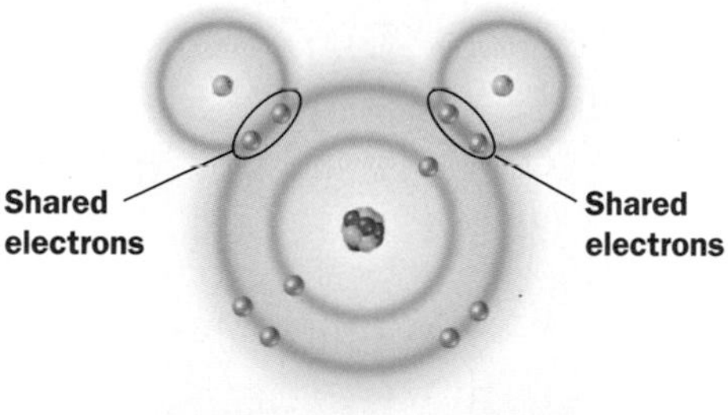

H_2O: A covalent compound

crater: bowl-shaped hollow in the ground, caused by a volcano or by a meteor strike **(239)**

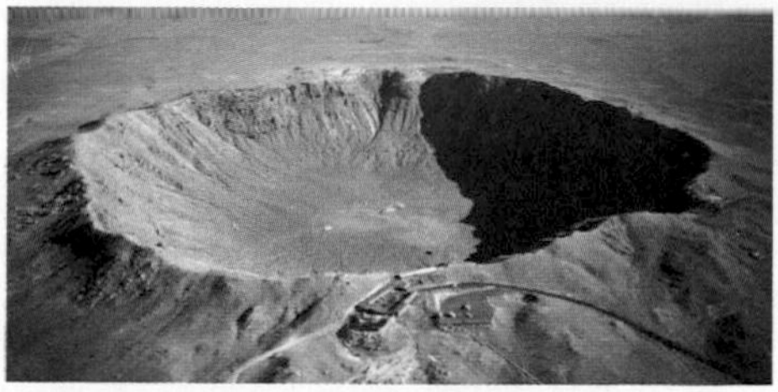

Meteor crater, Arizona

creep: a type of erosion in which soil and sediments move slowly downhill

crest: *See transverse wave* **(307)**

cross-cutting relationships: principle that states that when a rock formed from magma cuts through another rock, the rock formed from magma is younger than all the rocks it cuts through **(196)**

crucible: small porcelain pot used for heating substances **(030)**

crust: outermost, rocky layer of Earth **(177)**

crystal: solid made up of molecules arranged in a regular, repeating pattern

Halite crystal

crystal structure: how the particles in a mineral or chemical are arranged **(179)**

cumulo-, cumulus: thick clouds piled up in masses **(223)**

current electricity: the flow of electric charges through a conductor **(317)**

cyanobacteria: bacteria that make their own food through photosynthesis; also called **blue-green bacteria (157)**

cytoplasm: gel-like fluid that takes up most of the space inside a cell **(077, 078)**

D

data: collected information, the results of an experiment or other investigation; **quantitative data** include numbers, **qualitative data** are descriptive **(009, 386)**

day: time needed for Earth to complete one rotation around its axis (24 hours); also, the daylight period between sunrise and sunset **(233)**

decibel (dB): unit of measurement for the loudness of sound **(313)**

deciduous tree: tree that drops its leaves at the end of the growing season **(144)**

Deciduous tree in summer

Deciduous tree in winter

decimal: the base-10 number system; a **decimal fraction** is any number less than 1 that is shown using a base-ten system, such as 0.25, instead of using stacked whole numbers, such as $\frac{1}{4}$ **(378)**

decomposer: simple organism, such as bacteria or fungus, that breaks down dead organisms and waste, returning important nutrients to the environment **(133)**

decomposition: describes the process in which fungi and bacteria break down dead plant and animal materials and animal wastes, and release nutrients back into the environment **(138)**

deep-sea trench: long, narrow, extremely deep areas of world's oceans, that are formed where one lithospheric plate moves under another **(207)**

delta: a fan-shaped sediment deposit formed at the mouth of a river **(192)**

dendrite: short extension of the nerve cell body that receives stimuli from the axons; *See diagram at neuron* **(095)**

density: amount of mass (g) in a given volume (cm^3) of a substance or object; found by dividing the mass of the object by its volume **(068)**

dependent variable: factor whose value is the result you are testing; also called **responding variable (396)**

deposition: process by which wind, water, and gravity leave eroded sediments in new locations **(192)**

desert: dry climate that receives an average of less than 25 cm of rainfall per year **(147, 230)**

dew: water vapor from the atmosphere that has condensed into liquid water droplets on a surface **(226)**

dew point: air temperature at which dew will form under certain conditions **(226)**

diabetes (mellitus): condition in which the pancreas does not produce enough insulin to control blood sugar levels **(097)**

diameter: line segment passing through the center of a circle or sphere

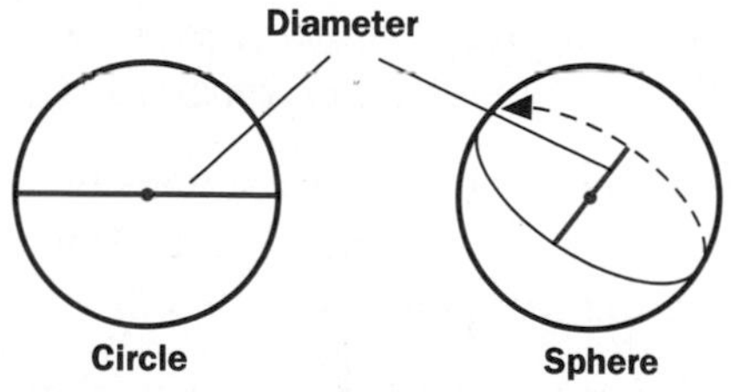

diaphragm: Human Body: large domed muscle that separates chest and abdomen and plays a major role in breathing; *See diagram at respiratory system* **(092);** Also, device that adjusts the amount of light entering a microscope **(049)**

dichotomous key: a system used for identifying plants, animals, rocks, or minerals, that is made up of a series of paired descriptions to choose between **(164)**

diffraction: bending of a wave through an opening or around the edge of an object

diffusion: Chemistry: movement of a molecule from an area where it is in higher concentration to an area where it is in lower concentration; Physics: scattering of light

digestion: process of breaking down food into a form the body can use; *See chemical digestion and mechanical digestion* **(089)**

digestive system: organ system that breaks down food into substances the body can use, and absorbs these substances **(089)**

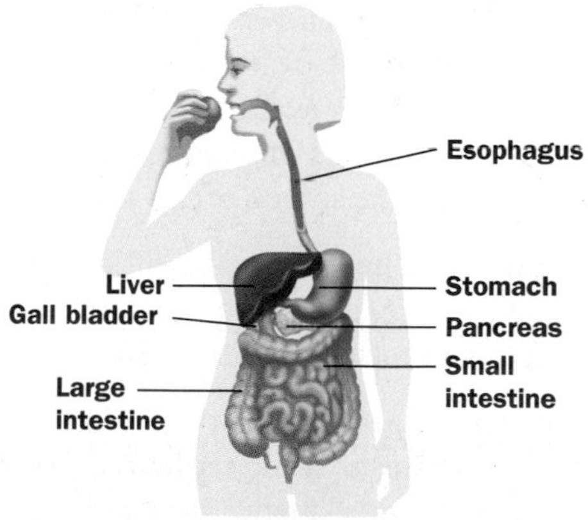

direct current (DC): flow of electricity through a conductor, in which electric charges move in only one direction **(317)**

displace, displacement: one substance or object moving another substance or object, or taking its place **(062)**

divergent boundary: forms where lithospheric plates are moving away from each other **(184)**

divide: ridge that separates two drainage basins **(193)**

DNA: deoxyribonucleic acid; the material found in a cell's nucleus, that determines the genetic traits of the organism **(115)**

doldrums: low air pressure band near the equator where there is little wind **(217)**

domain: largest grouping in the classification of organisms, above kingdom **(151)**

dominant: in a pair of alleles, the one that, if present, determines the trait **(122)**

Doppler effect: change in the apparent frequency of a wave, because either the source of the wave is moving toward or away from the observer, or the observer is moving toward or away from the source of the wave

double-pan balance: kind of laboratory balance, used with standard masses to measure mass **(065)**

drainage basin: area of land that drains water from higher land to lower land and into a stream; also called **watershed (193)**

dune: mound of sand that was deposited by wind

dung: dried animal feces; used as fuel in some parts of the world **(328)**; *See also coprolite* **(198)**

dwarf planet: an object that revolves around the sun, is large enough for gravity to pull it into a nearly round shape, but is not large enough to clear its area in space of other objects **(240)**

E

earthquake: energy travelling as waves passing through Earth, caused by a sudden shift along a fault line, or by volcanic activity **(186)**

echo: sound waves reflected off a surface

eclipse: when one solar system object passes between the Sun and another object, casting a shadow **(236)**

ecological succession: process by which one community of organisms slowly replaces another in an area; *See climax community, colonize* **(140)**

ecology: study of interactions of organisms with each other and their environment **(129)**

ecosystem: all the living populations in an area along with the nonliving parts of that environment **(129)**

efficiency: comparison of amount of energy used per amount of work done

egg: female sex cell; also an object that contains an animal developing from a fertilized sex cell (such as a bird or insect) **(106, 114)**

El Niño: unusually warm ocean current that occurs in the eastern Pacific near the equator, and shifts ocean current patterns **(229)**

electric charge: a property of the particles in an atom; may be positive (protons), negative (electrons), or neutral (neutrons) **(315)**

electric circuit: *See circuit* **(318)**

electric current: the amount of electric charge that moves past a certain point each second; measured in amperes (A) **(317)**

electric force: the attractive or repulsive force between charged objects **(315)**

electrical energy: form of energy that consists of a flow of electric charges through a conductor **(300)**

electricity: general term for interaction of electric charges **(314)**

electrolyte: substance that produces ions and conducts electricity when it is dissolved in water

electromagnet: magnet made by passing an electric current through a wire wrapped around an iron rod **(321)**

electromagnetic induction: the process in which electric current is generated by a changing magnetic field **(321)**

electromagnetic spectrum: full range of electromagnetic waves **(309)**

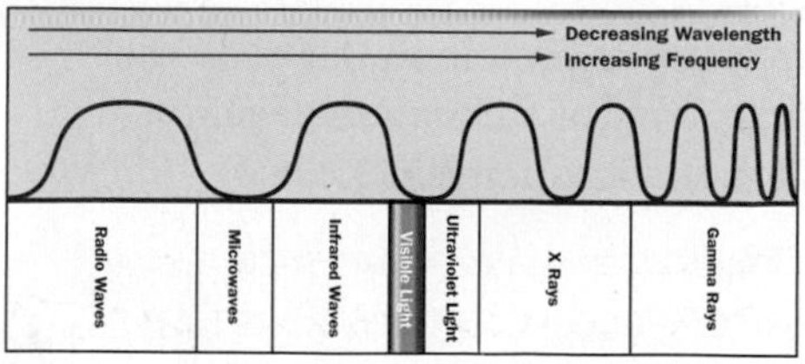

Electromagnetic spectrum

electromagnetic wave: form of energy that can travel through empty space as well as through matter; includes visible light, radio waves, X rays, and many other wavelengths **(305)**

electromagnetism: magnetic force caused by electric charges in motion **(321)**

electron: negatively charged particle found outside the nucleus of an atom **(256)**

electron cloud: in the electron cloud model of the atom, region around the nucleus where an electron may be found **(256)**

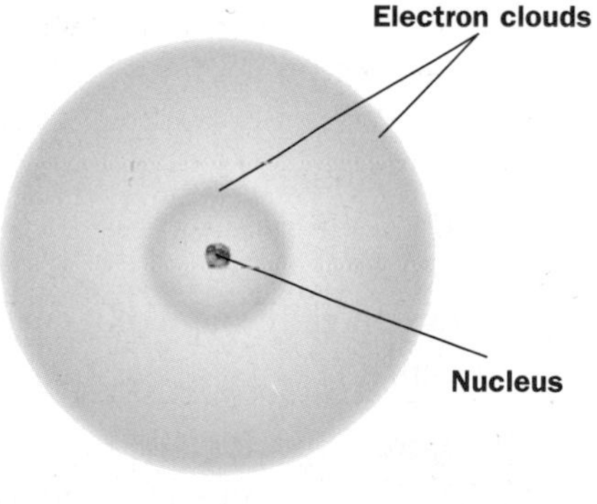

electron-dot diagram: way of using dots to show arrangement of outermost electrons in atoms; also used to show bonds between atoms **(268)**

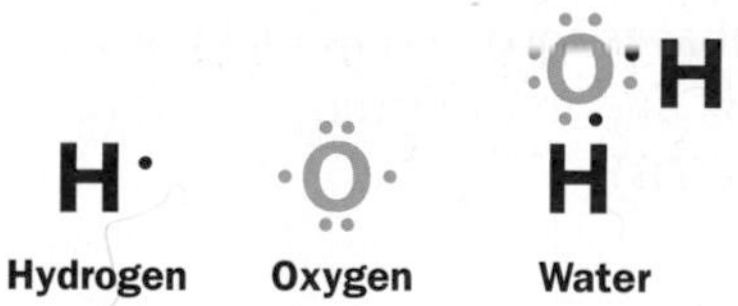

electronic balance: kind of laboratory balance used to measure mass **(066)**

elements: substances that are the building blocks of all matter; An element is made up of one kind of atom. **(260)**

elevation: height above average (mean) sea level; also called **altitude (172)**

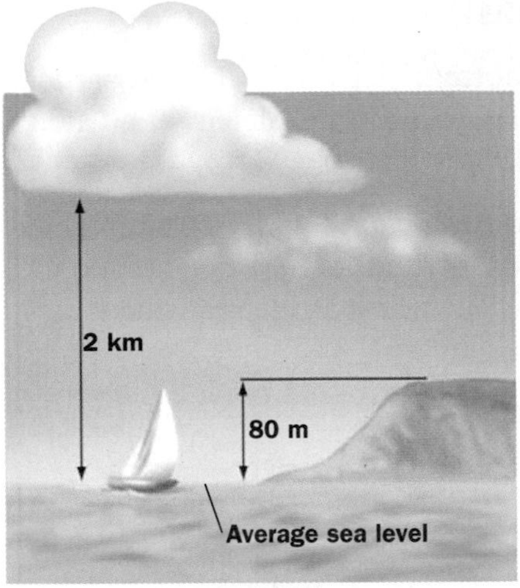

Elevation

embryo: an early stage of a developing organism.

endangered species: an organism that is in danger of extinction **(344)**

endocrine system: system of organs that controls body activities through chemical messengers (hormones) **(097)**

endoplasmic reticulum: structure in a cell that is involved in making proteins and transporting materials **(077, 078)**

endothermic: Biology: animal that keeps a constant body temperature, sometimes called **warm-blooded** or **homeothermic;** Chemistry: chemical reaction in which energy is absorbed

energy: ability to do work **(299)**

energy levels: the amount of energy carried by an electron in an atom; determines the electron's average distance from the nucleus **(256)**

energy pyramid: diagram that demonstrates the flow of energy through a food chain **(137)**

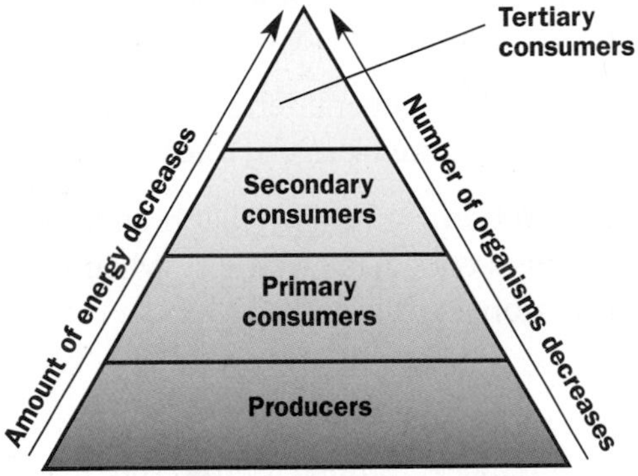

Energy pyramid

energy resources: resources that provide energy; include fossil fuels, biomass, geothermal energy, solar energy, hydroelectric energy, nuclear energy, and wind energy **(324)**

environment: surroundings and conditions in which an organism lives

enzyme: a protein in the body that helps control a chemical reaction, such as digestion **(079, 089)**

eon: largest division of geologic time, lasting many hundreds of millions of years **(200)**

epicenter: point on Earth's surface directly above the location (focus) of an earthquake **(186)**

epidermis: outer layer of a plant stem or of an animal (part of its skin)

epiglottis: flap of tissue at the top of the trachea, that prevents food from entering the lungs **(089)**

epinephrine: hormone that helps to prepare the body for emergency situations by increasing heart rate, blood pressure, and blood sugar levels; also called **adrenaline (097)**

epoch: smallest division of geologic time; lasts several million years **(200)**

equal-area projection: a map showing land masses with correct areas but distorted shapes **(168)**

equator: an imaginary line around the middle of Earth, halfway between the two poles **(169)**

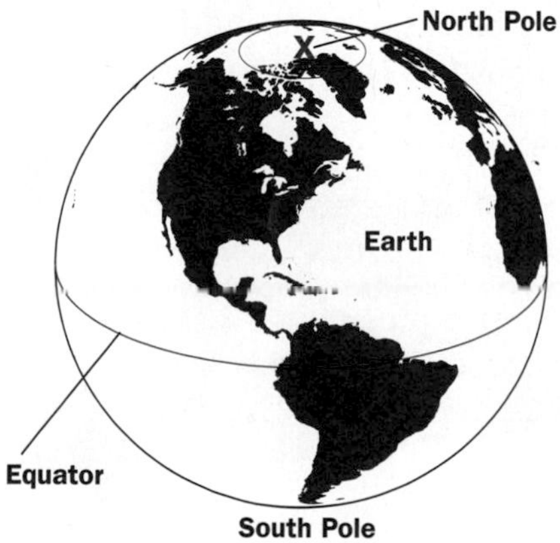

equinox: one of two days in the year when the hours of daylight equal the hours of darkness over Earth as a whole; **vernal equinox** marks the beginning of spring; **autumnal equinox** marks the beginning of autumn, or fall **(234)**

era: division of geologic time lasting several hundreds of millions of years; shorter than an eon, longer than a period **(200)**

erosion: movement of sediment by wind, water, ice, or gravity **(192)**

esophagus: tube that carries food from the mouth to the stomach; *See diagram at digestive system* **(089)**

estimate: an approximation or educated guess at a quantity, based on facts; also, the act of estimating **(053)**

estuary: regions where a river flows into the ocean, and fresh river water mixes with salty ocean water **(148)**

eubacteria: kingdom of single-celled organisms that lack a nucleus and live in a variety of environments **(157)**

eukaryote: organism made up of cells that have a membrane-bound nucleus and other organelles **(160)**

evaporation: change of matter from a liquid state to a gaseous state (vapor) **(216, 254)**

evolution: theory, based on scientific evidence, that describes how organisms change over many generations **(126)**

excrete: to eliminate waste from an organ or body; The waste itself is called an **excretion.**

excretory system: organ system that removes wastes from the body; The urinary system is part of the excretory system. **(090)**

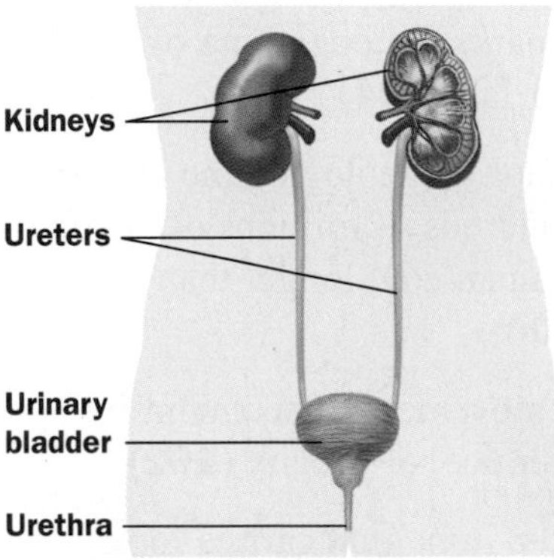

Urinary system

exoskeleton: a firm, supportive covering on the outside of certain organisms, including insects **(161)**

exosphere: outermost layer of Earth's atmosphere **(215)**

exothermic: Biology: animal whose body temperature changes with the temperature of its surroundings; sometimes called **cold-blooded** or **poikilothermic;** Chemistry: chemical reaction in which energy is given off, usually as thermal energy

experiment: series of steps that, under controlled conditions, produces data that test a hypothesis or prediction **(002, 008)**

extinct: condition in which there are no more living members of a species **(128, 340)**

extrapolation: estimate of a unknown value beyond a data set, made by assuming that unknown values follow the same trend as known values **(400)**

extrusive: igneous rock formed by lava cooling quickly at or near Earth's surface **(180)**

F

Fahrenheit (F): temperature scale commonly used in the United States, in which the freezing point of water is 32° and the boiling point is 212° **(071)**

family: Biology: division of organism classification below order and above genus, as in *Felidae* (cats) **(151);** Chemistry: *See group* **(265)**

fat: kind of organic compound that makes up part of a cell membrane, stores excess food energy for an organism, helps insulate an organism, and has many other roles

fault: Geology: crack within Earth's rocky crust, where rock has been fractured, and where rocks move past each other **(186);** Electricity: defect in an electrical circuit

fault-block mountain: mountains formed when rocks move along faults, leaving blocks of crust at different elevations **(187)**

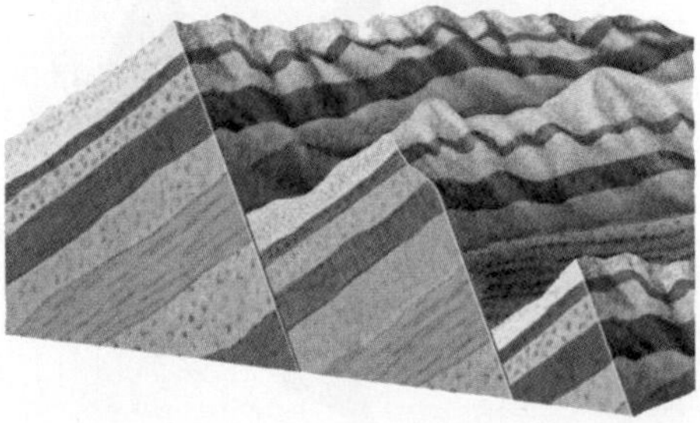

feces: solid waste eliminated by the body **(089)**

fertilization: union of a sperm cell with an egg cell **(114)**

fetus: a developing mammal, from the time its major organs are formed until birth **(106)**

field of view: area that is seen through a hand lens, microscope, or telescope **(050)**

filter paper: special paper used to separate solids from liquids **(048)**

fission: Biology: process in single-cell organisms, in which one cell splits into two or more cells; Chemistry/Physics: splitting of the nucleus of an atom **(327)**

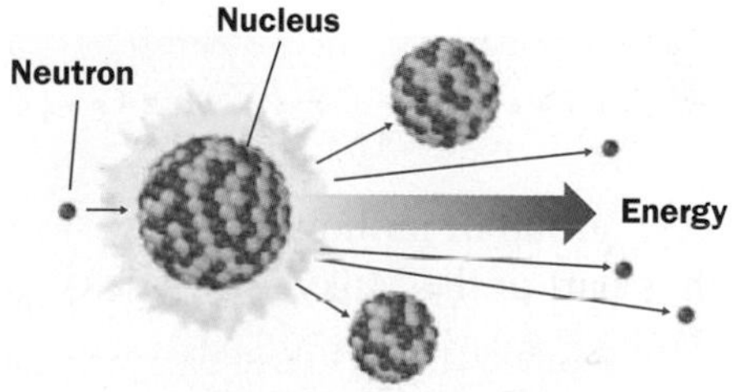

Fission of an atom

flask: a narrow-necked glass container **(047)**

flower: reproductive organ of a flowering plant **(108)**

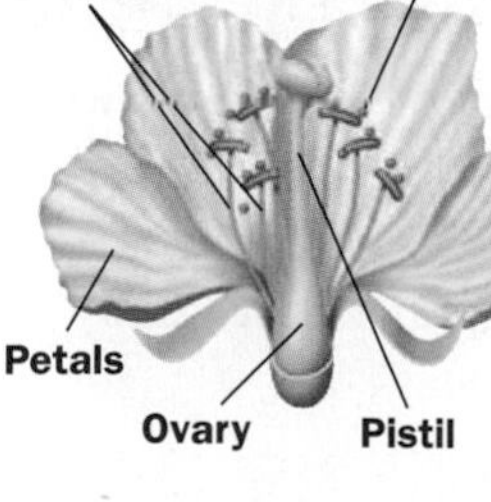

Parts of a flower

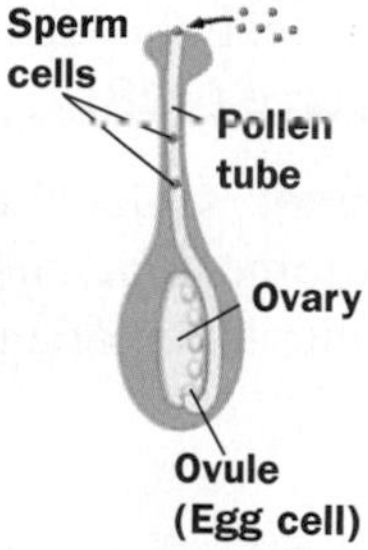

Fertilization

fluid: any material, liquid or gas, that can flow **(295)**

focus: Geology: point within the Earth where an earthquake took place **(186);** Optics: to adjust lenses of an instrument so that the image is clear and sharp **(049)**

folded mountain: mountains formed by the bending of rocks **(187)**

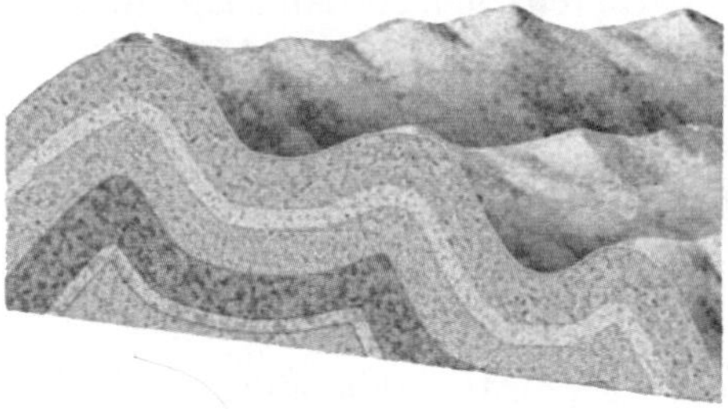

food chain: path of food energy from the sun to the producer to a series of consumers, in an ecosystem **(134)**

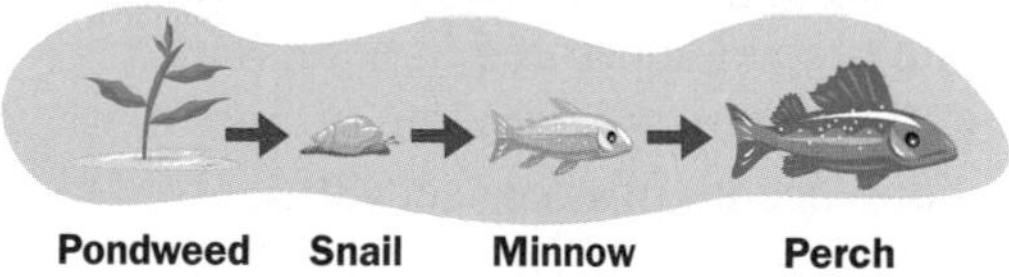

food web: in an ecosystem, arrangement of several overlapping food chains **(135)**

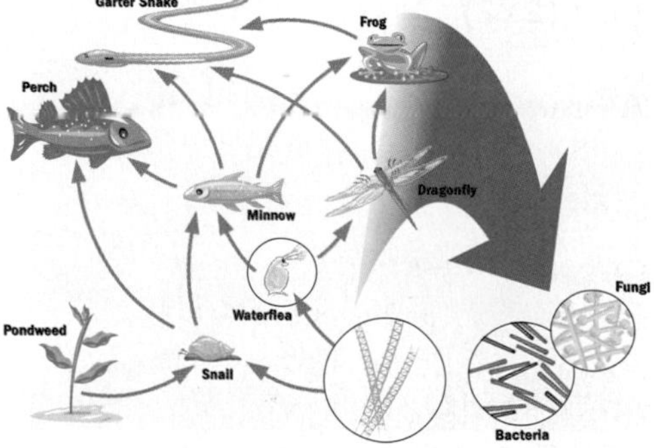

force: a push or a pull **(275)**

fossil: remains, impression, track, or other evidence of ancient organisms **(198)**

fossil fuels: fuels such as coal, oil, and natural gas; formed over millions of years from the remains of ancient plants and animals **(325)**

fracture: tendency of a mineral or rock to break in a certain shape that is not along a crystal plane **(179)**

fraternal twins: individuals born at the same time to the same mother, who developed from two different fertilized egg cells **(119)**

freezing point: temperature at which a substance changes from a liquid state to a solid state; same as melting point for that substance **(254)**

frequency: Physics: number of wave vibrations (oscillations) produced in one second, measured in hertz (Hz) **(306);** Statistics: number of times a value occurs in a data set **(384)**

friction: force that resists the motion of two surfaces that are touching each other **(279)**

front: place where two air masses of different temperatures and pressures meet **(222)**

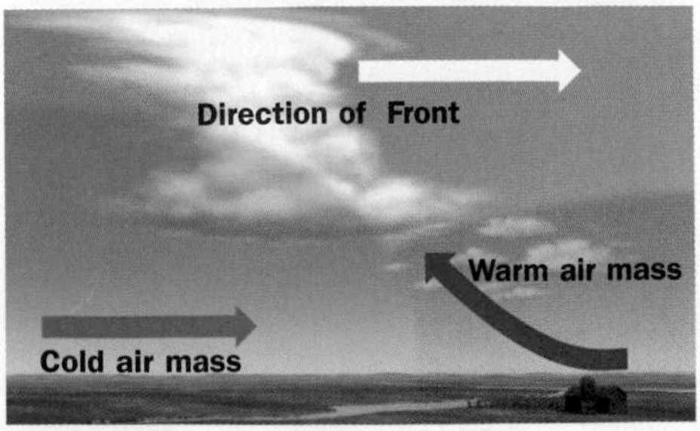

Cross-section of a cold front

fulcrum: point around which a lever turns; *See diagram at lever* **(292)**

fungi: single- or many-celled organisms that have cells walls, do not have chlorophyll, take food from the environment, and reproduce by budding or by spores **(155)**

funnel: cone-shaped object used to catch poured material and direct it into another container **(048)**

fusion: the combining of nuclei of lighter elements to form nuclei of heavier elements, such as hydrogen nuclei fusing to form helium nuclei; also called **nuclear fusion (245)**

G

galaxy: group of millions of stars; Earth is part of the Milky Way galaxy **(247)**

gall bladder: part of the digestive system; a sac that stores bile **(089)**

gas: matter that has no definite volume or shape, such as air **(253)**

gas giant: one of the large planets made mostly of gases; *See also outer planet* **(240)**

gasohol: gasoline with some amount of alcohol added; used as a fuel source **(328)**

gene: segment of DNA, found on a chromosome, that determines the inheritance of a particular trait **(116)**

generator: machine that converts mechanical energy into electrical energy **(328)**

genetic variation: differences in traits among organisms of the same species **(127)**

genetics: the study of how traits are passed from parent to offspring **(112)**

genome: all the genes that an organism has **(117)**

genotype: the set of genes carried by an organism *See also phenotype* **(123)**

genus: division of organism classification below family and above species, as in *Felis* (genus that includes house cats); *See also scientific name* **(151)**

geology: study of Earth's structure, composition, forces, history, and future **(175)**

geothermal energy: energy obtained from thermal energy inside Earth **(326)**

geotropism: *See gravitropism* **(111)**

germination: process in which a plant begins to sprout or grow **(108)**

gills: organs that take in oxygen that is dissolved in water **(106)**

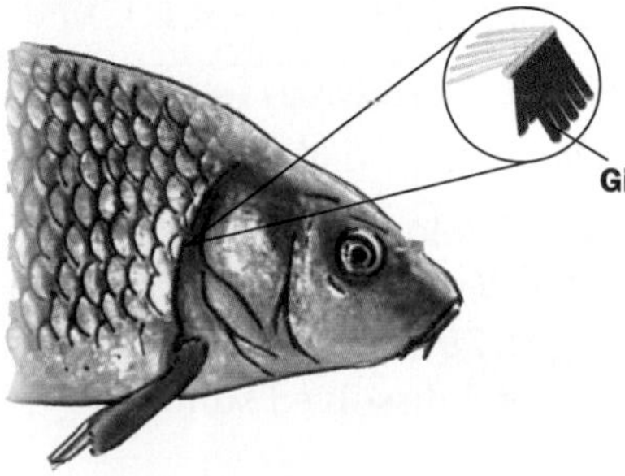

glacier: large mass of ice and snow that exists year-round and is involved in erosion **(192)**

glands: specialized organs that make substances that control and regulate body processes **(097)**

global warming: an increase in the world's average temperature, possibly caused in part by fossil fuel use **(349)**

global wind: a wind that blows steadily in the same direction across thousands of kilometers **(217)**

globe: a spherical (ball-shaped) map of Earth **(233)**

glucagon: substance made by the pancreas that causes blood sugar levels to rise **(097)**

glucose: simple sugar made by plants through the process of photosynthesis **(079)**

Golgi body: cell structure that helps package and distribute products within the cell **(077, 078)**

graduated cylinder: glass container with markings, used to measure volume of liquids **(060)**

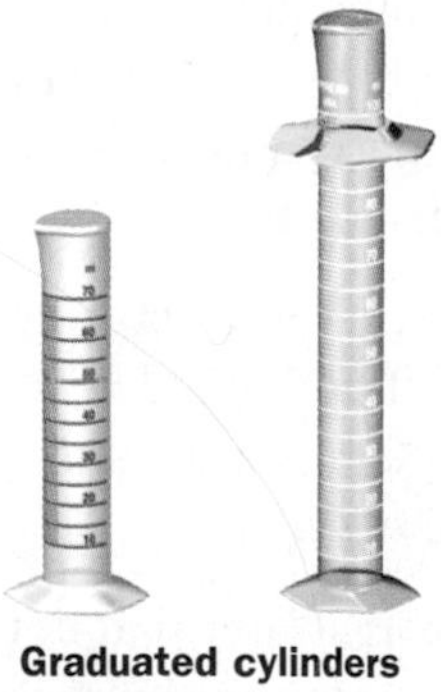

Graduated cylinders

gram (g): unit of mass used in the SI (metric) system **(063)**

graph: picture that shows relationships between sets of data **(390)**

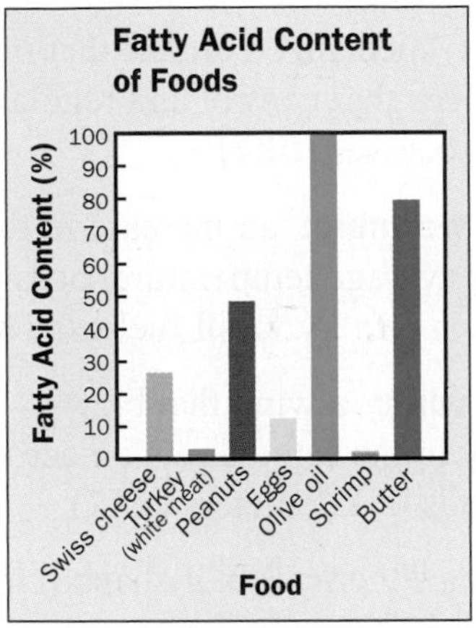

A bar graph

grassland: large land region in which the main types of plants are grasses **(146)**

gravitropism: growth of a plant in response to gravity; also called **geotropism (111)**

gravity: force of attraction between any two objects; *See law of universal gravitation* **(276)**

greenhouse effect: trapping of thermal energy in atmosphere when solar energy that was absorbed by Earth is re-radiated into atmosphere; also refers to global warming caused by an increase in gases (such as CO_2) that trap re-radiated energy **(349)**

ground-fault circuit interrupter: electrical outlet that stops current flowing if there is a ground (or short) in the circuit **(032)**

groundwater: water that collects in cracks and spaces in the rocks and sediments beneath Earth's surface; *See diagram at water table* **(353)**

group: column of elements in the periodic table, in which elements have certain properties in common; also called **chemical family (265)**

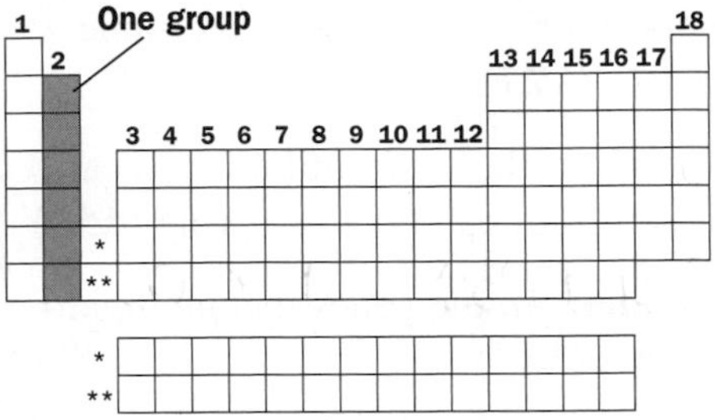

guyot: a smooth, flat-topped mountain on the ocean floor **(207)**

H

habitat: the place in an ecosystem where an organism lives **(131)**

half-life: amount of time needed for half of the radioactive atoms in a sample to decay to another form **(197)**

halogens: group of elements in the periodic table that are highly reactive nonmetals, including fluorine, chlorine, bromine, iodine, and astatine

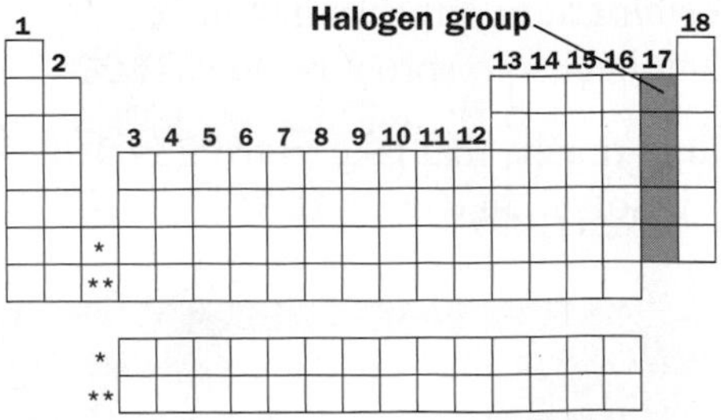

hardness: Geology: relative ability of a solid, such as a mineral, to resist scratching **(179)**; Hydrology: measure of the total dissolved solids in water

hazardous wastes: waste products that contain materials that may be harmful to living things; also called **toxic waste (045, 347)**

heart: part of the circulatory system; organ that pumps blood throughout the body **(093)**

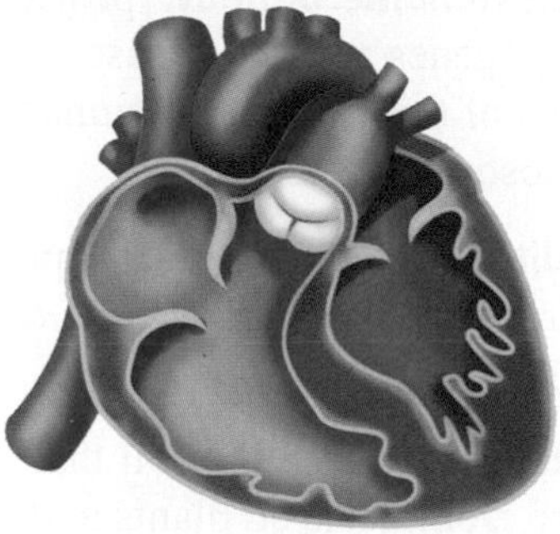

heat: transfer of thermal energy between substances that are at different temperatures; Also **thermal energy (302)**

heat energy: *See thermal energy* **(300)**

hemisphere: one-half of a sphere; Biology: the left or right half of the brain **(095);** Earth Science: half of Earth, divided at the equator (northern and southern hemispheres) or at the prime meridian and international date line (eastern and western hemispheres) **(169)**

herbaceous: plants with green fleshy stems rather than woody stems **(162)**

herbivore: an animal that feeds only on plants, such as a deer **(133)**

heredity: passing of traits from one generation to another **(121)**

hertz (Hz): measurement of wave frequency equal to vibrations per second **(306)**

heterotroph: an organism that obtains the energy it needs by feeding on other organisms **(159)**

hibernation: a deep sleep in which body systems reduce to minimal levels; Hibernation helps some animal species survive winter. **(110)**

hierarchy: graded system in which the most general or largest group or idea is at the top, and the most specific or smallest group or idea is at the bottom **(151)**

high: an area of higher air pressure, generally associated with clear weather **(224)**

histogram: kind of bar graph used to show the frequency of values within a set of data **(392)**

homeostasis: keeping conditions constant inside the body, as in keeping a steady body temperature **(084)**

homeothermic: *See endothermic*

homologous: corresponding in structure; In chromosome pairs, homologous chromosomes carry slightly different version of the same genetic information. **(114)**

horizon: the line where Earth and sky appear to meet; layers of soil with distinct properties **(191)**; line of separation between distinct time periods in a geologic record

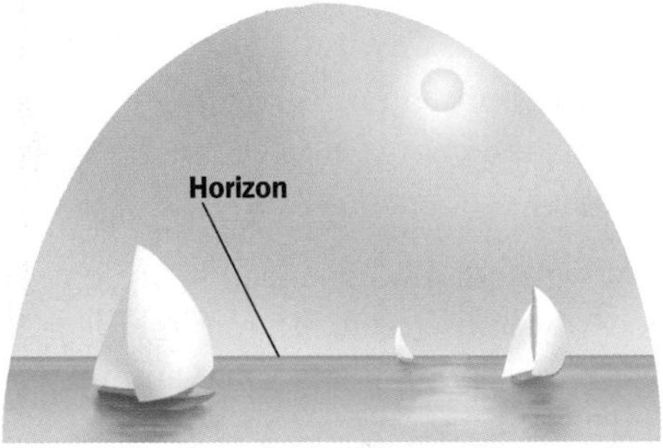

Horizon: where Earth and sky appear to meet

Soil horizons

horizontal: a surface or line that lies flat, side-to-side instead of up and down

horizontal axis: horizontal line marked with a scale that is used to place data points on a graph; sometimes called the x-axis **(390)**

hormone: a chemical released by a gland; controls a specific body function **(097)**

horse latitudes: latitudes between 30°–35°N and S of the equator, where winds are light or absent **(217)**

host: organism that supports a parasite **(132)**

hot spot: a place that is not at a plate boundary where magma rises to the surface; The Hawaiian islands and features in Yellowstone Park formed over hot spots.

Human Genome project: project to map the genes and DNA base pairs on each of the 23 pairs of human chromosomes **(118)**

humidity: amount of water vapor in the air; *See also relative humidity* **(226)**

humus: material in the soil that formed from decayed plants and animals **(191)**

hurricane: a huge, slowly-spinning tropical storm that forms over water and has winds of at least 119 km/h (74 mph)

Hurricane

hybrid: in genetics, an organism that carries both a dominant and recessive allele for the same trait **(122)**

hydroelectric energy: electricity generated using the power of falling water to turn turbines, usually associated with dams **(328)**

Hydroelectric dam

hypothesis: an idea that can be tested by experiment or observation **(006)**

I

ice wedging: breaking apart of rock when water in cracks turns to ice and expands **(189)**

identical twins: two individuals born to the same mother at the same time, who developed from a single fertilized egg **(119)**

igneous rock: one of the three main kinds of rock, made from cooled magma **(180)**

immune system: system that protects the body against disease **(098)**

imprint: fossil formed from an impression of an organism left in sediment before it hardens **(198)**

incinerator: a furnace made to burn trash **(346)**

inclined plane: simple machine that consists of a flat, sloping surface (ramp); *See also screw and wedge* **(289)**

Inclined plane

incomplete metamorphosis: describes the life cycle of an organism, such as a grasshopper, whose form does not change substantially through its life stages; *See also complete metamorphosis* **(106)**

independent variable: factor that affects the value of the dependent variable; in an experiment, you control the value of the independent variable; also called **causal variable (396)**

index contour: on a map, a contour line that is darker than nearby lines and has its elevation labeled **(173)**

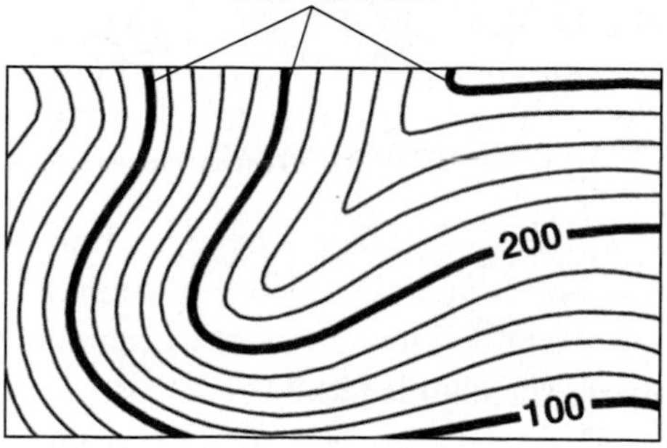

indicator: substance that changes color when it comes in contact with an acid or a base; Indicators are used to identify acidic and basic substances. **(264)**

inertia: an object's tendency to resist a change in motion **(284)**

infectious disease: an illness that is caused by a pathogen, such as a virus or bacteria. Many infectious diseases can be spread from one organism to another. **(099)**

inference: an explanation that is based on available evidence but is not a direct observation **(013)**

informed consent: describing an experiment and its potential risks and benefits, and asking permission, before allowing a person to participate **(361)**

innate behavior: inborn behavior that does not need to be learned **(110)**

inner core: innermost part of Earth, made of solid iron and nickel **(177)**

inner planet: one of the four planets nearest the Sun: Mercury, Venus, Earth, and Mars; also called **terrestrial planet (240)**

inorganic: Chemistry: matter that does not contain the element carbon; Life, Earth Science: matter that does not come from living things

insulator: a substance that does not transfer heat readily; also a substance that does not allow an electric current to pass through it **(317)**

insulin: substance made by the pancreas that reduces blood sugar levels **(097)**

international date line: an imaginary line on Earth at about the 180° meridian, through the Pacific Ocean; crossing the line changes the date **(169)**

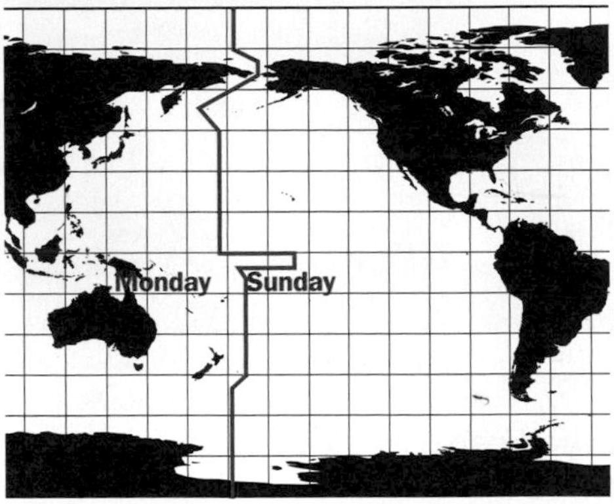

interphase: the stage before cell division begins, when the chromosomes of the cell make exact copies of themselves **(081)**

interpolation: estimate of an unknown or missing value within a data set that is made by assuming unknown values follow the same trends as known values **(400)**

intertidal zone: shoreline areas covered by water at high tide and not covered at low tide **(149, 209)**

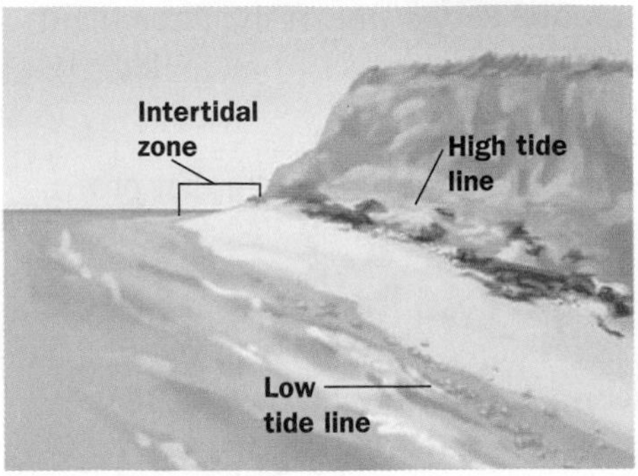

intestine: *See large intestine, small intestine* **(089)**

intrusive: igneous rock formed by magma cooling slowly beneath Earth's surface **(180)**

invertebrate: an animal without a backbone **(161)**

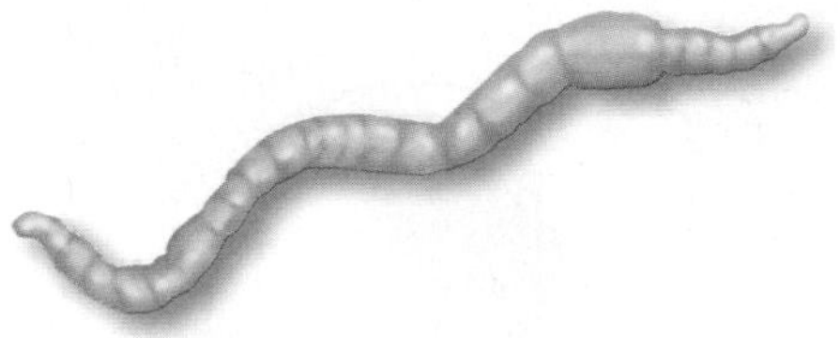

An earthworm is an example of an invertebrate.

involuntary muscle: smooth and cardiac muscle; not under conscious control **(087)**

ion: atom or molecule that has an overall electric charge due to loss or gain of electrons **(263)**

ionic bond: chemical bond in which one or more electrons from one atom are transferred to another atom; compounds formed this way are called **ionic compounds (263, 264)**

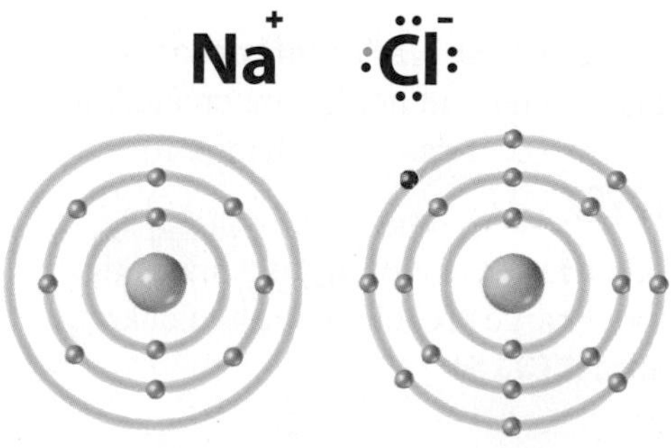

NaCl: An ionic compound

ionosphere: high layer of Earth's atmosphere, above 100 kilometers

isobar: line on a weather map that connects points of equal air pressure **(221)**

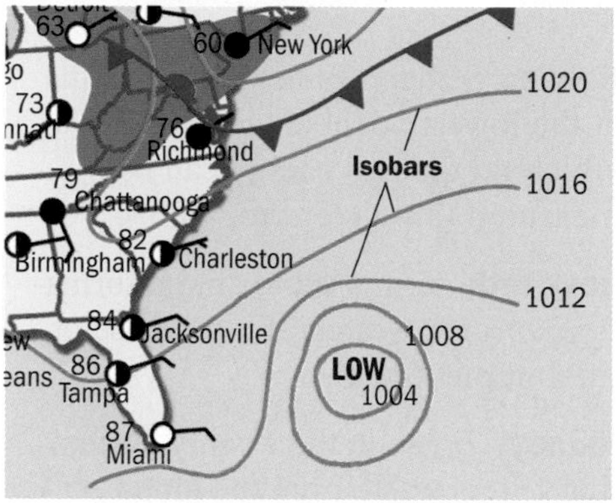

isotherm: line on a weather map that connects points that have equal air temperature

isotope: atoms of the same element with different numbers of neutrons in the nucleus, and thus different atomic masses; for example, carbon-12 and carbon-14 **(256)**

J

jet stream: narrow stream of high-speed wind high in the atmosphere, generally moving west to east in the Northern Hemisphere **(217)**

joint: Human Body: place where two or more bones meet **(086);** Geology: cracks in bedrock along which no movement has taken place

joules (J): SI unit of work and energy equal to 1 Newton-meter (1 N · m) **(287)**

K

Kelvin: SI temperature scale; begins at the lowest possible temperature, at which no thermal energy can be measured (absolute zero, -273°C)

keyword: term used to find information during a search of a database or the Internet **(422)**

kidney: organ in the urinary system that filters waste from the blood **(090)**

kinetic energy: energy an object or particle has because it is moving **(300)**

kingdom: second largest grouping in organism classification, as in the animal kingdom **(151)**

L

lab report: written record of a scientific investigation **(015)**

landfills: areas where solid waste (trash) is buried, in such a way that pollutants do not leak out **(346)**

landslide: form of erosion in which a large amount of the land surface suddenly moves downhill

large intestine: part of the digestive system where water is absorbed from solid waste **(089)**

larva: an early life stage of an animal, such as an ant or butterfly, that undergoes complete metamorphosis **(106)**

latitude lines: system of imaginary circles on Earth's surface that are used to describe position north and south of the equator; also called **parallels** **(169)**

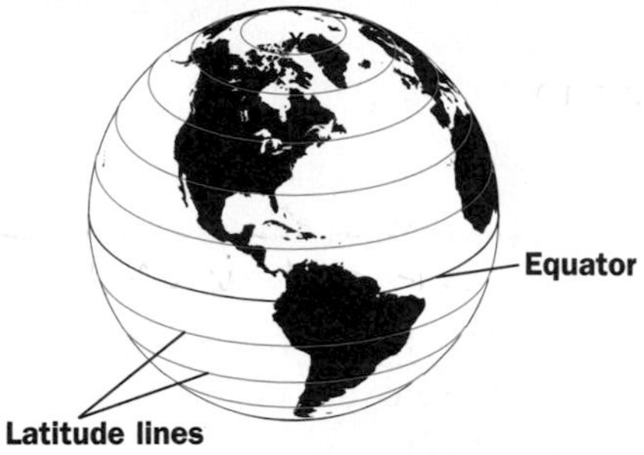

lava: molten rock material pushed up from a volcano or crack in the Earth; magma that has reached the surface **(180)**

law: a scientific explanation that describes how some part of the world or universe acts under certain conditions; also called **scientific law (002)**

law of conservation of energy: states that energy cannot be created or destroyed, it can only change form or be transferred **(300)**

law of conservation of mass: states that matter can neither be created nor destroyed, it can only change form **(270)**

law of electric charges: states that like charges repel and unlike charges attract **(315)**

law of reflection: states that a wave bounces off a surface at the same angle that it hits the surface **(311)**

law of universal gravitation: states that the force of gravity between two objects increases as the mass of the objects increases, and as the distance between them decreases **(276)**

lens: curved, transparent piece of glass or plastic that bends light rays to form an image

lever: simple machine made of a long rigid bar that rests on and turns around a support called a fulcrum **(292)**

lichen: a fungus and a photosynthetic alga (or a cyanobacterium) living in a cooperative relationship **(140)**

life cycle: all stages in the life of an organism **(106)**

lift: upward force on an object due to differences in fluid pressure above and below it; *See Bernoulli's principle* **(297)**

ligament: connective tissue that holds bones together at many joints **(086)**

light: a type of energy that humans can see; part of the electromagnetic spectrum; also called **visible spectrum (308)**

light-year: distance light travels in a vacuum in one year, equal to 9.46×10^{12} kilometers **(245)**

limiting factor: a condition or resource that keeps a population at a certain size, such as the amount of water available **(131)**

liquid: matter that has a definite volume but not a definite shape; for example, water **(253)**

liter (L): unit of liquid volume used with the SI (metric) system **(059)**

lithosphere: outermost layer of Earth's surface, which is rocky and solid; includes the crust and the rigid part of the upper mantle **(183)**

lithospheric plate: one of the pieces of Earth's surface, that is made up of the crust and the upper mantle **(183)**

liver: organ in the digestive system that produces bile and enzymes, breaks down toxins and wastes, and has many other functions **(089)**

loess: thick layer of silt that was probably deposited by wind, not water

longitude lines: system of imaginary half-circles on Earth's surface that end at the poles, used to describe position east and west, with 0° at the prime meridian; also called **meridians (169)**

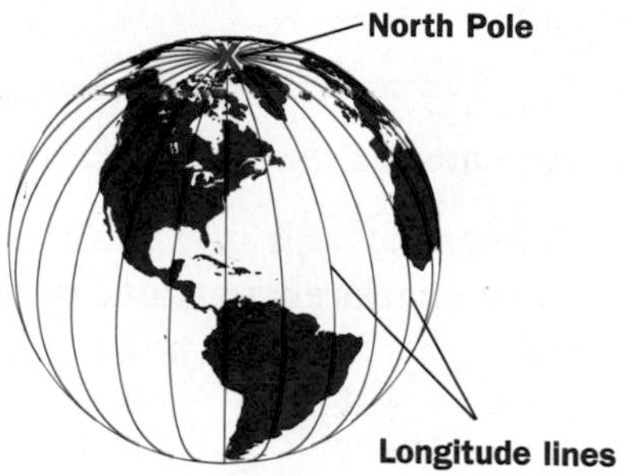

longitudinal wave: a wave that oscillates back and forth parallel to the direction it is traveling; where the wave pushes matter closer together is a **compression;** where the wave pushes matter farther apart is a **rarefaction (307)**

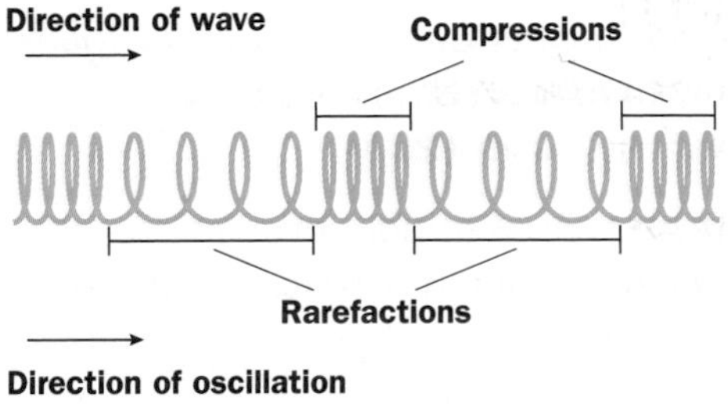

low: area of lower air pressure, generally associated with wet or overcast weather **(224)**

lunar eclipse: occurs when the moon passes through Earth's shadow **(236)**

lungs: pair of organs in respiratory system, where carbon dioxide and oxygen are exchanged; *See diagram at respiratory system* **(092)**

luster: how the surface of a mineral appears when it reflects light **(179)**

lymph node: lumps of tissue in which pathogens are filtered out of the bloodstream **(098)**

M

machine: *See simple machine* **(288)**

macrophage: type of white blood cell that attacks and engulfs pathogens **(098)**

magma: molten rock that makes up Earth's mantle and becomes igneous rock when it cools **(180)**

magnet: object that attracts iron **(320)**

magnetic field: region of magnetic force around a magnet **(320)**

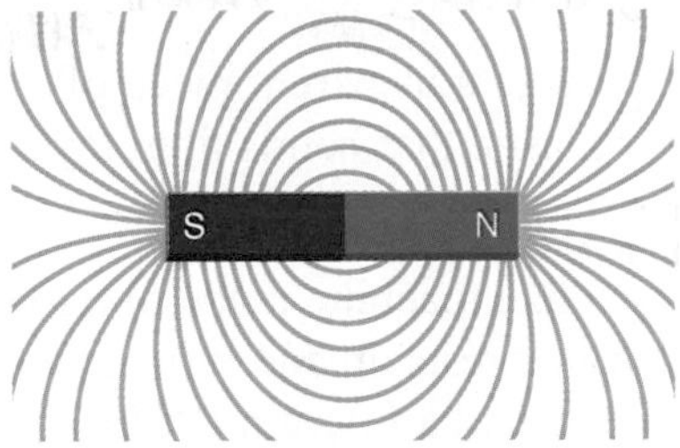

Magnetic field lines

magnetic force: the attractive or repulsive force that acts between magnetic materials **(320)**

magnification: power of a magnifying lens or set of lenses; also, total enlargement of an image seen through those lenses **(051)**

magnitude: strength or intensity of a property or event, such as the brightness of a star or planet **(246),** or the strength of an earthquake **(186)**

mammal: animals that have fur or hair, usually give birth to live young, and can nurse their young with milk **(106)**

mantle: a layer of Earth's surface, lying just below the crust and above the inner core **(177)**

map: Earth Science: flat picture of part or all of the surface of Earth or another planet **(166);** Genetics: to determine the sequence of DNA base pairs on a chromosome **(118)**

map legend: list or explanation of symbols on a map; also called **map key (171)**

map scale: way of showing how distances on a map relate to distances on Earth's surface **(170)**

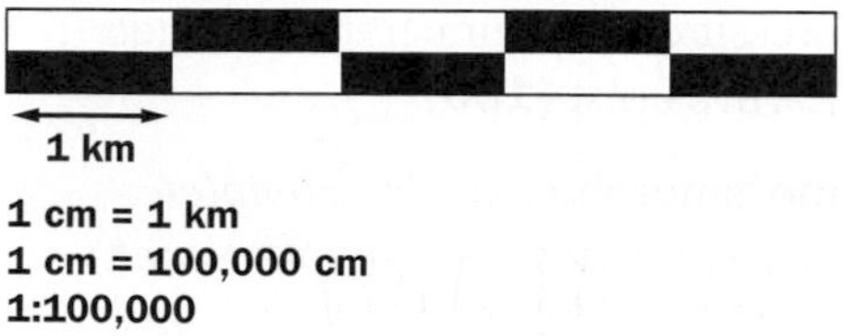

Map scales

map symbol: small drawings on a map that represent natural or human-made features **(171)**

maria: large, dark, and generally smooth areas on Earth's moon **(239)**

maritime polar: cool, moist air mass that forms over an ocean near a polar area **(221)**

maritime tropical: warm, humid air mass that forms over an ocean near tropical and subtropical areas **(221)**

mass: amount of matter in something; measured in grams (g) **(063)**

mass extinction: event in geologic history when many species of organisms died out over a short period of time **(128)**

material resources: natural resources that are used to make things, such as water, minerals, petroleum, and wood; sometimes called **raw materials (323)**

matter: the material that all objects and substances are made of; anything that has mass and takes up space **(250)**

mean: sum of all values in a data set, divided by number of values in the data set; sometimes called **average (384)**

mean sea level: average sea level, defined as an altitude of 0 **(172)**

measurement: a number and a unit that define a quantity, such as length, volume, or mass **(053)**

mechanical advantage: a description of how many times a simple machine multiplies the force put into it; It is found by dividing the output force (F_{out}) by the input force (F_{in}). **(288)**

mechanical digestion: process of breaking food into smaller pieces by chewing and mashing **(089)**

mechanical energy: energy an object has because of its motion or position **(300)**

mechanical wave: energy that travels through matter; examples include sound, ocean waves, and earthquake waves **(305)**

mechanical weathering: breaking up of rock by physical forces, such as the action of wind and moving water **(189)**

median: middle value in a data set, when the values are arranged in order from least to greatest **(384)**

medium: matter that a wave travels through

meiosis: cell division that produces sex cells (eggs or sperm), which have only half the chromosomes of the parent cell **(114)**

melting point: temperature at which a substance changes from solid state to liquid state; same as **freezing point** for that substance **(254)**

meniscus: curved surface of a liquid, such as water, where it meets the sides of its container **(060)**

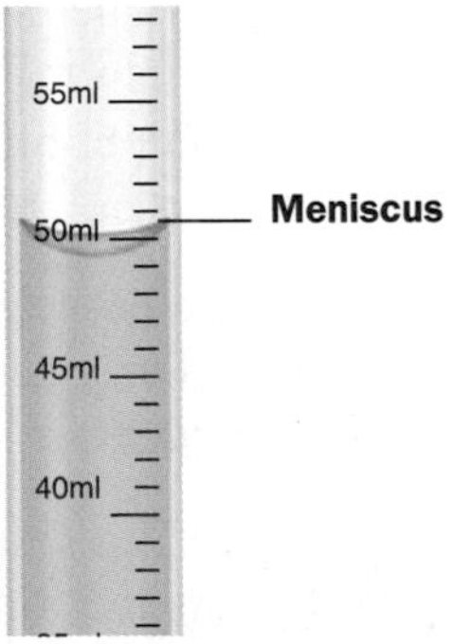

Mercator projection: map showing continents in correct shapes but incorrect areas **(168)**

meridian: *See longitude line* **(169)**

mesosphere: a layer of Earth's atmosphere located between 50–90 kilometers above the surface **(215)**

metabolism: cellular processes of making, storing, and transporting chemicals **(079)**; also, the sum of all these processes in an organism **(105)**

metals: elements, usually solid, with a shiny surface; metals conduct electricity and thermal energy well; examples include gold, iron, lead, copper, and silver **(331)**

metamorphic rock: rock that has been changed over time by high pressures and temperatures inside Earth's crust **(180)**

metamorphosis: *See complete metamorphosis, incomplete metamorphosis* **(106)**

metaphase: stage of cell division during which the chromosome copies line up in the center of the cell **(081)**

meteor: a piece of rock from space that enters Earth's atmosphere and burns, creating a bright streak of light across the sky; **meteorite** is a piece of that rock that lands on Earth **(243)**

meteorology: study of Earth's atmosphere **(212)**

meter (m): base unit for length in the SI (metric) system of measurement **(058)**

meter stick: a rod or stick one meter in length, used for measuring **(058)**

methane: flammable gas that forms from decaying organic matter; used as a fuel source **(328)**

metric system: *See SI system* **(055)**

microscope: an instrument that makes small objects appear larger **(049)**

microscopic: object or organism too small to be seen without a microscope **(076)**

mid-ocean ridge: undersea mountain range that forms where two parts of Earth's crust are pushing apart (diverging plate boundary) **(184, 207)**

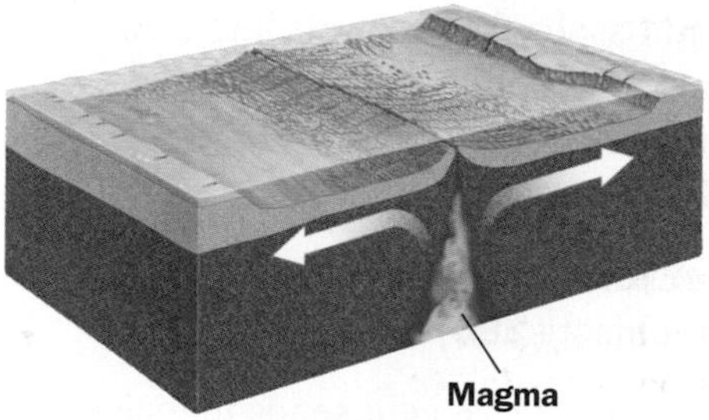

Mid-ocean ridge

migration: seasonal movement of animals from one place to another **(110)**

millibar: a unit of air pressure **(224)**

mineral: element or compound, formed by nature but not formed by living things, that has a specific crystal structure and physical and chemical properties **(179)**

mitochondria: structures in the cell that transform the energy in food into a form cells can use to carry out their activities **(077, 078)**

mitosis: during cell division, the process in which the material from the cell nucleus divides **(080)**

mixture: a combination of two or more substances that have not combined chemically and that can be separated by physical means **(271)**

mode: the value occurring most frequently in a data set **(384)**

model: *See scientific model* **(013)**

Moho: boundary between Earth's crust and mantle (short for Mohorovičić discontinuity)

Mohs' scale: a system listing ten minerals that the hardness of other minerals can be compared with **(179)**

mold: Biology: kind of fungus made up of threadlike branches that give the mold a fuzzy appearance; Geology: a kind of fossil, a space in a sedimentary rock that is shaped like a living thing that was once there; *See also cast* **(198)**

molecule: smallest particle of a substance that still has the properties of that substance **(261)**

moon: a natural object that revolves around a planet **(232)**

moon phases: regular changes in the Moon's appearance, as seen from Earth; *See also waning, waxing* **(235)**

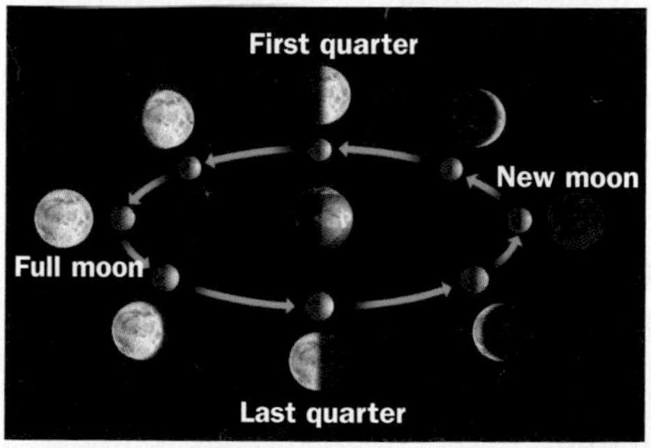

mouth: Biology: opening that animals use to take in food **(089)**; Geology: opening where one body of water enters a larger body, such as a river entering an ocean

multicellular: made up of more than one cell **(076)**

muscular system: all the muscles of the body, especially those involved in movement **(087)**

mutation: a random change in a gene **(127)**

mutualism: relationship between two species in which both species benefit **(132)**

N

natural gas: a fossil fuel; flammable, odorless gas (mostly methane) found in Earth's crust **(325)**

natural resources: resources that are used by humans, such as minerals, water, fossil fuels, and food sources **(323)**

natural selection: process by which organisms change over time as those with traits best suited to an environment pass their traits to the next generation **(127)**

neap tides: tides that are least extreme; happen twice a month, at first and last quarter moon phases

nebula: cloud of gas and dust in space, in which stars form

nekton: organisms living in water that swim freely and can swim against the current, such as fish **(210)**

nephrons: tiny filters in the kidney that remove liquid wastes from blood **(090)**

neritic zone: area of sea floor reaching from the shore to the edge of the continental shelf, to a depth of about 200 meters **(210)**

nervous system: system of organs and tissues that controls and coordinates the body's activities; *See diagram at central nervous system* **(095)**

net force: sum of all forces acting on an object **(280)**

neuron: nerve cell; sends messages through the nervous system **(095)**

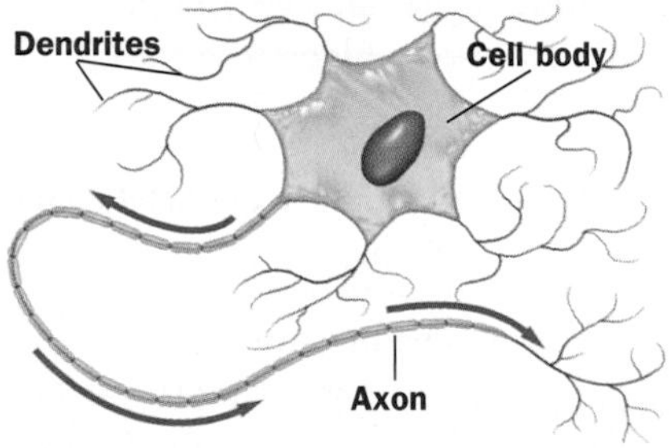

neutron: in an atom, particle with a neutral charge; located in the nucleus **(256)**

newton (N): SI unit of force **(275)**

Newton's laws of motion: three laws, developed by Isaac Newton, that explain the motions of objects **(283)**

niche: role that a species plays in a living community or ecosystem **(131)**

nimbo-, nimbus: any cloud that can produce precipitation **(223)**

nitrogen cycle: in the environment, the movement of nitrogen between the living and non-living parts of an ecosystem **(139)**

nitrogen fixation: transformation of nitrogen in the air into nitrogen compounds; carried out by certain bacteria **(139)**

noble gases: group of elements in the periodic table that generally do not react with other elements, and which are all gases; examples include neon and krypton

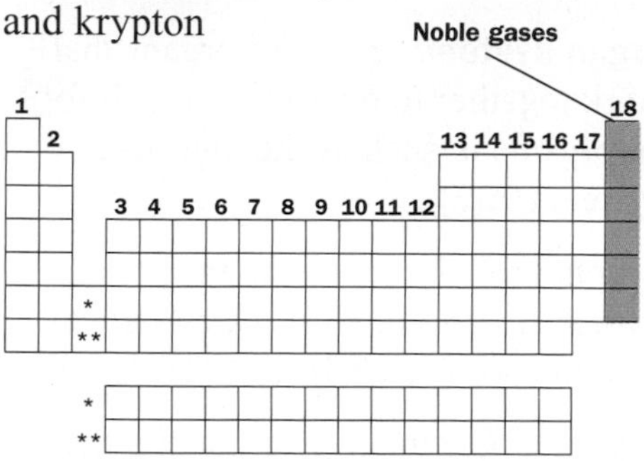

nocturnal: describes an animal that is mainly active at night; for example, a bat **(147)**

noninfectious disease: an illness that is not caused by a pathogen and cannot be spread from one organism to another **(099, 101)**

nonrenewable resources: natural resources that cannot be replaced once used, such as oil, coal, natural gas, and minerals **(323)**

non-sexual reproduction: *See asexual reproduction* **(114)**

nonvascular plant: a plant that does not have specialized tissue for moving water and food throughout the plant **(162)**

northern hemisphere: the half of Earth north of the equator

nuclear energy: energy contained in the center, or nucleus, of an atom **(327)**

nuclear membrane: structure that surrounds and protects the nucleus of a cell; also called **nuclear envelope** **(077, 078)**

nucleolus: small, round structure in the nucleus of a cell that helps direct how proteins are put together **(077, 078)**

nucleus: Biology: structure near the center of a cell that contains the cell's DNA **(077, 078);** Chemistry: center of an atom, made up of protons and neutrons **(256)**

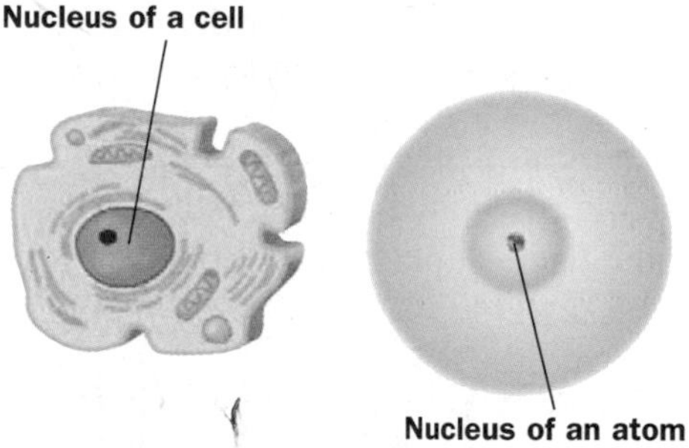

nutrient: substance that an organism needs in order to survive and grow

occluded front: formed in the atmosphere when a cold front overtakes a warm front, capturing the warm air mass between the two cold air masses **(222)**

ocean current: flow of water within the ocean that moves in a regular pattern **(203)**

oceanic crust: portion of Earth's outer crust that lies beneath the oceans; It is thinner, denser, and has darker-colored minerals than continental crust **(183)**

oceanography: study of the physical properties of oceans and seas **(201)**

ohm (Ω): unit of electrical resistance **(319)**

Ohm's law: an equation that describes the relationship among current, voltage, and resistance in an electric circuit: $I = \frac{V}{R}$ **(319)**

omnivore: an animal that feeds on both plants and animals; for example, a raccoon **(133)**

opaque: describes matter that light does not pass through **(311)**

open-ocean zone: ocean life zone reaching from the continental slope to the deepest plains and trenches **(149, 211)**

orbit: path an object in space follows as it revolves around another object, such as Earth around the sun or a satellite around Earth **(234)**

orbital plane: imaginary surface that contains an object's orbit **(233)**

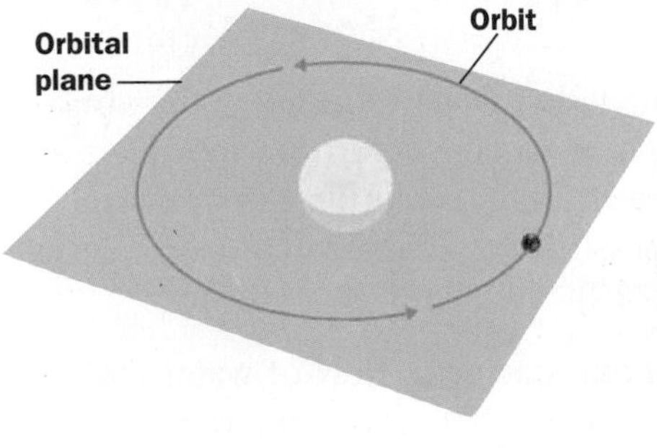

order: division of organism classification below class and above family, as in Carnivora, mammals that feed on other animals **(151)**

organ: in an organism, structure made of two or more different tissues which has a specialized function; for example, the lungs **(082)**

organ system: group of organs that work together to do a specific job for an organism, such as the digestive system **(082)**

organelles: structures in the cytoplasm of a cell that carry out cell activities **(077, 078)**

organic: Chemistry: compound that contains the element carbon; Life, Earth Science: material made of or by living things or once-living things **(180)**

organism: a living thing **(074)**

oscillate: to vibrate or swing back and forth, or up and down, from one extreme limit to another

osmosis: diffusion of water across a membrane, such as a cell membrane

outer core: layer inside Earth, between the mantle and inner core, which has some properties of a liquid **(177)**

outer planet: any planet beyond the asteroid belt; includes Jupiter, Saturn, Uranus, Neptune **(240)**

ovary: female part of a flower in which egg cells are produced **(114)**

ozone: form of oxygen that has three atoms in one molecule (O_3) **(214)**

ozone layer: region in Earth's upper atmosphere that blocks part of the sun's ultraviolet radiation **(350)**

P

pancreas: organ of the digestive system and endocrine system; makes enzymes that help in the breakdown of carbohydrates, and that help regulate blood sugar levels **(089, 097)**

Pangaea: ancient land mass believed to have broken up to form today's continents **(182, 199)**

parallel: General: lines that never touch each other; Earth Science: *See latitude line* **(169)**

Parallel lines

parallel circuit: circuit in which each load forms a separate circuit with the energy source; If one load stops working, the other loads keep working. **(318)**

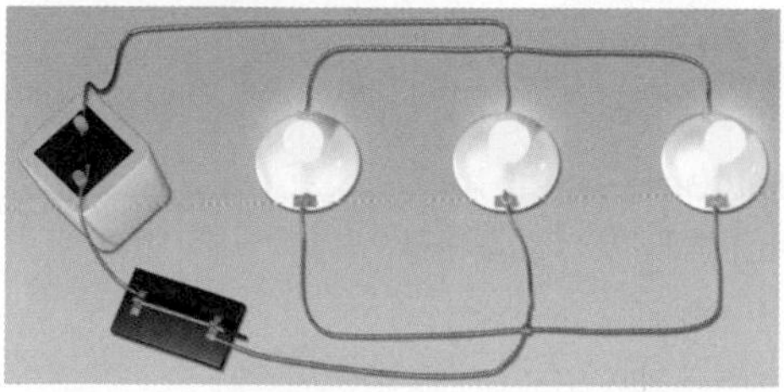

Parallel circuit

parasite: organism, such as a tick, that feeds on cells, tissues, or fluids of another living organism (the host) **(132)**

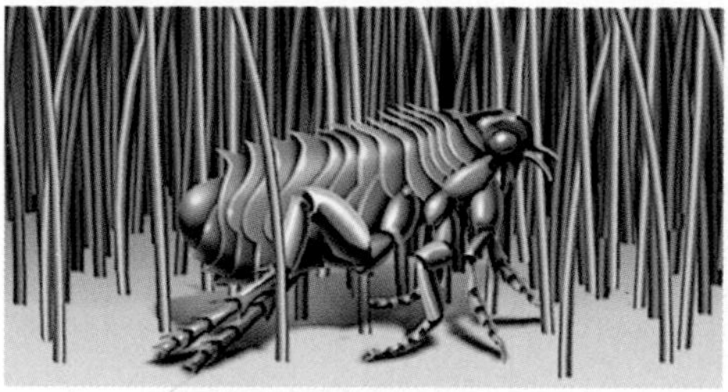

A flea is a parasite.

parasitism: relationship between species in which one species (parasite) benefits and the other (host) is harmed but not usually killed **(132)**

parathyroid glands: glands that produce hormones that control calcium levels in the blood **(097)**

part per thousand (ppt): way of describing how much of a substance is present in a mixture if the mixture is divided into 1000 parts, for example 35 parts per thousand salt in ocean water **(383)**

passive margin: continental margin without a plate boundary near it **(207)**

pathogen: agent of disease, such as a virus, bacteria, or fungus **(098)**

peat: partially decayed plant matter that forms a thick mat; used as a fuel **(328)**

percent: parts out of a hundred equal parts **(383)**

period: Chemistry: a row of elements in the periodic table arranged by atomic number **(265);** Geology: unit of geologic time lasting tens of millions of years, part of an era, and longer than an epoch **(200)**

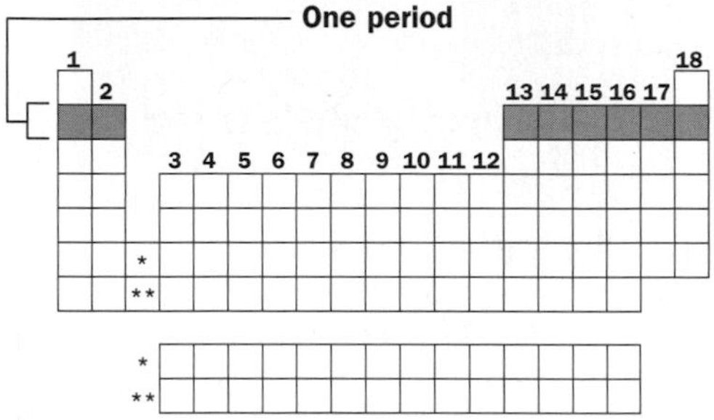

periodic table of elements: a chart where all elements are organized into periods and groups according to their properties **(265)**

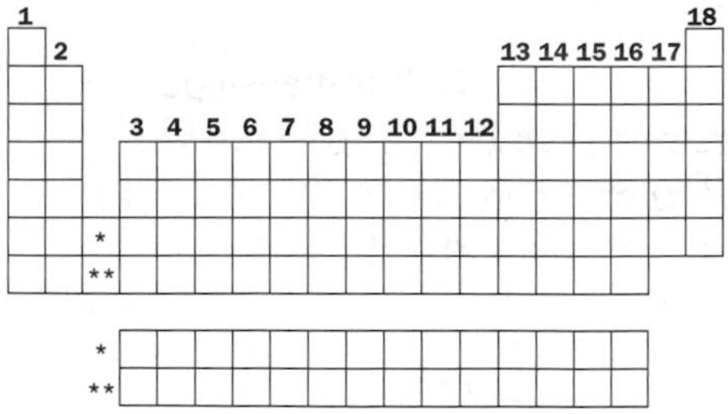

permafrost: layer of earth in the tundra biome that is frozen to a depth of about 1 meter year-round **(142)**

permeability: description of how well a rock or sediment lets water pass through

perpendicular: lines that are at right angles (90°) to each other

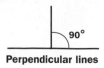

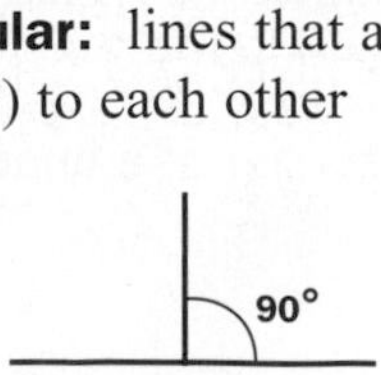

Perpendicular lines

petri dish: small covered dish used to grow bacteria and molds in the laboratory

petrified fossil: remains of living things that have been replaced by minerals and thus turned to stone **(198)**

petroleum: fossil fuel and material resource that formed deep in the Earth over millions of years from remains of ancient plants and animals; It is refined into products such as gasoline. **(325)**

pH scale: scale ranging from 0–14, used to describe how acidic (<7) or basic (>7) a substance is **(264)**

phase: Chemistry: *See state of matter* **(253);** Astronomy: *See moon phases* **(235)**

phenotype: the physical appearance of an organism; *See also genotype* **(123)**

phloem: plant tissue that transports sugar-rich sap from where it is made (the leaves), to where it is used and stored in other parts of the plant; *See diagram at vascular plant* **(162)**

photon: theoretical packet of light energy that behaves as a particle

photosynthesis: chemical process by which plants use light energy to make sugar from water and carbon dioxide **(079, 107)**

Sunlight (energy)

$$6CO_2 + 6H_2O \longrightarrow C_6H_{12}O_6 + 6O_2$$

carbon dioxide + water ⟶ glucose (sugar) + oxygen

Photosynthesis

phototropism: change in growth of a plant in response to light **(111)**

photovoltaic cells: devices used to convert sunlight to electricity; also called **solar cells (328)**

phylum: first division of organism classification below kingdom, as in Arthropoda **(151)**

physical change: occurs when one or more physical properties of a substance are changed; many physical changes can be undone by physical means **(252)**

physical map: map showing the land features of an area, such as rivers, lakes, mountains; *See also relief map*

physical property: property of matter that can be observed without changing the composition or identity of the matter **(251)**

physical science: study of matter and energy **(249)**

physical weathering: *See mechanical weathering* **(189)**

physics: study of energy, forces, and motion

physiology: study of all the internal functions of an organism **(104)**

pictogram: kind of graph that shows statistical information using pictures **(392)**

pie chart: a graph in the shape of a circle, where the size of each slice indicates a percent of the whole; also called a **circle graph (393)**

pioneer species: first organisms to live in an area **(140)**

pistil: female reproductive structure of a flowering plant; *See diagram at flower* **(114)**

pitch: how high or low a sound is; determined by the sound wave's frequency **(313)**

pituitary gland: gland that makes substances that control other glands and that affect growth, metabolism, and development **(097)**

placenta: in most mammals, organ responsible for the exchange of nutrients and waste materials between the mother and the developing fetus **(106)**

plankton: tiny plants and animals that live near the surface of water and cannot swim against the current **(149, 210)**

plasma: Human Body: the liquid part of blood that supports the other parts **(093);** Physics: the fourth state of matter, like a gas but consisting of charged particles (ions and electrons) and found mostly in stars **(253)**

plastics: chemical compounds that can be easily shaped into many different products, often made from refined petroleum **(331)**

plate boundary: the region where two lithospheric plates meet **(184)**

plate tectonics: theory that describes and explains the way that continents separated into today's land masses from one large ancestral land mass (Pangaea); also, the study of lithospheric plates, their movements, and Earth features that they affect **(182)**

platelets: cell pieces that help blood to clot where there is an injury **(093)**

plutonic: Refers to igneous activity beneath Earth's surface; *See also intrusive* **(180)**

polar: Earth Science: refers to the North or South Pole; Physical Science: refers to a material, such as a magnet or molecule, that has opposing forces on either side or end

polarized: describes light in which all waves are traveling the same direction and vibrating in parallel planes; Light is polarized by passing it through certain materials.

pollen: particles that carry male genetic material, from seed plants **(114)**

pollination: the transfer of pollen from the male part of a plant (stamen) to the female part (pistil) **(114)**

pollution: any change in the environment that is harmful to organisms **(348)**

population: Ecology: all the members of a species living in a particular area at a particular time **(130);** Statistics: the total group being analyzed

porosity: a measure of the amount of empty space in a rock or sediment

potential energy: stored energy an object has because of its position or shape **(300)**

power: how much work a machine can do in a unit of time; also, the numerical product of current and voltage in an electric circuit

precipitation: water falling from clouds in any form, such as snow, ice, raindrops, or drizzle **(216)**

predation: relationship between species in which one species (prey) acts as a food source for another species (predator) **(132)**

predator: animal, such as a lion, that kills and eats other animals (prey) **(132)**

prediction: a guess about what will happen under certain conditions, that is based on observation and research **(002)**

pressure: amount of force exerted on a given area by an object or substance; SI unit is the pascal (Pa) **(295)**

prevailing wind: a mid-latitude global wind that blows mostly in one direction **(217)**

prey: organism that is killed and eaten by another organism (predator) **(132)**

primary consumer: in a food chain, organism that eats plants, such as a rabbit **(134)**

prime meridian: longitude line of 0° that all other longitudes are measured by; passes through western Europe and Africa **(169)**

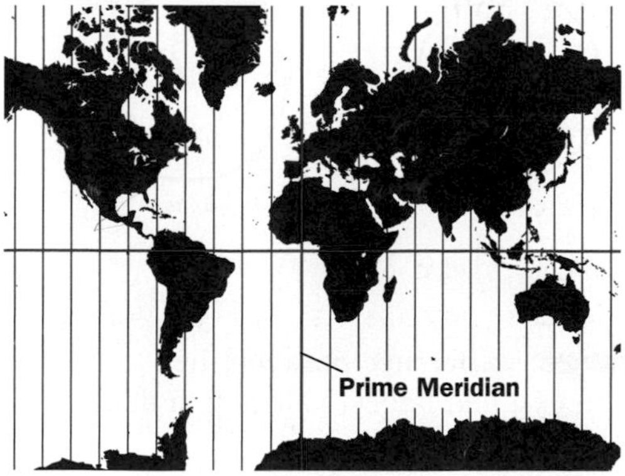

producer: organism that makes its own food, such as a plant or a photosynthetic alga **(133)**

product: compound or element that is the result of a chemical reaction **(269)**

Products

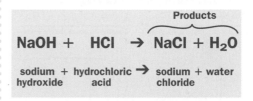

$$NaOH + HCl \rightarrow \underbrace{NaCl + H_2O}$$

sodium hydroxide + hydrochloric acid → sodium chloride + water

projection: any process used to transfer a spherical map (globe) to a flat map; also the map made by such a process **(168)**

prokaryote: one-celled organism that does not have a membrane-bound nucleus or organelles; includes all archaebacteria and eubacteria **(160)**

property: characteristic of a material that helps to identify or classify matter **(251)**

prophase: stage of cell division during which the genetic material shortens and thickens in the nucleus **(081)**

proteins: a class of organic compounds found in living things that are essential for life **(079)**

protists: one-celled or simple many-celled organisms, such as amoebas and algae **(156)**

proton: positively-charged particle located in the nucleus of an atom **(256)**

psychrometer: instrument used to measure moisture in the atmosphere **(226)**

pulley: simple machine consisting of one or more wheels with a rope wrapped around them **(294)**

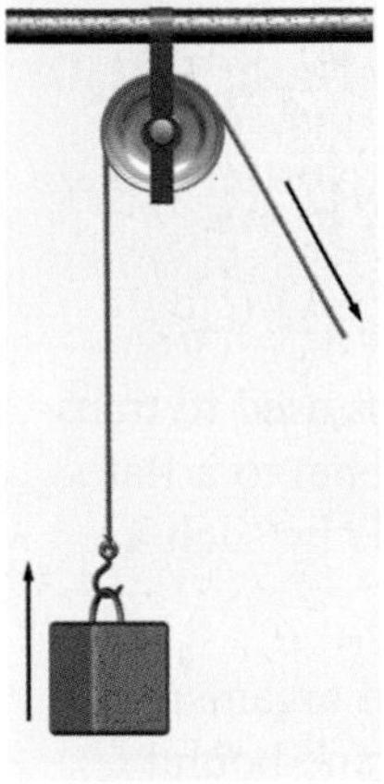

Fixed pulley

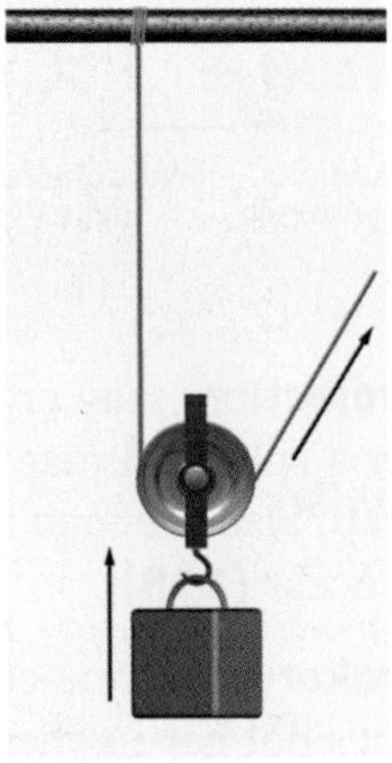

Movable pulley

Punnett square: in genetics, table used to predict what traits offspring will have, based on what traits the parents have **(123)**

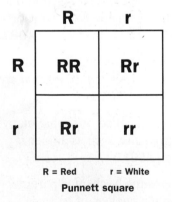

	R	r
R	RR	Rr
r	Rr	rr

R = Red r = White

Punnett square

pupa: stage in the life cycle of a metamorphic insect during which it changes from its larval to its adult form **(106)**

pure: in genetics: refers to an organism that carries two dominant or two recessive alleles for a given trait **(122)**

pyroclastic: ash, rocks, and similar solid material shot out from a volcano

R

radar: the use of reflected radio waves to determine the distance of an object and the direction it is moving **(219)**

radiation: transfer of energy in the form of electromagnetic waves **(304);** also high energy particles and rays emitted from the nuclei of radioactive elements **(197, 327)**

radioactive: element that gives off high-energy rays or particles **(197, 327)**

radius: distance from the center of a circle or sphere to its perimeter or surface

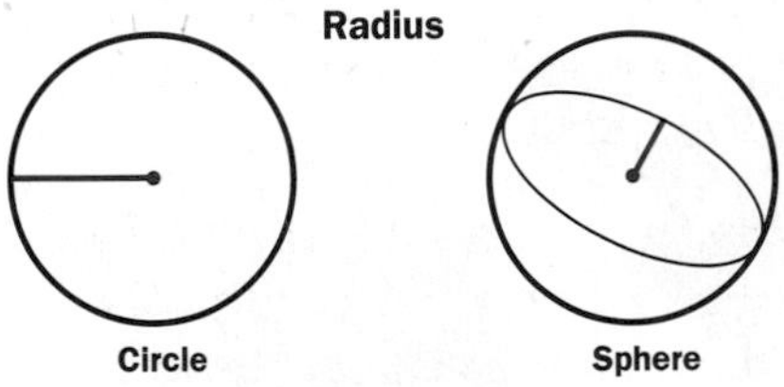

range: difference between the smallest and largest values in a data set **(384)**

rarefaction: *See longitudinal wave* **(307)**

rate: a comparison of a quantity to a unit of time, expressed as a fraction, such as 40 km/h **(381)**

ratio: relationship between two values that have the same unit **(382)**

reactant: compound or element that changes during a chemical reaction **(269)**

Reactants

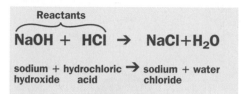

$NaOH + HCl \rightarrow NaCl + H_2O$

sodium hydroxide + hydrochloric acid → sodium chloride + water

reaction: *See chemical reaction* **(269)**

real image: image made by a lens which can be projected onto a screen

recessive: in a pair of alleles, the one that is masked if a dominant allele is present **(122)**

rectum: final section of the large intestine, ending in the anus **(089)**

red blood cell: cell that carries oxygen through the body **(093)**

refine: in petroleum processing, to separate petroleum into different substances **(325)**

reflection: bouncing back of a wave from a surface; in light, reflection from a smooth surface is **specular** reflection, from a rough surface is **diffuse** reflection **(311)**

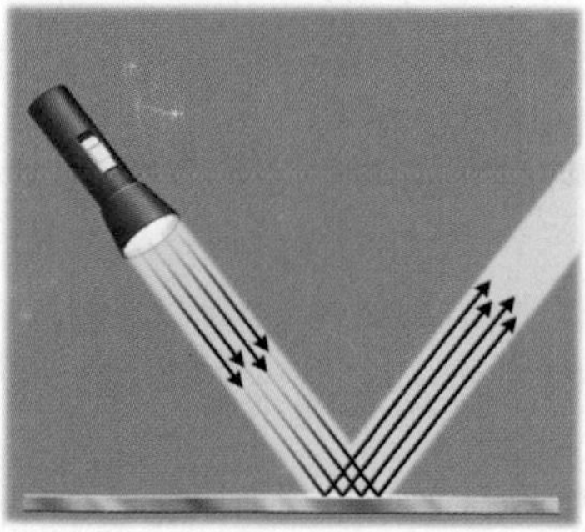

Specular reflection

Diffuse reflection

reflex: an animal's automatic response to a stimulus, such as jerking away from a hot surface **(095)**

refraction: bending of a wave as it moves across the boundary between one medium and another **(311)**

Refraction of light

relative age: method of describing the age of one object or event compared to another object or event **(197)**

relative humidity: amount of water vapor in the air compared to the amount in saturated air at the same temperature, reported as a percentage **(226)**

relief map: a physical map showing vertical features with a drawing, such as shaded mountains; *See also physical map*

renewable resources: natural resources that can be renewed or replaced by nature, such as food crops and solar energy **(323, 328)**

reproduce: to make more individuals of the same species from a parent organism or organisms **(113)**

reserves: supply of an energy resource, such as coal, petroleum, or natural gas **(325)**

resistance: measure of how much a material opposes the flow of electric current through it, measured in ohms (Ω) **(319)**

respiration: *See cellular respiration* **(079)**

respiratory system: organ system that takes oxygen into the body and releases carbon dioxide and water **(092)**

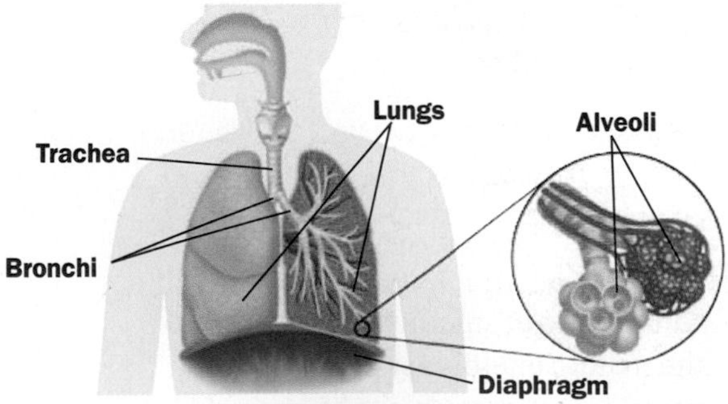

Respiratory system

revolution: one orbit of an object in space around another object in space, such as the moon around Earth **(234)**

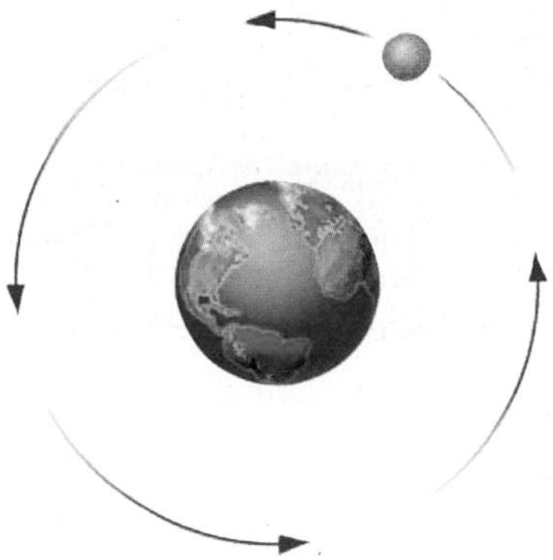

ribosome: structure in a cell where proteins are put together **(077, 078)**

Richter scale: way of measuring the severity of earthquakes, based on the energy released **(186)**

rift valley: valley that forms on land at a place where two plates are moving apart

Ring of Fire: string of volcanoes around the rim of the Pacific Ocean, resulting from plate boundary activity **(185)**

ring stand: piece of equipment used in laboratories to support beakers and other equipment **(034)**

risk-benefit analysis: identifying the possible negative (risk) and positive (benefit) results of a technology, before deciding to use it **(371)**

rock: hard and compact mixture of minerals that formed naturally **(180)**

rock cycle: process by which rocks, over geologic ages, can be changed into different kinds of rock **(180)**

rotation: spinning of a planet, moon, sun, or other object, around its axis **(233)**

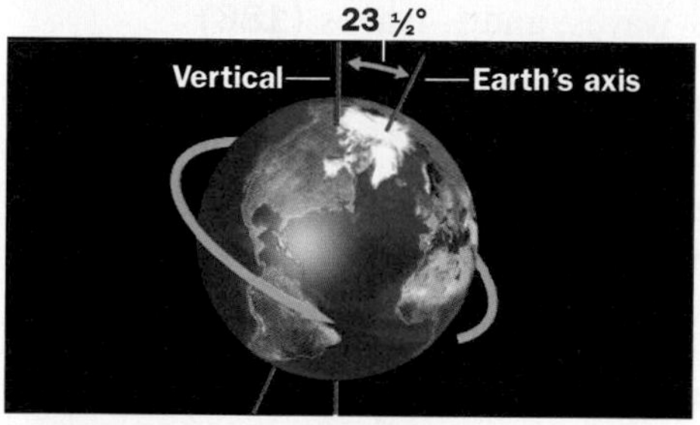

Rotation

S

safety goggles: safety equipment worn to protect the eyes from splashes and flying objects **(023)**

salinity: amount of dissolved solids in a solution, such as ocean water, usually measured as percent (%) or part per thousand (ppt) **(202)**

salt: ionic compound resulting from the reaction of an acid and a base, for example sodium chloride (NaCl), potassium nitrate (KNO_3)

sanctuary: *See wildlife preserve* **(344)**

satellite: object that revolves around a larger object in space; The moon is a natural satellite of Earth; the Hubble Space Telescope is an artificial satellite. **(239)**

saturated: containing as much of something as possible under certain conditions, for example: saturated air **(226)**, saturated solution, saturated fat

savanna: biome consisting of a grassland with scattered trees **(146, 230)**

scale: Graphing: series of equally-spaced marks that stand for equal intervals; Earth Science: *See map scale* **(170)**

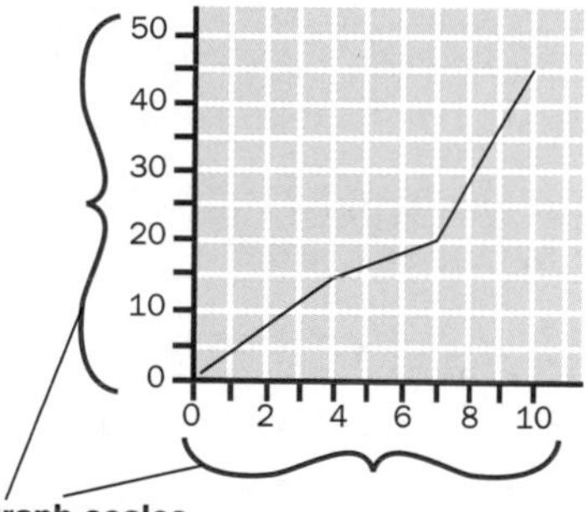

Graph scales

scavenger: organism, such as a vulture, that feeds on dead or decaying organisms **(133)**

scientific ethics: study of the impact of technology and science on human society **(358)**

scientific inquiry: efforts to understand and explain the natural world through observation and experiment **(002)**

scientific law: *See law* **(002)**

scientific model: simplified version of some part of the natural world that helps explain how it functions **(013)**

scientific name: the genus and species name of an organism; for example *Aplodontia rufa,* mountain beaver **(151)**

scientific notation: a way of writing extremely large or extremely small numbers; uses a number between 1–10 multiplied by a power of 10, such as 9.8×10^6, or 3.2×10^{-4} **(377)**

screw: a simple machine consisting of an inclined plane wrapped around a cylinder **(291)**

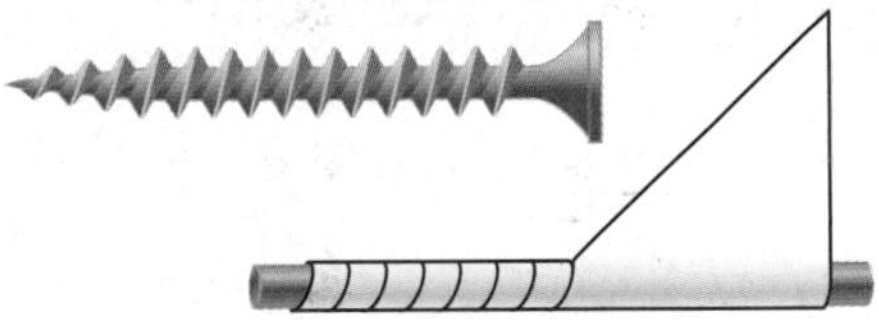

seamount: mountain that lies completely below the sea **(207)**

second (s): unit of time equal to $\frac{1}{60}$ of a minute **(070)**

secondary consumer: in a food chain, an organism that feeds on plant-eaters; also called a **predator** **(134)**

sediment: small pieces of material that have broken off of rocks and have been deposited by water, wind, or ice **(180)**

sedimentary rock: rock formed when sediment is pressed and cemented together naturally, over millions of years **(180)**

seed: structure able to sprout and develop into a plant; made of a plant embryo and its food supply **(108)**

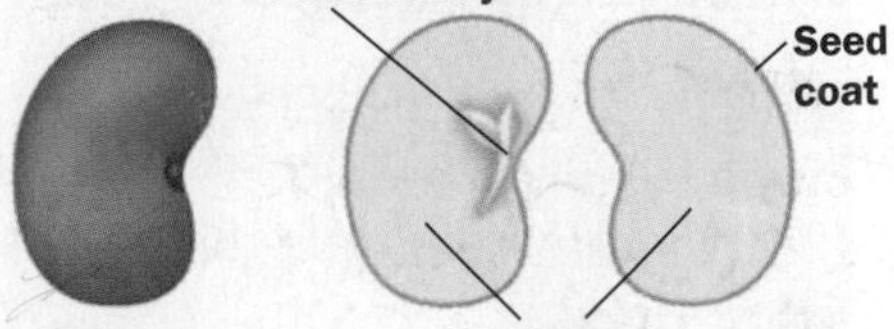

seismic wave: a wave of energy passing through Earth, caused by an earthquake; includes P-waves, S-waves, and L-waves **(186)**

sense organs: organs that gather information about the surrounding environment, including the eyes, ears, nose, mouth, and skin **(096)**

series circuit: circuit in which loads are arranged such that current must pass through each load to complete the circuit **(318)**

Series circuit

sexual reproduction: process in which two parents contribute genes to form a new individual **(114)**

SI system: system of measurement based on metric system that is used worldwide by scientists; includes meter, liter, and gram **(055)**

side effect: an unintended response caused by a medicine **(371)**

simple machine: a device that makes work easier by changing the size or direction of the force applied to it **(288)**

skeletal muscle: muscle that moves parts of the body and is under conscious control of the organism **(087)**

skeletal system: bones and cartilage (skeleton) that support a vertebrate's body **(086)**

small intestine: organ in the digestive system that completes digestion and absorbs nutrients **(089)**

smooth muscle: muscle found in many organs which is not under conscious control of the organism **(087)**

soil: mixture of rock, mineral particles, and organic matter that forms at Earth's surface **(191)**

solar eclipse: occurs when the moon passes between Earth and the sun, blocking the sun's light from Earth **(236)**

solar energy: energy from the sun in the form of heat and light **(328)**

solar system: the sun, its planets, and all other objects in orbit around the sun or planets **(238)**

solar wind: movement of charged particles from the sun through space **(242)**

solid: matter that has a definite shape and volume, such as a rock **(253)**

solstice: one of two days in the year when hours of daylight and hours of darkness are at their greatest and least; **summer solstice** marks the beginning of summer and the longest period of daylight; **winter solstice** marks the beginning of winter and the shortest period of daylight **(234)**

solubility: ability of a substance to dissolve in another substance, such as sugar dissolving in water; also, a measure of the amount of a substance that will dissolve in a certain volume of water **(273)**

solute: *See solution* **(272)**

solution: mixture in which the molecules of one substance, known as the **solute,** are dissolved in another substance, known as the **solvent;** The solute is present in a smaller quantity than the solvent. **(271, 272)**

Solution: After salt dissolves, a solution exists

solvent: *See solution* **(272)**

sound: energy that travels through matter as mechanical waves, and can be heard by the ear **(312)**

southern hemisphere: the half of Earth south of the equator

species: group of organisms that can mate and produce offspring that in turn can produce more offspring **(130);** also, most specific division of organism classification, below genus **(151);** *See also scientific name*

specific gravity: the density of a substance compared to the density of water **(179)**

specific heat: thermal energy needed to change the temperature of 1 g of a substance by 1°C

speed: distance traveled by an object in a given amount of time **(284)**

sperm: male sex cell **(114)**

spinal cord: bundle of nerves that goes from the brain stem down the center of the backbone **(095)**

spring tide: tides that are most extreme; occur twice a month, at full and new moon phases

stalactite: mineral deposit that hangs down from the roof of a cave **(190)**

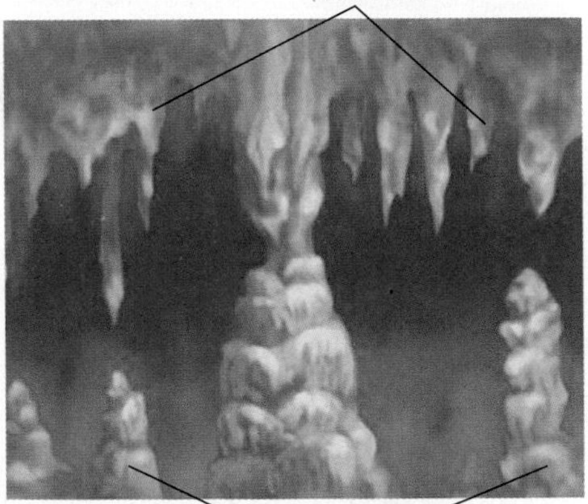

stalagmite: mineral deposit sticking up from the floor of a cave **(190)**

stamen: male reproductive structures of a flowering plant, which produce pollen; *See diagram at flower* **(114)**

star: huge object in space made up of gas and giving off light and heat from nuclear reactions; the sun is a star **(245)**

states of matter: the forms matter can take, as in liquid, solid, or gas; also called **phases of matter (253)**

static electricity: electricity in which electric charges build up on an object; the movement of the charge off the object is **electric discharge** or **static discharge (316)**

station model: a shorthand way of recording weather at a particular weather station, on a map **(219)**

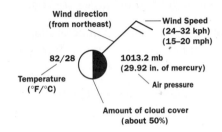

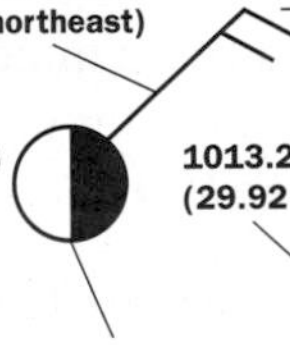

stationary front: boundary between two air masses where the masses are not moving **(222)**

steroid: a type of hormone that controls many body systems **(097)**

stimulus: anything that an organism can sense; usually refers to a change that causes an organism to do something in response; plural is **stimuli (109)**

stirring rod: glass rod used in the lab to stir solutions **(048)**

stomach: part of the digestive system, where food is stored and partially digested before it enters the small intestine **(089)**

stopper: rubber or cork plug used to seal test tubes and flasks **(047)**

stopwatch: kind of watch used to measure how long events last, in minutes or seconds **(070)**

strata: layers of sedimentary rock

stratosphere: a layer of Earth's atmosphere reaching from 16–50 kilometers above the surface **(215)**

stratus: clouds in layers with a flat base, usually at low altitudes **(223)**

streak: the color of a mineral in powder form, seen by rubbing the mineral on a streak plate; This property is used to help identify a mineral. **(179)**

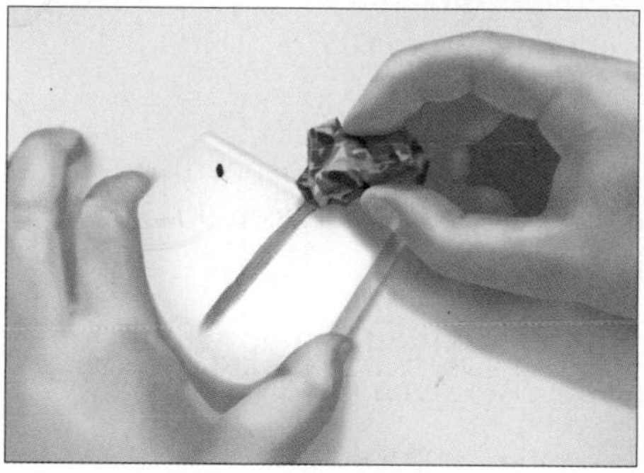

strike-slip fault: *See transform boundary* **(184)**

subduction: the process in which one lithospheric plate slides under another; occurs at converging plate boundaries **(184)**

sublimation: change from the solid state to the gaseous state, without first passing through the liquid state

submarine canyon: steep-sided valley cut into a continental shelf, often offshore from a major river **(207)**

subsoil: layer of soil below the topsoil **(191)**

subsurface current: an ocean current flowing beneath the surface, caused mainly by differences in water density **(206)**

succession: *See ecological succession* **(140)**

summer solstice: *See solstice* **(234)**

superposition: principle that states that in a series of sedimentary rock layers, the oldest are on the bottom and the youngest are on top, unless the layers have been overturned **(195)**

surface current: ocean current flowing at the surface, caused mainly by winds **(204)**

suspension: mixture in which particles of one substance are spread throughout another substance, and the particles are large enough to settle out **(271)**

symbiosis: a close relationship between two species **(132)**

T

taiga: a conifer forest biome located south of the tundra **(143, 230)**

taxonomic tree: a branching diagram showing the evolutionary relationships among groups of organisms **(163)**

technology: the use of scientific knowledge and processes to solve practical problems **(354)**

tectonic plate: *See lithospheric plate* **(183)**

telophase: final stage of cell division, during which the cell divides in half **(081)**

temperate: a mid-latitude (30–40°N or S) climate; Most temperate climates have seasons. **(230)**

temperature: measure of the average kinetic energy of the particles in a substance; measured in degrees Celsius (°C) or degrees Fahrenheit (°F) **(071, 302)**

tendon: connective tissue that attaches skeletal muscle to bone **(087)**

terminal speed: speed of an object that is falling through air when it has stopped accelerating; also called **terminal velocity (285)**

terrarium: closed container where plants and sometimes animals are kept, which is self-supporting as long as it has a source of light energy **(413)**

terrestrial planets: rocky planets in the inner solar system: Mercury, Venus, Earth, and Mars; also called **inner planets (240)**

tertiary consumer: in an ecosystem, a predator that feeds on other predators **(134)**

test tube: long, round, narrow glass container, sealed at one end, used in laboratories **(047)**

testable question: question that can be tested by experiment or observation **(416)**

theory: an idea that is the best explanation of many observations and helps make new predictions **(002)**

thermal energy: total kinetic energy contained in all the particles of a substance; also called **heat energy (301)**

thermometer: device used to measure temperature **(072)**

thermosphere: layer of Earth's atmosphere above ionosphere and below exosphere, between 90–300 kilometers **(215)**

thigmotropism: plant growth in response to touch **(111)**

threatened species: species that may become endangered if numbers continue to shrink **(344)**

thymus gland: gland that is involved in development of the immune system **(097)**

thyroid gland: gland that functions in making hormones that control chemical processes in the body **(097)**

tide: daily rise and fall of the oceans, caused mainly by the gravitational pull of the moon **(237)**

Low tide

High tide

tissue: in plants and animals, a group of cells that work together to do a specific job **(082)**

topographic map: map that shows the shape and elevation of the land surface using contour lines, and shows other land features using symbols and colors **(172)**

topography: features of a land area caused by differences in elevation; also called **relief (173)**

topsoil: upper layer of soil, often the richest in plant nutrients **(191)**

tornado: small, destructive, whirling, fast-moving storm that forms over land

toxic: refers to the effects of a poison or toxin

toxic waste: *See hazardous waste* **(347)**

trace fossil: mark or track of an ancient animal preserved in sedimentary rock **(198)**

trachea: part of the respiratory system, the windpipe; *See diagram at respiratory system* **(092)**

trade wind: global wind that blows nearly all the time in tropical areas **(217)**

tradeoff: accepting the drawbacks of a technology because of its benefits **(369)**

transform boundary: boundary between two lithospheric plates where the plates are sliding past each other **(184)**

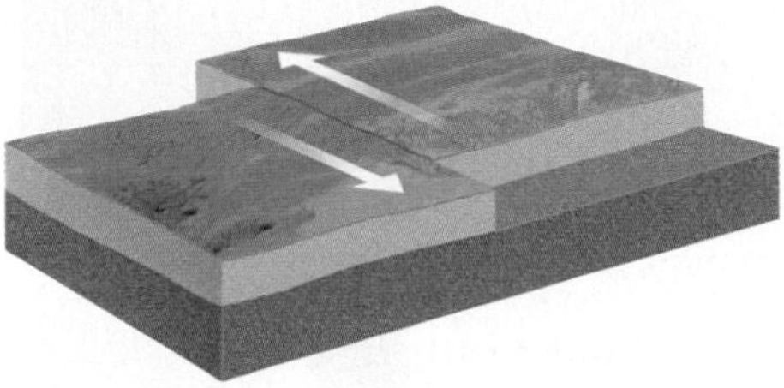

transformer: device used to change the voltage of an alternating current

translucent: describes matter that allows some, but not all, of the light that hits it to pass through, and that scatters some light **(311)**

transmission: passage of light through matter **(311);** also, sending of information or energy from one point to another

transparent: describes matter that allows light to pass through it easily **(311)**

transpiration: loss of water through a plant's leaves **(216)**

transverse wave: a wave that oscillates perpendicular to the direction it is traveling; highest point of wave is the **crest** and lowest point is the **trough (307)**

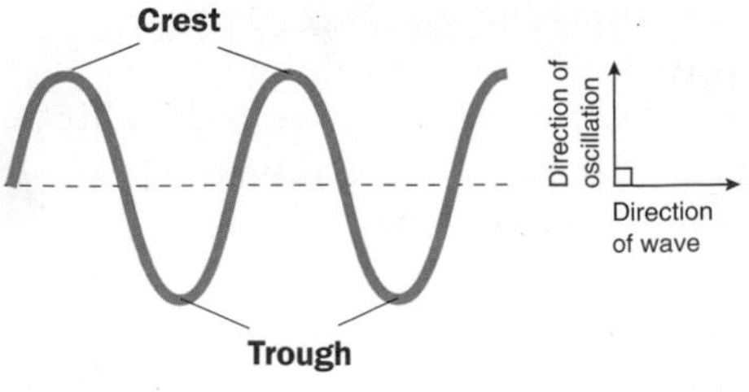

trend line: *See best-fit line* **(398)**

trial: one set of measurements or observations in an experiment **(009)**

triple-beam balance: laboratory scale with three bars that is used to measure mass **(064)**

tripod: a three-legged stand; some kinds are for laboratory use, others are for use in the field **(034)**

tropism: plant growth in response to a stimulus, such as phototropism, growing toward light **(111)**

troposphere: lowest layer of Earth's atmosphere, from the surface up to 16 kilometers; nearly all weather takes place here **(215)**

trough: *See transverse wave* **(307)**

trundle wheel: device for measuring distance consisting of a wheel that clicks when rolled forward a certain distance **(058)**

tsunami: a giant, dangerous ocean wave triggered by an earthquake, landslide, or volcanic eruption; sometimes called a **tidal wave,** but it has nothing to do with tides

tundra: a cold, dry, mostly treeless land biome located at high altitudes or at high latitudes **(142, 230)**

turbine: a machine that converts the mechanical energy of wind, moving water, or steam to electrical energy by using a generator **(328)**

U

ultraviolet radiation (UV): part of the electromagnetic spectrum, which is invisible to humans **(309, 350)**

unbalanced forces: occur when the net force on an object does not equal zero; results in the object changing its motion **(282)**

Forces on the cat are unbalanced.

unconformity: a place where rock layers are missing in the geologic record **(196)**

unicellular: made up of only one cell **(076)**

uniformitarianism: principle that states that the geologic processes of today were also operating in the past **(195)**

uplift: pushing up of Earth's crust by forces within Earth, such as the action of two lithospheric plates moving toward each other **(187)**

upwelling: subsurface ocean current that brings nutrient-rich water from the ocean bottom to the surface

ureter: in the urinary system, tube that passes urine from the kidney to the urinary bladder **(090)**

urethra: in the urinary system, tube that passes urine from the bladder to outside the body **(090)**

urinary bladder: in the urinary system, saclike structure that stores urine until it can be released **(090)**

urinary system: organ system that filters, stores, and releases waste products from the blood (urine); *See diagram at excretory system* **(090)**

urine: liquid waste filtered from the blood **(090)**

uterus: organ in a female mammal in which fertilized eggs develop into young **(106)**

V

vacuole: in a cell, fluid-filled structure that holds waste products or substances needed by the cell **(077, 078)**

valence electrons: electrons in the outermost energy level of an atom; in large part, they determine an element's chemical properties **(268)**

vaporization: change of matter from a liquid state to a gaseous (vapor) state; may occur at the boiling point, or at the surface of the liquid below the boiling point **(254)**

variable: In experiments: a condition that is changed in order to find out the effect of that change **(008);** In mathematics: part of an equation that can have different values, as opposed to a constant, which always has the same value

varieties: animals of the same species but with distinctly different traits, such as size and color; Dog breeds are different varieties of *Canis familiaris.* **(151)**

vascular plant: a plant that has specialized tissues for moving food and water throughout the plant **(162)**

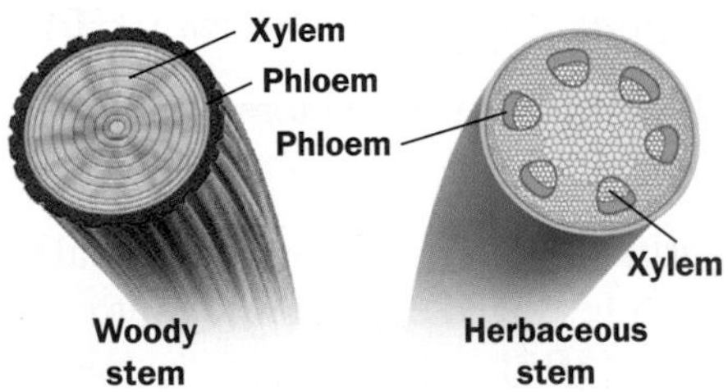

vein: in the circulatory system, vessel that carries blood toward the heart; *See diagram at circulatory system* **(093)**

velocity: an object's speed and direction at a given instant **(284)**

vernal equinox: *See equinox* **(234)**

vertebrate: an animal with a backbone **(161)**

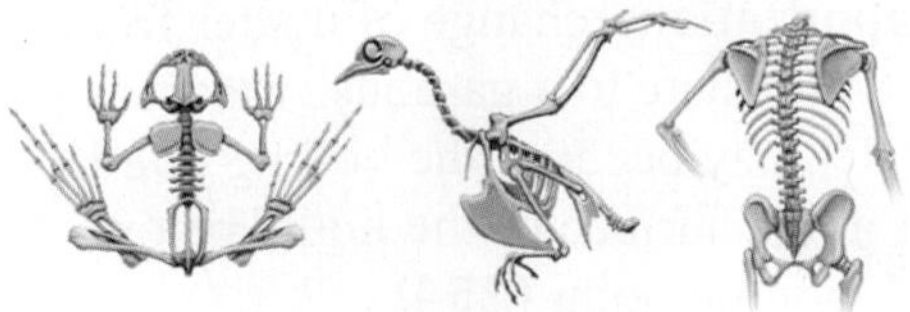

Examples of vertebrate skeletons

vertical: a line or surface that is up and down, not side to side

vertical axis: a vertical line marked with a scale that is used to place data points on a graph; sometimes called the y-axis **(390)**

villi: tiny fingerlike structures that line the small intestine and absorb digested food **(089)**

virtual image: image made by a lens or mirror which cannot be projected onto a screen

virus: a tiny particle that has characteristics of both living and nonliving things. Viruses cause some kinds of infectious disease **(100)**

visible spectrum: *See light* **(308)**

vitreous: describes a mineral with a glassy luster **(179)**

volcanic: *See extrusive* **(180)**

volcano: hill or mountain formed by material that erupts onto Earth's surface; caused by action of magma below surface **(187)**

voltage: potential difference between positively-charged and negatively-charged terminals of a battery, or between any two points in a circuit; measured in **volts (V) (318)**

volume: amount of space an object or substance takes up; measured in liters (L) or cubic centimeters (cm^3); *See also capacity* **(059)**

voluntary muscle: skeletal muscle that is under conscious control of the organism **(087)**

W

waft: to fan fumes from a chemical toward the face **(037)**

waning: moon phases from full moon to new moon, as the lit surface seen from Earth grows smaller **(235)**

warm front: leading edge of a warm air mass moving in to replace a cold air mass **(222)**

waste: trash; also any leftover, unusable material from the laboratory or from manufacturing or mining

water cycle: cycle in which water moves through the environment, through the processes of evaporation, condensation, and precipitation **(216)**

water table: beneath Earth's surface, the upper limit of soil that is saturated with groundwater

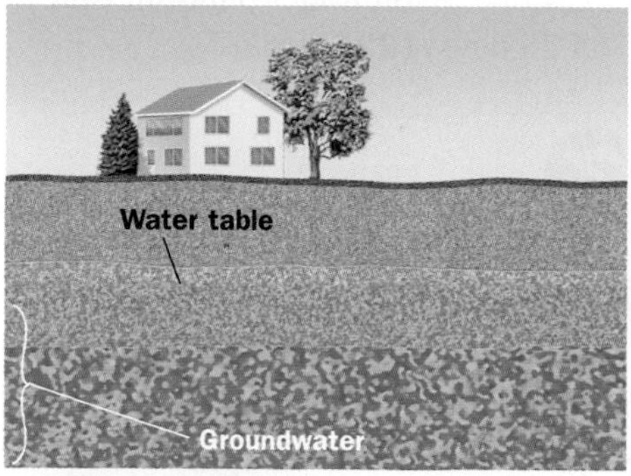

watershed: *See drainage basin* **(193)**

watt (W): unit of power, equal to one joule per second (1 J/s)

wave: a back-and-forth motion that travels from one place to another **(305)**

wave speed: distance a wave travels in a given amount of time **(306)**

wavelength: distance from any point on one wave to a corresponding point on the next wave, such as crest to crest or compression to compression **(306)**

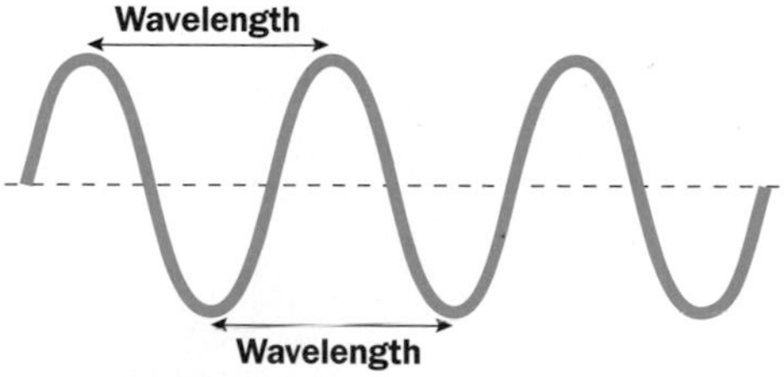

Wavelength of a transverse wave

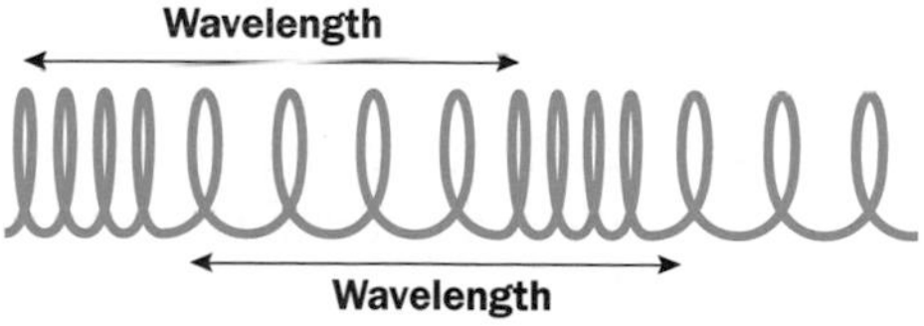

Wavelength of a longitudinal wave

waxing: moon phases from new moon to full moon, as the lit surface seen from Earth grows larger **(235)**

weather: conditions in the atmosphere, including humidity, cloud cover, temperature, wind, and precipitation **(218)**

weathering: process by which water, wind, and ice wear down rocks and other exposed surfaces; includes chemical and mechanical weathering **(188)**

wedge: simple machine consisting of an inclined plane that moves **(290)**

weight: a measure of the force of gravity on an object **(276)**

wheel and axle: simple machine made of a shaft (the axle) inserted though the middle of a circle (the wheel) **(293)**

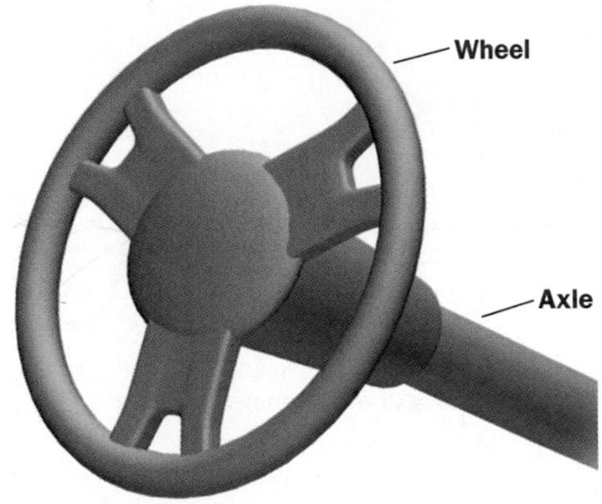

white blood cell: cell carried in the blood that helps fight infectious disease **(098)**

wildlife preserve: special area set aside as a habitat for wild animals and plants; also called **wildlife sanctuary (344)**

wind: movement of the air caused by differences in air pressure **(225)**

wind vane: device used to observe wind direction; also called **weather vane (225)**

winter solstice: *See solstice* **(234)**

woody plant: plant with stiff, sturdy stems, usually covered with bark **(162)**

work: occurs when a force is used to move an object through a distance; measured in **joules (J) (287)**

X

xylem: plant tissue that transports water from the roots up the stem to the branches and leaves; *See diagram at vascular plant* **(162)**

Y

year: period of time in which Earth makes one revolution around the sun (365.25 days) **(234)**

Z

zygote: a fertilized egg cell **(114)**

Index

A

B

C

D

E

F

I

J

K

L

M

P

Q

R

S

T

U

V

W

X

Y

Z

Credits

Writing: Kane Publishing Services, Inc.: Barbara Branca, Joseph Brennan, Claudia Cornett, Eliot Hoffman, Carl Proujan

Editorial: Great Source: Marianne Knowles, Sarah Martin, Susan Rogalski; Kane Publishing Services, Inc.: Linda Cernak, Jill Farinelli, Amy Goodale, Linda Zierdt-Warshaw

Design: Preface, Inc.; Great Source: Richard Spencer

Production Management: Preface, Inc.; Great Source: Evelyn Curley

Cover Design: Bill Smith Studios: Ron Leighton

Photo:

Cover

periodic table-PhotoDisc
fish- Corel
butterfly- PhotoDisc
shuttle- NASA
lightning- PhotoDisc
Earth- PhotoDisc
crowned crane- Wolfgang Bayer/Discovery Communications, Inc.
bucky ball- Ken Eward/Science Source/Photo Researchers
Einstein- Bettman/Corbis
amethyst geode- PhotoDisc

Scientific Investigation

019 Michelle Glidden/Science Service

Working in the Lab

051 Dr. E. R. Degginger/Color-Pic, Inc.

Life Science

087b Carolina Biological Supply Company/Phototake
087r Lester V. Bergman/Corbis
087t Carolina Biological Supply Company/Phototake
110l Gallo Images/Corbis
110r Zig Leszczynski/Animals Animals
118 CNRI/Phototake
119l Mary Kate Denny/PhotoEdit
119r PhotoDisc
128c Wolfgang Kaehler/Corbis
128l Ecoscene/Corbis
128r Lester V. Bergman/Corbis
132 Darlyne A. Murawski/NGS Image Collection

Earth Science

173 US Geological Survey
178 Science Photo Library/Photo Researchers, Inc.
179 Dr. E. R. Degginger/Color-Pic, Inc.
180b Dr. E. R. Degginger/Photo Researchers, Inc.
180c,t Dr. E. R. Degginger/Color-Pic, Inc.
186 Roger Ressmeyer/Corbis
189 George Turner/Photo Researchers, Inc.
192l Ecoscene/Corbis
192r Yann Arthus-Bertrand/Corbis
195 Tom Bean/Corbis
198b,c,r Dr. E. R. Degginger/Color-Pic, Inc.
198tc Simon Fraser/Science Photo Library/Photo Researchers, Inc.
198tl Phil Degginger/Color-Pic, Inc.
207 Tom Van Sant/Geosphere Project, Santa Monica/Science Photo Library/Photo Researchers, Inc.
210b Corbis
226 Dr. E. R. Degginger/Color-Pic, Inc.
239l Hale Observatory/Photo Researchers, Inc.
239r NASA Science Source/Photo Researchers, Inc.
240b NASA/Science Photo Library/Photo Researchers, Inc.
240t NASA
242 Dennis di Cicco/Corbis
247br,l David Malin/Anglo Australian Observatory
247tr AURA/NOAO/NSF

Natural Resources and the Environment

328l Dr. E. R. Degginger/Color-Pic, Inc.
328r Jim Goodwin/Photo Researchers, Inc.
331 Edifice/Corbis
341 Neil Rabinowitz/Corbis
342 John Bova/Photo Researchers, Inc.
343 PhotoDisc
344 Operation Migration, Inc.
348 Dr. E. R. Degginger/Color-Pic, Inc.
350 NOAA/Science Photo Library/Photo Researchers, Inc.

Science, Technology, and Society

356 Werner Forman/Corbis
357l Bettmann/Corbis
357r John Morrison Photography
361 Reuters NewMedia, Inc./Corbis
363 Dr. Jeremy Burgess/Science Photo Library/Photo Researchers, Inc.
366 Layne Kennedy/Corbis

Almanac

379c François Gohier/Photo Researchers, Inc.
379l NOAO/Science Photo Library/Photo Researchers, Inc.
379r Michael Freeman/Corbis

Yellow Pages

440b Hulton-Deutsch Collection/Corbis
440bc World Films Enterprise/Corbis
440bl Archivo Iconografico, S.A./Corbis
440c Richard T. Nowitz/Corbis

440tc Baldwin H. Ward & Kathryn C. Ward/Corbis
440tl Historical Picture Archive/Corbis
440tr Dennis di Cicco/Corbis
441bc Queen Elizabeth I in Coronation Robes, c.1559 (panel) by English School (16th century), National Portrait Gallery, London, UK/Bridgeman Art Library
441bl,br,c,cl Bettmann/Corbis
441cr Mary Evans Picture Library/Photo Researchers, Inc.
441tl Ecoscene/Corbis
441tr Michael Maslan Historic Photographs/Corbis
442bl Museum of the City of New York/Corbis
442br,c Bettmann/Corbis
443bl Christie's Images/Corbis
443br Joseph Sohm/Visions of America/Corbis
443cr Dr. E. R. Degginger/Color-Pic, Inc.
443l,tc PhotoDisc
443tr George Bernard/Science Photo Library/Photo Researchers, Inc.
444bc,br,cl,tl,tr Bettmann/Corbis
444bl Fredde Lieberman/Index Stock
444c Courtesy of NASA/JPL/Caltech
445bc,bl Corbis
445br Joseph Sohm/ChromoSohm/Corbis
445c,tr Bettmann/Corbis
445tc Jeremy Burgess/Science Photo Library/Photo Researchers, Inc.
445tl Steve Raymer/Corbis
446bl Hulton Archive
446br Corbis
446cl,t Bettmann/Corbis
447b,br Bettmann/Corbis
447bl,t Corbis
447br Bettmann/Corbis
447cr Laura Dwight/Corbis
448bl WildCountry/Corbis
448br Flip Schulke/Corbis
448cl,tl Bettmann/Corbis
448cr Charles O'Rear/Corbis
448t A. Barrington Brown/Photo Researchers, Inc.
448tr NASA
449bc,br David & Peter Turnley/Corbis
449bl Charles E. Rotkin/Corbis
449cl,tl Roger Ressmeyer/Corbis
449cr Reuters NewMedia, Inc./Corbis
449tr 1996 CORBIS; Original image courtesy of NASA/Corbis

Glossary

470 Dr. E. R. Degginger/Color-Pic, Inc.
475 CNRI/Phototake
477 Dennis di Cicco/Corbis
479l Charles & Josette Lenars/Corbis
479r Dr. E. R. Degginger/Color-Pic, Inc.
480c,l Dr. E. R. Degginger/Color-Pic, Inc.
480r Yann Arthus-Bertrand/Corbis
492 Phil Degginger/Color-Pic, Inc.
519 Jim Zuckerman/Corbis

Art:

All art that appears on the Title page and Table of Contents was created by Blake Thornton.

All charts, graphs, and tables were created by Preface, Inc.

Scientific Investigation

Stephen Durke: 004b, 006, 008b, 008c, 013b
Terry Guyer: 018b, 018c
Preface, Inc.: 002b, 002d, 015
Marty Roper: 016a, 016b
Dan Stuckenschneider: 013c
Blake Thornton: 001a, 001b, 002a, 002c, 002e, 004a, 005a, 005b, 008a, 009a, 009b, 010, 013a, 014, 017a, 017b, 018a, 019a, 019b, 019c, 019d

Working in the Lab

Stephen Durke: 029, 030b, 030c, 049, 051, 052a, 052b, 060a, 062a, 062b, 072
Terry Guyer: 027b, 033b, 034, 038, 039a, 039b, 040a, 040b, 042, 048, 058b, 058c, 058d, 060b, 070
Preface, Inc.: 021, 045
Marty Roper: 023b, 024a, 024b, 033a, 037, 065
Dan Stuckenschneider: 023a, 030a, 031a, 031b, 032a, 047a, 047b, 064, 066
Blake Thornton: 020a, 020b, 022, 025, 027a, 028, 036a, 036b, 041, 043, 044, 053, 054, 058a, 061, 068, 071

Life Science

Stephen Durke: 075b, 075c, 076b, 077, 078, 081, 082a, 084b, 087b, 093b, 095d, 098, 100, 101, 102, 106a, 111, 114a, 114b, 115, 116b, 117b, 138, 159, 160, 161b, 162a, 162b, 163b
John Edwards, Inc.: 141
Terry Guyer: 079, 082c, 087a, 089, 090, 092, 093a, 095a, 095b, 097, 142, 143, 144, 145, 146, 147, 148a, 148b, 153, 154, 155, 156, 157
Yuan Lee: 105, 106b, 106c, 125, 127a, 130, 131, 137, 139, 149a, 164
Dan Stuckenschneider: 086a, 086b, 107, 108, 110c, 110d, 114c, 122a, 140, 161a, 161c
Blake Thornton: 073a, 073b, 075a, 076a, 082b, 083, 084a, 095c, 096, 103, 104, 110a, 110b, 113, 116a, 117a, 121, 122b, 123, 126, 127b, 127c, 128, 133, 134, 135, 149b, 150a, 150b, 163a

Earth Science

Stephen Durke: 169b, 169c, 177, 200e, 200f, 202a, 222, 223, 233b, 233c, 234, 235, 236a, 236b, 237, 238a, 242
John Edwards, Inc.: 168a, 168b, 170a, 170b, 171, 182a, 182b, 185a, 193b, 199, 205b, 217a, 220, 230a, 230b
Terry Guyer: 179a, 180, 189, 190, 191, 196, 197a, 200a, 200b, 200c, 200d, 209, 210, 225, 228b
Preface, Inc.: 169a, 169d, 174, 185b, 238b, 245, 248b, 248c
Dan Stuckenschneider: 173a, 173b, 183, 184a,b,c,d,e, 186a, 187a,b,c, 193a, 205a, 207a,b, 215, 216
Blake Thornton: 165a, b, 169e, 172, 179b, 197b, 217b, 218, 228a,c, 233a, 239, 244, 248a

Physical Science

Stephen Durke: 253, 256, 258a, 258b, 258c, 261a, 261b, 263a, 263b, 293, 294, 304c, 316b, 317, 318a, 318b, 318c
Terry Guyer: 250b, 251, 264a, 264b, 277a, 285, 289, 290, 291, 295, 297a, 306, 307a, 307b, 312, 320a, 320b, 321a, 321b
Preface, Inc.: 254e, 309a, 309b, 315
Dan Stuckenschneider: 252, 254a, 254b, 254c, 254d, 269, 271b, 278, 301, 302, 303, 304a, 304b, 311a, 311b
Blake Thornton: 249a, 249b, 250a, 250c, 255, 271a, 273, 274, 275a, 275b, 276, 277b, 279, 280a, 280b, 281, 282, 283, 284, 286a, 286b, 287, 292, 296a, 296b, 297b, 299, 300, 316a

Natural Resources and the Environment

Stephen Brayfield: 324
Stephen Durke: 326, 327a, 338, 349, 351, 353
Terry Guyer: 325b, 325c, 331b, 343a, 343b
Preface, Inc.: 323a
Dan Stuckenschneider: 328, 330b, 334b, 342, 346b
Blake Thornton: 322a, 322b, 323b, 325a, 330a, 330c, 331a, 331c, 331d, 332, 334a, 336, 337a, 337b, 337c, 337d, 339a, 339b, 344, 346a, 347, 348, 350

Science, Technology, and Society

Preface, Inc.: 371
Blake Thornton: 354a, 354b, 359, 369, 370, 373

Almanac

Stephen Durke: 389, 413a
Terry Guyer: 409, 416, 433
Precision Graphics: 437a, 437b
Preface, Inc.: 401a, 413b, 421, 422
Blake Thornton: 374a, 381, 388, 405, 418a, 418b, 423, 424, 425

History of Science Timeline

Stephen Durke: 442b, 442c, 443b, 444a, 446c, 447a
John Edwards, Inc.: 446b
Preface, Inc.: 442a, 446a, 449
Dan Stuckenschneider: 443a, 445

Scientific Terms

Stephen Durke: 470a, 473b, 475, 479a, 479b, 482, 483b, 484b, 487a, 488a, 489b, 495b, 501b, 502, 503a, 503b, 504, 505a, 506, 507, 510, 513a, 514b, 518a, 518b, 524
John Edwards, Inc.: 495c
Terry Guyer: 469a, 469b, 472a, 473a, 474, 476, 478b, 481, 484a, 486a, 491, 492a, 492b, 493b, 494b, 495a, 498a, 498b, 500a, 512a, 514a, 516, 517, 519a, 519b, 520b, 523b, 523c
Yuan Lee: 489a
Preface, Inc.: 470b, 478a, 483a, 484c, 485, 494a, 496, 497b, 509
Dan Stuckenschneider: 469c, 477, 486b, 487b, 487c, 493a, 493c, 501a, 505b, 511a,b,c, 512b, 513b, 515, 520a, 522a, 522b, 523a
Blake Thornton: 471a, 472b, 487d, 487e, 497a, 521a